ANDERSON UNIVERSITY
INAR
JX1407 .E53 c.1-3,!
D1399459

Encyclopedia of AMERICAN FOREIGN POLICY

Encyclopedia of AMERICAN FOREIGN POLICY

Studies of the Principal Movements and Ideas

Alexander DeConde, *EDITOR*

Volume I

CHARLES SCRIBNER'S SONS · NEW YORK

Copyright © 1978 Charles Scribner's Sons

Library of Congress Cataloging in Publication Data

Main entry under title:

Encyclopedia of American foreign policy.

Includes index.
1. United States—Foreign relations
—Dictionaries. I. De Conde, Alexander.
JX1407.E53 327.73 78-5453
ISBN 0-684-155036-6

This book published simultaneously in the
United States of America and in Canada—
Copyright under the Berne Convention

All rights reserved. No part of this book
may be reproduced in any form without the
permission of Charles Scribner's Sons.

Acknowledgment is gratefully made to the American Council of Learned Societies for permission to use biographical material from the *Concise Dictionary of American Biography* (copyright © 1977, 1964 Charles Scribner's Sons) and *Dictionary of American Biography, Supplement 5* (copyright © 1977 American Council of Learned Societies).

1 3 5 7 9 11 13 15 17 19 V|C 20 18 16 14 12 10 8 6 4 2

Printed in the United States of America

Charles E. Wilson Library
Anderson College
Anderson, Indiana 46011

Ref.
JX
1407
.E53
v.1

Editorial Staff

Marshall De Bruhl	*Director*
Frederic C. Beil III	*Associate Editor*
David William Voorhees	*Associate Editor*
G. Michael McGinley	*Assistant Editor*
Leslie C. Henderson	*Editorial Assistant*
Elizabeth I. Wilson	*Associate Editor*
Joel Honig	*Associate Editor*
Helen Chumbley	*Proofreader*
Pauline Piekarz	*Proofreader*
Claire Sotnick	*Editor*

17 Dec 79, the Scribner Book Com., $120 (3 volumes) Library

Charles E. Wilson Library
Anderson College
Anderson, Indiana 46011

129155

CONTENTS

CONTENTS

CONTENTS

CONTENTS

CONTENTS

PREFACE

THE *Encyclopedia of American Foreign Policy* is a selective reference work containing essays of original scholarship by distinguished contributors commissioned to write them. The essays explore concepts, themes, large ideas, theories, doctrines, and distinctive policies in the history of American foreign relations, and range in coverage from broad concepts such as isolationism and national self-determination to specific topics such as the Monroe Doctrine and the Marshall Plan. Even collectively these articles do not attempt to cover chronologically the history of foreign relations. Excluded are conventional accounts of major episodes, such as the diplomacy of the American Revolution, the Louisiana Purchase, the War of 1812, or the Korean War, except as such topics fit within a conceptual analysis. With major conceptual topics, however, the editors have tried to be comprehensive. Since the decision to include some topics while excluding others depended ultimately on subjective judgments, even experts may disagree over the choices made, and doubtless some concepts that merit consideration may be missing.

The topical structure fits the purpose of the work, essentially to present to serious readers, among them students, academicians, government officials, journalists, and others an authoritative compendium of essays that analyze the development, application, and meaning of basic concepts in foreign policy. While this approach is not in itself exceptional, the manner of presentation is. In the extensive literature on American foreign policy no one up to this time has attempted conceptual analysis on a comparable scale. Many books, especially the better textbooks, give excellent chronological accounts of foreign relations, but few trace, analyze, and explain key concepts with consistency and unbroken continuity. Monographs treat a number of concepts, such as the Open Door, in depth. Yet they often present their findings in excessive details or technical jargon. While offering fullness where appropriate, the present studies explore their topics unweighted with heavy details and present them simply and clearly without the usual trappings of scholarship, such as footnotes. Based on the most recent scholarship, some essays explain concepts that have not previously been the subject of consistent investigation or systematic analysis. Other pieces deal with topics that have received considerable scholarly attention, but in all of them the syntheses and interpretations come from the contributors. Moreover, all the essays attempt in varying degrees to offer analysis within a meaningful historical context, and in a manner not readily available elsewhere. Although the authors and editors have worked to keep repetition to a minimum, some factual overlapping was unavoidable, and on occasion seemed necessary.

Intellectual overlapping, however, should be hardly discernible, particularly since the philosophical orientation of the studies covers a wide spectrum from right to left. The authors wrote with freedom, adhering to no standard methodology or ideological model. The only uniformity the editors desired was in syntax and format. Each author is among the foremost scholars in his field and each is a specialist in the area of his or her essay. While most are historians and Americans, the contributors represent a number of disciplines and come from several countries.

Most histories of foreign policy follow a chronological development and concentrate mainly on the exercise of power as discerned in official relations between countries. Research for such histories usually consists of tracing negotiations and the exchange of notes by prime ministers, presidents, secretaries of foreign relations, and ambassadors. Scholars of diplomacy rely heavily on official documents as sources. Diplomatic history, as a result, has often been narrow in focus, even when done well. In this volume, while traditional concern for diplomatic exchanges, exercise of power, and conflict between states remains central, the contributors often roam beyond areas of conventional scholarship. They examine relations between peoples within countries as they affect foreign policy and across national boundaries on both nongovernmental and official levels. They analyze concepts such as freedom of the seas and manifest destiny which defy precise definition; they scrutinize emotional influences such as ethnic loyalties, patriotism, and national honor and their impact on policy; they assess economic matters such as trade, embargoes, and tariffs as they influence the making of policy; and they probe the impact of social movements such as immigration and peace societies on people and the makers of policy.

While each essay is a unit within itself and stands on its own, each is also related to the others. The nature or extent of the relationship may be discerned not only through the reading of the articles but also through use of cross-references at the end of each essay. They are particularly useful for the reader interested in exploring nuances in related concepts and data, or in seeing a concept in one essay taken up in another and evaluated from another perspective. The selected bibliographies appended to each essay complement the cross-references and provide the reader with guides to the noteworthy literature on the subject so that he or she may pursue it in depth.

This work, in a sense, attests to the importance of American foreign policy in the contemporary world. While it should not be considered a substitute for conventional histories on the growth of American power in international politics, it is a comprehensive supplement of thoughtful analyses that enrich and clarify foreign policy and the concepts and rhetoric associated with it. In this and in other aspects, it is an undertaking unique in the historiography of American foreign relations.

Alexander DeConde

ALLIANCES, COALITIONS, AND ENTENTES

Warren F. Kimball

THE TRADITIONAL VIEW

AMERICAN reluctance to participate in alliances, coalitions, and ententes was traditional until World War II. According to the conventional wisdom, in 1778, out of sheer necessity, but remembering the colonial experience of being dragged into European wars, the Revolutionary leaders unhappily agreed to sign a political alliance with France. Some twenty years later, when that treaty seemingly forced the young American nation to choose between the two great antagonists in the Anglo-French conflict in Europe, the United States repudiated that alliance, fought a brief and undeclared war to make that repudiation stick, and then, embittered by the brief experience with "European-style" alliances, swore off such political activity forever. In his Farewell Address George Washington warned against "permanent alliances," and in an inaugural address Thomas Jefferson provided the slogan that Americans seem always to need for a policy—"entangling alliances with none." For a hundred and fifteen years, until World War I, the American nation refused to indulge in the kind of international alliance politics that characterized European diplomacy. Even then, once propelled into the Great War, the United States took the moral high ground and refused to accept full membership as an ally in the coalition against the Central Powers, opting instead for the label Associated Power. Disillusioned and angered by the selfishness that the European powers exhibited during the 1919 Paris Peace Conference, the United States attempted to withdraw from the international arena during the interwar period, only to be forced by Japanese and German aggression to come again to the rescue of the civilized world. The events of World War II forced the United States into what became a long-term alliance with Great Britain and a very short-term one with the Soviet Union. Then, as Cold War tensions mounted, the American government negotiated a series of defensive mutual security alliances aimed at protecting the "free" world against Russian (Communist) aggression.

Reluctant participation is clearly the tone of the entire story. Perhaps the thrust of generally accepted interpretations was best summarized by Thomas A. Bailey in his extraordinarily popular text *A Diplomatic History of the American People:* "The United States cannot afford to leave the world alone because the world will not leave it alone" (9th ed., p. 949). In other words, historians have treated coalition and alliance diplomacy as part and parcel of the story of America's traditional isolationism.

TERMINOLOGY

Before examining this conventional view, a brief discussion of terminology is in order. Although the American public has never drawn sharp distinctions between alliances, coalitions, and ententes, its leaders have frequently acted in a way that indicated that they understood the differences. Alliances are properly formal agreements between nations which call for specific joint action and responses to given political situations. They can be outlined verbally, but they are normally committed to paper and are, therefore, recognized in international law. Although alliances relate to wartime situations, they are usually concluded in times of peace and last for significant periods of time.

Coalitions bring to mind the various European joint efforts against France in the late eighteenth and early nineteenth centuries. Those wars saw various nations unite in military action against France frequently only after the fighting had actually begun. Short term and often not defined by written agreements, coalitions aim simply at the military defeat of a common enemy and do not relate to postwar considerations. Although the term is rarely applied, Russo-American cooperation during World War II against Nazi Germany was a coalition rather than an alliance. The only common ground was military victory over the enemy, and attempts by both nations to expand that limited relationship met with failure.

Entente, properly used, describes a far deeper relationship between nations than either alliance or coalition. An entente becomes possible only when two or more nations share a set of political goals and perceptions. The most obvious entente in American history has been the one that began to develop between Great Britain and the United States after the War of 1812. Frequently subjected to great strains, that entente was formalized as an alliance during World War II and the Cold War era. Such an entente is more a friendship than an alliance or coalition stimulated by sheer power politics, although the realities of international relations are never completely ignored.

REVOLUTIONARY DIPLOMACY—THE NECESSARY ALLIANCE

Historians have frequently argued that America's antipathy to political involvement with Europe originated with the colonial experiences, when European wars spread to the Western Hemisphere. Yet even a cursory glance at colonial newspapers indicates that the English settlers in America viewed the wars with France and Spain as their own. Historians agree that the colonials considered themselves Englishmen right up until the American Revolution began, and there is no evidence to show that this feeling did not extend to England's wars as well. Reluctance to pay war taxes proves nothing; taxes are generally unpopular at any time. The peace settlements negotiated by the English may have angered the colonists, but only because the treaties seemed to give more benefits to the French or Spanish than the American colonists thought necessary. Even after the Revolutionary War had begun in earnest, many American leaders could not bring themselves to negotiate any sort of alliance with their traditional enemy, France.

What American leaders sought was not isolation but rather situations that clearly benefited national interests. Born into a world of traditional alliances and coalitions, the new American nation chose to avoid such associations not out of any moral or philosophical judgments, although such rhetoric abounded, but because, at least temporarily, an independent policy seemed to promise greater rewards. Thomas Paine, often misinterpreted as recommending isolation, made his point clear in the pamphlet *Common Sense* (1776):

> Any submission to, or dependance on Great Britain, tends directly to involve this Continent in European wars and quarrels, and set us at variance with nations who would otherwise seek our friendship, and against whom we have neither anger nor complaint. As Europe is our market for trade, we ought to form no partial connection with any part of it. It is the true interest of America to steer clear of European contentions, which she can never do, while, by her dependance on Britain, she is made the make-weight in the scale of British politics.

Paine, who soon became impatient with the Revolution's conservatism, argued not for isolation but for a policy of impartiality designed to open all of Europe's markets to American trade. That policy, which soon stimulated America's strong support of neutral rights, hardly represented a new departure in foreign policy. The smaller nations of the world have always attempted to avoid choosing sides in struggles between the greater powers, although sheer geographic gravity made that rarely possible in Europe's history.

The debates among the Revolutionary leaders

over broad guidelines for American diplomats, discussions that culminated in the Model Treaty (or Plan) of 1776, illustrate the distinctions made by Paine. In spite of the precarious military situation, some argued for only a commercial connection with France. Led by John Adams, these men obviously feared that the presence of French troops in America would mean merely swapping one imperial master for another. Although Adams' statements were couched in the broad, sweeping terms so popular with Enlightenment thinkers, his objections stemmed from two factors: his practical appraisal of America's political weakness and economic needs and his intense distrust of French motives—a distrust he held in common with his fellow New Englanders. In spite of Americans' claims that they stood for a new approach to world politics—a *novus ordo seculorum*—they had adopted policies that were merely variations of the realistic power politics of the Europe they professed to scorn. When military necessity forced the Continental Congress to seek a military alliance with France in 1778, the terms of that treaty were not fundamentally different from alliances negotiated by European nations. The French intended the United States to become a permanent client-state of His Christian Majesty, a sentiment embodied in a clause stating that the alliance would last "from the present time and forever." A plea from the United States to Spain for a similar treaty of alliance was ignored.

Nor did the United States go about alliance diplomacy any differently than its European predecessors. The peace negotiations aimed at ending the Revolutionary War found the Americans as deceptive as France. Interpreting the alliance with France as selectively binding, Benjamin Franklin, John Adams, and John Jay negotiated an effective and separate treaty of peace with the British—a violation of their agreement with France. Although they justified their actions by pointing out that France had intended to betray the United States, their argument contrasts sharply with the self-righteous claims that America would practice a new diplomacy in which, to quote Adams, "the dignity of North America . . . consists solely in reason, justice, truth, the rights of mankind, and the interests of the nations of Europe." Ironically, Franklin—a man with long experience in the world of eighteenth-century diplomacy—opposed such a violation of treaty obligations, while Adams demanded that they open negotiations with the British.

Although the treaties of alliance and commerce with France represented no breakthrough into some sort of new diplomacy, American leaders, particularly the New Englanders, viewed the new nation's diplomacy as somehow flowing from values and purposes different from those of Europe. Distracted by the social implications that went with their repudiation of an aristocratic class, many Americans confused diplomatic forms with substance. Refusal to dress like European diplomats became equated with a refusal to indulge in European-style power politics.

That image proved to be longer lasting than the alliance with France. The rhetoric of America's uniqueness and exceptionalism, something common among young, intensely nationalistic nations, meshed neatly with the notion that the United States practiced a new form of diplomacy. In reality, the only thing new about America's diplomacy was that geography permitted it to remain aloof from the constantly shifting balance of power in Europe. Hence the decision not to join the League of Armed Neutrality was made because it was thought that the league offered no benefits to America, not because of any ideological opposition to taking sides.

By the mid-1790's, the French Alliance had become a detriment to the young republic. With the outbreak of the Wars of the French Revolution, soon to merge into the Napoleonic Wars, Presidents George Washington and John Adams feared that the United States would be drawn into a conflict in which it had no interest. Again myth overtook reality. French restrictions on American naval freedom appeared to be a direct retaliation for the refusal of the United States to live up to its treaty obligations, whereas the reality was that the French Directory believed that the recently negotiated commercial treaty between Britain and America (Jay's Treaty) contained secret clauses that amounted to a political alliance. The treaty contained no such political commitments, but the French argument struck home. When great powers go to war, neutrals can maintain their trade only at the risk of losing any claim to impartial economic policies. Although the United States did not sign Jay's Treaty as part of an anti-French policy, the French quite logically believed the opposite. Historians have argued that Washington's famous Farewell Address sprang primarily from domestic political considerations, but it was the awkward confrontation with France—including attempts by the French directly to influence American elections—which clearly stimulated his warning against alliances. Washington included a caveat which Americans soon forgot; he warned only against "artificial" connections with Europe, not ones that were natural and in the national interest. Since the Quasi-War with France followed soon after Washington's warning, Americans tended to view the address as an accurate prediction of the outcome of United States involvement in European alliances. The economic consequences that might have followed any American attempt to maintain real impartiality—something which would have required economic isolation—were forgotten.

JEFFERSONIAN REALISM

Thomas Jefferson obviously understood the difference between artificial and natural connections with Europe. His condemnation of "entangling" alliances referred to involvements in European politics, not to the defense of American interests. When, in 1802, France seemed about to occupy the Louisiana Territory, striking a wedge between the United States and land that many Americans assumed was destined to become part of the United States, Jefferson's thoughts turned to plans of alliance with Great Britain. The Louisiana Purchase made that unnecessary, and Jefferson then followed policies that subtly favored France in its conflict with the British. His reasoning was simple and logical: only the English had a fleet large enough to pose a military threat to the United States, hence they were America's only potential enemy of substance. But none of his talk of alliance or his attempts to play at a timid and small form of alliance politics came to public attention. With "no entangling alliances" already a tradition, domestic political considerations made Jefferson keep such thoughts to himself and his closest advisers.

After a brief period of peace beginning with the Treaty of Amiens (1802), the Napoleonic Wars started anew in 1803. Again the United States found itself caught between two great powers. As both England and France turned increasingly to economic warfare, American attempts to maintain business as usual were less and less successful. Frustrated in his attempts to negotiate arrangements which would permit American foreign trade to continue without harassment, Jefferson overestimated the value of that trade to the European powers and also turned to economic coercion. An embargo prevented all American ships from sailing to foreign destinations but drove home the lesson of America's economic dependence upon trade with Europe—a lesson statesmen have never forgotten.

IN ENGLAND'S WAKE—THE NINETEENTH CENTURY

The United States eventually became involved in the Napoleonic Wars. Logic demanded that the nation choose one side or the other, but tradition, past experience, and the intense national division over the foreign policies of Jefferson and his successor, James Madison, made the decision difficult. George Washington had already become the nation's father figure, and no leader could ignore such pronouncements as the Farewell Address with impunity. Moreover, the unhappy experience with the French Alliance made both politicians and the public cautious. More important, however, was the domestic political tug-of-war regarding foreign policy. Although President Madison and his supporters had strong sympathies for France, to have suggested an alliance with Napoleon would have confirmed the accusations of the Federalists, who claimed that the president had called for war to aid France, not to defend American interests. Since French violations of neutral rights had been as flagrant as those committed by England, that argument seemed plausible. So the United States entered the war against Britain, but without any alliance with France—a technique that the nation followed again in World War I, a hundred years later.

The combination of luck and domestic politics which kept the United States out of a formal alliance with France in 1812 also made it possible for war-weary England to extend remarkably generous peace terms to the Americans. In spite of an almost unbroken string of military defeats, the American public viewed the war as a great victory, thus adding to the tradition and myth that the United States need not and should not enter into alliances.

In the years immediately after the Treaty of Ghent (1815), the United States followed a foreign policy which took advantage of the European political situation. Designed and implemented primarily by Secretary of State John Quincy Adams, the policy took shrewd advantage of Europe's economic and psychological exhaustion following the defeat of Napoleon, of the Latin American revolts against Spain, of geography, and of the British desire to keep European power politics restricted to Europe. When the Latin American colonies revolted against Spain, the threat of intervention by the Holy Alliance (Russia, Prussia, Austria, and France) made Adams reconsider his earlier rejection of a British offer of an alliance. Nevertheless, Adams finally concluded, correctly, that England would act to keep other European countries out of the Western Hemisphere with or without an alliance with the United States, and he again spurned the offer. The British obtained a commitment from the French that they would not permit their fleet to be used for any transfer of Holy Alliance troops to Latin America. Once again American leaders had examined the possibility of entering into an alliance but had rejected that move; not because of tradition, but because a careful appraisal of the situation convinced them that such an alliance was simply unnecessary.

But it is out of such stuff that traditions are made. President James Monroe's Doctrine for the Western Hemisphere (1823) made British policy appear to be a function of American diplomacy. John Quincy Adams knew full well the emptiness of any threat from the Holy Alliance, but the American public treated the entire episode as proof of their nation's ability to solve its international problems without help. And so the United States proceeded through the nineteenth century armed with Washington's advice and a conviction that there was no need to play balance-of-power politics with the European nations.

British foreign policy continued to make such beliefs come true. Great Britain, busy in Europe and Asia, hoped to see the United States restricted in size and power, but never did the potential gains of such desires warrant the use of military force to ensure that they materialized. British leaders encouraged the Texans to remain independent after 1836, tried to hold onto the Oregon country, and hoped for a Confederate victory during the American Civil War, but whenever the United States government threatened to respond with force, the British backed away from the confrontation. Unwilling to fight the Americans, British statesmen repeatedly, if reluctantly, chose policies designed to make a friend of the United States.

At the same time two events served to fortify America's opposition to alliance diplomacy. The bloody and inconclusive Crimean War during the late 1850's seemed to demonstrate the bankruptcy of the European alliances, and the withdrawal of French troops from Mexico in 1867 indicated once again that the United States could itself deal with the "untrustworthy" European powers. The alliance system developed after 1871 by German Chancellor Otto von Bismarck only led American statesmen to condemn further such power politics.

THEODORE ROOSEVELT AND AMERICA'S DESTINY

By the end of the nineteenth century, American policymakers and political writers were convinced that alliances, coalitions, and ententes were all part of a dangerous concept of international relations. Convinced that alliances caused wars rather than prevented them, Americans looked upon the European political scene with contempt. Yet, at the same time, a small group of statesmen-politicians led by such ultranationalists as Henry Cabot Lodge, Albert

Beveridge, and Theodore Roosevelt, concluded that its size and economic power made it necessary for the United States to play an active role in international politics. As Theodore Roosevelt put it:

> We have no choice, we the people of the United States, as to whether or not we shall play a great part in the world. That has been decided for us by fate, by the march of events. We have to play that part. All that we can decide is whether we shall play it well or ill [Archibald C. Coolidge, *The United States as a World Power* (New York, 1912), p. 374].

With Roosevelt as president from 1901 through 1909, America had, for the first time as chief executive, a man who saw the nation's mission as much more than merely an example to others. Roosevelt—taking his cue from the social Darwinists, but adding an optimism based on the American experience—saw America's role in the world as unique and tinged with messianic destiny. He not only believed the United States was a nation with international responsibilities; he also unquestioningly embraced the idea that the fate of mankind depended upon America's willingness to accept those responsibilities. Roosevelt saw no need for anything less than American superiority in the Western Hemisphere, but he sought to avoid antagonizing Great Britain in the process. The community of Anglo-American interests had been growing since 1815, but not until Roosevelt's presidency did the government establish a strong, if unofficial, entente with Great Britain. Roosevelt's prejudice in favor of Anglo-Saxon "civilization" as well as his realistic appraisal of America's economic and military interests resulted in American influence invariably buttressing British goals in Europe. Roosevelt was not alone, as can be seen by such editorials as appeared in *Harper's Weekly* openly advocating American participation in the Anglo-French Entente. Although Roosevelt, largely because of domestic politics, did not heed such advice, he supported various British attempts to dominate the European balance of power, the best example being his secret diplomacy during the Moroccan crisis of 1905–1906.

The political situation in Asia concerned Roosevelt deeply. Convinced that the United States had to act like a Pacific Ocean power, he even expressed a vague desire for America to join the Anglo-Japanese alliance, which was designed to delineate British and Japanese interests in China and to halt Russian expansion in the area. Although such active participation in an alliance seemed politically impossible, Roosevelt attained that goal in part without any domestic struggle. His role as peacemaker during the Russo-Japanese War found him privately applying diplomatic pressure; yet the American public, still committed to nonentanglement, approved what appeared to be a role of disinterested and uninvolved organizer of a successful peace conference. From 1905 through 1908 American and Japanese representatives held almost continuous talks about other mutual problems. Although the discussions were frequently unpleasant, a special relationship developed between the two nations. Roosevelt firmly believed that Japanese–American cooperation—the beginnings of entente—would bring peace, order, and stability to East Asia; and, as part of that policy, he recognized Japanese spheres of influence in Korea and northern China.

Roosevelt committed the United States to an active role in international affairs—a commitment that had been growing out of American power as well as his actions—and put the nation on a path that could not be reversed regardless of the rhetoric of isolation and the natural desire to avoid the responsibilities that accompanied the thrill of world power.

THE TRAUMA OF WORLD WAR I

On 6 April 1917 the United States formally joined a wartime coalition for the first time in its history. In refusing actually to join the Anglo-French-Russian Alliance, President Woodrow Wilson hoped to avoid even an implied commitment to the many secret treaties that provided for the division of the spoils among the Allied Powers, although he also realized that American public opinion would support the idea of continuing some measure of aloofness from European political systems.

American entry into World War I supported Theodore Roosevelt's contention. Whether the cause was German submarine warfare, American national security, business investments in

Europe, or a desire to control events, the United States obviously if unknowingly had accepted his argument that it had to "play a great part in the world." Inspired by Wilson's rhetoric about a world safe for democracy, Americans set out upon their own "Great Crusade." After the defeat of Germany and its allies, the United States hoped to reform Europe and establish a permanent peace. Frustrated by the slow pace of reform at home, many Progressive Era reformers looked to Europe and the world for new opportunities.

Coalition diplomacy during the war reflected American distrust of Europe. It took the pressure of a German offensive to get American generals to coordinate their actions with a newly created Allied commander in chief, and even then the United States refused to permit its troops to come under foreign command.

Woodrow Wilson's historic proposal for a league of nations has rightfully dominated the history of the postwar period. Wilson's concept of collective security, however incompletely developed, clearly represents one of the few attempts by a major world statesman to find a workable substitute for the diplomacy of power politics—alliance, coalition, and entente. Wilson's proposal had a fatal flaw: it rested upon the creation of a homogeneous world economic–political system. The collective security approach required a remarkable degree of cooperation and trust among the major world powers, but such trust could develop only when they shared similar political and economic creeds, and that was not to be.

Instead, the peace settlements that followed World War I created a system of alliances and ententes by which the victors hoped to preserve the status quo. Although the United States refused a role in Europe when it rejected membership in the League of Nations, a proposed alliance with France against Germany might well have received Senate approval, but the Wilson administration lost interest in it following the rejection of the Treaty of Versailles. It soon became "traditional" again for Americans to speak disdainfully of Europe's power politics, never realizing that their government continued to display a strong interest in European events. In fact, American "observers" at the League's meetings frequently attempted to influence the deliberations, and throughout the 1920's and 1930's American policy paralleled that of Britain and France.

The peacekeeping system in Europe operated without overt American support, but the system for Asia sprang primarily from the efforts of the United States. The Washington Naval Conference of 1921–1922, called by Secretary of State Charles Evans Hughes, resulted in a series of treaties, each of which involved the United States in Asian power politics. The Five-Power Naval Disarmament Treaty was aimed directly at ending the naval arms race between Japan, Britain, and the United States. The Four-Power Treaty between Britain, Japan, France, and the United States replaced the old Anglo-Japanese Alliance with one that promised only consultations. Both agreements clearly implied American support for the status quo in the Pacific. The Nine-Power Treaty, which merely endorsed the Open Door in China, served to distract critics from the realities of the power relationships being established. American participation in this informal system had one limitation: there could be no prior commitments (entangling alliances?) requiring the use of either economic or military coercion.

The onset of the Great Depression in 1929 eliminated whatever slim chance there might have been of that system developing into a meaningful and long-term entente. Moreover, Germany, China, and the Soviet Union, all excluded from the power structure, soon mounted challenges that spelled the demise of the informal system that had spurned them. The 1930's saw most nations withdraw into themselves, but none more so than the United States. Embittered and cynical about their experience in Europe and the international community following the Great Crusade, Americans indulged in self-recrimination and vowed never again to try to "save" Europe from itself.

In spite of the rising tension caused by Nazi Germany during the early and mid-1930's, Americans opposed any participation by their government in European politics. President Franklin D. Roosevelt, although concerned about the actions of Adolf Hitler, chose to follow the lead of Britain and France. Those nations, eager to avoid a military confrontation, repeatedly asked the United States for firm commitments. The pattern held for all of Hitler's and Benito Mussolini's aggressive moves right up until war began. The remilitarization of the Rhineland in 1935, the Italian invasion of Ethiopia in 1936, the intervention in the Spanish Civil War beginning in 1936, German *Anschluss* with Austria in 1938, and the takeover of Czechoslovakia in 1939, all saw the United States draw away from Anglo-French requests for some sort of alliance. Inaction resulted as each blamed the other for a lack of leadership. Whether an alliance would have prevented a conflict with Germany is questionable; so is the claim that American support would have made the British and the French more courageous in their diplomacy. What is not questionable was the American attitude toward an alliance. The general public, the Congress, and most public leaders believed that alliances caused wars instead of preventing them, and they opposed any such arrangements for the United States.

THE RUDE AWAKENING—WORLD WAR II

Hitler's violation of the Munich Pact of 1938 opened the eyes of French and British leaders, and the outbreak of World War II in September 1939, following Germany's invasion of Poland, forced Americans to reconsider. Still, while they supported the Roosevelt administration's decision to permit the Allies to buy military supplies in the United States, few seriously considered an alliance and intervention. Memories of World War I were too strong. In spite of later claims that public opinion had limited his freedom of action, Roosevelt apparently agreed with the majority of Americans. He understood that Britain and France were fighting America's war, but saw no need for the United States to be anything except what he later labeled "the arsenal of democracy." The collapse of French resistance in June 1940 made the president willing to lend money, equipment, and technical aid to Britain (which culminated in the Lend-Lease Act of March 1941), but he remained convinced, even until early 1941, that a military alliance, and the shedding of American blood, might be avoided.

Hitler's invasion of the Soviet Union made Roosevelt less optimistic, for it raised the specter of a level of German strength that would necessitate American armed intervention, and by the fall of 1941 he had concluded that American intervention was necessary. But it took the Japanese attack on Pearl Harbor to bring the United States into the war. Only then did Americans begin to understand the degree to which an Anglo-American alliance—based upon firm entente—already existed. During 1941 the United States and Great Britain developed a remarkably close relationship at the level of military and logistical planning, based on the probability of an alliance.

Even with such close cooperation, the Anglo-American Entente, like almost all other ententes and alliances, was not an equal partnership. The British found themselves repeatedly in the position of the pleader, while the United States, with its vast economic strength, soon began to act like a senior partner. Only during the early stages of the war, when the overriding concern was the prevention of a defeat at the hands of Germany and Japan, did the two nations meet on equal ground. After it had become clear that victory was certain—roughly about the time of the Teheran Conference in December 1943—the United States more and more frequently forced the British to accept American decisions, particularly with regard to matters affecting the postwar situation.

Problems with what Churchill called the Grand Alliance fell into three categories: military strategy, politics, and economics. Disputes over military strategy found the Americans stubborn and rarely willing to compromise. Exhibiting a strong distaste for consistent British attempts to make war serve politics, particularly the preservation of the empire, American military leaders refused to consider any alternatives that did not combine the quickest and least costly path to victory. Except for the invasion of North Africa, Roosevelt refused to overrule his military chiefs of staff, and that one exception came more from his desire to get American troops into action than because he accepted Churchill's grand strategy. The Normandy invasion, the daylight bombing of Germany, and the invasion of southern France are only the most striking examples of America's insistence upon implementing its own military strategy.

As ever, economics and politics interacted. Economic diplomacy between Britain and the United States, at least as it related to the critically important questions of the structure of the postwar world, found the Americans rigid in their views. That rigidity was modified by the American desire for a postwar political alliance with Britain. Thus, the United States could and did demand that Britain eliminate the Imperial Preference System, which gave special trading benefits to members of the British Empire. The British realized that the system itself had outlived its usefulness; but when the Americans pressed Britain to give up its colonies, the Churchill government dug in its heels. Faced with that response, Roosevelt backed off, partly in order to preserve the wartime alliance, but more and more in the later stages of the war because of his commitment to an Anglo-American political alliance in the postwar world.

A good example of this interplay between economic and political desires is in the case of atomic energy. Early in the war the United States and Great Britain had agreed to work together to develop an atomic bomb. Initially, that cooperation was stimulated by fears that the Germans would develop the bomb first. But midway through the war, once the British had no more to offer, Roosevelt, at the instigation of his advisers, cut off the flow of information on atomic energy to England. They argued that Britain wanted to be privy to the secret in order to use atomic energy for commercial purposes after the war and that sharing nuclear knowledge would tie the United States to England politically—a reference to Britain's colonial problems. When Churchill protested vigorously, Roosevelt changed his mind. Not only had the president begun to worry about Britain's economic problems following the war, but he had come to assume Anglo-American alliance—and their atomic monopoly after the war.

The Anglo-American Entente was the deepest commitment made by the United States during World War II, but the coalition with the Union of Soviet Socialist Republics proved the most important—and the most difficult. Even during the early 1930's Franklin Roosevelt's attitude toward the Soviet Union had been one of practicality and persuasion, and once Hitler had invaded the Soviet Union, the president's nonideological stance made it easy to welcome the Russians as a military partner. Although Roosevelt has frequently been criticized as a political "fixer" rather than a man with an organized grand strategy, he clearly recognized the cardinal fact of the Russo-American coalition: if it defeated Germany and Japan (a certainty after the battles of Kursk, Stalingrad, El Alamein, and Midway—all by mid-1943), the Soviet Union would pose the major barrier to Anglo-American predominance in the postwar world. That left Roosevelt three simple but critical alternatives. First, he could include the Russians in the postwar power structure, hoping they would moderate their political and economic demands. Second, he could begin to confront Soviet power during the war by shaping military planning to meet postwar political needs. Third, he could firmly confront Soviet power late in the war, but only after military victory over Germany and Japan had been assured.

In spite of advice from many, including Churchill, Roosevelt based his policy on the principle that the United States was not fighting one war in order to lay the groundwork for the next. Roosevelt refused to follow the path of confrontation; but cooperation, during and after the war, did not mean simple compliance with every Russian political demand nor did it mean that Roosevelt expected postwar Soviet-American relations to be without serious tensions. He merely emphasized the positive approach in the hope that it would engender a similar response. Nor was the dire warning given Roosevelt about Soviet intentions timely, for most came late in the war and well after most of the basic military strategies had been carried out.

Roosevelt's strategy failed to take into account the magnitude of the Soviet Union's distrust of the capitalist nations as well as his own advisers' intense fear of communism. He was by inclination a believer in personal diplomacy, and the general lack of enthusiasm within the American State Department for a cooperative policy toward the Soviet Union forced Roosevelt to rely even more heavily on his own power and ability to shape events. More significantly, his conciliatory policies were not faithfully reflected by the American bureaucracy. Major changes in foreign policy can occur only when they generate the kind of national support which ensures that subordinates in the executive branch are actually thinking like the leadership. American policy toward the Soviet Union prior to World War II and the anticommunism of the Cold War show that Franklin Roosevelt's cooperative approach—a policy that foreshadowed the idea of "peaceful coexistence"—deviated from the norm of American foreign policy.

How the Soviet leaders, given their own ideological commitments and revolutionary experiences, would have responded to a totally candid and open Anglo-American policy during the war is uncertain. What is clear is that whenever Roosevelt hedged his bets—on the opening of a Second Front, on the Russian role in the occupation of Italy, on aid to left-wing partisan groups in Europe—Soviet leaders invariably accused the Anglo-Americans of playing political games. Although American policy toward Great Britain was frequently characterized by the same level of distrust as with the Russians, for example on the question of the Imperial Preference System, Soviet-American relations did not possess that community of interests that made it possible to transcend the differences. That, in essence, sums up the difference between an entente and a coalition.

The lesser partners in the Grand Alliance of World War II varied from such potential giants as China, to the small Central American states, to latecomers such as the newly constituted Provisional Government of the French Republic, which signed the Declaration of the United Nations in 1945. Intentionally vague, the declaration called only for mutual aid against the Axis nations and promised that no signatory would agree to a separate peace. Convinced that postwar questions were best left to personal diplomacy, Roosevelt refused to consider anything more substantial. American diplomacy during the war centered on the military defeat of the Axis, and relations with the less-important members of the United Nations were largely reserved to integrating their economic resources into the overall war production effort. Individual bureaucrats occasionally initiated and implemented policies that concerned America's postwar economic and political interests, particularly in Latin America, but such actions reflected traditional American attitudes, not any overall plan approved by the president.

Although Roosevelt's conception of a global balance of power—the Soviet Union, the Anglo-American Alliance, an Anglo-French association in western Europe, and eventually China—seems reflected in the Cold War power structure that soon developed, the president's vague ideas possessed a crucial difference: they emphasized cooperation, not distrust.

By the end of World War II, the United States seemed on the verge of a radical departure from past policies. With Harry S. Truman replacing Roosevelt in the White House, alliance diplomacy aimed increasingly at containing and defeating what appeared to be the new enemy, the Soviet Union. The nature of that Cold War determined part of the structure of America's alliance system, but other aspects of alliance diplomacy stemmed from traditional American attitudes.

THE AMERICAN ALLIANCE SYSTEM— AN UNAMERICAN TRADITION

Much has been made of the shift in 1945 and 1946 of some key Republicans, particularly Senator Arthur H. Vandenberg, from apparent isolationism to internationalism. Their approach toward alliance diplomacy demonstrates why that shift was really a logical progression. Isolationism had never argued against alliances per se, only against "entangling" ones. The atomic bomb, when added to America's conventional military strength and to the nation's demonstrable economic might, seemed to guarantee that any participation in alliances would be on American terms. Only the other nations would be entangled. Even the British, rhetorically an equal partner because of the sharing of nuclear weapons, quickly found that economics put them in a secondary role. Participation in the United Nations organization posed no problems, since pro-American states could dominate all voting. Moreover, the United Nations made internationalism appear somehow different from and more moral than balance-of-power politics. Alliances, however, appeared unnecessary until 1947, when clumsy Soviet attempts to influence domestic developments in

Greece and Turkey caused the president to announce the Truman Doctrine. A unilateral pronouncement rather than a negotiated alliance, the results were the same. The United States had committed itself to defend two distant nations—and by implication many more.

Those implications became fact in September 1947, when the Inter-American Treaty of Reciprocal Assistance, the first of many so-called mutual security agreements, came into being. The very label given such treaties—mutual security agreements—testifies to the long-lasting antipathy to the very word "alliance," although it was also a means of making such arrangements seem to fit the United Nations Charter. Although such a Western Hemisphere arrangement, dominated by the power of the United States, was part and parcel of the historic Monroe Doctrine, this particular treaty aimed primarily at preventing internal communist subversion—a concern that related directly to the Cold War.

As Cold War tensions increased, the United States resorted more and more to traditional balance-of-power politics in an attempt to maintain complete control. President Dwight Eisenhower and his secretary of state, John Foster Dulles, have usually been pictured as the architects of the American alliance system, but the bulk of those alliances came into being during the administration of Harry Truman and his secretary of state, Dean Acheson. Following the Berlin airlift and the establishment of Russian hegemony in Czechoslovakia, the keystone of what was to become a worldwide structure of alliances came in April 1949, when, at the instigation of the United States, eleven other nations in the North Atlantic area joined the United States in signing the North Atlantic Treaty. The role played by that treaty in the Cold War is told elsewhere in this volume; but much of America's conception of its own role within that treaty structure existed separately from Soviet-American tension. From the inception of the treaty, the United States used the North Atlantic alliance to pursue two frequently contradictory goals. The treaty was primarily aimed at the military and political containment of the Soviet Union, a function in which the United States, by virtue of its overwhelming military power, dominated all strategic planning. Since the conventional and small nuclear forces of Western Europe depended upon American nuclear weapons to act as the ultimate deterrent against any Russian aggression, the crucial decisions always lay with American leaders. Accordingly, the major NATO commands fell to Americans.

Yet that role as the military leader of the alliance became increasingly offset by American insistence upon Western European unity. At the time that the United States initiated the North Atlantic Treaty it had already begun implementing the Marshall Plan. Although ostensibly designed to promote European economic recovery, the Marshall Plan also added an economic facet to NATO. The long-term program supported by the United States called for economic and political unity among the Western European nations. In a transparent attempt to transfer their own federal system to Europe, Americans consistently demanded that Western Europe work together; first at the economic level and then, it was hoped, at the political level. American leaders spoke jejunely of a "United States of Europe" and frequently seemed to assume that, once European unification had occurred, the United States could pull back into the Western Hemisphere. This new reform movement—reminiscent of the Grand Crusade of three decades earlier—frequently clashed with American images of an evil and fanatical Soviet Russia, so powerful that only American military strength could defend the "Free World." Just as an economically stable Western Europe would eventually be able to compete with American business interests on an even basis, so the political/military strengthening of those nations inevitably meant that the United States would lose the total control of the North Atlantic Alliance that characterized the late 1940's and 1950's.

Initially, the North Atlantic Alliance exhibited great unity and strength under America's leadership, but only when the crisis was in Europe. So long as the Europeans feared Soviet expansion, either by force or subversion, they found NATO useful. But the Korean War, and American attempts to involve all its Allies, found the Western Europeans reluctant to translate a regional defense agreement into a worldwide crusade against communism. In spite of a United Nations resolution that sanctified America's "Police Action" in Korea, the contribution made by the other members of the North Atlantic Alliance was a token one.

Asia posed special problems for the United States. The victory of the communist forces in China in 1949 stimulated an immediate attempt by the Truman administration to contain communism in Asia. In 1951 the United States signed a peace treaty with Japan that provided bases and similar methods of integrating that nation into the American alliance system, even if the Japanese constitution—written by the American government—prohibited the development of any large-scale military forces. Less hypocritical were the mutual defense treaties the United States signed with its ex-colony, the Philippine Islands, and with Australia and New Zealand (the Pacific Security Treaty or, more usually, the ANZUS Pact). Yet those alliances too were a disappointment during the Korean War. Japan had no choice but to provide bases and similar logistical support, but the ANZUS Pact brought little in the way of concrete assistance to American forces.

By 1952 it should have been clear to American leaders that their conception of alliances against worldwide communism differed significantly from that of most of their allies. But the Eisenhower administration refused to reexamine the alliance system, choosing instead to expand it in two areas where the collapse of the European and Japanese colonial empires had left political chaos behind—Southeast Asia and the Middle East. Although specific events frequently stimulated the negotiation of specific alliances, the overarching purpose of the system was geographically obvious. The North Atlantic Treaty, which included Canada, Greece, and Turkey, in addition to the United States and Western Europe, blocked any Soviet expansion to the west, southwest, or north. The Southeast Asia Collective Defense Treaty, prompted by the collapse of French rule in Indochina and fear of the People's Republic of China, completed another portion of the *cordon sanitaire,* which also included Japan, South Korea, and the Republic of China on Taiwan (the last two each signed bilateral alliances with the United States shortly after the Korean Armistice of 1953). The containment ring around Russia and its supposed satellite, China, was nearly completed with the Baghdad Pact of 1955, which brought Iran, Iraq, Pakistan, Turkey, and Great Britain into alliance together. Although the United States never formally joined the alliance (renamed the Central Treaty Organization—CENTO—after Iraq dropped out in 1959 following a coup d'etat against the pro-British Hashimite monarchy), Congress and the president publicly committed America to aid the members in the event of aggression or externally supported subversion. There were large gaps in the geographic encirclement; India and Afghanistan, for example, refused all blandishments from the United States. Nevertheless, American schoolchildren during the 1950's and 1960's, their teachers, and their leaders all revelled in the illusory security of world maps, which imitated the ones that so delighted Englishmen in the nineteenth century. Only this time, the sun never set on an American empire and it was the enemy who were colored pink.

The enormous disparity in economic and military power between the United States and its Southeast Asian and Middle Eastern allies meant that their relationship was that of patron and client. Although Americans claimed to prefer liberal democracies as allies, they did not become involved in the domestic affairs of their clients unless there was communist subversion or aggression. The only criterion for an alliance with the United States became anticommunism. The liberal community in America justified actual or inferred alliances with dictatorships such as those in South Korea, Taiwan, Iran, and Spain because of the greater danger posed by militant, expansionist communism. Such nations had little choice but to accept American leadership, since American military and economic aid provided important props for their regimes.

THE SYSTEM CHANGES

Two events and two long-term developments in the late 1950's and in the 1960's forced major changes in America's alliance system. The events were the Suez crisis of 1956 and the Vietnam War; the developments were the steady relaxation of European fears of Russian aggression and the rise of mainland China as an effective world power.

The Suez crisis of 1956 found Great Britain and France, with Israel joining in for its own reasons, invading Egypt following that nation's nationalization of the Suez Canal. Ostensibly a fight to protect property, the Anglo-French action aimed at the restoration of their influence in the Middle East—influence that had begun to diminish rapidly in the face of rising Arab nationalism. Since the Middle East had not yet become a zone of confrontation between the United States and the Soviet Union, American leaders and the public viewed the Anglo-French action through their traditional prism of anticolonialism. Secretary of State Dulles publicly condemned the two European countries, and, in an ironically cooperative move, joined the Russians in applying intense pressure to force Britain and France to withdraw. Faced with such superpower unity, the two Western European nations had little choice; but the diplomatic defeat at the hands of their longtime ally rankled. British conservatives had nowhere else to go; but a few years later, under the leadership of newly elected President Charles de Gaulle, the French redefined their relationship to the North Atlantic Treaty Organization. Arguing that Korea and Suez had proven that the United States cared only about its own interests and could never be counted on to defend Western Europe (or anyone else), de Gaulle eventually pulled France out of virtually all the political aspects of NATO and withdrew French forces from the NATO military pool. Although the French promised to consider reintegrating their military forces if the need arose, the North Atlantic Alliance had obviously begun to deteriorate.

Still, the NATO alliance would have survived Suez and similar crises intact had the Western European nations continued to fear either massive subversion or outright military attack by the Soviet Union. But those fears, at their height between 1948 and the end of the Korean War, had steadily subsided. Russian-instigated subversion seemed less likely in the wake of the remarkable economic redevelopment of Western Europe, and all the members of the alliance simply assumed that the United States would retaliate with all necessary force in the unlikely event of open aggression. In short, the NATO alliance, like others, possessed a strength directly proportional to the size and immediacy of the jointly perceived threat to its members.

Another foundation of the North Atlantic Alliance, the Anglo-American Entente, also changed drastically in the twenty years following the end of World War II. The outward signs of that change came in such episodes as the *Skybolt* missile debacle. The United States forced the British to accept an American missile system over strong protests from the British military establishment and then failed to put the system into production. But the real problem was the increasing American contempt for the deterioration of the British economy. Although Americans and Englishmen continued to view the world through the same spectacles, the United States no longer looked for Britain to carry its share of the burden. Indeed, Britain appeared to be on the verge of economic and political collapse. Although fears of Britain's complete collapse were exaggerated, the United States refused to treat Britain as even a major partner—equal partnership having disappeared during World War II. Even the Conservative party in the United Kingdom was thus forced to rethink its relationship with Europe. The result—and the apparent end of the Anglo-American Entente—was Britain's decision, reaffirmed in 1975, to join the European Common Market.

THE 1970'S AND AFTER

The North Atlantic Alliance had, by the 1970's, changed significantly from what it had begun as in 1949, but it still remained an important part of international power politics. The curious combination of historical experience, liberal political institutions, and varying but compatible combinations of capitalism, socialism, and the welfare state that characterize Western Europe, Canada, and the United States, provided a vague sort of entente—even though many rejected the proposition that Russia and world communism posed a military threat.

In Asia the situation was far different. Although American leaders tended to believe, at least until the late 1960's, that the People's Republic of China took instructions from Moscow, United States policy still had to react to the reality of increasing Chinese power. Fears of another confrontation with China such as had occurred during the Korean War directed American efforts toward alliances that would guarantee that only Asians would confront

Asians. Supporters and opponents both likened such policies to that of the Roman Empire, which relied upon mercenaries to guard its frontiers. American troops remained in South Korea, but a massive military aid program made the Republic of Korea forces the first line of defense. The Japanese had proven surprisingly reluctant to rearm themselves, and the United States retained military bases in Japan.

The Southeast Asia Treaty Organization of 1954 (SEATO) represented an attempt by the United States to stabilize the political situation in that area by bringing Britain, France, Australia, New Zealand, Thailand, Pakistan, the Philippines, and the United States together after the collapse of French rule in Indochina. With Malaysia, the Philippines, and the nations of Indochina all struggling against communist-led guerrillas, America's alliance diplomacy sought to bolster the existing governments with military and economic aid. Although such aid helped maintain the status quo in Malaysia and the Philippines, the situation in Vietnam seemed to leave the United States no choice between direct military intervention or a communist victory. Working on the assumption that the entire alliance structure in Southeast Asia would collapse one country at a time—like "dominoes"—if Indochina came under communist domination, the United States guaranteed that very result by intervening unsuccessfully. Although the Southeast Asia Treaty remained in force, by the mid-1970's it had lost its effectiveness. Moreover, American requests to the SEATO and NATO nations for military or diplomatic support in Vietnam had met with even less success than during the Korean War. Clearly Western Europe saw no connection between their security and the spread of communism in Asia, particularly since they no longer had colonies to protect.

By 1976, the American system of alliances, so painstakingly constructed after World War II, lay in disarray. Arab nationalism, focused on the problems of the Palestinian refugees and the existence of the state of Israel, had effectively destroyed the Middle East Treaty. Although the ANZUS Pact remained, the defeat of American efforts in Vietnam and the rise of the People's Republic of China brought about American recognition of the Communist Chinese government and a scramble by nations from Australia to Japan to establish friendly relations with the Chinese. Latin America, once so obediently pro–United States in international affairs outside the hemisphere, now shifted to an increasingly anti–United States position as both the political Left and Right vied for public support. Outside of NATO, America's most entangling alliances were with the kinds of governments that the United States had condemned during World War II. Totalitarian regimes in Nationalist China, South Korea, Spain, and Greece all offered bases and staunch anticommunism in return for American economic and military aid. The key alliance, the North Atlantic Treaty Organization, still functioned, but the integration of Britain into Europe, the development of détente between the Soviet Union and the United States, the rise to prominence in many Western European countries of seemingly moderate and democratic Communist parties, and the reestablishment of the West German army as the most powerful in Europe outside the Soviet Union promised to force major alterations in the North Atlantic Alliance as well.

On paper, the Cold War alliance system appeared to be a radical departure from the early American proscription against entangling alliances. Actually, those alliances had never "entangled" the United States. Rather such agreements, whether explicit or implicit, had supposedly served American interests. George Washington might have disputed the argument that America's national interest demanded the worldwide containment of communism, but he would not have rejected on principle a system of alliances as the best way to achieve that goal. Like most American presidents, he was at home in the world of alliance diplomacy and power politics.

BIBLIOGRAPHY

Most material on alliances, coalitions, and ententes is buried in monographs and interpretive studies that are primarily concerned with other matters. Useful sources are Felix Gilbert's stimulating group of essays, *To the Farewell Address: Ideas of Early American Foreign Policy* (Princeton, 1961), which emphasizes the intellectual and ideological attitudes of the Founding Fathers. In *Entangling Alliance* (Durham, N.C., 1958) and the *Quasi-War* (New York, 1966) Alexander DeConde has investigated the French Alliance and its role in both foreign and domestic American politics during the 1790's. Thomas Jefferson's willingness to consider alliances as well as his overall efforts to work within a world dominated by European power politics is imaginatively discussed in Lawrence S. Kaplan, *Jefferson and France* (New Haven, Conn., 1967). Bradford Perkins, in *Prologue to War* (Berkeley, Calif., 1961), explains how the United States managed to enter the Napoleonic Wars without joining either side.

Two short but stimulating essays dealing with nineteenth-century Anglo-American relations are William H. Goetzmann, *When the Eagle Screamed: The Romantic Horizon in American Diplomacy, 1800–1860* (New York, 1966), and Norman Graebner, "Northern Diplomacy and European Neutrality," in *Why the North Won the Civil War* (Baton Rouge, La., 1960).

For the era of Theodore Roosevelt, Howard K. Beale, *Theodore Roosevelt and the Rise of America to World Power* (Baltimore, 1956), Archibald C. Coolidge, *The United States as a World Power* (New York, 1912) and Raymond A. Esthus, *Theodore Roosevelt and Japan* (Seattle, 1966), and *Theodore Roosevelt and the International Rivalries* (Waltham, Mass., 1970), amply illustrate the president's search for closer relationships with the other world powers.

America's attitude toward its European allies during World War I is repeated in all of the standard studies of American diplomacy during that period, although the items cited following the essay on Isolationism in this publication are the most useful. The concept of an informal system is put forth in Akira Iriye, *After Imperialism: The Search for a New Order in the Far East, 1921–1931* (Cambridge, Mass., 1965).

Of the many scholarly studies of American diplomacy during World War II, perhaps the best on Anglo-American relations is Robert E. Sherwood, *Roosevelt and Hopkins* (New York, 1950). A remarkably perceptive study of the anti-Hitler coalition is William H. McNeill, *America, Britain, and Russia* (London, 1953; New York, 1970). It is only slightly outdated by the vast amount of documentation which has become available since it first appeared.

The standard historical study of the North Altantic Treaty Organization is Robert E. Osgood, *NATO: The Entangling Alliance* (Chicago, 1962), although it must be supplemented by more recent studies. Henry Kissinger, *The Troubled Partnership* (New York, 1965), not only defends the continued utility of a revamped NATO, but is helpful for understanding the policies of the Nixon and Ford administrations. Richard Barnet and Marcus Raskin argue, in *After Twenty Years* (New York, 1965), that the alliance has outlived its usefulness and was, by the mid-1960's, contributing to increased world tension.

The broad sweep of alliance diplomacy is examined by ten experts in Arnold Wolfers, ed., *Alliance Policy in the Cold War* (Baltimore, 1959), and Richard Neustadt, *Alliance Politics* (New York, 1970). A recent study of the Sino-Soviet rift as it relates to American foreign policy is Harold C. Hinton, *Three and a Half Powers: The New Balance in Asia* (Bloomington, Ind., 1975).

[*See also* BALANCE OF POWER; COLLECTIVE SECURITY; DÉTENTE; ISOLATIONISM; PEACEMAKING; TREATIES.]

AMERICAN ATTITUDES TOWARD WAR

A. Russell Buchanan

AMERICAN attitudes toward war have varied according to time, circumstances, and the segment of the American people being considered. In view of the difficulties of appraising public opinion accurately, either with or without polls, a brief essay on American attitudes toward war must necessarily be impressionistic rather than definitive. One might start with a few generalizations. During periods of peace, Americans ordinarily have not been interested in war. One does not find "war" societies springing into existence as have "peace" societies. The American people have not subscribed to the thesis of Prussian military writer Karl von Clausewitz that war should be an instrument of national policy, to be employed when useful. When war did come to the United States, the American people on the whole supported it, not necessarily with enthusiasm but as a job to be done as soon as possible.

On the other hand, most Americans did not fall into the pure pacifist camp. If they did not believe in an eye for an eye neither did they advocate turning the other cheek. Possibly as late as World War I, Americans adhered to the doctrine of self-sufficiency for both the individual and the state. Consequently, in time of peace, Americans opposed conscription and a large standing army in the belief that they could lay aside their civilian duties and become soldiers when needed. Although not inclined toward war, many Americans supported the maintenance and strengthening of the nation's military defenses. It was perhaps natural for peace-minded groups to accuse defense organizations of being advocates of war.

If throughout American history there has been a thread of pacifism, it generally has attracted the active interest of only a minority of the people. In times of war, the voice of pacifism has been nearly silenced, and in times of peace, most Americans have been little interested in peace movements as such.

Since American attitudes have varied according to time and circumstances, it is important to examine them chronologically. During the colonial period, the bulk of American wars arose from two factors, the dependent status of the colonies in the British Empire and the presence of Indian populations on the frontier. Colonists accepted wars arising from imperialistic rivalries as a fact of life. They either participated in these conflicts or endured them while playing as inactive a role as possible. As the colonies grew in size and strength, their inhabitants became increasingly concerned with having some part in making the decisions for war or peace, as in the case of the French and Indian War. The colonists viewed war with the Indians as a matter of survival.

Pacifism, as such, had a small following in the colonial period. There were instances of resistance to specific threats of war, but these came over disagreement on policies or practices, not from opposition to war itself. Pacifists consisted primarily of those who objected to war on religious grounds. Leading the list were members of the Society of Friends, or Quakers, who looked on war, which killed human beings created in the image of God, as sacrilege. Consequently, they refused to bear arms. Quakers on the frontier sought with considerable success to conciliate the Indians. When these efforts failed, some, but not all, Quakers supported the use of force, not as war but as an extension of police power.

During the American Revolution, a small percentage of the population continued to oppose war on religious grounds, but there was also opposition from the sizable number of neutrals. In addition to the revolutionaries on one side and the Loyalists, or Tories, on the other, a large proportion of the population—perhaps as high as one third—endeavored to remain uncommitted to either side. For example, some farmers and merchants sold their goods to whichever army happened to be in control of the region. Still others, for personal, ideological, or other reasons, found it difficult to choose between loyalty to England and the causes for independence.

When the new nation came into being, peace was essential, not as a matter of political theory but of survival. The strains were great; the new states tried out one form of government under the Articles of Confederation before turning to the Constitution and embarking upon a federal form of government. There were heavy foreign pressures. The treaty of peace with England, although acknowledging American independence, did not solve all problems between Britain and its former colonies. Crises over maritime trade and the Anglo-American frontier kept alive a threat of renewed war. Relations with France, an ally during the Revolution, degenerated with the advent of the French Revolution. Feelings ran high between the two nations, and there were times when extremists called for war. The first American presidents, realizing how catastrophic a foreign war would be to the young nation, acted to maintain peace. President George Washington stressed these views in his Farewell Address. His successor, John Adams, found the principal threat to peace to come from France. Not a pacifist, Adams early in his administration had made a vigorous statement against France, urged and supported the building of military defenses, and backed the limited, unofficial, Quasi-War with France. Although he went along with this limited strife, Adams saw the dangers of full-scale war. Consequently, over sharp opposition, he sent a mission to Paris that negotiated the Treaty of Morfontaine in 1800, which avoided war and cut the entangling alliance with France.

Thomas Jefferson, elected president in 1800, continued to follow the uneasy path of peace. As it developed, international rivalries of Spain, France, and England aided him in his efforts. Although increased maritime problems took the United States to the brink of war with England, Jefferson believed in the efficacy of economic pressure. After a series of incidents, he took drastic steps and pushed through his Embargo Act of 1807, which prohibited American ships from sailing for foreign ports and placed a heavy bond on interstate trade. Jefferson conceived of the embargo as a means of making the nation more self-sufficient and partly as a device to keep the nation out of war. As an economic weapon the effort failed, but it remains as an interesting example of an effort to find a substitute for war. Jefferson was not an opponent of all war. In the vexatious dealings with the pirates of the Barbary States, after paying tribute for a time, Jefferson launched upon a limited undeclared war to terminate the nuisance. In other words, Jefferson used limited war as an instrument of national policy.

The War of 1812 was one of the most controversial of America's wars. Samuel Eliot Morison, in fact, expresses the opinion that it was "the most unpopular war that this country has ever waged, not even excepting the Vietnam conflict." It was largely a sectional war backed by the West and South and vigorously opposed by New England and New York. The government was unable to build its regular army to one-half its authorized strength or obtain more than 20 percent of the one-year volunteers sought. Even in the West, which had strongly favored war, volunteers were few in number. Yankee Federalists opposed the war, and there was extended opposition to it in other parts of the country. The most extreme step against the war was the calling of the Hartford Convention (1814–1815). There were charges that the purpose was secession, and its official objective was to turn over authority from the federal government to the states. Fortunately for the administration, the delegates actually sent to the convention were moderates and the convention did not meet until late in the war. General rejoicing at the conclusion of the war relegated the work of the Hartford Convention

Charles E. Wilson Library
Anderson College
Anderson, Indiana 46011

129155

to the background. Peace finally came, not from military successes but from Britain's other entanglements and its desire for peace in Europe. Although the peace was no victory for the United States, it did bring to an end the current Indian conflicts on the frontier.

In 1818 an example was set for a means of avoiding war. The Rush-Bagot Agreement between Britain and the United States provided for a limitation of naval armaments on the Great Lakes and Lake Champlain. The agreement did not go as far as it might have; it did not apply to land forces. It did give a start, however, to the concept of an unfortified boundary between the United States and Canada.

The War with Mexico (1846–1848) brought out a number of factors in connection with American attitudes toward war. In the first place, like the War of 1812, it was anything but popular. Involved were such issues as manifest destiny and the desire for western expansion, and mixed with these was the question of the further extension of slavery. Opinions on these matters produced deep divisions within the Whig and Democratic parties, the major parties of the time. The vote for the war bill, 174 to 14 in the House and 40 to 2 in the Senate, is misleading. Frederick Merk insists that the "explanation is found in a momentary hysteria on the part of the public which Polk converted into a stampede."

During the war, harsh criticism of it and of the administration continued. One result was that the Democratic Party while conducting a victorious war lost control of the House of Representatives in the election of 1846. Despite the outcry against the war and the vote against the party in power, even the sharpest critics in Congress did not attempt to obstruct the war effort by voting against military appropriations. How long such support would have continued was not brought to the test, for the United States was fighting a victorious and relatively short war.

Attention turned toward the war's outcome, and it is in this area that American attitudes did have an impact. During the conflict, opinions on war goals ranged from no gains to all of Mexico. The Treaty of Guadalupe Hidalgo (1848), negotiated by American diplomat Nicholas P. Trist, whom President Polk had already ordered home, was presented to the Senate by Polk because it gained the limited objectives for which he had been fighting, including California, and because he was not unaffected by the clamor for peace throughout the country. Frederick Merk concludes: "Dissent moderated the treaty by revealing the dangers of All Mexico and Manifest Destiny."

In a study of American attitudes toward war, the Mexican War was significant in that it produced an important document on dissent. Henry David Thoreau urged "the duty of civil disobedience" against a government that tolerated slavery and fought an unjust war. Thoreau, in other words, supported the concept of individual judgment on a nation's actions.

The Civil War (1861–1865) had Americans, once again, lining up for or against an impending conflict and then supporting the war when it came. Their concerns were with specific issues rather than with the question of war itself. The principal variation, of course, was that this was a fratricidal struggle; it was more difficult to accept with enthusiasm a war between brothers. Furthermore, the issues did not always divide cleanly between North and South. Although many Southerners had been strong unionists, they supported the Confederacy. The people in the border states, regardless of ideological beliefs, felt the impact of war most, since it was there that families were the most likely to break apart and that much of the fighting took place. As the war started, in each of the border states there were sharp struggles, ranging from political maneuvering to actual fighting, to determine which way the state would go.

Both the federal government and the Confederacy resorted to conscription. The South, with less total manpower, acted first, in April 1862. The conscription act was most unpopular with farmers, who objected to exemptions given tradesmen, professional people, and planters and overseers with more than twenty slaves. Still others considered the draft as an infringement upon states' rights. When introduced in the North, the draft provoked even more vigorous opposition, especially among immigrants, who felt that they had not come to the United States to enter military service. The most serious rioting occurred in New York City in July 1863.

The draft law in the North placed conscientious objectors in a difficult position. Quakers and others for religious reasons not only refused to serve in the armed forces but declined to take advantage of the portions of the draft law that permitted a person to avoid the draft either by finding a substitute or paying a commutation fee of $300. Apparently most federal officials had no desire to deal harshly with such persons, although the law toward religious conscientious objectors was strict. Such moderation was not extended toward those who opposed war on other than religious grounds.

As the war progressed, opposition toward its continuance grew. It is difficult to separate the desire for peace from other issues. A group known as Peace Democrats, or "Copperheads," came into being in the North. They vigorously criticized the Republican administration and in places were involved with secret organizations. The Republicans denounced them as traitors; but it appears that their actions were partisan rather than unpatriotic. In the election of 1864, caught between the demands for peace on the one hand and the cries for a more vigorous prosecution of the war on the other, Lincoln ran for reelection, not as a candidate of the Republican party but of a new National Union party, with a unionist Democrat, Andrew Johnson, as his running mate.

In the South, people of Unionist sentiments tended to support the war when it first started. As time went on and as war stringencies increased, antiwar feelings and actions grew in size and nature. Bands of deserters roamed large areas of the South robbing or plundering and finding shelter and support in the backcountry from folk who had no wish for what they considered a patrician war to preserve the institution of slavery. Secret peace societies began to spring up in the South in opposition to a continuance of the Confederacy. Other Southerners showed their dissatisfaction with the government by trading with the enemy. These factors contributed to a weakening of the Confederacy and helped the North achieve a military victory that brought the war to an end.

The Spanish-American War in 1898, as Frank Freidel has expressed it, "was too brief and too successful to be unpopular." The attitudes of the American people, however, played a role both in the war's beginning and in its aftermath. Americans had long been concerned over the lot of Cubans under Spanish rule. An unsuccessful revolution, reports of concentration camps into which large numbers of Cubans had been herded to keep them from supplying insurrectionists, and other incidents of cumulative importance influenced Americans into believing that something should be done for the Cubans. Newspapers, especially those of William Randolph Hearst and Joseph Pulitzer, helped whip this sentiment into a demand for war. Congress and President William McKinley felt the pressure, and, yielding to the demand, McKinley took the nation into war. After a brief conflict, to the surprise of many Americans, the United States emerged as a colonial power, with a protectorate over Cuba and title to Spain's Pacific empire, including the Philippines.

The debate between imperialists and anti-imperialists, which had been going on for some time, reached a high point in the battle over ratification of the Treaty of Paris (1898). Imperialism was in the air; old empires were standing their ground, and young ones, particularly Germany and Italy, were carving out new colonies. Many Americans felt that the industrialized United States should move in the same direction. Interwoven with economic convictions and the desire for status were Darwinian social concepts of survival of the fittest and ideas of the "white man's burden." Anti-imperialists seemed to have the greatest strength in New England. The Senate approved the Treaty of Paris with a margin of only two votes.

By the treaty Spain released its claims to the Philippines; the Filipinos still had to be convinced. Their leaders, like Emilio Aguinaldo, thought that the United States had been fighting to help Filipinos gain their independence. The result of American military efforts to take possession of the islands was a protracted, bitter insurrection.

In the nineteenth century there were numerous attempts to organize the peace movement in the United States. Several societies came into existence during the War of 1812, although only one survived the war period. This was the Massachusetts Peace Society, founded in 1815, which became part of the American Peace Society in 1828. A split developed in the new organization which would be characteristic of the principal difference among peace advocates. One group supported opposition to all war and an individual position of complete nonresistance to violence. Those with the other point of view were more moderate and became interested in gradual reform, political action, and attention to international relations. Then these peace advocates became involved with other social reforms, and further cleavages developed. The American Peace Society was inoperative during and after the Civil War.

In addition to general organizations, there were other movements directed toward specific ways of avoiding or minimizing the risk of war. The idea of arbitration appealed to some; on the national level, in 1874 both houses of Congress passed a resolution requesting the president to include arbitration clauses in future treaties. However, when Presidents McKinley and Theodore Roosevelt did propose arbitration treaties, the Senate rejected them; there were too many reservations regarding national honor and security.

The idea of arbitration led to the emergence of new organizations, such as the Lake Mohonk Arbitration Conferences held from 1894 to 1916. There were two main consequences of these organizations: first, careful studies were made of the implications of arbitration; second, people of great wealth became interested and, in effect, captured the peace movement and made it largely elitist in nature. During this period the search for peace led to the study and development of codes and the general body of principles of international law. For example, American peace groups supported the calling of the Hague Conference. As it developed, the conference became particularly concerned with the rules of warfare and neutral rights rather than the prevention of war.

Between 1914 and 1917, as the United States was drawing nearer to involvement in World War I, varying American attitudes emerged. On the one extreme were ardent supporters of England and its allies, who sought American aid to the Allies even if it meant entering the struggle. The other extreme, opponents of the war, included people of differing motives. There were the pacifists who objected to war of any kind, among whom were members of traditionally pacifist churches. In addition, socialists denounced war as a capitalistic struggle, fought by the laboring man. Pro-Germans also advocated peace, knowing that if the United States should enter the war it would be on the side of the Allies. In the middle was the great mass of the American people. At the outset there was little thought that the United States would be drawn into the war, although there was sympathy, without commitment, for the Allies. During the years of neutrality, this sentiment gradually solidified into a belief that entrance into the war was necessary.

In 1915, the preparedness movement gained headway when President Woodrow Wilson assumed its leadership, not as a means of taking the United States into war but as a safety measure. While people agreed that America should send support to the Allies, peace sentiment was still strong in 1916. Wilson's supporters in the campaign that year made much of the fact that he had kept the nation out of war, and his opponent, Charles Evans Hughes, was careful not to make the war an issue.

After Germany's resumption of unrestricted submarine warfare and Wilson's resultant severance of diplomatic relations with Germany, war appeared inevitable. The advocates of peace made a last desperate effort to keep the nation out of the conflict. Although at the time these people were accused of being pro-German, the charge seems unfounded. The pacifists who formed such groups as the Emergency Peace Federation included many intellectuals. One, David Starr Jordan, president of Stanford University, as a scientist attacked the idea that war resulted in the survival of the fittest. Instead, he argued, modern war slaughtered the fittest. In the last weeks the peace advocates concentrated on Washington and made strenuous efforts to persuade Congress to keep the country at peace. The tide was too strong, and the nation went to war. Jordan and many of the others accepted the verdict and supported their government.

In the period between World War I and World War II, the same alignments continued; there were small pacifist groups and there were supporters of international organizations, including the League of Nations and the World Court. The general attitude, however, was one of disinterest or apathy, stemming from disillusionment over the outcome of World War I and a concentration on domestic issues, first prosperity and later the Depression.

When World War II started, the picture in the United States bore some resemblance to that at the beginning of World War I. There were staunchly pro-Allied Americans who wished to aid the Allies and who would come to want the United States to enter the struggle. There were pro-Germans who realized that the only alternatives were neutrality or aid to the Allies and naturally sought the continuance of neutrality. There were also pacifists who opposed all war. The difference was that the great mass of Americans did not believe, as in 1914, that the United States would not become involved, but instead realized that involvement was a real possibility. President Franklin D. Roosevelt, unlike President Wilson, did not advocate neutrality in mind as well as in action, and it was clear from the beginning where American sympathies lay. The government first attempted to prevent involvement, but as the war continued, American aid to the Allies increased through such steps as the destroyer-base deal and, in the spring of 1941, the Lend-Lease Act, which made the United States in effect an economic belligerent. During the same period, the Neutrality Acts, which had been designed to keep the nation out of war, were altered to make possible greater aid to the Allies.

Opponents of American entry into World War II included a variety of persons and ideologies. In addition to pro-Germans, pacifists, and college students who signed the so-called Oxford Pledge not to fight, there were those who were represented by the America First Committee. This group argued that the nation or, some urged, the Western Hemisphere, should isolate itself and through increasing its own military strength protect itself from the rest of the world. Prominent businessmen, including Henry Ford, supported the group, and one of the principal speakers was Charles Lindbergh, who as a result of European visits was convinced of Germany's strength and that Britain's cause was already lost. Men like these were not pro-German and when war came to the United States gave it their full support.

The pro-Allied mass of Americans did not want war; they did not crave personal involvement, and the experience of World War I made them doubt that any good would come from the second conflict. On the other hand, they believed the cause of the Allies to be just and essential to the future well-being of the United States. Consequently, the nation began to build up its armed forces and its war machine.

The Japanese attack on Pearl Harbor, 7 December 1941, welded American opinion behind the war, and as a result there was probably stronger support for this conflict than for any other in American history. No significant opposition to the war developed once the United States was in it. There were, of course, individual dissenters, and conscientious objectors fell into a number of groups. Objectors on religious grounds did not all react in the same way. Some, like Seventh Day Adventists, were willing to engage in noncombatant duty. Others, like the Friends and Mennonites, carried on relief work as they had done previously. Still others went to conscientious objectors' camps or to jail. Some in the camps were willing to work, for example, in nearby agriculture. Others refused to do anything which in their opinion aided the war effort; the most extreme even resorted to hunger strikes to prove their point.

Generally, the government pursued a more liberal policy toward conscientious objectors than in World War I. For instance, it turned over operation of the conscientious objectors' camps to the pacifist churches. To a considerable degree, conscription was a local matter, and local boards differed in their handling of those who stated that they were conscientious objectors. Normally, there was little question about members of the well-known pacifist churches. The ones who had the greatest difficulty were those who objected to military service on other than religious grounds.

In the immediate postwar years, one could discern various attitudes bearing on war. In general, the people had become internationally minded and supported America's role in establishing the United Nations and becoming a member of it. At the same time, they did not favor disarmament, at least unilaterally, for victory in World War II convinced them of the necessity of maintaining military strength. Attitudes toward the atomic bomb changed. At first, people accepted the bombing of Japan as a military necessity. Then when descriptions of the effects of the bomb on Hiroshima came in, millions were horrified. Numbers of nuclear scientists began to lead in demanding an end to the further production of bombs. For a time they seemed to be making headway, until the Bikini tests occurred; a Gallup poll at that time indicated that people found the bomb to be less destructive than they had anticipated. Further, fear of atomic attack led to widespread support of armaments for protection, rather than of disarmament. Seeing these shifts of opinion, many scientists switched to an effort to obtain international control of nuclear energy. Development of the hydrogen bomb produced a further cleavage of opinion, between those who argued that scientists should aid in its development and those who opposed it on moral grounds.

Another idea that gained widespread support was world federation, which advocated going beyond a United Nations. Pacifists tended to be suspicious of world federation and expressed a belief that the same sort of people would still be in positions of power.

Pacifism rose and fell in popularity in the immediate postwar years. In 1946 Emily Greene Balch, a pacifist leader, won the Nobel Peace Prize, and the next year the award went to the American Friends Service Committee. Interest in peace movements declined; at the same time, however, there arose a new type of pacifist, mainly former conscientious objectors, who instead of joining old peace societies formed new ones. An example was the Committee of Non-Violent Revolution, which in 1948 joined the "Peacemakers," who established cells throughout the country. Inspired by Gandhi rather than Marx, they advocated disobedience as a course of action.

Pacifists devoted a good deal of time to obtaining the release of conscientious objectors still in prison and to ending compulsory military service. They started the practice of burning draft cards as a symbolic act. There was enough general opposition to a draft in peacetime to persuade Congress, in March 1947, to allow the wartime conscription act to expire.

The start of the Korean War seriously damaged the pacifist movement; even World Federalists supported the conflict as police action by the United Nations. That this was the McCarthy era was a large part of the story; peace activities were equated with communism. People became cautious and avoided association with any "causes."

The situation began to change after the middle of the decade. In 1957 scientists and others became concerned over nuclear fallout from tests in the Pacific. A new organization, SANE (National Committee for a Sane Nuclear Policy), combined efforts of pacifists and former supporters of world federation. Demonstrations followed; a few pacifists tried to sail into the bomb test zone, and others picketed federal buildings. In 1960 nonviolent action increased. Demonstrators boarded a few nuclear submarines as a protest, and others started a two-year vigil in front of Fort Detrick, Maryland, known as the germ warfare center. Students, who for some time had not exhibited much interest in peace movements, began to take part. They joined in massive demonstrations against racial segregation and at other times against nuclear armaments.

Although President John F. Kennedy continued a policy of increasing the nation's armaments, he gave pacifists hope by backing the organization of an arms control and disarmament agency. In 1963 they were also encouraged by the announcement of a Soviet-American accord on a nuclear test ban treaty.

With the advent and escalation of the Vietnam War, attitudes became blurred toward war in general and this one in particular. The Vietnam War was one of the most divisive conflicts in the nation's history. Being an undeclared war, it came upon the American people before they were aware of the implications of individual decisions or of the increasing extent of the involvement. Presidential administrations did not really explain such decisions as the following: to defend the French, to replace the French in Vietnam, to support President Ngo Dinh Diem and then turn against him, to increase the number of military advisers, to start air warfare, to engage in ground operations and expand them greatly. Supporters of government policies became "hawks," opponents became "doves," but millions did not take a definite stand.

One side believed in the domino theory; communism was on the move, and if one Southeast Asian country fell the rest would topple like dominoes in a row. Some, like President Kennedy, feared that if the United States lost face in the Far East, McCarthyism would rise again on the domestic scene.

Opposition to the war contained many elements. There were pacifists who opposed all war. There were activists who objected to the war for a variety of reasons, and they came to call the conflict not only mistaken but immoral. Among many charges, they pointed to young Americans who had no interest in the struggle being called upon to fight and die. They decried the modern "conventional" methods of fighting, denouncing the war as immoral and its methods as atrocious. In time others joined; included were politicians who took the arguments into the political arena, hoping to make the war a principal issue in the election of 1968. Senator Eugene McCarthy aroused the excitement of young people but failed to win the nomination in the bitter shambles of the 1968 Democratic Convention in Chicago. Another, Senator Robert Kennedy, was building up a large following until, like his brother President Kennedy and the Reverend Martin Luther King, he was assassinated.

By 1968 the Vietnam War had become more than a limited engagement in the Far East—a part of America's foreign policy, it had become a major domestic issue that threatened to tear the nation apart. The rising protest against continuance of American participation in the war forced President Lyndon B. Johnson to announce that he would not run for reelection. In the election of 1968, the war did not emerge as a clear-cut issue between hawks and doves; by the time of the voting both major candidates were promising that they would end American involvement.

Republican candidate Richard M. Nixon promised that he would terminate the war "with honor." Elected to the presidency, his plan of "Vietnamization"—the replacement of American troops with South Vietnamese troops—produced a divided response among Americans. Many committed to peace thought that this procedure was too slow and that Vietnamization would not work. Others, who had voted for Nixon and who also wanted the war to end, waited more or less patiently for the president to make his moves. Meanwhile, Nixon was making an important shift in policy away from the attempt to contain China. In addition to attempting to negotiate with Hanoi, he began to make overtures to the Chinese government. By the end of 1969, about 20 percent of the American troops had been withdrawn from South Vietnam. In the spring of 1970, North Vietnamese and Vietcong forces moved into Cambodia. Since he felt this action threatened American troop withdrawals from South Vietnam, President Nixon decided upon a limited invasion of Cambodia. The move created a tremendous reaction in the United States, and Nixon found that he had failed to convince the American people of the need for the attack. There were meetings and demonstrations throughout the country; four student demonstrators were killed by National Guardsmen at Kent State.

President Nixon tried to bring reassurance by announcing on 6 May that all United States ground forces would be out of Cambodia by 30 June and that penetration of Cambodia would not exceed twenty-one miles. These promises did not satisfy an aroused Congress, which on 30 June, the day of American troop withdrawals from Cambodia, passed the Cooper-Church amendment, which prohibited the use of funds for military operations beyond the time and space limits that Nixon had announced. Members of the Senate were expressing concern not only over the extension of the war but also the steady increase of executive power, and they demonstrated their concern by repealing the Tonkin Gulf Resolution of 1964, which had given the executive a virtually free hand. Although Nixon verbally challenged the actions of Congress, he did not actually test them, and American troops pulled out of Cambodia.

Public opinion divided sharply over Nixon's actions toward the Vietnamese war. His prolongation of withdrawal to give the Saigon government time to prepare for its own defense made sense to some, but all chafed under the dragging out of a war that continued to exact American casualties.

President Nixon's overtures to China, and his visit to China in 1971, had wide support and indirectly helped bring American involvement in the Vietnam War to an end. In October 1972 American and North Vietnamese delegates in Paris signed an agreement for a cease-fire.

Before withdrawal finally came, Nixon made one more move that produced a strong reaction in the United States. When the North Vietnamese appeared to be changing their position on some of the points in the agreement, President Nixon ordered a renewal of air bombardment of North Vietnam. Congressional leaders were among those calling for an immediate cessation of bombing, and they discussed again the dangers of excessive executive power. Nixon, in response, cut back the bombing as chief negotiator Henry Kissinger continued his bargaining. He negotiated a new agreement, and American involvement began to come to an end. President Nixon appeared to have weathered the storm and won a landslide reelection victory in November 1972. One of the factors involved was general relief that the United States was at last practically out of the war. The mood throughout the country was strongly for peace. What it would become in the future would again be a matter of time, circumstances, and the segment of the American people examined.

In recent years the American people have been concerned primarily with domestic matters: Watergate, the election of President James E. Carter, inflation, and numerous aspects of the energy problem. They have been interested secondarily in foreign affairs, including Soviet-American rivalry, the reopening of relations with China, problems of the Mideast, and Africa. Throughout, the impulse toward peace remains strong; and while sympathies are shown toward various peoples and causes, the American people firmly oppose American military involvement that might lead either to another Vietnam or to a third world war.

BIBLIOGRAPHY

See Thomas A. Bailey, *The Man in the Street: The Impact of American Public Opinion on Foreign Policy* (New York, 1948); Leo Bogart, *Silent Politics: Polls and the Awareness of Public Opinion* (New York–London–Sydney–Toronto, 1972); Charles Chatfield, ed., *Peace Movements in America* (New York, 1973); Merle Curti, *Peace or War: The American Struggle 1636–1936,* 2nd ed. (Boston, 1959); Staughton Lynd, ed., *Nonviolence in America: A Documentary History* (Indianapolis–New York–Kansas City, 1966); Samuel Eliot Morison, Frederick Merk, Frank Freidel, *Dissent in Three American Wars* (Cambridge, Mass., 1970); Lawrence S. Wittner, *Rebels Against War: The American Peace Movement, 1941–1960* (New York–London, 1969); and Quincy Wright, *A Study of War,* 2nd ed. (Chicago–London, 1965), with a commentary on war since 1942.

[*See also* ANTI-IMPERIALISM; THE COLD WAR; CONSCRIPTION; DISSENT IN WARS; IMPERIALISM; MILITARISM; PACIFISM; PEACE MOVEMENTS; PUBLIC OPINION.]

ANTI-IMPERIALISM

E. Berkeley Tompkins

THE United States had its origin in the struggle for empire of several Old World powers; and the nation was born out of a reaction against British imperial tyranny. In this context one might, perhaps, plausibly argue that the United States has an extensive heritage of anti-imperialism. On the other hand, it must be noted that territorial expansion of several kinds played a very prominent role in the United States during the nineteenth century, and the American people in this period displayed an ambivalent attitude vis-à-vis imperialism and its manifestations.

From the comparatively small nation hugging the eastern seaboard which was created by throwing off the shackles of British imperialism at the end of the eighteenth century, the United States steadily expanded westward in a series of diplomatic and military maneuvers, which in the context of the history of Europe and Asia could only be regarded as empire-building. The acquisition of Florida, the Louisiana and Oregon territories, Texas, and the vast region ceded by Mexico after the Mexican-American War created a huge continental empire. Still, in the heady aura of manifest destiny in the mid-nineteenth century, there were those who maintained this was too small a territory, and in hyperbolic rhetoric called for the acquisition of more and more land, regardless of the desires or feelings of the indigenous inhabitants. In the 1850's land-hungry politicians and others advocated, and not infrequently demanded, the acquisition of Mexico, Central America, Cuba, Hawaii, Haiti, and the Dominican Republic; and a number of the arguments and counterarguments of American imperialists and anti-imperialists were first enunciated at this juncture.

Cursory feints, however, toward the acquisition of insular possessions prior to the Civil War proved abortive. The times and public opinion were not yet ripe for this newer kind of imperialism involving the seizure of overseas territory. Moreover, the many complex domestic problems that ultimately resulted in the Civil War temporarily turned attention and energy away from overseas expansion. Thus, at mid-century the most important problem for the United States was not extension of the national domain, but, rather, the need to keep the existing territory from being ripped asunder. The Union was preserved, but only as the result of a lengthy internecine struggle, which left the people of the nation physically enervated, emotionally exhausted, financially burdened, and in no mood to undertake risky foreign ventures.

There were some men even in this fallow period of imperial endeavor who wished to revivify national interest in a broad expansionist policy. For example, Secretary of State William Seward sought to match his Alaskan coup by further extending American hegemony; but he was frustrated in this desire and lamented that "public attention . . . continues to be fastened upon the Domestic questions which have grown out of our late Civil War. The public mind refuses to dismiss these questions even so far as to entertain the higher but more remote, questions of national extension."

In the ensuing two decades, the nation experienced a profound transformation, which set the stage for the great debate over American imperialism that occurred at the turn of the century. During this period the United States changed from a predominantly agricultural nation preoccupied with the development of a virgin continent to a vigorous industrial colossus seeking new markets abroad. Competition for markets led to competition for colonies, and the United States sought to emulate the older European empires. This trend received further intellectual stimulation from the widespread acceptance of the tenets of social Darwinism, which maintained that nations, like biological organisms, must engage in a primordial struggle leading to the "survival of the fittest." By 1890 the stage was set economically, politically, and emotionally for a major alteration in American policy, and the surge of specific events in the final tumultuous decade of the nineteenth century caused abstract imperial theory to be put into actual practice by the United States government.

This dramatic change in American foreign policy elicited a strong adverse reaction. This reaction, anti-imperialism, developed concomitantly with the growth of imperialist sentiment in the United States. Although the tangible symbols of America's insular empire—Hawaii, the Philippines, Samoa, Guam, and Puerto Rico—were not acquired until the last two years of the century, the ideological struggle between the imperialists and anti-imperialists began almost a decade before the Spanish-American War and lingered on, although diminished in intensity, for a number of years afterward.

Thus, from approximately 1890 to 1904 anti-imperialism was a significant phenomenon in American history. Much of the controversy between the imperialists and anti-imperialists in this era was manifested in the form of an extended and vigorous debate, with charges and countercharges, presentations and rebuttals filling the nation's journals and echoing in the halls of Congress. The anti-imperialists felt that this issue was, in the words of George F. Hoar, one of their leaders in the Senate, "the greatest ever discussed from the beginning of our government"; and they believed that they were fighting to preserve the very life of the nation as a democratic republic. The anti-imperialists contended that imperialism represented a flagrant violation of the fundamental principles on which the government of the United States was based. They emphasized that the United States viewed itself as the champion of liberty, democracy, equality, and self-government and that imperialism constituted a direct denial of the universal validity of these tenets.

The anti-imperialists believed strongly in the traditional American policy of avoiding foreign entanglements, which had its genesis in Washington's Farewell Address and Jefferson's First Inaugural. They doubted the validity of the imperialists' confident and sweeping predictions of the course of universal destiny. They questioned the inherent value of an expanding military establishment and decried the growth in the 1890's of chauvinism and jingoism.

The initial departure from traditional American foreign policy was occasioned by increasing American involvement in the affairs of Samoa, which resulted in a treaty, signed in June 1889, providing for a tripartite (with Germany and Great Britain) condominium that would control the formerly independent island kingdom. The anti-imperialists denounced this move as a "dangerous departure" from "tried and true" United States policy and predicted that it would set a dangerous precedent. They were proven right in 1893 when an attempt was made to annex the Hawaiian Islands.

The gentlemen who headed the State Department in the early 1890's, James G. Blaine and John W. Foster, strongly favored American annexation of Hawaii and labored assiduously, if discreetly, to bring it about. John L. Stevens, the American minister in Hawaii, aided a revolution that in January 1893 deposed the Hawaiian monarch and instituted a nonrepresentative government of American sugar planters who favored annexation by the United States. An attempt was made to railroad a treaty of annexation through the Senate, claiming principally that the islands would be a great military and economic asset to the United States. A determined group of anti-imperialists, however, frustrated the plans of the outgoing Republican administration to obtain passage of the treaty before Grover Cleveland's return to office.

In his first inaugural in 1885, Cleveland had made it quite clear that he was unalterably opposed to "a policy of acquisition of new and distant territory," and the two most important members of his new cabinet in 1893, Secretary of State Walter Q. Gresham and Secretary of the Treasury John G. Carlisle, shared Cleveland's anti-imperialist views. The Democratic administration's opposition to imperialistic moves received vigorous support in the nation's leading journals from a group of intellectuals, academicians, and jurists, which included Theodore D. Woolsey, E. L. Godkin, Carl Schurz, Eugene T. Chamberlain, Frederic R. Coudert, William M. Springer, James Schouler, George T. Curtis, and Thomas M. Cooley.

A series of events, however, in another island halfway around the world from Hawaii, was to bring the question of imperialism to the fore once again several years later. Cuba had been coveted by American expansionists for many years. Half a dozen presidents—most notably James K. Polk and Franklin Pierce—had contemplated annexation. With the return of expansionist ardor in the 1890's, Cuba once again was frequently mentioned as a logical target for annexation. In July 1895 *American Magazine of Civics* conducted an extensive symposium on the subject of Cuban annexation, which revealed that there was a wide diversity of national opinion on the subject. One of the most significant matters debated at this time was the question of whether the United States should accord belligerent rights to the insurgents who were seeking independence from Spain. The imperialists favored intervention in Cuba as a prelude to annexation, and the anti-imperialists opposed it for the same reason. The anti-imperialists' consistently greater respect for the amenities of international law undoubtedly also influenced their support of strict neutrality on the part of the United States.

Although rising and diminishing in intensity, the debate between the American imperialists and anti-imperialists continued throughout the 1890's. In a notable article, "The Menace of Pseudo Patriotism" (*North American Review* [February 1897]), Edward Chapman castigated the chauvinism of the imperialists and their journalistic abettors and presented an epitome of the anti-imperialist position. Foreseeing some such incident as the sinking of the *Maine,* he warned that "in an international crisis, when great issues hang in the balance and popular excitement runs high, a democracy contains no more dangerous element than that which would stimulate so-called patriotic passion to gain a vote or sell a newspaper." Chapman and his fellow anti-imperialists were concerned that the jingoes might convince the nation to follow the siren song of imperialism. "Nothing," he cautioned, "can more surely militate against the fulfillment of our national mission than our adoption of that military imperialism which is leading the nations of Europe into a labyrinth of increasing complexity and difficulty."

Such views, however, had less influence than the saber rattling of Henry Cabot Lodge, Alfred T. Mahan, and Theodore Roosevelt. Having entered office on a platform that called for a "firm and vigorous" foreign policy, control of the Hawaiian Islands, an isthmian canal, strategic naval bases, and demonstrative action vis-à-vis Cuba, President William McKinley—goaded by more belligerent members of his party and by the "yellow press"—led the nation into war against Spain in April 1898. On 1 May, just one week after the formal declaration of a war supposedly initiated solely to liberate Cuba, Commodore George Dewey steamed into Manila Bay and annihilated the Spanish fleet there. One of the principal by-products of this phenomenal action was a reawakening of interest in the annexation of the Hawaiian Islands.

Declaring "we need Hawaii as much and a good deal more than we did California; it is Manifest Destiny," McKinley arranged for a treaty of annexation, which was submitted to the Senate in June 1897. The traditional reluctance, however, to acquire territory overseas would not allow the administration to muster the two-thirds majority in the Senate to ratify the treaty. Therefore, in the spring of 1898 it was decided to seek approval for annexation through a joint congressional resolution, which requires only a simple majority for passage. It was at this point that Admiral George Dewey's overwhelming victory at Manila Bay brought the long debate over Hawaiian annexation to a climax; for the imperialists' most persuasive argument was that the islands were vital to the nation's new sphere of imperial interest in the Pacific.

The question of Hawaiian annexation marked a crucial turning point in the struggle between the imperialists and anti-imperialists, and both sides marshaled their forces accordingly. The imperialists' range of arguments was much narrower than their opponents' and came down basically to the contention that the islands were of great strategic and military value. The anti-imperialists countered with a host of negative arguments. They immediately offered critiques of the claim that Hawaii was a military necessity. They pointed out the great distance of Hawaii from the mainland and argued that it would be more of a liability than a military asset, since it would be a difficult outpost to defend.

The anti-imperialists claimed that annexation of any territory would pervert the lofty motives with which the United States had entered the war, and observed that President McKinley at the inception of the hostilities had specifically disavowed a desire for the acquisition of overseas possessions. Extending their arguments beyond the war, per se, they objected to annexation on the ground that it would require a permanent military establishment along European lines and that a large army and navy were opposed to American tradition and would require huge military expenditures and greatly increased taxes.

In the course of the congressional debates, the anti-imperialists constantly reiterated their fear that annexation would be, in the words of Senator William B. Bate of Tennessee, "the commencement of indefinite extension of our territory." They contended, moreover, that Hawaiian annexation would constitute "a dangerous precedent," and they predicted that if the United States took Hawaii, Spain's colonies would be next on the list.

The anti-imperialists felt that the causes of the war with Spain should have taught the United States something about the deleterious effects of colonialism. They contended, furthermore, that imperialism was a "dangerous departure" from traditional American foreign policy, which they viewed as proven by long experience to be beneficial. One element of American foreign policy that the anti-imperialists believed would be particularly jeopardized was the Monroe Doctrine. For example, Congressman John C. Bell of Colorado claimed that the acquisition of overseas territory would operate "ipso facto as a renunciation of our further intention to maintain the Monroe Doctrine and would proclaim that we had joined the horde of European greed in attempting to absorb as many of the weaker powers on earth as possible."

It was argued that the adoption of imperialism constituted a renunciation not only of traditional American foreign policy but also of the basic principle of American polity that governments derive their just powers from the consent of the governed. The anti-imperialists believed that it was immoral to govern subject peoples, and those who had earlier been active in the abolitionist movement often compared imperialism to slavery. On the other hand, neither the imperialists nor anti-imperialists advocated United States citizenship for the peoples of the islands. While the principal leaders of the anti-imperialist movement in the United States—the officers of the Anti-Imperialist League—were among the staunchest friends of the non-white races in the United States of their era, a noticeable element in the congressional objection to Hawaiian annexation was racial. This was founded partly on prejudice, partly upon the pragmatic consideration that the United States already had a plethora of unresolved racial problems, and partly on the extant United States laws that excluded Orientals.

To a certain extent the racial issue was related to the objection that colonialism would be detrimental to American labor, and Samuel Gompers, the president of the American Federation of Labor, complained that it would "threaten an inundation of Mongolians to overwhelm the free laborers of our country." Likewise, American agricultural interests, particularly in the South, feared the possible detrimental effect upon the domestic sugar industry.

While the debate over imperialism centered upon the nation's foreign affairs, many anti-imperialists were greatly disturbed by what they felt would be the unfavorable reverberations upon the domestic scene, and they frequently stressed the point that adoption of colonialism would divert attention from a host of pressing domestic problems.

Finally, a consistent anti-imperialist argument over a period of many years was that the Constitution did not provide for the acquisition of colonies and that the whole imperialistic apparatus was unconstitutional. In the particular case of Hawaiian annexation, there was the additional argument that the very means of effecting it, that is, the joint resolution, was an evasion of the regular constitutional process.

Neither law nor logic, however, could hold

sway against the emotional surge in favor of imperialism generated by the war with Spain. The passage of the joint resolution for the annexation of Hawaii, which established a definite precedent soon to be followed in the acquisition of other insular dependencies, was effected by a considerable margin in the House on 15 June 1898 and in the Senate on 6 July. By that time the question of Hawaiian annexation had been vigorously debated for over five years, and the major and minor points on both sides had been skillfully presented many times by able and articulate spokesmen. The new and decisive element interjected in 1898 was the war, which provided the requisite catalyst for the inception of the overseas empire.

Although various individuals in Congress, the press, and elsewhere had for almost a decade fought the drift of the nation toward imperialism, it was not until the summer of 1898 that a concerted movement to organize the opposition to colonialism found formal expression in the creation of a number of "anti-imperialist leagues" in major cities throughout the nation. At the apogee of the movement (1898–1900) these leagues claimed a following of over 700,000 people scattered throughout forty-five states and five territories. It was, however, the original organization founded in Boston in November 1898 by a group of prominent New England intellectuals and reformers, and known throughout most of its twenty-two-year existence (1898–1920) as the Anti-Imperialist League, which provided the real spearhead of the anti-imperialist movement in the United States. An analysis of the fifty-two officers of the original Anti-Imperialist League reveals the essence of the nature of the cause.

Some commentators have viewed the anti-imperialist leaders as a disparate group, but actually, while atypical of the general American population, they had much in common with one another. To begin with their most obvious characteristic, they were all male. The number of well-educated men is remarkable. At a time when less than one percent of the population had a college education, 73 percent of these gentlemen had college degrees (largely from Harvard and Yale), and 50 percent of them had graduate training. From an occupational standpoint they were also exceptional. The great majority were professional people. Lawyers predominated; almost half of the league's officers had been admitted to the bar, and this group included such outstanding attorneys as George F. Edmunds, Edwin B. Smith, Henry W. Rogers, Moorfield Storey, and James C. Carter—the latter two both serving as president of the American Bar Association. The league's officers included some of the nation's most distinguished clergymen, such as Henry C. Potter, Episcopal bishop of New York; Leonard W. Bacon; Charles H. Parkhurst; and Theodore L. Cuyler. There were also many famous editors, who were particularly articulate and demonstrative in their critiques of imperialism, including Samuel Bowles of the *Springfield Republican,* Herbert Welsh of *City and State,* Patrick Ford of the *Irish World,* Emil Preetorius of the *St. Louis Westliche Post,* and Herbert Myrick, the foremost editor of agricultural publications in the country. The anti-imperialist cause was especially vigorously supported in the nation's universities, and the league's officers included such leading educators as Hermann Eduard von Holst of the University of Chicago; Felix Adler of Columbia; William Graham Sumner of Yale; Henry W. Rogers, president of Northwestern University; and David Starr Jordan, president of Stanford.

The typical anti-imperialist was a white, Anglo-Saxon Protestant, from an upper middle class, fifth or sixth generation American family, who had a strong belief in traditional values. The anti-imperialists were very serious, idealistic men, whose basic creed involved a particularly strong belief in liberty, political equality, and self-government—to all of which imperialism was antithetical. They essentially wished to preserve the political ideas and foreign policy goals that were a product of the late eighteenth century. Economically they were overwhelmingly advocates of free trade and "sound money." Politically they were divided into four general groups. First, there were the regular members of the Republican party, including notable men like George S. Boutwell, George Franklin Edmunds, and John Sherman. Second, there was a particularly large representation of the liberal wing of the Republican party—the so-called mugwumps, including Thomas Wentworth Higginson, Samuel Bowles, Carl Schurz, and Moorfield Storey. Both of these groups had originally been drawn to the Republican party by its opposition to slavery, and they strongly equated abolitionism with anti-imperialism. A third group was composed of apostate Republicans who styled themselves independents, such as Charles Francis Adams, Jr., and Edward Atkinson. The fourth political group of importance consisted of members of the economically conservative wing of the Democratic party, such as Grover Cleveland, John G. Carlisle, and Winslow Warren. Finally, the most salient characteristic of the anti-imperialist leaders was their intense devotion to a host of interrelated reform movements, including abolitionism, pacifism, and civil service reform; but they viewed anti-imperialism as their most significant crusade.

From 1898 to 1900 these eminent and gifted men flooded the country with anti-imperialist literature; held hundreds of meetings, conferences, and rallies to oppose colonialism; provided speakers for all occasions; raised many crucial questions; and contributed importantly to public thinking on the subject. They deplored the probable effects of imperialism upon the American economy, fiscal structure, national institutions, and political principles; and they emphasized the myriad problems inherent in the adoption of a colonial policy.

After their failure to stop the annexation of Hawaii, the next crucial test for the anti-imperialists was the ratification of the Treaty of Paris, which called for the annexation of the Philippines, Guam, and Puerto Rico. It was submitted to the Senate in January 1899. The question of annexing the Philippines raised the same issues as Hawaii, except that these islands were even farther away and had a larger and more diverse population, greater linguistic, racial, cultural and religious differences, and no former ties with the United States. Although the majority of the opponents of the Republican administration's policy naturally were Democrats, the leader of the opposition to the treaty was one of the most respected elder statesmen of President McKinley's own party—Senator George Frisbie Hoar of Massachusetts. Surprisingly, at the final hour, William Jennings Bryan, who had been stumping the country denouncing the administration's imperialistic policy, urged his followers to support the ratification of the treaty, and with this added fillip, it passed by the narrowest of margins, thereby creating a true American overseas empire.

Frustrated in their attempt to block the takeover of the Philippines by defeating the Treaty of Paris, the anti-imperialists sought to turn the election of 1900 into a referendum on imperialism that might reverse the administration's policy. A combination of personalities, ideologies, and events, however, doomed this attempt to failure. Although the anti-imperialists labored assiduously, it was to no avail, and the selection of William Jennings Bryan as the Democratic standard-bearer muddied the political waters. It has been suggested by some commentators that the officers of the Anti-Imperialist League were ineffective in this election because of their diverse political backgrounds. They were, however, men who largely placed principle above party; therefore, many of them in remaining loyal to their principles were not disturbed by shifting party allegiance. But in the election of 1900 they were hampered not so much by conflicting political ties, as by conflicting principles and ideologies. Although many of them doubted Bryan's sincerity, they were pleased by his espousal of anti-imperialism. But they abhorred his flamboyance, economic radicalism, and curious behavior vis-à-vis the Treaty of Paris; and this greatly weakened the effectiveness of the anti-imperialists in this crucial election.

The election of 1900 marked the zenith of the debate over imperialism in the United States. The debate continued, but with gradually and steadily diminishing intensity. Each year after the turn of the century witnessed the demise of an increasing number of the original leaders of the movement; and their places were not filled by men of comparable stature and devotion to the cause. Moreover, the infirmities and lessening vigor of advancing years greatly reduced the effectiveness of the original leaders. The numbers and strength of the anti-imperialist organizations also steadily declined after 1900. The weaker ones naturally dissolved first, and by 1904 the original league was the only viable organization left in the field.

The remaining anti-imperialists continued to agitate for Philippine independence and for better treatment of the Filipinos in the interim. Whenever an incident such as Theodore Roosevelt's backing of the Panama revolt in 1903 gave them an opportunity, they did what they could to rally their forces and reawaken interest in the anti-imperialist cause. But as time went by, there was comparatively less need for their strictures. By 1905 imperialism had lost much of its tinseled appeal for the American people, and Moorfield Storey, the president of the Anti-Imperialist League, commented that "the wave of imperialism which reached this country in 1898 and for a while threatened to drown our people's faith in the great principles of free government has spent its force and the tide is ebbing fast." The current of public opinion drifted more strongly in the direction that the anti-imperialists desired, and by 1908 David Haskins, the long-time treasurer of the league, could correctly claim that "the enthusiasm for colonies is dead."

The "custom house interventions" by the United States in Santo Domingo, Nicaragua, and Honduras briefly rekindled some of the old fires and received cursory, if occasionally vehement, criticism from the Anti-Imperialist League, but no large sustained campaign was mounted against these moves, principally because no attempt was made to annex these areas, as had been done in the case of Hawaii and the Philippines. The latter remained, as it had always been, the fundamental interest of the anti-imperialists. A statement issued in 1916, for example, proclaimed that "the Anti-Imperialist League maintains with faith and courage its special work of obtaining, by the establishment of Philippine independence, relief from the anomalous and dangerous responsibility of holding and defending remote possessions." The passage in August 1916 of the Jones Act (the Organic Act of the Philippine Islands) granting the Filipinos a greater measure of self-government and providing for eventual independence was applauded by the anti-imperialists. Although they would have preferred immediate independence, they felt that the principles for which they had labored so long and earnestly had now been officially vindicated.

The Anti-Imperialist League lingered on in a formal sense until 1920, but in its latter stages it was merely a single group of aging Bostonians who issued sporadic communiqués and met annually to repledge their personal allegiance to a cause that was once the cynosure of national politics.

Viewed in perspective, anti-imperialism as a philosophy and later as a movement, while unsuccessful in its immediate aims, had a meaningful role in American history in the decade between 1892 and 1902. At a time when the United States was initiating a major change in its foreign policy, the anti-imperialists insisted, in the best democratic tradition, that the matter should be thoroughly debated; and they forcefully and repeatedly pointed out the myriad grave problems, of both a philosophical and pragmatic nature, which stemmed from the adoption of an imperialist policy. Their constant agitation eventually had a cumulative effect, especially when combined with the bitter practical experience of subduing and governing the Philippines. In a way, their experience was like that of a number of minor parties in American history which have been rejected by the voters but whose ideas have ultimately won wide acceptance.

Compared to the major European nations that built colonial empires, which they maintained over a long period of time, the acquisition of colonies by the United States was both limited and relatively short-lived; and the principal colony, the Philippines, was granted independence voluntarily. As in almost every major historical question, multiple factors were involved in the limitation and eventual renunciation of imperialism by the United States, but the contributions of the anti-imperialists must certainly be given their full measure of credit.

Although anti-imperialism as a concerted movement was a significant factor in American history for a relatively brief period of years, ideas and arguments which it engendered have been resuscitated and reiterated periodically (for example, during the debate over Vietnam) and today form an integral part of American foreign policy.

BIBLIOGRAPHY

The primary source material on anti-imperialism is extensive because the issue was debated in Congress and principal newspapers for more than a decade. The principal repositories of anti-imperialists' papers are the Library of Congress (for example, Schurz, Storey, Andrew Carnegie, John Sherman, Grover Cleveland, and others), the Houghton Library of Harvard University (the papers of Godkin, T. W. Higginson, and William James) and the Massachusetts Historical Society (the papers of George F. Hoar, Edward Atkinson, and Charles Francis Adams, Jr.).

The two major works on the subject are Robert L. Beisner, *Twelve Against Empire: The Anti-Imperialists: 1898–1900* (New York, 1968); and E. Berkeley Tompkins, *Anti-Imperialism in the United States: The Great Debate: 1890–1920* (Philadelphia, 1970, 1972). The latter is the most extensive treatment and contains the only comprehensive bibliography available on American anti-imperialism (pp. 297–331).

See also Donald M. Dozer, "Anti-Expansionism During the Johnson Administration," in *Pacific Historical Review,* 12 (1943); J. A. S. Grenville and George B. Young, *Politics, Strategy and American Diplomacy, 1873–1917* (New Haven, 1966); Fred H. Harrington, "The Anti-Imperialist Movement in the United States, 1898–1900," in *Mississippi Valley Historical Review,* 22 (1935); Fred H. Harrington, "Literary Aspects of American Anti-Imperialism," in *New England Quarterly,* 10 (1937); David Healy, *U.S. Expansionism: The Imperialist Urge in the 1890's* (Madison, Wisc., 1970); Walter LaFeber, *The New Empire: An Interpretation of American Imperialism, 1860–1898* (Ithaca, 1963); Ernest R. May, *American Imperialism: A Speculative Essay* (New York, 1968); Richard H. Miller, ed., *American Imperialism in 1898* (New York, 1970); Milton Plesur, *America's Outward Thrust: Approaches to Foreign Affairs, 1865–1890* (DeKalb, Ill., 1971); Daniel B. Schirmer, *Republic or Empire* (Cambridge, Mass., 1972); E. Berkeley Tompkins, "Scylla and Charybdis: The Anti-Imperialist Dilemma in the Election of 1900," in *Pacific Historical Review,* 36 (1967), and "The Old Guard: A Study of the Anti-Imperialist Leadership," in *Historian,* 30 (1968); Richard E. Welch, "Senator George Frisbie Hoar and the Defeat of Anti-Imperialism, 1898–1900," in *Historian,* 26 (1964); Richard E. Welch, *Imperialists Vs. Anti-Imperialists* (Itasca, Ill., 1972); and Leon Wolf, *Little Brown Brother* (London, 1961).

[*See also* American Attitudes Toward War; Colonialism; Imperialism; Isolationism; Manifest Destiny.]

ARBITRATION, MEDIATION, AND CONCILIATION

Calvin D. Davis

SINCE the earliest days of the Republic, Americans have been interested in developing peaceful methods other than negotiation for settling international disputes. Arbitration, judicial settlement, mediation, and conciliation have all appeared in connection with important chapters in the diplomatic history of the United States. Of these methods arbitration has been the most important. In fact, it was a major aspect of American foreign policy before World War I and was of profound influence upon American thinking about international organization before that war.

International arbitration may be defined as the settlement of a difference between states through the decision of one or more individuals or a tribunal or court chosen by the parties to the dispute. An arbitrator may be the chief of state of a nation not concerned with the dispute, an ambassador, a minister, or other official, or even a private individual. When a monarch or a president is an arbitrator he usually does not act personally; indeed, he delegates most responsibilities to the appropriate legal authorities of his government. When the parties to an arbitration decide to establish a tribunal, they may choose judges from their own nationals and then agree upon another individual to act as umpire. Sometimes they ask the head of another government to choose an umpire, or leave the choice of an umpire to the arbitrators already appointed. In several nineteenth-century cases no individuals were designated as umpires. Arbitrations may be concerned with questions of international law or facts. When arbitrations are primarily concerned with facts, as in pecuniary claims or boundary cases, the group of arbitrators is generally called a commission, but no precise distinction can be drawn between commissions and tribunals. An arbitral decision is called an award, and it may be set aside if there are reasons to believe that it was not given in good faith or was not in accord with international law or the preliminary special agreement, usually called a *compromis,* concluded by the parties to the arbitration.

Historians and anthropologists have discovered arbitral customs and institutions in many cultures. The city-states of ancient Greece developed fairly elaborate arbitral procedure; on occasion they organized groups of arbitrators similar to modern international tribunals. During the Middle Ages popes, princes, jurisconsults, and even city governments acted as arbitrators. Arbitration was less important during late medieval and early modern times, but it never disappeared altogether from international relations. Occasionally European governments made use of it when trying to resolve American questions. In fact, some aspects of the first problem in the diplomatic history of the European conquest of the Western Hemisphere—the location of the dividing line between Spanish and Portuguese interests—suggest later arbitral practices. When Portugal challenged Spain's rights in the lands Columbus had discovered, King Ferdinand asked Pope Alexander VI to confirm the Spanish title. The pontiff obliged, issuing in 1493 a series of bulls in which he drew a line between the imperial claims of the two countries. The

Portuguese protested the papal decision, and in 1494 Spain and Portugal, in the Treaty of Tordesillas, moved the line westward and agreed that a commission of surveyors and mariners should locate the line. While the two governments never set up the commission, the provisions of the treaty calling for such a body are evidence that commissions were of some importance in international relations at that time.

Commissions appeared occasionally in connection with England's colonial problems during the seventeenth and eighteenth centuries. The Treaty of Westminster, which Cromwell concluded with the Dutch at the end of the First Anglo-Dutch War in 1654, referred claims concerning the East Indies and the Americas to a commission. Apparently this commission met but failed to arrive at a decision. England and France in 1686 referred disputes over American matters to a commission, but it disbanded after outbreak of the War of the League of Augsburg. The Anglo-French treaties of Ryswick in 1697 and Utrecht in 1713 and the Treaty of Seville concluded by Britain, France, and Spain in 1729 provided for commissions to deal with American problems. All failed. After the War of the Austrian Succession, Britain and France established a commission for American questions. Again, failure. Certainly, the performances of commissions during the colonial era should have encouraged no one to believe that arbitration would be of large importance in later American history, yet that series of failures kept the idea alive. After the United States won independence, there were many problems which American and British diplomats found difficult to settle through negotiation, and they turned to commissions almost as a matter of course.

The United States and Great Britain for the first time agreed to use arbitration in their relations with each other when they concluded their first commercial treaty, usually called Jay's Treaty, in 1794. That treaty provided for three joint commissions to deal with disputes over boundaries, compensation due British creditors for obligations incurred by Americans before the Revolution, and questions arising from Britain's treatment of American shipping in the war with Revolutionary France then in progress. The commission for maritime matters decided several questions, and the boundary commission also attained some success. It identified the Schoodiac River as the St. Croix, the river which was supposed to be part of the boundary between Maine and British territory according to the treaty of independence. But the debt commission broke up in an angry exchange, and it was necessary for the two governments to resume negotiations. According to a treaty concluded in 1802, the United States paid Britain a lump sum and the controversy came to an end.

The Treaty of Ghent, signed 24 December 1814, like Jay's Treaty, provided for three joint commissions. Only one commission completed its assignment, determination of the ownership of islands in the Passamaquoddy Bay. One commission tried to determine boundaries between British territory and the United States from the St. Lawrence River to the Lake of the Woods; it agreed upon a boundary through the Great Lakes but failed to determine the line from Lake Superior to the Lake of the Woods. The third commission was supposed to decide the boundary from the St. Croix to the St. Lawrence, but it failed to reach accord. The two governments thereupon referred the dispute to William I of the Netherlands. That monarch failed to find a clear basis for a decision but in 1831 made an award anyway, giving the United States and Britain what he believed to be equitable shares of a wilderness. The United States refused to accept this award, protesting that the king had not acted in accord with the agreement referring the controversy to him. While arbitration had failed in this instance, the case was of considerable importance, for it clearly established the principle that arbitrators should abide by the terms of a *compromis* or other preliminary agreements. (The American government probably erred in refusing to accept the award, for the Webster-Ashburton Treaty in 1842 gave the United States less territory than it would have received according to the king's decision.)

The United States and Britain meanwhile had had one other arbitration in connection with the Treaty of Ghent. The two powers were supposed to restore all property, both public and private, which they had seized from each other during the War of 1812. The treaty specifically mentioned slaves, but the British failed to return all American slaves under their jurisdiction at the close of hostilities. After many protests from Washington, British leaders agreed that an arbitrator should deal with the matter, and the two governments referred their dispute to Alexander I of Russia. The emperor decided that Britain had failed to meet its obligations and should pay an indemnity. Upon his recommendation the United States and Britain concluded a convention setting up a commission to decide the amount due the United States. After elaborate proceedings the commissioners decided that the indemnity should be $1,204,960, and, in a convention concluded 13 November 1826, the British government accepted this decision.

During the last half of the nineteenth century the United States and Britain both made increasing use of arbitration. The United States had arbitrations with Brazil, Chile, Colombia, Costa Rica, Ecuador, Haiti, Mexico, Paraguay, Peru, Denmark, France, Portugal, and Spain. Britain, too, entered into many arbitrations with Latin American and European states, but the two English-speaking countries continued to have more arbitrations with each other than with other powers. Several minor but difficult Anglo-American controversies were settled by arbitration during the 1850's and 1860's; after the Civil War, arbitration became a major feature of relations between Washington and London.

The nineteenth century's most important arbitral decisions concerned Anglo-American controversies arising from the Civil War. British shipbuilders had built warships for the Confederacy, a practice stopped by London only after vehement protests from Washington. But British authorities acted too late to prevent the sailing of several ships, among them the *Alabama,* the most notorious commerce raider of the war. When the *Alabama* and her sister ships began destroying Union merchant ships, many American shipowners transferred their ships to foreign registry, Britain receiving the largest number of registrations. The American merchant marine almost disappeared. As the war closed, influential Americans fulminated against British misdeeds. Senator Charles Sumner of Massachusetts charged that Britain was really responsible for prolonging the war for two years and demanded a large indemnity. Britain, too, had grievances, for British shipping had sustained considerable damages at the hands of the Union. As charges and countercharges were exchanged by intemperate speakers on both sides of the Atlantic, diplomats found negotiation of a settlement extremely difficult. Finally, in a treaty signed at Washington on 8 May 1871, the two governments agreed to arbitration of their Civil War claims and two other difficult matters, the boundary through the San Juan waterway between Vancouver Island and the United States and the compensation due Britain for recent concessions to the United States in the fisheries off Newfoundland and Canada.

The two governments used all the best-known forms of arbitration to resolve their four disputes. They made their most elaborate preparations for claims concerning the *Alabama* and the other commerce raiders, establishing a tribunal of five members in Geneva, Switzerland. Each of the two parties appointed an arbitrator, as did Brazil, Italy, and Switzerland. Presenting its case, the United States demanded payment of indirect claims, i.e., damages sustained as a result of the prolonging of the war through actions of the raiders. The tribunal denied this demand, but in a decision announced 14 September 1872, it awarded the United States $15,500,000 for actual destruction of ships and cargoes. Other American maritime claims against Britain and British claims against the United States were referred to a commission of three members, appointed by the United States, Britain, and Spain. Meeting in Washington, the commission soon decided against American claims but, in a decision announced 25 September 1873, awarded the British $1,929,819. Meanwhile the United States and Britain had referred the San Juan waterway boundary dispute to German Emperor William I, who announced his decision on 21 October 1872, an award essentially in accord with American contentions. A commission of three members—an American, a Briton, and a Belgian—handled the fisheries case in sessions at Halifax. The commission announced on 23 November 1877 that the United States should pay Britain $5,500,000.

Of the four arbitrations, that of the *Alabama* claims was by far the most important. No other arbitration has so stimulated imaginations. While it is no doubt true, as Woodrow Wilson wrote, that the award "ended, not a controversy but a judicial process at the end of a controversy," many individuals convinced themselves that in this instance arbitration may have been a substitute for war. Long before the Civil War, arbitration had attracted the attention of people anxious to find ways of ridding mankind of the curse of war, and to such people the decisions of the Geneva tribunal seemed proof of what arbitration could accomplish. The spokesmen and journals of the American Peace Society, the Universal Peace Union, and many other peace organizations found in the Geneva arbitration topics for countless lectures and articles.

Even before the Geneva tribunal announced its award there were earnest recommendations that Britain and America negotiate treaties between themselves and with other nations in which they would recognize an obligation to resort to arbitration rather than war. Charles Sumner, on 31 May 1872, introduced a resolution in the Senate declaring that

> . . . in the determination of international differences Arbitration should become a substitute for war in reality as well as in name, and therefore coextensive with war in jurisdiction, so that any question or grievance which might be the occasion of war or of misunderstanding between nations should be considered by this tribunal.

A British peace leader, Henry Richard, on 8 July 1873, secured passage of a similar resolution in the House of Commons, and Sumner on 1 December of that year introduced another resolution urging arbitration in the Senate. While the two governments took no actions in response to these resolutions, the idea of treaties of obligatory arbitration continued to gain adherents. American and British peace advocates were probably unaware that Latin American governments almost as a matter of course included promises of arbitration in many of their treaties, and most Americans had probably forgotten that the Treaty of Guadalupe Hidalgo (1848), which ended the Mexican War, contained an article by which the United States and Mexico agreed to arbitration of differences in connection with the treaty. The peace movement in the United States and Britain gave little attention to developments in Latin America; it focused attention upon Anglo-American relations. If the United States and Britain were to conclude a permanent arbitration treaty, they would set an example for the rest of the world, peace leaders reasoned.

It was not until the 1890's that there came many new opportunities to advance the ideas of arbitration enthusiasts. During that decade, marked as it was by naval building, imperial rivalries, and war, arbitration nonetheless seemed to emerge as a major feature of international relations, and the American government was at the forefront of this development. As the period began, President Benjamin Harrison's secretary of state, James G. Blaine, brought together in Washington during late 1889 and early 1890 the First International Conference of American States. This conference recommended a number of proposals to promote hemispheric unity, among them a plan by which the American republics would have referred to arbitration all disputes that diplomacy could not settle, excepting questions of independence. Blaine called this agreement "the first and great fruit" of the conference, but he rejoiced too soon. No government ratified the agreement.

Even before it was apparent that the Pan-American arbitral plan would fail, the United States was concluding an agreement with Britain for arbitration of an acrimonious dispute. Endeavoring to stop the indiscriminate killing of fur seals in the Bering Sea by both British subjects and American citizens, State Department officials grasped at mistaken translations and interpretations of Russian documents which seemed to prove that sovereignty over the sea had passed to the United States with the acquisition of Alaska. The Coast Guard seized Canadian ships and arrested their crews. Britain protested vigorously. Blaine's successor, John Watson Foster, negotiated an agreement by which the two powers established a tribunal in Paris to hear the case. In an award announced in 1895 the tribunal upheld Britain's contention that the Bering Sea was part of the high seas and thus not subject to the police actions of any government in time of peace. It became necessary for the State Department to resume negotiations to save the seals.

The Bering Sea tribunal had barely completed its labors when a serious Anglo-American quarrel arose over arbitration in another matter. The United States had long urged arbitration of the border dispute between Venezuela and British Guiana, but the British government, fearing that such an arbitration would encourage demands for changes in boundaries of other British colonies, repeatedly rejected American suggestions. Late in 1895 President Grover Cleveland's new secretary of state, Richard Olney, convinced himself and the president that Britain was very possibly claiming territory without real justification and was, therefore, about to violate the Monroe Doctrine. The secretary sent stern messages to London. Lord Salisbury, who was both prime minister and foreign minister, responded with a statement that sounded much like a schoolmaster explaining a few simple facts to a student with little intelligence. The Monroe Doctrine was not "public law," as Olney claimed, it was simply a statement made by a distinguished American statesman. Salisbury was accurate enough, but Americans insisted that the Monroe Doctrine had a larger meaning which other nations should recognize. Cleveland sent Congress a special message which resounded with appeals to honor and patriotic duty. In both America and Britain there were calls for war. After a few days calmer counsel prevailed. The British government decided that arbitration, after all, was the best way out of the crisis and concluded a treaty with Venezuela by which the two countries established a tribunal in Paris to determine the boundary. To the irritation of many Americans, the tribunal, in an award announced in 1899, largely upheld the British position.

In addition to the proceedings at Paris the boundary controversy had another important result for arbitration. Shocked by the emotional excesses of the recent crisis, British and American leaders at last yielded to the pleas of peace spokesmen for a treaty of arbitration. Secretary Olney and the British ambassador, Sir Julian Pauncefote, negotiated a treaty according to which their governments were to agree that for a five-year period they would settle territorial and pecuniary claims through arbitration. The treaty made no exception for national honor, but it provided an elaborate procedure for setting up tribunals and handling appeals which should have been adequate safeguards for the interests of both parties. Optimists believed the treaty could be a first step towards a permanent world tribunal. Olney and Pauncefote signed the treaty on 11 January 1897, and Cleveland and his successor, William McKinley, both urged ratification. Unfortunately, partisan politics, dislike for Britain, and fear of a departure from the traditional policy of avoiding entangling alliances influenced many senators. After approving amendments that would have deprived the treaty of any real force, the Senate on 5 May 1897 declined consent for ratification.

Great was the disappointment of arbitration enthusiasts, but there soon came another opportunity for their cause. The Russian foreign ministry, on 24 August 1898, sent a circular note to all governments with diplomatic representation in St. Petersburg. Emperor Nicholas II proposed a conference to consider limitation of armaments. The United States was quick to accept, although there was no interest in Washington in limiting or reducing armaments, and some influential people suspected a connection between the Russian proposal and the recent American victory in the war with Spain. When the Russians added improvements in the laws of war and arbitration to the agenda, American officials became more interested. Secretary of State John Hay instructed the American delegates to work for agreement on these subjects, and he told them to present a plan for a permanent international tribunal modeled on the Supreme Court of the United States.

Upon request of Nicholas II, Queen Wilhelmina of the Netherlands provided the conference with a meeting place at The Hague. Representatives of twenty-six governments were present for the opening session on 18 May 1899, at one of the Dutch royal palaces, the House in the Wood. In addition to the delegates, peace workers gathered at The Hague, anxious to encourage the "Peace Conference," as they called it, to make large initiatives for peace. To many people the term Peace Conference soon seemed a misnomer, for the conference spent much of its time discussing war. It failed to agree to any reduction in armies and navies or their budgets but did adopt declarations against poison gas, needlessly cruel bullets, and the throwing of projectiles or explosives from balloons or similar devices. It was more successful in its work with the laws of war. It framed two conventions about this subject, one of which was a codification of the laws of land warfare and the other a convention extending the Geneva convention of 1864 (popularly known as the Red Cross convention) to naval warfare. While humanitarians hailed these conventions, another document, the Convention for the Pacific Settlement of International Disputes, was more interesting to peace workers. This convention summarized experience with arbitration, mediation, and commissions of inquiry and made several significant innovations in the application of these methods to the resolution of international differences.

No part of the conference's work required more diplomacy than Title IV of the Pacific Settlement convention, "On International Arbitration." The American delegates soon discovered that there was little chance for adoption of their plan for a permanent tribunal, and they decided not to press for its acceptance. Instead, they supported a plan offered by Pauncefote, the chairman of the British delegation. The British proposed that each signatory power name two jurists to a list and that parties to an arbitration should choose judges from that list. The Russians also advanced a plan, proposing that five powers be given authority to name one judge each and that these judges should always be ready to act as arbitrators. Both plans called for an administrative bureau at The Hague. The chairman of the American delegation, Andrew D. White, and the delegation secretary, Frederick W. Holls, worked closely with the British and Russians to secure an acceptable compromise. For a time German objections threatened to defeat their efforts; and it required much persuasion before the German government agreed to support a plan believed somewhat weaker than the original British and Russian proposals. The conference then agreed that each signatory power should select "four persons at the most, of known competency in international law, of the highest moral reputation, and disposed to accept the duties of Arbitrator." These people were to be members of a permanent international institution, the Permanent Court of Arbitration. A bureau at The Hague would maintain their names on a list and carry out all administrative responsibilities. Powers wishing to enter into arbitrations could choose arbitrators from the list, but there was no requirement that they do so.

Efforts at incorporating obligatory features into the convention largely failed. The Germans, in particular, opposed obligatory arbitration, and without their support little was possible. The completed convention included, however, a statement that the signatory powers recognized arbitration "as the most effective, and at the same time the most equitable, means of settling disputes which diplomacy has failed to settle," and article 27 declared that the signatory powers would "consider it their duty, if a serious dispute threatens to break out between two or more of them, to remind these latter that the Permanent Court is open to them." This provision, based on a French proposal that Holls had warmly supported, was the subject of serious disagreement within the American delegation. The naval delegate, Captain Alfred T. Mahan, the famed historian of sea power, argued that the article could lead to conflict between the Hague convention and the Monroe Doctrine. Debate within the delegation ceased only when White read a statement to the conference that in signing the convention the United States was in no way departing from its traditional policies toward Europe or the Americas.

Many of the framers of the Peaceful Settlement convention were as concerned with good offices and mediation as with arbitration. When a government extends an offer of good offices to powers in controversy or at war, it makes its diplomatic services and facilities available to them. When a power acts as a mediator it takes an active part in negotiations, acting much as a middleman. In actual practice it is difficult to distinguish between good offices and mediation, and the First Hague Conference did not make such a distinction, but it did recognize the need to guarantee their benevolent character. Too often such offers had been viewed as unfriendly interventions, sometimes for good reasons. Americans remembered how the imperial French government during the Civil War had been unsympathetic to the Union cause and had, at an inconvenient moment, offered mediation. The Peace Conference sought to prevent such problems in the future by including in the convention a declaration that powers that were strangers to a dispute had the right to offer good offices and mediation even during hostilities and that the exercise of this right could "never be regarded by either of the parties at variance as an unfriendly act." The convention was as careful in its treatment of recipients of offers of good offices and mediation. Article 6 declared that offers of good offices and mediation "have exclusively the character of advice, and never have binding force," while article 7 stated that mediation could not interrupt, delay, or hinder mobilization or other preparations for war.

Article 8 of the mediation section was in a class by itself. The result of a proposal by Holls—other delegates referred to it as *La Proposition Holls*—it provided for what was called "special mediation." According to its terms each party to a conflict could choose another power to act in its place. For thirty days the disputing powers would cease all communication about their controversy and let their seconds make an effort at settlement.

In addition to the articles on mediation and arbitration the conference included provisions in the convention for commissions of inquiry. It was already an accepted practice to promote international conciliation by appointing commissions to ascertain facts. Such commissions were not expected to make recommendations for settlement, but they were expected to make reports that could aid quarreling governments to work out their differences. There was, however, no generally accepted procedure for establishing commissions. Cleveland had appointed a commission to gather evidence during the Venezuelan boundary controversy, and while the commission did much good work the fact that it was constituted by only one party to the dispute was lost on no one. Obviously, such one-sided arrangements should be avoided in the future. The Hague convention provided that commissions should be organized according to a procedure similar to that by which arbitral bodies could be constituted from the list of the Permanent Court of Arbitration and that the commissions should confine their activities to the determination of facts. They would present reports to the conflicting powers but those powers would retain full freedom to interpret the findings of the commissions.

During the fifteen years following the Peace Conference of 1899 the Convention for the Pacific Settlement of International Disputes was of considerable importance in international relations, and no country displayed more interest in the convention and the Hague Court than the United States. American statesmen made promotion of the court an important part of foreign policy. Upon the suggestion of President Theodore Roosevelt the United States and Mexico gave the court its first case, a dispute over whether the cession of California to the United States had ended Mexico's obligation to give financial support to an ancient fund for the conversion of the California Indians, the Pious Fund of the Californias. The court carefully examined a large quantity of historical evidence and, on 14 October 1902, rendered an award stating that Mexico was still obligated to support the fund.

Within a few months after the Pious Fund award the Permanent Court of Arbitration was hearing a much more important case. After Britain, Germany, and Italy blockaded Venezuelan ports in late 1902 and early 1903 to force Venezuela to honor financial obligations due their nationals in that country, other governments asked that the claims of their nationals in Venezuela also be paid. The question then arose as to whether the blockading powers should have preference when the payments began. Roosevelt saw another opportunity for the Hague Court. Upon his suggestion a court was again constituted from its list of arbitrators, and the interested powers began a long and complicated arbitration. The court finally announced, on 22 February 1904, an award stating that the blockading powers should have preference, a disappointing decision to many of the warmest friends of the court, for it seemed to reward violence.

Before World War I broke out, the Hague Court rendered awards in twelve other cases, two of them involving the United States. The Treaty of Washington of 1871 and the Halifax commission had failed to put to rest all difficulties over the North Atlantic fisheries, and the American and British governments referred their controversy to the Permanent Court in 1909. The court, on 10 September 1910, announced an award that upheld most British contentions but which was so carefully stated that the Americans as well as the British believed justice had been done. A few weeks after making this award, the court, on 25 October, made an award in another case involving the United States, the Orinoco Steamship Company case, a dispute between a company owned by American citizens and the Venezuelan government. The award was substantially in accord with the position of the United States government.

The provisions of the Pacific Settlement convention for commissions of inquiry and good offices and mediation were not used as often as the arbitration sections from 1899 to 1914, but they were of importance in connection with the most serious armed conflict of the era, the Russo-Japanese War. When Russia's Baltic fleet, en route to the Far East, fired into a British fishing fleet off Dogger Bank on the night of 21–22 October 1904, having mistaken the fishing boats for Japanese torpedo boats, there was a furor in Britain, and high officials in London talked of using force to stop the Russian fleet. Anger subsided when the Russian government suggested establishment of a commission of inquiry under terms of the Hague convention. Four admirals—one each from Russia, Britain, France, and the United States—were appointed to a commission that carefully investigated the matter. Upon receiving the commission's report the Russian government paid damages and the matter was closed.

As the war passed its decisive stages, peace movement spokesmen hoped that powers signatory to the Hague convention would remember its provisions for good offices and mediation, and they were elated when President Roosevelt mediated a settlement, the Peace of Portsmouth of 1905. The American president made no use of the language of the Hague convention, but it is probable that that document influenced him, for at one time he suggested that the Russians and Japanese hold peace negotiations at The Hague.

Many peace spokesmen in America and Europe believed Roosevelt's efforts to improve the Hague system would prove as important in the long run as his mediation of the Russo-Japanese conflict. The president in 1904 promised the visiting Interparliamentary Union that he would call another Hague peace conference, and in October of that year Secretary of State Hay sent out a circular suggesting a new conference. Later, Roosevelt stepped aside in response to a Russian request that Nicholas II have the honor of calling the conference officially, but the United States took an active role in the conference.

The Second Hague Peace Conference, which met in 1907, was much larger than the 1899 conference, for it included delegates from most Latin American countries. The Latin Americans were present because the United States asked for their inclusion. Indeed, Latin American policy was one of the most important considerations of the United States at the conference, but Secretary of State Elihu Root and the president did not forget the old dream of a world court. The chairman of the American delegation, Joseph Hodges Choate, and another American member, James Brown Scott, struggled valiantly to secure establishment of a new tribunal, the Court of Arbitral Justice, which would have stood alongside the Permanent Court of Arbitration but would have been a truly permanent court, always in existence and ready to hear cases. Unfortunately, it proved impossible to agree upon a system of appointing judges without offending smaller powers which could not have continuous representation. As the conference closed, the Court of Arbitral Justice was only a project attached to a *voeu* (formal wish) that the powers signatory to the Final Act bring the court into existence as soon as they agreed upon the selection of judges and several details of the court's constitution.

The negotiation of arbitration treaties and treaties of conciliation were other important aspects of the diplomacy of peace from 1899 to 1914. Britain and France in 1903 negotiated a treaty of arbitration, and peace movement leaders then urged the United States to follow this example. Roosevelt and Hay yielded to their pleas, and Hay, in 1904 and 1905, negotiated treaties with France, Switzerland, Germany, Portugal, Great Britain, Italy, Spain, Austria-Hungary, Mexico, and Sweden and Norway. To the anger of Roosevelt and Hay, the Senate in advising ratification insisted that the preliminary arbitration agreements be actual treaties and therefore subject to the ratifying process. Roosevelt thereupon refused to proceed further, but Hay's successor, Root, was convinced that treaties amended so as to meet the Senate's requirements would be better than none. He prevailed upon the president to consent to negotiation in 1908 of a new set of treaties. The Senate found these treaties more to its liking and approved ratification.

It would have been well if President William

Howard Taft and his secretary of state, Philander C. Knox, had been as cautious as Root in dealing with the Senate, for they would have been spared a large disappointment. Knox negotiated arbitration treaties with Britain and France in 1911 which made no exceptions for such considerations as national honor. The treaties merely stated that any matter which was justiciable would be arbitrated. Since whether or not a dispute was justiciable was subject to varying interpretations, it seemed that the treaties contained adequate safeguards for the interests of the governments concerned, but the Senate saw the matter in a different light. Believing that the treaties could limit the nation's freedom of action, the Senate refused consent for ratification.

President Woodrow Wilson's first secretary of state, William Jennings Bryan, was less interested in arbitration than his immediate predecessors, although he negotiated renewal of the Root treaties. He was more impressed with the conciliatory effects of commissions of inquiry, and believed that their development could be carried much farther than the Pacific Settlement convention had done. He hoped for treaties of conciliation incorporating new ideas about investigating commissions. Soon after the Wilson administration took office, he advanced what he called the president's peace plan. He urged nations to agree to refer their disputes to investigating commissions for six months or a year. While awaiting the reports of the commissions they would refrain from going to war or increasing their armaments. The signatories of the treaties would be free to accept or reject conclusions of the commissions or to go to war, but Bryan was confident that the period of waiting could have a cooling-off effect and would help avert war. He negotiated twenty-nine treaties according to this plan, and twenty of them were ratified. Sadly, this initiative for peace was interrupted by the outbreak of World War I.

The declarations of war in 1914 also interrupted American efforts to bring the Court of Arbitral Justice into existence and to ensure the meeting of a third Hague peace conference. Since the conference of 1907 American diplomats had been conducting quiet negotiations with the British, French, and Germans to establish the Court of Arbitral Justice without waiting for the consent of all powers that had participated in that conference. While these negotiations had reached no definite conclusion, in 1914 there were some reasons to hope for success. Negotiations for a third Hague peace conference were even more promising. The 1907 conference had recommended that another conference meet after an eight-year interval, the same as between the first two conferences. To many peace spokesmen and theorists, the conference seemed to be developing into a permanent institution. A periodic world conference and a world court with judges always ready to hold sessions—these were the institutions necessary for a viable world organization, they believed. In the United States the peace societies and the new Carnegie Endowment for International Peace brought pressure to bear upon Wilson and Bryan to use their influence to bring about the meeting of the conference, and this the president and the secretary of state agreed to do. Planning for the conference had made considerable progress when war began in 1914.

The Hague period of modern internationalism ended abruptly with the declarations of war. The Pacific Settlement convention and the treaties of arbitration and conciliation were brushed aside as the armies of the warring nations hastened to secure strategic positions. Four years later, as the war moved toward its close, European nations and the United States advocated a world organization. Occasionally there were recommendations that the new world system be founded on the work of the Hague Conferences, but at Paris, in 1919, Wilson and other internationalists planned the League of Nations with little reference to the conferences of 1899 and 1907. But the Hague idea of a world court survived. The Council of the League of Nations in 1920 convened a small conference of legal experts at The Hague to draft a statute for a world court, the Permanent International Court of Justice. Taking the draft Hague Convention for a Court of Arbitral Justice as the basis of its deliberations, the conference soon framed an acceptable statute. Giving judges of the Permanent Court of Arbitration responsibility for nominating judges for the new court, the conference solved the problem that had prevented realization of the court project thirteen years before. The court was inaugurated in 1922 and continued to function until the end of 1945.

The United Nations then made changes in the court statute, and the court reappeared in 1946 as the International Court of Justice.

Arbitration and conciliation treaties, like the idea of a permanent court, survived World War I and the Paris Peace Conference. During the 1920's numerous treaties of these types were concluded, and arbitrations as well as the more judicial proceedings of the Permanent International Court of Justice were of some importance throughout the era between the world wars. After World War II they continued to have their roles in international relations, but at no time since World War I have the ideas of arbitration and international adjudication seemed to offer mankind the bright hope arbitration enthusiasts saw in them during the late nineteenth and early twentieth centuries. This is not to say that the ideas and dreams of the pre-1914 peace movement should be discounted altogether. The institutions the leaders of that movement so desired now exist. In time the society of nations may yet develop the will and the spirit necessary to make them effective instruments for the prevention of war.

BIBLIOGRAPHY

For the basic concepts and terminology of arbitration, mediation, and conciliation as they were understood early in the twentieth century, see Montague H. Crackanthorpe, "Arbitration, International," in *Encyclopaedia Britannica,* II (Cambridge, 1910), 327–330, and Lassa Oppenheim, *International Law: A Treatise,* II (London, 1906).

The best general surveys of the history of arbitration are John Bassett Moore, "International Arbitration: Historical Notes and Projects," in *The Collected Papers of John Bassett Moore,* II (New Haven, 1944); and chapter 5 of Percy E. Corbett, *Law in Diplomacy* (Princeton, 1959). Helen May Cory, *Compulsory Arbitration of International Disputes* (New York, 1933), describes the development of its special topic from 1820 to 1931.

The promotion of arbitration by the peace movement is carefully discussed in Merle Curti, *Peace or War: The American Struggle 1636–1936* (New York, 1936), and Warren F. Kuehl, *Seeking World Order, The United States and International Organization to 1920* (Nashville, Tenn., 1969). For analyses of important peace ideas, see Sandra R. Herman, *Eleven Against War: Studies in American Internationalist Thought, 1898–1921* (Stanford, 1969); C. Roland Marchand, *The American Peace Movement and Social Reform, 1898–1918* (Princeton, 1972); and David S. Patterson, *Toward A Warless World: The Travail of the American Peace Movement, 1887–1914* (Bloomington, Ind., 1976).

There has been considerable writing on arbitration in American foreign relations from the Civil War to World War I. Recent scholarship on the Washington treaty and the Geneva arbitration can be found in Martin Duberman, *Charles Francis Adams: 1807–1886* (Boston, 1961), and Adrian Cook, *The Alabama Claims: American Politics and Anglo-American Relations, 1865–1872* (Ithaca, N.Y., 1975). Nelson M. Blake, "The Olney-Pauncefote Treaty of 1897," in *American Historical Review,* 50 (1945), is a study of the Senate's rejection of an arbitration treaty. Calvin D. Davis, *The United States and the First Hague Peace Conference* (Ithaca, N.Y., 1962), contains a detailed account of the negotiation of the Convention for the Pacific Settlement of International Disputes. Calvin D. Davis, *The United States and the Second Hague Peace Conference: American Diplomacy and International Organization, 1899–1914* (Durham, N.C., 1976), describes the establishment and development of the Permanent Court of Arbitration, the attempt of the Second Hague Peace Conference to establish a stronger world tribunal, and the efforts of American diplomacy to further development of the Hague Conferences and Court into a permanent world system. John P. Campbell, "Taft, Roosevelt, and the Arbitration Treaties of 1911," in *Journal of American History,* 53 (1966), discusses the failure of the last important American effort to conclude obligatory arbitration treaties before World War I.

For arbitration in the period between the world wars, see Robert H. Ferrell, *Peace in Their Time: The Origins of the Kellogg-Briand Pact* (New Haven, 1952). For modern legal scholarship on arbitration, see Pieter Sanders, ed., *International Arbitration: Liber Amicorum for Martin Domke* (The Hague, 1967), and W. Michael Reisman, "The Multifaceted Phenomenon of International Arbitration," in *Arbitration Journal,* 24 (1969).

[*See also* Balance of Power; Internationalism; International Law; International Organization; Pacifism; Pan-Americanism; Peacemaking; Peace Movements; Treaties.]

ARMED NEUTRALITIES

I. Mugridge

ONE of the recurrent and most difficult problems attached to all wars is that of the relations between belligerents and neutrals. In land wars the question is not of such magnitude, although Switzerland is probably the only nation to have arrived at a satisfactory solution. In naval wars, however, in situations where maritime commerce and other activities are involved, the question of the relationship between belligerents and neutrals, that is, of neutral rights, has long been debated, almost always with inconclusive results.

The question of neutral rights in wartime is almost always discussed, especially by neutrals, within the context of international law. It is usually claimed that such international law is supported by principles established by earlier treaties or practice or both, and that it is an expression of some accepted view of maritime conduct in wartime, which should therefore guide the behavior of belligerents and neutrals alike in their relations with one another.

The problem is that international law has no validity beyond that accorded to it in particular situations by particular nations. It only exists either when nations agree that it does or when they can uphold their conception of it by whatever means are appropriate. In a narrower context, the problem with stating and attempting to uphold neutral rights at sea is that, in the end, neutrals have no rights except those that they can maintain by their own action, in which case they often cease to be neutrals, as the Dutch discovered in the War of American Independence. Again, the example of the Swiss is instructive. They have preserved their neutrality inviolate for hundreds of years by the simple but effective expedient of placing themselves in such a position that a challenge to their neutrality would not be worth the cost.

The introduction of principles to regulate relations between belligerents and neutrals has never been motivated by anything other than self-interest. Since at least the seventeenth century, the world has been afflicted with declarations, opinions, judgments, and conventions on neutral rights in seaborne commerce. If one strips away the philosophical disguises, legal circumlocutions, and endless casuistry, what remains is really very simple: neutrals have constantly been trying to trade with some or all of the belligerents in a given war while some or all of these belligerents have been trying to stop neutral trade with their enemies. For example, the cause of most of the problems concerning the West Indies, and the French islands in particular, during the War of American Independence was the clear and avowed intention of the French to assist the Americans and the equally firm intention of the British to stop this. What mattered in this situation was not declarations of neutral rights or expressions of principle but the possession of the force required to carry out national policy.

Despite this, there has developed during the last three hundred years a great body of pronouncements on neutral rights as both neutrals and belligerents have sought to regulate their relations and to justify their self-interested conduct by appeals to principle and to precedent. No nation has been absolutely consistent in the principles and doctrines to which it appealed and on which it acted; and this has been as true of the United States as of any other nation.

In his *The Diplomacy of the American Revolution* (1935), still the standard work on the topic, Samuel Flagg Bemis noted that, in espousing unequivocally the principles of the Armed Neutrality of 1780 and in embodying some of these principles in the Treaty of Paris, the

United States established what he called "the American doctrine of freedom of the seas." This doctrine, which he recognized as being rooted in past practice, was by no means American nor has it been one to which the United States has consistently adhered. During the Civil War the British in particular tried, which was unusual for them, to uphold the principle of free ships, free goods; but the government of Abraham Lincoln refused to do anything but cling to the old British doctrine of continuous voyage. In the two major wars of the twentieth century, the neutral rights of American shipping were one of the causes of contention between the United States and Germany, but in neither case was the real neutrality of the nation clearly established. More recently, it might be maintained that one of the ingredients of the Cuban missile crisis was the unwillingness of the United States to uphold the principle of freedom of the seas when such an action would seriously have threatened its security. This is not meant to apply any extreme strictures on the actions of the United States in successive crises, but merely to point out that its governments, like those of other major and minor powers over the years, have been motivated by self-interest rather than by continuous adherence to principle.

An examination of the conduct of the maritime powers in time of war, however, indicates that the body of international maritime law, ephemeral and even illusory as it may be, has yet had considerable influence on their actions.

In his *Colonial Blockade and Neutral Rights, 1739–1763* (1938), Richard Pares noted that the classic age in the struggle between land power and sea power occurred in the middle years of the eighteenth century and that one of the results of this was that the same period became the classic age in the development of the international law of war at sea. During the years of the two great colonial wars, the War of the Austrian Succession and the Seven Years' War, important doctrines on contraband, blockade and colonial trade were defined by English and continental jurists in a long series of opinions in prize cases and the like. These definitions were, in turn, embodied in governmental pronouncements and treaties to build up reference points for the future. As Pares noted at the close of his work, ". . . for Admirals, for Foreign Ministers, and for judges, [these wars] were the dress rehearsals for greater struggles to come." By implication at least, this view was taken up much later by Max Savelle in his massive work, *The Origins of American Diplomacy* (1967), in which he examined the international history of the European colonies in America, and particularly those of Great Britain, from 1492 to the end of the Seven Years' War.

At the beginning of this war, as both Pares and Savelle noted, the neutrals assumed that free ships made free goods and that they would be able to continue their lucrative trade with the belligerents as if nothing had happened. This was, however, not the British view of the situation. In response to the neutral position, the British produced what came to be known as the Rule of the War of 1756, which drew a distinction between trading with the enemy and trading for the enemy. The former was to be regarded as permissible so that trade that would have been carried on in peacetime would remain free and uninterrupted during war. The latter, however, was not permissible and, during war, the British reserved the right to interfere with any trade in war matériel that would not have existed in peacetime. As 1757 and 1758 progressed, however, it became obvious to the British that even this rather strict rule was being continuously evaded by transferring contraband from one ship to another. The response to this problem was to promulgate a supplementary order that became known as the doctrine of continuous voyage. This rule laid down the principle that for a confiscatable cargo to begin a voyage in one ship and then to continue "in the ship of a friend" made no difference, for the British government would regard such a voyage as a continuous one. In other words, it was the cargo and not the ship that mattered.

On these principles, the British government and its navy rested its actions throughout the Seven Years' War. From their point of view, it was a simple problem: in Pares' words, "English trade had nothing to gain from the vindication of neutral rights." In addition, the British war effort might be placed in considerable jeopardy by adherence to the principles being espoused by the French foreign minister, Étienne François, Duc de Choiseul, in his attempts to win over the neutral powers. These powers did not, however, take the same view of the problem as the British. Although Choiseul and his agents discovered that the neutral position was by no means a united one, there was yet sufficient feeling of grievance against Great Britain among all the neutral powers in Europe to make the construction of a maritime league of neutrals a serious proposition. The British desired to establish overwhelming power at sea and were not altogether unsuccessful in their attempts to do so.

It was to the creation of such a league that the French government, posing as the champion of the neutrals, bent its energies in the early years of the war. It was a difficult and, of course, ultimately fruitless task, but in many ways it provided the model for the League of the Armed Neutrality of 1780.

There were precedents for a league of neutrals, especially in northern Europe where, as early as 1690, Denmark and Sweden had combined to try to enforce their concept of neutral rights. The Baltic was indeed the area where a league of neutrals stood the greatest chance of success. It could easily be closed to the shipping of nations refusing to respect neutral rights, much to the disadvantage of, in particular, the British who at this time were beginning to rely increasingly on Baltic naval stores. The Danes, however, also relied heavily on the income they gained from dues collected on the Sound and the Baltic trading nations as a group were growing more dependent on their naval stores industries. Nevertheless, the French concentrated on this area, especially in view of the agreement on neutral rights signed by Denmark and Sweden shortly before hostilities began.

But French efforts were to fail through the weakness of the neutral position, the unwillingness of the British to recognize claims not already granted by treaty, and the resultant reluctance of the neutrals to make a firm commitment to a maritime league. Not only was the Baltic project doomed almost from the beginning—the Danes, for example, would never actually say that free ships made free goods—but attempts to put together a wider league met with equal reluctance to participate. Whatever their long-term interests might have appeared to dictate, whatever blandishments the French used on them, the neutrals, and the Danes and the Dutch in particular, always lacked sufficient confidence in their own ability or that of the French to uphold the principles with which they were flirting. They were always too reliant on British friendship, or at least noninterference, in maintaining their overseas trade to give unequivocal assent and support to a league that might oblige them to sacrifice concrete gain for abstract principles. By the spring of 1759, Choiseul had—apart from a rather half-hearted effort in the summer—given up the attempt.

In many ways, as Pares noted, the events of the Seven Years' War were a rehearsal for later wars. In the War of American Independence and later struggles, both neutrals and belligerents appealed to the body of maritime law developed in the years up to 1763. As in the past too, efforts to set up a maritime league of neutrals, a concept that became a reality only in a limited sense, foundered on the rock of national self-interest as did later attempts. In one important respect, however, the league of 1780 differed from attempts made by Choiseul and the French to bring together a group of neutral powers in the 1750's. It may be this difference that goes a long way to explain the success it had, if not in limiting the belligerents' interference with neutral shipping, then at least in providing a certain amount of mediation and service in bringing the American war to a close.

The League of the Armed Neutrality, formed in the spring and summer of 1780, was the first genuine league of neutrals formed because of complaints of the neutral powers against the major belligerents—with the possible exception of the United States. Although, in this respect as in others, the United States was of rather limited importance to anyone except Great Britain, France, and Spain, there is some evidence that the activities of American privateers were partly responsible for the movement to form a league of neutrals.

From the beginning of the war, Great Britain, still supremely, though as it turned out misguidedly, confident in the ability of its navy to hold the world at bay, had reverted to the maritime doctrines it had espoused in the past; and its actions had provided a constant source of complaint for the Danes and the Swedes as well as the Dutch and, later, the Russians. After the entry of France and Spain into the war in 1778, France made attempts to conciliate the neutrals as it had done in the Seven Years' War. Spanish policy hovered somewhere between the two. Whatever the avowed policies of the belligerent powers, however, they all, in varying degrees, offended the neutrals and produced a growing sense among them that some kind of joint expression of disapproval and firm resolve to take action was necessary to protect their interests.

Ultimately, leadership in this project was provided by Catherine II of Russia who, under pressure both from Great Britain to enter an alliance and from the northern powers to help protect their neutrality, found her own shipping becoming more subject to interference from the belligerents. The result was the declaration of 1780, identifying the principles by which Catherine proposed to act and the means—commissioning a substantial portion of her fleet to go "wherever honour, interest and necessity compelled"—by which she proposed to enforce those principles. Broadly, these principles were that neutral shipping might navigate freely from port to port and on the coasts of nations at war; that the property of subjects of belligerent states on neutral ships should be free except when it was classed as contraband within the meaning of the Anglo-Russian Treaty of 1766; and that a port was assumed to be blockaded only when the attacking power had rendered its ships stationary and made entry a clear danger.

Through the summer of 1780 other neutral powers issued similar declarations and the belligerents protested that they had always treated and always intended to treat Russian shipping according to these principles. By August, Denmark and Sweden, by almost identical agreements, had joined Russia in conventions establishing an Armed Neutrality; and, beginning with the Dutch in January of the following year, most of the major neutrals of Europe acceded to the league before the end of the war. Of these powers, only the Dutch were obliged, at least partly because of their joining the league, to go to war with Great Britain. In this case, Catherine and her allies agreed to regard the Dutch as neutrals in their dealings with France and Spain to mitigate the effects on them of war with the British. Even so, the Dutch suffered severely from the war which, in spite of repeated attempts at mediation by Catherine and other members of the league, dragged on into the early summer of 1784 before Great Britain and the United Provinces finally signed a treaty of peace.

What, in the end, did the league achieve? It is probably true that its existence made little, if any, difference in the attitude or practice of the British navy in dealing with neutral shipping. Indeed, in the case of the United Provinces, adherence to the league was at least partly responsible for a far more serious situation than that nation might otherwise have faced. Any slackening in British depredations on the neutrals in general was perhaps due more to the declining effectiveness of the British navy, to the ineptitude of those running the war effort, and to the appearance of France and Spain on the rebel side than to the unity and effectiveness of the league. It is nevertheless undeniably true that the British government was seriously worried by the steadfast attachment of Catherine and most of her allies to the league convention and that the threat of war with the whole of Europe, while perhaps never a great one, was taken rather seriously in the early 1780's.

The mediation of Catherine and Joseph II of Austria, who had joined the league in October 1781, was also, to a large extent, responsible for producing treaties of peace between Great Britain and first France and then Spain in the fall of 1783. Again, Catherine and her allies were interested primarily in Europe and they did not seek to influence the Anglo-American peace settlement.

This was probably the limit of the achievements of the first Armed Neutrality. It had little or no influence on American affairs and diplomacy in general, beyond the threat it imposed on the British. For the United States as for other nations, it provided a set of principles of maritime law that were useful when they became convenient or necessary but that were to be discarded when neither of these conditions existed. At the end of the war, Charles James Fox, the British foreign secretary, proposed drawing up a treaty embodying the principles of armed neutrality, but his plan came to nothing. Ten years later, with Europe once again at war, Sweden and Denmark signed a convention renewing the provisions of the armed neutrality; but Catherine had already concluded an alliance with Great Britain which, by virtue of the fact that one of its objects was to destroy French commerce, deliberately ignored the principles of the league.

In the words of Isabel de Madariaga, the idea of a league of neutrals "flickered into brief life again in 1800" before it was finally abandoned. At that point, Napoleon Bonaparte, first consul of the French Republic, was anxious to construct a continental alliance against Great Britain, whose opposition to his designs was proving intransigent. One of the major weapons that he was attempting to use was a league of neutral powers, particularly those of northern Europe, who were angered by British refusal to recognize the rights of neutral commerce.

In this endeavor, Bonaparte found an ally in Paul I of Russia, whose inclination, at the turn of the century, was to persuade the French government that the interests of both powers were best served by an alliance and by a resolution to cooperate in an effort to keep the peace. As the year 1800 wore on, as the French and the Americans settled the differences that had virtually brought them to war, and as Bonaparte removed the last great continental obstacle to a general peace by smashing the Austrians at Hohenlinden in December, the project began to take concrete form.

By mid-December 1800, Norway, Denmark, Sweden and Russia had signed separate conventions with France to further their "disinterested desire to maintain the inalienable rights of neutral nations." Bonaparte had earlier declared that he would not make peace with the British while they refused to respect the neutral rights not only of these powers, but also of the United States. It was his hope to attach the Americans to the league and this was particularly so after the accession to the presidency of Thomas Jefferson early in 1801.

But this was not to be. Both Jefferson and his secretary of state, James Madison, were cautious about entering into a firm attachment with a league in which, in the words of one of the American envoys in Europe, "the silly powers of the north" had responded to "this interested and politic cry of France against Great Britain." They recognized too that the situation could be turned to their advantage if the Baltic trade were denied to the British; and they were suspicious of Bonaparte's designs in the Western Hemisphere and fearful of the seriousness with which the British government clearly took the league.

So they hung back; and, while they did, the league collapsed. In the spring of 1801, two events destroyed it. Late in March, Paul I, the main prop of the league, was assassinated. Ten days later the British demanded that the Danes abandon the league or disarm; and, when this was refused, Horatio Nelson indicated the view his government held of neutral rights by destroying the Danish fleet in the harbor at Copenhagen. These two events finished the league, for the new czar, Alexander I, refused to maintain the policies of his father.

The League of the Armed Neutrality of 1780 had, because of the temporary concurrence of a number of factors, some effect on the course of the War of American Independence and, more particularly, on the European policies that surrounded it. A weakened Great Britain, faced with rebellious colonies and declarations of war by the major European powers, was in no position to resist effectively a league that eventually contained all the other major European powers. For once, an unusual show of neutral strength and unity had an effect on European politics, although even this did not extend fully to all the members and particularly to the Dutch.

The effectiveness of the league, however, had nothing to do with the principles it had espoused, with their justice or their strength. It had to do with the strength of the league's members and the comparative weakness of the major object of its existence. In 1800, when such a situation did not exist, this fact was illustrated graphically by the collapse of the second League of the Armed Neutrality. On this occasion, admittedly helped by a fortunate accident of Russian politics, the British, strong and confident, led by a resolute and able prime minister and served by a brilliant and fearless admiral, struck hard at the league's weakest link and destroyed it. Unable to maintain the rights they claimed, the neutrals returned to conciliation of Great Britain. They had learned a severe lesson—and so, watching them, had the government of the United States.

BIBLIOGRAPHY

The best short treatment of the Armed Neutrality of 1780 is in chapters 11 and 12 of Samuel Flagg Bemis, *The Diplomacy of the American Revolution* (New Haven, 1935). The most comprehensive treatment of events surrounding the establishment and working of the Armed Neutrality is Isabel de Madariaga, *Britain, Russia and the Armed Neutrality of 1780* (New Haven, 1962). While this work is subtitled "Sir James Harris's Mission to St. Petersburg During the American Revolution," it goes beyond the confines of this title with a well-constructed and indispensable account of its subject. Its bibliography also provides the most comprehensive treatment of the field. David M. Griffiths, "An American Contribution to the Armed Neutrality of 1780," in *Russian Review,* 30 (1970), is a short but valuable essay that examines American influence on the formation of the first Armed Neutrality.

The two major works on the eighteenth century mentioned in this essay are Richard Pares, *Colonial Blockade and Neutral Rights, 1739–1763* (Oxford, 1938), supplemented by Max Savelle, *The Origins of American Diplomacy* (New York, 1967). The latter contains perhaps the most complete bibliography of the international relations affecting the colonies in the mid- to late eighteenth century.

Among the primary sources for the Armed Neutrality, an excellent starting point is Sir Francis Piggott and G. W. T. Ormond, eds., *Documentary History of the Armed Neutralities 1780 and 1800* (London, 1919), which contains not only an excellent collection of documents, but also an interesting introduction, and a chronological account of the events surrounding the Armed Neutrality. A similar collection is James Brown Scott, ed., *The Armed Neutralities of 1780 and 1800* (New York, 1918), which, along with a good collection of documents, contains a lengthy selection of extracts from works on international law bearing on the work's main subject.

A comprehensive treatment of the second Armed Neutrality and its influence on United States policy is to be found in Alexander DeConde, *The Quasi-War* (New York, 1966).

[*See also* BLOCKADES AND QUARANTINES; FREEDOM OF THE SEAS; INTERNATIONAL LAW; NEUTRALITY; TRADE AND COMMERCE.]

ASYLUM

William O. Walker III

"MAN'S search for a place of refuge is an old one," writes S. Prakash Sinha in his study, *Asylum and International Law.* Cities in ancient Greece often granted asylum to refugees from other lands. Centuries later, ecclesiastical law recognized church asylum as the inherent right of a fugitive, but the rise of the sovereign state severely limited and ultimately abolished that concept. In *The Law of Nations* (1758), Emmerich de Vattel provided the basis for sovereignty in international law through his idea that a state could not be legally bound without its consent.

By the latter half of the eighteenth century, European jurists generally agreed that a state possessed a discretionary right to extend or refuse refuge to a fugitive in its territory. In fulfillment of treaty obligations, most states customarily extradited those persons accused of political offenses against another state. After the French Revolution, however, political offenders, as opposed to common criminals, frequently received territorial asylum. Following the defeat of Napoleon, Switzerland became a prominent place of refuge as European monarchical regimes turned increasingly conservative and curtailed internal dissent. At no time, though, did the granting of asylum become a principle supported by international law. It remained simply a nonlegal custom, with the frequency of usage dependent upon traditional practices and immediate circumstances. Therefore, asylum cannot be understood solely in legal terms since it primarily reflects broad, national goals defined by considerations of public and foreign policy.

Asylum has been viewed functionally as either "diplomatic" or "territorial." Diplomatic asylum refers to a grant of refuge for a political offender by a foreign embassy or legation within a host country. The apparent, attendant immunity from local sovereignty is based upon "exterritoriality," a fictional principle of international law propounded in the seventeenth century by the Dutch jurist Hugo Grotius, who at one time sought refuge in France as a political fugitive. As Sinha points out, the practice of diplomatic asylum "is not of a concordantly general nature and . . . has not been accepted by states as obligatory." For instance, during the Spanish Civil War, the United States embassy in Madrid, a possible base for activity against the government, refused to extend diplomatic asylum or temporary refuge to Spanish citizens. On the other hand, Chile granted asylum in its embassy and found relations with the Spanish Republic strained.

Because diplomatic asylum has not acquired an obligatory status in international law, few nations outside Latin America accord it. Historical conditions explain the granting of asylum there. As in Spain and Turkey during the nineteenth century, government instability and internal disorder have existed throughout Latin America since independence, thereby prompting the extension of diplomatic asylum to political offenders, many of whom participated in revolutionary movements. Also, governments during the revolutionary era adopted the practice in order not to jeopardize diplomatic recognition accorded by major foreign states. In five separate conferences, from Montevideo in 1889 to Caracas in 1954, the American republics, with the exception of the United States and Peru, concluded a series of treaties constituting an attempt to provide a juridical basis for diplomatic asylum. The two most widely adopted conventions, formulated at

Havana in 1928 and Montevideo in 1933, did not impose an obligation to extend asylum, but recognized the right to grant it based upon customary usage.

In direct contrast, both the United States and Great Britain historically have condemned diplomatic asylum. The United States views the practice as subject to much abuse that tends to aggravate the conditions bringing it into being. It is only granted when conditions of extreme disorder exist and lives are consequently endangered, such as during the Boxer Rebellion in China. A modification of this general policy existed until the 1920's in United States embassies and legations in Latin America where asylum was extended on the basis of local toleration for the grant. This situation changed as the United States refused to ratify any of the inter-American conventions on asylum. Foreign Service regulations set down precise guidelines on the extension of diplomatic asylum by American representatives abroad: refuge granted shall usually be terminated if the host country objects or upon "satisfactory assurances from the established national government that the refugee's personal safety is guaranteed against lawless or arbitrary actions and that he will be accorded due process of law."

The other kind of asylum, territorial, also known as political, refers to a grant of refuge by a receiving nation to such refugees as that state may choose to admit within its geographical borders. The recognition of national sovereignty in international law provides the basis for extending territorial asylum. General acceptance of the practice began in Europe after 1830. That a state has no duty to extradite fugitives, except under treaties to which it is a party, reinforces the right to grant territorial asylum. It has traditionally played a role during wartime as neutral territory offered asylum for private property; for public enemy property, including war matériel, cash, and provisions; for private citizens of enemy countries; and for enemy land, air, and naval forces. Prisoners of war and enemy soldiers come within the final category.

AN OPEN DOOR FOR REFUGEES

The response of the United States to the search for refuge goes beyond the mere implementation of carefully defined diplomatic procedures. The extension of territorial asylum more clearly reveals the nature of American asylum policy than does the occasional grant of diplomatic refuge. Asylum constitutes therefore an ad hoc reaction to the exodus of people from their homes. Whatever limitations that approach may have, the United States has demonstrated a generous and receptive attitude toward foreign exiles in the two centuries since independence. Prior to the end of World War I, immigrants and refugees of primarily European extraction entered this country without fear of legal exclusion.

At the time of the Stamp Act crisis, John Adams invoked the unique sense of mission he and his contemporaries associated with the history of the colonies. Blessed by the will of Providence, the United States stood for "the emancipation of the slavish part of mankind all over the earth." As true as the colonials desired that sentiment to be in 1765, it had not always been the case either in law or practice. Non-English immigrants, including French Huguenots, Germans, and Scotch-Irish, endured some hostility from the original settlers and their descendants until they were appreciably assimilated.

The first instance remotely similar to modern grants of territorial asylum occurred at the time of the Revolutionary War when five thousand Hessian soldiers settled in America. Some of the troops—being offered free land by the Continental Congress—deserted the British and moved into established German communities in Pennsylvania, New York, and Virginia. In contrast, the earliest refugees from abroad sought asylum with the new nation during the French Revolution. Predominant among these émigrés were aristocrats and royalist sympathizers. Also, the slave revolt in Santo Domingo in 1791 prompted the flight of perhaps ten to twenty thousand white Frenchmen to the United States within three years. Congress even appropriated $15,000 in 1794 to assist their settlement. As a group the French exiles left few lasting traces of their years in the United States; and by the end of the decade, as Federalist animosity nearly erupted into war with France, many of them returned to their former homeland.

Belief in the ideal of asylum or uncertainty about the kind of foreigners who might seek refuge and possibly settle in the United States played an important role in congressional deliberations over naturalization laws during the 1790's. At one point a five-year period of residence was required before immigrants or refugees could become citizens; xenophobic Federalists increased the waiting period to fourteen years in 1798. Four years later the mandated time between arrival and eligibility for citizenship reverted to five years. After 1914, restrictive immigration laws would be used to keep out unwanted foreigners, often including refugees.

At least thirty million people came to the United States from Europe between 1815 and 1914. Most of them arrived with hopes for material advancement; only a small percentage were actually refugees seeking asylum. Even the refugees were encouraged to partake of the material, spiritual, and political benefits of American society. By the middle of the nineteenth century, for American citizens asylum meant more than temporary refuge. Asylum, as Rush Welter notes, was intended to help "other peoples overcome the burden of their history while still protecting the United States from involvement in the evils Americans had left behind." This view of asylum, consistent with the earlier encomium of John Adams, presumed that many émigrés simply would not desire to return to their homelands. In large measure, Americans had thereby managed to obscure the distinctions between refugees and immigrants.

Real differences continued to exist, however. The liberal German revolution of 1848 and 1849 provided the United States with its largest and most prominent group of refugees during the century. Reasonably wealthy and well educated, more than four thousand "Forty-Eighters" fled to the United States seeking personal safety and hoping to engender support for another effort at revolution back home. Unlike immigrants, they at first had no intention of establishing permanent residence, although most of them did so after failing to receive the desired assistance.

Revolutionary cadres from Europe found little more than sympathy in the United States, although some modest attempts to provide assistance were made. In one case, Italians in New York City in 1848 organized a militia unit to help insurgents fight the Bourbon monarch. With the downfall of the Roman Republic, a new wave of political refugees came to the United States, including Giuseppe Garibaldi who arrived in July 1850. He lived and worked briefly in New York, but moved on to Central America by April 1851. During that year popular support for the Young Italy movement of Giuseppe Mazzini reached its peak. For its part, the American government feted certain leading revolutionaries, the Hungarian Lajos Kossuth being the best known, but rejected all attempts to turn expressions of support into commitments for action.

Throughout the remainder of the 1800's and into the next century, the need for territorial asylum continued to exist. In Hungary freedom of expression all but disappeared. Also, the intermittent pogroms in the wake of the assassination of Alexander II made the life of Russian Jews intolerable; aid came solely from Jewish relief agencies set up in a few countries to assist emigration. Those individuals who actually fled to the United States from southern and eastern Europe comprised only a small percentage of the nearly eight million Italians, Slovaks, and Russians arriving between 1890 and 1920. Consequently, the plight of refugees did not seem as urgent as in the period 1848–1850.

QUALITATIVE EXCLUSION

By 1900 the nation's long-standing open-door attitude toward foreigners had started to change. Excluding certain aliens from the country appeared to be a judicious policy amid the welter of modernization. The popularity of the eugenics movement and the suspicion of aliens fostered by patriotic, veterans, and fraternal organizations coalesced in a widespread campaign for Anglo-conformity. The dyspeptic red scare of 1919–1920 and subsequent forced repatriation of some immigrants made Americans skeptical of potential political refugees from Europe and highlighted the drift toward "qualitative exclusion" of foreigners, to use the apt phrase of Maldwyn Allen Jones. In practice, these developments curtailed the liberal extension of asylum that had existed until that time. Since the government did not accord a different legal status to territorial asylum than to immigration, restrictions upon the admission of foreigners made more difficult the entry of refugees. Exclusion occurred along with the appearance of the first large-scale, forced migration of the century; in the aftermath of World War I, a million and a half Russians were living abroad. Their transient condition was a phenomenon that would be endemic throughout the century.

The fate of the wartime refugees was left in the hands of the League of Nations during the 1920's. The office of the High Commissioner for Refugees performed creditably under the direction of Norway's Fridtjof Nansen despite numerous economic and political obstacles. When Nansen died in 1930, the United States was supporting his efforts only through voluntary contributions of charitable organizations.

The American government was not prepared to deal with large numbers of refugees. It did not recognize the legality of asylum under international law and rarely granted diplomatic asylum. Territorial asylum was extended only if a refugee could reach the United States, but to do so an individual had to meet qualifications set down in the various immigration laws. A provisional statute in 1921 and the Johnson-Reed law of 1924 based admission to the United States upon the 1890 census. Under that system northern Europeans were allowed into the country in numbers that were disproportionate to their desire or need to emigrate, but southern and eastern Europeans found entry more difficult than before. Another change in the immigration quota system in 1929 further limited the chance for settlement of European refugees in the United States. The so-called national origins scheme halved the annual German quota to fewer than twenty-six thousand persons and nearly doubled the generally unused British quota to sixty-five thousand. Also working against individuals most in need of a place of asylum were administrative regulations that levied head taxes and excluded from entry contract labor, people diagnosed as mentally ill, and those who in the determination of American consular officials might become a public charge. The United States seemed to be making refuge, because of its inclusion within immigration statutes, conditional upon an individual's wealth or renown.

Given the economic crisis of the time, exclusion may have been the only politically tenable position. President Herbert Hoover surely overstated the case, however, when he said in October 1932, "With the growth of democracy in foreign countries, political persecution has largely ceased. There is no longer a necessity for the United States to provide an asylum for those persecuted because of conscience." In 1935 there were still more than a million and a half refugees throughout Europe. The efforts of the League of Nations and charitable organizations alone could not alter their situation. Yet governments in Europe were finding it burdensome to assist the League. France, which long had served as a temporary shelter for homeless persons, reluctantly adopted a policy of *refoulement,* or forcible expulsion of refugees whose allotted time of residence had elapsed. An effort was made during the civil war in Spain to extend diplomatic asylum to beleaguered Spanish nationals whose lives were in danger. Fourteen nations, none a major power, took part in the action.

Some Americans became alarmed at the worsening conditions for refugees in Europe, but most attempts to translate concern into assistance proved unavailing. Several crucial barriers existed: exclusionist sentiment had been increasing for fifty years; the depression continued to be the primary fact of life in the country; and there were renewed doubts about the assimilability of foreigners, especially Jews. At the same time, because of a widespread belief that the United States had participated needlessly in World War I, there existed an aversion to further involvement in European political affairs.

As a result of the interplay of these conditions, the vast majority of Americans stood by as "Aryanization" continued apace in Germany and persecution of Jews worsened in the aftermath of *Kristallnacht* in November 1938. Over three-fourths of the people then responding to a Gallup opinion poll remained opposed to entry into the United States of larger numbers of Jewish refugees. A share of the responsibility for this situation must rest with the government. Concerning the president and the Jews, Saul Friedman writes that Franklin D. Roosevelt "consistently avoided acknowledging their singular persecution between 1933 and 1945." European Jews had no more chance of gaining asylum than did serfs in feudal times who were excluded from the practice of territorial asylum.

Nonetheless, some persecuted Europeans managed to escape Nazi Germany's grasp. One group of individuals receiving special assistance was composed of intellectuals, many of whom were Jewish. American officials invoked a section of the 1929 national origins law providing for nonquota immigration of persons capable of teaching in institutions of higher learning. Yet even the arrival of the refugee intellectuals, except for such internationally renowned figures as Albert Einstein, Thomas Mann, and Paul Tillich, to name only three, provoked controversy. Some academics feared for their own positions. That fear never became a reality, in part because of the establishment of facilities such as the Institute for Advanced Study at Princeton and the availability of private funding for special projects at American universities. As generous as this reception was, most other potential émigrés had no access to similar assistance, thus lending credence to the conclusion that the extension of asylum was related to the quality of persons benefiting from the grant.

ASYLUM SINCE WORLD WAR II

By the end of the war in Europe, nearly six million Jews had been killed. For those who survived, but who were still confined to the camps, problems remained. For instance, the mandate of the United Nations Relief and Rehabilitation Agency did not specifically cover Jews—only those "displaced persons" who could be defined as "Allied nationals" or as former enemy nationals in immediate danger of persecution. Before their needs could be met adequately, thousands of Jews died of starvation; others received insufficient supplies of food and clothing.

This situation underlined the deficiencies in the international approach to asylum and the treatment of refugees. The denial of a place for asylum within international law failed to respond to the needs of refugees and potential émigrés. Either the legal status of asylum had to be altered or international agencies and individual countries had to make special provisions to deal with refugees. Although both measures were taken to an extent, the latter proved to be more effective.

The United States employed executive orders and amendments to immigration statutes along with other legislative means to assist refugees. Late in September 1945, President Harry S. Truman ordered special arrangements to be made for homeless Jews still suffering in Europe. He next issued an executive order on 22 December that ultimately admitted more than forty-one thousand refugees and displaced persons to the United States. Then in 1948 Congress passed the Displaced Persons Act, under which more than four hundred thousand persons entered this country by the end of 1952.

The newly created United Nations also helped in ameliorating the plight of refugees. Organized on the initiative of the United States and Great Britain, the International Refugee Organization (IRO) began a program of planned migrations that lasted from 1947 to 1952. The IRO moved more than a million people to Australia, Canada, Latin America, and the United States; it fed and housed an even larger number of persons who remained in Europe. Of great help, too, in relieving Europe's burden of caring for so many refugees was the settlement in Palestine by 1951 of more than three hundred thousand Jews.

In the midst of the ongoing effort to find homes for stateless people, the relationship between asylum and international law received renewed attention. Legal questions regarding asylum primarily have concerned the right of the state to grant, rather than that of the individual to receive, asylum. Under the positivist doctrine of international law, the consent of states is necessary to determine the content of the law and to what subjects it applies. In practice, international law has evolved so that it applies exclusively to states; individuals cannot derive any rights therefrom. Yet the spread of constitutionalism and popular government in the nineteenth century brought with it the belief that individuals have the right to rebel against oppressive governments. The related question then arose whether people whose well-being was uncertain could be guaranteed freedom from persecution.

Legally, of course, no country could be compelled to grant asylum. The United Nations, however, sought to assist potential refugees. Article 14 of the Universal Declaration of

Human Rights, approved by the General Assembly on 10 December 1948, provides:

> 1. Everyone has the right to seek and enjoy in other countries asylum from persecution.
> 2. This right may not be invoked in the case of prosecution genuinely arising from non-political crimes or from acts contrary to the purposes and principles of the United Nations.

Although it is possible to argue otherwise, there exists in Article 14 no intention to assume either a legal or moral obligation to grant asylum. Such an interpretation would have forced changes in the immigration laws of most nations and would have amounted to a limitation upon national sovereignty. At most, Article 14 therefore serves as a means of extending respect for the practice of granting asylum.

Earlier in 1948 several Latin American states acted in a similar, expansive vein. Article 27 of the American Republics Declaration of the Rights and Duties of Man, adopted at an inter-American conference held at Bogotá, Colombia, provides: "Every person has the right, in case of pursuit not resulting from ordinary crimes, to seek and receive asylum in foreign territory, in accordance with the laws of each country and with international agreements."

About the same time a federal court in the United States reaffirmed traditional restrictions on the extension of asylum. The ruling in *Chandler* v. *United States* (1949) held: "But the right is that of the state voluntarily to offer asylum, not that of the fugitive to insist upon it." As was true of the Universal Declaration of Human Rights, the court's ruling emphasized the difficulty in reconciling the historical role of nations with the protection of individual rights within a framework of international law. A United Nations conference held at Geneva in 1951 endeavored to minimize the legal problems associated with asylum by adopting the Convention Relating to the Status of Refugees. Various provisions of the convention define the rights and duties of a refugee in the receiving country as well as the obligations of that country to a refugee. The United States has not become a party to the convention.

Even were asylum accorded a legitimate place in international law, disputes would likely continue over the nature of offenses for which asylum could be granted. The statutes of most nations, including the United States, fail to define the terms "political offender" or "political offense," nor are they clarified in extradition treaties. For example, the Immigration and Nationality Act of 1952 exempts, without further explanation, people convicted of "a purely political offense" from those aliens ineligible for admission to the United States. It seems clear, however, that the murder of a public official does not fall within the purview of generally acknowledged political offenses. Nor are the actions of anarchists deemed to merit asylum since, in theory, anarchists oppose all forms of government.

Asylum acquired a greater political importance in the years after World War II than the foregoing discussion of its legal and administrative role indicates. By early 1946 it was evident that the Soviet Union and the United States held fundamentally incompatible ideas regarding the composition of the postwar world. Asylum policy, as implemented by the United States, served the purposes of postwar anticommunism. Syngman Rhee returned to Korea after thirty-five years' exile in the United States to head the anticommunist government in South Korea. Also, the United States successfully embarrassed the Soviets with its assistance to displaced persons and refugees in Europe and Asia. The International Refugee Organization, the United Nations Korean Reconstruction Agency, and other resettlement programs depended heavily upon American funding for their existence. Accordingly, they became tied to broader political considerations in the early years of the Cold War. As Alona E. Evans concludes, a grant of "political asylum is predicated in substantial part upon considerations of public policy."

The numbers of refugees needing asylum increased dramatically in the 1950's. An average of more than two hundred thousand people fled to West Germany each year. Along with the refugees there were numerous indigenous nationals who desired to leave their homes and settle elsewhere. Since the International Refugee Organization and other agencies were not equipped to handle the situation, the United States proposed the creation of the Intergovernmental Committee for European Migration at the Brussels Conference on Migration late in 1951. The task of the migration committee was to move both normal migrants and refugees to countries affording resettlement opportunities.

The major effort of the migration committee in the first years of operation came in the aftermath of the rebellion against Soviet domination in Hungary in October 1956. The organization helped ninety-four thousand Hungarians to resettle. The United States, having given unwitting encouragement to the revolt with broadcasts over Radio Free Europe, also rendered needed assistance to the refugees. By using visas provided by the 1953 Refugee Relief Act (the Hungarian quota was subscribed through 1990), the United States took in nearly thirty-eight thousand exiles by the end of 1957. A presidential directive of 1 December 1956, authorizing the admission of twelve thousand Hungarians on parole, or temporary admission, under the 1952 Immigration and Nationality Act, also proved helpful.

Two other occurrences in the decade further illustrate the close link between the course of international politics, the treatment of refugees, and the extension of territorial asylum. Arising out of both the flight of many people to West Germany and the situation in Hungary, the Soviet Union, with the assistance of its East European allies, initiated an extensive repatriation campaign. The mildest tactic employed was amnesty for the émigrés and an appeal to religious ties with their homelands. In one instance in East Berlin, a Committee for Return to the Motherland was set up to issue pleas for return home from the families and friends of those who had fled to the West. The Soviets tried more direct measures in the United States. Diplomatic officials brought to the attention of the Immigration and Naturalization Service legal or procedural deficiencies in the status of refugees on parole in the United States. At one point the intrusive activities of the Soviet Union moved the Department of State to declare *persona non grata* several members of the Soviet delegation to the United Nations and staff members of the embassy in Washington, D.C.

The other occurrence reemphasized one of the basic problems associated with the lives of refugees in the postwar era, that of determining whether they qualified for asylum in a foreign nation. The West German Federal Constitutional Court described the problem in 1959: "The 'politization' of large spheres of life and the utilization of criminal law for securing and carrying out social and political revolutions have blurred the boundary line between 'criminal' and 'political' offenses in many states."

If nothing else, the vast number of stateless or quasi-stateless people, perhaps one hundred fifty million in 1961, attested to the complexity of the situation. Relief organizations and individual governments therefore had an obligation to act responsibly. This seemed especially true of the United States which, as John Stoessinger writes, "by footing the largest part of the [relief] bill, has enjoyed a veto power over life and death."

The postwar involvement of the United States in the matter of territorial and diplomatic asylum was not as passive as considerations of international law or the encouragement of flight and subsequent reception of foreign exiles suggest. The Cold War policies of the United States at times created the need for asylum in various regions of the world. Nowhere was this process more evident than in Cuba after Fidel Castro seized power. Had the United States not severed relations with Cuba and not tried to overthrow the Castro regime, it seems plausible that fewer Cubans would have left their homes for refuge abroad. The exile of many Cubans was doubtlessly self-imposed, but the diplomatic quarantine of Cuba followed by the missile crisis in 1962 in all probability convinced numerous others that they should emigrate.

The Cuban exiles were fortunate. American officials, if not all the citizens of Florida, were prepared to provide sanctuary for them in the Miami area. By July 1961, nearly sixty-six thousand Cubans were living in the United States as refugees. As the nation of first asylum, the United States assumed a large economic burden. Geographical proximity to Cuba posed a greater problem, however. In short, the laws of the country and the Cuban policy of the Kennedy administration were incompatible. Under neutrality legislation it is a criminal offense to raise hostile forces to fight a foreign country with which the United States is not at war. The various attempts to remove Castro from power partly by the use of Cubans previously tendered asylum ostensibly violated neutrality statutes.

The government possessed the ability to control the actions of refugees under provisions in the immigration laws. Of approximately sixty-six thousand Cuban refugees, more than one-half were classified as nonimmigrants who were technically deportable. Five thousand others were parolees residing in the country on a temporary basis. Although the government did not legally try to stop the anti-Castro activity, by 1965 the situation had stabilized enough for the United States and Cuba, through the Swiss embassy in Havana, to exchange diplomatic notes establishing procedures for the continued exodus of refugees.

The Cuban experience led to a reconsideration of the place of asylum within the immigration laws of the United States. In 1965 Congress amended the 1952 law to eliminate the national origins quota system and made special provision for the admission of refugees. Under the new law, a maximum of 170,000 immigrants per year, excluding special cases and the relatives of citizens, were eligible for entry. More than one hundred thousand people from the Western Hemisphere could qualify each year as special immigrants. (A new law greatly reduced that number as of 1 January 1977.) Another 10,200 could receive conditional admission if they met certain requirements, which included having fled a communist or communist-dominated state or the general area of the Middle East; having fled on account of persecution or fear of persecution for reasons of race, religion, or political opinion; being unwilling to return home for the same reasons; and being a non-national of, but having applied for entry to, the United States in Austria, Belgium, France, West Germany, Greece, Hong Kong, Italy, or Lebanon. Those persons conditionally in the country were liable to summary deportation, but after living in the United States for two years could obtain the status of permanent resident at the discretion of the attorney general.

By 1965 changes in immigration laws that took the issue of asylum into account were long overdue. This does not imply that American policy toward refugees after World War II was ignoble or parsimonious; at least a million exiles entered the country between 1945 and 1965. Yet special attention to the plight of refugees marked an important change in American policy. Never before had asylum been so clearly distinguished from immigration in the nation's laws. (The United States, of course, still did not admit the legality of asylum under international law.) The law of 1965 explicitly addressed the contemporary needs of large numbers of refugees. Indeed, the statute amounts to tacit admission by the United States that its foreign policy throughout the Cold War helped to bring about conditions that resulted in many people leaving their homes.

Such a crucial admission, albeit by implication, would seem to entail special responsibilities for the American government. In the case of the Vietnamese refugees, thousands of whom streamed into Saigon just prior to its fall in April 1975, the United States responded insufficiently to the situation. Families were broken up; and children, many of whom were not orphans, were taken from their country under American auspices. The very real tragedy of "Operation Babylift" cannot be minimized, but the numbers were small compared to the total of 135,000 Vietnamese who eventually came to the United States. The extension of asylum arose primarily out of two policy considerations: to provide humanitarian assistance, if possible, and to reassure the allies of the United States of the continued worldwide American commitments to them.

The contradictory effects of the American response to the situation faced by Vietnamese refugees symbolized the postwar history of asylum. Attempts to provide a place of refuge for stateless persons became increasingly reflective of broader policy considerations, most of which were dictated by the course of the Cold War. The resulting changes in American immigration laws and the expanded efforts of international resettlement agencies, often on the initiative of the United States, undoubtedly had a salutary effect for countless people. Administrative and legislative means had thereby circumvented the traditional legal limitations upon the extension of asylum and given due recognition for the first time in the century to the issue of forced migration. Although it was still possible to exclude exiles from entry into the United States, admission policy no longer seemed to be predicated upon qualitative exclusion. The American standard of asylum had not reverted to what John Adams believed it to be 200 years earlier, nor to the nationalistic optimism of the 1840's and 1850's, but it still offered genuine hope to many foreigners.

BIBLIOGRAPHY

The best source on the status of asylum within international law, and the most available source for the writings of Alona E. Evans, is the *American Journal of International Law.* Martin A. Bursten, *Escape From Fear* (Syracuse, N.Y., 1958), is a journalistic account of American aid for Hungarian refugees in 1956–1957. Alexander DeConde, *Half Bitter, Half Sweet* (New York, 1971), is a thorough study of Italian-American cultural exchange. Robert A. Divine, *American Immigration Policy, 1924–1952* (New Haven, Conn., 1957), details the development of restrictionist immigration legislation in the twentieth century. Richard R. Fagan, Richard A. Brody, and Thomas J. O'Leary, *Cubans in Exile* (Stanford, Calif., 1968), is a strong, analytical study of the flight of Cubans from their homeland in the early 1960's. Laura Fermi, *Illustrious Immigrants* (Chicago, 1968), gives a descriptive account of the flight of prominent European intellectuals to the United States in the 1930's. Saul S. Friedman, *No Haven for the Oppressed* (Detroit, Mich., 1973), has the best analysis of the failure of the United States to assist European Jews in the 1930's and 1940's. Manuel R. Garcia-Mora, *International Law and Asylum as a Human Right* (Washington, D.C., 1956), is an impassioned attempt to find a place for individual rights within modern international law. Maldwyn Allen Jones, *American Immigration* (Chicago, 1960), is an extensive historical survey. Arthur D. Morse, *While Six Million Died* (New York, 1968), is an accusative account of the role of the United States in the extermination of Jews by Nazi Germany. Malcolm J. Proudfoot, *European Refugees: 1939–52* (Evanston, Ill., 1956), is a detailed survey of population movements. C. Neale Ronning, *Diplomatic Asylum: Legal Norms and Political Reality in Latin America* (The Hague, 1965), gives a thorough survey of the history of diplomatic asylum in Latin America. S. Prakash Sinha, *Asylum and International Law* (The Hague, 1971), is an excellent survey of the development of asylum in relation to international law. John C. Stoessinger, *The Refugee and the World Community* (Minneapolis, Minn., 1956), has a solid overview of the problems involved in the settlement of refugees after World War II. Philip Taylor, *The Distant Magnet: European Emigration to the U.S.A.* (New York, 1971), is an important survey of social history from 1830 to 1930. The United States Department of State, *Digest of International Law* (Washington, D.C., 1968), gives a brief, important overview of the legal status of diplomatic and territorial asylum in international politics. Rush Welter, *The Mind of America, 1820–1860* (New York, 1975), is an excellent intellectual history with important implications for the study of asylum. Carl Wittke, *Refugees of Revolution: The German Forty-Eighters in America* (Westport, Conn., 1952), is a scholarly account of the flight of German liberals to the United States after 1848.

[*See also* ETHNICITY AND FOREIGN POLICY; INTERNATIONAL LAW; NATIVISM.]

BALANCE OF POWER

A. E. Campbell

THE balance of power appears at first sight a simple concept. It has been defined as "a phrase in international law for such a 'just equilibrium' between the members of the family of nations as should prevent any one of them from becoming sufficiently strong to enforce its will upon the rest." Yet the phrase has always been of more use in political polemic than in political analysis. Like other phrases with a strong emotional appeal it is vague, and it would lose its appeal if it were more precise. Its obscurities are several, but the most important is that it blends the descriptive and the normative. The condition is one, the term "balance" implies, toward which international life is forever tending. That is the descriptive element. But the condition is also one that may be upset, and right-thinking statesmen should constantly be on the alert to preserve or restore it. That is the normative element. These two elements reinforce each other. Because such a balance will be established in any event, it is sensible and moral to work toward it. Because men work toward it, it will be more readily established. Difficulties arise if either element is weakened. At what point is it right to abandon an old balance and accept a new one? Can a balance exist if men are unconscious of the need to maintain it?

Behind all the interpretations of the balance of power lies the appeal to realism in the conduct of international affairs. Realism remains the best, perhaps the only persuasive, argument for restraint; and it is common ground that the doctrine of the balance of power is a device to promote restraint, whether men argue that lack of restraint is wrong, or dangerous, or ultimately bound to fail. In that sense the balance of power in international affairs is clearly related to the idea of checks and balances within a government, which is equally a device to impose restraint on men who might otherwise, seduced by power, abandon it.

The international balance received its classical exposition during the eighteenth century, about the time at which, largely during the struggle for independence of the American colonies, the idea of checks and balances within a government was elaborated. Although linked, the doctrines had important differences. The international balance existed, if at all, among similar entities, the recognized powers, who placed in the scale weights of the same kind—military power actual or potential. It was the lack of any precedent and effective authority among nations that made the balance of power necessary. The threat of war maintained the balance, and sometimes war was needed to restore it. By contrast the domestic balance refined by the Founding Fathers was not among powers of the same sort, but among powers of different sorts. All these were derived from the people, who might limit, redistribute, or withdraw what they had given. And few men believed that domestic society rested on the perpetual threat of strife.

It is not an accident that the doctrine of the balance of power—alike in international and in domestic politics—received its classic and most rigorous statements at a time when foreign policy was largely a matter for rulers who could use the war-potential of their states for their own aggrandizement. It was because a ruler had to be able to wage effective war that he had to be allowed the armed force that contributed to his domestic control. British reliance on a navy rather than on a standing army was, and was known to be, important to the growth of

British liberties—and later to American liberty. In a sense, therefore, the international balance of power was needed to check the pretensions of rulers who lacked any effective domestic check.

Many of the early American leaders, however, held the belief that in their new world a more just—a more perfect—society than that of Europe could be formed. Historians may differ about the degree to which that implied a regard for democracy. The tyrant people was hardly less to be feared than the tyrant king. But that sensible, rational men—of property and standing—could cooperate for the common good, few doubted. To balance the servants of the public against each other was both a political safeguard and a political convenience, rendering excess less likely and vigilance less demanding. It was not a political necessity of the same order as the international balance of power. Americans quickly came to believe, and continued to believe through most of their history, that sound domestic institutions must bring sound foreign policies with them.

The balance of power, however, although it may act to restrain the actions of those who believe in the doctrine, is in the first instance a device to restrain others. Should not Americans, very conscious that other states were not founded on their own good principles, have been ready to consider contributing to the maintenance of an international balance when appropriate, more rather than less because their own domestic principles were sound? There is little evidence that they did consider doing so, and that fact may throw light on the limitations of the doctrine.

The revolutionary war itself provides an example of the balance of power in operation. A desire not to be involved in the European balance, not to be a weight in the British scale, had played an important part in the American demand for independence. It was the readiness of the allies in the coalition against Britain to abandon each other, and the readiness of Britain to calculate relative gains and losses, that made the outcome possible. Behind the behavior of all the parties in the American war lay a tacit agreement that American independence was acceptable—the Americans wanted to be removed from the British scale, the French and Spaniards wanted the colonies removed from the British scale, but on their side the British were finally convinced that that removal would not have disadvantages only. Such calculations may imply a large element of uncertainty as to how the independent United States would behave—why should their independence weaken Britain more than their continued existence as disaffected colonies?—but in the event few of the negotiators had any doubt as to the only possible conclusion of the war.

For a short time after independence, Americans remembered that the European balance of power had played some part in their victory. George Washington's famous injunction against "excessive partiality for one foreign nation and excessive dislike of another" would hardly have been necessary had there been no Americans who wanted to align themselves either with Britain or with France. It would not have been uttered had American interests clearly required an alignment with either side. Yet in the political debates at the end of the eighteenth century there was already a large ideological element. Washington was not merely arguing that a due regard for the balance of power requires powers to hold themselves aloof until it is clear that the balance is about to tip, and then to place in the scale only such weight as is needed to adjust it. He was urging his countrymen not to take sides in European quarrels whose outcome could not affect the United States.

So well did they learn their lesson and follow his injunction that at a later stage in the Napoleonic war Americans seemed to have little or no interest in the issues of the war. Neutral rights, and no doubt a free hand in the Americas, were what concerned them. Neither the possibility that Napoleon might come to dominate the world, which loomed so large to many Britons, nor the possibility that he might overthrow the archaic monarchies of Europe and bring in a new order, which seemed to others an exciting prospect, affected Americans to any great extent.

By that time the doctrine of the balance of power had ceased to interest Americans, and so it remained for a full century. Most students would contend that a balance of power existed in the world of the nineteenth century and perhaps worked more effectively than ever before or since, and that whether they chose to recognize the balance or not, Americans were beneficiaries of it. Americans then gave little weight to that proposition, and they were right. They quickly discovered a doctrine, or a practice, that served their needs better than any contribution to a balance of power. This was the American withdrawal from the affairs of Europe—in certain matters only—enshrined in the Monroe Doctrine of 1823. Attacking the international system, the British radical Richard Cobden could use as one of his chief arguments the fact that *"America, with infinite wisdom, refuses to be a party to the 'balance of power'* " (Cobden's emphasis).

If Americans could so largely ignore the existence of the balance on which their security finally rested, it follows that the balance was more stable than it has often been. This is, clearly, a balance in one sense, and perhaps in the most obvious sense—forces resting in equilibrium without perpetual adjustment and still more without fundamental readjustment. When the balance of power is most noticed, it is because it must be maintained—that is, because it is in perpetual danger of tipping too far to one side or the other. What, then, are the conditions of stability such that they can even be neglected? American experience suggests that they are the introduction of what might be called an element of friction into the balance, something that operates on neither side, but inhibits movement or makes it more difficult.

It was this friction that the geographical distance of the United States from the power center of Europe introduced, so that for Americans the balance of power was always less delicate. Until the era of modern communications, this distance clearly made it more difficult for the United States to intervene in a European quarrel. Both more resources and more time were needed to sustain effective intervention. On the other hand, the converse was equally true. While it might be arguable that the complete overthrow of the European balance, and the dominance of Europe by one power or group of powers, would endanger the security of the United States, it was also arguable that that dominance would have to be more complete than it was ever likely in practice to be. The balance in Europe would have to be tipped far past the point at which the security of some European states was endangered before there could be any threat to the security of the United States. As Abraham Lincoln put it, rhetorically enough, in an address before the Young Men's Lyceum of Springfield, Illinois, on 27 January 1838: "All the armies of Europe, Asia and Africa combined, with all the treasure of the earth (our own excepted) in their military chest; with a Buonaparte for a commander, could not by force, take a drink from the Ohio, or make a track on the Blue Ridge, in a trial of a thousand years."

This meant that American reluctance to be drawn into the quarrels of Europe was for long a realistic one. Americans could benefit from the balance of power without being fully conscious of it. The European states made little effort to involve the United States in their concerns. The well-known claim made in 1826 by George Canning, then British foreign secretary, to have "called the New World into existence, to redress the balance of the Old," was confined in practice to denying France "Spain with the Indies." With that accomplished, there was an agreement (so general that it could be ignored) that there was no effective and inexpensive way of using American support in a European quarrel; nor, per contra, of using European support in an American quarrel. For most of the nineteenth century Britain was the only major power that had serious differences with the United States. Difficulties arose over Canada, over Britain's remaining Caribbean possessions, and over trade, but the British always concluded that such differences should be settled—if need be even by British surrender—without attempting to involve other powers. They were not prepared to call in the Old World to redress the balance of the New.

Perhaps this became most obvious at times when it looked as if the United States might not continue to dominate North America. In 1842 and 1843 it was widely supposed that Britain would guarantee the independence of Texas in return for the abolition of slavery there—as a preliminary to attacking slavery in the United States. "The present attempt upon Texas is the beginning of her operations upon us," wrote Secretary of State Abel P. Upshur. It came to nothing. Still more obviously, during the Civil War the Confederacy hoped for European recognition and even intervention. The hope rested on several grounds, but clearly implicit was the belief that a restored American union could not be in the interest of Europe. Nor was it. But none of the European powers—among whom Britain was the key—had sufficient interest in creating an American balance to justify the European risks that the effort would entail. The relative remoteness of America meant that the effort would have had to be greater than the rewards justified, and great enough to entail unacceptable risks nearer home. It remained possible, and it was easier and safer, to exclude the United States from a European balance, rather than to draw the Americas into an enlarged world balance.

Social change in the nineteenth century, however, was to reveal certain limitations in the doctrine of the balance of power. Some advocates of the balance have defended it on the ground that it maintains peace, or, at all events, sets limits to wars—a proposition supported to some extent by the American revolutionary war. Others have contended, with Edmund Burke, that the balance "has been the original [origin] of innumerable and fruitless wars" and "ever has been, and it is to be feared always will continue a cause of infinite contention and bloodshed." To such critics the purpose, or at any rate the desirable result, of the balance was the maintenance not of peace but of liberty. As many have pointed out, there is something inconsistent about the notion of going to war to preserve peace. One must calculate that continuing peace will result in some undesirable consequence, before war is justified. Loss of freedom is the most persuasive such consequence.

The ninteenth century saw the growth of romantic nationalism and democracy, and with it the demand of peoples for some voice in policy. In some areas rulers could behave as before, but increasingly the aggrandizement of princes was felt to have natural limits and was overshadowed by other forms of state activity. Within Europe, transfers of territory were found to cause more trouble than they were worth unless they were accompanied by wholesale transfers of population, a resource more acceptable in the twentieth century than in the nineteenth. The great revolution in nineteenth-century Europe, the unification of Germany—the unification of Italy had no equal consequences—was tolerated partly because its effect on the balance of power was not immediately foreseen, but partly also because it was held to be an expression of nationalism that could not justly be opposed, rather than mere Prussian aggrandizement—so that it would increase stability rather than lessen it. In a war of the ordinary sort, by contrast, there were natural limits to what the victor could gain, and the destruction of a rival nation lay outside them. As that was accepted, it became possible to argue that defense itself, the most traditional and urgent duty of the nation-state, might have unacceptable consequences for the quality of life within the state. There seemed better ways than conquest to increase wealth and power. With the modern revolution in technology, and with the ever-increasing role of government in the lives of citizens, discussions of the balance of power took on a new dimension.

Thus, when World War I broke out, although all parties made some play with the need to maintain or protect the balance of power (which, of course, they interpreted variously), none of them could argue that governments, or princes, were behaving in the way which one would expect. German apologists had to contend that Germany was surrounded by malevolent foes and that the survival of Germany was at stake. The Allies had to contend not merely that Germany was too powerful for comfort, but that German militarism threatened a European civilization which would otherwise be peaceable. The argument, in short, could not be cast in terms of the balance of power.

Americans were presented with a dilemma. It was not, in the first instance, a dilemma of policy. Clearly the United States was not immediately threatened. The great growth of American power during the nineteenth century, if it made the policy of fortress America less necessary, made it no less appealing. It was hard to argue that the victor in the European war, whatever the outcome, would turn on the United States. Americans were therefore forced toward moral judgments about the merits of the war. Some indeed argued that what was going on was an old-fashioned struggle for the balance of power, of a sort which revealed how politically backward even the most advanced of European states were, and of a sort with which the United States had no concern. Others accepted the argument that German militarism was the root of the trouble. Historians will long continue to debate the causes that finally brought the United States into the war, and their merits, but it is clear that no balance of power argument would have sufficed. A balance of power argument would have kept the United States neutral. (With the advantage of hindsight it might be argued that since the United States was the beneficiary of a balance of power in Europe likely to be upset, the proper American course was to intervene delicately to tip the balance back to the point at which it had been—and no more. Yet because the balance was bound to shift, war or no war, as the whole history of Europe in the 1920's and 1930's was to show, that kind of intervention could not have been temporary and would have required a degree of anxious vigilance over the long term which could have been neither sustained nor justified.) Neutrality, defended on grounds of self-interest and its morality, or intervention, defended on moral grounds, were the only serious alternatives and the only alternatives debated.

The decision for war was President Woodrow Wilson's, and in taking it he was much moved by the realization that if the United States did not participate in the war it would have no voice in the settlement that followed it. As part of the settlement Wilson was determined to establish an international concert—the League of Nations—which would bring about a better world order. Wilson's hostility to the balance of power was intense, and it was widely shared by Americans of his day. In an address at the Guildhall, London, on 29 December 1918, Wilson stated that

> the center and characteristic of the old order was that unstable thing which we used to call the "balance of power"—a thing in which the balance was determined by the sword which was thrown in the one side or the other; a balance which was determined by the unstable equilibrium of competitive interests; a balance which was maintained by jealous watchfulness and an antagonism of interests which, though it was generally latent, was always deep-seated.

Wilson made an automatic connection between the balance of power and spheres of influence, to which he was equally opposed. That connection is characteristic of much American thinking on the subject; its consistency with adherence to the Monroe Doctrine is clearer to Americans than to others.

The approach of World War II presented Americans with a dilemma of a different sort. The Great Depression diverted attention from international affairs, but increasingly Americans could not avoid being drawn into efforts both to mitigate the depression itself and to mitigate the political consequences that seemed to follow. The whole structure of reparations and war debts set up at Versailles would alone have required American involvement. The rise of aggressive regimes in Italy, Germany, and Japan, together with the long-cherished hope that they might be rendered more moderate by well-calculated economic concessions, or by democratic strength and solidarity, or a combination of these, ensured it. By contrast with the years before World War I, few Americans doubted on which side their sympathies lay. Whatever their fears of communism, the Soviet Union was quiescent, and the actions of the Nazis deprived their claim to be a bulwark against communism of all appeal. Secretary of State Cordell Hull (1933–1944) shared completely Wilson's dislike of the balance of power, and had learned it in the same school; but such views, although they became influential again later, were irrelevant in the 1930's, when it became ever clearer—certainly to President Franklin D. Roosevelt—that the important contest was not among rival states but between dictatorship and democracy.

Paradoxically the desire of Europeans, especially the British, that the United States should become part of the balance of power—that the New World should be called in to redress the balance of the Old—and the fact that Americans had little doubt on which side their sympathies lay, did almost nothing to make policy decisions easier. The arguments, both within the American government and between Americans and British, are a fascinating and complex field, on which much work remains to be done. But in essence a dispute developed among the Allies—even before the alliance was formed—over who should contribute how much to the common cause. The residue of American security, which was very great, together with well-founded doubts as to whether the interests of the United States might not be better served if some accommodation were reached in Europe without American intervention—doubts shared by some European statesmen, such as Neville Chamberlain—meant that American activity was diplomatically ineffective. A slow process of economic support for the Western democracies did begin, and might in time have drawn the United States into the war, but Hitler had the good sense to avoid the mistakes of his predecessors, and he was at great pains to avoid giving the United States an occasion for belligerency. That occasion was, of course, provided by Japan.

Some exponents of balance of power theory have argued that the theory requires that nations should match, if need be by war, any increase in a rival's power, actual or foreseen, even in the absence of any aggressive act. But all the evidence suggests that even when nations have adequate cause for war, they do not go to war unless they also have an occasion for war. The occasion, the indicator that the right moment for war has arrived, is vital. Of course, occasions for war can often be manufactured when they are needed; but they are hard to manufacture, or even to identify, for a nation that disposes of such great reserves of security as the United States. One important argument is missing—the argument that if the nation does not fight now, it will be too late to fight tomorrow. It is that argument—with its corollary that opponents must be supposed to know how sensitive one's position is, and that therefore their threats are not accidental but evidence of real intention—which identifies most clearly the occasion for war. At Pearl Harbor the Japanese faced the United States with an affront such as no nation could possibly let pass. The Germans had been most careful to avoid an affront. (In World War I, on the other hand, when by reviving their unrestricted submarine campaign they deliberately took the risk of American intervention, a good many Americans could still be found to argue that the affront was not great enough to justify war in the absence of a real threat. The cause of neutral rights and of democracy had to be invoked.)

Just as a nation needs a signal to begin a war, so it needs a signal to stop, and that signal is often even harder to give or to detect. Because statesmen in the modern world are seldom wholly cynical, they commonly feel that war has been forced on them. As a war continues they begin to raise their demands to include compensation for losses incurred. It is therefore hard to identify the point at which agreement for a truce can be reached, short of the final defeat of one side. Every success by either side leads it to think that final victory may be possible, every defeat that this is not the moment to negotiate. It is the intellectual difficulty of translating the theory of the balance of power into a workable policy in a specific situation that, more than anything else, ensures that this theory is seldom of use when the time comes for negotiation.

These generalizations are supported by American practice in two world wars, yet American practice was not different from that of any other nation. Neither Britain nor France paid any special heed to the balance of power during either war. No way could be found of ending either without the complete defeat of one side. After each war the recourse was not to some restored balance, but to a congress system. The experience of the League of Nations suggested to the Allies in 1945 that no security structure was worth anything unless the great powers agreed, and that the right of veto might as well be formally accepted. If the five powers were not in agreement, the hope was at best for stalemate, by the agreed inactivity of four if one stood out. As always at the end of a war, what was in men's minds was peace, rather than either liberty or justice.

In neither war, then, did the United States enter for considerations of the balance of power. In both, the entry of the United States so quickly and completely tilted the balance of power in favor of the side it joined that had the United States been regarded as an element in the balance, the wars in the form they took would never have broken out. After World War I, the United States withdrew in disillusionment. After World War II that recourse was not open, although many in the Truman administration feared it and worked to prevent it. It took time before it became apparent, either to Americans or to any others, that the balance had been shifted permanently during, and to some extent as a result of, the war. It took time before it was realized that Britain would not recover, that France was not a world power, and that non-communist China would not become the guardian of the Far East. Yet paradoxically, while the postwar hope of a concert gave way, just as it did after the Congress of Vienna, to an ideological confrontation, the balance of power was being restored.

It has often been argued that the balance of power is really an imbalance of power. If the balance is to work at all, there must be at least three parties, such that any two can overpower the third, should its activities become too threatening. More than three are better; but three is the minimum. The idea of balance as implying some sort of equality gives way readily to the idea of balance as superiority of force on the side of the existing order. The balance between two powers or groups—sometimes called the "simple" balance—is altogether too unstable. It requires a degree of vigilance, of preparedness, of national concentration on defense, which is ultimately intolerable. Just such a balance, of course, the Cold War implied, and it should come as no surprise that the rhetoric of the Cold War, on both sides (although recent attention has been given to that of the West) did not speak of balance at all, but looked to victory. That is a characteristic of the simple balance.

It was well recognized that the United States and the Soviet Union were in direct and unique competition. The appalling consequences of nuclear war introduced a new kind of stability. The so-called balance of terror or balance of deterrence ensured that each nuclear power was anxious not to give the other power any sort of signal that would justify an attack, and was also anxious not to identify such a signal. This caution was compatible with, and even required, an arms race. It was not by accident that for a time the chief danger to stability was thought to arise in an area—Western Europe—where nuclear power could not be used with any advantage, yet which was regarded as vital. Talk of tactical nuclear weapons showed more wishful ingenuity than realism, and much of the American emphasis on strategic nuclear superiority derived from the knowledge that only such superiority could counter Soviet geographical advantages in Europe.

If compatible with an arms race, the American-Soviet balance was also compatible with an ideological struggle waged with vigor on both sides. It is false to claim, as some revisionist historians now do, that the Cold War was started and maintained only by the United States; and that the Soviet Union, much weakened by the world war, was pursuing merely the traditional aims of Russian policy. (Those aims had been opposed by Great Britain for a century, and it is odd to find the Left arguing that a policy of old-fashioned imperialism is acceptable, and, in essence, advancing the doctrine, if not of the balance of power, at least of spheres of influence.) The ideological struggle reflected the knowledge of both great powers that they contended in a fast-changing world; and the Cold War began to lose intensity, not when the protagonists decided to abandon it, but when world circumstances changed and new elements began again to contribute to the balance, lacking nuclear capacity, it is true, but disposing of real force. It became almost conventional to speak in terms of a world of five poles—the United States, the Soviet Union, Europe, China, and Japan—to which perhaps the oil-producing states should be added. These poles differ from the great powers of old in that they are not of the same sort. Two only are nuclear in any serious sense. Other differences readily suggest themselves. It is as a consequence of this development that serious discussion of the balance of power is again taking place.

Secretary of State Henry Kissinger, a student of Metternich and Bismarck, naturally introduced the concept of balance into his discussions of foreign policy; he would not have done so if the preconditions had not been there. Yet, while he spoke of Soviet policy as "heavily influenced by the Soviet conception of the balance of forces" and as "never determined in isolation from the prevailing military balance," he was more apt to speak of American policy as seeking a "balance of mutual interests" with the Soviet Union and as moving toward détente through a "balance of risks and incentives." Such language was chosen with an American audience, and with the preconceptions that Kissinger believed Americans to have, in mind. Nevertheless it shows two elements almost wholly lacking in classic balance of power theory: the recognition that nations may now offer domestic rewards and suffer domestic penalties in the conduct of international relations, and the conviction that the domestic penalties will be too great without an agreement on restraint—deliberate if tacit—by the opponents. The balance of power is seen not as replacing cooperation, but rather as requiring it.

The history of modern international relations, and of the American part in them, then, suggests a certain pattern. There is some sort of basic preference for a balance among nations, as the only alternative to a single world structure that has always seemed in practice to imply the dominance of one state or group. That preference has survived the important shift from a world of very slow social change to a world of awesomely fast social change. It has not prevented wars nor served effectively to restrain any state that sees advantage from an active policy; it means only that at the eleventh hour, coalitions form to oppose serious attempts at world dominion. In this process the United States has played an appropriate part, allowance made for the great security provided until lately by its geographical position.

The practical preference for an international balance does not always give rise to anything that can be called a theory of the balance of power, nor even to the use of the term in political discussion. At times when the balance is a "simple" balance—as during the Cold War or the years immediately preceding World War I—there is little discussion of a concept to which appeal cannot usefully be made, and what discussion there is, is apt to be critical. Equally, a period of great international complexity and uncertainty does not seem to be one which a theory of the balance of power can helpfully elucidate. Somewhere between these extremes the greater flexibility provided by a "complex" balance allows the idea of a balance, as something desirable and as a positive interest of the contending parties themselves, to be advanced. Because the balance is at its most stable when men need not consider its maintenance or even its existence, the discussion of balance is at best an indicator of strain in international affairs; but it may indicate the least amount of strain that mankind is likely to achieve.

BIBLIOGRAPHY

The balance of power still lacks a full history. In its absence the work that must stand at the head of any bibliography is F. H. Hinsley, *Power and the Pursuit of Peace* (Cambridge, 1963). Herbert Butterfield, "The Balance of Power," in Herbert Butterfield and Martin Wight, eds., *Diplomatic Investigations* (London, 1966), and two essays by Martin Wight, "The Balance of Power," in Butterfield and Wight, op. cit., and "The Balance of Power and International Order," in Alan James, ed., *The Bases of International Order* (London, 1973), are elegant and perceptive essays, historical in approach. E. B. Haas, "The Balance of Power as a Guide of Policy-Making," in *Journal of Politics* (1953); Hans J. Morgenthau, *Politics Among Nations* (New York, 1962); and Arnold Wolfers, *Discord and Collaboration* (Baltimore, Md., 1962), adopt the approach of political science. L. Dehio, *The Precarious Balance* (London, 1963), surveys four centuries of the European power struggle, while E. V. Gulick, *Europe's Classical Balance of Power* (Ithaca, N.Y., 1955), focuses on the struggle against Napoleon and the Congress of Vienna. The works touching on American attitudes are legion, but Arthur S. Link, *Wilson the Diplomatist* (Baltimore, Md., 1957), is a small classic on the American statesman who gave most thought to this problem. Moorhead Wright, ed., *Theory and Practice of the Balance of Power 1486–1914* (London, 1975), is a convenient short selection of European writings.

[*See also* ALLIANCES, COALITIONS, AND ENTENTES; THE COLD WAR; COLLECTIVE SECURITY; IDEOLOGY AND FOREIGN POLICY; ISOLATIONISM; NATIONAL SECURITY; PROTECTORATES AND SPHERES OF INFLUENCE.]

THE BEHAVIORAL APPROACH TO DIPLOMATIC HISTORY

J. David Singer

WHEN it comes to the ability to understand and predict events of importance, students and practitioners of American diplomacy manifest a fair degree of ambivalence. On the one hand, we find many bold efforts to explain why certain events unfolded as they did, and on the other, we find frequent statements to the effect that these phenomena are so complex as to defy comprehension. According to Henry Kissinger, one of the more celebrated practitioner-scholars, such understanding is often "in the nature of things . . . a guess." Or, as Robert Bowie put it, "The policy maker works in an uneasy world of prediction and probability." And George F. Kennan put it still another way: "I can testify from personal experience that not only can one never know, when one takes a far-reaching decision in foreign policy, precisely what the consequences are going to be, but almost never do these consequences fully coincide with what one intended or expected."

While there is truth in these statements, such uncertainty may not necessarily inhere in the phenomena we study. It may well be, rather, in the ways in which that study is conducted. At the risk, then, of suggesting that students of diplomatic history—American and otherwise—have plied their trade with less than a full bag of tools, let me address here a number of ways in which the behavioral approach might usefully supplement the more traditional procedures.

By behavioral approach, I do not mean to say that we should pay more attention to the *behavior* of individuals, factions, and nations than to their *attributes* and *relationships* or to the regional and global environment within which such behavior occurs. If anything, diplomatic history seems to be overly attentive to behavioral phenomena, and insufficiently attentive to the background conditions and ecological constraints within which these phenomena occur. Rather, I mean here a fuller utilization of what we might learn from the *behavioral sciences*. Normally, this label includes psychology, anthropology, sociology, economics, and political science, but the range of disciplines embraced is less interesting to us here than is the range of methods, concepts, and findings that we might borrow from those who labor in those particular vineyards.

SOME PURPOSES OF HISTORICAL RESEARCH

One way to examine those possibilities would be in the context of the various purposes and goals that diplomatic historians might set for themselves. For some, the purpose of research is to locate and present the facts alone: what happened, in what sequence, under what conditions, and who was involved? Others go a step further and try to put those facts into graceful narrative. More typically, we seek not only to tell the story, but to do so in an interpretive fashion. This involves both a selection from among all the facts (which is, in truth, what we *all* do, since it is almost inevitable) and an interpretation of them. In interpretive history, once we are persuaded as to the facts, we make certain inferences from them: causes, motives, and likely consequences, as well as missing facts.

Some historians (even some diplomatic historians) consider these missions too modest, and tend to be more ambitious. Among these, there are of course the "grand theorists," who offer up wide-ranging interpretations of several sets of events, telling us just what it all means, in terms reaching from the plausible to the outrageous. A small but growing number are, however, beginning to redefine their mission, albeit in a less pretentious direction. Instead of offering sweeping inferences from a limited and selected set of facts, these historians are moving toward the generation of knowledge that may be not only more complex, but more useful than that to which we have been accustomed.

TYPES OF KNOWLEDGE AND RELATED METHODS

The most distinctive characteristic of the behavioral approach is its emphasis on reproducible knowledge. This approach does not belittle or ignore knowledge and evidence of a more intuitive or subjective sort, but it does recognize the very real limits of such knowledge. Without insights and suspicions as to certain historical patterns, there would be no place to begin, no hypotheses to test, and no theoretical models to formulate. But in recognizing the impermanence and contestability of subjective knowledge, the behavioral approach seeks methods that might avoid some of those liabilities. These methods are of several types and are best understood in connection with the types of knowledge sought.

Let me begin, then, by suggesting that historical knowledge may be distinguished by two very different sets of criteria. The first are essentially theoretical and substantive in nature: are we indeed getting at the relevant combination of variables in our search for explanation? The second are epistemological: assuming that we *are* on a promising substantive and theoretical path, what is the quality of knowledge that we think has been acquired or that we hope to acquire? Leaving the matter of the *relevance* of our knowledge aside for the moment, let me focus on the *qualitative* dimensions of our knowledge. One possible way of evaluating the quality of historical knowledge is to first reduce it to its component assertions or propositions, translate these (if need be) into clear and operational language, and then ascertain where each such proposition or cluster of propositions falls along each of three dimensions.

The first, or *accuracy,* dimension reflects the degree of confidence that the relevant scholarly community can have in the assertion at a given point in time; this confidence level is basically a function of the empirical or logical evidence in support of the proposition, but may vary appreciably both across time and among different scholars and schools of thought at any particular moment. The second qualitative dimension reflects the *generality* of the proposition, ranging from a single fact assertion (of any degree of accuracy) to an assertion embracing a great many phenomena of a given class. Third is the *existential-correlational-explanatory* dimension: is the assertion essentially descriptive of some existential regularity, is it correlational, or is it largely explanatory? With these three dimensions, an epistemological profile of any proposition or set of propositions can be constructed and a given body of knowledge can be classified and compared with another, or with itself over time.

For many of us the objective is to move as rapidly as possible on all three dimensions. We seek propositions in which the most competent, skeptical, and rigorous scholars can have a high degree of confidence, although these propositions may have originally been put forth on the basis of almost no empirical evidence at all. They will be propositions that are highly "causal" in form, although they may have been built up from, and upon, a number of propositions that come close to being purely descriptive. And they will be general rather than particular, although the generalizations must ultimately be based on the observation of many particular cases. As to the accuracy dimension, a proposition that seems nearly incontrovertible for decades may be overturned in a day, one that is thought of as preposterous may be vindicated by a single study or a brilliant insight, and those that have stood at the "pinnacle of uncertainty" (that is, a subjective probability of .5) may slowly or quickly be confirmed or disconfirmed. Moreover, a statement may enjoy a good, bad, or mixed reputation not only because of its inherent truthfulness or accuracy, but merely because it is not in operational language and is therefore not testable.

Shifting from the degree-of-confidence dimension to that of generality, little needs to be said. The assertion (of whose accuracy we are extremely confident) that World War I began on 29 July 1914 is less general than the assertion that more European wars of the past century began in the months of April and October than in others, and this in turn is less general than the assertion (which may or may not be true) that all wars since the Treaty of Utrecht have begun in the spring or autumn. Theory (defined here as a coherent and consistent body of interrelated propositions of fairly high confidence levels) must be fairly general, and no useful theory of any set of historical events can be built upon, or concerned only with, a single case. As Quincy Wright reminds us: "A case history, if composed without a theory indicating which of the factors surrounding a conflict are relevant and what is their relative importance, cannot be compared with other case histories, and cannot, therefore, contribute to valid and useful generalizations. On the other hand, a theory, if not applied to actual data, remains unconvincing. . . ." (In the same article, he also noted, "Comparison would be facilitated if quantifications, even though crude, are made whenever possible.")

Existential Knowledge and Data-Generating Methods. When we leave the accuracy and the generality dimensions and turn to the third proposed dimension along which a piece or body of knowledge may be described, we run into greater conceptual difficulty. A set of distinctions that I have found useful is that alluded to above: existential, correlational, and explanatory types of knowledge. Existential knowledge is essentially a data set, or string of highly comparable facts. If, for example, we are told that one army had 1,248 men killed or missing in a given battle and that the enemy had "also suffered heavily," we would have something less than data. Similarly, statements that the United States has had two separate alliances with France since 1815, running a total of forty-seven years, and that American alliances with England and Russia have been nearly the same in number and longevity as those with France, would be something less than data. That is, data provide the basis for comparison and generalization across two or more cases, situations, nations, etc., and permit the generation of existential knowledge.

Of course, existential knowledge would not be very useful to the diplomatic historian if restricted only to phenomena that are readily quantified. Most of the interesting phenomena of history are of the so-called qualitative, not quantitative, variety, and it is usually assumed that the world's events and conditions are naturally and ineluctably divided into those two categories. Many phenomena that are thought to be "qualitative in nature" at a given time, turn out to be readily quantifiable at a later date. In the physical world, examples might range from the difference between yellow and orange to the amount of moisture in the air; these were originally believed to be qualitative concepts. In the biological world, one thinks of metabolic rate or genetic predispositions. Likewise, in the world of social phenomena a good many allegedly qualitative phenomena turn out to be quite quantitative. Some illustrations might be the "linguistic similarity" of two nations, the extent to which nations gain or lose diplomatic "importance" after war, the changing "cohesion" of work groups, or the national "product" of given economies.

Of course, it is one thing to think of a way to measure or quantify a phenomenon that has been considered nonquantifiable and quite another thing to demonstrate that the measurement is a *valid* one. That is, we may apply the same measuring procedure to the same phenomenon over and over, and always get the same score; that demonstrates that our measure is a *reliable* one. But there is no way to demonstrate that it is a valid one—that it really gets at the phenomenon we claim to be measuring. The closest we come to validation of a measure (also known as an index or indicator) is a consensus among specialists that it taps what it claims to be tapping, and that consensus will rest upon (*a*) the "face validity" or reasonableness of the claim; (*b*) the extent to which it correlates with a widely accepted alternative indicator of the same phenomenon; and (*c*) the extent to which it predicts some measurable outcome variable that it is—according to an accepted theoretical argument—supposed to predict.

Quantification, however, may take a second, and more familiar, form. That is, in addition to assigning a numerical value to each observation of a given phenomenon, one can quantify by merely (*a*) assigning each such case or observation to a given nominal or ordinal category, and then (*b*) counting the number of observations that fall into each such category. The nominal category pertains to a set of criteria which are used to classify events and conditions; an ordinal category refers to the criteria used to rank them. To illustrate, generalizing about the American propensity to form alliances might require distinguishing among defense, neutrality, and entente commitments. Once the coding rules have been formulated and written down in explicit language (with examples), a fairly naive student assistant could go through the texts and contexts of all American alliances and assign each to one of those three categories.

The same could be done, for example, if one wanted to order a wide variety of foreign policy moves and countermoves, in the context of comparing the effects of different strategies upon the propensity of diplomatic conflicts to escalate toward war. The judgments of a panel of experts could be used to ascertain which types of action seem to be high, medium, or low on a conflict-exacerbating dimension. Of course, the earlier distinction between the reliability and validity of measures is quite appropriate here. There might be almost perfect agreement among our experts that economic boycotts are higher on such a dimension than ultimata, since the latter are merely *threats* to act. But if one examined a set of diplomatic confrontations and found that those in which boycotts were used seldom ended in war whereas those characterized by ultimata often did end in war, one might be inclined to challenge the validity of the ordinal measure.

So much, then, for existential knowledge. Whether merely acquired in ready-made form from governmental or commercial statistics, or generated by data-making procedures that are highly operational and reproducible, propositions of an existential nature are the bedrock upon which we can build correlational and explanatory knowledge.

Correlational Knowledge and Data Analysis Methods. Although many diplomatic historians will be quite content to go no further than the acquisition of existential knowledge, there will be others who will not only want to generalize, but also to formulate and test explanations. To do so, it is necessary to begin assembling two or more data sets and to see how strongly one correlates with the other(s). Correlation or covariation may take several forms and may be calculated in several ways, depending on whether the data sets are in nominal, ordinal, or interval (that is, cardinal number) form.

In general, a correlational proposition is one that shows the extent of coincidence or covariation between two (or more) sets of numbers. If these sets of numbers are viewed as the varying or fluctuating magnitudes of each variable, the correlation between them is a reflection of the extent to which the quantitative configuration of one variable can be ascertained when the configuration of the other is known. Or, in statistical parlance, the coefficient of correlation, which usually ranges from +1.00 to −1.00, indicates how accurately one can predict the magnitudes of all the observations in one data set once one knows the magnitudes in the other set of observations. Even though the measured events or conditions occurred in the past, we still speak of "prediction," since we know only that those phenomena occurred, but do not know the strength of association until the correlation coefficient has been computed.

Another way to put it is that the correlation between two sets of data is a measure of their similarity, whether they are based on pairs of simultaneous observations or ones in which variable Y was always measured at a fixed interval of time after each observation or measurement of variable X. If they rise and fall together over time or across a number of cases, they are similar, and the correlation between them will be close to +1.00; but if Y rises every time X drops, or vice versa, they are dissimilar, giving a negative correlation of close to −1.00. Finally, if there is neither a strong similarity nor dissimilarity, but randomness, the correlation coefficient will approach zero. There are, of course, many different measures or indices of correlation, usually named after the scholar who developed and applied them, and while we cannot examine any of them in great detail, we can discuss two of them briefly.

Although any correlation coefficient can be calculated with pencil and paper, a slide rule, or a calculator, the most efficient method is the electronic computer, which can be programmed so that it can automatically receive two or more sets of data along with instructions as to which correlation formula to use, and almost instantaneously produce coefficient scores. Looking, then, at the very simple "rank order" correlation, we note that it is used to calculate the similarity or association between two sets of ranked data. It is particularly appropriate when we can ascertain only the orderings, from high to low or top to bottom, of our two data sets, and cannot ascertain with much confidence the distances or intervals between those rank positions. The rank order statistic is also especially appropriate for checking the validity of two separate measures or indicators and ascertaining whether they "get at" the same phenomena.

To illustrate, if we suspect that a fairly good index of a nation's power is simply the absolute amount of money it allocates to military preparedness—regardless of its population, wealth, or industrial capability—we might investigate how strongly that index correlates with an alternative measure. And, since power is itself a vague and elusive concept, we might decide to derive our second measure by having the nations ranked by a panel of diplomatic historians. When these two listings—one based on a single, simple index and the other based on the fallible human judgments of scholarly specialists—are brought together, we then compute the rank order correlation between them. The results of any such computation can in principle, as we noted earlier, range from +1.00 to −1.00, with 0.00 representing the midpoint. If there is absolutely no pattern of association between the two rankings, we say there is no correlation, and the figure would indeed be zero. Further, if each nation has exactly the same rank position in both columns, the rank order correlation between the two variables is +1.00, and if the orders are completely reversed (with the nation that is at the top of one column found at the bottom of the other, and so on) it would be −1.00. None of these three extreme cases is likely to occur in the real world, of course, and on a pair of variables such as these, a rank order correlation of approximately +0.80 is pretty much what we would expect to find when the computation has been done.

The above illustrates how a rank order correlation might be used to estimate the similarity between two different rankings. While a high positive correlation would increase our confidence in the validity of military expenditure levels as a measure of power, we assumed no particular theoretical or causal connection between the two data sets. Now, however, suppose that we believed (that is, suspected, but did not know with very much confidence) that the war-proneness of a nation was somehow or other a consequence of its level of industrialization. If we only know how many wars a nation has been involved in during a given number of decades, we have a rather crude indicator of its war-proneness. Such a number does not discriminate between long and short wars; wars that led to a great many or very few fatalities; and wars that engaged all of its forces or only a small fraction. Thus, we would be quite reluctant to say that a nation that fought in eight wars is four times more war-prone than one that experienced only two military conflicts in a given period. We would even be reluctant to say that the difference between two nations that participated in six and four wars respectively is the same as that between those nations that fought in seven and five wars. In sum, we might be justified in treating such a measure of war-proneness as, at best, ordinal in nature.

Suppose, further, that our measure of industrialization is almost as crude, based, for example, on the single factor of iron and steel production. Even though we might have quite accurate figures on such production, we realize that it is a rather incomplete index, underestimating some moderately powerful nations that have little coal or ore and therefore tend to import much of their iron and steel. In such a case, we would again be wise to ignore the size of the differences between the nations, and settle for only a rank order listing. Depending on the magnitude of the resulting coefficient of correlation (computed by such measures as Spearman's *rho*) between these two rank orderings, we could make a number of different inferences about the relationship between industrialization and war-proneness. The nature, and grounds for, such inferences will be discussed below, but let us first look at a slightly different type of correlational statistic.

Suppose now that we were working with much better indices than those used in the two illustrations above, and that we could measure our variables with considerably greater confidence. That is, we now have a basis for believing that our indicators or measures are not only valid (and that has no bearing on the statistical tests that can be applied to a variable) but reliable and quite precise. If one variable were the amount of money spent for the operation of IGO's (international intergovernmental organizations) in the international system each half-decade, and the other were the number of nation-months of war that ended in each previous half-decade, and such interval scale data appeared to be very accurate, we could employ a more sensitive type of statistical test, such as Pearson's product moment correlation.

The reason that a product moment type of correlational analysis is more sensitive is that its computation does not—because it need not—ignore the magnitude of the differences between the rank positions on a given pair of listings. Whereas rank order data merely tells us that the nation (or year, or case, or observation) at one position is so many positions or notches above or below another, interval scale data tell us how much higher or lower it is on a particular yardstick. The magnitude of those inter-rank distances carries a lot of useful information, and when our data are of such a quality to give us that additional information, it is foolish to "throw it away." Thus, when the measures of our variables permit, we generally use a product moment rather than a rank order correlation. As we might expect, certain conditions regarding the normality of the distributions, independence of the observations, randomness of the sample, etc., must be met before we can use this more sensitive measure of statistical association, but we need not go into those fine points here.

Once we have computed the rank order or product moment correlation coefficient between any two sets of measures, several inferences about the relationship between the variables become possible, providing that one additional requirement is met. If the correlation score is close to zero, we can—for the moment, at least—assume that there is little or no association between the variables, and tentatively conclude that (*a*) one measure is not a particularly good index of the other (when validation of a measure is our objective); or (*b*) that one variable exercises very little impact on the other (when a correlational proposition is our objective). If, however, the correlation coefficient is about 0.50 or higher, either positive (+) or negative (−), we would want to go on and ask whether the above-mentioned requirement has been met.

That requirement is that the correlation be high enough to have had a very low probability of occurring by chance alone. That is ascertained by computing (or looking up in a standard text) the "statistical significance" of the correlation. When we have very few pairs of observations (or cases) in our analysis, even a correlation as high as 0.90 can occur by sheer chance. And when we have a great many cases, even a figure as low as 0.30 can be statistically significant. To illustrate with what is known as the Z-test, statisticians have computed that a product moment correlation would have to be as high as 0.65 if the association between 12 sets of observations were to be thought of as having only a 1 percent probability of being mere coincidence. Conversely, if there were as many as 120 cases, they calculate that a correlation as low as 0.22 would also have only a 1 percent probability of being mere coincidence. In statistical parlance, we say that for a given number of cases, a given correlation score is "significant at the 1 percent (or 2 percent or 5 percent, etc.) level."

Once we have ascertained that the strength of a given correlation, as well as its statistical significance, is sufficiently high (and the evaluation of "sufficiently" is a complex matter, still debated by statisticians and scientists) we can then go on to make a number of inferences about the predictive or the explanatory association between the variables being examined. The nature of those inferences and the justification for them will be explored in the next section. Suffice it to say here that when two variables are strongly correlated, and one of them precedes the other in time, we have a typical form of correlational knowledge, but are not yet able to say very much of an explanatory nature.

Explanatory Knowledge and Causal Inference. It should now be quite clear that operational classification and enumeration, combined with statistical analysis of the resulting data sets, can eventually produce a large body of correlational knowledge. Further, it should be evident that correlational knowledge can indeed provide a rather satisfactory basis for foreign policy prediction, despite the limitations noted above. But the major limitation lies in the difference between predictions based on correlations from the past, and predictions based on theories. Without a fairly good theory (which, it will be recalled, is more than either a hunch or a model) our predictions will often be vulnerable on two counts.

First, there is the problem that has often intrigued the philosopher of science and delighted the traditional humanist. If the decision makers of nation *A* have a fair idea what predictions are being made about them by the officials of nation *B,* they can often confound *B* by selecting a move or a strategy other than the one they think is expected. A good theory, however, has built into it just such contingencies, and can often cope with the "we think that they think that we think, etc." problem. Second, a good theory increases our ability to predict in cases that have no exact (or even approximate) parallel in history. That is, it permits us to first build up—via the inductive mode—a general set of propositions on the basis of the specific cases for which we do have historical evidence, and then to deduce—from the theory based on those general propositions—back down to specific cases for which we do not have historical evidence.

If theories are, then, quite important in the study of foreign policy, how do we go about building, verifying, improving, and consolidating them? To some extent, the answer depends on one's definition of a theory, and the word has, unfortunately, disparate meanings. To the layman, a theory is often nothing more than a hunch or an idea. Worse yet, some define theory as anything other than what is real or pragmatic or observable; hence the expression that such and such may be true "in theory, but not in practice." The problem here is that—and this is the second type of definition—a number of scientists also imply that same distinction by urging that a theory need not be true or accurate, as long as it is useful. To be sure, many theories do turn out to be useful (in the sense that they describe and predict reality) even though they are built upon *assumptions* that are not true. One example is in the field of economics, where some very useful theories rest on the assumption that most individuals act on the basis of purely materialistic, cost-versus-benefit calculations. We are fairly certain, of course, that a great many decisions are made on the basis of all sorts of noneconomic and nonrational considerations, but somehow or other, the market or the firm nevertheless tends to behave *as if* individual shoppers, investors, etc., do make such calculations. The important point here is that the theory itself is not out of line with reality, but that the assumptions on which it rests may be untrue without weakening the predictive power of the theory.

This leads, then, to the need for distinguishing between theories that are adequate for predictive purposes and those of a more comprehensive nature that seek to not only predict, but to explain. While the dividing line between them is by no means sharp and clear, we can nevertheless make a rough distinction between those theories that are supposed to tell us *what* happens, or will happen under certain conditions, and those that tell us *why* it happens. Even in economics, it is recognized that the predictive power of its major theories can be improved, and their explanatory adequacy markedly enhanced, by looking into and rectifying the psychological or other assumptions on which they rest.

Thus, even though our short-run needs may be served by theories that are merely predictive, our concern here is with theories that are capable of explaining why certain regularities (and deviations therefrom) are indeed found in the affairs of men. To repeat the definition we suggested earlier, a theory is a logically consistent body of existential and correlational propositions, most of which are in operational and testable form, and many of which have been tested and confirmed. This definition requires that all of the propositional components in the theory be, in principle at least, true; further, if the theory is to explain why things occur as they do, the propositions underlying it must also be true. Given these stringent requirements, it is little wonder that we have so little in the way of explanatory theory in the social sciences.

THE BEHAVIORAL APPROACH TO DIPLOMATIC HISTORY

SOME BEHAVIORAL CONCEPTS

Shifting now from some of the *methods* associated with the behavioral approach, one of the more serious obstacles to a richer and more subtle understanding of diplomatic history may well be the rather restricted set of *concepts* that we use in seeking to put together our predictive and explanatory models. To a considerable extent, our concepts are limited to those used by the practitioners, their spokesmen, and the journalists who cover diplomatic events. And, I would suggest, these people are no more likely to provide the concepts by which to theorize and comprehend our phenomena than is the boy with his finger in the dike likely to help us develop a theory of hydraulics. Are there in the behavioral science literature some concepts that might provide us with new insights or suggest more powerful ways of thinking about diplomatic history?

Let me illustrate the extent to which I think that there are such concepts by first noting certain very general orientations and then turning to a few more specific and potentially useful concepts. First, there are several conceptual schemes that have developed to such a degree that they might qualify under the rubric of "theories"; indeed, they are so labeled by many of those from whose disciplines they emerge. Perhaps most promising is that set of notions that we have come to call general systems theory. Proceeding from the assumption that there are structural similarities in different fields, and correspondences in the principles that govern the behavior of entities that are intrinsically widely different, this approach seeks to identify those similarities and correspondences (as well as dissimilarities) that might be found in the universes of all the scientific disciplines. In its search for an integrated theory of behavior, the general systems approach postulates the existence of a system, its environment, and its subsystems. Some of the key concepts employed are feedback, homeostasis, network, entropy, and information, reflecting a considerable intellectual debt to cybernetics. By thinking of the states as subsystems within the international system, which in turn has a particular environment of physical and social dimensions, we are provided with a rather fruitful taxonomy which suggests, in turn, a fascinating array of hypotheses. Within the same context, the idea of homeostasis is particularly suggestive to those of us concerned with balance, stability, and equilibrium in the international system.

Another set of concepts that seems to offer real promise is that employed in the theory of games. The clearest model postulates two or more players (individuals, groups, states, coalitions, etc.) pursuing a set of goals according to a variety of strategies. If the goals are perceived by the players as incompatible, that is, only one player may win, we have a so-called "zero-sum" or win-lose game, with the players tending to utilize a "minimax" strategy. If, however, they perceive a possible win-win outcome, their strategies tend to deviate sharply from the conservative minimax pattern, in which they place prime emphasis on minimizing their maximum losses. The appropriateness of such a model for bipolar international relations seems rather evident.

We now turn from these very general conceptual schemes to some of the more limited concepts found in the specific behavioral disciplines. Looking first at psychology, let us consider for example the ways in which we might think of diplomatic influence. From learning theory, stimulus-response theory, and the concepts associated with reinforcement, we might adapt and modify a wide range of models that could ultimately shed useful light on this central aspect of international relations. To illustrate: Is a major power more likely to shape the policies of a weaker neighbor by punishment, reward, denial, threat, promise, or calculated detachment? Or in seeking to explain the way in which public opinion in a given state ultimately influenced a certain policy decision, we might find some valuable suggestions in reference-group theory, the concepts of access and role-conflict, or some of the models of communication nets. To take another problem area, if one were concerned with the emerging attitudinal characteristics of the international environment, such notions as acculturation, internalization, relative deprivation, self-image, or consensus might prove to be highly productive.

Or consider the discipline of sociology, from which many contemporary researchers in foreign affairs have borrowed heavily. If we seek to better understand the foreign policy of the United States or any other nation, we may want to think of the international system (regional or global) as similar to other social systems, but with national states—rather than individuals or groups—as the component units. Such systems manifest certain characteristics, and as these change, the behavior of the component units might also be expected to change. For example, certain social systems are highly stratified at certain times, in the sense that people who rank high on wealth are also high on education, prestige, and political power. Under such conditions, one might expect more conflict because the underdogs are deprived on every dimension. Might it also be that when the *international* system is highly stratified—with a few nations ranking at the top in wealth, resources, population, military capability, industrial output, and diplomatic status—the likelihood of sharp conflict goes up?

Remaining with sociological concepts, but shifting down from the systemic to the unit level of aggregation, certain individuals tend to be much more mobile than others, and as a result may acquire power more easily, or perhaps experience more conflict. That is, lateral mobility—by which we mean the rate at which individuals move in and out of certain cliques or associations—may also apply to nations, reflecting the rate at which they move in and out of blocs, alliances, or international organizations. Similarly, rapid vertical (upward or downward) mobility might be expected to get nations, as well as individuals, into more conflict than if they occupied a constant niche or moved up or down very gradually.

In the same vein, the concept of status inconsistency and its relationship to "deviant" behavior might merit closer examination. For example, if an individual ranks high on education or some other status-relevant dimension, but low on political influence, he should—according to some sociologists—show a fair amount of deviant behavior. Do *nations* that rank high in certain prestige or status dimensions but low in power, manifest more odd and unpredictable behavior than those that are status-consistent?

To take our final example from the discipline of economics, consider the concepts of monopoly and oligopoly, reflecting the extent to which a given market is dominated by one firm, or a handful of firms. The concentration of economic power may have its parallel at the international level, with a regional, functional, or global system manifesting a high degree of concentration as one or two nations enjoy most of the trade, industrial output, energy consumption, or military might in that system. The consequences of such high concentration, among firms or among nations, could be quite profound in its effects on such phenomena as conflict and cooperation, vertical mobility or stagnation, or the formation and dissolution of coalitions.

The range and variety of concepts that have been developed in the behavioral sciences is impressive indeed, as is the extent to which those concepts have often helped to differentiate, clarify, synthesize, or explain phenomena that had hitherto been quite baffling. In the next section, while concentrating on the matter of findings, a number of additional concepts will be mentioned.

SOME BEHAVIORAL FINDINGS

Turning now to the third possible sector in which the behavioral science approach might enhance our comprehension of diplomatic history, let us consider briefly some of the *findings* that emerge from these disciplines. By findings, of course, we mean either existential or correlational propositions that seem to enjoy some standing in their home disciplines, and on the basis of which, explanatory theories might be articulated.

One can hardly exaggerate the importance of these findings for diplomatic historians, and of course, for practitioners. That is, those of us who are interested in foreign policy rest many of our interpretations, analyses, and predictions on behavioral science propositions that may or may not be accurate. We do so in two ways. First, we often extrapolate from the individual to the group or national level of aggregation, assuming that what holds for the individual will also hold for the collectivity. Given the examples offered in the previous section, I can have no quarrel with the pursuit of such analogies, but as I hope was made clear, this is for purposes of speculation and hypothesis only. That is, in the absence of evidence to the contrary, it is probably economical to assume that if, for example, individuals tend to be more cooperative in the face of reward rather than in the face of punishment, so will corporations or nations.

On the other hand, there are some fundamental differences between individuals and collectivities, and we ignore these at our peril. The primary difference, of course, is that individuals (or, more precisely, rational, intelligent, and informed ones) can be thought of as purposive, problem-solving entities, trying to maximize their particular values. Collectivities, on the other hand, exactly because they are made up of such individuals—each pursuing a mix of private and public goals—cannot be so conceived. The group or organization will, almost inevitably, pursue a range of goals reflecting a compromise and amalgam of the often incompatible goals of its more powerful individuals and subgroups. Thus, it is essential that we be sufficiently familiar with the findings of such microsocial disciplines as psychology, and the macrosocial ones of economics, sociology, and political science. Unless we know something of the discontinuities between the individual and the collective levels of aggregation, we may be guilty of the most naive extrapolation.

But that is only half of the problem. The second way in which we rest our analyses and predictions on behavioral science findings is more direct, with many of our models depending heavily upon the accuracy of our assumptions about individual and collective behavior. This dependence is quite heavy whether our focus is upon public opinion, elite recruitment, executive-legislative relationships, bureaucratic responsibility for policy execution, or the decision process itself. In each of these areas of activity, individuals and groups—with considerable propensities toward regular and consistent behavior—are playing key roles, and to the extent that we remain unaware of the findings that reflect those regularities and consistencies, we seriously limit the accuracy and completeness of our analyses.

Rather than select some limited number of existential and correlational propositions from the behavioral sciences and summarize the evidence in support or contravention, let me follow a more efficient strategy and merely suggest where we might turn for a large number of these findings. The most general source is, of course, the *International Encyclopedia of the Social Sciences* (1967), which replaces the 1930–1935 edition. The *Encyclopedia* is something like this particular treatise in that each section is written by a leading authority, and virtually all topics in the field are covered. Embracing nearly a dozen disciplines, however, rather than only part of one, it runs to sixteen volumes plus an index.

In it, one finds summaries of the existential and correlational knowledge on such concepts as: acculturation, aggression, anxiety, avoidance, business cycles, charisma, coalition formation, cognitive dissonance, mass communication, cybernetics, conformity, conditioning, conflict, cultural diffusion, decision making, defense mechanisms, demography, deviant behavior, diplomacy, disarmament, dominance, dreams, ecology, economic equilibrium, elites, ethnology, ethology, evolution, family structure, fatigue, fertility, forgetting, frustration, geopolitics, gestalt, motivation, homeostasis, identity, ideology, imperialism, income distribution, influence, inflation, interest groups, interpersonal interaction, kinship, land tenure, language, leadership, learning, legitimacy, loyalty, migration, social mobility, monopoly, norms, national character, neurosis, oligopoly, pacifism, paranoid reactions, perception (ten separate articles), personality, persuasion, pluralism, prejudice, prestige, propaganda, psychoanalysis, public opinion, punishment, race relations, reciprocity, reference groups, response set, roles, sanctions, self-image, sex differences, social stratification, stereotypes, stress, sympathy and empathy, thinking, traits, utilitarianism, utility, voluntary associations, voting, wages, war, and worship.

(One also finds in the *Encyclopedia* articles on such methodological matters as: content analysis, contingency table analysis, curve-fitting, experimental design, multivariate analysis, statistical distributions, factor analysis, field work, forecasting, game theory, historiography, hypothesis testing, index construction, statistical inference, Markov chains, observation, panel studies, probability, rank correlation, scaling, simulation, spectral analysis, statistical inference, survey analysis, time series, typologies, and validity.)

Another very general source, although

slightly outdated, is *Human Behavior: An Inventory of Scientific Findings* (Berelson and Steiner, 1964). After discussing the six most frequently cited procedures for generating the findings they report, the compilers then go on to summarize what they consider to be the more interesting propositions to have emerged from research in the behavioral sciences. The substantive topics covered are behavioral development (meaning biological, emotional, and cognitive change as individuals mature); perceiving; learning and thinking; motivation; the family; small face-to-face groups; organizations; institutions; social stratification; ethnic relations; mass communications; opinions, attitudes, and beliefs; the society; and culture.

Then there are collections of articles, summarizing the correlational and explanatory knowledge in the specific disciplines or problem areas. Among the more relevant for our purposes are the following, all of whose titles begin with *Handbook of: Personality Theory and Research* (Borgatta and Lambert, 1967); *Political Psychology* (Knutson, 1973); *Psychiatry* (Solomon and Patch, 1971); *Small Group Research* (Hare, 1962); *Psychoanalysis* (Herma and Kurth, 1963); *Social and Cultural Anthropology* (Honigmann, 1973); *Social Psychology* (Gardner and Aronson, 1968); *Sociological Information* (Tolman and Hull, 1894); *Socialization Theory and Research* (Goslin, 1969); *Abnormal Psychology* (Eysenck, 1973); *Clinical Psychology* (Wolman, 1965); *Communications* (Schramm, 1973); *Ethnography* (Leyburn, 1931); *General Psychology* (Wolman, 1973); *Modern Personality Theory* (Cattell and Dreger, 1974); and *Organizations* (March, 1965).

There are two other anthologies that not only summarize a good many concepts and findings from these related disciplines, but select and organize the articles on the basis of their applicability to specific topics in international affairs. These are *Man and International Relations* (Zawodny, 1966) and *Human Behavior and International Politics* (Singer, 1965).

Even "closer to home" are two collections that bring together the findings of research in foreign policy and international politics. Most recent of these is *The Comparative Study of Foreign Policy: A Survey of Scientific Findings* (McGowan and Shapiro, 1973), in which the compilers seek to interpret and integrate the results of empirical investigations in the context of 118 general propositions. Of a different genre is *Beyond Conjecture in International Politics: Abstracts of Data-Based Research* (Jones and Singer, 1972). Here, the compilers attend only to published articles in English that generate, or rest upon, reproducible evidence. No effort is made to interpret, integrate, or evaluate the 150-odd studies that are covered, but they are very systematically arranged. Further, each is abstracted in accordance with a checklist that includes the following: query, spatial-temporal domain, outcome variable, predictor variable(s), data sources, data-making operations, data preparation and manipulation, data analysis procedure, findings, and related research. Since the first volume covers only research up to 1970, a second volume is now in preparation, and will bring the coverage up to 1974.

CONCLUSION

There are several ways in which one might react to the foregoing information and suggestions. One might, for example, paraphrase that observer who told us that "history is bunk," and assert that "social science is bunk." Less frivolously, one might see little value in trying to apply the behavioral sciences to the study of diplomatic history, concluding that the investment will far exceed the likely gain. For those who conclude otherwise, it may nevertheless appear to represent a radical break with traditional style, and thus one that should not be taken lightly.

Not only can we benefit considerably by attending to the behavioral sciences, but to do so represents only a logical extension of practices and procedures that for decades have been the stock in trade of historians. First, we note that the scientific method has been utilized for centuries in the solution of all sorts of physical and biological problems. But for a variety of reasons ranging from religious taboos and superstition to the allegedly greater complexity of social phenomena, men have shied away from (if not vigorously resisted) its application to the study of social problems. That orientation has, however, been gradually eroded, partly through the work of courageous and creative scholars and partly because of the increasingly obvious need to replace folklore with knowledge.

In addition to the fact that social science is

merely an extension of a given intellectual style already well established in the study of physical and biological phenomena, it is also quite nonrevolutionary in that it is little more than an extension of certain problem-solving processes that have always been used. While it is clearly an extension, the fact is that man has used a combination of logic and sensory observation for centuries in coping with social problems. In trying to understand what people did under certain conditions, and why they did it, philosophers, kings, merchants, and soldiers have often employed a rudimentary form of scientific method. That is, they have tried (*a*) to identify and classify a variety of social events and conditions; (*b*) to ascertain the extent to which they occurred together or in sequence; and (*c*) to remember those observed co-occurrences.

But since they seldom have used *explicit* criteria in classification, they often placed highly dissimilar events and conditions in the same category; and since they seldom used *constant* criteria, they often forgot which criteria they had used for earlier classifications, with the same garbled results. Moreover, because one could not put social events on a scale, or measure the length and breadth of a social condition, their basic belief that social phenomena were not tangible, and therefore not measurable, was reinforced. This failure to measure and scale further reinforced the philosophic notion that whereas physical (and later, biological) phenomena were inherently quantitative, those of a social nature were inherently qualitative. Given this widespread belief, there was of course little effort to develop either the instruments of observation or the tools of measurement.

For centuries, then, men could study social phenomena in a no more reliable or accurate fashion than if they had studied physical ones without yardsticks, balance scales, or telescopes. To put it another way, they used the primitive essentials of scientific method, but ignored the critical refinements. Instead of aiding and enhancing their natural capacities to observe, remember, and reason, they made a virtue of these very frailties and inadequacies by arguing that the incomprehensibility of social phenomena was inherent in the events and conditions themselves, rather than in the grossly inadequate methods they used in that effort to comprehend. Modern social science, then, is nothing more than an application of methods already found useful in the other sciences and an extension and refinement of the basic methods we have always used. To repeat the familiar cliché, we have been "speaking prose" all along, but prose of a rather poor quality.

In sum, it is very difficult to quarrel with Collingwood's early recognition (1922) of the intellectual similarity between history and science:

> The analysis of science in epistemological terms is thus identical with the analysis of history, and the distinction between them as separate kinds of knowledge is an illusion. . . . When both are regarded as actual inquiries, the difference of method and of logic wholly disappears. . . . The nineteenth century positivists were right in thinking that history could and would become more scientific.

BIBLIOGRAPHY

Bernard Berelson and Gary Steiner, *Human Behavior: An Inventory of Scientific Findings* (N.Y., 1964); Robin G. Collingwood, "Are History and Science Different Kinds of Knowledge?" in *Mind* (1922); *International Encyclopedia of the Social Sciences* (N.Y., 1967); Susan D. Jones and J. David Singer, *Beyond Conjecture in International Politics: Abstracts of Data-Based Research* (Itasca, Ill., 1972); Patrick McGowan and Howard Shapiro, *The Comparative Study of Foreign Policy: A Survey of Scientific Findings* (Beverly Hills, 1973); Bruce Russett *et al., World Handbook of Political and Social Indicators* (New Haven, 1964); J. David Singer, ed., *Human Behavior and International Politics: Contributions From the Social-Psychological Sciences* (Chicago, 1965); Melvin Small and J. David Singer, "Formal Alliances, 1816–1965: An Extension of the Basic Data," in *Journal of Peace Research,* 3 (1969); Charles Taylor and Michael Hudson, *World Handbook of Political and Social Indicators,* 2nd ed. (New Haven, 1972); Wladimir Woytinsky and Emma Woytinsky, *World Population and Production* (N.Y., 1953); Quincy Wright, "Design for a Research Proposal on International Conflicts," in *Western Political Quarterly,* 10 (1957); and Janusz Zawodny, *Man and International Relations: Contributions of the Social Sciences to the Study of Conflict and Integration* (San Francisco, 1966).

[*See also* DECISION-MAKING APPROACHES AND THEORIES; PUBLIC OPINION.]

BIPARTISANSHIP

C. David Tompkins

A DEFINITION of bipartisanship in foreign policy, which includes executive-legislative cooperation, must by its very nature be diffuse and varied depending upon the situation, personalities involved, and needed action. Not even its chief practitioners could agree on its title. Franklin D. Roosevelt's secretary of state, Cordell Hull, wanted to classify close executive-congressional cooperation as "nonpartisan" because he refused to share credit with the Republicans. Michigan senator Arthur Vandenberg sought acceptance of the term "unpartisan," by which he meant policy developed above partisan purposes and for the national interest. Political scientist H. Bradford Westerfield prefers the term "extrapartisanship," which he defines as a presidential resolution "to associate in active collaboration with his Administration's conduct of foreign relations enough influential members of the opposition party to prevent its lines from solidifying against basic administrative foreign policies, while at the same time the President's position as leader of his own party is used to mobilize support for those policies to the limited extent that it can safely be done without causing the opposition to consolidate its counteraction" (*Foreign Policy and Partisan Politics* [New Haven, 1955], p. 16). Significantly, only President Franklin D. Roosevelt and John Foster Dulles preferred the term "bipartisanship," which has become the most widely accepted and used term.

As used herein, bipartisanship is the formulation of foreign policy that presupposes that the president will provide the overall parameters defining the national interest. Hopefully he provides the leadership and direction in implementing a positive policy. This policy would be carefully developed by himself, his advisers, and the State Department, working closely and providing complete information to leaders in the Senate and House, but especially to the chairman and members of both parties who serve on the Senate Committee on Foreign Relations. By its nature, bipartisanship assumes that responsible leaders who share confidence and mutual respect will study, examine, and, finally, jointly formulate the foreign policy that the State Department and the president must execute, but that generally depends upon persistent congressional support from one administration to another.

The president must be willing to consult with leaders of both parties, especially those senators who can assist the administration in gaining broadly based support. He must appoint members of both parties to serve on United States delegations to important international conferences. He must be amenable to modifications, amendments, revisions, and changes in treaties or legislation as well as in the administration of such policies to help win the widest support in Congress and in the body politic. Bipartisanship fails to preclude differences and partisan advantage but should, as much as possible, secure general agreement on a course of action before it becomes the victim of partisan squabbling with the hope that the United States can present a unified voice in international relations.

Bipartisan foreign policy also assumes that an involvement-minded policy, unlike isolationism, is pursued which gives authority to the president but requires from him candor with Congress so as to assure its support in the form of funds and military forces, which may be needed to implement the national interest. Obviously, bipartisanship cannot apply in all situations and even during its heyday following World War II was not used as a means of developing policy in several Asian crises. The purpose of bipartisanship is, in the last analysis, to formulate the most informed and broadly based policy for United States leadership in an unstable world faced by the dangers of nationalist uprisings, rising consumer expectations, and the constant threat of a nuclear holocaust. Congressional, particularly senatorial, support is essential. Bipartisanship would appear critical to a president, especially when confronted with domination of both houses of Congress by the opposite party. Close staff work between the Senate Committee on Foreign Relations, the State Department, and presidential advisers must accompany changes in policy. The cooperation between the administration and Congress must also withstand the strains of political campaigns, which recur every two years. Sharing, compromising, and finding areas of agreement upon which to build policy must be maximized.

At its best, bipartisan foreign policy functions as part of the American democratic process in that popular opinion is reflected in the willingness of the House and Senate to harness power to support policies initiated by the president in consultation, not only with his advisers, but also from the input offered by the representatives of the people acting through the congressional machinery. In addition, that policy must be based on generally agreed-upon principles and assumptions, which are shared by the president and congressional leaders, including those of the opposition party.

Bipartisanship served as the model for the making of American foreign policy from the entry into World War II until the mid-1960's, when the Vietnam debacle destroyed the Cold War consensus and the spirit of consultation and shared responsibility for America's external affairs. President Franklin D. Roosevelt felt that bipartisanship would never succeed and Secretary of State Cordell Hull held a narrow view of cooperation with the Senate to secure approval of a United Nations charter. Congress, however, sought during World War II to establish a working relationship with the administration to provide support for American leadership in the postwar world. Thus, step by step during the war, culminating in the Senate's approval of the United Nations Charter, bipartisanship became the prevalent policymaking method, reaching its apogee during 1947–1948 under the Republican-controlled Eightieth Congress. Thereafter, bipartisanship continued to serve, with a few exceptions, to secure broadly based support in Congress for the major thrust of America's foreign policy.

Before World War II, executive-legislative conflicts had often characterized the making of foreign policy. Alexander Hamilton and Thomas Jefferson had argued vigorously over America's policy toward revolutionary France; New Englanders had resisted national efforts during the War of 1812; charges of mendacity had characterized the critique of President James K. Polk's leadership during the Mexican-American War; the anti-imperialists had challenged William McKinley's Spanish-American War policies and the acquisition of colonies; and partisan struggles between President Woodrow Wilson and Congress prevented American membership in the League of Nations in 1919–20.

What changed dramatically during World War II, a shift neither understood nor appreciated by Roosevelt and Hull, was the attitude of the American people. They were willing, as they had not been earlier, to assume their country's burden of responsibility in world affairs. The realization that positive measures would be needed to prevent a third world war convinced them that their leaders, regardless of party, must cooperate to best serve the national interests abroad. This change culminated in United States participation in most major international events resulting from the war. It also meant that America could never return to the simple days preceding World War II, when the popular will dictated a limited role by the country, the president, and the State Department in international affairs.

The change in the mood of the people, reflected particularly in Congress, now supported full participation in the previously shunned international power politics. Apparently Americans realized that there should be no repeat of the rejection of the League of Nations, and that the United States had to assume the leadership in forging a postwar international peacekeeping organization. This shift in public opinion may have reflected a sense of guilt for refusing to join the League of Nations, a move that some thought could have prevented war in Europe and Asia. Never again should America isolate herself from responsibility in safeguarding peace. Americans also experienced a guilt syndrome because the isolationists had dominated American foreign policy down to the outbreak of the war. In order to achieve full participation in world events, Americans demanded that partisan politics be removed from foreign policy so that the United States could speak with a single voice in foreign affairs. Politicians, presidents, senators, and the members of the House of Representatives were to work to develop policies that would receive broadly based support.

The people seemed also to desire strong presidential leadership in the conduct of foreign affairs, with the active support of Congress, mainly to prevent another war. The war experience had been so painful that Americans were willing to make sacrifices in the form of economic aid for the rebuilding of Europe, and to provide funds for defense against the Soviet Union. Seemingly the people were ahead of the politicians in their willingness to support collective security. In contrast to past experience in American diplomacy, the people demanded cooperation between party leaders in and outside of Congress and close collaboration between the administration and Congress.

Secretary of State Cordell Hull failed to understand the mood of the American people. He shared their ambition for a postwar international organization and realized the need for Senate cooperation, but his vision reached only the point of recreating a League of Nations-type organization with American leadership as well as membership. He did not appreciate the extent of the people's support for programs—with funds and troops, if necessary—to maintain world security interests.

Similarly, Franklin D. Roosevelt, who was never fully committed to State Department planning for a postwar international organization, held a fuzzy conception of what the postwar world should be. Roosevelt, however, did believe in cooperation among the big powers and summit diplomacy to maintain the peace. He believed that such cooperation had won the war and that big-power agreement would prevent another war. He never thought that the American people would support the stationing of American troops abroad and the rebuilding of Western Europe. Roosevelt thought that only full cooperation would suffice as nonpartisan cooperation within Congress; he wanted to run foreign policy himself without congressional interference.

Both Hull and Roosevelt were suspicious of close cooperation with congressional leaders of both parties, especially with Republicans who had caused them grief in fighting the Great Depression, in gaining approval of the reciprocal trade agreements, and in preparing the United States for war in the late 1930's. In a sense, the departure of both Roosevelt and Hull at the end of World War II was fortunate. The American public apparently would not have tolerated the harsh partisan and executive-legislative conflicts that had followed the Civil War and World War I.

It was in this climate of popular demand for unity in winning the war and in keeping the peace that the bipartisan foreign policy model was slowly and painfully hammered out during World War II. Despite halting starts and the president's indecisiveness, the bipartisan method of making foreign policy prevailed over the traditional pattern of political partisanship and congressional-administrative struggles.

Although the several bipartisan committees established by Hull were of little consequence, Congress reflected measurable public opinion by supporting participation in an international organization to preserve peace. On 21 September 1943 the House of Representatives gave its approval in a resolution offered by J. William Fulbright. A resolution sponsored by Tom Connally of Texas provided in general terms for Senate support.

Even before the passage of the Connally resolution, the leadership of the Republican party had gathered on Mackinac Island, Michigan. Under the tutelage of Senator Arthur H. Vandenberg of Michigan and Governor Thomas E. Dewey of New York, the conferees devised a compromise resolution, which was acceptable to most Republicans, and favored the formation of an international organization after the war. At this point Republicans were ahead of the president and his party.

BIPARTISANSHIP

A good example of the working model of bipartisan foreign policy arose after the White House announced American participation in the United Nations Relief and Rehabilitation Administration (UNRRA), a vehicle for providing European relief after the war. Policymakers conceived UNRRA because Congress had placed restrictions on the use of lend-lease funds after hostilities ceased. Several senators on the Foreign Relations Committee objected to vast expenditures and postwar commitments by executive agreement. Subsequently, a subcommittee worked closely with the State Department during the summer of 1943, negotiated differences, and produced a document acceptable to the Senate and the State Department. Both sides felt a sense of satisfaction and victory. The State Department and the Foreign Relations Subcommittee agreed that American participation should be contingent upon approval by a majority vote of both houses of Congress of the amended agreement and subsequent congressional appropriations.

The resolution of the UNRRA controversy marked a step toward bipartisanship in that the executive branch and the Senate sought to achieve through consultations an understanding acceptable to both branches of government. Although some senators bragged about the changes they wrote into the agreement and Roosevelt never acknowledged this cooperation, the creation of UNRRA represented a micromodel of bipartisanship. On 14 February 1944 the Senate Committee on Foreign Relations voted 16-1 for the amended UNRRA draft, and it was subsequently approved by the whole Senate.

Despite Hull's reluctance to consult the Senate on many foreign policy issues, he realized that any postwar international organization would require approval by two-thirds of the senators present and voting. To prevent a repetition of the Senate's rejection of the League of Nations, Hull early in the war decided to appoint nonpartisan committees to prepare proposals for a peacekeeping organization. The most important was the committee led by Leo Pasvolsky, which drafted a charter for the United Nations. Roosevelt gave a half-hearted approval for continued planning and permitted Hull to share the proposed charter with a select group of senators who became known as the Committee of Eight. They met several times from 25 April through 8 June 1944, and Hull tried to obtain committee approval for the proposed charter. The senators remained adamant in their refusal to endorse a document to which the president was not yet committed and which had not been disclosed to other countries. The Committee of Eight would have been willing to issue a joint statement on postwar intention but would not give a blank-check approval of a draft charter. Although Hull thought he had failed, these consultations were precursors of evolving bipartisan foreign policy and executive-legislative cooperation. Before policy was publicly promulgated, the concept of discussion between the State Department and the Senate Committee on Foreign Relations became an important aspect of postwar policymaking, and became regular during 1945.

Despite the failure to reach agreement on the draft of the United Nations Charter, both Hull and Vandenberg worked closely so that the issue of a postwar peacekeeping organization would not become embroiled in the 1944 elections. With limited success Hull tried to persuade Roosevelt not to make partisan speeches regarding foreign policy. On the Republican side, Vandenberg persuaded both Thomas E. Dewey, the Republican nominee, and his chief foreign policy adviser, John Foster Dulles, to minimize the use of foreign affairs for campaign purposes. Hull eventually invited Dulles to the State Department to be briefed on both the meetings at Dumbarton Oaks and general policy. These meetings proved fruitful when the two men agreed upon a joint statement to keep partisanship on foreign policy out of the campaign.

Up to this point Senators Connally, Vandenberg, and Warren Austin, and Hull, Dewey, and Dulles agreed on the need for an international organization to keep the peace, but Roosevelt remained silent as to his commitment to the idea. Unaware of how deeply American public opinion demanded a method to prevent another war, Roosevelt permitted Wilson's experience with the League to guide him. Roosevelt remained convinced that the isolationists and Republicans could not be trusted and would oppose him when the day of decision arrived; he certainly did not abide with the notion that the Republicans should gain political advantage by agreeing with a proposal that should be credited to the Democrats. Roosevelt suspected that a new international organization, like the League, would fail. He likewise remained convinced that a regional defense system would be necessary because, from his view of history, the people would never agree to station troops abroad nor assume the financial burden necessary to rebuild Europe and protect it. He refused to commit himself to the United Nations draft until he had met with Winston Churchill and Josef Stalin at Yalta. Roosevelt still hoped to continue the wartime cooperation among the Allies who had won the war and could preserve the peace.

Into this general malaise stepped Vandenberg. In an address to the Senate on 10 January 1945, marking another step in the establishment of bipartisan foreign policy, he rejected isolationism and pledged cooperation if the administration would clarify its plans for the postwar world with candor. Vandenberg announced that he would support the evolving United Nations. To further guarantee the peace and allay Russian distrust of the West, he called for a four-power military alliance to prevent another war and to insure that Germany would not rearm. More importantly, he suggested maximum consultation and cooperation between the administration and the Senate in charting the course and development of institutions in which the United States would provide leadership for the postwar world. Applauded by his fellow senators, Vandenberg stated the convictions of the American people, most of whom demanded an end to partisanship in foreign policy matters and cooperation within an international organization. Vandenberg's speech received praise in thousands of letters he received and in nearly one thousand editorials.

Initially the White House reacted coldly to the speech, fearing that it represented an isolationist ploy of a lateral action to defeat Roosevelt's leadership and policies. For that reason, the next day Roosevelt summoned the members of the Senate Committee on Foreign Relations to the White House to meet with him. In a most candid manner the president gave his analysis of the war scene and future problems and answered questions, thus creating a new sense of confidence in his leadership. The long-term reaction to Vandenberg's speech surfaced when Roosevelt invited Vandenberg, Connally, and the former Republican governor of Minnesota, Harold Stassen, to serve as delegates to the United Nations Conference on International Organization. Roosevelt also appointed John Foster Dulles as a consultant to the delegation. Congressmen Sol Bloom of New York and Charles A. Eaton of New Jersey were to serve as delegates. Roosevelt realized that he would need Republican support regardless of which type of international organization emerged from the San Francisco deliberations, which he planned to attend. Roosevelt liked Vandenberg's proposal for a four-party alliance. To illustrate to Great Britain and the Soviet Union the solidarity of American political leaders on the postwar peace, Roosevelt took fifty copies of Vandenberg's speech to the Yalta Conference for distribution.

Before the United States delegation embarked for San Francisco, where delegates from the Allied countries were to create the new international organization, several changes took place within the White House and State Department which helped the developing bipartisanship. Cordell Hull left the State Department because of illness on 29 November 1944. He was replaced by Edward R. Stettinius, Jr., an able administrator who, despite his lack of experience in foreign affairs, would prove most cooperative with the senators. Of course, Roosevelt would remain his own secretary of state until his death on 13 April 1945.

The succession of Harry S. Truman to the presidency portended well for bipartisanship. Truman knew the senators as friends and had respect for their abilities. As a former member of the Senate establishment he well understood the benefits of working closely with Senate and House committees, and as a new president he needed all the support and advice he could garner.

Unlike Roosevelt, Truman willingly permitted the delegates to debate the American position on issues that remained to be settled at San Francisco. In retrospect it appears unlikely that Roosevelt would have appointed a bipartisan delegation, and allow it to arrive at an independent stand on the remaining unsettled issues. Before his death Roosevelt had planned to lead the delegation and would probably have reserved for himself the making of major decisions, seeking merely the passive assent of the United States delegation. Instead, Truman, overwhelmed with his official responsibilities as president, permitted and supported the delegation's demands at the conference for the trusteeship of a few islands and bases to protect the United States strategically. He sent his adviser Harry Hopkins to the Union of Soviet Socialist Republics to persuade Commissar Stalin to go along with Roosevelt's understanding that there should be unrestricted debate in the Security Council and General Assembly, thus placing such discussion outside the veto. The delegation successfully incorporated Articles 51–54 into the Charter, providing for regional defense arrangements. The result of this bipartisan cooperation at San Francisco was that Senators Connally and Vandenberg agreed that a simple majority affirmation of the United Nations Participatory Act by both Houses of Congress would constitute approval of the United Nations Charter. This legislation passed the Senate by a vote of 82–2. As H. Bradford Westerfield observed: "It was a full bipartisan effort in the respect that consultation was decidedly prior to decision and that the administration did not merely pick and choose amenable members of the opposite party leadership." American adherence and commitment to the United Nations marked the completion of the bipartisan foreign policy model, which, with variations arising on account of necessity, remained the mode of making certain foreign policies.

President Truman furthered the bipartisanship system by appointing Senators Connally and Vandenberg as delegates to the first meeting of the General Assembly of the United Nations. The two leaders also served as delegates to the Council of Foreign Ministers, which convened to write peace treaties for the Balkan States and Italy. John Foster Dulles was appointed to serve as a State Department adviser at several meetings of the Council of Foreign Ministers. Long-standing internationalist and Republican Warren Austin represented the Truman administration as a delegate to the Inter-American Conference on Problems of War and Peace near Mexico City, which resulted in the Act of Chapultepec (1945). Bipartisan support also resulted in approval of the loan to Great Britain and American adherence to the World Court.

The Cold War consensus that solidified under Truman intended to get tough with the Russians regarding their policies, especially in Eastern Europe. Secretary of State James F. Byrnes, who initially sought to continue the process of cooperation with the Soviet Union in settling German and Eastern European questions, was pressured by both the president and Senate leaders to recognize the impossibility of cooperation with the Russians. Eventually Byrnes also pursued anti-Soviet policies to prevent the spread of communism. Later he resigned and Truman convinced George C. Marshall to become secretary of state.

In the national leaderships there existed an agreement that the spread of communism was not in the best interests of the United States. Differences with the Russians over the terms of Yalta and Potsdam caused a change in American policy. American leaders agreed that internal subversion and aggression from outside a nation's boundaries had to be contained by military action if necessary. The Cold War consensus prevailed until the American defeat in Vietnam, détente with the Soviet Union, and friendship with China—causing a reevaluation of American foreign policy.

Bipartisan foreign policy reached its high point during 1946–1949, when Truman, Byrnes, Marshall, and Dean Acheson worked closely with Senators Connally and Vandenberg to provide a unified national leadership. The Republican sweep of House and Senate elections in 1946 meant that Truman's Democratic administration would be forced to deal with a Republican-dominated Congress and that Vandenberg, a recent convert from isolationism, would serve as chairman of the Senate Committee on Foreign Relations. From the onset, Vandenberg pledged that he would strive to lead his party in support of Truman's postwar policy.

Easily winning the 1946 congressional elections on a platform for reducing the federal budget, the Republican-dominated Eightieth Congress was not receptive to requests for additional appropriations to support American foreign policy. Despite the Republican pledge to reduce taxes, Truman summoned leaders of both parties to the White House on 27 February 1947 to discuss the situation developing in both Greece and Turkey. The British had advised the secretary of state in a note on 21 February that because of its depressed economy, Britain could no longer carry the burden of stabilizing the civil war in Greece. The Greek government was fighting communist guerrillas financed by Russian satellite states. Should the Greek communists win, Turkey would be surrounded by communist governments. Prompted by the desire to keep Greece and Turkey out of communist control, Truman and the State Department decided to assume Britain's burden in the Eastern Mediterranean. With the appointment of General George C. Marshall as secretary of state, there was a significant shift in the State Department, from concern about trade and tariffs to the broader problems of European reconstruction. Through bipartisan cooperation on a crisis-reaction basis, the administration decided to provide economic and military aid to both Greece and Turkey.

Under Secretary of State Dean Acheson, at a White House conference of administration and congressional leaders on 27 February, pleaded for speedy action by Congress. At a subsequent meeting on 10 March Vandenberg urged the president to address a joint session of Congress and tell the people about the possibility of a communist takeover of one or both nations, accompanied by a detailed description of the implications for America's future security. At the same time, Vandenberg pledged his cooperation and predicted that his fellow senators would support the administration if they understood the gravity of the situation. Vandenberg also received assurances from the State Department that it would answer any questions posed by members of the House and Senate. These numbered over 400, were boiled down to 111, and the State Department provided answers pointing to the need for immediate American action.

Accordingly, Truman addressed Congress on 12 March 1947, requesting $400 million in aid for Greece and Turkey. Of greater long-term significance, he annunciated the Truman Doctrine, which provided for American support of "free peoples who are resisting attempted subjugation by armed minorities or by outside pressures . . . to assist free peoples to work out their destiny in their own way." Truman also stated that "help should be primarily through economic and financial aid which is essential to economic stability and orderly political process."

Although Vandenberg endorsed the Truman Doctrine, a radical shift in American foreign policy, he made this a personal commitment and not one representing the positions of the Republican party or the Senate Foreign Relations Committee. He nonetheless worked feverishly to gain unanimous support for the foreign aid bill for Greece and Turkey. It was reported out of committee on 23 April 1947, and approved by the House Foreign Affairs Committee two days later. In the debate that ensued, the bill was attacked by left-wing Democrats as being too anti-Soviet and by right-wing Republicans as requiring too large an expenditure and as a violation of America's isolationist tradition. Vandenberg criticized the administration for not consulting with congressional leaders while the policy evolved and for handling the question on a crisis basis. He also criticized the administration for not referring the matter to the United Nations, calling it a "colossal blunder." Debated through March and April, the bill was defended by Vandenberg, who had made a persuasive speech in favor of its passage. The House voted 287–108 and the Senate 67–23 favorably and agreed by voice vote on 15 May 1947 to the conference report that Truman signed into law on 22 May.

The spirit of bipartisanship continued as the president appointed Dwight P. Griswold, former Republican governor of Nebraska, as chief of the Greek aid mission. Congress provided the necessary appropriations, and on 22 March 1948 Vandenberg submitted another aid bill for Greece and Turkey, which the Senate approved by voice vote on 23 March 1948. The House incorporated the aid bill into the Foreign Assistance Act (Marshall Plan) of 1948.

Truman further demonstrated his commitment to bipartisan foreign policy when he appointed a balanced delegation of Democrats and Republicans, composed of Senators Vandenberg and Connally, former Senator Warren R. Austin, and Representatives Sol Bloom and

Charles Eaton, to the Inter-American Conference for the Maintenance of Continental Peace and Security. It convened near Rio de Janeiro to implement the Act of Chapultepec by a formal alliance, the first such commitment by the United States since the Franco-American alliance of 1778. Meeting from 15 August to 2 September 1947, the delegates agreed that an attack on any American state would be repelled by military force if necessary and pledged to develop appropriate machinery for inter-American cooperation. This idea was eventually implemented by the Organization of American States. Senator Vandenberg led the fight for unanimous approval by the Senate Foreign Relations Committee and formal approval by the Senate on 8 December 1947. Seventy-two senators voted affirmatively; there was only one dissenting vote. The process of close consultation and collaboration between the Senate and the administration had produced what Vandenberg, a long-term defender of the Monroe Doctrine, declared was the "most important document in the life of the new world."

Meanwhile, as legislation for aid to Greece and Turkey wound its way through Congress, the administration realized that the Greek-Turkish crises were symptomatic of a greater need for American cooperation in the rebuilding of a war-devastated Europe. To develop a program designed to deal with the economic needs of those countries, the Truman administration urged cooperation of the congressional leadership from the inception of a program of mutual assistance.

Secretary of State Marshall believed the collaboration of the Soviets in rebuilding Europe was unattainable. He therefore used the occasion of an honorary doctorate granted him at the Harvard University commencement on 5 June 1947 to outline the need for a cooperative American-European venture for the recovery of Europe. Reports from Under Secretary Acheson and Assistant Secretary William L. Clayton, and George M. Kennan's informal Policy Planning Committee, strengthened Marshall's resolution to act. Marshall spoke of the necessity for a cooperative program to deal with a Europe ravished by floods, droughts, starvation, unemployment, inflation, and destroyed trade and monetary systems, coupled with a severe winter with inadequate coal for heat, and the breakdown of the steel and grain industries. While the proposal may also have had an anticommunist motivation, its main concern, as expressed by the president, the State Department, and the congressional leadership, was the suffering peoples of Europe. In his address Marshall summoned European leadership to devise a plan and urged the American people to accept the challenge to restore Europe.

Even before the Harvard address, Vandenberg had protested the rumors of some massive American "New Deal" for Europe alluded to in a speech in Mississippi by Under Secretary Acheson, and in remarks by Senator Alben W. Barkley and news columnists. Furious at not being consulted, Vandenberg met with Marshall and Acheson at Blair House within two weeks after Acheson's Mississippi speech to secure what he, as chairman of the Senate Committee on Foreign Relations, felt was necessary background information. At the meeting, as reported by Acheson and Joseph M. Jones, Vandenberg listened to the State Department explanation that a piecemeal aid program, such as the Greece-Turkey crisis, must be replaced by a long-term education of Congress, the American people, and European leaders for the reconstruction of Europe.

Vandenberg agreed to the Marshall Plan, but more importantly attempted to convince fellow Republicans to approve bills for interim aid grants of $350 million for Austria, Hungary, Poland, Italy, Trieste, China, and Greece. Approved unanimously by the Senate committee, the Marshall Plan was agreed to by both houses on 21 May 1947, and signed by the president on 31 May. Vandenberg also used his talents as a bipartisan legislator for the authorization of $587 million, as suggested by Truman when he called for a special session of Congress, to assist Austria, China, France, and Italy.

The Marshall Plan developed within a context of bipartisanship. At an early stage in the collaboration Vandenberg suggested to Marshall, Acheson, and the president that nonpartisan committees should study the European economic crises, suggest programs, and analyze their impact on the American economy. In announcing the forming of three committees at a joint congressional meeting at the White House in June 1947, Truman credited Vandenberg with the idea. The president appointed Secretary of Commerce Julius Krug to head a committee to report on available American resources, E. G. Nourse to detail the impact of a foreign aid program on the American economy, and W. Averell Harriman to chair a nongovernment, bipartisan committee to study the best methods for dealing with the European crises.

Thereafter, Vandenberg worked closely with Marshall and the banker Robert A. Lovett, who on 1 July 1947 replaced Acheson as under secretary of state. More than 200 congressmen traveled to Europe to investigate the situation, and the press began an instructive campaign to set the stage for Truman's message of 19 December 1947, requesting enactment of legislation for the Marshall Plan. Following presidential leadership, the Senate and House hearings ended before 1 March 1948, when Vandenberg launched the Senate debate on the Marshall Plan by praising the president, State Department, and his colleagues for their cooperative efforts, and pleading for the quick adoption of the plan. Under British and French leadership, following a refusal by the Soviet Union to cooperate, European leaders designed their cooperative proposals in response to Marshall's call for European initiative in planning recovery.

In his drive for approval, Vandenberg persuaded the administration to scale its requests for a twelve-month period and thus secure House and Senate approval for an appropriation of $5.3 million, a feat which was a high point in Vandenberg's career and a victory for the Truman administration. It was an unlikely result that only Vandenberg, as the leader of the loyal opposition, could have devised. He persuaded the administration to submit to the Brookings Institution the question of whether the State Department or a new organization with a separate administration should run the program. The result was a recommendation for a separate agency, the European Cooperative Administration. After opposing William Clayton and former Under Secretary Dean Acheson for the ECA post, Vandenberg convinced Truman to appoint Paul G. Hoffman as chief administrator of the European Recovery Program. Vandenberg knew that other Republicans such as Dwight D. Eisenhower, Henry L. Stimson, John J. McCloy, John Foster Dulles, Herbert Hoover, Styles Bridges, and Paul Hoffman shared his commitment to bipartisanship in American foreign policy and deserved a measure of the credit for its success. In addition, the Marshall Plan brought to Western Europe a prosperity greater than it had known before the war.

Even before the appropriations for the ECA, Vandenberg and others concluded that the economic recovery of Europe would require an integrated system of security against possible communist aggression. In the wake of the communist coup in Czechoslovakia and the Berlin blockade, Great Britain, France, Belgium, the Netherlands, and Luxembourg signed the Brussels Mutual Defense Pact in March 1948. Because of Soviet vetoes within the Security Council of the United Nations, Vandenberg conferred with Under Secretary Robert Lovett to devise a Senate resolution calling for a United States–European security system "within the charter, but outside the veto." In other words, the senator wished to use Articles 51–54 of the Charter, which permitted regional defense systems similar to the Rio Alliance of the American States. This Vandenberg Resolution also developed as a response to a series of bills submitted to Congress to amend the United Nations Charter. After consulting with Marshall and Dulles, Vandenberg completed his resolution on 11 May 1948. It provided for a reaffirmation of peace and security through the United Nations; removal of the veto; development of regional collective arrangements for self-defense, to which the United States could adhere by proper constitutional procedures; and an agreement that all signatories would intervene militarily in the event of armed aggression against any of the other participating nations. The Senate Committee on Foreign Relations approved the Vandenberg Resolution unanimously on 19 May 1948. It won Senate approval by a margin of 64–6 on 11 June, and was subsequently approved by the House. Within one month after passage of the Vandenberg Resolution, Lovett began secret negotiations that would lead to the North Atlantic Treaty Organization. His efforts progressed under the cover of the 1948 presidential election.

As in 1944, Dewey won the Republican

nomination and Truman was renominated by the Democratic party. Vandenberg played the major role in writing the Republican national platform, essentially praising bipartisanship and Truman's foreign policy. Vandenberg delivered only one campaign speech in support of Dewey, after which Truman summoned him to the White House to praise his statesmanlike support of bipartisanship. The Democrats were split on the left by Henry Wallace's bid for the presidency with a platform that attacked the anti-Soviet bias of bipartisan foreign policy, and on the right by Strom Thurmond of South Carolina, who campaigned on an anti–civil rights stance in defense of states' rights. Confident of victory, Dewey endorsed an interventionist foreign policy.

During the campaign, Dulles accompanied Marshall in September 1948 to the Council of Foreign Ministers in Paris in order to insure that the United States spoke with one voice in foreign policy. In the last minutes of the campaign Truman attacked the "Do-nothing 80th Congress." In doing so he squandered the wide support he had enjoyed from Republicans led by Vandenberg and which he would need if he won reelection. Truman's victory brought Democratic control of both houses of Congress. This respite from bipartisanship offended Vandenberg, but subsequently in the national interest, Republicans and Democrats rejoined forces to cooperate in approving American participation in the North Atlantic Treaty Organization.

During the election campaign, Under Secretary of State Lovett had worked to develop a draft of a proposed treaty. He began to meet several times each week with Senator Tom Connally, the new chairman of the Foreign Relations Committee, and Senator Vandenberg. Lovett proposed two ideas; namely, that an attack on any treaty member would be regarded as a military attack on all treaty members, and that each treaty member would initiate "military or other action" at once. Initially the senators requested the word "military" deleted for easier Senate approval. Public opinion, however, both in the United States and in Europe led to replacement of the original wording, which called for American adherence to an alliance with a commitment to use military forces to repel any outside aggression, specifically from the Soviet Union and its Eastern European satellites. Secretary Acheson met several times with the committee. Promulgated on 18 March 1949, the treaty was signed by Great Britain, France, Canada, Belgium, Italy, the Netherlands, Luxembourg, Iceland, Denmark, Norway, Portugal, and the United States on 4 April 1949. It was sent to the Senate on 12 April, and after executive and public hearings was reported out of committee unanimously on 6 June. After weeks of debate, the Senate, on 21 July 1949, gave its consent, without amendments, by a vote of 82–13. Eventually Greece, Turkey, and the German Federal Republic joined NATO.

Building the NATO alliance served as another example of bipartisan foreign policy. The senators on the Foreign Relations Committee charged that the administration had not been candid when it failed to inform both the senators and the public of the essentially military nature of the treaty. They also insisted that proper constitutional procedure be followed in bringing the nation into NATO and in any declaration of war. The president must not be allowed to bring the country into a war on his own. The senators' fears of unilateral executive action were shortly confirmed when on 25 July 1949 Truman sent a message to Congress requesting funds to arm NATO signatories. Acting in a bipartisan manner, Congress appended amendments regarding the size of the appropriations, presidential discretion in their use, and the sales of munitions. Then, as in the future, the administration gained bipartisan approval for the requested arms. Congress was particularly willing to approve appropriations requested by the administration during the Korean War.

Although bipartisanship was the primary method of developing foreign policy, especially in areas where the administration needed congressional support or funding to implement existing policies, its implementation for the remainder of the Truman administration waned. In several areas partisan fighting was stronger than it had ever been. Senator Joseph McCarthy, a Republican from Wisconsin, attacked Truman's foreign policy as treasonous, and others blamed him for the triumph of communism in China, and for blundering leadership during the Korean War. Yet even in these partisan times, Truman appointed Dulles to negotiate a peace treaty with Japan. Other factors that help explain the fissures in bipartisanship include the electoral victory of Truman in 1948, so he appeared overconfident in his relations with Congress, which became strained despite the fact that the Democrats controlled both houses. For example, he appointed Dean Acheson secretary of state without consulting congressional leadership, and did not consult Congress before announcing his Point Four Program. The administration also lost a valuable ally for garnering Republican support with the death of Vandenberg in 1951.

Moreover, even at its zenith, bipartisanship had not applied to all areas of American foreign policy. The Democrats and the Republicans could not, for example, agree on policy toward the Chinese civil war. Vandenberg frequently complained that the Senate Committee on Foreign Relations was not consulted with regard to defense appropriations; policies regarding Germany, Iran, Japan, Latin America, the Middle East; or on general United Nations policy.

During the administrations of Dwight D. Eisenhower and John F. Kennedy, the bipartisan approach to foreign policy was sustained by the willingness of both to call party leaders for consultation during major crises. Eisenhower found it easy to work with Democratic legislative leaders, especially Senators Walter George of Georgia and Lyndon B. Johnson of Texas. Eisenhower experienced little Democratic opposition because he and Secretary of State Dulles embraced the Cold War consensus and consulted with the congressional leadership regarding important political decisions. Except for the abortive Bricker amendment, which would have restricted the power of the president in making executive agreements, bipartisanship prevailed.

President Kennedy followed the same course of action in consulting Republican and Democratic congressional leaders who responded favorably to presidential leadership, especially in crises over the Berlin Wall and Soviet missiles in Cuba. This bipartisan legacy in foreign affairs passed to Kennedy's successor, Lyndon B. Johnson.

In the presidential campaign of 1964 the candidates used the bipartisan model. A consensus seemingly supported the idea that the Truman Doctrine should not be implemented in all situations, especially in South Vietnam, where a conservative government was battling left-wing insurgents. Johnson promised not to intervene with American troops. Barry Goldwater, the Republican candidate, urged a strong stand against a communist takeover of South Vietnam. This defiance of the consensus may have cost Goldwater considerable support. Following the election and the escalation of the Vietnam war, the public no longer sustained the containment policy. Congressional leaders and others attacked Johnson's policies and ended the quarter century of bipartisan foreign policy.

With the election of Richard M. Nixon as president, the appointement of Henry Kissinger as national security adviser, and the winding down of the Vietnam war, bipartisanship appeared to have some chance of revival because of the mutual respect of Kissinger and the chairman of the Senate Committee on Foreign Relations, J. William Fulbright. But Fulbright's loss of office, and foreign policy crises that aroused partisan popular emotions precluded a new era of bipartisan cooperation.

Insofar as both houses of Congress presumably reflect prevailing public opinion with regard to presidential leadership in foreign affairs, bipartisanship can be adjudged to be democratic within the confines of the constitutional system. Lyndon B. Johnson, Richard M. Nixon, and his successor, Gerald R. Ford, frequently found themselves in open confrontation with a truculent Congress; and wherever policy resulted from collaboration between the Congress and the administration, bipartisanship prevailed.

In late June 1975 the Commission on the Organization of the Government for the Conduct of Foreign Policy, headed by Robert D. Murphy and established by legislation in July 1972, presented its formal report in which the major commission recommendations called, in effect, for the reestablishment of bipartisan foreign policy. The crux of the Murphy report suggested that the president provide the overall objectives of American foreign policy to the public and Congress so that other nations would understand the United States position in world affairs; that foreign policy be more orderly and open, with input by those inside and outside of government; and that Congress should be consulted, receiving complete information so it can more effectively discharge its role as both critic and supporter of the administration's general policies. Congress would need better leadership, more information, and a more controlled organization if it were to discharge its foreign policy responsibilities effectively. Above all there should be a cooperative spirit and working machinery to reduce congressional-executive confrontations over policy. Finally, this cooperative approach to American foreign policy was also frequently advocated by President-elect James E. Carter during his successful 1976 campaign for the presidency.

BIBLIOGRAPHY

H. Bradford Westerfield, *Foreign Policy and Party Politics* (New Haven, 1955), analyzes Congress and the making of American foreign policy from Pearl Harbor down to the Korean War. Malcolm Jewell, *Senatorial Politics and Foreign Policy* (Lexington, Ky., 1962), is a crucial study of Senate voting patterns, demonstrating that bipartisan foreign policy prevailed under both Truman and Eisenhower. Cecil V. Crabb, Jr., *Bipartisan Foreign Policy: Myth or Reality* (Evanston, Ill., 1957), remains useful despite his harsh treatment of bipartisan foreign policy. Howard Bliss and M. Glen Johnsen, *Beyond the Water's Edge: American Foreign Policies* (New York, 1975), is a brief, but insightful study of bipartisanship and its underlying Cold War consensus. Paul Y. Hammond, *Cold War and Détente: The American Foreign Policy Process Since 1945* (New York, 1975), is perceptive, especially on the relationship between the executive and Congress in determining the U.S. response to international events. *Commission on the Organization of the Government for the Conduct of Foreign Policy* (Washington, D.C., 1975) indicates the desirability of a bipartisan foreign policy. Roger Hilsman, "Congressional-Executive Relations and Foreign Policy Consensus," in *American Political Science Review* (1958), is persuasive on the need for a close working relationship between the executive and Congress in making foreign policy. The U.S. Senate Committee on Foreign Relations, *Review of Bipartisan Foreign Policy Consultations Since World War II,* 82nd Congress, 1st session, Senate document no. 87 (Washington, D.C., 1951), is a survey of the record of bipartisanship.

[*See also* CONGRESS AND FOREIGN POLICY; EXECUTIVE AGENTS; POLITICS AND FOREIGN POLICY.]

BLOCKADES AND QUARANTINES

Frank J. Merli
Robert H. Ferrell

BLOCKADES and quarantines have always been attractive concepts to the American people and government, for if properly defined they have seemed a way of restricting war and even of preserving peace. In time of war a narrowly drawn blockade might clearly ward off a conflict and allow a neutral nation, perhaps the United States, to carry on its foreign relations and trade much as before. In time of peace a proper quarantine might prove sufficient to discourage a quarreling nation from employing military force. "Blockade" is not necessarily synonymous with war, for according to international law there can be pacific and also belligerent blockades. Most blockades, of course, have been instituted in wartime. "Quarantine," essentially a twentieth-century expression, in recent years has tended to replace blockade, a word stretched beyond all reason during the two world wars. Moreover, the international organizations created after each world war have anticipated the prevention of conflicts through the cordoning off of "aggressor" nations by multilateral action and not by the traditional bilateral maneuvers involving a blockade. Then, too, in the Cuban missile confrontation of 1962 between the United States and the Soviet Union, lawyers at the State Department used the word "quarantine" as a circumlocution, because it seemed less provocative than blockade, and also because it would not automatically invoke inconvenient rules and practices of the not too distant past.

The law of blockade, that is, the rules governing proper legal practice, originated in the early struggles for supremacy among the maritime nations of Europe in the fifteenth and sixteenth centuries. During that time belligerents hacked and hewed, by sea as by land, and neutrals constantly found themselves involved in quarrels, whether they wished to be or not. Early in the seventeenth century a compromise of sorts emerged between neutrals and belligerents, in which the latter undertook to define carefully the list of items that were contraband and subject to capture. They also agreed that blockades could not merely be proclaimed: acceptable practice would require that a port be cordoned off by the stationing of naval vessels at its entrance. As originally conceived, a blockade might be likened to a maritime equivalent of a land siege. When a port was properly blockaded an investing belligerent could prohibit all trade with that port, including that of neutral nations. The idea apparently appeared first in a treaty of 1614 between the Netherlands and Sweden. A refinement of the concept of effective blockade appeared in a Dutch announcement or *Placaart* of 1630, issued after consultation with private jurists and judges of the courts of admiralty. Its first article declared: "Neutral ships and goods passing in or out of the ports of the enemy in Flanders; or being so near them, that there can be no doubt but they will go into them, shall be confiscated: Because their High Mightinesses continually beset those ports with ships of war, in order to hinder any commerce with the enemy." Interestingly enough, the drafters of this rule justified it as "an ancient custom, warranted by the example of all princes"—a useful, if not entirely accurate, assessment of prior practice. The "law" of blockade, however, unlike other branches of international law, owed less to statutory enactments and more to the customs and precedents of naval officers and admiralty lawyers as they sought to bend the definitions of blockade to accommodate national interests, especially the need for victory in war.

In the early modern period of European history, with its frequent maritime wars, new rules of blockade rapidly evolved, and as they grew they acquired increasing importance as effective instruments of naval coercion. But those rules never remained static. They required frequent adjustment to new circumstances, technological innovation, and modified strategic concepts. More importantly, over the centuries, blockades had to be adapted to the exigencies created by new definitions of the nature of war.

From the mid-seventeenth century onward development of concepts of blockade expanded rapidly and soon the nations of Europe had agreed on some basic rules governing their use. Hugo Grotius, the father of international law, had set out a rule that foodstuffs, so-called provisions, should be treated as contraband only when an attempt was made to introduce them into a blockaded port *in extremis,* and this humane refinement had received general approval from naval authorities. For their part, legal theorists generally agreed that international law recognized no right of access to ports effectively closed by naval squadrons. When the United States drew up a model treaty of commerce in 1776 for submission to foreign nations, it overlooked an article defining blockades, but soon remedied that omission. American statesmen took inspiration from the attempted Armed Neutrality of 1780. Catherine the Great sought to bring together some of the European neutrals in the general war then raging, to unite them in a pact of armed neutrality to enforce an expanded definition of neutral rights in wartime. Russia proposed that ". . . the denomination of a blockaded port is to be given only to one which has the enemy vessels stationed sufficiently near to cause an evident danger to the attempt to enter." Though little came of Catherine's initiative, the government of the United States incorporated this proviso into its Treaty Plan of 1784, and it sought international recognition of this principle.

In the seventeenth and eighteenth centuries the practices of nations vis-à-vis blockade tended to follow their treaty obligations, and those treaties spelled out a wide variety of reciprocal rights and duties that would become operative in time of war. Naturally, a good many of the arrangements concerned the proper implementation of the rules of blockade, for nations that were neutral had no wish to become embroiled in the quarrels of their neighbors. It might be said that no branch of international relations had received more attention than the search for a viable definition of blockade, one that would protect the rights of neutrals without too seriously impeding the war efforts of belligerents. Part of the reason for a certain tolerance on the subject stemmed from necessity: the naval powers of that day, Britain and Holland, depended upon Scandinavian sources of naval stores. Prudence dictated a circumspect policy toward the northern neutrals of Europe, while the conditions of warfare made such a policy easier to pursue. In that time of limited war, full-scale blockades were rarely imposed, for men-of-war and privateers usually found it more profitable to waylay merchantmen that might be subject to seizure and condemnation in a prize court (with consequent enrichment of the captors). In prize law, problems of blockade violation remained largely a subdivision of the law of contraband until the era of the wars of the French Revolution. In the 1790's British Admiralty officials began to pay closer attention to the problems posed by blockade. The altered circumstances of the time required new approaches, and all concessions toward neutrals had to be reevaluated.

The struggle that engulfed Europe from 1793 to 1815 ushered in a new era of international relations. Changed conditions of warfare required the belligerents to impose heavy restrictions on trade with the enemy. Almost at once Great Britain and France narrowed their definitions of neutral rights; and as the struggle between them intensified, both nations demonstrated that they would take whatever measures seemed necessary to defeat the enemy. At one point the French proclaimed that there were no neutrals; the British echoed that sentiment. According to one commentator, international law, if it existed at all, had been known only "through the declamations of publicists and its violation by governments." Whatever the cynicism of that mot, it accurately reflected the views of an age caught up in revolutionary upheaval.

When the wars of the French Revolution led Britain to an assault on America's presumed right of unfettered trade with all the nations of the world, belligerent as well as neutral, Secretary of State Thomas Jefferson drew up a strong protest. The provision order of 1793 had instructed British naval commanders to bring in for preemptive purchase all neutral ships en route to French ports with cargoes of corn, flour, or meal. By this arbitrary redefinition of contraband, by an order that would keep American grain out of French markets in Europe and in the West Indies, by a decree that arrogantly restricted American produce to the ports of Britain or her allies, the infamous provision order threatened the new nation's honor and interests. The threat led Jefferson to a spirited defense of America's canons of commerce and international law. After denouncing the British order as contrary to the law of nations and asserting that food could never be classified as contraband, he acknowledged a "single restriction" on the right of neutrals to use the seas freely: ". . . that of not furnishing to either party implements merely of war . . . nor anything whatever to a place blockaded by its enemy." Jefferson thus put his finger on an important point, for if food could be classified as contraband, as an implement of war, British cruisers could legally seize it on American ships. If an order in council could declare entire islands of the West Indies or the entire coast of France blockaded, then Americans could carry nothing whatever to those places.

In the practice of the times a legal blockade "entitled the blockading power to intercept all commerce with the blockaded port and to confiscate ships and cargoes of whatever description attempting to breach the blockade." As a nation that lived largely by export of foodstuff, America had a vested interest in the outcome of arguments on the fine points of international law, but Jefferson could not bring the British around to his view. Nor could John Jay when, in 1794, he went to London to draw up a commercial treaty and to resolve a number of simmering disputes, including claims for damages that had grown out of the British attacks on American commerce. In part, Jay sought to bring the British around to Jefferson's definition of neutral rights, to get them to agree that foodstuffs could never be classified as contraband (although they might be captured on ships attempting to enter a blockaded port). In these negotiations the Americans also desired British assent to the definition of effective blockade incorporated in the Armed Neutrality of 1780. Unable to obtain these arrangements, Jay had to be satisfied with a British promise to indemnify American citizens for captured articles, "not generally regarded as contraband," and for assurances that vessels approaching a blockaded port would be turned away rather than captured, if the captain had no prior knowledge of such blockade. Beyond these innocuous concessions the British refused to go.

Meanwhile, on the French side during the 1790's matters became so trying for the United States that a quasi war broke out in 1798, largely because of French interference with American commerce. Lasting two years, the war ended with the Treaty of Mortefontaine (better known as the Convention of 1800), which contained a Napoleonic affirmation of neutral rights, including a narrow definition of blockade. No altruism dictated such a concession; in all probability Napoleon sought to embarrass the British for their provision order and for other executive acts of the British cabinet that both interfered with his supplies and irritated neutrals by their arbitrary nature. Or he may have sought to lure the United States into another league of armed neutrals that was then forming in Europe.

The Peace of Amiens (1802) momentarily brought peace to Europe, but when war resumed barely a year later, the concept of neutral rights and the definition of blockade again came in for heavy pummeling by both belligerents. Horatio Nelson's victory at Trafalgar in October 1805, and Napoleon's at Austerlitz in December of that year, made England supreme on the sea and France supreme on land. As Napoleon moved from triumph to triumph thereafter, as he consolidated his hegemony over the Continent, the British sought to bring him down with ever more restrictive maritime regulations. The military stalemate required full-scale economic war, which spelled trouble for the neutrals. The British had already tightened up on neutral trade with French colonial possessions by invoking the Rule of 1756—a diktat that forbade in wartime trade not allowed in peacetime—to cut neutrals out of the profitable French carrying trade.

But blockade proved the most potent weapon in the arsenals of both belligerents. Upon becoming prime minister in 1806, Charles James Fox sponsored an order-in-council that declared the coast of Europe, from Brest to the Elbe, in a state of blockade (although its prohibitions were absolute only between the Seine and Ostend). But whatever its leniencies, whatever concessions it might allow neutrals, it amounted to a paper blockade, one unsupported by ships stationed off the ports in blockade. Even the mistress of the seas did not have sufficient ships to cordon off so extensive a portion of seacoast, but by cruising off enemy coasts and by crisscrossing trade routes, the Royal Navy hoped to capture neutral vessels—whatever their cargo might be—en route to blockaded ports.

The French, in turn, responded with the Berlin (1806) and Milan (1807) decrees. These imperial enactments placed the British Isles in a state of blockade, and any ship submitting to search by British cruisers or complying with regulations requiring a stop at a British port, the French considered denationalized and lawful prize. Essentially a set of domestic French regulations, Napoleon's continental system remained legal in territories under French control, in the dominions of its allies, or in consenting neutral countries. Although the system amounted to "a fantastic blockade in reverse," its main purpose was not blockade but the ruin of British commerce, as Napoleon himself admitted. "It is by dominating all the coasts of Europe that we shall succeed in bringing Pitt [the Younger, then prime minister] to an honorable peace," he had written in 1800, but "if the seas escape us, there is not a port, not the mouth of a river, that is not within reach of our sword." By denying his adversary access to continental markets, the emperor hoped to destroy British power.

Faced with competing blockades (the British, for their part, desired only to push their own goods onto the Continent, contrary to Napoleon's desire), confronted with ever more restrictive practices on the part of the European belligerents, the neutral United States twisted and turned, without finding a satisfactory resolution of its dilemma. On one occasion President Jefferson told the French minister in Washington that "we have principles from which we shall never depart. Our people have commerce everywhere, and everywhere our neutrality should be respected. On the other hand we do not want war, and all this is very embarrassing." The situation called for action, but action risked war. Under such circumstances, and given the peaceful proclivities of the Jeffersonians, it was tempting to resort to ingenuity; the more so because Napoleon had cunningly remarked in the Milan Decree that its provisions would not be enforced against neutrals who compelled Britain to respect their flag. The president sponsored a series of legislative enactments, including the embargo of 1807–1809, which, through unfortunate timing, coincided with the apogee of Napoleonic power. The baleful effects of the embargo helped convince some Federalists in Boston and elsewhere that the president was in league with the emperor. Nothing could be further from the truth. The European situation remained beyond the influence of American stratagems, no matter how ingenious, as Jefferson and his successor James Madison learned.

The British openly violated their own blockade of Europe by a system of licenses encouraging neutrals to carry both British and colonial goods through the French self-blockade, albeit after those goods had passed through British hands at a profit. In 1807 some 1,600 such licenses were granted; and by 1810 the number had reached 18,000. By that time Russia had deserted the continental system, opening the Baltic to neutral and British trade. Unable to control the periphery of his system, in Spain, Portugal, and Russia, Napoleon took his Grande Armée to Moscow and disaster. The object of that campaign, of course, was to force the Russians back into the system and to reconstruct his continental blockade. Shortly before this great effort commenced, the United States, with its sixteen assorted ships of war, entered the conflict against England. Soon the British blockaded ports in the American South and West, although they carefully refrained from blockading New England, where there was much disaffection with Mr. Madison's war. Merchants who carried foodstuffs for British troops received passes through British squadrons. For two months after the declaration of war the British consul in Boston licensed cargoes. Nor did American participation in the war do much to clarify the rules of blockade, and these problems passed to subsequent generations.

The wars of 1793–1815 clearly demonstrated the perhaps irreconcilable difference between belligerents and neutrals over use of the flexible doctrines of blockade. For the belligerents, especially the naval powers, blockade was a weapon which, if used imaginatively, could do much to bring the enemy to its knees; for the neutrals, blockade constituted a danger to trade and a means of involvement in the war. For to the extent that a neutral acquiesced in "unlawful" definitions, that nation decreased its impartiality by actions that gave sustenance to one side while denying it to the other. Conversely, a too vigorous assertion of neutral rights might involve the nation in war. While clear-cut blockade practices, that is, generally accepted standards of effectiveness and legality, would enhance opportunities for neutral trade and profit, the blockadee (if one may use such a term) would thereby be aided in his war effort, thwarting the purpose of the blockade. On the other hand, the imprecisions inherent in formulations satisfactory to all, hence to none, provided loopholes that required no great legal legerdemain to stretch meanings to fit the exigencies of a particular war. By selecting from an assortment of precedents and practices, a belligerent could easily define the rules of blockade so as to make neutral commerce a victim of the drive for victory.

When the British sought to close the Continent to neutral trade or to control that trade in their own interest by whatever arbitrary or quasi-legal means they might devise, their higher objective, the destruction of Napoleon's war-making capacity, took precedence over abstract, poorly defined, and largely unrecognized neutral rights and theoretical definitions of how the Royal Navy might or might not use one of its most powerful weapons. In like manner, when Napoleon's continental system came into conflict with American views of proper conduct, the emperor proved no less ingenious or heavy-handed in bending practice to fit his military or economic objectives. Between the infringements of the British and French, Americans had little to choose. Caught between implacable forces in the war that raged over Europe for nearly a generation, Americans struggled to define and defend principles for which the world, at that dangerous time, could find no use. When war threatened the safety of the state, right gave way to might. In its life-or-death struggle for national existence, Britain could not countenance interpretations of blockade that interfered with the pursuit of victory. Failure to understand that fact of international life did much to embroil the United States in a war it did not really want.

But with the close of the Napoleonic wars in 1815, attendant upon Waterloo and the emperor's banishment to St. Helena, there followed almost a century when, with the possible exception of the Crimean War, no major conflict involving neutral rights took place in Europe or the world. The important wars of the nineteenth century, from 1815 to 1914, were either civil wars—such as the Taiping rebellion in China (1850–1864) or the American Civil War (1861–1865)—or land wars of relatively short duration—the Franco-Prussian War (1870–1871). Commentators on the law of war therefore had ample opportunity to refine their concepts and to sharpen their definitions. Statesmen of the time, especially American leaders, stressed the need for a new, more reasonable international order. As secretary of state, Madison had set the lines of this litany when he denied the legality of a British blockade of the entire islands of Martinique and Guadeloupe. In 1803 he told the British chargé d'affaires in Washington that international law required the presence of sufficient force to render "access to the prohibited place manifestly difficult and dangerous." In defense of this doctrine—and for the sake of American exports of food and naval stores—he added: "It can never be admitted that the trade of a neutral nation in articles not contraband, can be legally obstructed to any place, not actually blockaded." In 1824 Secretary of State John Quincy Adams ventured a new definition of a legal blockade, one that required "ships stationary or sufficiently near" the place prohibited, so that there was "evident danger" in attempting an entry. Then, during the Mexican War (1846–1848) the United States again affirmed its opposition to nominal blockades by telling the neutral British that according to

American rules, "no Mexican port was considered blockaded unless a force was stationed sufficiently near to make trade with that port dangerous."

It was curious, then, that the United States refused to adopt the 1856 Declaration of Paris by which the major European powers at the end of the Crimean War attempted to promulgate a new code of neutral rights. That set of rules included a revised definition of blockade: "Blockades, in order to be binding, must be effective—that is to say, maintained by a force sufficient really to prevent access to the coast of the enemy." Although that article clearly coincided with traditional American views, other portions of the declaration did not measure up to Washington's expectations of what a proper code of conduct should be. During the war, with the fighting mainly on land and hardly touching neutral commerce, the maritime powers, France and England (then allied against Russia), realized that privateers, that is, legalized private ships of war, might prove attractive to the Russians in some future war. Having renounced use of such vessels during the war, the victorious allies sought in peace a formal international prohibition against their use. Part of the price for such an abolition was adoption of a more liberal view of neutral rights; and the powers of Europe, including Great Britain, subscribed to the rules set out at Paris. Hence the ideal statement about blockade. But the American government, like the Russian, found fault with the new code. With its small navy, the United States might find future utility in use of private vessels of war and was therefore reluctant to surrender their use. Until belligerents were willing to afford a total immunity to all private property at sea, the Americans did not want to abolish privateering. They sought, rather, to trade off American acceptance of the article abolishing privateers for European recognition of the principle of immunity for private property at sea during wartime. Those efforts failed. In time, however, the government of the United States recognized the Paris formula on blockade as conforming to American principles of international law, and by 1914 all the nations of the world (except the United States and Venezuela) had signified adherence to the formulations of the Declaration of 1856.

Failure to sign that accord did not enhance America's status as a champion of expanded neutral rights or as a proponent of the need for clear limits to the implementation of blockades. Nor was the American position advanced by the circumstances of the Civil War, a conflict that became so heated—the need to contain the rebellious South being so pressing—that Washington officials proved willing to abridge the national record on the rights of neutrals, particularly in the use of blockade theory and practice, if only such abridgment would bring victory. Indeed some observers and later historians even have argued that the United States had been a champion of neutral rights when it had a small navy and little military power; but when it marshaled the most effective army and largest navy, it jettisoned the principles of an earlier generation in favor of a more expedient approach.

In retrospect the Civil War seems to have been so large an anomaly in American life that no easy judgment can be made on whether Abraham Lincoln and his aides forsook the principles of the Founding Fathers to save the Union. For the president and his secretary of state the fundamental international problem during the war was to preserve the neutrality and if possible the goodwill of Great Britain. Blockade measures against the South therefore had to be arranged so as to put maximum pressure on the Confederacy without provoking British reprisals. To be sure, other European neutrals occasionally encountered difficulties, such as Spain because of its ownership of Cuba, from whence blockade-runners sometimes passed, or Denmark because of the proximity of the Virgin Islands to the Confederate coast; but their involvement never reached crisis proportions. The Mexican government frequently complained about actions by Union captains off Matamoros, contrary to the Treaty of Guadalupe Hidalgo (1848), which forbade any blockade of the Rio Grande. But the British response to problems generated by the war always concerned Union leaders most, for they realized that Britain's international position, its merchant fleet and naval strength, gave Her Majesty's government a vital interest in transatlantic affairs. For example, when the British almost from the outset of the war failed to push any blockade cases with the American government, that forbearance provided Lincoln's administration with a helpful leeway in manhandling aid for the South coming in by sea, or any effort by Southerners to ship cotton abroad in order to import the arms and supplies needed to prosecute the war. Britain's lack of militancy on issues concerning blockade became so marked by the second year of the war that the federal government in Washington enjoyed virtual carte blanche in its implementation of measures to seal off the South from outside supplies.

At the outbreak of war the Lincoln administration made a slip, when on 19 April 1861 it proclaimed a blockade of Southern ports from South Carolina to Texas and then eight days later of the ports of North Carolina and Virginia. The president should have declared the ports closed. Proclamation of the blockade was a presumption that the South enjoyed belligerent status and might merit international recognition as an independent nation. British officials in London felt that, in any event, they could not look upon some five million people as pirates or as engaged in unlawful combination, and on 13 May they issued a neutrality proclamation, which included a warning to British subjects against the violation of any blockade established by either belligerent. Some months later, in July, Lincoln tried to amend the legal faux pas by saying that the blockade was "in pursuance of the law of nations" against a domestic insurrection: "A proclamation was issued for closing the ports of the insurrectionary districts by proceedings in the nature of blockade." These changes in legal terminology did not result in European withdrawal of recognition of Confederate belligerent status.

Later, debate would focus on the effectiveness of the Union blockade or on the "proceedings in the nature of blockade." Some writers have contended that Union efforts were effective, but one twentieth-century Southern historian has argued that the blockade was a sieve. He calculated that blockade-runners made over eight thousand trips to the South. He further points out that, in the early stages, the Union did not have sufficient ships to give even a semblance of effectiveness to its declaration. Naturally, the porous nature of the blockade invited attempts to run into Southern ports with profitable cargo. Many of the adventurers who tried their hand at the business were "retired" British naval officers and other subjects of Her Majesty, the Queen. So many Britishers took part in blockade-running that Lord John Russell, the British foreign secretary, offhandedly quipped that Englishmen would, "if money were to be made by it, send supplies even to hell at the risk of burning their sails." Throughout the war, profits remained high; a return of 1,000 percent upon investment was not uncommon. Even in 1864, a captain who ordinarily made about $150 per month might earn $5,000 in the same period. A popular toast celebrated the blockade-runners' thankfulness to everyone: "The Confederates that produce the cotton; the Yankees that maintain the blockade and keep up the price of cotton; the Britishers that buy the cotton and pay the high price for it. Here's to all three, and a long continuance of the war, and success to blockade-runners."

Still, the blockade was effective enough for the British government, despite a considerable pressure against the move, to recognize its existence. Lord Russell, who can hardly be described as pro-North in outlook, eventually concluded that the Union blockade had to be considered "generally effective against foreign trade." His minister in Washington, Lord Lyons, regarded it as more than a mere paper blockade, noting that if it were "as ineffective as Mr. Jefferson Davis says . . . he would not be so very anxious to get rid of it." From reports of the commander of their North American station, the British carefully monitored the performance of Union blockading squadrons, and not until early 1862 did they formally accept the blockade. In February of that year Russell told Lyons that there were enough Union vessels on blockade duty to prevent access to Southern ports or "to create an evident danger" to ships seeking to enter them.

Another Southern wartime hope—that the need for cotton would force European powers to press Lincoln's government to relax its blockade—also proved illusory. As it turned out, King Cotton proved a weak champion and an inept diplomat. By chance the crop of 1860, one of the largest on record, had been shipped to Europe before the war started, and by the time a shortage developed, in the winter of

1862–1863, the South's military position was too precarious to warrant European intervention in American affairs.

One additional facet of the Civil War blockade merits mention. Too much can be made of the importance of the prize cases tried during and soon after the war and of their part in defining the American interpretation of the legal limits of blockade, and yet some interesting ramifications of wartime approaches to such problems emerge from a study of those cases. Four captures of ships made during the first months of the war raised questions about the right of the federal government under international law to establish a blockade of its own ports during an insurrection, and of the right of the president to do so in the absence of a congressional declaration of war. Attorney General Edward Bates was advised to delay the cases until the president could appoint more politically reliable justices to the Supreme Court. After three Lincoln appointees joined the Court, the government's position on the utility of the blockade was barely upheld in 1863, by a vote of five to four. The five cooperative justices made up in ardor what they lacked in support from their less certain brethren; and the dissenters no doubt blanched to hear that they had taken the "wrong" side of an issue involving "the greatest civil war known in the history of the human race," and that their negative arguments had threatened to "cripple the arm of the government and paralyze its power by subtle definitions and ingenious sophisms."

In one of the prize cases, that of the *Springbok,* the courts ruled that any cargo ultimately intended for a blockaded port could be captured whenever it left the territorial waters of its port of origin. This rule applied, the court said, "even if the cargo was to be transshipped at an intermediate port, and the vessel in which it was found when captured was not the one which was to carry it to a blockaded port." In this case the court assigned a penalty for a breach of blockade "to a guilty cargo in an innocent ship." The court, in effect, ruled that the cargo was on a continuous voyage from its port of origin to a blockaded port. Acceptance of this definition by American courts greatly increased the power of the Union navy in intercepting supplies en route to the South. Such rulings went far toward making a blockade of Confederate ports almost unnecessary by substituting what amounted to a paper blockade of neutral ports in the Caribbean and Mexico.

The case of the *Peterhoff* raised a question of the shipment of contraband overland, from Matamoros, Mexico, across the Rio Grande to Brownsville, Texas. The Union navy found itself with a perplexing problem in Matamoros, which had scarcely half-a-dozen visiting vessels a year, before the war. This hardly vibrant entrepôt welcomed more than 200 ships by 1864. Union captains hesitated to move against a neutral port, but they took ships en route to it, the *Peterhoff* being one of their more famous captures. After the war the case of the *Peterhoff* came before the Supreme Court; on appeal Chief Justice Salmon P. Chase roundly affirmed America's traditional record of respecting neutral ports and internationalized rivers such as the Rio Grande; he also asserted that the nation did not favor paper blockades. Release of the ship seemed a reasonable price for so many reassuring affirmations.

In another ploy to increase the efficacy of the blockade, Union officials even refused clearances to suspicious cargoes from their own ports or required the posting of heavy bonds to assure that such cargoes were intended for peaceful purposes. (During the war, suspiciously large amounts of clean-burning anthracite coal, a key component of successful blockade-running, were being shipped to British ports in Canada and the Caribbean.) The British chargé d'affaires complained about these export restrictions, remarking that the congressional enactment that sanctioned them was "a cheap and easy substitute for an effectual blockade." These practices so irritated British merchants that in 1864 Lord Richard Lyons, the British minister, threatened that Her Majesty's government might have to reconsider its recognition of the legality of the Union blockade. Secretary of State William H. Seward knew that, so late in the war, such an action could not serve the British interests, so he ignored the minister's protest; and for the remainder of the war the Union continued to use all the legal and economic weapons that it possessed to defeat the South.

During the half-century from the close of the Civil War to the opening of World War I, there were only one or two refinements in the concept of blockade. As noted, the Franco-Prussian War provided no opportunities for the expansion of old definitions or the creation of new ones. The Boer War and the Spanish-American War were local conflicts—the one a civil war, the other a splendid little one. In the course of operations before Manila, prior to the capture of that city in 1898, Admiral George Dewey came to dislike the pretensions of a German admiral who happened to be in the harbor, and there is some evidence that Dewey told his German opposite that he wanted to "damn the Dutch." But that was hardly a refinement of blockade; nor did anything of a novel nature accompany use of blockades in the Caribbean, although the closing off of Santiago was one of the last presubmarine close-in blockades, while the one at Havana, which began on 22 April 1898, had a closer connection with strategic considerations than with economic ones. The Americans believed that they could not storm Havana harbor without risking heavy losses in ships, a development that might preclude command of the sea.

More important developments took place in the contretemps before the ports of Venezuela in 1902, when Britain, Germany, and Italy instituted a pacific blockade to collect the debts owed by Venezuela to European creditors. The United States served notice that there was no right to interfere with vessels of third parties, that is, the Americans; whereupon the blockading powers announced that their blockade "created *ipso facto* a state of war," and they gave themselves belligerent rights. When the affair went to the Permanent Court of Arbitration, the tribunal carefully skirted questions about the legality of the blockade of Venezuelan ports, but it decided in favor of the blockading powers in adjudicating the claims of the creditors. Shortly thereafter the nations of the world made another illustrious, if inconsequential, pronouncement about blockade. The second Hague Peace Conference (1907) had sought to establish an International Prize Court, but the delegates could not agree on the rules of prize law. To fill this gap a conference met in December 1908 in London, where after two months the delegates signed the London Declaration. Its provisions on blockade demonstrated once again the great difficulty in arriving at a satisfactory definition of that term; indeed, the men of the twentieth century did little better than their nineteenth-century counterparts at Paris. Unable to agree upon terminology that would be acceptable to all and recognizing the need for a "certain imprecision," the delegates merely reaffirmed the illegality of paper blockades and said that for a blockade to be binding it had to be effectively maintained by an "adequate" naval force. No government ratified the treaty, and during World War I, when the United States attempted to pressure the British into accepting its principles, the refusal highlighted a basic ambiguity of international life. Despite the best intentions, a power at war will wish to retain loopholes in its commitments to other nations so as to permit maximum use of major offensive and defensive weapons.

The theory and practice of blockade entered its final stage—previously there had been the formative period in the seventeenth and eighteenth centuries, the trial and testing of the wars of the French Revolution and Napoleon, and the somnolent period from 1815 to 1914—when the major nations of Europe joined in the Great War (1914–1918), and when, with the entrance of the United States in 1917, the conflict became a world war. By the time of the opening campaign along the Marne, when the French and a small British contingent slowed the German armies and the war turned from movement to position, several forces and factors had made the narrow definitions of the London and Paris declarations all but obsolete—inoperable except in the most minor situations. Those formulations could not serve the conditions of twentieth-century war. There was the growth of a network of transportation across all modern countries—rivers and canals, railroads, and more recently the macadamized roads and highways for motorized travel; there was the appearance of the new navies of steel and steam epitomized by the launching of the British battleship *Dreadnought* in 1906; and there was the virtually finished conversion of merchant shipping from sail to steam. The new network of transportation made enemy ports of less consequence than before, as goods could be shipped in and out via nearby neutrals. The naval revolution made it unnecessary for warships to catch the wind in their sails before they moved out against blockade-runners or illicit neutral traders. Merchant shipping itself now could operate apart from trade routes and could quite literally turn up anywhere instead of having to find prevailing winds. Then, too, the industrialization of much of Western Europe, especially of Germany, the prime antagonist of the Allies, gave a new dimension to blockade—the right sort of blockade might destroy German industry, or at least severely cripple it. And as if blockade in the traditional sense of Grotius and Cornelius van Bynkershoek would have had much chance at all in the twentieth century, there came the invention of practical submarines and of highly reliable mines, just prior to the outbreak of war in 1914. Small wonder that World War I virtually ended blockade as it had been known.

In several instances the old, traditional blockade of close-in surveillance of enemy ports was practiced during World War I, but these operations, carried out in reasonable conformity to the strictures of the London Declaration, occurred in secondary theaters of naval activity—the Mediterranean, China, and Africa. Where things really mattered—the blockade off the European coast and in the North Sea—the British at least made a formal effort to maintain that the old rules still roughly applied. Their foreign secretary, Sir Edward Grey, indulged in frequent long explanations to the American ambassador in London and to the secretary of state in Washington. He assured them and reassured them that any changes the British government had been compelled to make in traditional rules of blockade stemmed not from a spirit of innovation but from the need to adjust old definitions to new circumstances. He implied that nothing really had changed.

In fact, the purposes of a blockade during the war were assisted by other measures not given that name, and the belligerents were usually careful in avoiding use of that term to describe their actions. The outstanding examples of such measures were the German declarations of war zones and the British designations of mine areas, military areas, and danger zones. It was a piquantly interesting fact that every one of the belligerent resorts to what might be described as measures of quasi blockade was adopted via the principle of international law known as the law of retaliation.

It is hardly necessary to explain in detail how the British and German blockades operated during World War I. The Germans first used mines, giving notice of their intent to do so in August 1914; the British countered in November by closing the entire North Sea because of mine fields. In a proclamation of 4 February 1915 the Germans announced unrestricted submarine and mine warfare, and the following month the British and French retaliated by declaring their intent to detain and take into port all ships "carrying goods of presumed enemy destination, ownership, or origin." To the Americans, Grey described that move as a blockade, and the United States government took his note as a formal notice of the establishment of a blockade and sought to get the Allies to respect neutral ports and vessels according to traditional standards of international law. In responding to the strictures of Washington officials Grey took the stand that the March order amounted to "no more than an adaptation of the old principles of blockade to the circumstances with which we are confronted." A decade later in his memoirs he was to write more candidly, "The Navy acted and the Foreign Office had to find the argument to support the action; it was anxious work." And well done. The order in council of 11 March 1915 was one of the most powerful weapons in the British system of economic warfare against Germany. With the order the Allies gained all the advantages that would have come from a formal declaration of blockade of German ports—and without the inconvenience of stationing "adequate" naval forces off the ports. Also, when the Royal Navy acted under that mandate it succeeded in reducing the flow of supplies to the enemy via neutral ports, while at the same time significantly cutting down on Germany's overseas trade. If the Allied pursuit of victory impinged too closely upon the interests of neutrals, if American shippers complained too loudly about innovations or illegalities, the lawyers at the British Foreign Office had little trouble finding arguments to support the work of their navy. Ironically, they found quite a few in the practices of the Union navy during the American Civil War.

One of the more interesting adjuncts to the

British system of blockade closely paralleled a technique used by the North in its efforts to subdue the South, although there is no evidence that the British borrowed the idea from the Americans. From 1861 to 1865 Union officials sought to cut off supplies to the Confederacy by requiring exporters to obtain licences, which, of course, could only be procured upon evidence that the cargoes in question had a bona fide neutral use. During World War I the British played a variation of this theme in order to make their restrictions more palatable to neutrals. Their system, called navicerting, worked thusly: A neutral exporter, say an American interested in perfectly legal, noncontraband trade with a Scandinavian country, applied to British authorities (usually a consul) for permission to send his ship through naval cordons guarding approaches to European coasts. If he convinced them of the innocence of his venture they issued a navicert, a sort of commercial passport, which in most cases assured noninterference with his ship and cargo. The innovation conferred enormous advantage on the British, for in effect it transferred control of a large measure of neutral trade "from the deck to the dock."

The Allies introduced other refinements in their practice of blockade. They censored neutral mail to discover firms trading with the enemy, and then blacklisted them and subjected them to various harassments, such as depriving them of coal or denying them repair facilities. In the case of the *Kim* a British prize-court judge accepted statistical evidence to establish a presumption that American goods consigned to a Danish port were actually on a continuous voyage to Germany. The prize courts also made a slight but significant alteration in procedure when they transferred the burden of proving the innocence of a cargo to the claimant. With such pressures the British secured neutral cooperation with their system of economic control. The alternative, to be sure, was not to cooperate, but the Allied supremacy at sea meant that noncooperation had unpleasant consequences: detention of cargo, expensive and time-consuming legal proceedings, confiscation of goods, and the denial of facilities needed to conduct business.

All the while the German blockade of Britain moved back and forth from observance of rules of cruiser warfare (meaning that submarines would not sink on sight, would visit and search and if necessary make provision for the safety of passengers and crew) to the waging of unrestricted submarine warfare, with its barbaric killing of noncombatants. With a poor harvest in the United States in 1916 it appeared possible to prevent other grain from entering the British Isles, and in that hope the German government at the end of January 1917 announced unrestricted submarine warfare and knowingly brought the United States into the war, believing that their submarine blockade would bring victory before the Americans could raise and transport an army to Europe.

That the Allied long-range blockade of Germany was effective must admit of little doubt. Its effect upon the enemy, however, took far longer than expected. During the great German offensive in the spring of 1918, the troops were astonished at the quality of the equipment of the routed British army, and also at the relative luxury in which French civilians were living. In the last weeks of the war the German home front virtually caved in. The military forces, of course, had been defeated first—there may be no doubt about that. But the civilians had been standing in line for months and years, and the word *Ersatz* had become a commonplace. When the prospect of peace clearly emerged during the diplomatic exchanges of October 1918, the German civilians came to believe that they had suffered too long. In this sense the British blockade at last placed an impossible burden on the already overtaxed and, indeed, defeated armies. Continuation of the war into 1919, which otherwise might have been possible, was too harrowing to contemplate.

In examining the operation of the blockade during World War I there remains the practice of the United States once it had entered the war. Popular wisdom at the time and later had it that the Americans turned their principles of neutral rights around as soon as they became a belligerent. Such was not the case, however. There appears to have been only two clear-cut and rather minor violations of international law by the American government. Use of embargoes, bunker control, and the blacklist were all unquestionably legal, involving only domestic jurisdiction and municipal law. The task of enforcing the blockade remained in British hands; the American navy took no prizes. It is true that a great barrier of over 70,000 mines was laid from Scotland to Norway. During its period of neutrality, the United States had reserved its rights on the question of British and German mining of the seas, and so, technically at least, the Americans did nothing startlingly novel by constructing that huge mine barrier in 1918. Naval fears about possible incursions into neutral waters dissipated when the Norwegians closed the gap in the barrage by mining their own waters. In the pre-armistice negotiations with the British about their insistence upon reserving freedom of the seas from discussion at the peace conference (because they feared that it might outlaw the right of blockade) Woodrow Wilson assured them that "Blockade is one of the many things which will require immediate redefinition in view of the many new circumstances of warfare developed by this war." There was, he said, "no danger of its being abolished."

In the decades since the Armistice of 1918 the word "blockade" has gone out of style, although it occasionally reappears. A more popular term, "quarantine," has tended to replace it. The belief has been that the new world organizations, the League of Nations and the United Nations—not to mention the Kellogg-Briand Pact (1928), by which most of the nations of the world renounced and outlawed war—virtually ensured that neutrality in the old sense was gone forever, replaced by collective security.

The record of the League of Nations in this regard was probably too short to be conclusive. Article 16 of the Covenant of the League provided for sanctions, and the first assembly of that organization created an International Blockade Committee, which issued a cautious report in 1921. The committee felt that "to pronounce an opinion in regard to the naval blockade and the right of search" was outside the scope of its work because more study was needed on those subjects. It also noted that a number of great exporting countries (the Soviet Union, the United States, and Germany) remained outside the League; and in a curious bit of logic the committee concluded that its name was a misnomer, since application of Article 16 did not involve imposition of blockades in the traditional sense.

In the 1930's there was talk, in and out of the League, about quarantining aggressors. Membership in the League did not seem to make much difference in the results of the talk, for there were virtually no results. League members hesitated to include an oil embargo among the measures invoked against Mussolini's adventure in Ethiopia in 1935–1936, for the Duce said that he would consider an oil embargo an act of war. In 1937 Franklin D. Roosevelt spoke in Chicago about quarantining aggressors, but then gingerly withdrew the idea when it aroused a storm of protest from his fellow citizens. In that troubled decade before the outbreak of World War II there was plain evidence that neutral thoughts had not disappeared. In 1932 the United States ratified a Pan-American Convention that reaffirmed the belligerent right of visit and search. The neutrality acts (1935–1941), passed by Congress to keep the country out of war, went into great detail about neutral rights and duties, including those that involved blockades. The acts implied that for the United States the League's new order would not function. Nor did it.

During World War II the United States again was forced to confront the problems of blockade, both as a neutral and as a belligerent. While neutral, American officials took an indulgent stand in regard to British blockade measures and sought to avoid repetition of the same arguments that had occurred during World War I. Of course the United States reserved its rights under international law, but in practice it reached a cozy accommodation with British restrictions, including a much expanded version of the navicert system. Then, as a belligerent, the nation found frequent occasion to expand the utility of blockade as a weapon of victory. For example, when the United States Navy achieved dominance in the Pacific, it instituted a tight cordon around the Japanese home islands, in order to cut off imports, and enforced that blockade with the chilling efficiency of its submarine fleet. Clearly, the demands of total war imposed a need for new permutations of what the legal profession calls the latent law of blockade—the belligerent who possesses effective command of the sea is entitled to deprive his opponent of the use of it. The drafters of the Dutch *Placaart* of 1630 would have understood that need.

But what had been appropriate to the period of total war proved inappropriate to the era of limited wars that plagued the world after 1945. Once more the United States devised modifications in its utilization of blockade. These postwar variations have been called "special function blockades," and they have had a wide use, in Vietnam, Korea, and even in Cuba. No extended discussion of their use is possible, but a glance at one or two of them may clarify still another dimension of the American method of blockade. Because of its predominant naval power during the Korean conflict, the United States imposed a close-in blockade of all Korean ports and coasts that was reminiscent of the practice of earlier eras. In Vietnam other tactics were used to interdict the flow of supplies to enemy contingents operating in South Vietnam. To prevent the introduction of war matériel by sea, the South Vietnamese, with the aid of American naval craft, conducted what might be described as a self-blockade. During this time they practiced all the traditional techniques of visit and search off their own coasts and in their own territorial waters. Perhaps a more interesting case was the mining of Haiphong harbor and the internal waterways and coastal waters of North Vietnam by American aircraft in the spring of 1972. By this process of air interdiction of seaborne supplies the United States hoped to carry out the purposes of a blockade, and it took extreme care to minimize the danger to neutral commerce. The navy even observed the ancient custom of allowing a grace period for neutral vessels to leave the coast and harbors before the mines were activated.

The most important invocation of a "special function" blockade occurred in the Caribbean in October 1962. The Soviet attempt to alter the strategic balance of power by placing nuclear missiles in Cuba provoked a vigorous response from the United States—but one that would avoid the risk of escalating the crisis. After careful review of his options, John F. Kennedy responded with a quarantine, a limited naval blockade of Cuba. Thus the United States relied on one of the oldest weapons in its arsenal to avoid resorting to more deadly ones. In his speech to the nation (21 October 1962) the president announced his intent to initiate "a strict quarantine of all offensive military equipment under shipment to Cuba" and to turn back all ships found to be carrying offensive weapons, "from whatever nation or port." His proclamation (24 October) ordered American forces to interdict delivery of such matériel to Cuba, and the navy set up a quarantine line around the eastern and southern approaches to the island. The president carefully coordinated his naval maneuvers with those on the diplomatic front, so as to leave room for compliance by the Russians with these restrictions on their freedom of the seas. The imaginative response to that crisis and its successful resolution again demonstrated the protean possibilities of concepts of blockade and quarantine, or "proceedings in the nature of a blockade," as flexible instruments of national policy.

BIBLIOGRAPHY

The literature on blockades falls into three categories, each with its specialized studies: law, naval strategy, and diplomacy. No satisfactory treatment of the interrelatedness of these divisions has appeared, although historians are beginning to batter at the walls that have compartmentalized approaches to the subject. For the European background, see Max Savelle, *The Origins of American Diplomacy: The International History of Anglo-America, 1492–1763* (New York, 1967). Although he has no index entry for blockade, Savelle has an important chapter on "The Impact of the New World of the Colonies Upon the Evolution of the Theory and Practice of International Law." Another treatment of the evolution of a key portion of international law is the older and still useful Francis Deak, ed., *Neutrality: Its History, Economics, and Law*, 4 vols. (New York, 1935–1936). A handy compilation of documentary material has been put together by Carlton Savage, *Policy of the United States Toward Maritime Commerce in War*, 2 vols. (Washington, D.C., 1934). A much fuller, although still usable, collection is John B. Moore, *Digest of International Law*, 8 vols. (Washington, D.C., 1906).

For the ideological dimension of the early debate on neutral rights and expanded commerce in wartime, see Felix Gilbert, *To the Farewell Address: Ideas of Early American Foreign Policy* (Princeton, 1961); Paul Varg, *Foreign Policies of the Founding Fathers* (East Lansing, Mich., 1963); and James Field, *America and the Mediterranean World, 1776–1882* (Princeton, 1969). For the era of the American Revolution and the Napoleonic Wars, see A. L. Burt, *The United States, Great Britain, and British North America From the Revolution to the Establishment of Peace After the War of 1812*

(New Haven, 1940). On the Civil War era, see Stuart Bernath, *Squall Across the Atlantic: American Civil War Prize Cases* (Berkeley–Los Angeles, 1970), which makes international law not only intelligible but interesting to the layman. Another work that details the British response to the Civil War, especially Union attempts to keep the Confederacy from acquiring a navy in Britain, is Frank J. Merli, *Great Britain and the Confederate Navy* (Bloomington, Ind., 1970), a portion of which deals with the complexities of keeping blockade-runners out of Southern hands.

On the period from the end of the American Civil War to World War I, see M. R. Pitt, "Great Britain and Belligerent Maritime Rights from the Declaration of Paris, 1856, to the Declaration of London, 1909" (Ph.D. diss., University of London, 1964). World War I spawned a voluminous literature on neutral rights, freedom of the seas, and blockade. On the latter subject, see Marion C. Siney, *The Allied Blockade of Germany, 1914–1916* (Ann Arbor, Mich., 1957). See also David Trask, *Captains and Cabinets: Anglo-American Naval Relations, 1917–1918* (Columbia, Mo., 1972). For the legal problems raised by submarine war, see W. T. Mallison, *Studies in the Law of Naval Warfare: Submarines in General and Limited Wars,* International Law Studies (Washington, D.C., 1968). For a contemporary assessment of the blockade, written by a member of the Allied Blockade Committee, see Maurice Parmelee, *Blockade and Sea Power: The Blockade, 1914–1919, and Its Significance for a World State* (New York, 1924).

Details of the role played by American submarine units in enforcing the blockade of Japan during World War II have recently been revealed in Clay Blair, *Silent Victory: The U.S. Submarine War Against Japan* (Philadelphia–New York, 1975). For all other aspects of the navy's role in the war, consult Samuel Eliot Morison, *History of United States Naval Operations in World War II* (Boston, 1947–1962). On the mechanics and implementation of economic war, two volumes in the British series, History of the Second World War: United Kingdom Civil Series, merit special attention: C. B. A. Behrens, *Merchant Shipping and the Demands of War* (London, 1955); and W. N. Medlicott, *The Economic Blockade,* 2 vols. (London, 1952). For purposes of the present essay, the two most useful commentaries on the events of October 1962 are Abram Chayes, *The Cuban Missile Crisis* (New York, 1974); and the reminiscence of the chief of naval operations, Admiral George W. Anderson, in *Proceedings* of the Naval History Symposium held at Annapolis, 27–28 April 1973. For the complexities of the legal dimension of this subject, see Sally V. Mallison and W. Thomas Mallison, Jr., "A Survey of the International Law of Naval Blockade," in *Proceedings of the United States Naval Institute,* 102 (1976). [*See also* Economic Foreign Policy; Freedom of the Seas; International Law; Neutrality; Trade and Commerce.]

THE CHINA LOBBY

Warren I. Cohen

"CHINA lobby" is a pejorative phrase first applied in the 1940's to a disparate collection of Chinese and Americans who tried to influence the people and government of the United States on behalf of the Nationalist regime of Chiang Kai-shek and in opposition to the Chinese Communists. Opponents of aid to the Nationalists commonly used the term to imply that Chiang's American supporters were paid and that their activities were coordinated by Chiang and other officials of his government or members of his family. A second usage implied the existence of an organization of Chinese Nationalist officials and American Rightists joined to stimulate anticommunism in the United States. Americans most commonly associated with the China lobby were noted publisher Henry R. Luce; Alfred Kohlberg, a retired New York importer; Frederick C. McKee, a wealthy Pittsburgh manufacturer and philanthropist; Republican congressman Walter H. Judd of Minnesota; and Republican senators William F. Knowland of California and Joseph R. McCarthy of Wisconsin. The lobby was presumed to have tremendous influence in American politics. It has been credited with forcing a reluctant Truman administration to continue aid to Chiang during the Chinese civil war, preventing recognition of the People's Republic of China and barring it from the United Nations, and blocking the distribution of a book exposing the operations of the China lobby.

Although the Chinese Nationalist regime employed American lobbyists and public-relations operatives and had the support of the American Right in the struggle against communism in China, support for Chiang's China cannot be written off as either hired or right wing. In the United States popular support for Chiang—or more precisely, opposition to communist control of China—was broadly based, including liberals and conservatives; Democrats and Republicans; and Southerners, Northerners, Easterners, and Westerners. Popular antipathy toward the Chinese Communists derived from a widespread and profound distaste for communism and from traditional sympathies for the heathen Chinese. But it was the Korean War—especially the intervention of the People's Republic of China in the war—that brought about the results for which Chiang's supporters worked in the late 1940's and early 1950's. Without the Korean War, the limited public interest in Asian affairs and the reality of the communist victory in China might well have led to an early accommodation between the United States and the regime of Mao Tse-tung, despite the efforts of the friends of Nationalist China.

Pressure group activity on behalf of the Nationalist regime dates back to the Nationalist revolution (1925–1928), when Chiang Kai-shek was struggling to unite China with Soviet and Chinese Communist assistance. Fearing intervention by the American and other governments, a group of American missionaries and educators, led by men like A. L. Warnshuis, secretary of the International Missionary Council; J. Leighton Stuart, president of Yenching University (Peking); and Roger S. Greene of the China Medical Board of the Rockefeller Foundation, worked to alert policymakers, congressmen, and the public to the need for an accommodation with Chinese nationalism. Links between Chiang's government and American missionaries and reformers continued into the 1930's as Madame Chiang Kai-shek and other

American-educated Chinese leaders sporadically attempted to gain American assistance in the modernization of China. Major lobbying activities did not begin, however, until after the outbreak of the Second Sino-Japanese War in 1937.

Of the various groups that were organized to influence American policy on behalf of China between 1937 and 1941 the most important was the American Committee for Non-Participation in Japanese Aggression, also known as the Price Committee. In 1938, appalled by the inaction of the American government in the face of Japanese aggression in China, Frank and Harry Price, sons of the famous missionary P. Frank Price, called together a small group of men, including an American employed as a propagandist for the Chinese government. To campaign against the flow of American supplies to Japan, they created an organization that soon received financial support from the Chinese government. There is no evidence that the formation of the committee was inspired by Chinese authorities, but given the relations between the two, especially during the early stages, this possibility cannot be ignored. Furthermore, the Chinese government considered itself entitled to reports.

Despite the initial role of the Chinese, the Price Committee subsequently attempted to restrict contributors to Americans and to sever potentially embarrassing ties to Chinese officials. One member who was employed by the Chinese government and required to register as the agent of a foreign principal resigned from the committee. Roger Greene and Henry L. Stimson served respectively as chairman and honorary chairman; Harry Price, as executive secretary; and Walter Judd, a former medical missionary, proved to be its most effective speaker. Frederick McKee and Geraldine Fitch, wife of the well-known missionary George A. Fitch, were also important members of the organization.

The central program of the Price Committee called for an embargo on supplies of military value to Japan. Beginning in 1939 it worked closely with key figures in the American government, especially with Stanley K. Hornbeck of the Department of State and with Stimson, who became secretary of war in 1940. Individual members, like Greene and McKee, were also active and influential in the most important of the pressure groups espousing collective security. The activities of these friends of China may have been responsible for President Franklin D. Roosevelt's decision in July 1939 to notify Japan of the intention of the United States to terminate the commercial treaty between the two nations, thus facilitating economic sanctions. With access to Roosevelt and other top administration officials, Greene and Price may have shaped a number of important government actions, such as credits to China for the purchase of trucks and the National Defense Act of 1940, which gave Roosevelt authority to control exports. Similarly, these lobbyists on behalf of China mobilized public opinion behind administration efforts to help China, and indeed generated pressures designed to push Roosevelt faster than he wanted to move. In the autumn of 1941 their warning against a Far Eastern Munich made a modus vivendi with Japan extremely difficult.

After the United States entered World War II, many groups emerged to raise money for China, enlisting men and women who had participated in the Price Committee's efforts. Most of these groups were brought together under United China Relief, a kind of holding company that attempted to coordinate private aid to China. Typical of the new groups that were organized during the war was the American Bureau for Medical Aid to China (ABMAC), with which Greene was involved and in which Kohlberg played a major role. All of these organizations reminded the American people of the long suffering of their Chinese allies, filled the country with stories of Chinese resistance and heroism, and, to simplify their story, personified China in the figures of Generalissimo and Madame Chiang Kai-shek. From the *Weekly Reader* to the newsreels and the public prints, these glamorous figures appeared as the spirit of Free China, with greatly exaggerated references to their dedication to democracy and to the Four Freedoms that Roosevelt had offered as symbols of the ideals for which Americans fought.

From 1937 on, as Americans who believed China to be worthy of American support exercised their right to attempt to influence the policies of their government, various Chinese officials worked toward the same end. The

Chinese ambassador, Hu Shih, made strenuous efforts to obtain aid for his country; and he was supported by a host of other officials, most prominent among them Madame Chiang's brother, T. V. Soong. Madame Chiang was herself probably the most effective propagandist for her country: an attractive, American-educated Christian who made marvelous copy for the mass media. Lin Yu-tang, a well-known popularizer of Chinese culture, also spent the war years in the United States on a diplomatic passport, advertising the virtues of Chiang's regime to the American people. These and similar Chinese activities were sometimes irritating to American officials who resented pressures to do more for China, but the Chinese were not known to be violating any laws and were engaged in practices whose legitimacy was sanctioned by custom in the United States.

Chinese officials and American friends of China naturally came together frequently to discuss China's needs and strategy for various campaigns. Again, there was nothing improper about this sort of cooperation. Most of the American participants were not acting as agents for the Chinese government and those who were did so openly and legally. They shared a concern for China, and their countries were allies in war, sharing an interest in the effort to defeat Japan. Problems developed only as questions arose as to whether Chinese and American interests remained congruous, as questions arose as to whether Chiang's regime represented the best interests of the Chinese people.

In 1943 the cohesiveness that Japanese aggression had produced among Americans interested in China began to wear away. The initial friction between the Chinese and American governments had come about because of the Chinese share of lend-lease material, and American friends of China generally shared Chinese dissatisfaction. But in 1943 the focus was shifting to the Chinese war effort and to tensions between Chiang's regime and the Chinese Communists—tensions that threatened to erupt into civil war and already prevented Chinese forces from devoting their full attention to the Japanese invader. More and more criticism of Chiang was heard in American government circles and leaked to the press. A few knowledgeable Americans began to argue in favor of sending aid to the Chinese Communists, who seemed more willing to fight against Japan and more committed to democratic principles than were Chiang's Nationalists. Among China's American friends a growing number despaired of Chiang's repressive tendencies, brooded over corruption in his regime and, although apprehensive of the Chinese Communists, wondered if the American government might find an alternative to its total support of Chiang.

On a trip to China in 1943 Kohlberg was troubled by criticisms he heard of Chiang's regime—criticisms that did not appear to him to be justified. Increasingly he brooded about the source of these charges. Increasingly the Chinese government became fearful of the effects on American support if a corrupt and repressive image prevailed. Lin Yu-tang and Hu Shih publicly and privately contended that communist agents were responsible for the attacks on Chiang. Hu Shih maintained that American scholars affiliated with the Institute of Pacific Relations (IPR) depended on Chinese researchers who were in fact communists. Greene was troubled by the publication of articles that appeared to substantiate Hu Shih's argument. Kohlberg gradually became convinced of a communist conspiracy to deceive the American people, convinced that the Institute of Pacific Relations, the center of East Asian studies in the United States, was an instrument of this conspiracy.

As Chiang's regime and some of its staunchest American friends, such as Judd and Fitch, tried to preserve the idealized image of the early war years, Kohlberg attacked the IPR. A man of great energy and considerable wealth, Kohlberg conducted a one-man campaign to purge the IPR of alleged communist domination. His initial charges in 1944 were ignored, but he persisted tirelessly, gaining support from professional ex-communists and Red-baiters who helped him to formulate charges and to obtain broader publicity for his effort. In particular, George E. Sokolsky, a widely syndicated Hearst columnist with strong ties to the House Un-American Activities Committee, helped Kohlberg with contacts and provided a broad hearing for his accusations.

At the end of World War II China faced civil war, and American efforts to mediate failed.

THE CHINA LOBBY

The few Americans interested in East Asian affairs fell into two main categories. One group argued that American interests would be served best by a scrupulous neutrality, allowing Chiang and his communist enemies to work toward their own resolution of China's problems. Another group contended that the interests of the United States would be served best by providing whatever aid short of troops was necessary to maintain Chiang in power. Members of the former group generally warned that the communists enjoyed greater support among the Chinese people and would ultimately triumph. They contended that American aid to Chiang left him unwilling to compromise while peace was possible and would prolong the war and the agony of the Chinese people once the conflict began. The latter group generally mistrusted the Chinese Communists, fearing they would serve Soviet rather than Chinese interests and bring misery to the Chinese people. They argued that a communist-controlled China would be a negation of the ends for which the United States had fought in the Pacific. As fear of the Soviet Union increased in the United States in the late 1940's, anticommunist sentiment grew apace, and more and more Americans became receptive to the arguments of Chiang's supporters—that is, to the China lobby.

In the late 1940's the two major organizations calling for American aid to Nationalist China were the American China Policy Association and the Committee to Defend America by Aiding Anti-Communist China. The American China Policy Association was founded by Kohlberg; John B. Powell, one of the best-known American journalists in China during the 1920's and 1930's; and Christopher Emmett, a writer with decidedly liberal pretensions. The members worked to reveal what they considered the insidious nature of the Chinese Communist movement and, within the matrix of intense anticommunist feeling, the association began on a moderate note. Soon, however, it was dominated by Kohlberg, who was himself becoming increasingly irresponsible in his charges against diplomats and scholars critical of Chiang Kai-shek.

The Committee to Defend America by Aiding Anti-Communist China was run by Frederick McKee. McKee had long contributed to liberal causes and to the collective security wing of the peace movement. Since the late 1930's he had contributed both time and money in China's behalf, joining existing groups and organizing his own. Unlike Kohlberg, McKee did not become involved in extremist activities. Restrained and responsible, McKee was easily overshadowed. Membership in the Kohlberg and McKee organizations overlapped, but McKee was able to muster the support of several prominent men not identified with Chinese affairs, such as James A. Farley and labor leader David Dubinsky.

If the Kohlberg and McKee operations could claim some degree of respectability, there were other operations that could not. The Chinese embassy in Washington and a variety of more or less independent entrepreneurs like T. V. Soong and his brother-in-law, H. H. Kung, lobbied frenetically for aid. Although their operations appear to have remained within the law, there is evidence of some sleight of hand within the embassy, resulting in the disappearance of large sums of money, the disappearance of senior Chinese military officers attached to the mission, and the appearance of Chinese documents revealing some of their operations and including extravagant claims of success with American congressmen. These activities had no discernible effect on American policy, and only the Chinese government seems to have been swindled.

Another unsavory but legal Chinese activity was the employment of William J. Goodwin as a lobbyist. In the 1930's Goodwin had distinguished himself by his affiliation with the Christian Front and with the American fascists Gerald L. K. Smith and the Reverend Charles E. Coughlin. Like the Chinese operatives in the embassy, Goodwin was probably most effective at obtaining money from the Chinese government while claiming to be influencing American politicians.

A majority of congressmen in both houses were sympathetic to the Chinese Nationalist cause and willing to vote for aid to Chiang in his fight against the communists. There is no evidence that any of these congressmen had been bought by the Chinese government or by Kohlberg or McKee. Virtually all of these people equated the Chinese Communist movement with Soviet totalitarianism and looked with regret upon the likelihood of such oppression being levied upon their erstwhile Chinese allies. Most of these congressional supporters of the Chinese Nationalists were not committed to Chiang or his regime but rather to what they saw as a worldwide struggle against international communism. Furthermore, if the administration asked for funds to protect endangered Greeks and Turks against communist subversion, why not aid the Chinese as well? Having once conjured up fears of an international communist conspiracy for world domination, the Truman administration failed to convince Congress or the American people that China could be or had to be written off. When providing aid for a beleaguered Europe, Congress forced the administration to continue aid to Chiang Kai-shek and anticommunist China.

Despite congressional and public sympathy for Chiang, and the intimidating efforts of Kohlberg and his allies in the Hearst press, when the communists drove Chiang from mainland China, the Truman administration was prepared to recognize the People's Republic of China and to allow it to take the Chinese seat in the United Nations. Even in early 1950, when Kohlberg and Sokolsky found an ally in Senator Joseph R. McCarthy, the Truman administration proceeded with plans to thwart them and to come to terms with reality. The outbreak of war in Korea and the subsequent confrontation between troops from the United States and troops from the People's Republic of China accomplished what Kohlberg and his friends and the Chinese Embassy could not have accomplished by themselves. It created a climate of opinion in the United States in which Kohlberg's charges of treason in high places could be taken seriously and in which an accommodation with the People's Republic of China proved impossible.

Ironically, it was Democratic senator Pat McCarran of Nevada, an archconservative whose reelection McKee had earlier tried to prevent, who chaired the congressional committee that investigated the Kohlberg-McCarthy charges against the Institute of Pacific Relations. The 1952 hearings were used to discredit and intimidate American critics of Chiang Kai-shek. But from 1951 to 1953 it was McCarthy—advised by Kohlberg, Sokolsky, and Roy Cohn—who succeeded in driving some of the State Department's ablest men from Chinese affairs and from the Foreign Service. Whether from McCarran or McCarthy, Kohlberg or Sokolsky, the story was always the same: China had been lost to the communists because disloyal Americans had prevented Chiang from receiving the aid with which he could have won; and American boys died in Korea because they had been betrayed by disloyal and stupid liberals who had turned China over to the communists. It was not until the marked change in the climate of opinion that came with revulsion against the war in Vietnam that some of the men vilified during the McCarthy era were vindicated.

By 1952 the legitimate concern some Americans had for the future of China had been transformed into an instrument with which the extreme Right tried to destroy liberalism in the United States. Sokolsky, whose earlier writings showed him to be unusually well informed about the history of the Chinese Communist movement, consistently misled his readers, in keeping with his assumed role as a spokesman for the extreme Right. The success that he and his colleagues enjoyed in discrediting Dean Acheson, George C. Marshall, John S. Service, and Owen Lattimore demonstrated the validity of George Washington's warning about the consequences of "excessive partiality" for a foreign nation. In the 1950's, when criticism of Chiang Kai-shek invited charges of disloyalty to the United States, foreign service officers and scholars were intimidated, with a consequent crippling of both national policy and scholarship.

There were reactions against the work of Chiang's friends even at the height of their power, but to no avail. The Truman administration tried to neutralize them in 1951, promising friendly senators that it would cooperate in an investigation of the China lobby. In Congress, however, there was little interest in the investigation and the administration's own effort could turn up nothing to stimulate interest on Capitol Hill or in the press. In April 1952 the *Reporter* published two long articles that named some of the participants (Kohlberg, McKee, and Goodwin), implied more shady dealings than could be proven, and provided less than a model example of investigative reporting. Nonetheless, the articles contributed to the notoriety of the China lobby, and there were reports that mysterious Chinese were buying enormous quantities of the issues of the *Reporter* in which the articles appeared. In April 1952 Republican senator Wayne L. Morse of Oregon introduced into the Senate Chinese documents outlining the plans of the Nationalist regime to influence American policy. Some of the documents referred to cooperation with Goodwin, Judd, and Knowland, who was sometimes referred to as the senator from Formosa. Although the authenticity of the documents was never proven, the Chinese embassy admitted that they were cables sent from its offices, but denied that the counselor of the embassy had sent them, as alleged by Morse. There was little to be learned from the documents, which contained merely evidence of the deceits the embassy was practicing on its principal—and its agents were practicing on it.

After the Korean War, the question of which Chinese regime was entitled to the seat in the United Nations arose and a powerful new pressure group was created to retain the seat for Chiang's rump regime. Beginning with a petition drive, a Committee of One Million Against the Admission of Communist China to the United Nations emerged in 1953. After collecting the requisite million signatures, including those of prominent Democrats and Republicans, the organizers disbanded in 1954, only to reorganize as the Committee of One Million in 1955. Liberal Democratic and Republican senators lent their names to the new committee, including Democrats Paul Douglas of Illinois, William Proxmire of Wisconsin, and Hubert H. Humphrey of Minnesota, and Republican Thomas H. Kuchel of California. As with earlier organizations, anticommunism rather than approval of Chiang's regime explains the widespread support for the Committee of One Million, run by Marvin Liebman, an ex-communist.

In 1960 Ross Y. Koen, a young professor in California, prepared to publish his dissertation, *The China Lobby in American Politics,* but the book was not distributed. The Chinese embassy reportedly threatened legal action against the publishers for defamatory statements in the book, and it was widely assumed that the power of the China lobby had succeeded in frightening them. That power continued to seem impressive as President John F. Kennedy shied away from a rapprochement with the People's Republic, secretly promising Chiang that the United States would veto any effort to seat the communist regime in the United Nations. Lyndon Johnson's presidency brought no hope of change, although McCarthy, Kohlberg, and Sokolsky were dead, men like Judd and Knowland had lost their national offices, and the reality of the Sino-Soviet split had finally penetrated the American consciousness.

The election of Richard M. Nixon in 1968 provided no expectation of new directions in American policy toward China. Nixon, the personification of the cold warrior, had been close to many of Chiang's staunchest supporters and had repeated many of the same inflammatory and unsubstantiated accusations that Kohlberg had levied. But slowly and cautiously the Nixon administration moved to improve relations with the People's Republic, and in July 1971 presidential adviser Henry Kissinger suddenly turned up in Peking. A few months later a stunned world watched Richard Nixon and Mao Tse-tung exchanging pleasantries in Mao's study. In 1972 the United States facilitated the admission of the People's Republic to the United Nations and acquiesced in the expulsion of Chiang's government. There was hardly a whimper of opposition—and that from a few supporters of the president who felt they had been betrayed. The day of the China lobby had passed.

BIBLIOGRAPHY

Stanley D. Bachrack, *The Committee of One Million: "China-Lobby" Politics, 1953–1971* (New York, 1976). Dorothy Borg, *American Policy and the Chinese Revolution, 1925–1928* (New York, 1947), includes references to the activities of Americans sympathetic to the Chinese Nationalist cause during the 1920's. Warren I. Cohen, "The Role of Private Groups in the United States," in Dorothy Borg and Shumpei Okamoto, eds., *Pearl Harbor as History* (New York, 1973), discusses the lobbying activities of a number of groups and individuals between 1931 and 1941. Donald J. Friedman, *The Road From Isolation* (Cambridge, Mass., 1968), is a useful study of the American Committee for Non-Participation in Japanese Aggression; it should be supplemented by the Cohen article cited above. Joseph Keeley, *The China Lobby Man* (New Rochelle, N.Y., 1969), is a biography of Kohlberg and epitomizes his exploitation by the American Right. Ross Y. Koen, *The China Lobby in American Politics* (New York, 1974), is a comprehensive account of Chinese Nationalist and pro-Nationalist activities in the United States during Truman's term as president. Koen is better at describing the impact of these activities than at explaining how the Chinese and their American friends functioned. A. T. Steele, *The American People and China* (New York, 1966), is a valuable survey of American attitudes toward China, especially after 1937. John N. Thomas, *The Institute of Pacific Relations* (Seattle, 1974), is an unsympathetic study of the organization with a useful chapter on Kohlberg.

[*See also* CONGRESS AND FOREIGN POLICY; FOREIGN AID; IDEOLOGY AND FOREIGN POLICY; MISSIONARIES; PUBLIC OPINION.]

THE COLD WAR

George C. Herring

THE phrase "Cold War" was originally coined by the American columnist Walter Lippmann to describe the emerging conflict between the United States and the Soviet Union and the condition of neither war nor peace that followed World War II. This Soviet-American struggle originated in the latter stages of World War II, became increasingly dangerous in the 1950's and early 1960's, and gradually subsided during the decade from the Cuban missile crisis of 1962 to the 1972 summit meeting between Leonid Brezhnev and Richard Nixon. The Cold War bears many of the features of traditional power struggles among nation-states. Its ideological dimension and its global scope have given it a measure of distinction, however, and it has been unique in that the major contestants, each possessing enormously destructive nuclear weapons and increasingly sophisticated delivery systems, have chosen to wage the conflict through client-states and by diplomatic means, propaganda, and threats of force rather than by resorting to war.

Since the onset of the Cold War, official spokesmen and historians have debated its causes. Soviet apologists placed responsibility on the United States, arguing that American "ruling circles" during and after World War II employed economic and atomic blackmail and mobilized the reactionary forces of Europe and Asia to destroy the Soviet Union and undermine the "democratic" revolutions it supported. American publicists blamed an aggressive Josef Stalin, who exploited the chaos of war to impose communism on Eastern Europe and whose relentless drive for world domination forced the United States to initiate a global policy of containment.

Cold War orthodoxy held sway in both nations for nearly two decades, but in the late 1960's American revisionists challenged the official viewpoint. The revisionists argued that Stalin's goals were determined by Russia's legitimate security needs and were restricted to the establishment of a sphere of influence in Eastern Europe and checks on Germany's revival as a military power. In their eyes, the United States was the aggressor. American officials rejected Stalin's reasonable demands, employed various weapons to deprive the Soviet Union of the fruits of victory, and when this failed formed an anti-Soviet bloc among the Western European nations. Revisionists disagree among themselves when assessing the sources of American policy. Moderates view the change from a sympathetic and flexible Franklin D. Roosevelt to an aggressive and doctrinaire Harry S. Truman as the crucial factor. Radicals contend that American hostility toward the Soviet Union was dictated by the requirements of an expansive capitalist economy. Revisionists generally agree, however, that the United States must bear primary responsibility for the Cold War.

Revisionism has provoked a much-needed reassessment of the origins of the Cold War, but many of its arguments remain unconvincing. While persuasively modifying the orthodox interpretation of Soviet foreign policy, revisionists have underestimated the difficulties of dealing with Stalinist Russia. Their analysis of American foreign policy is also narrowly drawn. While properly pointing out the American actions that appeared provocative to the Soviet Union, they have ignored the extent to which Roosevelt—and even Truman—went to accommodate the Russians. They have placed American policy in a rigid mold, which does not take into account the ambiguities and frequent contradictions. Most important, their implicit assumption that different American policies might have averted the Cold War minimizes the larger historical forces that brought the two nations into conflict.

From the perspective of nearly thirty years, the Cold War appears a logical, if not inevitable, consequence of the power realignment wrought by World War II. That conflict destroyed the old balance of power, leaving Germany and Japan crushed and impotent and reducing Great Britain and France to second- or even third-rate powers. Once-proud empires crumbled under the pressure from emergent nationalist movements, and the war left worldwide turmoil and instability.

Only the United States and, to a lesser extent, the Soviet Union, emerged with the power to determine postwar settlements, but these nations were divided by conflicting ideologies. Soviet dogma taught suspicion of capitalist nations and stressed that genuine peace could come only after the inevitable triumph of the revolution. Americans regarded communism as antithetical to their most basic values and principles, and feared the Soviet commitment to world revolution. The uneasy and sometimes openly hostile relations between the two nations from 1917 to 1941 reinforced these suspicions and fears.

Hitler's invasion of Russia in June 1941 brought the United States and the Soviet Union, along with Great Britain, into a military partnership, but the Grand Alliance was based on nothing more than mutual need against a common enemy. From the beginning, the alliance was subject to enormous strains. Conflicts over strategy and unfulfilled expectations fed old suspicions and aroused new fears. Despite President Roosevelt's herculean efforts, the United States fell far behind its supply commitments to the Soviet Union. Having assured Stalin that they would open a second front in France in 1942 or early 1943, Roosevelt and British Prime Minister Winston Churchill postponed the invasion, first until 1943 and then until 1944. Soviet publicists accused the Allies of deliberately holding back assistance to weaken the Soviet Union, thus allowing themselves to dictate the terms of the peace. The Americans and British, on the other hand, were deeply annoyed by the seeming ingratitude of the Russians and their unwillingness to concede the difficulties that delayed aid to the Soviet Union and the opening up of a second front. Relations improved as victory came into sight, but despite much brave rhetoric about friendship and postwar cooperation, the Allies never overcame their old suspicions.

Most important, they disagreed sharply on the way the postwar world should be constructed. Twice invaded and laid waste by Germany in the twentieth century and gripped by historic fears of invasion from east and west, the Russians sought to protect their security by the establishment of a sphere of influence in the areas along the western border of the Soviet Union. Stalin's minimum war aims included absorption of the Baltic States and the creation of pliant governments in Poland and other Eastern European nations that could stand as a buffer against future invasions. A Germany rendered incapable of repeating the invasions of 1917 and 1941 formed another central objective.

Distrustful of European power politics since the days of its own revolution, the United States sought the creation of a new order based on liberal principles. There should be no territorial aggrandizement; colonial empires and spheres of influence should be eliminated; and all peoples should have the right to determine their own form of government. Security in the postwar era would be provided by an international organization, modeled on the League of Nations, in which each nation would have a voice and through which the rights and integrity of all would be protected. The United States also called for a new order in international economics, in which all areas of the world would be open on a nondiscriminatory basis to trade, investment, and access to raw materials.

Given their divergent approaches toward the peace, it is not surprising that the United States and the Soviet Union failed to resolve major postwar issues. Throughout the war, Eastern Europe was the most controversial problem. By the end of 1944 the Red Army had swept across much of Eastern Europe and Stalin had used his military position to effect political settlements favorable to the Soviet Union. He excluded the United States and Britain from arrangements in Bulgaria and Rumania; facilitated the triumph of Tito (Josip Broz), the partisan leader in Yugoslavia; and assisted the organization of Polish communists into a liberation committee, which he subsequently recognized as the government of Poland.

Soviet moves in Eastern Europe aroused great concern in the United States. Representatives of East European ethnic groups and Roman Catholic leaders protested the betrayal of self-determination. Business leaders complained of Soviet seizure of American property. State Department officials warned that if Stalin were permitted to dominate Eastern Europe he might be tempted to extend Russian influence further. Roosevelt himself was deeply divided. Unwilling to risk a break in the alliance by challenging Stalin directly, he nevertheless could not ignore the protest that was building around him. At the Yalta Conference in February 1945 Roosevelt sought to persuade the Russian leader to permit three-power consultation in the liberated nations and to agree to changes in the Polish government. After hours of discussion, the Big Three finally negotiated several vague agreements that subsequently caused bitter controversy.

In the weeks after Yalta, conflict over Eastern Europe intensified. Soviet intervention in Rumania provoked American protests, and the three-power commission established to implement the Yalta accord on Poland quickly reached an impasse. Roosevelt's untimely death on 12 April added to the tension. The new president, Harry S. Truman, attempted to follow his predecessor's policies, but he was suspicious of and less sympathetic to the Soviet Union. He finally acquiesced in Soviet preeminence in Poland, but only after a long period of heated controversy. He refused to recognize Soviet-sponsored governments in Rumania and Bulgaria. By the end of the war, Eastern Europe had brought great discord into the alliance. American officials feared that the Soviet conquest of Eastern Europe might represent only the first stage of a broader pattern of expansion. American protests reinforced traditional Russian fears.

The all-important German problem caused further divisions. To prevent a German revival, the Soviet leaders advocated a punitive peace, including heavy reparations. Initially, Roosevelt sympathized with this point of view, but by the end of 1944 American leaders began to have second thoughts. They were reluctant to destroy the German economy, which they regarded as the key to the economic recovery of Europe, and they feared that the elimination of Germany as a major power would leave Western Europe vulnerable to Soviet penetration. Through extended negotiations from Yalta to Potsdam, the Allies were able to resolve only partially the great range of issues involving Germany.

Soviet intervention in the Far Eastern war and the nuclear explosions over Hiroshima and Nagasaki brought an unexpectedly early end to the war, but the Allied victory did not bring peace to the world. Defeat of the enemy removed the most substantial tie binding the nations together. They had agreed upon the structure of a new international organization, the United Nations, but the workability of that body hinged upon their ability to collaborate. Neither nation had abandoned hopes of creating a lasting peace, but the leaders were increasingly suspicious of each other. Eager to create a postwar world to their own liking and conscious of the vast economic and military power at their disposal, American officials began to regard the Soviet Union as the greatest obstacle to their plans and feared that Stalin, like Hitler before him, had vast expansionist ambitions. On the other hand, the Soviet leader's insecurity was magnified by the task of reconstruction, American possession of the atomic bomb, and continuing American protest against the Soviet position in Eastern Europe.

During the next eighteen months, the Cold War began to take form. Both nations continued to try to resolve outstanding problems, but they achieved little. It took more than a year, four stormy "peace" conferences, and hours of bitter argument before treaties could be arranged for the lesser Axis nations: Italy, Rumania, Bulgaria, and Finland. A treaty for Austria would not be concluded until 1955; and on the most difficult issue—Germany—there would be no treaty at all.

The joint occupation of Germany added to the tension. The United States became increasingly reluctant to subsidize the German economy while the Russians stripped their zone of its wealth, and in April 1946 American occupation authorities suspended reparations deliveries to the Soviet Union. As they became more skeptical of the likelihood or desirability of four-power agreement on Germany, American officials determined to go their own way, developing plans to merge the American and British zones and to allow Germany a measure of economic recovery and independence.

Clashes over occupation policies developed across the world. Roosevelt had agreed at Yalta that the Kuriles should be turned over to Russia, but the Truman administration subsequently rejected Soviet demands for a role in the occupation of the Japanese home-islands. The two nations could not agree on a postwar arrangement for Korea, and that country remained divided into two zones. Stalin withdrew Red Army forces from Manchuria only after vigorous American protests and after assisting the Chinese communists to secure key positions. The retention of Soviet forces in Iran long after the withdrawal date provoked forceful Anglo-American protests and precipitated a showdown in the first session of the United Nations. Stalin eventually backed down, and the United Nations weathered the first of many crises, but the name-calling and tense atmosphere produced by the clash established a characteristic of postwar international relations.

By the latter part of 1946, each nation had concluded that the other represented a grave threat to its security. The Truman administration accepted an explanation of Soviet behavior best articulated by the career diplomat and Russian expert George F. Kennan. Kennan argued that the Soviet leadership was inflexibly committed to a policy of expansionism on the basis of its ideological convictions and in order to maintain a stranglehold over the Russian people. His somber analysis seemed to be borne out in Russian actions. The conquest of Eastern Europe, the maintenance of forces in Iran and Manchuria, and evidence of atomic espionage in the United States and Canada seemed to confirm Stalin's limitless ambitions. The conclusions were inescapable—Soviet demands must be resisted, and Soviet expansion contained.

Patterns in Soviet policy are more difficult to assess. As Kennan suggested, Stalin may have found in the Cold War a convenient means of limiting alien influences in Russia and maintaining his own power. More likely, the Soviet leader's security concerns, magnified by ideological preconceptions and by the Russian tradition of seeking security through expansion, moved him to exploit the opportunities created by the war to extend Russian influence into peripheral areas. During the war he may have concluded that the United States would not stop him, but when the Truman administration began to pose obstacles, it confirmed his suspicions of Western hostility and aroused his fears for Russian security. By the end of 1946 the Soviet leadership had concluded that the United States threatened its vital interests.

In the final analysis, debate on the question of responsibility for the Cold War is unproductive and futile. American leaders most probably exaggerated the scope of Stalin's ambitions, and American actions—the denial of postwar economic aid, protests over Eastern Europe, and the mere possession of the atomic bomb—probably appeared provocative to the Soviet Union. The United States might have done better to acquiesce in Soviet influence in Eastern Europe, an area in which its own interests were marginal; but history and experience had not prepared American leaders to act with such restraint, and domestic political pressures compelled a hard line. Nor can it be proven that a more accommodating American posture would have decisively altered the outcome. When viewed over the long perspective, the Cold War was the result of broad historical forces that neither nation could control. The destruction of Europe and the confrontation of two expansive nations that were sharply divided ideologically placed severe limits on the capacity of the great powers to establish a lasting peace.

It was only a short step from the acceptance of mutual enmity to the division of Europe—and ultimately much of the world—into two hostile blocs. From 1947 to 1950 the United States and the Soviet Union moved rapidly to consolidate control over the regions that they occupied at the end of the war. Each nation perceived its policy as defensive, the United States the containment of communism, the Soviet Union the prevention of "capitalist encirclement." But the steps that were taken were interpreted by the adversary as offensive, reinforcing fears and hardening attitudes.

The United States took the initiative, filling

the vacuum left by British withdrawal from the Mediterranean and binding Western Europe to itself through economic assistance and a military alliance. Responding to an internal insurgency in Greece, which Washington mistakenly interpreted as part of a Soviet grand design for conquest of the Mediterranean region, President Truman in March 1947 proclaimed the Truman Doctrine, the first stage in the policy of containment. Declaring that the United States must defend "free peoples everywhere" against communist subversion and military threats, Truman proposed $400 million in military and economic assistance for Greece and Turkey. Fearing that the economic collapse of Western Europe, followed by political upheaval, would open irresistible opportunities for communist penetration of an area traditionally considered vital to American security, the administration shortly thereafter launched the Marshall Plan. Named for Secretary of State George C. Marshall, the program eventually provided Western Europe with more than $12 billion in economic assistance and integrated its economies closely with that of the United States.

The Truman Doctrine and the Marshall Plan apparently confirmed Russian fears of an aggressive capitalist offensive, and Stalin moved in a heavy-handed manner to solidify his Eastern European buffer zone. In February 1948 Soviet collaborators overthrew the Czech government, which had attempted to maintain a precarious neutrality between East and West. Stalin tried everything short of armed attack against Yugoslavia to bring the dissident dictator Tito into line, and replaced Władysław Gomułka as head of the Polish Communist party with the more pliant Bolesław Bierut. In the summer of 1947 the Soviet Union established the Cominform, an "information office," the real purpose of which was to enforce ideological purity among the communist parties of Eastern Europe. In January 1949 the Soviet Union created the Council for Economic Mutual Assistance, a mutual aid program that gave the Kremlin tighter control over the satellite economies.

Both the United States and the Soviet Union considered Germany the key to Europe, and the jockeying for position there provoked in 1948 the most serious Cold War crisis up to that time. Convinced by the summer of 1947 that the Soviet Union did not wish a German settlement, the United States pressed forward with plans to unify and reconstruct the Western zone, and used the lure of Marshall Plan funds to bring the British and French into line. Stalin feared nothing more than the prospect of a revived Germany, and to compel the West to withdraw, or accept a German settlement on his terms, he cut off passenger and freight access to Berlin, which was isolated within the Soviet zone. General Lucius Clay, the American military commander in Germany, urged the use of force to break the blockade, but the Truman administration responded much more cautiously. For over a year the United States airlifted into Berlin sufficient supplies to sustain the population. His gambit checked, Stalin eventually dropped the blockade, and despite much talk of war and several incidents that could have provoked hostilities, the crisis eased. But the division of Germany hardened rapidly. In 1949 the Soviet Union proclaimed the formation of the German Democratic Republic and the United States and its allies, the Federal Republic of Germany. For the next fifteen years a divided Germany and an isolated Berlin would remain the most volatile trouble spots in the Cold War.

The formation of military alliances completed the division of Europe. It is now evident that the Soviet Union did not contemplate military action against Western Europe and that the United States had no designs against Eastern Europe. But by 1949 these fears had come to dominate policymaking in Washington and Moscow. Viewing the Czech coup and the Berlin blockade from the perspective of Hitler's invasion of Czechoslovakia just ten years before, American officials fearfully anticipated a Soviet assault against Western Europe. In 1949 the United States joined with eleven European nations to form the North Atlantic Treaty Organization, a mutual defense alliance to deter Soviet aggression. Several years later the Russians countered with the Warsaw Pact (1955), a defense alliance binding the Soviet Union and its Eastern European satellites.

By 1949 the Cold War had crystallized. Each side viewed the other as a threat not simply to its vital interests but to its way of life and had taken frantic measures to protect exposed positions. Negotiations had stopped, and diplomacy was reduced to the exchange of shrill ideological blasts. Europe was divided into two hostile blocs. The United States and the Soviet Union began preparations for a war that seemed by this time a real possibility. After 1948, Soviet defense spending rose dramatically as Stalin attempted to develop the conventional military power necessary to counter American nuclear superiority. By April 1950 the Truman administration had formulated NSC-68, a defense plan that projected a military budget as high as $50 billion to enable the United States to meet any communist challenge "promptly and unequivocally."

Within each nation Cold War orthodoxy was vigorously enforced. Stalin launched a wave of terror to repress dissent in all areas of life within the Soviet Union and in the satellites. The Truman administration initiated a loyalty program for government employees and gradually tightened its implementation. The Soviet explosion of an atomic bomb in 1949, and investigations of a Russian espionage network that had allegedly penetrated the top echelons of the American government, set off irrational fears in the United States. The anticommunist hysteria culminated in the 1950's in the phenomenon known as McCarthyism, a witch-hunt—named for its chief practitioner, Senator Joseph McCarthy of Wisconsin—that brought harassment of dissenters and a growing conformity in American politics and intellectual life.

The victory of Mao Tse-tung's forces in the Chinese civil war extended the Cold War into the Far East. Stalin's relations with the Chinese Communists had never been cordial and on occasion had been openly hostile, but the Soviet leader could not pass up the opportunities created by Mao's triumph. Close ties with China would help balance American power in Japan. Perhaps fearful of a resurgent China, even under communist leadership, Stalin may also have hoped to influence the future course of Mao's revolution. He quickly recognized the new government, ceded old rights in Manchuria, and granted the Chinese credits.

The extension of communism into China had profound effects in the United States. It reinforced official and popular fears of the global scope of communist ambitions and of the seemingly vast capacity of communist minorities to overthrow established governments. Republicans charged that the administration had betrayed Chiang Kai-shek by withholding vital military aid, and some extremists even claimed that communist agents within the United States government had determined America's China policy. The Truman administration had hoped to disengage from the Chinese civil war, but the political uproar that followed the fall of Chiang made impolitic any attempt to reach an accommodation with Mao's government or indeed any negotiations with communist nations. American Far Eastern policy was set in a rigid mold that would not be broken for more than two decades.

The outbreak of war in Korea in 1950 intensified Cold War divisions. By supporting the North Korean invasion of South Korea, Stalin apparently hoped to pressure the United States to leave Japan, and he acted in the certainty that the United States would not intervene, an assumption that seemed to be borne out in official American statements. As was so often the case in the early Cold War, however, the two sides badly misread each other's intentions. Truman and his advisers interpreted Stalin's probe as the first stage of an all-out communist offensive in the Far East. Already under fire for the "loss" of China and recalling the 1930's when unchecked aggression had led to a general war, they concluded that the invasion must be met by force, and after little internal debate sent naval, air, and ground forces to support the South Koreans.

The Korean War ended in a stalemate, but it had far-reaching implications for the future of the Cold War. The United States suffered heavy casualties, and the frustrations of the limited-war, no-victory strategy heightened domestic anxieties and strengthened militant anticommunism. Continued Soviet support for the North Koreans and Chinese intervention in the war confirmed Washington's suspicions that the United States now faced a tightly unified, monolithic communist "bloc," directed by Moscow and bent on world domination. In the aftermath of Korea, the Truman administration shored up containment in Europe by enlarging American troop commitments, expanding European forces, and planning for the rearmament of West Germany. At the same time the containment policy was extended to Asia. The

Japanese Peace Treaty of 1951 provided for a continued American military presence. The United States assumed a commitment to defend Chiang's exile government on Formosa, and began to extend massive aid to the French in their effort to suppress a communist insurgency in Indochina.

As the Cold War intensified, the Soviet Union and the United States rebuilt the military machines that had been demobilized after World War II and initiated a nuclear arms race. The Russian defense budget soared to wartime levels, and by 1953 the Soviet armed forces numbered nearly five million men. As a result of Korea, American defense expenditures, including foreign aid, rose to more than $50 billion in 1952, and the armed forces, which had fallen to a low of about 1.5 million personnel in 1948, increased to more than 3.5 million by 1952. By 1951 the Soviet Union had developed a small stockpile of about sixty atomic bombs, and that same year the United States tested a thermonuclear hydrogen bomb. By the early 1950's, both nations had assumed a war footing, an enduring feature of the Cold War.

The advent of a Republican administration in Washington in January 1953 and the death of Stalin in March of the same year introduced new leaders and eventually new patterns into Soviet-American conflict. It appears that in his last years Stalin had grown concerned with the dangers of war and had initiated a reconsideration of Soviet policy. The power struggle that followed his death consumed the energies of the aspirants for his mantle, and made a relaxation of tensions with the West even more important. The new collective leadership initiated significant changes, playing down talk of world revolution and an irreconcilable struggle between communism and capitalism; easing repression in Eastern Europe; and offering to negotiate with the United States on a number of outstanding international problems, including Germany.

The United States did not test the sincerity of the Soviet overtures. The Eisenhower administration had taken office after waging a bitter campaign on a militant anticommunist platform. Secretary of State John Foster Dulles had condemned Truman's policy of containment as "negative, immoral and futile," and had promised a vigorous offensive to "liberate" captive nations from communist enslavement. The administration was not eager for war and in its first years sharply reduced the defense budget. "Liberation" was quickly abandoned, if indeed it had ever been taken seriously. But Eisenhower and Dulles distrusted the Russians, and in any event the persistence of the red scare within the United States made negotiations impolitic. The United States agreed to end the Korean War and to neutralize Austria, and Eisenhower met with Soviet leaders at the summit in 1955. But this was the extent of the reconciliation.

The Cold War soon settled into a pattern that would last for nearly a decade. The United States and the Soviet Union were the dominant powers in a bipolar world, and Soviet-American conflict was the preeminent factor in world politics. The development by both sides of thermonuclear weapons of growing destructive capacity made war unlikely, if not unthinkable, and what Winston Churchill called the "delicate balance of terror" imposed restraints upon both Moscow and Washington. The intense ideological battles of the Truman-Stalin years abated somewhat. Nikita Khrushchev, who finally emerged the top figure in the Soviet hierarchy, increasingly spoke of "peaceful coexistence," and Eisenhower projected an image of moderation and peace. In reality, however, the struggle continued. Neither leader felt secure enough either in relation to the adversary or within his own political system to make the sort of concessions that were necessary for meaningful negotiations. Still viewing the other as a dangerous threat, each nation worked vigorously to prevent the erosion of strategic positions already established and to extend its influence into areas that remained uncommitted. The Cold War became, in George Lichtheim's phrase, a series of "competitive attempts to alter the balance of power . . . without overt resort to force."

Positions in Europe hardened during the 1950's. The Eisenhower administration did not seriously consider Soviet proposals for a reunified, neutralized Germany, instead moving to perfect the institutions of containment created by Truman. Over strong British and French opposition Secretary Dulles rammed through a European defense plan calling for the integration of West Germany into the North Atlantic Treaty Organization and for partial German rearmament. The Soviet Union responded by creating the Warsaw Pact, in which East Germany was incorporated. The division of Germany, and of Europe, was sealed.

Both nations moved to check threats to their respective spheres of influence. Soviet tanks put down incipient revolts in East Berlin in 1953 and in Hungary in 1956, and diplomatic pressure, backed by the threat of force, was sufficient to repress an uprising in Poland. The United States employed its power more subtly but no less effectively. The Eisenhower administration intervened in Iran in 1953 to unseat a government deemed inimical to United States interests, and encouraged a counterrevolution in Guatemala to force out a government that had nationalized United States property and secured arms from the Soviet bloc.

In the mid- and late 1950's, however, the Cold War moved into new arenas. As positions in Europe and East Asia stabilized, the great powers increasingly turned their attention to the Third World, the newly independent nations of the Middle East, Southeast Asia, and Africa, which were struggling to develop viable economies and to establish national identities. The United States and the Soviet Union came to regard these new nations as testing grounds in the struggle between their two systems and as pawns in the global struggle for power, vigorously competing for their allegiance by massive propaganda campaigns and generous offers of economic and military assistance. Khrushchev undertook goodwill junkets to such neutralist nations as India, Burma, and Indonesia; Soviet publicists offered Russian achievements in industrialization as a relevant model to the new nations; and the Soviet Union established a foreign aid program that would grow steadily during the 1950's. The United States lured a number of Southeast Asian and Middle Eastern nations into mutual security pacts, and extended substantial economic assistance to neutralist states such as India. The most ambitious American undertaking was in South Vietnam. Following the French withdrawal in 1955, the Eisenhower administration sent scores of advisers and spent billions of dollars in the effort to create an independent noncommunist state that could stand as a bulwark against communist penetration of Southeast Asia.

Soviet-American competition in the Third World produced the first of many explosive confrontations in the Suez crisis of 1956. When the United States withdrew an offer to assist Egypt in constructing a gigantic dam on the Nile, the Egyptian leader, Gamal Abdel Nasser, nationalized the Suez Canal. Dependent on the Mediterranean lifeline, Britain, France, and Israel subsequently launched military action against Egypt. The Soviet Union backed Nasser, and Khrushchev even threatened to use nuclear weapons against the western allies. Fearful that the Soviet Union might exploit the crisis to extend its influence in the Middle East, the Eisenhower administration forced Britain and France to withdraw. The crisis ended, but Soviet-American rivalry in the Middle East intensified. The Russians expanded their assistance to Nasser and sought to gain influence in other Middle Eastern nations. The United States enunciated the Eisenhower Doctrine, which offered aid to any Middle Eastern nation threatened by communism.

In the late 1950's the Soviet Union launched a vigorous global offensive, ultimately bringing about the most dangerous period of the Cold War. America's refusal to intervene in Hungary and its indecisiveness in the Suez crisis may have persuaded the Soviet leadership that Eisenhower was weak and irresolute. Khrushchev was apparently under great pressure from the more militant Chinese, with whom serious ideological differences were developing, and from hard-liners within the Soviet bureaucracy. Major Soviet breakthroughs in rocketry, the launching of the first earth satellite in 1957, and the development of a "missile gap," presumably in favor of the Russians, injected a new note of confidence into Soviet foreign policy. In an attempt to win diplomatic victories that would secure his own position within the Soviet hierarchy and the Soviet Union's position within the communist world, Khrushchev adopted an increasingly aggressive policy. He reopened the explosive Berlin question, threatening to settle it on his own terms if the United States did not negotiate. He intensified the offensive in the Third World, widening Soviet involvement in the Middle East and Southeast Asia and establishing political and economic ties with a number of newly independent nations in Africa. More ominously, he moved into the Caribbean, an area traditionally within the American sphere of influence. When the United States severed relations with the leftist government of Fidel Castro, the Soviet Union began extending to Cuba substantial loans, technical assistance, and military aid, and Khrushchev provocatively announced that the Monroe Doctrine was dead.

The Soviet offensive stimulated an American counteroffensive. Eisenhower had stood fast on Berlin and was preparing to take action against Castro, but the scope and force of Soviet aggressiveness and the apparent threat posed by the Soviet Union's missiles and nuclear capacity aroused growing uneasiness in the United States. When the Democrat John F. Kennedy came into office in 1961, he pledged to reinvigorate an American foreign policy that he charged had been weak and indecisive, and to rebuild American military power, which had become inadequate for the challenge of the Cold War. Kennedy and his advisers deliberately avoided the moral absolutism of Dulles, fancying themselves "tough-minded realists," but their rhetoric was even more militant and they committed themselves to meet the Russian challenge forcefully. In their view the United States had a moral obligation to defend freedom against communist aggression; the very existence of the United States depended upon how effectively they met the challenge. "Everytime a country, regardless of how far away from our own borders . . . passes behind the Iron Curtain," Kennedy himself warned, "the security of the United States is thereby endangered."

Tensions mounted dangerously throughout 1961. The United States and the Soviet Union backed opposing factions in civil wars in tiny, landlocked Laos and in the Congo in Africa. The United States attempted to overthrow Castro, a move that ended disastrously at the Bay of Pigs, when Cuban exile forces, trained by the Central Intelligence Agency, were destroyed by Castro's soldiers. The Kennedy administration also drastically stepped up aid to the government of South Vietnam, which was threatened by an internal insurgency supported by communist North Vietnam. At a summit meeting in June, Khrushchev reaffirmed Soviet support for wars of liberation across the globe and issued a new ultimatum on Berlin. Two months later the East Germans constructed a steel and concrete wall to seal off East Berlin from West Berlin. More certain than ever of hostile Soviet intentions and under rising pressure from right-wing critics at home, Kennedy ordered a massive increase in American military spending, placing particular emphasis on outstripping the Soviets in missile construction and on developing the conventional forces to fight "brush-fire" wars in the Third World.

The buildup of tension culminated in the Cuban missile crisis of 1962, the most dangerous confrontation of the Cold War. Fearful that the United States would soon have an insurmountable lead in missiles and under fire from critics within his own government and the Chinese, Khrushchev by placing medium-range missiles in Cuba sought to balance American nuclear power cheaply and quickly and to secure leverage for dealing with Berlin and other issues. Certain that acquiescence in Khrushchev's daring gambit would shift the fragile global balance against the United States and tempt the Russians to further adventures, Kennedy instituted a "quarantine" of Cuba and demanded that Khrushchev dismantle the missile sites. For over a week the great powers stood precariously on the brink of nuclear war. Ultimately, Khrushchev backed down, preferring the certain humiliation of defeat to the chance of a disastrous war. The crisis ended as the United States was completing plans for an invasion of Cuba.

In the years after the missile crisis, the Cold War entered into a transitional phase characterized by confusion and uncertainty. Old patterns of conflict persisted and in some areas assumed extremely dangerous proportions. At the same time, however, the United States and the Soviet Union made deliberate attempts to scale down mutual hostility and to avoid confrontations that might threaten nuclear war. More significant over the long run, both powers found their ability to control world events challenged as the bipolar world of the 1950's gave way to a more complex polycentric world, in which nationalism prevailed over ideology and new centers of power emerged.

The most noticeable immediate effect of the

missile crisis was a relaxation of Soviet-American tensions. Both nations withdrew from the brink sobered by the experience. The inflammatory rhetoric toned down, the five-year crisis over Berlin eased, and competition in the Third World abated. A hot line was established so that Soviet and American leaders could communicate directly in time of crisis, and in 1963 the two nations agreed to ban atmospheric and underwater testing of nuclear weapons.

Old patterns of behavior were not easily altered, however, and although the Cold War abated, it by no means ended. The strategic arms race took on ominous new proportions. Khrushchev fell from power shortly after the missile crisis, and his successors, determined that the Soviet Union must never again be caught in a position of strategic vulnerability, initiated a crash program to catch up with the United States. During the 1960's both nations developed more sophisticated weapons systems, including antiballistic missiles, which could neutralize conventional rockets, and missiles that could hurl multiple nuclear warheads toward a number of predesignated targets.

In areas of vital interest the great powers continued to use military power to check revolts that might weaken their position to the advantage of the adversary. Kennedy's successor, Lyndon B. Johnson, sent marines into the Dominican Republic in 1965 to suppress a revolution that had allegedly come under communist control. The new Soviet leaders, Leonid Brezhnev and Aleksei Kosygin, sent tanks into Czechoslovakia in 1968 to overthrow a government whose liberal tendencies appeared to threaten the solidity of the Warsaw Pact.

Old trouble spots continued to hold out the possibility of confrontation. The United States and the Soviet Union provided massive aid to Israel and Egypt respectively, and the volatile situation in the Middle East replaced Berlin as potentially the most dangerous area in the world. From 1965 to 1968, moreover, the Johnson administration launched a full-scale war in Vietnam, initiating regular bombing raids over North Vietnam and sending a half million men to maintain the embattled government of South Vietnam. The Soviet Union responded by sharply increasing its assistance to Hanoi.

In areas where the Cold War persisted, however, the great powers seemed to accept new ground rules. The interventions in the Dominican Republic and in Czechoslovakia provoked no crises—indeed neither nation attempted to exploit the other's predicament for propaganda purposes. Each seemed to acknowledge, at least tacitly, the legitimacy of the other's freedom of action within its own sphere of influence. In instances where the nations competed, moreover, they did so on the basis of an unwritten agreement to avoid confrontation. When a war between Egypt and Israel in 1967 appeared likely to provoke great power intervention, Johnson and Kosygin used the hot line to impose a cease-fire. While escalating the war in Vietnam, the Johnson administration carefully avoided actions that might provoke Russian intervention.

At the same time, dramatic changes in the world power structure speeded the demise of the Cold War. The missile crisis catalyzed a trend underway for some years—the breakup of the power blocs that had been constructed after World War II. By the early 1960's, historic conflicts of interest and growing ideological differences had brought the Soviet Union and China into bitter conflict. Khrushchev's failure to consult the Chinese during the missile crisis brought the dispute out into the open, and within several years the two communist giants had mobilized troops along their long common border. The Sino-Soviet split divided communist parties across the world into opposing camps, introducing complex new factors into world politics.

The rise of nationalism also eroded the American alliance system. Kennedy's unilateral action in the Cuban crisis reinforced Charles de Gaulle's determination to take an independent course in world affairs. In the mid-1960's France vetoed British entry into the Common Market, opened independent initiatives with West Germany, and pulled out of the North Atlantic Treaty Organization. No longer fearful of a Soviet invasion and rapidly becoming an economic power in its own right, Western Europe took an increasingly independent line in the late 1960's. West German Chancellor Willy Brandt, mayor of West Berlin during the crises of 1958–1961, opened independent discussions with the Soviet Union; cultivated economic and political ties with Eastern Europe; and settled the boundary dispute with Poland that had been a source of contention since the Potsdam Conference of 1945.

These fundamental changes in the international system, combined with severe domestic problems, forced American and Soviet leaders to seek a further relaxation of tensions. The war in Vietnam would eventually cost the United States more than 55,000 dead and $100 billion. By 1969 it had raised critical economic and political problems and compelled a reassessment of policies that had gone unchallenged for more than twenty years. Massive military expenditures caused a runaway inflation that undercut postwar prosperity and aroused growing discontent. The war also became a great moral issue, polarizing American society as no other issue had since slavery a century before. As it dragged on, seemingly without end, critics began to question not simply the merits of American intervention in Southeast Asia but the entire set of assumptions upon which the containment policy had been based.

More than anything else, the war in Vietnam induced the Republican administration of Richard M. Nixon to seek détente with the Soviet Union. Economic and political necessity compelled Nixon to extricate the United States from Vietnam and to reduce military expenditures and overseas commitments. Soviet help could be decisive in ending the war, and a stabilization of the arms race and a general relaxation of tensions were required to cut the defense budget. Nixon and his chief foreign policy adviser, Henry Kissinger, also hoped to exploit Sino-Soviet tensions to the benefit of the United States, and looked to an expansion of trade with both communist powers to ease America's economic problems. There is more than a touch of irony in the fact that Nixon, cold warrior nonpareil of the 1940's and 1950's, initiated overtures toward détente with the Soviet Union and the normalization of relations with China.

The Soviet leadership found good reasons for accepting Nixon's approaches. By 1969 Brezhnev had established within the Kremlin a position that was secure enough to permit a new direction in foreign policy. While the United States had been mired down in Vietnam, moreover, the Soviet Union had undertaken a massive buildup of missile and naval power, and for the first time in the Cold War faced the United States from a position of strategic parity. The emergence of a hostile China along the Soviet Union's eastern flank required an easing of tensions in the West, and the new policies pursued by France and West Germany afforded an opportunity to encourage European independence from the United States and weaken the North Atlantic Treaty Organization. Like Nixon, Brezhnev also viewed détente as a means of dealing with domestic problems. The military buildup had produced severe dislocations in the Soviet economy, leaving a shortage of consumer goods that threatened domestic unrest and causing the Russians to fall far behind the West in the application of new technology to industry. Facing a choice of basic domestic reforms, which could threaten the dominance of the party, or of expanded East-West trade, Brezhnev apparently chose détente as the most satisfactory means for dealing with his several problems.

The turnabout on both sides produced dramatic results. By the end of 1971 the European issues that had given rise to the Cold War appeared closer to resolution than at any previous time. Brandt's demarche brought major breakthroughs on Berlin and Germany, since 1945 the very symbol of Cold War divisions. The Soviet Union guaranteed access to West Berlin, defusing the most explosive problem. West Germany and the Soviet Union concluded a treaty regularizing their relations, and the United States recognized East Germany. These agreements "made explicit what had been implicit in the policies of the two superpowers," Hans Morgenthau has written, ". . . the recognition by all concerned of the territorial boundaries established at the end of the Second World War."

A Nixon-Brezhnev summit meeting in the summer of 1972 brought further results. For the first time leaders of the two great powers publicly renounced the Cold War. They also agreed to a statement of principles pledging consultation and the avoidance of confrontation in times of international crisis, and concluded a major commercial treaty. A strategic arms limitation agreement prevented the further deployment of ballistic missile defenses, restricted the improvement of antiaircraft missiles, and froze offensive missiles at their 1 July 1972 levels.

The effect of détente was evident in other areas. In the spring of 1972, when Nixon initiated a massive bombing campaign in North Vietnam and mined Haiphong harbor, the Kremlin was conspicuously silent, and Brezhnev subsequently put pressure on the North Vietnamese to accept a cease-fire in Indochina permitting American withdrawal. After a brief and apparently grave threat of confrontation, the United States and the Soviet Union collaborated in arranging a cease-fire following yet another war in the Middle East in the autumn of 1973.

Over the next few years, both nations persisted in their efforts to expand the horizons of détente. An agreement signed at Vladivostok in November 1974 added to the 1972 arms limitation treaty by restricting the number of strategic launchers and multiple independently targeted reentry vehicles (MIRV's) available to each. At Helsinki in the summer of 1975, the Soviet Union secured its long-sought goal of Western recognition of the status quo in Europe in return for vague promises to permit a freer flow of people, information, and ideas between East and West. Between 1972 and 1976, the United States and the Soviet Union concluded more than fifty agreements on matters ranging from cooperation in the exploration of outer space to the underground testing of nuclear power for peaceful purposes, and established a variety of cultural exchange programs.

The Helsinki and Vladivostok accords were of limited practical significance, however, and détente increasingly ran up against deep-seated mutual suspicions and conflicts of interest. The arms limitation talks bogged down in sharp disagreements over the applicability of the Vladivostok restrictions to the Soviet Backfire bomber and American cruise missiles. Heated conflict over the Angolan civil war in the winter of 1975–1976 revived the possibility of a major confrontation, at least temporarily, and brought into the open basic differences over the meaning of détente. Congressional determination to avoid another Vietnam checked American involvement in Angola, but the Soviet Union sent arms and advisers, and Cuba sent some 8,000 troops to support the faction that eventually emerged victorious. When Secretary of State Kissinger warned that Soviet intervention in Angola threatened collaboration with the United States in other areas, Russian spokesmen hotly retorted that détente could not be "interpreted as a ban on popular national liberation struggles against colonial oppression."

Nixon and Kissinger had oversold the benefits that the United States would secure from the new relationship with the Soviet Union, and Nixon's resignation as a result of the Watergate scandal and the apparent breakdown of Soviet-American cooperation unleashed powerful political forces in the United States that threatened further progress in détente. When Congress insisted that the 1972 trade treaty be conditional on the Soviet Union's more lenient treatment of its Jewish population, the Kremlin angrily rejected an agreement Nixon and Kissinger had regarded as the very underpinning of détente. In the aftermath of Angola, Democratic and Republican critics alike charged that Nixon and his successor, Gerald Ford, had jeopardized the security and global interests of the United States by giving away too much without demanding anything in return. Such was the political backlash by early 1976 that Ford was compelled to state publicly that he would no longer use the word "détente."

The future of Soviet-American relations was shrouded in uncertainty by the end of 1976. Messianic impulses in both nations had diminished, and the shrill propaganda tirades had abated. Neither nation had withdrawn into isolationism, but both seemed to be shaping new policies characterized by greater restraint. Brezhnev appeared to be shifting from Khrushchev's globalism to a form of continentalism, which focused on building Soviet power in Eurasia. The post-Vietnam direction of American policy remained unclear, but it seemed evident that containment, at least as applied on the global scale of the 1950's and 1960's, had ended. The possibilities of global conflict thus appeared reduced, but fundamental ideological differences remained; each nation retained far-flung interests it considered vital, and the Angolan affair suggested how quickly the old tensions could resurface. Both nations had admitted the importance of arms control, but old weapons were being improved and new weapons developed faster than limits were being imposed, and the proliferation of nuclear weapons to the Third World raised ominous long-range threats to bilateral agreement. The uncertain political situation in China following the death of Mao Tse-tung, the advent of a new Democratic administration in Washington, and the aging of the Soviet leadership further clouded the picture.

Dramatic changes in the international system brought additional uncertainty. The increasingly serious economic problems in the United States, Japan, and Western Europe introduced new and potentially dangerous destabilizing factors and raised the possibility that at some future point the Soviet Union might attempt to exploit what Soviet ideologues referred to as the "aggravated and intensifying crisis of world capitalism." The assertiveness of Third World leaders and the use of cartels to exploit western dependence upon critical raw materials such as oil opened the possibility of sustained conflict, even war, between the developing nations and the advanced industrial nations, with uncertain implications for Soviet-American relations.

"We find ourselves, at the moment, in an international landscape curiously devoid of familiar landmarks," Alastair Buchan has written. Indeed, such were the changes in world politics that the future appeared more confusing than at any time since before World War II. The postwar era had passed, but the structure and patterns of the new era were not yet evident. Détente itself symbolized the untidy new period of international relations that followed the verities of the Cold War. It appeared unlikely that Soviet-American relations would revert to the extreme hostility and unchecked global competition of the 1950's, but it seemed equally doubtful that détente would blossom into a close friendship or fruitful collaboration. At best, it portended a complex and ambiguous new relationship with elements of both cooperation and conflict. Moreover, the vast changes in world politics and the emergence of new issues and problems suggested that Soviet-American relations, whatever their form, would evolve in a new and very different international context. The Cold War, at least as it was known in its most clearly definable form, appeared to be a passing epoch in world history.

BIBLIOGRAPHY

Zbigniew Brzezinski, "How the Cold War Was Played," in *Foreign Affairs,* 51 (1972), is a useful analysis that seeks to determine dominant patterns during the various phases of the Cold War. Alastair Buchan, "The Emerging International System: A European Perspective," in *International Interactions,* 1 (1974), attempts to show how recent developments have altered the structure of international politics and the behavior of nations since the heyday of the Cold War. John C. Campbell, "Soviet-American Relations: Détente and Dispute," in *Current History* (October 1975), is a thorough and balanced assessment of détente as of late 1975. Louis Halle, *The Cold War as History* (New York, 1967), is a balanced treatment, written from the "realist" perspective, which concludes that the Cold War was inevitable. Gabriel Kolko, *The Politics of War: The World and United States Foreign Policy, 1943–1945* (New York, 1969), and Gabriel and Joyce Kolko, *The Limits of Power: The World and United States Foreign Policy, 1945–1954* (New York, 1972), provide a detailed radical indictment of American foreign policy during the early stages of the Cold War. Walter LaFeber, *America, Russia and the Cold War, 1945–1971* (New York, 1972), reflects the influence of revisionism, but is perhaps the most balanced assessment. John Lukacs, *A New History of the Cold War* (New York, 1966), is a stimulating interpretative study that places the Cold War in a broad historical setting and emphasizes the societal and ideological influences on the Soviet-American relationship. John W. Spanier, *American Foreign Policy Since World War II* (New York, 1971), is an able statement of the conventional American interpretation of the Cold War. Robert W. Tucker, *The Radical Left and American Foreign Policy* (Baltimore, Md., 1971), is the fullest and most effective critique of revisionism. Adam B. Ulam, *The Rivals: America and Russia Since World War II* (New York, 1971), is a provocative, interpretative study, written by one of the foremost analysts of Soviet foreign policy.

[*See also* American Attitudes Toward War; Collective Security; Containment; Détente; The Eisenhower Doctrine; Ideology and Foreign Policy; The Marshall Plan; The Nixon Doctrine; Nuclear Weapons and Diplomacy; The Truman Doctrine.]

COLLECTIVE SECURITY

Roland N. Stromberg

COLLECTIVE security may be defined as a plan for maintaining peace through an organization of sovereign states, whose members pledge themselves to defend each other against attack. The idea emerged in 1914, was extensively discussed during World War I, and took shape rather imperfectly in the 1919 Covenant of the League of Nations and again in the Charter of the United Nations after World War II. The term has subsequently been applied to less idealistic and narrower arrangements for joint defense such as the North Atlantic Treaty Organization.

The term "collective security" was not used until the 1930's and is a slogan; more accurate is "security for individual nations by collective means," that is, by membership in an international organization made up of all or most of the states of the world pledged to defend each other from attack. "Collective security" is a handier term, and it entered deeply into the international vocabulary when from about 1931 to 1939 many hoped, in vain, that the League of Nations through its machinery for collective action might avert war by checking the "aggression" of the revisionist powers, Germany, Italy, and Japan.

Although the modern idea of collective security was born in 1914, it has roots in the distant past. Elements of collective security were present in some of the leagues of ancient Greek states; likewise in the experiment of the Holy League in Renaissance Italy (1495). China saw some unsuccessful experiments in cooperative leagues of independent states in the seventh and sixth centuries B.C., prior to a period of bitter warfare ending in the victory of one state that imposed unity. In his *De recuperatione sanctae terrae* (*ca.* 1306) Pierre Dubois produced a plan of this sort in Europe; and in the seventeenth century Maximilien de Béthune, duc de Sully, produced a more famous plan, which proposed keeping the peace by general pledges to defend the territorial status quo. Similar schemes flourished in the eighteenth century, when such philosophers as Immanuel Kant and Jeremy Bentham were among the authors of "plans for perpetual peace." Among the Romantic utopists of the earlier nineteenth century was Comte Henri de Saint-Simon. The little world of Swiss independent cantons proved an interesting laboratory for such experiments. The Arab League today shows some affinities to this model. Although it seldom worked effectively, collective security as a "universal alliance" of all the states within a given international system (which in former times could embrace a particular area such as China, Greece, Italy, or Switzerland) is a basic, archetypal mode of international relations, lying somewhere between total state egoism (in which states may be allied with each other in hostile or "balance of power" groupings subject to alteration) and a federated or unitary superstate that has managed to absorb the lesser sovereignties.

Nevertheless, in the nineteenth century, the classic era of nationalism, Europe found little room for collective security. The great nineteenth-century "peace movement" looked mainly in other directions. Quite vigorous in the decades preceding the outbreak of war in 1914, this world peace movement put its emphasis on arbitration, disarmament, and the growth of international law by voluntary agreement. In accordance with the spirit of the times, people felt that progress toward peace would come gradually and voluntarily. The long era of European peace embracing most of the period from 1815 to 1914, and especially 1871–1914, was not favorable to the consideration of drastic plans. Most people complacently assumed that the Western world had set its feet firmly on a path that led slowly but inevitably to the extinction of war. The Hague Peace Conferences of 1899 and 1907 reflected this outlook. Leading spokesmen of the pre-1914 period rejected a "league of force" as impracticable and too extreme, although in the 1900's there was some discussion of a European "league of peace" pledged to nonaggression and arbitration of disputes. Thus, for example, the French socialist Jean Jaurès suggested such a league in 1900.

In the realm of practical statecraft, the "concert of Europe" invoked from time to time was a nebulous conception without any permanent organization or specific constitution. A general congress of all the European powers might be assembled to deal with a particular crisis, as happened in 1856 and 1878, but this was really only an extension of the methods of traditional diplomacy, in which states negotiated with each other through their appointed agents of foreign policy. Multistate conferences of a more restricted membership, including the signatories to a particular treaty or convention, might also be held on an ad hoc basis, as, for example, the Algeciras Conference of 1906 that dealt with the Moroccan crisis. In such meetings of the powers there was at most a faint foreshadowing of a permanent and regularized international league or society.

The shock of August 1914 forced total reconsideration. The old ways of diplomacy—rival alliances and balances of power—appeared to have failed. One could no longer believe in the path of steady progress toward international order. Bolder remedies were needed if civilization were not to be destroyed by devastating wars. Numerous schemes soon proposed basic reorganization to end the "international anarchy" which, a consensus held, had been responsible for the coming of the war. The most important of these plans, beginning with Sir James Bryce's proposals in 1914 and including the American-based League to Enforce Peace, as well as the Fabian Society plan, asked the nations of the world to join a league or association of nations, and in so doing to agree to submit their disputes to arbitration or mediation before going to war, and to apply penalties or "sanctions" to any member state that resorted to war without so doing. As Bryce put it, "The League shall undertake to defend any one of its members who may be attacked by any other State who has refused to accept Arbitration or Conciliation."

These theorists assumed that the hour was not ripe for a world state, and that sovereign states cannot be coerced, but they hoped that states would voluntarily accept and honor such a pledge in the cause of peace. Some critics thought that these collective security proposals did not go far enough, since states could still in the end resort to war; others felt they went too far, since no great power could or would bind itself in advance in any significant way.

Uncertainty also existed about who should belong to the league, especially with reference to the enemy powers in the ongoing war; about the mode of representation; and about the method of identifying aggression and responding to it. The discussion was far-ranging and tended to expose as many difficulties as it resolved. Underlying it was the urgent feeling that somehow the scourge of war had to be eliminated, under pain of the extinction of civilization, and that the old idea of "selfish nationalism" was bankrupt. Yet informed people also knew that nationalism was far from a spent force and that no chance realistically existed to set up a world superstate. Collective security hoped to establish a halfway house on the road to true world government. Its advocates frequently cited the analogy of a vigilante stage of law enforcement, one in which, prior to the arrival of formal government, settlers suppressed crime by forming a posse or voluntary citizens' organization.

During World War I many organizations and individuals contributed to the formulation of plans for a league of nations. In the United States the League to Enforce Peace included ex-president William Howard Taft, Harvard president A. Lawrence Lowell, and a host of other prominent citizens. Lord Bryce or his colleague G. Lowes Dickinson may best be given credit for initiating the entire discussion, but an extensive British debate also featured books by Leonard Woolf and H. N. Brailsford among others; a committee headed by Sir Walter Phillimore eventually produced an official British plan. The numerous plans varied in details, but all sought to unite the major states of the world in a permanent organization, in which they would be represented as states and which would have power to deal with their disputes and prevent war. The broad concept of a "league to enforce peace" was endorsed "not only by pacifists and thinkers, but by practical statesmen." It was the great idea of 1914–1918, although skeptical criticism was not lacking even then.

Although there was some interest in collective security in France and in the neutral countries (the Netherlands, for example), the ideas that were to be incorporated into the League of Nations came mainly from Anglo-American sources. It is a mistake to attribute these ideas preeminently to President Woodrow Wilson, as is frequently done. Wilson showed relatively little interest in any explicit plan for a league based on collective security principles until quite late. At Paris he played a part in framing the League Covenant but received assistance from his aide Colonel Edward M. House, American adviser David Hunter Miller, British advisers Lord Robert Cecil and Sir Cecil Hurst, and South African leader General Jan C. Smuts. Wilson did of course become an earnest and tireless advocate of the League of Nations Covenant.

This Covenant, drawn up at Paris in 1919 and made part of the Treaty of Versailles imposed on a defeated Germany, was an incongruous amalgamation of the various ideas discussed during the war and was destined to have a disappointing life. Article 10, the most controversial and debated provision, seemed to demand of member states an obligation to "preserve as against external aggression the territorial integrity and existing political independence of all members of the League." But in fact the League through its Council (upper chamber) could only request them to act, not force them to do so. Some of the issues that were to plague collective security thus arose early: Is it possible to get binding commitments from states to suppress any future forcible alteration of the status quo? Is this even desirable, since the status quo may not be just or reasonable, at least not to everybody?

Although the French (for obvious reasons) asked for the creation of an international army under control of the League of Nations, this idea received no serious support. Frightened by the specter of American soldiers being summoned to fight on foreign soil at the behest of an alien organization, the Senate refused to ratify the Treaty of Versailles. Thus the United States did not become a member of the League; nor was the new, outcast Russian socialist state a member. Also excluded at first were the defeated powers of World War I. The League thus began life with serious, if not fatal, handicaps. In 1924–1925 the security-conscious states—such as Poland and Czechoslovakia, which had profited by the peace settlement, or France, which most feared any revision of it—unsuccessfully tried to clarify and tighten the security obligations of members.

It thus became evident that the League would have to function in ways other than as an agent of collective security standing guard against revision of boundaries. In the 1920's Geneva became instead a place of diplomacy and conciliation, along with more modest forms of functional international cooperation. Germany's entrance into the League in 1926 signaled this change of perspective. For a number of years little was heard about plans to suppress war by joint military action; much was said of the uses of the League to help cultivate habits of negotiation and peaceful settlement of disputes between nations. "Collective security" lay dormant. The events of the 1930's revived it.

American opinion in the 1920's strongly opposed any political involvement in the quarrels of Europe and was all but unanimous in rejecting an obligation to act as policeman in areas outside the Western Hemisphere. The treaties of peace executed after the war had become unpopular, and many regarded them as unjust and unlikely to last. The United States participated in most of the nonpolitical activities of the League of Nations and also played a leading part in the movement to "outlaw war" by voluntary renunciation, which culminated in the Kellogg-Briand Pact (1928), but it exhibited an almost pathological fear of any commitment that might entail the possible use of armed force in some "foreign quarrel." (Intervention in the small Caribbean countries lying at the doorstep of the United States might be another matter, although there was also a reaction against this sort of "imperialism.") This fear of repeating what a large majority of Americans now regarded as the terrible mistake of having entered World War I receded only slowly in the 1930's under the threat of a renewal of war in Europe and Asia. Initial American reaction to rumblings of conflict from 1931 on was to reaffirm vows not to be duped again by appeals to "save the world" by marching off to fight in Europe. The Great Depression intensified these feelings by intruding much more urgent questions of domestic recovery and reform. Isolationism reached its peak in 1934–1936, when legislation attempted to cut ties between the United States and all belligerent countries in the event of war, without discriminating between "aggressor" and victim.

The international disturbances of the troubled 1930's began with the Japanese extension of military control over Manchuria in 1931. This was followed by the Italian campaign in Ethiopia in 1935 and Adolf Hitler's demands that the "fetters of Versailles" be smashed and that the German nation be allowed *Lebensraum* ("living space") for expansion. In 1936 Germany reoccupied the Rhineland and in 1938 annexed Austria. Czechoslovakia followed in 1939. Faced with this determined assault on the post-World War I boundaries, diplomats in Western Europe and in the Soviet Union, which joined the League in 1934, sought to make the machinery of the League an effective tool of war prevention by means of collective action against "aggression." The attempt was not successful. Although Japan received a verbal rebuke from the League in 1933 for its behavior in Manchuria, it simply resigned from the League and did not end its forward policies in China, which may even have been stimulated by what was construed in Japan as a hypocritical insult.

Following the eloquent appeal of Ethiopian Emperor Haile Selassie for aid, the League, under British leadership, tried to organize economic sanctions against Italy in 1935, but this did not prevent the Italian conquest of Ethiopia and probably helped move Mussolini closer to Hitler's side. The embargo was not sufficiently enforceable to be effective. This fiasco, which ended in a British-French retreat from high principles to offer Italy a compromise deal (the Hoare-Laval proposals), did much to diminish enthusiasm for collective security through the League of Nations. Direct negotiations between the major European powers during the tense crises of 1938–1939 bypassed the machinery of the League.

Many came to believe that a more vigorous and less selfish support of the League might have checked the aggressions of Japan, Italy, and Germany, and prevented World War II. In much of the literature on the origins of the war collective security appeared as the opposite of "appeasement," which had gambled and failed to win the goodwill of Germany by yielding to its demands. The lesson that one should never appease (yield to) the demands of an aggressive "criminal" nation became deeply engraved in the public mind during the grim years when Hitler's appetite only grew with eating. And the dishonor of the 1938 Munich "appeasement" did not prevent war the following year. Popular, too, was a similar thesis applied to Japan's expansion in the Pacific. Between 1938 and 1941 American opinion shifted dramatically toward the view that isolationism, or the avoidance of American responsibility to keep the world secure from aggression, had been a fearful blunder. To this was added the belief that the United States should have followed Wilson's vision, joined the League of Nations, upheld collective security, and thus prevented World War II.

Critics were to cast doubt on this interpretation insofar as it involved the assumption that the League represented anything more than the sum of its parts. The League obviously commanded no military power of its own. If England, France, the Soviet Union, and the United States could not see their way to thwarting Hitler's goals at the risk of war, as a matter of national interest, the League could not help them. If they would not help the League, it was impotent. The League might at most supply convenient machinery or a meeting place, but what really mattered was the will to resist, which was notably lacking in the democracies in these years. Some argued that the idea of collective security was even an obstacle to a firm policy, because public opinion at times, as in England in the mid-1930's, tended to look upon collective security and the League as a substitute for national power. Evidently some people thought that if only the problem of stopping the dictators could be turned over to Geneva, nothing need be done by the separate nations. This clearly was a dangerous illusion.

World War II brought a surge of hope that a revised League of Nations, now supported by the United States and the Soviet Union and profiting from the lessons of the 1930's, might serve as the basis for a new international order. Because the League of Nations had become discredited, especially in the eyes of the Soviet Union, which was expelled from the League in 1940 for attacking Finland, it was necessary to create a new world organization. With strong support from American public opinion, the United Nations was officially established in 1945 after earlier conferences and discussions. It differed in some particulars from the League of Nations but reflected the same basic philosophy of collective security. In order to make it more effective, the United Nations Charter placed more power in the hands of the five major states, which were given veto powers and permanent representation in the upper chamber, the Security Council, which had exclusive jurisdiction in security matters. Initially the Security Council also had six nonpermanent members. (This was later expanded to ten.) Based according to the Charter on "the principle of the sovereign equality of all its members," all of which pledged themselves to "refrain in their international relations from the threat or use of force against the territorial integrity or political independence of any state," the United Nations endowed the Security Council with "primary responsibility for the maintenance of international peace and security," charging other members with a duty to "accept and carry out the decisions of the Security Council." Seven of the eleven votes were declared necessary to decide substantive issues, including the votes of all the permanent members—the United States, the Soviet Union, China, France, and the United Kingdom. The Security Council "shall determine the existence of any threat to the peace, breach of the peace, or act of aggression" and decide what to do, including taking "such action by air, sea or land forces as may be necessary to maintain or restore international peace and security." The idea of the "four policemen" (China, the Soviet Union, Britain, and the United States), each maintaining peace in its area of the globe, was one popular formulation of this big-power conception of collective security, which encountered some criticism from the smaller countries but appeared practicable as a continuation of the wartime alliance against the Axis.

Once the war was over, amity dissolved in quarrels between the United States and the Soviet Union. Their continued goodwill and cooperation was a condition for United Nations success. The spreading post-1945 Cold War between the Soviet and American-West European blocs ensured the failure of collective security and rendered the United Nations increasingly irrelevant except as one arena for the power struggle between the two blocs.

Critics of collective security pointed out at this time that as a plan of war prevention it suffers from the defect of assuming the problem already solved. It assumes that the great majority of the world powers are naturally peaceloving, and that war is caused only by the occasional transgressions of a bad nation, led into wickedness by unusual circumstances. If this is true, the problem of war is not so great in any case. Put concretely, if the superpowers could keep on friendly terms and cooperate for world peace, all would be reasonably well; if they could not, then no collective security plan could work. Under Cold War conditions, collective security's inclination to use force to defend peace—always something of a paradox—became a positive menace.

In 1950 the United States took the lead in persuading the United Nations Security Council to condemn the aggression of North Korea against South Korea, in a land left divided by the post-1945 Soviet-American rift. The apparently fortuitous absence from the Security Council at that time of the Soviet Union, which otherwise could have vetoed the resolution, facilitated this decision. A major war ensued in Korea, as United Nations forces, of which the great majority were American, turned back the North Korean "aggressors" and then invaded the North, only to encounter Chinese intervention. The paradox of calling war on this scale a peaceable "police action" struck home forcibly. Not everyone was persuaded that the North was the aggressor, although there seemed clear evidence that it did launch an overt attack in 1950. Border incidents and provocations in an unnaturally divided land had been going on for several years; and the United Nations forces, commanded by an American general, Douglas MacArthur, seemed less those of the United Nations than of the United States. The armistice negotiated in 1953, which left the North-South border in Korea not far from where it had originally been, underscored the futility of the enterprise, if one thought of it as "punishing the aggressor." Although initially it was hailed as a successful application of collective security, and many continued to believe in resisting the expansion of communist power, the Korean War tended to discredit collective security. There was little enthusiasm for more actions of this sort.

In 1956 the United Nations nevertheless played a significant part in the Suez crisis, and a United Nations Expeditionary Force helped to police the armistice. United Nations forces went into the Congo in some strength in 1961 under conditions of chaos and strife in that recently liberated former Belgian colony, there being on this occasion a rare meeting of minds between the Soviet Union and the United States. Once again leaders spoke of "putting out a brush fire" before it became a major conflagration. The United Nations force in the Congo suffered from divided counsel reflecting the divergent aims of the various interests involved: East, West, and Third World. The action was hardly a success and resulted in fresh disillusionment with use of the United Nations as a military force. From this time on, "crisis management" took the form of direct negotiations between the powers concerned, or special conferences, with the United Nations usually playing a peripheral although often useful role as supplier of truce-observing teams. The situation was not unlike that of the League of Nations in the 1920's.

The most traumatic international conflict of the 1960's, the Vietnam War, also had an anticollective security fallout. The motives for American entry into Indochina initially included a feeling, derived from the collective-security complex of ideas, that aggression was being checked in the spirit, if not exactly the letter, of the United Nations Charter. The organization of the North Atlantic Treaty Organization in 1949, and its subsequent development into a close military alliance of most of the states of noncommunist Europe with Canada and the United States, had been a reaction to the Soviet threat to Europe (real or imagined). American ideologists justified it as something more than an old-fashioned military alliance based as of yore on the realities of power in a world of hostile blocs. The North Atlantic Treaty Organization was called "collective security," and somewhat uneasily squared with the United Nations Charter by an appeal to Articles 51 and 52, which referred to the validity of "collective self-defense" via "regional arrangements." It was argued that the paralysis of the United Nations, resulting from Soviet noncooperation, forced recourse to such arrangements. In the wake of NATO's apparent success in "containing" Soviet expansion in Europe, American policy sought to create other regional security groupings, including a relatively ineffective Southeast Asia Treaty Organization (SEATO) and the Central Treaty Organization (CENTO) in the Middle East.

The North Atlantic Treaty Organization paved the way for thinking of regional resistance to communist expansion as "collective security." Behind the designs of North Vietnam to unite a war-divided country under its leadership, many saw the expansion of a monolithic Asiatic communism centered in China, and they invoked the lesson of the Hitler years: Draw the line and fight rather than allow "appeasement" to erode your position. (A similar logic had appealed to British Prime Minister Anthony Eden at the time of the Suez crisis, when he and French leaders detected what they saw as another Hitler in Egyptian leader Gamal Abdel Nasser.) The initially small American involvement in Southeast Asia, joined by some forces from other SEATO members, swelled into the nightmare of major war as the conflict steadily escalated, creating a formidable backlash of public opinion against the war in the United States and elsewhere. In the general hysteria the initial aims of the intervention were almost forgotten; but it is safe to say that some of the key themes of collective security suffered severe damage in the revolution of opinion resulting from the Vietnam War (1957–1975). The so-called Nixon Doctrine announced an American withdrawal from unlimited commitments to serve as policeman in remote places. It may be added that during the

Vietnam War the United Nations was almost altogether excluded from important negotiations. At various times each side brought complaints of "aggression" before the Security Council—Laos in 1959 against Hanoi, Cambodia in 1964 against the United States and South Vietnam, the United States later the same year against Hanoi—but these resulted in no action and were employed chiefly for propaganda purposes. Both the Geneva accords of 1954 and the Paris Conference peace settlement of 1973 completely ignored the United Nations. This was unquestionably a blow to the prestige of the United Nations, although optimists might point out that the admission of Red China to the United Nations in 1971 made it a more ecumenical body. Exclusion of mainland China from the United Nations had prevented use of that organization in matters involving Chinese interests.

"Collective security" is still frequently used to describe the North Atlantic Treaty Organization. In this usage it merely means military cooperation between allied states, or having allies for defense against a common enemy. Similarly in the Russian-dominated East European zone, "collective security" refers to the Warsaw Pact. Needless to say, "security" and "cooperation for security," as for example in the Conference on Security and Cooperation in Europe (1973–1974), are common terms. But in its original sense, of a new plan for world peace based on a "universal alliance" and pledges to suppress war by joint action of all its members against aggression, collective security seems to have become a casualty of recent history. This failure is reflected in frequently reiterated expressions of concern about the waning of the United Nations, its "crisis of relevance," its tendency to become a backwater, ignored in the major crises and world decisions—a fact often blamed, in the words of former United Nations Secretary-General U Thant, on "the growing tendency for States to revert to a reliance on force as a means of resolving their international differences" (1970). Bitterness or chagrin may be directed against the United Nations itself, more often against the "selfishness" of powers who do not give it necessary support.

Revision of the Charter as a means to improvement no longer arouses much enthusiasm; the roots of the problem are recognized as going deeper. Changes in the Charter included enlarging the Security Council, but the five permanent members and the veto power remain the same. Paralyzed by the vetoes of the superpowers, the Security Council diminished in importance. Today its concept of a dictatorship of a few big powers seems especially outmoded in view of the flood of new, smaller states that has much more than doubled United Nations membership since 1960. In the 1950's the General Assembly asserted its own right to recommend action in support of peace and security (Uniting for Peace resolution); but it can only recommend, and the possibility of securing global unanimity on any of the military conflicts that spring up grows increasingly dim as ideological unity shrinks. The many new states of the Third World, products of the tide of decolonization, are both independent-minded and unstable. Realists regard the goal of a strong United Nations army as increasingly ethereal.

"Peacekeeping" is increasingly distinguished and dissociated from collective security, the stress being placed not on a large United Nations army capable of crushing an aggressor, but on small, noncombat units, serving only with permission of the host country and acting as observers of truces or as buffers along sensitive frontiers. Although disputes and financial problems plagued even these forces, they served useful functions in Cyprus and New Guinea, and on the Israeli-Egyptian border (intermittently). But this, to repeat, was a swing away from the collective security conception.

One may study the problems encountered by the idea of collective security in connection with many of the major episodes of recent diplomatic history, barely outlined here: the background of World War II, the Cold War, the North Atlantic Treaty Organization, the Korean War, the Suez crisis, the Congo, Vietnam, and other recent events. (Of much significance is the bypassing of United Nations channels in many of the other crises of the last two decades, such as the Berlin crisis, the Cuban missile crisis, Middle East wars for the most part, Biafra, and Bangladesh.) One may also note, however, that the collective security idea itself has proved less successful (to say the least) than its adherents initially hoped.

It may be suggested first, and perhaps most

fundamentally, that collective security failed to find a compromise between national and world sovereignty because sovereignty is inherently indivisible. In the last analysis sovereign states cannot be fully bound by pledges to act in some hypothetical future case, especially where such pledges involve the risk of war. Plans for collective security demand such ironclad commitments, or the system decays into just another instrument of national policy (as the United Nations has tended to become). United Nations actions do not supersede politics among nations; they become a branch of these politics. The United Nations only mirrors the existing international society. National sovereignties remain the basis of world politics, and in the last analysis these sovereignties will agree to cooperate only so far as this serves their interests. Such cooperation may indeed accord with their interests at times, but there is no assurance that it will. The larger powers (who after all must bear the major burdens of enforcing peace under a collective security system) have never been willing to give an unconditional commitment to carry out the commands of the world organization; they have always reserved for themselves some escape hatch. They have never been willing to set up an international army of any significant strength, under direct control of the League or United Nations without strings attached. That is to say that it still is a world of nationalism and national states. If a world superstate could somehow be set up, this would obviate and supersede collective security, which in theory is a hypothetical stage somewhere in between. In Karl Mannheim's terminology collective security is a "relative utopia"—one that tries to be realistic but retains elements of fantasy.

An army under the direct control of the international organization, one that could be used without asking permission of the various member states, seems necessary to collective security; otherwise, as has been the case, it must make ad hoc requests for military contingents, which the various governments may or may not choose to honor depending on their interests. If it had its own army, the United Nations would already be a world government, possessing sovereign powers over the subordinate member units.

One of the illusions of collective security, as was observed, seems to be that conflict is relatively rare, is a product of criminality, and can readily be recognized as "aggression" and as such suppressed by the great majority of law-abiding, peaceloving peoples. But conflict, one may argue, is both much more endemic in the world and much less possible to categorize as good and evil than this theory concedes. Aggression has proved much more difficult to identify and to define than collective security plans foresaw. In such clashes as those between Israel and the Arab states, North and South Vietnam, North and South Korea, India and Pakistan, and perhaps most others, there is great difficulty in ascertaining who in fact struck the first blow, as well as a certain aridity in making this the crux. Does aggression include indirect attacks such as subversion and propaganda? How far back in time should one carry the feud? What states were ever at war, as Coleridge mused long ago, and did not each charge the other with the aggression? Historians still debate the responsibility for World War I and most other wars. In this respect Hitler's unashamed *Realpolitik* of 1936–1941 was a rarity in the history of wars. Although some have argued that any "breach of the peace" ought to be a signal for a "police action" by the world organization, regardless of who is responsible, or have suggested formal tests such as willingness to submit the dispute to an arbitrator or mediator, in fact the validity of the theory seems to depend on clear criteria of aggression. But attempts to reach a satisfactory definition of aggression failed in long years of debate first in the League and then in the United Nations, whose Special Committee on Defining Aggression struggled fruitlessly for years. Some argued that a definition is undesirable, since it could not cover all the contingencies and would be "a signpost for the guilty and a trap for the innocent." States might find themselves in the position of having to act against a friend or defend a foe. The reality of international relations in a world of particular sovereignties thus again confuses and thwarts the ideal of a pure collective security system. (After twenty-four years of effort, the United Nations Special Committee in 1974 did finally agree on a tortuous definition of aggression, but one too full of exceptions to be very helpful.)

There is also the argument of redundancy. A workable collective security order is one in which most of the powers are in harmony, and which has enough unity to agree on basic definitions, for example, of justice and aggression. It is significant that the idea has come into play in state systems marked by considerable underlying cultural unity, as in ancient China or modern Europe. But if there is this much unity, there is hardly any need to install a system of collective security, for the problem will virtually solve itself. To create the formal institution of a League of Nations or United Nations does not alter the existing order of power and international relations.

Insofar as collective security is based on a firm defense of existing borders, it is open to criticism on the ground that this freezes the status quo. This raises the problem of justice. Many states will not accept the justice of existing boundaries, which probably reflect the results of the most recent war and may contain arrangements clearly unacceptable to the losers. Many groups fervently advance claims for revision of frontiers at all times, today, for example, the Arabs and Pakistanis. Collective security thus is in danger of being labeled the selfish policy of satiated or victor states. (Germany consistently viewed it in that light between the world wars.) One must allow for some method of revising existing boundaries or one has condemned a dynamic world to immobility, which clearly is impossible. Proponents of collective security may urge "peaceful change," but how is this to come about? Their theory contains no specific answer. In a world without a single government possessing laws and courts that are binding on and acceptable to all, war must remain a possible last-resort remedy for injustice. Here we impinge upon arguments against pure pacifism and confront again the nonexistence of world government. It may be noted that recent fashionable support for wars of revolution and "liberation" runs counter to collective security's immobilism. Those who believe that there is indeed a "just war" for national independence, recovery of a region forcibly seized in the past by another state, overthrow of an oppressive government, or some other such compelling cause, will defend the right to resort to it rather than submit indefinitely to an unjust peace. (In the late 1960's and early 1970's the United Nations General Assembly, with a Third World majority, voted that nations should wage war on the "racist" government of Rhodesia, not for violating any frontier, but for being unjust.)

Insofar as it is based on guaranteeing frontiers, collective security assumes not only that these frontiers are just but also that they are well defined. Some writers have observed that collective security was more suited to the classical European state system than to much of the world today, where boundaries are ill defined or even nonexistent, and where civil wars, wars of secession, wars of "liberation"—sometimes with outside aid—are the most usual types of violent conflict.

Finally, there is the basic dilemma of collective security being—if it is effective—a waging of war to prevent war. War by any other name, including "police action," is still war. Of course, the advocates of collective security hoped that vigilant international police work performed in time would nip a potential war in the bud—stamp out the brush fire before it became a raging inferno. But experiences such as Korea and Vietnam suggest that well-intentioned interventions of this sort may result not in diminishing war but intensifying it. Intervention by outside powers, even if acting in the name of an international organization, is, after all, not usually apt to reduce a conflict. In principle, collective security abolishes neutrality; no state may stand aside and observe, all must become involved to stop a war. (The 1930's saw a considerable debate on the implications of the new doctrine for traditional neutrality.) But the venerable principle of neutrality may be valuable in confining the scope of a war. To abandon it may involve the risk of widening wars.

In this connection the "limited war" theorists and strategists advise accepting the inevitability of war while seeking to keep it as confined and limited as possible, rather than trying vainly to abolish it. Collective security has been accused of unrealistically demanding the total suppression of war, and, in its anxiety to achieve that goal, blowing up every skirmish into an international crisis.

Many scholars, and innumerable others, believe that the United Nations discredited itself—rather than gaining accolades—by waging war in Korea and the Congo. It has not wished to repeat the experiment. The same may be said of the United States in regard to acting as an agent of world order in Vietnam-type situations.

These objections can certainly be countered by other arguments; they are not all unassailable. The United Nations remains in existence and is a useful forum for debate. There is far less ideological unity today than in its earlier days, since it is no longer dominated by the Euro-American countries. Earnest discussions are held from time to time on how to restore it to a significant role in "peacekeeping." But the criticisms have called seriously into question the workability of collective security, perhaps the chief idea of this century addressed to the problem of war. It was born of the shock of 1914 and nourished by the further horror of World War II. Its goal was laudatory—to bring an end to the "international anarchy" of blindly competing states acknowledging no limitations on their powers except those of brute force. Recognizing the existence of nationalism as a powerful fact not likely soon to be extinguished, followers of collective security conceded to realism that dreams of a world state are as yet wholly premature; they tried to build on the foundation of independent sovereignties a society or league of nations to which these sovereign powers would offer their voluntary cooperation, in the common interest of suppressing war. In the last analysis such a compromise between national and international sovereignty seems impossible—the gulf is unbridgeable. Those who are unprepared to accept continuing prospects of rivalry between nations and peoples, mitigated only by diplomacy and leading intermittently to war, must face the formidable task of creating a world community able to support a world government. The term "collective security" has declined in usage in recent years; it is now chiefly applied to cooperation among members of armed alliances such as the North Atlantic Treaty Organization, a debasement of its original meaning.

BIBLIOGRAPHY

Marina S. and Lawrence S. Finkelstein, comps. and eds., *Collective Security* (San Francisco, 1966), is a handy collection of readings. Richard N. Current, "The United States and 'Collective Security': Notes on the History of an Idea," in Alexander DeConde, ed., *Isolation and Security* (Durham, N.C., 1957), is semantically helpful. Roland N. Stromberg, *Collective Security and American Foreign Policy* (New York, 1963), and "Uncertainties and Obscurities About the League of Nations," in *Journal of the History of Ideas* (January–March, 1972), mix analysis with history. On the earlier history of the idea, see S. J. Hemleben, *Plans for Peace Through Six Centuries* (Chicago, 1943). Warren F. Kuehl, *Seeking World Order* (Nashville, Tenn., 1969), is a history of the American approach to international organizations to 1920. A general history of collective security in practice seems to be lacking; one case study of interest is William E. Rappard, *Collective Security in Swiss Experience 1291–1948* (London, 1948). From the many studies of collective security in action in this century, the following may be suggested: Bruce Williams, *State Security and the League of Nations* (Baltimore, 1927); Reginald Bassett, *Democracy and Foreign Policy: A Case History: The Sino-Japanese Dispute 1931–1933* (London, 1968); Dean Acheson, *The Korean War* (New York, 1971); Ernest W. Lefever, *Uncertain Mandate: Politics of the United Nations Congo Operation* (Baltimore, 1968); and Lincoln P. Bloomfield, *The United Nations and Vietnam* (New York, 1968). See also Inis L. Claude, *The United Nations and the Use of Force* (New York, 1961); Lincoln P. Bloomfield, *The United Nations and U.S. Foreign Policy* (Boston, 1960); Ernest B. Haas, *Collective Security and the Future International System* (Denver, 1968); and Alan James, *The Politics of Peacekeeping* (New York, 1969).

[*See also* ALLIANCES, COALITIONS, AND ENTENTES; THE COLD WAR; CONTAINMENT; THE DOMINO THEORY; INTERNATIONAL ORGANIZATION; NEUTRALITY; PACIFISM; REALISM AND IDEALISM; SANCTIONS.]

COLONIALISM

Edward M. Bennett

COLONIALISM began as a descriptive term and subsequently assumed a pejorative connotation. In recent times most studies of the subject have focused their attention on attacking both the idea and its practitioners but have also tended to confuse it with imperialism to such a degree as to blur the lines of distinction between the two. It is necessary to discuss imperialism in the context of colonialism and to make the differences clear. For example, it is possible to be imperialistic without having colonies, but it is not possible to have colonies without being an empire. Thus in the case of the Soviet Union, which has exercised rigid controls over the economies of its small neighbors and forcefully absorbed within its structure Latvia, Lithuania, and Estonia, the Russians have practiced imperialism but not colonialism. If Stalin had succeeded in holding Manchuria under his control at the end of World War II, the Soviet Union would be also a colonial power. The United States, however, must be judged a colonial power because it holds American Samoa and has control of the strategic trust area of the Pacific, although the areas are not inclined to move toward independence and have sought instead territorial status.

A state possessing territories not incorporated within its borders, the native inhabitants of which are not granted the full rights or privileges of citizenship of the possessing state, is a colonial power. There is, however, a difference between colonizing an area and colonialism per se. For example, in the American experience colonialism did not exist while the United States was annexing contiguous areas on the continent of North America, for the areas being colonized were recognized as territories destined to be incorporated into the United States as an integral part of the nation.

While there were numerous efforts by various presidents and secretaries of state to make the United States a colonial power in the nineteenth century, none succeeded in adding territory not destined for statehood until the United States formally annexed the Midway Islands in the Pacific Ocean on 28 August 1867, after their discovery in 1859 by the American N. C. Brooks. This was not, however, a true colonial venture because the American purpose was to provide a way station and fueling stop en route to the Far East. The United States made no effort to develop the islands economically or politically or to populate them with colonists. Therefore, another definition of colonialism is that there must be a conscious effort on the part of the possessing power to develop or exploit the area in the interest of the possessor and to provide some form of government or control through colonial administrative machinery. This does not mean that the colonial power must necessarily neglect or abuse the interests of the native inhabitants of the territory taken as a colony, although more often than not such neglect and abuse does occur. It does mean, however, that the colonial nation has the power to impose its rule over the area and to assert its economic preeminence without resistance from the inhabitants of the area.

Probably no region under colonial administration received more considerate treatment by the mother country than Great Britain's colonies in North America, partly because they were peopled in the main by British subjects transplanted for the purpose of developing raw materials and markets for England. Where a colonial administration was imposed on an already existing and alien population, treatment of the native residents was less benign and generally considered more degrading by those thus possessed, depending on their level of civilization and organization at the time of conquest or occupation. For example, in the areas where Islamic or Oriental culture, religion, and laws had existed for a thousand or more years there was often fierce resistance to being subjected to colonial status, whereas in parts of Central Africa, New Guinea, and Borneo, where the native inhabitants were primitive in their development, the resistance was less prolonged or nonexistent.

If the American colonists were treated more as equals than most, they also resented more than most that they were not accorded exactly equal status with Englishmen who had not immigrated to the colonies. Therefore when they rebelled and gained their independence, they had a particular dislike for the very concept of colonialism. Representatives of the new United States wrote their prejudices into the Constitution in 1789, insisting that new acquisitions must become states after securing sufficient population and complying with the laws of the land. This anticolonialism continued as the preeminent view of Americans and their government until the end of the nineteenth century when the new manifest destiny seized the popular imagination and propelled the United States into the race for colonies.

When John L. O'Sullivan coined the term "manifest destiny" in 1845, it referred to the "destiny" of the United States to occupy and develop the American continent because of her superior institutions and form of government. Relative to its later counterpart, the "old" manifest destiny provided a modest program for the development and population of contiguous areas to the then existent United States. The new manifest destiny at the end of the nineteenth century bespoke a certain arrogance, since it claimed for Americans a superior system of government, a superior culture, and a superior race destined to carry mankind to the highest pinnacle of achievement. Many of the adherents of this philosophy extolled Yankee capitalism as part of the superior culture.

A man worthy of the task of educating the nation to the needs of expansion appeared in the form of Captain Alfred Thayer Mahan, whose major work, *The Influence of Sea Power Upon History, 1660–1783* (1890), extolled the virtues of a big navy as the route to national greatness—which required colonies to extend the defense perimeters of a great nation, and a merchant marine to carry trade to and from the colonies that would be defended by the navy. Mahan's great fear was a forthcoming contest with a rising China, and by means of its navy he wished to put the United States in a position that would keep China confined to the Asian continent. In numerous books, articles, speeches, and through his classes at the War College in Newport, Mahan bombarded Americans with his perception of the need for colonies. Ironically, while his impact was great in the United States, before World War I it was possibly even greater in Germany and Japan. Mahan was not nearly as interested in colonies for their commercial value as for their strategic value, but commerce became a selling point to attract a broad segment of the American public.

Social Darwinism added a sinister bent to the American urge for colonial expansion. American exponents of this pseudoscientific philosophy espoused by the Englishman Herbert Spencer adapted the concept of the survival of the fittest to the new manifest destiny, urging the spread of the Anglo-Saxon race and system of government to the less-fortunate peoples of Asia and the Far Pacific. Such proponents of expansion for security motives as Theodore Roosevelt might stress the strategic value of port facilities in the Philippines, but they were drowned out by the more flamboyant spokesmen like Senator Albert Beveridge, who demanded annexation of the whole Philippine archipelago. Roosevelt warned President William McKinley that it was feasible to hold a military naval base to protect American interests in Asia, but possession of the whole of the Philippines would be a commitment that the American people would not support in the long run. His advice was ignored. Again in 1907 Roosevelt referred to the Philippines as an Achilles' heel, which should be given at least nominal independence at the earliest possible moment.

Various answers have been proposed for why Americans, with an anticolonial bias deeply ingrained in their political system, turned to colonialism; or, in other words, what the cause was of the development of the new manifest destiny. Obviously social Darwinism and the hold that it established on the opinionmakers in the United States provides one of the many answers. Richard Hofstadter ascribed

America's outward thrust for colonies to what he called the psychic crisis. In *The Paranoid Style in American Politics and Other Essays* (1965) he argued that the severity of depressions of the period created fears about radicalism that caused the upper middle and upper classes in the United States to look for some diversion from internal crises, and they found relief by focusing on the expansionist issue. Restless energies, which had concentrated on internal development in the first century of American history, turned in some degree to external adventures, such as Frederick Jackson Turner feared they would with the closing of the frontier in 1890. Missionary enthusiasts saw fields available for the spread of Protestant doctrine. Idealists dreamed of lifting the yoke of European monarchists from the Western Hemisphere and then also from Asia. Some proponents of the Spanish-American War hoped to reunite the North and the South through this uplifting national endeavor. A search for markets motivated some enthusiasts for annexation of the Philippines. A desire to be included among the nations of great powers, which required colonial possessions in the late nineteenth century, proved yet another component to the expansionist movement. But Hofstadter's main emphasis in the psychic crisis rested on internal stimuli for external policy, not the least of which was the contest for political position as each of the major parties struggled to become the repository of public confidence.

In a perceptive study of Sino-American relations pertaining to Manchuria in the period 1895–1911, Michael H. Hunt examined the forces that worked toward American involvement in China. He stressed the misperceptions that guided both powers' views of one another and their vital interests. He saw racism or ethnocentrism along with excessive provincialism as contributing factors on both sides, keeping China and America from seeing their true interest. Contrary to a number of writers who attempt to discover a carefully developed imperial plan underlying American moves in Asia at the end of the nineteenth and beginning of the twentieth centuries, Hunt found American imperialism to be ill-defined or haphazard in its goals. Many policymakers dreamed of cooperation with China in preserving and developing Chinese nationalism and of profiting by trade with this emergent nation. Opportunities for such cooperation existed but foundered on mistrust and misunderstanding.

An important conclusion that emerged from this study was Hunt's observation that while imperialism was in part a motivating force for a number of Americans promoting United States involvement in Manchuria, with some even demanding territorial concessions, the government dragged its feet on implementing imperial plans, did not stand firm on economic penetration, laid its faith in the open door, and criticized China for the failure of American policy. The Americans asked why the Chinese did not stand up to the powers trying to carve out spheres of influence, especially when the Americans gave them the Open Door policy to use as a weapon to deny special rights, while the Chinese asked why the Americans did not help to enforce the open door with more than words. Hunt also reenforced much of Hofstadter's argument concerning the importance of the psychic crisis as an influence on American foreign policy and the impetus to "look outward" as an escape from domestic problems.

George F. Kennan, the historian-diplomat, argued cogently for the idea that the legalistic-moralistic tradition of the United States accounted for adventures in imperialism without commensurate understanding of the burdens or responsibilities of empire by most Americans and some policymakers, especially President McKinley and his third secretary of state, John Hay. Hay, who assumed office on 30 September 1898, the day before the peace commission met in Paris to determine the settlement of the Spanish-American War, spoke the language of the new manifest destiny: "No man, no party, can fight with any chance of final success against a cosmic tendency; no cleverness, no popularity avails against the spirit of the age." Hay was a determined annexationist, but more significantly he was the author of the Open Door policy, proclaiming the need and obligation of the powers involved in Asia to maintain the open door to trade in China and the maintenance of China's territorial integrity. Later historians accused Hay of fomenting through the Open Door policy a kind of imperialism, one that denied the need for territory and promoted instead economic exploitation of areas not strong enough to resist it.

Kennan said Hay did not understand the

far-reaching commitments assumed under the Open Door policy. It was part of the effort to ensure American participation in the external world by legalism and appeal to the moral conscience of Americans defending China against the assault of the great powers at no cost save legal definition of the obligations of the powers. This is probably true as far as it goes, but it also was intended to guarantee the entrance into the Asian world of American power and influence through a door Hay and others considered to have been opened by the acquisition of the Philippine Islands. That he became disillusioned by the inability and ineffectiveness of the United States to win support for the open door does not in any way diminish his responsibility for it. Hay opened not a door but a Pandora's box with his policy, which the United States was to pursue through a tortuous maze to participation in the Pacific phase of World War II.

Marilyn Blatt Young, in her study of American China policy from 1895 to 1901, corroborated much of Kennan's viewpoint on the inefficacy of open-door diplomacy, the difficulties inherent in the legalistic-moralistic perspective that permeated the Department of State, and the tendency to be more concerned with chauvinistic interests than national interests. In addition she pointed out the difficulties that plagued both China and the United States because of the view each held of the other as barbarians and the attendant implications of racism stemming from the perception of social Darwinism, which gained credence in the late nineteenth century. If imperialism was the American objective, it was so poorly contrived and so reliant on rhetoric and half-baked schemes failing of genuine government support as to be ineffectual.

Kennan was one of the early and chief spokesmen for the realist perspective in assessing right conduct in America's foreign relations and ascribing colonial expansion to a lack of realism in the formulators of the policy. Hay, Beveridge, Henry Cabot Lodge, and others who promoted the idea of empire for the United States failed to take into consideration, according to Kennan, the pervasive influence of anticolonialism in the United States, and failed to advertise the cost of empire to the American people, who were unwilling to bear the expense of defending what they had won by war or annexation. Believing that the Filipinos would welcome them with open arms, Americans were flustered and embarrassed when they were greeted instead with open rebellion. As soon as the empire had been acquired, agitation began to get rid of it, with mixed results. Incorporated territories (Alaska, Hawaii, Puerto Rico) were retained without much question. Where there was a desire to adhere to American protection (for example, American Samoa), responsibility was ultimately accepted (February 1929); but the Philippines demanded independence, and by means of the Tydings-McDuffie Act (1934) were promised independence in 1944, which was postponed until 1946 because of Japanese occupation of the islands during World War II. The Virgin Islands, purchased from Denmark in 1917, became an American territory, while other islands which were too small for incorporation but important strategically, continued as possessions, such as Wake and Johnston islands. The last territories considered for annexation by an incorporation agreement were part of the Trust Territory of the Pacific Islands under United States supervision as a United Nations trusteeship, including the Marshall, Caroline, and Marianna islands. Parts of the latter two asked for incorporation in 1975, and their disposition was still not determined in late 1977.

Realist and traditionalist historians have usually judged that the United States entered the colonization business by the back door at the end of the nineteenth and beginning of the twentieth centuries and could not wait to exit by the same route because being a colonial power was embarrassing and outside the American tradition. For example, in the traditional school, Samuel Flagg Bemis, Thomas A. Bailey, and Julius W. Pratt hold such views, while among the realists Norman A. Graebner and George F. Kennan would agree to the extent that colonialism was not and did not become a part of the American tradition. Another group of historians, the New Left, have argued that colonialism was a conscious expression of American capitalism, which had always been the determining force in American foreign policy and merely reached a conscious level of expression in colonialism. William Appleman Williams argued that colonialism was merely one phase of American imperialism, which became passé when it was discovered that economic imperialism that penetrated other areas by the force of dollars was superior to the actual possession of the territories that the United States wished to dominate. According to Williams and those of his persuasion, dollar diplomacy became the preeminent source of imperialism because it was easier to maintain, less embarrassing, and made it possible to eliminate the bother of colonial administration. But colonialism itself was merely an extension of the American experience and not an aberration.

One of the most respected historians associated with the New Left, Walter LaFeber, has argued that there was no break in tradition. While he emphasized the economic forces behind the new manifest destiny, he recognized that other forces played a part in promoting it. He insisted that colonialism was part and parcel of the American experience, all of which was preparing the way for the surge to overseas colonial possession as a natural extension of the colonial spirit developing from the outset in America. One of the few historians normally classed in the realist tradition, Richard W. Van Alstyne, agreed with at least part of the New Left assessment that there was no break in the American pattern of expansion. According to Van Alstyne the westward movement itself was an imperial endeavor preparing the way for further imperialism when the continent was filled or occupied.

These examples could be extended to include a number of other prominent diplomatic historians who have sided with the innocent victim-of-circumstances view of American colonial expansion versus the concept of the planned and persistent imperial thrust. Thus the debate over how and why the United States became a colonial power at the end of the nineteenth century rages on, with definitive answers lying in neither camp.

It seems prudent to assume that like all significant events in the world's development there were many causes for American colonialism. Economic determinists assess greed or material benefits deriving from colonial possession as the determinate cause. This does not explain the correspondence of such advocates of the colonial experiment as Mahan and Theodore Roosevelt, who laid stress on the importance of prestige and great-power status for the United States resting on the needs of security, which is or should be the primary consideration underlying the motivation for formulators of foreign policy.

Realist historians tend to examine colonialism as the result of some elements of the psychic crisis; the security motives; the spread of American industry and commerce; emotional appeals to liberal humanitarian objectives; social Darwinism; nationalism; and "egoistic nationalism," a term applied by the political scientist Robert E. Osgood to explain positions taken by Lodge and Beveridge, who flamboyantly expressed American national destiny without carefully examining the consequences. The traditionalists have been more inclined to focus on the idea of the aberration of anticolonial liberal democratic ideals. In some degree they are all correct, but because the realists take into account a multiplicity of factors arguing for colonial expansion and the retreat from colonialism that followed, they would appear to provide the most complete explanation.

Of course, there are also Marxist interpretations carried to the level of prediction by Lenin, who argued that imperialism was the highest stage of capitalism, which would lead to the most flagrant exploitation of proletarians and to the ultimate collapse of capitalism as imperial rivalries led to struggles for markets terminating in enervating wars. What Lenin did not foresee was the Soviet Union's entrance into the imperial grouping through such practices as the economic exploitation of the states under its sway. While condemning the United States and other Western powers, historians of the Marxist persuasion first rationalized Soviet behavior and claimed there was not exploitation, or else dropped Russia as the exemplar of Communist or Marxist principles and raised Communist China as a new model. Marxists and other economic determinists have also tended to lump together the Western colonial powers in defense of one another's interests and in support of racism, as in the case of American support of France in Algeria and Indochina, and of South Africa and Israel. This ignores Franklin D. Roosevelt's frequently expressed anticolonialism. It also overlooks such changes in position as the Department of State's shift in recent years concerning American support of South Africa.

Ironically while racism or ethnocentrism

has undeniably played a determinant role in both colonialism and imperialism and the powers that practiced them have been justly criticized for the practice, those who were its victims have generally not illustrated a much better record in their treatment of other races over whom they have been able to establish control. Fostered by the efforts to break free of colonial domination, virulent nationalism has led to extremist attitudes on the part, for example, of Arabs toward Jews, and Jews toward Arabs; of neighboring African tribes struggling to achieve preeminence over other tribes inside the borders of new states; of Chinese toward Tibetans and Indians; and of Indians toward Pakistanis and Pakistanis toward Indians. While this list is incomplete, it is still impressive of the evidence that the power to abuse is confined to no particular race. Perhaps the problem lies not in racism per se so much as in the corrupting influence of absolute power over another people. Some historians have attempted to identify racism as a phenomenon of one socioeconomic group exclusively or to whites versus other races, as though the problem would be eliminated if the world were socialist or the whites lost influence to the other races. They have not met the real challenge, which is that abuse rests with unrestrained power.

Ethnocentric behavior is a form of racism, which has permitted the Japanese to treat others of the yellow race as inferior when they held imperial control of the Chinese and the Koreans, and the Chinese to do the same when they have held similar power over Tibetans. The same phenomenon has permitted various tribal groups in Africa to persecute other tribes and the others to retaliate in kind. Ethnocentrism has permitted Great Russians to maintain that their "little Slav brothers" inside and outside Soviet borders need special tutelage by their betters. What made racism identifiable with colonialism and imperialism was the unrestrained power of the colonial and imperial nations to abuse those over whom they held dominance. The decline of colonialism has not eliminated the problem, for the nationalism that grew in a virulent strain in the places formerly under colonial control has bred a similar virus.

Admittedly there are still areas that may be defined as colonial possessions, but generally they are headed for either incorporation within the possessing state, autonomous status within some sort of confederation like the British Commonwealth, or independence. For example, in some cases there is the fiction of independence or autonomy such as the forced adherence of Latvia, Lithuania, and Estonia to the Soviet Union: the continued possession of Samoa by the United States; French colonial administration of Martinique, St. Pierre, and French Guiana; and British control of such places as Hong Kong and the Falkland Islands. There are, however, very few vestiges of colonialism left.

This, however, does not mean the end of imperialism, which has taken many forms. Economic penetration of underdeveloped areas has become a competitive replacement for colonialism and is absorbing the energies of the former colonial powers including the Soviet Union, which holds most of the areas formerly under the Russian empire in a grip of economic and political dominance as firm at least as in the declining years of that empire. Added to this form of exploitation of resources and capital control is a new element—the oil-rich Arab states that have recently emerged from colonial status and have exhibited all the symptoms of nationalism and desires for political power which they condemned in their former imperial masters. Colonialism is virtually dead, but imperialism continues as those nations with the economic or military power to perpetuate it have refused to give up the practice.

BIBLIOGRAPHY

Stewart C. Easton, *The Rise and Fall of Western Colonialism* (New York, 1964), provides a useful examination of the motives and processes of colonial expansion and development in the nineteenth century, and traces the reasons for the decline of colonialism and what happened to the colonial areas through 1964. Norman A. Graebner, ed., *Ideas and Diplomacy: Readings in the Intellectual Tradition of American Foreign Policy* (New York, 1964), argues that the new colonialism at the end of the nineteenth century was as much motivated by a quest for prestige as economic advantages and that strategic position for security was always a part of the American strategy. Michael H. Hunt, *Frontier Defense and the Open Door: Manchuria in Chinese-American Relations, 1895–1911* (New Haven, Conn.–London, 1973), focuses on the attempts of the Chinese to use the United States to bolster defense of China's frontiers. Hunt notes that racism and ethnocentrism warped the views on both sides and aided in preventing a rapprochement which both nations desired. George F. Kennan, *American Diplomacy: 1900–1950* (New York, 1960), a series of lectures for the Walgreen Foundation at the University of Chicago in 1950, provides a realist viewpoint on the development of American foreign policy at the turn of the century and is highly critical of the legalistic-moralistic perspective of the policymakers of the era. Walter LaFeber, *The New Empire: An Interpretation of American Expansion, 1860–1898* (Ithaca, N.Y., 1963), is more inclined to credit motives other than economic as contributing factors to America's colonial experiment, but argues that the empire was consciously acquired as a part of the traditional role of expansionism in American history. Julius W. Pratt, *Expansionists of 1898* (Baltimore, 1936), the first important study that submitted the war and the imperial thrust to a multicausationist analysis, follows a number of works that claim that the business community fomented and fostered the Spanish-American War and American colonialism. E. Berkeley Tompkins, *Anti-Imperialism in the United States: The Great Debate, 1890–1920* (Philadelphia, 1970), is a careful tracing of the debate over whether the United States should assume an empire. Tompkins concludes that the decision was rendered after the fact by the neglect of the United States and the embarrassed retreat from colonial possession. Richard W. Van Alstyne, *The Rising American Empire* (Chicago, 1960), argues that imperial expansion was part of American historical development and disagrees with the traditionalists that it was a departure from tradition. He assigns the tradition to other than economic motives, although economics were important. Charles Verlinden, *The Beginnings of Modern Colonization* (Ithaca, N.Y., 1970), trans. by Yvonne Freccero, is a good description of the beginnings of colonialism in the fifteenth century and offers some explanations for its development in Western civilization. William Appleman Williams, *The Roots of the Modern American Empire: A Study of the Growth and Shaping of Social Consciousness in a Marketplace Society* (New York, 1969), presents the United States as imperialistic from its inception and the colonial expansion at the end of the nineteenth century as a further expression of the traditional posture of an economically oriented society. Marilyn Blatt Young, *The Rhetoric of Empire: American China Policy, 1895–1901* (Cambridge, Mass., 1968), does not believe the Open Door policy was effective, in part because the Department of State did not limit application of the policy to the extent that the United States was willing to enforce it. She acknowledges that some American policymakers might have had some vague idea of imperial penetration of China, although it was too ill defined and poorly planned to be effectual.

[*See also* ANTI-IMPERIALISM; IMPERIALISM; ISOLATIONISM; MANDATES AND TRUSTEESHIPS; MANIFEST DESTINY; OPEN DOOR INTERPRETATION; THE OPEN DOOR POLICY.]

CONGRESS AND FOREIGN POLICY

Bruce Kuklick

According to the usual analysis, Congress and the president struggle with one another in making United States foreign policy. Despite the growth of executive power in the twentieth century, commentators have assumed that this struggle is essential to a republic's foreign affairs and defines American diplomacy. The distinctive feature of a democracy is that public opinion allegedly informs its international policies, for better or worse. Elected by the people and ultimately subject to their will, the legislative branch is the most significant conduit for the expression of public opinion; consequently, Congress must have an impact on diplomacy. Moreover, the legislature's popular ideas often conflict with those of the president's experts in the State Department who are insulated from the people and concerned with subtleties unknown to the average voter. Both critics and apologists have accepted this analysis. Some scholars have lamented the division of power because they think that the pursuit of the national interest becomes subject to the whims of provincial legislators at the mercy of an ignorant citizenry. Other scholars have lauded the situation because it demonstrates that democracy in the United States is not a sham and that the people do have a voice in decision making.

There is much truth in this vision of congressional-executive strife. In the formative period of the republic Congress displayed a concern about overwhelming executive power. A committee of secret correspondence established by the Continental Congress in 1775 first supervised American external relations. In 1777 the name of the committee was changed to the Committee for Foreign Affairs. This committee went out of existence in 1781 when Congress appointed Robert R. Livingston first secretary for foreign affairs; John Jay succeeded him and served until the Constitution of the new government went into effect in 1789. During these early years it is clear that Congress considered the control of foreign relations—conceived in terms of treaty-making power—as coming under its purview. Fearful of the abuse of executive power, Congress would act as both legislature and executive. In the Constitutional Convention there was a distinct shift in favor of a separate executive authority. In fact, the powers finally delegated to the president are mostly in the diplomatic field. The Founding Fathers appear to have wanted to grant the executive some initiative but simultaneously to have the Senate act as an informal advisory council to the president in formulating foreign policy and in drafting treaties. The office of secretary of state was simply conceived as that of a secretary, whose duty was to keep the great seal and with it to certify state papers.

The Constitution itself partitions responsibility in the sphere of diplomacy, supporting the notion that Congress and the president fight for the control of foreign policy. Through his appointees the president has the right to transact business with other countries, but he makes his appointments with the advice and consent of the Senate, and the Constitution is silent concerning the branch responsible for deciding with which countries the United States will have official relations. Moreover, although the president can avoid dealing with Congress by concluding executive agreements with other nations, the Senate must approve treaties by a two-thirds vote of members present. In respect to the use of force there is a deliberate and explicit overlapping of responsibilities. The president is commander in chief of the armed forces, but only Congress can declare war. Finally, there are myriad ways in which a determined Congress can harass the executive. All appropriations, including those for the implementation of foreign policies, must originate in the House of Representatives. In carrying out its domestic legislative duties, Congress may pass tariff, immigration, or neutrality bills that impinge on the president's freedom of action; and congressional investigations, hearings, and power of subpoena can embarrass or even intimidate the executive.

Despite the constitutional evidence, this conventional analysis of congressional-presidential strife is formalistic because it ignores the basic truth that a nation's foreign policy reflects the values of the culture that makes a nation a cohesive entity. The socioeconomic elite shapes these values, and members of this group actually determine "the national interest," the foreign policy to be pursued. Composed of the upper economic strata and the socially prestigious with a sense of noblesse oblige, and those who have successfully aspired to power, the membership of the elite is more or less homogeneous in its values. It agrees on the way of life that defines the culture of the United States and the principles of American foreign policy. These people occupy the strategic governmental positions in both the executive and legislative branches; they run the military and control the media; and they command the business and industrial concerns with interests in international affairs.

In most instances the executive branch, which has the initiative in diplomacy and is officially and primarily involved in deciding international policy, is able to deal with other nation-states with the support of Congress and other wielders of power. But if there is dispute within the elite concerning the nature of the national interest, Congress is an obvious forum where subordinate and dissatisfied elements can make their views heard and, perhaps, their policies dominant. While the executive branch and its supporters have always had the preponderance of strength in any conflict, Congress' constitutional prerogatives assure that it can be a major adversary to the president. Many congressmen represent constituencies of the elite that may or may not be satisfied with the conduct of foreign affairs. In other cases influential segments of the elite directly affect legislators by means of various lobbying techniques; they indirectly affect legislators via the press and, more recently, via radio and television.

Within this framework of analysis, the role of Congress in diplomacy is clear. It is a natural vehicle in which disgruntled members of the elite can voice their displeasure with American diplomacy. In a healthy, vigorous polity, frequent although not acrimonious congressional activity and debate will signal this displeasure. Partisan politics, differences in the locus of institutional power, and personal idiosyncrasies may each also contribute to congressional-executive friction. Except in extraordinary cases the disputes will be like family quarrels; they will assume certain premises and will not substantially influence American international relations.

Leading congressmen have implicitly substantiated this view by their vacillating opinions on the nature and scope of legislative authority. Congressmen may at times sanctify legislative claims, but the same men who are apparently committed to congressional privileges have also asserted the supremacy of the executive when he is fighting for policies they endorse or is engaged in a foreign-relations fight with the opposition party. It has become an axiom of American politics that the ideas of politicians on the locus of governmental authority depend much more on the changing positions they occupy than on a commitment to abstract constitutional niceties.

In the early years of the republic there was conflict over international policy, but this conflict did not yet reflect disputes between the executive and the legislature over diplomatic authority. Rather, conflict reflected the shifting sectional, commercial, and political alignments that characterized the maturing American democracy. During the early years of the nineteenth century, Jefferson's foreign policy was a matter of great controversy, but debates over it involved loyalty to the nascent political parties and not to the branch of government in which a politician served. The elite was also divided in its support for the War of 1812, but this time sectional interests were the paramount determinant of policy differences. Several years later when Congress investigated General Andrew

Jackson's exploits in Florida, the cause was not legislative-executive acrimony but, mainly, attempts to injure Jackson as a public figure. Similarly, John Adams' political enemies consistently opposed him for personal reasons while he was president (1825–1829); but the locus of authority in the making of diplomacy was not contested.

The first major confrontation between the legislature and the executive took place in the 1840's. During that period there was an expansionist consensus within the elite; but factional fights in the Whig and Democratic parties, arguments over the use of force in securing additional territory and over citizenship for "colored races," and the slavery question almost made this consensus nominal. Although the United States fought a war with Mexico to achieve the expansionist goals of the James K. Polk administration, the president clashed bitterly with disaffected members of the elite with congressional representation.

The Texas issue had been prominent in American politics since the 1830's, when Texas had won de facto independence from Mexico; but slavery, financial troubles in both the United States and Texas, and Mexican hostility to annexation all stood in the way of Texas statehood. In 1843 and 1844 President John Tyler safely assumed that he had a senatorial consensus for a treaty of annexation because powerful Americans feared British influence in Texas and hoped for commercial gain. But the Senate did not act until May 1844, after the party nominating conventions. A member of a minority faction of the Whig party, Tyler had acceded to the presidency upon the death of William Henry Harrison and was soon without a party. The Whigs nominated Henry Clay who was against immediate expansion. The Democrats were more split, and when their leading contender, Martin Van Buren, also opposed immediate annexation, the party nominated the little-known but dedicated expansionist Polk. The Senate vote against Texas annexation (35–16) reflected these divisions. Northern and Southern Whigs voted against it, as did Van Buren Democrats. Party and factional politics, not disagreement on the principles of American foreign policy, kept Texas temporarily out of the Union.

Polk won the November election, and Tyler interpreted the results as a victory for immediate annexation. Although realizing he could not get a two-thirds vote in the Senate, Tyler knew annexation had greater support than the earlier Senate vote indicated. Resorting to some adroit political maneuvering, he outwitted senatorial opponents by the expediency of a joint congressional resolution for annexation; it passed the House, and the Senate by 27 to 25. Before the end of his term in March 1845 Tyler began to implement the resolution, and Polk carried on Tyler's policies when he took office a few days later.

Texas became a state before the end of the year but the battle over foreign policy had just begun. The Mexican government was hostile to annexation, and a dispute over the Texas-Mexico border inflamed this hostility. Moreover, even at the risk of war, Polk was determined to take advantage of Mexican weakness and to acquire the disputed territory and, he hoped, the Mexican lands in all the Southwest. After fruitless negotiations with Mexico, he ordered General Zachary Taylor, in a series of moves in the first part of 1846, to advance through the disputed territory up to the Mexican border, finally blockading the mouth of the Rio Grande—an act of war. In the aftermath the Mexicans attacked a small American force and won an initial skirmish, but by the time this news reached Washington, Polk had already prepared most of a war message to Congress. The alleged shedding of American blood "on American soil," as Polk usefully described the Mexican attack, assured support in both houses. Congress voted overwhelmingly in favor of war and appropriated the funds necessary to conduct it.

The president's message again displayed his ability to outwit Congress. Many Whigs and some dissident Democrats disapproved of Polk's policies, but they could not oppose the president without being charged with disloyalty and unwillingness to support American combat troops. Moreover, the Democrats successfully employed a variety of parliamentary tactics to muzzle debate. Finally, the Whig opposition was itself divided because as Taylor progressed from victory to victory, he appeared as a likely winner for the Whigs in the presidential election of 1848.

After more fighting and complex negotiations, Polk submitted a treaty to the Senate in early 1848; it gave the United States the contested land and also secured for it the great territory of New Mexico and Upper California. Some Northern Whigs condemned the war and the treaty as a cover for the slave conspiracy to augment its power. The "Continental Democrats," who wanted all of Mexico, the argument went, desired slave territory and states. This explanation misreads the concerns of those who promoted the war and large annexation. Southern Whigs condemned the war, as did some Southern Democrats; Mexico had abolished slavery and there were doubts about its feasibility in the territory. As John C. Calhoun of South Carolina expressed it, annexation of Mexico would permit people of a "hybrid race" to become citizens of the Union. It became so clear that Mexican territory would be "free soil" that even a few abolitionists supported the war as a battle for the expansion of freedom.

Polk's purpose in waging war was not to expand slavery but to expand the geographic domain of the nation for the good of American commerce and trade. He believed that the continued political well-being of the United States depended on the growth of its economic interests in the territories. These interests were not necessarily proslavery, as the priority Polk felt for California and the Pacific ports demonstrates. War with Mexico was a means to acquire land on the Pacific and an important border on the Rio Grande.

The American elite accepted some version of Polk's nationalist-expansionist vision. His opposition objected to the president's notion of how expansion would occur. The Senate debate about the treaty illustrates this fact. A group of Whigs, fearing that the expansion of slavery could not be dissociated from Polk's kind of expansion, voted against it; so too did a group of Democrats who wanted to add more Mexican territory. In the context of debate, however, Polk represented a "moderate" opinion that won the support of the elite. The two groups of malcontents, whose arguments were more theoretical than practical against Polk's proposals for expansion, could neither work together nor win over converts, and the Senate approved the treaty 38 to 14.

Although incidents surrounding the Mexican War have not been of overwhelming importance to historians of American diplomacy, they do illustrate a recurring set of themes. First, there was broad agreement among the elite on the goals and principles of American foreign policy—the commercial and political expansion of the Union. Second, whatever the disagreement on the exact means of achieving these goals, this sort of expansion had already become traditional American policy and was to endure into the twentieth century. Third, the Mexican problem demonstrated the president's initiative in foreign affairs and his ability to frustrate opponents. Finally, the prewar, war, and postwar diplomacy evidenced the capacity of disappointed segments of the elite working through Congress to stall the executive and to moderate, if not alter, his policy.

The next important battle between legislators and the executive occurred after the Spanish-American War in 1898. It followed a pattern similar to that of the struggle that took place during the Mexican War. Throughout the 1890's Spain's inability to govern Cuba effectively and without bloodshed created a widespread feeling among decision makers at all levels that something had to change. Spanish misrule put Cuba at the mercy of other powers, disturbed American interests there, and offended the American sense of decency. Of course, the crucial question was what positive steps should be taken under the circumstances. If the United States were to intervene in any way, what would happen to the "mongrel Cuban people," who surely could not become citizens? Even in this perplexing situation, Congress passed a concurrent resolution in 1896 in support of native insurgents fighting to throw off Spanish governance. The new administration of William McKinley shared these sentiments but was more circumspect in voicing or acting on them, having, as it did, ultimate authority in the matter. At the end of 1897, in his annual message, the president urged that Spain be allowed to carry out its new reform program but noted that its failure might require American intervention. Four months later there was unanimity in the elite outside the executive on the need for action. Almost all Democrats and many Republicans in the House and Senate pressed the president, as did newspapers and other shapers of opinion, especially those in the business community.

Some scholars have argued that McKinley was a weak man who yielded to these pressures. On the contrary, the president was a shrewd and astute leader. He had stated more than once that Spain must bring peace to Cuba or be chastised; that is, he basically accepted the analysis of the rest of the elite. His concern was timing. When he believed that the Spanish were no longer in control in Cuba, he acted, with a united nation behind him. In mid-April 1898 he sent a war message to Congress, and on 22 April the United States was at war with Cuba.

The Spanish empire was ripe for picking. Americans were victorious not only in the Spanish possessions in the Caribbean but also in the Pacific. When the Senate had to solve the practical problem of how the United States should exercise its new powers, there were disputes. In its vote for war, the legislature had debated whether its recognition of Cuban independence should include recognition of the republican Cuban government. The administration's view—that the United States should not recognize the government—prevailed, but the debate signaled things to come. If diplomats could not support Cuban self-government, then someone else must govern the Cubans. Could a democracy like the United States aggrandize colonies to itself? The Teller Amendment (1898), a resolution prepared by Senator Henry M. Teller of Colorado and adopted by Congress, further muddied the waters. It specifically rejected American annexation of Cuba, although it left that possibility open in respect to Spain's other holdings.

All those who determined American policy agreed on the need for the political and commercial expansion of the United States. They also agreed that American expansion should not proceed in the fashion of European colonialism. The United States would create a new kind of empire; commercial expansion by American businessmen abroad would carry with it other American ideals. There was no need to control alien peoples politically; this was un-American and unnecessary. Given contact with Americans and time to evolve, other nations would gradually adopt a democratic way of life. The problem that the elite faced was how to realize these ideals. Although the primary focus of decision makers was the commerce of the Far East, the defeat of Spain would give the nation control of strategic waterways in the Caribbean, and in the Pacific the Philippines provided a base to enable the United States to defend its rights in China. How would the country practically dispose of its new island possessions?

One group, represented by Assistant Secretary of the Navy Theodore Roosevelt and Senator Henry Cabot Lodge of Massachusetts, came close to urging that European methods should be used in the New World. Another group loosely organized around the Anti-Imperialist League feared that annexation of lands with nonwhite populations would destroy the republic. It was unthinkable that these "inferior peoples" could be made citizens, and to rule them as subjects would subvert the principles of democracy. This part of the elite had substantial strength in the Senate. When McKinley sent it a treaty with Spain that provided for the acquisition of colonial territory, this group aired its views; its primary concern was annexation of the Philippines, whose people were unqualified for self-government.

The administration and leading senators had cooperated in drafting the treaty, and the Senate approved it 57 to 27. Victory, however, went not to the Roosevelt-Lodge element but to the administration and congressional middle-of-the-roaders who wanted to avoid both that extreme and that of the anti-imperialists. Feeling the problems of guiding the Filipinos, the centrists voted for annexation as the best possible solution in a bad situation; they did not relish the prospect of ruling subject peoples. The arrangements for Cuba specified by the Teller Amendment best expressed their views. In the form of the Platt Amendment (after Senator Orville H. Platt of Connecticut) these views became an appendix to the Cuban constitution. The United States gave Cuba independence but reserved the right to intervene in its affairs to preserve Cuban independence and a republican government. Cuba was also to sell or lease to the United States land for coaling and naval stations.

The victors in the administration and in Congress had to compromise their desire for commercial expansion alone, but they agreed to only the minimal trappings of colonialism. In so doing they achieved the ends to which the entire elite subscribed and they demonstrated the cooperation of legislature and executive in policymaking.

The most celebrated instance of conflict in foreign affairs occurred twenty years later when the Senate rejected Woodrow Wilson's Versailles Treaty after World War I. Wilson was an arrogant and self-righteous man convinced of the need for presidential leadership and unable to tolerate opposition. His domestic program, the New Freedom, had intended to use the federal government to restore a mythic nineteenth-century state of laissez–faire. So far as Wilson was concerned, the League of Nations at the heart of the Versailles Treaty would make this vision a reality all over the globe. He saw a union of coequal democracies whose open economies would combat the root sources of war; the reformed capitalism under which they would operate would steer between the moribund and belligerent capitalism that characterized Europe and the revolutionary socialism that gripped Russia. Essentially, Wilson's League internationalized the Far Eastern policy of the open door promulgated under McKinley. The liberal capitalism that the League would institutionalize was to maximize American economic power within a stable democratic framework.

Important segments of the elite, including influential members of the Republican party—Henry L. Stimson, William Howard Taft, and Charles Evans Hughes—supported Wilson's notions. Another group following Theodore Roosevelt and led by Henry Cabot Lodge, now chairman of the Senate Committee on Foreign Relations, was more pessimistic about the prospects of world order. These men were also concerned with American expansion, but they thought that nothing could prevent economic rivalry and that a strong defense system emphasizing a large navy was imperative. The critical element of their beliefs, however, was the view that it was unnecessary for the United States to commit itself to stabilizing conflict across the globe. Political and military intervention might occur, but policymakers should unilaterally be able to determine the need for intervention according to American interests at the time. Limiting American freedom of action in advance gained nothing. This was the principle at issue in the fight over the League: Article 10 of the treaty called for a moral commitment by the United States to stop aggression, and Wilson chose to interpret it in such a way that it was plausible for some to believe that he was usurping, or at least curtailing, the war powers of Congress.

Senate debate over the treaty raised many other issues, but the paramount problem was executive prerogative. Even so, Wilson had a large group backing him; and because Wilson and Lodge held similar substantive views of American interests, the treaty could have been expected to receive Senate sanction. There was, however, personal animosity between the two men, and Lodge played on Wilson's intolerance to opposition, skillfully using his position in the Senate to put together an anti-Wilson coalition. Burkean pessimists like Lodge dominated one part; on the same side was a more liberal group, led by William E. Borah of Idaho and Hiram Johnson of California, who feared that a League would contaminate the United States with European imperialism. Wilson aided this coalition. He took no steps to strengthen the segment of the Republican leadership sympathetic to his goals, and he refused to conciliate his moderate opponents in Congress. As a result he sapped the power of his supporters and drove many of them to the Lodge side. Senate defeat of the treaty represented not so much a turning away from a global open door but the personal humiliation of Woodrow Wilson.

Many commentators have seen the defeat of the League as a critical instance of legislative-executive conflict because America's nonparticipation in it was a significant cause of World War II. If Congress had listened to Wilson, according to the argument, collective security might have stopped Hitler's aggression. During the 1920's, however, policymakers followed the internationalist economic outlook espoused by proponents of the League. Although Republican diplomats earned the label "isolationists" in this period, the phrase applied only to their political interest in Europe, and there was little occasion to test this interest. Believing in a peace that would reintegrate Germany into the European system, Wilson had backed a punitive settlement at Versailles in a spasm of vindictive moralism. He later hoped to use the League to bring a liberal Germany into the community of nations. During the 1920's there was a consensus on this key Wilsonian issue among the American elite, and policymakers used economic strategy to secure a politically healthy and strong Germany. This consensus carried over into the early 1930's. American cooperation with the League at the time indicated, again, that the gap between Wilsonians and their nominal opponents was not wide.

In the first years of the Franklin D. Roosevelt presidency there was agreement that Americans should go no further than this minimal cooperation. A special Senate committee led by Gerald P. Nye of North Dakota stirred up concern about involvement in future European wars by castigating United States involvement in World War I. The committee's findings gave impetus to a series of neutrality acts designed to prevent entanglements that might lead once more to American involvement in Europe. Although this legislation created friction between Roosevelt and the Congress, what troubled the president was not so much the substance of the laws but their circumscription of executive discretion. At issue was not the policy the United States should pursue but which element of the elite should make the policy. From 1919 to 1936 congressional and administration diplomatists concurred on the blend of economic expansionism and limited political internationalism that the United States should adopt, and this policy was a close relative to what Wilsonianism would have amounted to in practice.

From the late 1930's until American entry into World War II in 1941, there was again conflict within the decision-making elite over policy, and opposition to Roosevelt's diplomatic stance centered in Congress. "Isolationists," composed of a rump group of those who had been most intransigent about the League and many others fearful of American military involvement in Europe, objected to Roosevelt's pro-Allied stance, which, they argued, would eventually bring the United States into the war against the Germans. As leader of the diplomatic "interventionists," Roosevelt overwhelmed his opponents and gained public favor for his ideas before Pearl Harbor, although the isolationists were powerful enough to force the president to work deviously for his goals. Fearful of the congressional hold on the electorate, Roosevelt had to "do good by stealth," as even his defenders admit. He circumvented the prerogatives of the Congress by broad use of executive powers; he came close to lying in describing his intentions; and he also came close to creating incidents to rally public opinion around the interventionists. Nonetheless, so far as the isolationists were politically potent, they could not have defended their ideas for long against the forces of the administration.

Roosevelt's diplomats argued that a nazified Western Europe would pose a direct threat to the security of the American way of life. Politically and economically, they believed, the United States was dependent on democratic capitalist supremacy in Europe. The isolationists countered that the United States could survive and prosper if diplomats concentrated on unifying the Western Hemisphere. In fact, the Western Hemisphere was not a viable political-economic unit in 1941. The commercial systems of many of the Latin American countries required trade with Western Europe that the United States could not duplicate. To permit German domination of Europe would ultimately affect the American interest in Latin America, something that no one contemplated. To be sure, the United States could use its power to restructure these trading arrangements drastically and so orient the Latins away from their particular dependencies on Western European trade. This strategy called for a reorganization of the American economy and, probably, a state trading system, and no one wanted that either. As contestants for policymaking power, the isolationists could not in any event have ultimately emerged victorious, able to undertake a policy different from that of the interventionists, for they shared the same premises.

The coming of World War II showed Roosevelt at his worst. During the war he had a united elite behind him, and in planning for the peace he tried to ensure that he would not repeat Wilson's "mistakes." Consequently, the administration sought congressional cooperation in working out postwar programs. Harry Truman was not as conscious of Wilson's "errors" as Roosevelt, but he was more concerned that foreign policy be consensual and also stressed consultation with Congress.

The war provided the internationalists

with unbeatable reasoning. As Wilson foretold, World War II had come because the United States had acted irresponsibly after World War I; to prevent a third world war the United States must assume its responsibilities. Roosevelt and more importantly Truman and his cadre of policymakers used this argument against the isolationists. Interventionist victories in Congress through 1950 measured executive success.

American support for the United Nations is a weak guide to the activist political and economic posture of the United States after 1945, but it had great symbolic significance at the time. By assiduously cultivating Senate Republican leadership—most importantly Senator Arthur H. Vandenberg of Michigan—the Democratic administration secured an 89 to 2 Senate vote in favor of the United Nations Charter. This was the first victory for what became known as bipartisan foreign policy. With the help of Vandenberg and the strong Democratic leadership in the Senate under Tom Connally of Texas, the executive determined policy essentials in the early years of the Cold War. During this period Truman scored a number of apparent triumphs: the doctrine that bears his name, the Marshall Plan, and the North Atlantic Treaty Organization (introduced in the Senate by the Vandenberg Resolution).

There was, however, a serious weakness in the internationalism of the late 1940's. Its theoretic long-range goal was surely transformation of the communist system, but the practical aim of its practitioners was the economic and subsequent political rehabilitation of Western Europe. This strategy, however, was understood only by experts in the executive branch. Congressional support was gained by exaggerating the threat of militant communism; in fact, many in the House and Senate would have refused to vote for economic policies that they regarded as handouts. Lack of support for what it realistically wanted to achieve forced the administration to rely more and more on anticommunist rhetoric in passing its foreign policy.

The long-range consequences were disastrous. By overemphasizing the anticommunist strain of its diplomacy, the State Department left itself open to the charge that it was not acting in Asia, where the threat of communism was greatest. On many occasions Secretary of State Dean Acheson attempted to bypass this criticism—voiced more and more by congressional Republicans—by attempting to reassert the overriding importance of Western Europe to the United States. But Truman, Acheson, and their associates had created a climate in which this seemed more excuse than explanation; for the public and critical congressmen anticommunism, not Western Europe, was the priority of United States foreign policy. And Mao Tse-tung's defeat of the Kuomintang under Chiang Kai-shek in 1949 gave credibility to the notion that Truman and Acheson were not acting on their often-expressed anticommunist policies. When North Korea invaded South Korea in June 1950, congressional critics contended that the weakness of Truman administration diplomacy caused the outbreak of fighting.

During this time Senators John W. Bricker and Robert A. Taft of Ohio, William F. Knowland of California, and Kenneth Wherry of Nebraska led the attacks on Democratic policies. The House also interested itself in foreign policy as Representative Richard M. Nixon of California made a national reputation by flailing the Democrats. The often vicious charges coupled with the rise of McCarthyism—named after Senator Joseph McCarthy of Wisconsin—have led commentators to conclude that there was a distinction of principle between congressional Republicans and administration Democrats. This is a mistake. Much of the criticism was simply partisan. The Republican party muted its criticism when Dwight D. Eisenhower took over in 1953, although the diplomacy of his secretary of state, John Foster Dulles, duplicated Acheson's. Dulles concentrated on Western Europe and refused to involve the United States heavily in Asia. While he satisfied those fearful of communism in the Far East, he did so without acting. He merely intoned an anticommunism the style of which was almost that of religious fundamentalism, and he cleared the State Department of those with variant and more urbane styles. Moreover, while the Truman administration planted the seeds of its own decay by justifying its politico-economic policies in anticommunist terms, it thought this exaggeration a small price to pay. Truman and Acheson shared the vision of a totalitarian communist menace and shaped their decisions, finally, to bring about its demise. They differed from their opponents in having a more subtle and varied series of responses to the menace and in having a pressing set of practical goals. The ends of administration Democrats and congressional Republicans were the same.

Nothing illustrates this consonance better than the administration's response to the Korean War. Although Acheson had declared Korea outside the American defense perimeter, officials did not hesitate to commit the United States to war after the North Korean attack. Both the executive and the legislature viewed communism as a monolithic force; Moscow must get the message that Americans would no longer tolerate its expansion. Although congressmen complained that had the president acted wisely ealier, he would not have had to act heroically in 1950, they backed the American commitment. Some months later when General Douglas MacArthur decided that he could reunite Korea and score a victory for the West, the administration agreed. Truman and Acheson thought MacArthur untrustworthy, but they relished the idea of an inexpensive coup. MacArthur himself was a hero to congressional Republicans, and the general had dreams of glory that would carry him far beyond military command of the Pacific. When his reunification strategy proved impossible and Truman removed him, many pundits predicted that the administration would not survive. The boom for the old soldier did not last. After hearing MacArthur's views in detail, the decison-making elite quickly rallied around the administration, and even most of its vitriolic enemies in Congress cooled in their practical support for the general.

Whether or not a battle over principle, the fight between the legislature and the executive over anticommunist diplomacy was short-lived. From 1949 to 1952 there was much acrimonious debate, but then Eisenhower's victory silenced congressional critics. For all its troubles the Truman administration had created a framework in which Congress and the president operated harmoniously in working out foreign policy. Throughout the 1950's and much of the 1960's there was little opposition to executive initiative. Having formulated an acceptable public language for stating his policies, the president was free to do as he pleased in foreign affairs. It seemed that Truman had strengthened executive power and co-opted opponents by creating an intense homogeneity within the decision-making elite and a predisposition to leave policy to the president. Nonetheless, Truman had made it almost impossible for policymakers to speak candidly on international relations—especially for Democrats, a militant anticommunism was prerequisite in all discussions, and this limited options. For example, it was forbidden to speak of the diplomatic recognition of Red China. This sort of limitation indicated that executive discretion in foreign affairs existed within narrowly defined boundaries; that branch responded to congressional fears. The war in Vietnam demonstrated that to a large extent the crusading anticommunism that the China lobby had used to discredit Truman made the Asian adventurism of the 1960's feasible to Truman's Democratic heirs.

Here was a strange example of the homogeneity of view within the elite. Its eastern, and largely Democratic, segment was concerned with Europe, but that group ran the war in Vietnam. It has become a commonplace that Lyndon B. Johnson yielded to the sophistication of the Harvard-educated talent that he inherited from John F. Kennedy. These men, "the best and the brightest," carried out the fantasies of the congressional China lobby. So far as action is a measure of belief, they too saw part of the American destiny in the Orient. In fact, in the aftermath of the war, policymakers argued with one voice that the principles at stake in American involvement in Vietnam were sound—the United States was obligated to stop the spread of communism and wars of liberation. Diplomats claimed that the trouble was that the United States erred in the application of policy, used a set of techniques that were self-defeating, and misjudged its own public opinion and the will of the enemy. From Korea to Vietnam, Democrats in the executive and Republicans in the legislative branch agreed on basics; their feuds were in-house squabbles. Moreover, the president's power remained intact into the 1970's. In spite of disaffection with the Vietnam War that both branches finally felt, the presidents—in this case Johnson and

Nixon—continued to hold the reins in foreign affairs. Even when domestic scandals caused the disintegration of the second Nixon administration, the president continued to score apparent successes in the international arena. Henry Kissinger, initially Nixon's foreign policy adviser and then secretary of state under both Nixon and his successor, Gerald R. Ford, enjoyed undisputed leadership in formulating foreign policy.

The defeat in Vietnam and the weakening of executive leadership as a result of the Watergate scandals did lead Congress to attempt to limit the executive's war-making powers. And along with this went a critique of one-man diplomacy. But in the broad context of the growth of presidential power in the twentieth century—especially in international affairs—these events appeared as significant as the neutrality legislation in the 1930's. In the long run it was doubtful that executive power would be compromised; in the short run the essence of the dispute was not the principles of policy but who should formulate the principles. The second half of the twentieth century witnessed the tacit consent of the decision-making elite to accord the executive undivided responsibility in the diplomatic sphere.

BIBLIOGRAPHY

Richard W. Leopold's influential text, *The Growth of American Foreign Policy: A History* (New York, 1965), is organized around the theme of executive-legislative conflict and presents the best statement of the standard analysis. A classic rendering of the argument that policy has been mishandled because of congressional interference is George Kennan, *American Diplomacy, 1900–1950* (Chicago, 1951). The limited nature of recent displeasure with presidential autonomy in foreign policy may be measured by analyzing Arthur Schlesinger, Jr., *The Imperial Presidency* (Boston, 1973). A case study illuminating the most intense congressional-executive rivalry is Richard M. Fried, *Men Against McCarthy* (New York, 1976). Useful on modern developments is James A. Robinson, *Congress and Foreign Policy-Making,* rev. ed. (Homewood, Ill., 1967).

[*See also* Anti-Imperialism; Bipartisanship; The Constitution and Foreign Policy; Dissent in Wars; Elitism and Foreign Policy; Executive Agreements; Isolationism; Presidential Power in Foreign Affairs; Public Opinion; Treaties.]

CONSCRIPTION

Thomas C. Kennedy

CONSCRIPTION, the compulsory enrollment of men for the performance of military duties, is a policy of long standing in American history. It has also been the object of frequent controversy over the means of its implementation and the ends contemplated for those individuals who were drafted for military service.

The statutes of nearly all the thirteen colonies (beginning with Virginia in 1629 and with the exception of the Quaker colony of Pennsylvania) imposed a military obligation upon all able-bodied men ranging from sixteen to sixty years of age. Before the War for American Independence, about two hundred acts embodying the principle of compulsory service in militias were passed by colonial legislatures. These militias were intended for defense against the French or Spanish and their Indian allies on the frontier.

Those colonies, including Pennsylvania, which sought to sever political ties with Great Britain, adopted the policy of drafting "citizen soldiers" to wage war against the British, their Indian allies, and Hessian mercenaries. Despite the "minuteman" mystique of a widespread voluntary commitment to fight for independence from the crown, many problems were encountered in securing enough well-trained soldiers to serve with the Continental army—problems that would appear in nearly every war in the history of the United States.

On 18 July 1775 the Continental Congress resolved that state legislatures organize all able-bodied men between the ages of sixteen and fifty into militia units that would support the Continental army of volunteers. But under the Articles of Confederation, Congress lacked the authority to exact compliance. Some states, such as Virginia, encountered open, and occasionally violent, resistance in their efforts to draft men for militia service. Further, there were instances when, in order to avoid the draft, an individual could hire a substitute or pay a fine for not answering the call. Bounties were also resorted to as an inducement to enroll volunteers. Yet, according to one estimate, about one-half of the militia troops who served during the Revolutionary War deserted. As a result, the number of soldiers in the Continental army varied from 47,000 to as low as 2,000.

On the eve of the nation's birth, then, a number of controversial themes associated with conscription had appeared that would be revived in future debates concerning the raising of armed forces: the principle of compulsory versus voluntary enlistment; the inequities in the selection of those who would have to fight; the issue of central versus local, that is, state, authority; and the adequacy of a large volunteer professional army versus a citizen army (militia or National Guard) plus a small regular army to be used only in times of emergency.

Given the problems he encountered in prosecuting the war against the British, George Washington in 1783 reflected on how to reduce these problems in the future. He personally objected to the idea of a large standing army in peacetime, believing that it could be "dangerous to the liberties of a Country," and because "Our distance from the European States in a great degree frees us of apprehension, from their numerous regular forces and the Insults and dangers which are to be dreaded from their Ambition. . . ." In expressing such sentiments, Washington formulated two basic points that would be reiterated in the continuing dialogue on the nature of the military establishment in the United States: (1) a great concern for the freedoms of civilian society, and (2) a general sense of security owing to the absence of truly strong nations on the North American continent. He recommended, however, that on the principle "every Citizen who enjoys the protection of a free Government, owes . . . his personal services to the defence of it," that a small regular army of fewer than 3,000 men be established, which would be reinforced by a national militia of all able-bodied men between the ages of eighteen and fifty. They would be "in such a condition as that they may appear truly respectable in the Eyes of our Friends and formidable to those who would otherwise become our enemies. . . ." In short, Washington regarded conscription as an aspect of deterrence in the foreign policy of the infant nation.

A small standing army, national in scope, was sanctioned by the Constitution of 1787, with the states still retaining full control over their militia units. The principle of antimilitarism was clearly set forth in provisions that called for civilian supremacy over the military, especially the notion of the president as a civilian commander in chief who was responsible to Congress. In translating this constitutional mandate into policy, Congress approved the Militia Act of 1792. This legislation, however, did not grant the federal government authority to supervise state militias. Since members of the militias had to furnish their own equipment, and since those who refused to participate in militia programs were not subjected to stipulated penalties, the idea of an effective national militia became what has been called a "phantom citizen army."

During the War of 1812 the military value of the Militia Act of 1792 was confronted with its first major test and, on balance, was found wanting. The real burden of day-to-day fighting was shouldered by the regular army. To be sure, it was supported by thousands of enrolled militia; but they served for varying tours of duty, some as brief as one to twelve weeks, and often without distinction.

Following the British attack on the nation's capital in August 1814, the James Madison administration regarded the military manpower situation as grave enough to warrant a conscription proposal of 40,000 militiamen to serve for two years. This proposal represented "the first instance in which a central government in a federal state claimed the authority to reach down without regard to state boundaries, into the homes of the citizenry and to force the able-bodied men to enter the national army."

The administration's bill encountered stiff congressional opposition, led by Daniel Webster of Massachusetts in the House. In an impassioned antidraft speech (9 December 1814) Webster not only rejected the bill as unconstitutional, but insisted it was "incompatible with any notion of personal liberty." The latter idea would repeatedly be proclaimed by the majority of future anticonscription spokesmen.

Shortly after Webster's speech a report of the Hartford Convention objected to the proposal as "destructive of the liberties of the people." Another major concern of the convention's participants was the issue of states' rights, for it was feared that the central government's unlimited power of conscription "would permit it to take control over all militiamen and thus destroy the rightful power of the several states." Word of the Treaty of Ghent (December 1814), ending the War of 1812, was received before the bill could be submitted to a full vote of the House and Senate. Thus, a bona fide congressional ruling on conscription would not be rendered until the Civil War.

In the interim the Mexican War furnished the next important test of the adequacy of America's military posture. In addition to the troops of the regular army, volunteers and organized militia units proved to be sufficient to secure victory. The option of serving a twelve-month tour of duty rather than for the duration of the war, however, found thousands of volunteer troops resigning at critical times. This was most notable in the case of General Winfield Scott losing the effective manpower of two companies and seven of his eleven regiments (about 4,000 men) when he was within a few days of reaching Mexico City.

In spite of the growing sectional tensions of the 1850's, "neither the North nor the South made any detailed plans for manpower procurement." When the Civil War became a reality, leaders on both sides believed that it would be of short duration and that traditional means of securing military personnel (the small regular army, organized militia, and volunteers) would bring success to their cause. But the magnitude and indecisive nature of the conflict during the first year shocked the Confederacy and the Union into the adoption of conscription.

The South led the way on 16 April 1862, by passing the first bill in American history that gave a central government authority to conscript troops, even from state militias. The action of Jefferson Davis' administration was a measure not only of the seriousness of manpower requirements, but was fraught with a supreme irony: secession had been justified, in part, on the principle of the supremacy of the sovereign state. This contradiction in Southern political theory was not overlooked by the governors of Georgia and North Carolina, who obstructed or thwarted the efficient operation of the draft. Even the South's vice-president, Alexander Stephens, along with other Confederate officials, opposed the principle of conscription.

But it was the North's conscription act (3 March 1863) that elicited the greatest protests, including the bloody New York City draft riot of 13–16 July 1863, which has been described as "the most violent episode of civil insurrection in American history." As was true of less violent demonstrations against this legislation throughout the North, the New York riot was aimed against the manifest inequities of the draft, particularly the possibility of hiring a substitute, which necessarily resulted in greater jeopardy and hardships for the poor males in Northern society. The Union's draft law also raised the question, for the first time in a significant fashion, of conscientious objection to military service on religious grounds. While no provision was included for such a status in the original act, an amendment was added in February 1864 which allowed individuals who objected for religious reasons to be released from combat service. Instead, they had the options of hospital duty or the payment of a $300 commutation fee, which would be earmarked for the care of wounded soldiers.

The resort to the draft, of course, was intended to preserve the Union, not to defend the country from possible foreign invasion. But James Gordon Bennett, the editor of the *New York Herald,* initially an opponent of the bill for its alleged unconstitutionality, perceived possible diplomatic implications shortly after its passage. On the assumption that a greatly enlarged army would be raised through conscription, he believed this would have the effect of convincing both the Confederacy and Great Britain that the North possessed the strength and determination "to supress the rebellion even in the face of foreign intervention."

The conclusion of the Civil War ushered in a three-decade period of decreasing interest in military affairs. This was due to a greater concern with Reconstruction, settlement of the Great Plains West, and economic expansion, accompanied by few foreign threats to the security of the United States. Accordingly, the regular army averaged about 26,000 men, and participation in the organized militia diminished appreciably.

Similar to the Mexican War, the Spanish-American War resulted in notable territorial acquisitions. As in the earlier conflict, the regular army, volunteers, and units from the organized militia (that is, the National Guard) amply met the manpower needs required to wage the brief "splendid little war." Indeed, two-thirds of the 225,000 men who were prepared to free Cuba and the Philippines from Spanish rule never had to leave the United States. Although American army and naval forces had little difficulty in defeating Spain, a number of administrative and structural deficiencies in the army were revealed during the war. Consequently, Secretary of War Elihu Root promoted a number of reforms to modernize the army and place it "on the soundest footing in its peacetime history."

The beginning of World War I in the summer of 1914, however, raised the question of whether America's forces-in-being were enough to ensure the defense of the nation against potential threats from the war in Europe. In December 1914 President Woodrow Wilson assured Congress that the nation could still rely on volunteers backed by the National Guard. He pointedly rejected the idea of any program that might result in a large standing army that could turn the United States into a "military camp." The majority in Congress and among the people, until April 1917, concurred with the president's judgment that peacetime conscription in the form of universal military training was unnecessary. But the problems of maintaining America's neutral posture in the face of British and German violations of maritime rights encouraged a preparedness program. The upshot was increased naval appropriations and, in the National Defense Act of 1916, the enlargement of the number of men who could voluntarily enlist in the regular army or National Guard units.

Before April 1917 the public dialogue on the appropriate size of the American army and the principle of voluntary versus compulsory military service almost always focused on what would be an adequate army to defend the nation and its overseas territories. But in November 1916 Charles Eliot, president emeritus of Harvard University, published an article recommending universal military training. He related it to what he believed should be an ongoing concern with foreign policy goals. "The United States," he wrote, "having become an industrial and commercial world power, needs to have all the seas and oceans of the world open for its foreign trade in times of peace, and so far as is practicable in time of war also." Eliot asserted that the Atlantic and Pacific oceans could no longer guarantee America's security. He then urged the establishment of "a Navy powerful in every respect, and an Army in reserve visibly strong in numbers and visibly prepared for immediate service" against "any military Power which might assail" the United States "for purposes of conquest or ransom." Such an army and navy would also avoid "the great waste of lives and money which has taken place at the beginning of every war in which the United States has been engaged since the government was organized."

On 6 April 1917, when the House of Representatives endorsed Wilson's request for a declaration of war against Germany, the administration sent a conscription law to the Congress. Opposition to the draft was not as strong as in the War of 1812 and the Civil War. But the traditional objection to compulsory service at the behest of the federal government did have its advocates who, like Speaker of the House Champ Clark, may have felt there was "precious little difference between a conscript and a convict." The bill nonetheless was approved by substantial majorities in both Houses and signed by the president on 18 May 1917.

There was some resistance to, or evasion of, the draft—over 300,000 men were involved. On the whole, however, the registration and induction of draftees was successful, even if there were no important combat contributions to the European theater of war until the spring of 1918. The lessons of the bitter experiences of the Civil War draft—the way in which it was administered and its numerous inequities—had been heeded and avoided. This resulted in the conscription of nearly three million men who constituted about two-thirds of America's armed forces in World War I, a stark contrast to the six percent who were draftees in the Civil War. But there were many sincere conscientious objectors who, in the atmosphere of the "great crusade" and the anti–civil liberties mood of the nation, were jailed (sometimes under inhumane conditions) until two years after the armistice and did not have their civil rights fully restored until 1933, when President Franklin D. Roosevelt granted them a Christmas amnesty. The constitutionality of the conscription bill was also challenged during the war. It was upheld by the Supreme Court in *Arver* v. *U.S.* (January 1918) as a legitimate exercise of the war-making powers of the Congress and as not contrary to the prohibition of involuntary servitude under the Thirteenth Amendment.

The desire to "return to normalcy," to abide by the biblical injunction to "beat swords into plowshares," and the traditional antimilitarist spirit effectively ruled out serious consideration during the 1920's of any universal military training program. This attitude prevailed throughout much of the 1930's, when the economic and social dislocations wrought by the Great Depression absorbed the thoughts and energies of the majority of Americans. But the aggressive warfare of the Axis Powers in Asia and Europe finally set the stage for a major debate on conscription during peacetime. This was a debate, moreover, in which the possible bearing of a large conscript army on present and future foreign policies was more candidly and frequently discussed than ever before in American history.

The initial major step toward enlarging the military strength of the United States was signaled by President Franklin D. Roosevelt's request of Congress in January 1938 for a substantial increase in military and naval appropriations. Coming soon after the president's quarantine-of-aggressors speech (October 1937) and the inability to secure House passage of the Ludlow amendment to the Constitution requiring a national referendum before a declaration of war (except in case of attack), this call for additional military expenditures encountered vigorous opposition from many quarters. In two days of testimony before the House Committee on Naval Affairs, historian Charles A. Beard charged that the president's recommendation could lead to "aggressive warfare in the Far Pacific or the Far Atlantic." He also ridiculed speculations in which "Fascist goblins of Europe are pictured as marching across the Atlantic to Brazil."

A similar verdict was rendered by four members of the committee, whose minority report on the bill questioned the need for three more battleships at a cost of $75 million each. Also challenged was the administration's contention that the legislation was intended solely for defensive purposes. They charged that it was diplomatic in nature and not just naval defense, concluding: "If this bill is passed the President will have a blanket authorization after Congress adjourns to apply the universal-quarantine policy and Asiatic interventionist policy." The objections to naval expansion notwithstanding, the bill passed both houses of Congress in May 1938. This decision seemed to have the consent of a majority of Americans. In the early summer of 1938, 74 percent of those polled by the Gallup organization favored naval expansion.

The issue of conscription for the army still had not been faced. With the beginning of World War II in September 1939, the regular army of 180,000 men was extremely small (about 15 million men served in all the armed services in the course of the war). In December 1939 the Gallup poll suggested that only 37 percent of the populace approved of a program of universal military training. But the German offensive in the spring of 1940, culminating in the surrender of France in June 1940, found 64 percent of those interviewed (in a poll published on 23 June 1940) in favor of such a measure. Possibly encouraged by this sign of uneasiness over German military success, in the second week of July 1940, President Roosevelt sent a message to Congress asking for the enactment of a conscription bill, a request subsequently endorsed by Wendell L. Willkie, Roosevelt's Republican opponent in the election of 1940.

This sense of bipartisanship concerning an issue bearing on national security and foreign policy encountered significant opposition. The critics included pacifists; some isolationists; and prominent leaders in the religious, academic, journalistic, and labor communities who feared the militaristic, allegedly antidemocratic, and aggressive warfare implications of the draft law. Supporters of the measure disputed the validity of these views and argued that the nation should not wait for an attack before adopting adequate defense measures. The result of the debate was the passage of the Selective Training and Service Act (Burke-Wadsworth bill) by decisive majorities in the summer of 1940. On 16 September Roosevelt signed the bill into law—the country's first peacetime conscription legislation. On that same day the selective service agency was established to mobilize the nation's manpower. The text of the bill avowed defensive purposes only and called for a maximum of 900,000 men to be inducted at any one time; the duration of service was to be limited to one year; and draftees could not serve outside the Western Hemisphere. The legislation was also more liberal than previous conscription proposals in that it permitted conscientious objectors, whose "religious training and belief" forbade participation in any warlike activity, to engage in some alternative service under civilian, not military, supervision. The 1940 bill was amended in August 1941 to extend by eighteen months the term of service of the initial draftees, a controversial proposal that saw the House give its approval by only a one-vote majority.

The total nature of World War II, plus the widespread acceptance of the idea that the United States would have to play a leading role in maintaining world peace after the defeat of the Axis Powers, encouraged a public discussion about the implementation of a universal military training system even before the surrender of Germany and Japan. The intensity of the debate was heightened by a growing sense of insecurity stemming from the development of new weapons of war, such as long-range airplanes and rockets, plus the advent of the nuclear age.

Opponents of such a program argued that it

was premature to consider compulsory military service in peacetime before the war had ended. They questioned whether postwar conscription of any type was essential to world peace and believed it would be inconsistent with the principles of the Atlantic Charter (1941). Peace groups contended, moreover, that "the passage of Universal Military Training would surrender the goals of the war and lead to future conflicts." Assuming the unconditional surrender of all the Axis Powers, other critics wondered against what nations a large standing army presumably would be needed for defense. The implication was that our current allies, most notably the Soviet Union, seemed the only possible "enemies."

Congress would not agree to a universal training program, but did approve extension of the selective service system into the postwar period. The renewed acceptance of the idea of peacetime conscription stemmed from three major factors: (1) the necessity for occupation forces in defeated nations; (2) growing concern about U.S.–Soviet cold war tensions; and (3) a change in the traditional view of conscription. In regard to the latter, Arthur A. Ekirch, Jr., observed:

> In general, American public opinion followed the lead of the [Truman] administration. Under the impact of World War II, the American people largely discarded the antimilitarist convictions of the past. . . . The task of securing a genuine internationalism, based on the ideals of peace and world patriotism, instead of militarism and war, was to be the chief heritage and the continuing problem of the postwar years [*The Civilian and the Military* (1956), p. 270].

The 1940 draft act, as extended, was allowed to expire on 31 March 1947, soon after President Harry S. Truman asserted his doctrine that would implement a policy of containing what were believed to be Russian expansionist ambitions toward Greece and Turkey. The administration hoped to replace the selective service with a program of universal training. Once again, neither the Congress nor the American people were prepared to take such an unprecedented step. A Selective Service Act, however, was passed and then signed into law by the president on 24 June 1948, the very day Stalin began the Berlin blockade. In the same month the Senate approved U.S. affiliation with regional security pacts, an endorsement that was implemented in America's membership in the North Atlantic Treaty Organization the following year.

The 1948 draft law was close to its expiration date when the Korean War began in June 1950. Congress renewed the act for one year, after which it placed the selective service system on a permanent basis in 1951. Thereafter, for more than a decade, "renewals of the legislation provoked only brief, cursory debate."

By the mid-1960's, the nation's deepening military involvement in the Vietnam War provoked bitter criticism of the conduct of the war (particularly after the Communist Tet offensive of February 1968) and the nature of American foreign policy in Asia. It also called into question the legitimacy of the draft itself. Complaints that had been voiced occasionally in the 1950's were expanded, especially the policy of deferments for occupational or academic status, with its built-in greater draft risks for racial minorities and lower socioeconomic groups. These concerns, although very real, were only the tip of the iceberg. More important were the fundamental doubts about the legality and morality of America's participation in the war.

Nevertheless, many of the objections to the war were centered on resistance to the draft, which saw thousands of young American men choosing exile in Canada or Sweden, the public burning of draft cards, and the destruction of records in some selective service offices. By the fall of 1967 a number of groups that had been engaging in uncoordinated activities against the draft organized "the resistance" for the express purpose of challenging the selective service system.

From 4 December to 7 December 1966 a conference on the problems of the draft was held at the University of Chicago. Of diverse political persuasions, the participants included distinguished individuals from the military, congressional, and academic communities. Numerous recommendations were made, such as a lottery or some form of national service as an alternative to the draft. On balance, most contributors questioned the need for the continuation of the draft in terms of national defense, foreign policy goals, fairness, and cost. Moreover, in view of certain experiences stemming from the Vietnam War by the late 1960's—a high desertion rate, a breakdown in discipline reflected in racial confrontations, significant drug addiction, and occasional violence against both commissioned and noncommissioned officers—some career army officers were not averse to the prospect of eliminating the draft in favor of a professional army. In the presidential campaign of 1968 Richard M. Nixon discussed the possibility of ending the draft, as had Senator Barry Goldwater in his bid for the presidency in 1964. The acceptance of such an idea by the late 1960's, then, was not confined to liberals or radicals on the Left, but spanned the political spectrum.

The postwar pattern of heavy reliance on conscription was finally set aside when Secretary of Defense Melvin Laird announced on 27 January 1973 (the day the agreement ending the Vietnam War was signed in Paris): "I wish to inform you that the Armed Forces henceforth will depend exclusively on volunteer soldiers, sailors, airmen and Marines. Use of the draft has ended." This executive action did not mean that the selective service system was abolished, or that those who were registered were relieved of any potential military obligation. But by 1976 the federal agency had been cut back considerably in budget (by 80 percent to less than $7 million in fiscal 1977) and in personnel (from 2,000 to about 100 employees), who continued to plan for emergency preparedness procedures. Moreover, no further draft cards were issued owing to the decision to rely on the National Guard and reserve troops to support the regular army forces of about two and one-half million during the early stages of any crisis that might require additional manpower mobilization.

In the year of America's bicentennial as a nation, then, it had set aside the active program, if not entirely the principle, of conscription in peacetime. This policy was certainly in accord with the traditional ideal of a maximum of individual freedom in a democratic society. It was also a pragmatic policy; the country probably would not condone diplomatic commitment and military involvement to the extent that marked relations in Southeast Asia in the 1960's and early 1970's. Whether dependence upon an all-volunteer armed forces can fulfill the requirements of national defense and foreign policy goals desired by the government and people of the United States undoubtedly will be determined by ever-changing international events and how they affect the national interest.

BIBLIOGRAPHY

The United States Selective Service has issued reports of the director and special monographs on various aspects of its policies and operations since 1942 (Washington, D.C.). Other primary sources are the papers, letters, and memoirs of presidents and other political figures who held office when conscription and other forms of military manpower procurement legislation were contemplated. The *Congressional Record* contains the views of congressmen and senators on such legislation. Valuable in compiling this brief survey were Robert E. Summers and Harrison B. Summers, comps., *Universal Military Service* (New York, 1941); Julia E. Johnson, comp., *Peacetime Conscription* (New York, 1945); and John O'Sullivan and Alan M. Meckler, eds., *The Draft and Its Enemies: A Documentary History* (Urbana, Ill., 1974). Special studies that were consulted for diversity of opinion include John F. Leach, *Conscription in the United States: Historical Background* (Rutland, Vt., 1952), a strong endorsement of the principle and policy of conscription; Arthur A. Ekirch, Jr., *The Civilian and the Military* (New York, 1956), an indictment of trends the author perceived toward "a garrison state" following World War II; James M. Gerhardt, *The Draft and Public Policy: Issues in Military Manpower Procurement, 1945–1970* (Columbus, Ohio, 1971), a balanced appraisal of the administrative, political, financial, foreign policy, and of public opinion problems associated with conscription; and Michael Usem, *Conscription, Protest and Social Conflict: The Life and Death of a Draft Resistance Movement* (New York, 1974), a sociological analysis. The conflicting views and proposals presented in December 1966 at the University of Chicago conference on the draft are in Sol Tax, ed., *The Draft: A Handbook of Facts and Alternatives* (Chicago, 1967). The debate is sharply drawn in Thomas Reeves and Karl Hess, *The End of the Draft: A Proposal for Abolishing Conscription and for a Volunteer Army* (New York, 1970); and Harry A. Marmion, *The Case Against a Volunteer Army* (Chicago, 1971). Works on conscientious objection to conscription prior to the Vietnam War may be found in Hi Doty, *Bibliography of Conscientious Objection to War* (Philadelphia, 1954). For studies in the late 1960's and early 1970's consult Gordon C. Zahn, *War, Conscience, and Dissent* (New York, 1967); and Murray Polner, ed., *When Can I Come Home? A Debate on Amnesty for Exiles, Antiwar Prisoners, and Others* (Garden City, N.Y., 1972).

[*See also* AMERICAN ATTITUDES TOWARD WAR; THE COLD WAR; CONGRESS AND FOREIGN POLICY; DISSENT IN WARS; MILITARISM; NATIONAL SECURITY; PACIFISM; PEACE MOVEMENTS; PRESIDENTIAL POWER IN FOREIGN AFFAIRS.]

CONSENSUS HISTORY AND FOREIGN POLICY

Lloyd C. Gardner

THE term "consensus history" usually refers to a trend that developed after World War II in writings about American history. Consensus historians supposedly were reacting against the Progressive tradition, which had dominated the field for more than three decades, and which had reached its height with the publication of Charles and Mary Beard's *The Rise of American Civilization* (1927). The Beards' discussion centered on conflict (class, sectional, and racial) as the principal theme in American history. Where Progressive historians saw ideological divisions and bitter antagonism, the consensus writers found instead a remarkable degree of social and political cohesiveness in America's past, especially when compared with the European experience.

But like many phrases that historians bandy about, "consensus history" proves elusive when one attempts to pin it down to specifics. For one thing, consensus historians did not agree among themselves about the sources or the meaning of America's conflict-free experience. Were there really no issues in American politics worthy of the name, or was the consensus really built upon evading the issues by a series of temporary expedients? And what about the Civil War? Did the consensus break down in that instance, or was the war fought because a blundering generation of politicians failed to contain the near-psychotic outbursts of an abolitionist minority? Was American imperialism at the turn of the century based on the cheerful, assertive spirit of Horatio Alger, or determined by the gloomy dictates of Freudian maladjustment? Consensus historians argued both sides of each of these questions.

As is often the case, therefore, it is far easier to talk about what the consensus historians disagreed with than to demonstrate a consensus within their own writing. Richard Hofstadter's justly famous *The American Political Tradition* (1948) is sometimes taken as a beginning point for consensus history, although other works (including some of Hofstadter's later writings) probably have an equal claim. However that may be, Hofstadter's debunking of Progressive myths, his insistence upon seeing Jefferson and his heirs not as ideological opponents of Hamiltonian capitalists—knights of the sacred plow, as it were—but opportunists who succeeded in blurring the issues to their own advantage, quickly made his volume one of the most influential and widely read texts of the entire postwar era.

While Hofstadter deplored the consensus that he saw in the past as a form of intellectual bankruptcy, that is, the domination of political thought by popular mythology, others found in it reason for celebration. Later, Louis Hartz described *The Liberal Tradition in America* (1955), which he ascribed to the complete absence of a feudal system in the nation's past: "It is not accidental that America which has uniquely lacked a feudal tradition has uniquely lacked also a socialist tradition." In *People of Plenty* (1954) David Potter wrote about the American character and its shaping by economic abundance. In Potter's view, abundance was not an unmixed blessing, but its problems and discontents were different in both quantity and quality from those confronting other societies: "Our democratic system, which, like other systems, can survive only when its ideals are realized, survived because an economic surplus was available to pay democracy's promissory notes."

Another way of looking at consensus history is to replace it within the postwar context out of which it emerged. It then becomes a Cold War phenomenon. This is an oversimplification, of course, but it suggests a relevant line of inquiry. Faced with a powerful ideological challenge, American historians (and other intellectuals) reacted by proclaiming the immunity of their country to Marxist historical materialism. Interestingly enough, Hofstadter's critique originated in a Marxist tradition, but it centered on idols of American leftists. And in later essays Hofstadter specifically ruled out the possibility of a Leninist interpretation of American imperialism. Other consensus historians simply assumed that the absence of a feudal tradition or the presence of material abundance protected America from socialist diseases. The more the Soviet Union insisted upon the class struggle, the more Americans would deny it.

In an era of "total diplomacy," as Secretary of State Dean Acheson once described his times, consensus history (whatever the historians themselves intended) served the cause. The Progressive tradition, which had come close to idealizing protest movements as a substitute for the European proletariat, had to be abandoned. It was even posited that the most famous of these movements, Populism, which perhaps came the closest to uniting workers and agrarians or sharecroppers in a single political party, was actually a forerunner of McCarthyism—without question the most reactionary and self-defeating of the anticommunist crusades the nation endured during the early Cold War years.

That was really standing Progressive historiography on its head. Having erased all those conventional assertions of Populist moral superiority and political wisdom, the consensus historians drew a new line starting from the narrow and revivalistic rhetoric they insisted revealed the true nature of Populism in the 1890's, then tracing it through the nativistic resurgence of rural America in the 1920's, to put the final dot on the frustrated modern-day inhabitants of Sinclair Lewis' *Main Street* and the surrounding area. (Comparative historians noted similar phenomena among anticapitalist peasant movements in late nineteenth-century Japan and China. In their haste to condemn American Populists, consensus historians perhaps missed the wider significance of their own insights. But they would not have welcomed evidence that suggested that American agrarian protests had something in common with those in other developing countries and were directly related to the painful transition to modern capitalism. Such a discovery would tend to undermine the all-important consensus argument that American political institutions and economic development were unique. For a brief discussion, see the bibliographical essay at the end of this article.) Not only was the American Left deprived of a serious tradition, but it was blamed for inculcating a rightist movement of serious proportions by its foolish insistence upon making the Know-Nothing Populists into heroic harbingers of socialism.

Later researchers found much evidence to dispute this interpretation, and to reestablish the Populists as reasonable men and women who posed rational (whether reformist or radical was another question) alternatives to contemporary modes of economic behavior and organization. But the consensus historians had started everyone thinking about this, as well as other problems, once thought settled. Sometimes the results were unexpected. This was especially true in the area of American foreign policy. Critics of the Cold War discovered in consensus viewpoints a possible foundation for a new understanding of the history of the nation's foreign relations.

Traditional interpretations had emphasized the abrupt changes in mood and policy in the conduct of American foreign policy over the years. If there was a consensus among diplomatic historians, it centered on this point: It almost seemed as if the United States were stuck in a revolving door, forever being pushed into internationalism but spinning back just as fast into isolationism. The Progressive movement in American historical writing had had but little impact upon foreign policy specialists. In large part the explanation was that diplomatic history, as a separate field of study, attracted few scholars, and precious few more students, before World War II. A "course" in American diplomatic history might be offered now and then, perhaps as the second half of a history of the West, but it was regarded as a luxury. Doctorates in American diplomatic history were rarer still, and most of the published work in the area was undertaken by men who started out in something else.

The first edition of Thomas A. Bailey's *A Diplomatic History of the American People* appeared in 1940. No other diplomatic history text has ever approached its popularity, although the field has become relatively crowded in recent years. Superbly written, the book often overcame even bad classroom teaching to interest college students in long-neglected foreign policy subjects. Various specific interpretations of events and trends changed from edition to edition, but the author's point of departure remained the same: "The American people themselves, by expressing their attitudes and desires, decide fundamental policies or objectives. The executive branch, by framing specific courses of action, provides implementing policies or tactics."

The task that Bailey set himself, as did other diplomatic historians concerned about their country, as much as or more than their academic speciality, was the education of the public so that the revolving-door effect would not destroy every initiative the nation's farsighted leaders developed in response to the better instincts of the people. The struggle was always against isolationism. Interestingly, isolationism was, in turn, always associated with the less noble attributes of the American character: smugness, complacency, selfishness, and even indolence, or unwillingness to bear the burdens that circumstances, or God, had plainly intended Americans to carry. For this generation of diplomatic historians, really the first group large enough to be called a generation, World War I and the struggle to secure American entrance into the League of Nations were the central events of their times.

Woodrow Wilson's effort to "practice what he preached" in foreign affairs generally received high marks in these works, and was almost always contrasted favorably with Theodore Roosevelt's bullying Big Stick treatment of the smaller republics of the Western Hemisphere and William Howard Taft's unseemly enlistment of Wall Street bankers in support of dollar diplomacy. But Wilson failed grievously. Samuel Flagg Bemis summed up the disappointment felt by diplomatic historians: "In his successful attempt to get the League of Nations written into the treaty [of Versailles], Woodrow Wilson had made great concessions from his principles to the national interests of Great Britain, France, Italy, and Japan. Now he would not make necessary concessions to his political opponents at home."

While Wilson's Calvinist stubbornness in dealing with Republican senators (and some from his own party) was often cited in accounts of the defeat of the Versailles treaty in America, those same concessions—cited by Bemis—to the national interests of European powers and Japan had also lost the president votes in the Senate. There thus appeared a real dilemma in the midst of the newly developing tradition in American diplomatic history. Since the objectives of American foreign policy were assumed to be (with a few embarrassing exceptions such as the Mexican War) peace, prosperity, and humanitarianism, how could Wilson have compromised with the national interests of other powers and yet have retained the support of his idealistic followers at home?

During World War II the dilemma fell with full force on Franklin Delano Roosevelt. One set of advisers urged the president not to have anything to do with "secret treaties," the bargains that America's allies in World War I had made among themselves and to which Wilson had to make concessions at Paris. A lesser number wished him to deal frankly and openly with his allies on the basis of a mutual recognition of spheres of influence. Undoubtedly, Roosevelt felt tremendous pressure. His offhand remark that it had been a mistake to keep written records of the Big Four discussions at the Paris Peace Conference more than implied a recognition of the two-way pressure bearing down on him during the Big Three meetings of World War II.

Wilson's ghost sat beside Roosevelt at Teheran and Yalta. Sometimes it reminded him that, having taken the lead against the Axis Powers ideologically, he could not fall short of "self-determination" for all nations. At other moments it seemed to be cautioning him against repeating Wilson's mistakes. Roosevelt's inclination to compromise, and the realization that other nations did have national interests, led him to accept a flawed solution to several questions that would later become major Cold War issues. He passed off many of these compromises as temporary expedients, as though he wanted to hide them from everyone.

In his public statements, however, the president always insisted that the peace he sought, and the peace he was achieving with the aid of the Soviet Union and Great Britain, was a Wilsonian peace. After Yalta, in his last major address to Congress, the president asserted that the Big Three decisions at the meeting spelled the end "of the system of unilateral action and exclusive alliances and spheres of influence and balances of power and all the other expedients which have been tried for centuries—and have failed."

Picking up on Roosevelt's assurances, Bailey wrote: "Soviet darkness gradually enshrouded Rumania, Bulgaria, Albania, and Hungary, as Moscow-manipulated stooges took command. Washington, appealing to Stalin's unredeemed pledges at Yalta, lodged repeated protests with Moscow against coercion and intimidation. But in Soviet thinking security ranked higher than capitalistic conceptions of honor." Bemis, however, came down hard on the other side, raising the matter of secret agreements at Yalta and Roosevelt's ultimate responsibility for negotiating them and their consequences. Bemis wrote:

> To be sure, in return for these concessions Stalin pledged support to the Chinese Nationalist Government and democratic principles in the liberated states in Eastern Europe and elsewhere—just as Chamberlain received guaranties from Hitler at Munich not to advance any farther in Europe after taking part of Czechoslovakia. Perhaps placing this promise of Stalin's on record for these principles was a most important moral factor in the great issues that were to follow. Nevertheless, in its aftermath of deception, Yalta was in a sense equivalent to another Munich [*A Short History of American Foreign Policy and Diplomacy* (New York, 1959), p. 601].

The Wilson-Roosevelt dilemma is reflected in the writing of American diplomatic history, and in the basic assumptions historians share with policymakers about the sources and nature of the nation's political system and the direction it is going. We have already touched upon one of these: the battle against isolationism. From the time of the revolution, it is argued, the United States preferred and pursued an "isolationist" foreign policy. The Monroe Doctrine was no exception to this generalization, since it proclaimed to the world that America and Europe were separate—and should forevermore remain so. The War of 1812 and the Mexican War were like the Monroe Doctrine in that they were undertaken either to disengage America from Europe or to expand the area of security on the nation's borders.

World power was an unwanted obligation, thrust upon the United States at the turn of the century. In fact, all the major influences upon the nation's foreign policy have been external. Throughout most of its history the United States has been reacting to outside events, not seeking involvement in the outside world's affairs. Only when physically endangered or actually attacked has the United States responded to its leaders' call to arms; otherwise it has preferred to remain at home.

With great reluctance, then, Americans fought in two world wars, bravely (if perhaps foolishly), without giving much thought to "international politics." But the battle against isolationism still had to be won. Senator Arthur Vandenberg admonished President Harry S. Truman in 1947 that he had to scare hell out of the country if he expected Congress to provide funds for Greece and Turkey in their efforts to resist Russian pressure and subversion. In what became known as the Truman Doctrine speech, the president declared that "it must be the policy of the United States to support free peoples who are resisting attempted subjugation by armed minorities or by outside pressures."

The original draft of the Truman Doctrine speech had contained references to the raw materials located in the area, but the president had these references taken out, fearing that his speech would read too much like an investment prospectus. It was not that Truman feared giving a propaganda bonanza to leftist critics so much as he was concerned about the need to convince Congress that Greece and Turkey were only part of a worldwide crisis. Anything that focused attention on details detracted from his purpose and would give the isolationists something to haggle about, thereby preventing prompt action.

Perhaps the most interesting aspect of the episode of the Truman Doctrine was the way in which both diplomatic historians and foreign policy spokesmen turned around references to the Monroe Doctrine in order to supply precedent for this startling new departure.

By common consent both internationalists and isolationists took the Monroe Doctrine as a statement of nonintervention, and took pride in its bold anticolonialism. Isolationists, however, could point out that President Monroe had promised to stay out of Greek affairs, and allow Europe to deal with that revolution, just as he expected Europe to stay out of American affairs and not seek to restore Spanish rule in Latin America.

In the months before Pearl Harbor, Dexter Perkins, another distinguished member of the original "group" of American diplomatic historians, proposed a modern interpretation of the Monroe Doctrine, which would be taken up again as the Cold War developed after the defeat of the Axis Powers. Perkins wrote in the *Yale Review* (July 1941):

> In the great debate between isolationists and advocates of aid to Britain, what have we to learn from the declaration of 1823? Superficially, the case may seem stronger for the isolationists. Monroe's message seems to draw a sharp line between the New World and the Old. It emphasizes the cleavage of the continents.
>
> But there is, it might be maintained, another side to the matter. The message of 1823 was one of the great pronunciamentos of the nineteenth century in the cause of free government as against despotism. It was a paean of praise of the democratic system. It drew a line of cleavage not only between geographical areas but between political systems, between republicanism and despotism.

Viewed from this angle, Perkins argued, the Monroe Doctrine "wears an aspect not so pleasing to the friends of isolation." While it was true that at the time of Monroe's declaration the ideal set forth in the message was almost exclusively an American ideal, during the course of the next one hundred years Great Britain had moved steadily in that direction. Great Britain had moved closer, to put it another way, to the ideological area of the Monroe Doctrine, and, therefore, deserved all the admiration and aid the United States could give to prevent a German triumph in Europe.

Truman made good use of this theme to justify American military aid to Greece and Turkey. Speaking at the annual Jefferson Day dinner on 5 April 1947, the president drew an appropriate parallel:

> When we hear the cry of freedom arising from the shores beyond our own, we can take heart from the words of Thomas Jefferson. In his letter to President Monroe, urging the adoption of what we now know as the Monroe Doctrine, he wrote: "Nor is the occasion to be slighted which this proposition offers of declaring our protest against the atrocious violations of the rights of nations by the interference of any one in the internal affairs of another."

The Perkins-Truman reformulation of the Monroe Doctrine seemed to work well for Europe, but what about Asia? Could the president have it both ways? Could he justify intervention in one area on the basis of Russian machinations and aggressiveness, yet allow a Communist victory in the Chinese civil war? Put another way: What, or where, were the limits of this new corollary to the Monroe Doctrine? The later history of the Cold War demonstrates how difficult it was to come to grips with this methodological and practical issue.

Neither diplomats nor scholars fared very well in the effort to resolve the problem. The closest anyone came was the word "containment." Taken from the private and published writings of George F. Kennan (especially "The Sources of Soviet Conduct," in *Foreign Affairs* [July 1947]), containment was shorthand for the author's argument that the United States should meet Russian aggression "by the adroit and vigilant application of counter-force at a series of constantly shifting geographical and political points." The containment policy, as Truman's approach soon became known, had the advantage that it satisfied commonly held beliefs about American foreign policy that were in most textbooks of the era. For example, it could be maintained that resistance to Soviet expansion was no different from containment of the German menace in World War I or stopping the Axis advance in World War II.

Of course the essential connection was that in each instance the United States was responding to an external challenge, thus fulfilling the dictum that America rests in quiet isolationism until forced into action. Presumably, containment also allowed choices as to where and how to apply the needed counterforce to thwart Russian ambitions. The only trouble was that there was hardly a place in the world that, viewed from the right perspective, lacked strategic value. Even Antarctica could not be abandoned, insisted some planners, at least not in the face of an imagined Soviet takeover.

Actually, a critique of containment as it applied to Asia had been delivered many years earlier, in 1938, when Secretary of State Cordell Hull explained why it was impossible for the United States to permit Japan to succeed in China. "In our opinion," he began, "an endeavor by any country in any part of the world to establish itself in favor of a preferred position in another country is incompatible with the maintenance of our own and the establishment of world prosperity." China's "loss" to communism set off the first major foreign policy debate of the Cold War. The answers found in textbooks were simply no longer sufficient: the battle against isolationism had at last been won. Something more was needed—a new consensus history to replace the old outworn orthodoxy.

If any work in diplomatic history occupies the same high place as Hofstadter's *American Political Tradition* in domestic history, it would have to be George Kennan's *American Foreign Policy, 1900–1950*. Kennan's book—actually a series of lectures delivered at the University of Chicago—departed sharply from the traditional view. What had once been seen as a noble and generous effort to bring about a decent world order now became a quixotic and meddlesome interference in other people's business. "I see the most serious fault of our past policy formulation," said Kennan, "to lie in something that I might call the legalistic-moralistic approach to international problems. This approach runs like a red skein through our foreign policy of the last fifty years."

Kennan riddled Wilson's legacy, called into question the nation's Asian policies from the Open Door to Pearl Harbor, and raised the problem of whether a democracy could conduct a consistent, realistic, foreign policy. Coming as it did in the aftermath of the China debacle and in the midst of the Korean War, the scholar-diplomat's book offered historians a way out of the impasse that had been reached by the traditionalists.

Moreover, the realist approach to American diplomatic history fit in well with the consensus view of political developments since 1789. In both interpretations serious issues took second place to symbols. Thus Kennan's discussion of John Hay and the origins of the Open Door policy concluded: "The formula had a high-minded and idealistic ring; it would sound well at home; it was obviously in the interests of American trade; the British had been known to advocate it—still did, so far as he knew—and it was hard to see what harm could come from trying it on the other powers." Without inquiring too closely into all the implications of what he was about to do, John Hay started the United States on the road to Pearl Harbor.

Kennan's critique appealed to some traditionalists because it supplied a ready answer to right-wing accusations that the United States had sold out China to the communists. For others, statements like the following were too extreme: "Behind all this, of course, lies the American assumption that the things for which other peoples in this world are apt to contend are for the most part neither creditable nor important and might justly be expected to take second place behind the desirability of an orderly world, untroubled by international violence." That was close—too close for many—to saying that the United States was an imperialist power, a high-minded imperialist power, to be sure, but nevertheless one which was prepared to enforce its particular vision upon the world.

Kennan's book even appealed to a relatively small group of left-wing critics who found in it the first systematic review of the nation's recent foreign policy that did not begin with the assumption that America never took the initiative but was always acted upon by other nations. Republican charges that containment was little better than appeasement or surrender on the installment plan, the fate of foreign service officers who had tried to tell the truth about China, and the general climate of the early 1950's made Kennan's conclusions seem more radical by comparison than they actually were. Where Kennan stopped—with a scalding comment on American diplomacy as the product of "the legal profession in our country" groping for an international framework compatible with Anglo-Saxon jurisprudence—leftist observers only began.

But if the traditional approach to the study of American foreign policy had become ensnarled in a trap of its own making (the "new" Monroe Doctrine), the realists also had difficulties to overcome. In the writings of Hans

Morgenthau national interest appeared even more clearly to be opposed to Wilsonian moralisms than was the case in *American Diplomacy, 1900–1950.* But how does one go about defining "national interest"? Kennan believed the open-door policy was unrealistic; Morgenthau saw it as the expression of a real interest in preventing the domination of China by a foreign power.

Realists seemed to want American statesmen to behave as if they were Europeans, vitally concerned with nuances in the balance of power. In reply, Dexter Perkins, in *Foreign Policy and the American Spirit* (1957), stressed examples of realism or "pragmatism," which demonstrated that Americans were not slaves to general theory or abstraction in developing their foreign policy. "On the whole, such a diplomacy as ours is sufficiently realistic to deal with the actual world and sufficiently idealistic to derive great strength from its idealism." America had made mistakes, added Perkins, but these were minor when compared with those made by the great dictators of the twentieth century. "Such statements as those of Monroe and Truman are characteristic of American foreign attitudes, in the breadth of their generalization, in the instinct for bold and sweeping assertion. But characteristic, too, is the American instinct for the practical, the retreat from theory when retreat becomes convenient or necessary."

Perkins' restatement of the orthodox, or some call it the "nationalist," position helps to explain why the realists did not achieve predominance in the field. The traditionalists may have encountered problems along the way, but they knew that the realists were wrong in applying European standards to American diplomacy and mistaken in assuming that principle and pragmatism were at odds in its conduct.

Meanwhile, the consensus historians incorporated realist insights into their own work. It is difficult to say if Hofstadter's essay on "Manifest Destiny and the Philippines" (1952) was influenced much, if at all, by Kennan's writing, but certain themes emerge which seem to have common roots. As in *The American Political Tradition,* Hofstadter used the war with Spain and the subsequent annexation of the Philippines as examples of how the Progressive historians had got things turned around. It was not the rich, capitalistic Easterners who wanted the war, but Bryan's yawping Populists. Not that the Eastern elite was guiltless, for it manipulated serious protests against internal conditions into this safe outlet. Thus he wrote in "Manifest Destiny and the Philippines":

> An opportunity to discharge aggressions against "Wall Street interests" coolly indifferent to the fate of both Cuban *insurrectos* and staple farmers may have been more important than the more rationalized and abstract linkage between a war and free silver. The primary significance of the war for the psychic economy of the nineties was that it served as an outlet for aggressive impulses while presenting itself, quite truthfully, as an idealistic and humanitarian crusade.

Hofstadter found that Americans "showed a conspicuous and symptomatic inability to distinguish between interests, rights, and duties." The theory of the "psychic crisis of the 1890's," as Hofstadter called it, thus encompassed what would be called the realist view—and went beyond it. Unlike the traditional interpretation, both the consensus and the realist theories discounted the battle against isolationism as the central event in the drama of American foreign relations, and as the major focus for scholarly inquiry. Both were concerned instead with the internal sources of America's behavior toward the outside world.

Realist interpretations, however, dismissed Marxist models of imperialism (as did traditionalists, of course) as totally irrelevant to the American experience. So did Hofstadter. Yet he hedged a bit. While he maintained that anyone who approached American imperialism with preconceptions no more supple than those of Lenin would find himself helpless in the face of contradictory evidence, he remained fascinated by the relationship between the depression of the mid-1890's and the public mood. As between Marx and Freud, however, Hofstadter chose the prober of the unconscious and the irrational.

Over the next few years, after the appearance of Kennan's lectures in book form and Hofstadter's essay on the acquisition of the Philippines, historians undertook a far-reaching reassessment of American imperialism, both narrowly conceived in relation to the

Spanish-American War and broadly understood as expansionism. That no new synthesis was achieved was indicated by the title of one of the last books published in this "series"—Ernest R. May's *American Imperialism: A Speculative Essay* (1968). Perhaps the important thing was that Americans were speculating about the past more than ever before. However that may be, the consensus historians had helped to reopen important historical questions.

One direction these new inquiries took was pioneered by William Appleman Williams in *The Tragedy of American Diplomacy* (1959). Although Williams was to become famous as a "revisionist," his book could be read as a consensus study of American expansion and diplomacy. Rejecting the notion of a sharp division between imperialists and anti-imperialists at the turn of the century, Williams posited a "consensus" among American leaders on the question of expansion, as evidenced by the general acceptance of and support for the Open Door policy. Whatever John Hay's personal motives or quirks, the demand for equality of treatment in the China market reflected neither an overweening moralism nor a pervasive psychic crisis. Instead, the Open Door policy was a rational plan for economic advantage without onerous colonial responsibilities.

But it was more than that. The Open Door policy also involved a way of looking at the world that most Americans understood and shared. It was anticolonial and liberal; it satisfied the American's image of himself. Most important, it reunited political belief and economic institutions, divided in other interpretations. On the Populists, the favorite "test" of consensus history, Williams took a new position, one that he developed over the years in several later books. He did not doubt the seriousness of their situation, nor the genuineness of their protest; but neither did he see them as protosocialists, except for a small minority. Instead, as he concluded in the *Roots of the Modern American Empire* (1969), Populists were participants and leaders in the formulation of the social consciousness that produced the Open Door policy.

Having analyzed the weaknesses of capitalist society, the farmers, or agricultural businessmen, moved beyond protest to the world marketplace.

> Agricultural businessmen strongly approved the Open Door policy promulgated later in 1899 even though, in the narrow sense of policymaking, it was very largely formulated by metropolitan leaders. The reason for that support is apparent. The policy represented the essence of the outlook, attitudes, and specific proposals that the farm businessmen had been promoting for more than a generation. It was their policy in the deepest sense of being a manifestation of the social consciousness they had developed and molded [pp. 442–443].

It remained for someone to make an explicit link between consensus history and the rapidly developing new interpretations. In a final chapter to *The Liberal Tradition in America* (1955) Louis Hartz discussed "liberal absolutism," which alienated the United States not only from antiliberal states like the Soviet Union, but also from "socialist" governments in Western Europe. American progressivism, argued Hartz, alone of all reform movements in the West, was preoccupied with attaining a Horatio Alger world.

> It is interesting how Wilson's world policy reflected his domestic Progressivism. One can, to be sure, make out a case in realpolitik for that policy: its stress on free trade and equal opportunity for nations was remarkably well suited to America's new economic supremacy enhanced now by a merchant marine and a strong position in foreign markets. But the common reliance on a free play of interests in the domestic and the international spheres is too obvious to go ignored. Wasn't Wilson smashing the Austro-Hungarian Empire into bits much as he would smash an American trust? [pp. 295–296].

Hartz traced the hysterical anticommunism of the A. Mitchell Palmer raids (1919–1920) and the McCarthy era to the same absence of a feudal tradition that he saw as the determining force in the development of American politics. The notion that one could solve the problem by deportation, as in the Red Scare of the early 1920's, was a manifestation of liberal absolutism at its very worst. It was also, concluded N. Gordon Levin, the opposite side of the Open Door policy. Levin's *Woodrow Wilson and World Politics* (1968) received favorable reviews from scholars identified with nearly every point of view. "Wilsonians laid the foundations of a modern American foreign policy," Levin wrote in the introduction to his study, "whose main thrust, from 1917 on, may be characterized as an effort to construct a stable world order of liberal-capitalist internationalism, at the Center of the global ideological spectrum, safe from both the threat of imperialism on the Right and the danger of revolution on the Left."

Borrowing freely from Hartz and Williams, Levin suggested the existence of an American liberal imperialism-internationalism not unlike that which some writers have discovered in late-nineteenth-century European thought. The most interesting of these books to date, Bernard Semmel's *Imperialism & Social Reform* (1968), appeared in the same year as Levin's work on Wilsonian world views. Semmel's study suggested that future efforts to follow up on Levin's ideas in a comparative framework might provide some interesting results.

The consensus history that began appearing around 1950 profoundly influenced the development of the study of American foreign policy. The traditional, textbook view remains dominant, but even that "consensus" has undergone considerable reexamination and does not stand unchallenged. The notion that American foreign policy is best explained as a struggle between isolationists and internationalists has yielded to a broader understanding of the forces at work, which shape the dimensions and directions of the nation's relations with the world.

BIBLIOGRAPHY

In writing this essay, Christopher Lasch's foreword to the twenty-fifth anniversary edition of Richard Hofstadter, *The American Political Tradition* (New York, 1974), and Hofstadter's own Preface, written in 1967, were extremely useful. Thomas Bailey, "Confessions of a Diplomatic Historian," in The Society for Historians of American Foreign Relations, *Newsletter,* 6 (1975), provides additional confirmation for my conclusions about the background of the first generation of diplomatic historians and the premises of their work. A convenient and useful collection of differing views on the history of American foreign policy has been provided by Jerald A. Combs, ed., *Nationalist, Realist, and Radical: Three Views of American Diplomacy* (New York, 1972).

Hofstadter's treatment of the Populists provoked several responses, the most important of which was Michael Paul Rogin, *The Intellectuals and McCarthy: The Radical Specter* (Cambridge, Mass., 1967). The agrarian question and developing capitalism is the subject of Barrington Moore, Jr., *Social Origins of Dictatorship and Democracy* (Boston, 1966); see also E. J. Hobsbawm, *Primitive Rebels* (New York, 1959). These books are important as different approaches to a key problem that becomes important in consensus attitudes about American foreign policy.

The original work of the consensus historians on late nineteenth-century America and the Progressive era has been extended in two directions by Robert Wiebe, *The Search for Order* (New York, 1967), and Gabriel Kolko, *The Triumph of Conservatism* (Glencoe, Ill., 1963). Realist interpretations of American foreign policy, in addition to those of Kennan and Morgenthau, include Robert Endicott Osgood, *Ideals and Self-Interest in America's Foreign Relations* (Chicago, 1953); Stanley Hoffmann, *Gulliver's Troubles: The Setting of American Foreign Policy* (New York, 1968); and Louis Halle, *Dream and Reality: Aspects of American Foreign Policy* (New York, 1958). Howard K. Beale, *Theodore Roosevelt and America's Rise to World Power* (Baltimore, 1956), is noteworthy because it demonstrates the conversion of a progressive historian to a realist-consensus position. An interesting reevaluation of a consensus-realist approach to the foundations of American diplomacy (Felix Gilbert's highly influential *To the Farewell Address: Ideas of Early American Foreign Policy* [Princeton, 1961]) is James Hutson, "Intellectual Foundations of Early American Diplomacy," in *Diplomatic History,* 1 (1977).

In conclusion, there are three books that suggest possible future trends that will appeal to all traditions. In comparative history, Arno J. Mayer, *Politics and Diplomacy of Peacemaking* (New York, 1965), is a multinational study of the "great event" (the Paris Peace Conference) and the politics of each nation that attended the congress. On the role of ideology in American foreign policy, see Joan Hoff Wilson, *Ideology and Economics: U.S. Relations With the Soviet Union, 1918–1933* (Columbia, Mo., 1974), a highly stimulating study of the hierarchy of ideas and values and needs in the shaping of a foreign policy. Dorothy Borg and Shumpei Okomoto, *Pearl Harbor as History: Japanese-American Relations 1931–1941* (New York, 1973), is a pioneering effort to bring together historians of two countries to study every aspect of their relations in a given period.

[*See also* Bipartisanship; The Cold War; Elitism and Foreign Policy; Peacemaking; Politics and Foreign Policy; Public Opinion; Realism and Idealism; Revisionism.]

CONSORTIA

Warren I. Cohen

As generally found in world affairs, consortia are multinational cooperative ventures designed to cope with some common problem, ostensibly apolitical. The best-known consortia, the so-called China consortiums, were banking syndicates—combinations of banking groups from several countries. Lacking adequate capital for export, the United States did not serve as a lender in international financial operations until the twentieth century. When it did begin to take part, American bankers proved to be imperfect instruments for national policy.

In the early years of the twentieth century a number of American financial institutions accumulated capital for which they sought foreign markets. J. P. Morgan and Company, Kuhn, Loeb and Company, and National City Bank of New York were prominent among firms interested in investing funds outside the United States. Opportunities for domestic investment were still plentiful: the United States remained a capital-importing nation, and Europe remained the world's banker until World War I. Opportunities for greater profit, however, were believed to exist abroad, and American bankers became deeply involved in the financial affairs of countries such as Mexico, Cuba, Haiti, the Dominican Republic, and Nicaragua. To a lesser extent, some bankers and industrialists were interested in East Asia, especially China. China was attempting to modernize, preferred American capital to European or Japanese, and the Chinese government was a better credit risk than a number of American state governments.

There were, however, other kinds of risks involved in investing in China. The Caribbean was an American lake, dominated by the growing power of the United States, and investors were confident that the American government would protect their interests in Caribbean countries. But in China all of the great European powers and Japan struggled for advantage, sometimes political as well as economic. With rare exception the American government had shown itself disinclined to become involved in Chinese affairs, unwilling to give American businessmen support comparable to that which their European and Japanese competitors might reasonably expect from their own governments. As a result, little American capital could be found in China in 1909, when William Howard Taft became president of the United States.

Taft was eager to expand American influence and power, and his administration was noted for its use of "dollar diplomacy" to achieve its ends. Taft not only continued Theodore Roosevelt's support of American economic interests in Latin America, but also backed enterprises in places as remote as Turkey. The most striking contrast between the policies of Taft and Roosevelt could be found in East Asia, where Taft refused to acquiesce in Japanese expansion in Manchuria. He believed that Chinese and Americans shared a mutual interest in preventing Japanese hegemony over China's northeastern provinces and that the development of American economic interests in that region would serve the interests of both nations—perhaps all nations. Several schemes for forcing American capital into Manchuria, most notably the "neutralization" plan of Secretary of State Philander Knox, a scheme for internationalizing Chinese railways, failed; but in China proper the Taft offensive met with one apparent success: American bankers were awarded a share in a loan for the building of the Hankow-Canton or Hukuang Railway and allowed to join what became known as the consortium.

A group of American banking firms had come together in the last year of the Roosevelt administration to explore investment opportunities in East Asia, but had not acted in the absence of interest in the White House or on the part of the secretary of state. When Taft and Knox insisted, early in 1909, that the United States be allowed to participate in the financing of the Hukuang, the existing banking group was formally designated the American group and called upon to play the American role—if the British, French, and German groups, and their respective governments, as well as the Chinese government, would honor the American demand.

In June 1909, as a syndicate of British, French, and German bankers was about to conclude negotiations with the Chinese, Knox filed a formal protest, reminding the Chinese government of assurances it had given in 1904 that the United States would be able to share in any loan to build the Hukuang. Choosing to see the exclusion of the United States as an unfriendly act, Knox threatened to discontinue the remission of Boxer indemnity payments. Responding to American pressures, the Chinese urged the British, French, and German bankers to share their concession with the Americans. Almost a year of haggling over the terms of American participation followed, featuring the personal intercession of President Taft and the Department of State's refusal to permit the American group to accept anything less than a full quarter share of all components of the project. The American group, recognizing that its share of the bond issue that would ensue from the Hukuang loan would likely require listing in European exchanges, was willing to compromise with the European bankers in order to retain goodwill and preserve their own profits. The Department of State, however, was far more concerned with American prestige and influence, presumably contingent on the American group's participating on a basis of absolute equality. Finally, in May 1910, an agreement was signed between the three European banking groups and the American group that not only permitted the Americans to share in the Hukuang loan, but brought them into the banking syndicate. As of the signing of the agreement, bankers of Great Britain, France, Germany, and the United States were united in a four-power consortium, committed to sharing equally all future business in China.

But the creation of the consortium did not lead to the immediate consummation of the Hukuang loan. To the consternation of the bankers, the Chinese government backed away, fearful that coming to terms with the consortium would exacerbate mounting unrest in China and lead to a revolution. Opposition to foreign control of China's railways was growing among educated Chinese and there was, in addition, a desire by provincial gentry to prevent central control of railways. The consortium bankers insisted that a preliminary agreement was binding upon the Chinese and asked for and received diplomatic support from their governments. The American minister to China, William J. Calhoun, was greatly embarrassed by instructions that he demand that the Chinese conclude the loan negotiations. He argued that it was undignified, "unworthy of civilized powers," to force a loan on an unwilling government. But Calhoun's protests were brushed aside, and the American government joined in the pressures to which the Chinese succumbed in May 1911. As the Peking government anticipated, conclusion of the £6 million loan led to increased violence in the provinces and ultimately to revolution.

Even Calhoun was willing to drop his opposition to the loan if the loan operations were essential to continued cooperation between the United States and its new European partners in China. In Washington this cooperation was deemed vital to the furtherance of American interests in China. Participation in the loan was a wedge for American investments, which would lead to expanded American trade, greater public attention to East Asia, and a greater role for the United States in the political affairs of the region. By forcing the consortium to admit American bankers, the Taft administration assumed it had reserved a place at the table at which the future of China would be played out. As long as the game promised to be profitable, the bankers of the American group demonstrated a grudging willingness to play the pawn.

While negotiations over the American role in

the Hukuang loan were underway, the American group had responded favorably to a Chinese request for another large loan, partly for currency reform and partly for Manchurian development. The Chinese hoped that by turning to the American bankers they could obtain better terms than were available from European bankers—that they could play off the American bankers against the Europeans. To Knox the Chinese proposal held the dual promise of American hegemony over Chinese finances and an opportunity to penetrate Manchuria in order to fulfill the goal of checking Japanese expansion there. The American banking group, however, brushed aside the visions of both the Chinese and the Department of State by insisting on offering the new loan to the European bankers. Again the problem was the shortage of capital in the United States, which necessitated an international listing of the bond issue for the loan to be floated successfully. If the American group offered the currency loan to the European groups, the Europeans might prove less disagreeable about having been forced to offer the American group a share in the Hukuang loan and allow the American group to list the bonds of both its loans on European exchanges. Profits for the American bankers would thus be assured. The Chinese were indignant, but once Knox was converted he bludgeoned them into permitting the currency loan to be taken over by the consortium. The currency loan was never issued, however, because the revolution began.

The creation of the four-power consortium worried the Japanese and Russian governments, especially when they learned that part of the currency loan was earmarked for use in Manchuria. The Russians attempted to block the loan and, failing at that, they tried unsuccessfully to destroy the consortium by urging the French—to whom they were closely tied, politically and economically—to withdraw. Ultimately the Russians accepted French assurances that their interests in Manchuria could best be served if they too joined the consortium. As early as November 1910, while the Russians were still being obstructive, the Japanese concluded that their interests could be protected most readily from within and expressed an interest in membership in the consortium.

Knox was willing to allow both the Russians and the Japanese to have a share in the loan business, but not in the management of the consortium. The bankers of the consortium were not eager to share their profits with new partners. Both the British and American governments tried instead to reassure the Russians and Japanese by specifying the particular Manchurian enterprises for which the consortium would provide funds, trying to demonstrate the absence of any intention to threaten the existing interests of the two Manchurian overlords. But the Russians and Japanese continued to fear that the Chinese intended to allow the consortium a monopoly on development loans in Manchuria and were still opposed to the terms of the currency reform loan in October 1911 when the revolution began.

As Ch'ing rule of China disintegrated and warfare spread along the Yangtze, the American government surrendered its hope of using the consortium or other forms of dollar diplomacy against Japan and Russia in Manchuria. With China less able than ever to protect its own interests in the frontier regions of the empire, Knox and his assistants concluded that American interests could be furthered only by cooperating with Japan and Russia, settling for an equal opportunity to trade in Chinese provinces under their control. The British Foreign Office reached similar conclusions, joining Knox in recommending that Japan and Russia be invited to join the consortium. Both France and Yüan Shih-k'ai, strong man and later president of the Chinese Republic, agreed; but the American bankers, reinforced by the Germans, both government and bankers, opposed Russian participation.

As Yüan's regime began to assert itself over the country, his prime minister, T'ang Shao-i, notified the consortium's representatives in Peking of his interest in a £60 million loan to enable the government to reorganize, pay off advances, and proceed with development projects. In return for an option on the reorganization loan, the consortium bankers agreed to an immediate advance on the currency loan. A few days later the consortium bankers learned that the Chinese had concluded another loan, with a Belgian syndicate that included the Russo-Asiatic Bank—the main instrument of the Russian equivalent of dollar diplomacy. To the Russian government and to bankers of England and France who were excluded from the consortium, the opportunity to disrupt the consortium's efforts to monopolize China's financial transactions proved irresistible. Similarly, the Chinese were delighted to find other bankers to play off against those who combined in order to dictate the terms under which China could obtain foreign capital. The consortium bankers were outraged and broke off negotiations with Yüan's government.

The few bankers involved in the consortium, of whatever nationality, wanted a monopoly over all Chinese loans. Their governments, especially the British and American governments, were uneasy about the demands of their bankers and were more interested in establishing and preserving order in China and in using economic cooperation as a base upon which political cooperation in China could be built. The governments were more receptive to Chinese requests for a relaxation of the foreign controls that the consortium bankers demanded and were ready to admit Japan and Russia to the organization if that was necessary to facilitate operations in China proper. In addition, European political considerations made pacification of Russia imperative to France and Great Britain. Consequently, the French and British governments pressed for the admission of Japan and Russia to the consortium, appeasing the consortium bankers by forcing British and French participants in the Belgian loan to withdraw, which led to cancellation of that transaction.

Although Japan and Russia were both interested in joining the consortium, they stipulated the exclusion of Manchuria and Mongolia from the scope of the organization's operations. The British and French governments were willing to accept the Russo-Japanese terms and in May 1912 Knox assented, but it was June before a formula agreeable to all concerned could be discovered. In June 1912 the six-power consortium came into existence, and more money was advanced to Yüan's regime. Yüan used the money to consolidate his position against his enemies, especially against Sun Yat-sen's supporters in the south and in parliament.

As Yüan sought more money, the banking groups were caught up by the political machinations of their governments in the selection of foreign advisers to oversee the expenditure of the monies loaned. European politics prevailed as Britain, France, and Russia supported each other's proposals to the detriment of German suggestions. Yüan became increasingly irritated with the consortium, his political opponents anxiously opposed further loans, and the American bankers wearied of the entire process. The American minister to China had never been comfortable with the loan operations and by 1913 Sir John Jordan, the British minister, considered the consortium arrangements to be of benefit to the one British bank involved, but detrimental to British interests generally. To the American bankers there appeared little prospect for reasonable profits. The American government had abandoned hope of playing an important role in Manchuria. Only the principle of cooperation, to which the State Department had dedicated itself, remained. In 1913 the new American president, Woodrow Wilson, did not consider cooperation with European or Japanese imperialists a virtue, and he refused the American group the support it no longer wanted. In April the American role in the consortium was terminated.

Wilson mistrusted the Wall Street bankers of the American group, and he mistrusted their foreign partners. He suspected the consortium of seeking to take advantage of China's weakness to infringe on Chinese sovereignty and to profit at the expense of the Chinese people. He wanted to help China, but was determined to find another way. Yüan was pleased, hoping that an American loan on better terms would soon be available. But American money was not forthcoming, and Yüan, desperately in need of money, concluded the reorganization loan with the remaining five members of the consortium. His position thus strengthened, Yüan was able to crush a rebellion led by Sun's Kuomintang (Nationalist Party).

By April 1915, with Europe embroiled in warfare, Wilson recognized Japan's intent to dominate China, as evidenced by the Twenty-one Demands (1915). To check Japanese imperialism and further American interests in China, he designed his own version of dollar diplomacy. Although hostile to the American group because of its monopolistic practices and attempts to infringe on Chinese sovereignty, Wilson was very much interested in the use of American capital to further the process of Chinese modernization. He failed, however, to elicit interest among other American bankers and, in response to a request from the Chinese government in 1916, Wilson asked the American group to consider a loan to China.

The member banks wanted to disband the American group but were held together by their inability to rid themselves of their share of the Hukuang loan. They responded negatively to Wilson's proposition, refusing to compete with the consortium and willing to consider a loan outside the scope of the consortium only if the American government would offer a guarantee that China would fulfill its obligations. The government would not offer a guarantee, and appealed instead to the bankers' patriotism. But the bankers would lend to China only as a business proposition, and the matter was dropped.

When an American bank outside the American group entered into a loan agreement with the Chinese in 1916, the other consortium banking groups protested angrily. Wilson rejected the protests, warning the British, French, Japanese, and Russian governments against excluding American bankers from participation in Chinese affairs. With most of these governments anxious to avoid conflict with the United States while involved in a life-and-death struggle with the Central Powers in Europe, their bankers could count on little support against an invasion of American capital. There was one hope: British, French, Russian, and Japanese bankers expressed a desire to see the United States rejoin the consortium, to co-opt the United States and contain the financial offensive the American bankers were now presumed capable of launching.

In March 1917 the American group notified the Department of State that it favored accepting the invitation to rejoin the consortium, contending that the time was ripe for advancing American commercial prestige. But Wilson was unyielding: loans should be made directly to China and not through the consortium. The president recognized the overtures from the consortium as an attempt to prevent independent American action.

By June 1918 the Wilson administration was forced to concede failure in its efforts to find American capital for investment in China. Fearing that the Japanese, in the absence of American or European competition, would monopolize Chinese economic affairs, Wilson agreed to allow the American group to join its old associates in a new consortium. The American group was to become more inclusive, admitting to membership banking groups throughout the country, and it would pledge not to undermine Chinese sovereignty. In return Wilson agreed to announce that the group was offering a loan to China at the suggestion of the government.

The Wilson administration had returned to the conception of an international banking consortium because no other means could be found to move American capital into China. The American initiative for a new consortium was intended to serve the same purpose independent American loans would have served: the containment of Japanese economic expansion to preserve opportunity for American expansion in China. Given Wilson's faith in the "liberal exceptionalism" of the United States, he readily assumed that American expansion, unlike the Japanese variety, would be salutary for China—that Chinese and American interests were congruent.

For the American group, Thomas W. Lamont of J. P. Morgan and Company met with representatives of the British, French, and Japanese banking groups in May 1919, at the Paris Peace Conference. Lamont proposed and reached rapid agreement on the American plan for pooling all future business in China and for pooling all existing loan agreements and options involving public subscription except those relating to industrial undertakings upon which substantial progress had been made. The efficiency of cooperation and the expectation of the exclusive support of their governments were attractive to the bankers.

In June, however, the Japanese group reported that its government insisted on excluding from the consortium agreement all rights and options held by Japan in Manchuria and Mongolia, where Japan had "special interests." The Japanese expected the United States to consent to the exceptions on the basis of Secretary of State Robert Lansing's recognition of Japan's "special interests" in his 1917 agreement with Viscount Ishii Kikujiro. Once Japan's sphere in Manchuria and Inner Mongolia was thus protected, the Japanese government viewed the consortium with favor, as a means of improving relations with the United States and as an instrument for checking the anticipated torrent of American capital.

The purpose of the consortium, as understood in Washington and London, however, was to eliminate special claims to spheres of influence and to open all of China to cooperative international development. Not only the Wilsonians, but also Lord Curzon, Great Britain's secretary of state for foreign affairs, considered economic imperialism an anachronism in the face of the nationalist movement that was sweeping over China. When the French government expressed fear that refusal to grant the reservations Japan requested would result in the Japanese finding friends outside the circle of their wartime allies, Curzon insisted that the Japanese request was inadmissible and expressed confidence that they would back down in face of the unanimity of the British, French, and American groups supported by their governments.

Months passed as the Japanese and American governments exchanged mutually unsatisfactory counterproposals. In February 1920 Lamont went to Tokyo in an attempt to break the deadlock. One area for possible compromise existed, and the State Department had focused on it in December 1919: Japan's existing economic interests ("vested" interests in Manchuria and Mongolia) could be conceded, excluded from the scope of the consortium. Both sides moved slowly toward this position. To prod the Japanese government, Wilson authorized a threat to reveal the secret protocol of the Lansing-Ishii agreement, in which Ishii had committed Japan not to seek privileges in China at the expense of other powers.

As the negotiations proceeded, Lamont proposed an exchange of notes between the American and Japanese groups defining the attitudes of foreign bankers toward Japanese economic interests in Manchuria and Mongolia, specifying what would or would not come within the scope of the consortium. Lamont's plan would allow for the acceptance of existing economic facts without giving official governmental recognition. Only the consortium would recognize Japan's economic interests. The American and British ambassadors to Japan liked Lamont's proposal, but the Department of State rejected it and suggested that Lamont reach an agreement on the basis of specific enterprises the Japanese wanted to exclude from the consortium's focus. The American government would not accept a reference to the exclusion of any region of China. Lamont was angered by State Department scruples; but, insisting that Manchuria was in fact dominated by the Japanese and unattractive to nationals of the other banking groups, he was able to reach agreement with his Japanese counterpart on the department's terms.

In April 1920 the Japanese government, in a last effort to strengthen the consensus within the leadership, bid once more for veto power over railway construction in Manchuria. If further concessions could be won from Japan's prospective partners, opposition to the agreement within Japan might be stilled. The effort alone might satisfy dissidents within the cabinet that the government had done all that was possible. But the American and British governments held firm and the Japanese appeared to retreat.

In the following month the Ministry of Foreign Affairs gave the American ambassador, Roland Morris, a "draft reply" to the American rejection of Japan's last set of reservations, claiming that the earlier note had not been presented for the purpose of raising new conditions but simply to avoid future misunderstandings. The Japanese government would not insist on explicit American assurances but would accept the general assurances offered previously and refrain from insisting upon discussion of the veto power it sought initially. The Japanese were satisfied to make known to the American government their interpretation of the questions at issue.

Lamont and the American ambassador were pleased, interpreting the Japanese position as complete acceptance of the position taken by the American government and supported by the British and French governments. But J. V. A. MacMurray, chief of the State Department's Division of Far Eastern Affairs, argued that the Japanese had retracted nothing. MacMurray claimed that the Japanese note reemphasized Japan's claim to a veto on railway construction in Manchuria and had further placed on record their understanding that American assurances regarding Japan's right of self-preservation meant American recognition of that veto power. But MacMurray was overruled; the Department of State accepted the Japanese draft, and the consortium negotiations were concluded.

MacMurray was probably correct when he contended that the Japanese, in addition to receiving explicit acceptance of all of their existing and some of their projected economic interests in Manchuria and Mongolia, had established a strong basis for arguing that the United States had conceded to Japan veto power over railway construction in Manchuria. Certainly that was the view that prevailed in official Japanese circles. But MacMurray's superiors in the Department of State had concluded that the choice was between accepting the conditions obtained or surrendering the idea of the four-power consortium. To the American government there appeared no alternative means of preserving American interests in China. After March 1920, when the Senate for the third time rejected American membership in the League of Nations, the consortium offered the best, perhaps the only, basis for cooperation with the powers in China.

With the formation of the consortium in 1920 and the subsequent agreements reached at the Washington Conference (1921–1922), Great Britain, France, Japan, and the United States were committed to cooperation among themselves in assisting with the modernization of China. The consortium bankers were to provide the Chinese government with the funds it needed to build railroads and other major productive enterprises. But in the six years that followed the Washington Conference, China suffered from almost constant civil strife and, despite prompting from the American and British governments, the consortium did nothing to assist China's economic development: no loans were granted. The British frequently referred to the consortium as a financial "blockade," designed to prevent the Chinese government from obtaining funds it would presumably misuse.

Similarly, American businessmen anxious to develop or expand their interests in China failed to obtain needed capital. They did not lack support from the American government, within which the Departments of Commerce and State competed to build up American economic interests in China. But American entrepreneurs in China, like the Chinese government, found the consortium an obstacle.

The core of the problem was the divergence between the interests of the Department of State and those of Lamont and his fellow bankers. The department wanted the consortium to provide capital for China's development—to help in the creation of a strong modern China in which American interests would thrive. For the bankers, the remote promise of China could not compete with the more immediate promise of Japan. In 1923 the House of Morgan floated a $150 million loan for the Japanese government, and other smaller loans followed in the mid-1920's. American capital that might have been available to China was lent instead to the Japanese and some of it, by indirect means, by being "laundered" or simply by freeing other capital, facilitated the expansion of Japanese interests on the Asian mainland. Because the Japanese were competing with the Chinese for American capital, they could use their position in the consortium to discourage loans to China. The American group, led by Lamont, accepted this process. In short, one of the two competitors for capital worked in collusion with the potential lender to deny capital to the other. However permissible among businessmen pursuing profit, it was not consistent with the ends of public policy. Conditions in China, however, left the Department of State no means for changing the direction of the flow of capital. Lamont proved to be remarkably skillful in leading State Department officials to believe that he shared their views but was held back by partners less interested in helping China.

Twice during the early years of the consortium's existence the ability of Lamont and his colleagues to avoid lending money to the Chinese was tested. In both instances, in 1922 and in 1923, the American, British, French, and Japanese ministers to China and the Peking representatives of all four banking groups recommended that the loans be granted. In both instances the diplomats and group representatives argued that the consortium could not afford to reject Chinese overtures. But in neither instance could Lamont be moved, supporting or being supported by the head of the British group or the Japanese government in his opposition to taking up the Chinese business.

For the next two years, until the violence subsequent to the May Thirtieth Incident radically changed the context, Lamont and his British counterpart, with at least the public support of their governments, sang in praise of the success of the consortium's negative effort. They had stopped wasteful borrowing by the Chinese government, and their cooperation had a salutary effect on relations among the powers in China. Despite dissatisfaction with the inactivity of the consortium, the American and British governments were anxious to have it remain in existence. For the United States and Great Britain the consortium appeared to have assisted in checking the expansion of Japan's economic hold over China. For the British, continued Anglo-American cooperation in East Asia was itself a valuable end. And the Japanese indicated no dissatisfaction with the consortium, supporting a motion in 1924 to renew the agreement in perpetuity. France, the fourth party to the consortium agreement, appeared to its partners to be apathetic, unreliable, and forever bargaining for some trivial advantage, but supportive of the others when the agreement was renewed.

Although after 1923 there was never again serious consideration of a loan from the consortium to any Chinese regime, the organization continued to exist, at least in theory, until a decision in 1946 that the Japanese attack on American and British forces in 1941 constituted abrogation of the agreement. The persistence of the consortium through the 1930's is remarkable because of the constant desire of the American group to withdraw and because of the determination of the British government to end the agreement in 1937. One stubborn man, Stanley K. Hornbeck of the Division of Far Eastern Affairs, Department of State, continually blocked dissolution, with an assist from the Japanese army in the summer of 1937.

The American group's desire to be rid of the consortium, voiced regularly by Lamont, reflected the leadership's conviction that there was no money to be made out of China and that continuation of the organization was not worth the bother or expense. From 1920 on, Lamont argued that there was no market for Chinese securities in the United States—that the American investor would not touch Chinese bonds until the Chinese demonstrated stability and paid off earlier loans, especially the Hukuang Railway loan, on all issues of which they had defaulted in 1925. After the Banking Act of 1933 prohibited banks of deposit from underwriting or offering securities, Lamont explained to the Department of State that his own firm and most members of the American group could no longer participate in loan operations even if they were to become feasible on a business basis. But for over a quarter of a century, Lamont deferred to the State Department's desire to maintain the consortium. Not until January 1946 did he succeed in getting the department to concede unequivocally that no useful purpose would be served by continuing the consortium, with or without the American group in it.

Despite their failure to get the consortium to lend money to China, officials of the Department of State fought to keep the organization in existence. Certainly it was not because American economic interests prospered. Lamont and his colleagues were concerned with their own profits and not with the expansion of the trade of their countrymen or with abstract conceptions of national interest. Sino-American trade remained static in the 1920's and rose slightly only in percentage terms for a few years in the early 1930's. The increase in American investments in China was not impressive. The American group hindered rather than helped the development of American economic interests in China, as the Department of Commerce found when it tried to advance the prospects of American corporations.

Ultimately, men like MacMurray and Hornbeck fought to retain the consortium as a means of keeping the United States involved in East Asia, in the affairs of China. This had always been the fundamental purpose of a policy of cooperation with those powers earlier and more profoundly committed to activism in China. Without hitching a ride, the State Department's East Asian specialists, from John Hay's adviser, William W. Rockhill, through Hornbeck, feared not only that the United States would be deprived of an opportunity to expand its interests in their region, but also that interest in the area to which they were committed would cease to exist in the United States. The promise of American expansion in China, however remote the reality, had become their raison d'être. The consortium, however inadequate, was the only vehicle they had for much of the interwar period.

Formed in 1919, the International Committee of Bankers on Mexico (ICBM) provides an interesting comparison with the second China consortium. Once again Lamont was the central figure on the American side, and once again the bankers demonstrated that they would act independently of other business interests or the wishes of their government in pursuit of their ends. The ICBM, however, never loomed as large in the plans of the Department of State's Division of Mexican Affairs as the China consortium did in the visions of MacMurray and Hornbeck.

Claiming pressure from European bankers, Lamont solicited the approval of the Department of State for the organization of an international committee of bankers in 1918. In 1919 approval to bring together American, British, and French banking groups concerned with investments in Mexico was granted by the department, with the proviso that control of the committee's policy remain in American hands. Swiss, Dutch, and Belgian banking interests were subsequently given token representation on the committee.

The primary concern of the bankers was to protect the holders of Mexican securities, especially those of the Mexican government. Lamont and his colleagues were at best marginally concerned with the primary issue dividing the American and Mexican governments in 1920: interpretations of Article 27 of the Mexican constitution and its effect on the claims of American oil companies. Fearing debt repudiation, the bankers were unsympathetic to Washington's tactic of withholding recognition from the Mexican government as a means of forcing it to respect the property rights and claims of the oil companies. Whereas the government of the United States wanted all American claims against Mexico to be settled simultaneously, the International Committee of Bankers on Mexico exhibited few inhibitions about negotiating a separate settlement of Mexico's foreign debt.

Restrained initially by the Department of State, Lamont obtained approval to begin negotiations with the administration of Alvaro Obregón in 1921. In June 1922 the Lamont–De la Huerta agreement was reached, recognizing $500 million of indebtedness and arranging for eventual payment. This arrangement paved the way for the Bucareli agreements between the Mexican and United States governments in 1923, ameliorating the differences between the two and leading to recognition of Obregón's regime.

In the years that followed, Mexico had difficulty meeting the schedule established in the Lamont–De la Huerta agreement, and in 1925 Lamont negotiated a new agreement. Payment remained irregular, however, and negotiations between the ICBM and the Mexican government continued throughout the 1920's and 1930's. In 1930 considerable friction arose between Lamont and the American ambassador to Mexico, his former partner Dwight Morrow. Morrow and the Department of State insisted that a separate agreement between the bankers and the Mexican government was contrary to the interests of both the United States and Mexico. Choosing on this occasion to understate the connection between the ICBM and the Department of State, Lamont insisted that he had reached a private arrangement with the Mexican minister of finance, and was not asking for the department's consent. Unable to sway Lamont or the Mexican ambassador to the United States, Morrow warned the Mexican government that the United States did not see the agreement with Lamont as a constructive step toward financial stability. The Mexican government capitulated, assuring Morrow it would not submit the agreement to Congress except as a package comprising provisions for all of Mexico's debts. A final settlement between the ICBM and Mexico was not obtained until November 1942 in the Suarez-Lamont agreement ratified by the Mexican Congress and the foreign bondholders.

Legal problems kept the International Committee of Bankers on Mexico in existence until at least 1948, when its unrecorded demise appears to have occurred. It did not have any political significance after 1930, when it alienated the Department of State. The department was not kept informed of subsequent negotiations between Lamont and Mexican authorities.

The International Committee of Bankers on Mexico resembled the China consortium in that both consisted of groups of bankers from several nations, brought together with the approval of their governments, but ultimately indifferent to the interests of their governments or of other businessmen. The bankers of the ICBM were concerned with their own particularistic interests: any benefit derived from their activities by their governments or other peoples was incidental.

The ICBM differed strikingly from the China consortium in its relationship to the governments of the members' groups. The committee was formed at the initiative of the bankers, and only the government of the United States indicated a deep concern for its activities. There were no international political problems because none of the other countries that were represented had political interests in Mexico. All accepted American hegemony in Mexico, in contrast to the response to Japan's claims to hegemony over Manchuria. The government of the United States had other interests in Mexico and many other ways to exercise influence there. It never saw the committee as an important instrument of policy. After the friction between the Department of State and Lamont in 1930, only the bondholders cared about the future of the committee.

BIBLIOGRAPHY

Dorothy Borg, *The United States and the Far Eastern Crisis of 1933–1938* (Cambridge, Mass., 1964), contains an account of Hornbeck's views and of the fate of the second consortium during the 1930's. Roy W. Curry, *Woodrow Wilson and Far Eastern Policy* (New York, 1957), describes Wilson's initial attitude toward the American group and explains the Wilson administration's decision to create a new consortium. Frederick V. Field, *American Participation in the China Consortiums* (New York, 1931), is a clear and detailed description of both the old and new consortiums. The analysis of the problems of the old consortium is superior to the discussion of the new consortium; in the latter case, Field relied too heavily on Lamont for information. Thomas W. Lamont, *Across World Frontiers* (New York, 1951), is a charming but unreliable account. Karl M. Schmitt, *Mexico and the United States, 1821–1973* (New York, 1974), includes reference to the International Committee of Bankers on Mexico in a chapter devoted to land and oil controversies. Walter U. Scholes and Marie V. Scholes, *The Foreign Policies of the Taft Administration* (Columbia, Mo., 1970), contains an excellent discussion of workings of the first consortium, based on multiarchival research. It is also important for the context of Taft's East Asian offensive. Robert F. Smith, *The United States and Revolutionary Nationalism in Mexico, 1916–1932* (Chicago, 1972), provides a thoughtful analysis of the problems of a less-developed country in a world in which international law is interpreted by advanced capitalist countries. Smith effectively uses the Lamont papers. Joan Hoff Wilson, *American Business and Foreign Policy, 1920–1933* (Lexington, Ky., 1971), provides a useful context for the workings of the second consortium and the ICBM, but Wilson did not have access to the Lamont papers.

[*See also* Dollar Diplomacy; Economic Foreign Policy.]

THE CONSTITUTION AND FOREIGN POLICY

Alfred H. Kelly

THE Constitution is not specific upon the subject of foreign policy. Nowhere in the document is there any formal grant of power upon the matter; instead, the Constitution appears to take for granted that control over foreign relations is vested in the national government. Beyond this it contents itself with a series of specific but fragmentary provisions touching various aspects of the conduct of foreign relations. In no sense do these add up to a comprehensive disposition of the subject, or even to an answer as to where the locus of power within the national government with respect to the conduct of foreign policy finally lies.

Thus, Article II, Section 2, of the Constitution gives the president the authority, "by and with the Advice and Consent of the Senate, to make Treaties, provided two thirds of the Senators present concur." Another provision, the so-called "supremacy clause," in Article VI, makes treaties, along with the Constitution and acts of Congress, the "supreme Law of the Land." Article II, Section 2, confers upon the president the authority to "appoint Ambassadors, other public Ministers and Consuls . . .," with the advice and consent of a majority of the Senate; and Article II, Section 3, enjoins the president to "receive Ambassadors and other public Ministers," presumably from foreign states.

Elsewhere, in Article I, Section 8, the Constitution bestows upon Congress the power to declare war. (Nowhere does it make any mention of the power to decide upon the termination of wars, or to decide upon a policy of neutrality as an alternative to war.) Article I, Section 8, also gives Congress the power to "regulate Commerce with foreign Nations . . ." and "to define and punish . . . Offences against the Law of Nations." And Article II, Section 2, confers upon the Supreme Court original jurisdiction in "all Cases affecting Ambassadors, other public Ministers and Consuls . . .," while it generally lodges in the federal courts jurisdiction in "Controversies between a State, or the Citizens thereof, and foreign States, Citizens, or Subjects."

The Constitution also imposes a few specific prohibitions, none of them in practice very important, which by implication, at least, touch upon the conduct of foreign policy. Thus no state may, without the consent of Congress, "enter into any Agreement or Compact . . . with a foreign Power, or engage in War, unless actually invaded," or in "imminent Danger" thereof. Furthermore, no holder of any "Office of Profit or Trust" under the United States may "accept of any present, Emolument, Office, or Title, of any kind whatever, from any King, Prince, or foreign State," without the consent of Congress.

In spite of the Constitution's relative silence, the proposition that the government of the United States is endowed by it with all the necessary attributes of sovereignty and power to formulate foreign policy and conduct relations with other nation-states has been accepted from the time of the Philadelphia Convention in 1787—both by commentators, such as Joseph Story and Edward S. Corwin, and by the courts. In *The Federalist,* Number 43, Alexander

Hamilton wrote that "no constitutional shackles can wisely be imposed" upon those aspects of national power having to do with "the safety of nations." And in an early Supreme Court decision, *Penhallow* v. *Doane* (1795), Justice James Iredell declared that between 1776 and 1789 comprehensive sovereignty in the field of foreign affairs had resided in the several states, but that with the ratification of the Constitution it had become lodged in the national government.

In a parallel opinion Justice William Paterson took a different view of the matter. He argued that sovereignty in the conduct of foreign policy had passed from Great Britain to the new nation in its collective capacity by virtue of the Declaration of Independence, so that the national government under the Constitution had merely inherited a power earlier lodged in the Confederation Congress. In 1936 Paterson's interpretation received powerful support in *United States* v. *Curtiss-Wright Export Corporation,* the much-controverted decision of the Supreme Court. This case dealt with the constitutionality of an embargo that President Franklin D. Roosevelt had laid upon the export of arms to Bolivia and Paraguay, during the Chaco War. The president had imposed the embargo in accordance with the provisions of a joint resolution of Congress.

In a remarkable opinion Justice George Sutherland pointed out that federal power in the field of foreign affairs differed radically from that with respect to internal matters. He observed that internal federal power had been carved from "the general mass of legislative powers then possessed by the states"; but this was not at all true of the control of foreign policy, which had never been in the possession of the states. Instead, before the Revolution, general power over foreign affairs had been lodged with the British crown, while with the Declaration of Independence, "the power of external sovereignty had passed . . . to the colonies in the collective and corporate capacity as the United States of America." The power over foreign affairs was "older than the Constitution" and had been inherited by the Constitution from the Confederation. It did not depend upon any direct grant of authority to the federal government in the Constitution itself.

It followed, Sutherland concluded, that the power of the national government to formulate and execute foreign policy was larger and more comprehensive than any specific grant of sovereignty to the president, to Congress, or to the federal courts. It was not to be circumscribed by any theory of delegated sovereignty. It was instead an expression of the broad and comprehensive character of nationhood itself.

Regardless of whether one accepts Sutherland's view of the origins of federal sovereignty in the field of foreign policy, there can be little doubt that his description of its comprehensive character comes close to an accurate statement of the reality of the matter. This is not to say that there are not substantial constitutional limits upon the exercise of national power in the domain of foreign policy. There are indeed such. But it is the comprehensive character of the authority of the national government that is most impressive.

Sutherland's second major point in his *Curtiss-Wright* opinion is more controversial. He argued that the principal repository for the sovereign power of the United States in foreign affairs is the president. The usual constitutional limits sharply circumscribing and delimiting the delegation of legislative power to the executive—which the Court only lately had emphasized in successive cases invalidating the National Industrial Recovery Act (1933) and the Bituminous Coal Conservation Act (1935)—did not apply in the field of foreign policy, since the president, Sutherland said, already possessed a general residual power in this area independent of any grant from Congress.

Sutherland's contention that the president possesses something like a comprehensive prerogative power in the field of foreign policy more extensive than any specific delegation of authority to him set forth in Article II was not new. Alexander Hamilton had argued to the same end in his "Pacificus" articles, nearly 150 years earlier, at the time of the Genêt crisis with France. Hamilton had pointed out that Article II, Section 1, of the Constitution declared that "the Executive Power shall be vested in a President of the United States of America." Hamilton contended that this language was not merely a convenient description of the title of the new republic's principal executive officer, but also a formal bestowal upon the president of the whole body of governmental authority commonly thought of as executive in character.

Hamilton did not confine his notion of a comprehensive executive prerogative to foreign affairs, although his essay had arisen out of the crisis in that area. But few presidents in the course of the next century—with the possible exception of Abraham Lincoln in the crisis of the Civil War—ventured to assume the possession of anything like a comprehensive presidential prerogative in internal matters.

On the other hand, in the twentieth century a series of presidents—from Theodore Roosevelt and Woodrow Wilson to Franklin D. Roosevelt, Harry S. Truman, and John F. Kennedy—on occasion have assumed the existence of something like such a power in their attempts to deal with the successive crises of war and economic catastrophe, which the nation at one time or another has confonted. In the *Steel Seizure Case* (1952), however, the Supreme Court, in a six-to-three decision, denied categorically that any such power resides in the executive. But notwithstanding Justice Hugo Black's categorical denunciation of presidential prerogative, it is the Hamilton-Sutherland theory of the matter that for the most part has prevailed in the field of foreign policy.

By no means, however, has the resultant presidential power over foreign policy been absolute or unconditional. On the contrary, the Senate's role in the ratification of treaties; congressional control of the purse strings; the allocation by the Constitution to Congress alone of the power to declare war; the weight of public opinion as it makes itself felt through the press, the party process, and elections have all at one time or another constituted important limits upon the executive conduct of foreign affairs. One may conclude that the initiation of foreign policy has long since come to rest almost entirely in the executive, but both the formulation of policy and its day-to-day conduct are subject to the limitations that the Constitution and the democratic political process impose.

More immediately, the authority of the executive in the field of foreign affairs has evolved historically from the following three specific grants of power in the Constitution itself: the president's power to send and receive ambassadors and ministers to and from foreign states, his authority as commander in chief of the armed forces, and his power to make treaties by and with the advice and consent of a two-thirds majority of the Senate.

It is from the Constitution's grant of authority to the executive to send and receive diplomatic emissaries that the president's power to bestow recognition upon foreign governments (or, conversely, to withhold such recognition) has been derived. The power of recognition, assumed by President George Washington in the Genêt crisis in 1793, has been exercised by presidents since that time and has never been challenged seriously.

In the twentieth century the president's power to grant or withhold recognition has on occasion become a prominent instrument of policy. Thus from 1913 to 1921 Woodrow Wilson, adhering to a theory of democratic legitimacy with respect to Latin American countries, refused to grant recognition to governments in that region which had come into power through revolution or violence when lawful constitutional means of achieving political change existed. Again, in 1920, Wilson, through Secretary of State Bainbridge Colby, declared that the United States would not recognize the Soviet Union, on the ground that the U.S.S.R. was dedicated to the revolutionary overthrow of other governments in the state system. During the next thirteen years successive presidents adhered to the resultant policy of isolation from the Soviet Union.

Franklin Roosevelt's decision, implemented in the so-called Litvinov agreements of 1933, to enter into diplomatic relations with the Soviet Union was an exercise of the same constitutional power. Also in the same constitutional category were Franklin Roosevelt's decision to withhold recognition from the Japanese puppet-state of Manchukuo; President Truman's decision after World War II not to recognize the People's Republic of China, and his concomitant refusal to grant recognition to several of the Communist satellite states of Eastern Europe; and President Richard M. Nixon's decision in 1972 to extend what amounted to diplomatic recognition to the People's Republic of China.

The Supreme Court has held that recognition or nonrecognition of a foreign government is an act of presidential discretion binding upon all departments of the government, including the courts. "We take judicial notice of the fact," said the Court in *United States* v. *Belmont* (1937), a case dealing with the validity of the Litvinov agreements, "that the President of the United States recognized the Soviet Government, and that normal relations were established [in 1933] between that government and the Government of the United States. The effect was to validate, so far as this country is concerned, all acts of the Soviet Government here involved from the commencement of its existence." Again, in *Baker* v. *Carr* (1962), Justice William J. Brennan included presidential recognition or nonrecognition of foreign governments as within that category of "political questions" ordinarily to be regarded as outside the purview of judicial review. "Recognition of foreign governments," Brennan declared, "so strongly defies judicial treatment that without executive recognition a foreign state has been called 'a republic of which we know nothing.' "

The Supreme Court has held also that the president may at his discretion grant a pretended foreign government the status of belligerency; this falls short of full recognition but it does recognize such a government's legal status for purposes of de jure war. This was the status, said the Court in the *Prize Cases* in 1863, which Lincoln's proclamation of a blockade of the seceded Southern states had conferred upon the Confederacy.

Again, in 1936, President Franklin Roosevelt, by means of a proclamation of neutrality, conferred belligerent status upon the rebel regime of General Francisco Franco in Spain. The president thereafter carefully refrained from formal recognition of Franco's regime as the government of Spain until it had secured full de facto control of the Spanish state, a policy in accord with well-recognized principles of international law.

Formal emissaries sent abroad by the president to permanent diplomatic posts—ambassadors, ministers resident, and chargés d'affaires—are subject to confirmation by a majority vote of the Senate. Only occasionally have such nominees met rejection. A celebrated instance occurred in 1831, when Vice-President John C. Calhoun and certain of President Andrew Jackson's other political enemies succeeded in defeating Martin Van Buren's nomination to be minister to England, a political faux pas that was to play its part in Van Buren's eventual elevation to the presidency.

Presidents have on numerous occasions sent trusted confidants abroad on special diplomatic missions without submitting their names to the Senate for confirmation. Thus, Woodrow Wilson sent Colonel Edward M. House to Europe in the winter of 1915–1916 to negotiate on intimate terms with the British, French, and German governments. A generation later Franklin Roosevelt used his friend Harry Hopkins in the same fashion. Neither president sent the name of his confidential emissary to the Senate for confirmation.

Nor do presidents customarily send to the Senate the names of emissaries to peace negotiations, international conferences, and the like. This practice arose out of the Senate's refusal in 1813 to confirm James Madison's nomination of Albert Gallatin as a special commissioner to negotiate peace with Great Britain, on the ground that his projected status as an envoy extraordinary was incompatible with his duties as secretary of the Treasury. Thereafter presidents pointedly refrained from requesting Senate confirmation for diplomats in this category. For example, President James K. Polk did not send to the Senate the name of Nicholas Trist, whom he appointed in 1847 to negotiate peace with Mexico. In 1898 President William McKinley followed the same practice in initiating peace negotiations with Spain, as did Wilson in 1919 in designating the four men who were to accompany him to Versailles. President Truman also failed to send to the Senate the names of any of his delegates to the San Francisco United Nations Conference in 1945, although the mission included two senators, Arthur Vandenberg and Tom Connally.

More potent as an instrument of foreign policy than the power to send and receive diplomatic emissaries has been the president's constitutional position as commander in chief of the armed forces. Karl von Clausewitz, the German analyst of the theory and philosophy of war, remarked more than a century and a half ago upon the intimate relationship between foreign policy and war. He defined war as an extension of diplomacy by other means. American presidents have taken full advantage of this intimacy to employ the armed forces as a major diplomatic weapon, with or without congressional support. Frequently this has meant resorting to armed intervention against foreign states, or even to undeclared wars, sometimes of considerable duration, without authority from Congress.

President John Adams initiated this policy in 1798, when, after France had rebuffed an American diplomatic mission in the XYZ affair, he broke off diplomatic relations and inaugurated an undeclared naval war at sea. Again, between 1801 and 1815, Presidents Jefferson and Madison waged a series of protracted undeclared naval wars against the Barbary States of the Mediterranean for the purpose of suppressing their piratical depredations on American commerce. At no time did either president request any formal declaration from Congress.

More impressive as an instance of the president's capacity to capitalize upon the intimate relationship between diplomacy and war was President Polk's conduct early in 1846, when he sent an army under General Zachary Taylor to the Rio Grande to support John Slidell's mission to Mexico City, where Slidell was attempting to maneuver that nation into a cession to the United States of California and New Mexico. Polk thus made virtually certain that should the negotiations at Mexico City fail, he could seize upon a border skirmish in the disputed strip between the Nueces River and the Rio Grande as a suitable pretext for war. This is precisely what occurred.

Between 1901 and 1921 Presidents Theodore Roosevelt, Taft, and Wilson intervened repeatedly in the Caribbean to protect what they perceived to be the national interests of the United States. More immediately, they intervened with military forces to support Roosevelt's "police power" corollary to the Caribbean doctrine, to back up Wilson's policy of nonrecognition as an instrument of democratic legitimacy, or to rescue one republic or another from what was seen to be an intolerable state of chaos and anarchy. Highlights were Roosevelt's use of four cruisers and a marine landing force in November 1903 to effect the separation of Panama from its mother state of Colombia as a preliminary to canal negotiations; the armed interventions in Cuba in 1906, 1912, and 1917 under the terms of the Platt Amendment (which did have treaty status); Wilson's decision to land the marines at Vera Cruz in 1914 in order to expedite the fall of the Huerta regime; the large-scale invasion of Mexico in 1916 by National Guard units under General John J. Pershing in pursuit of the "bandit" General Pancho Villa; and Wilson's intervention with the marines in Haiti in 1915 to protect lives and property from conditions of total anarchy. (The Haiti intervention was the prelude to an American occupation lasting until 1934.) One authority has calculated that from 1789 to 1950 successive presidents resorted either to de facto war or to armed intervention short of war for diplomatic purposes on no fewer than 140 distinct occasions.

In the period since 1940 presidential resort to armed force as an instrument of foreign policy has assumed an order of magnitude unknown in an earlier era. On at least three occasions—in 1941, 1950, and 1964—presidents on their own authority have involved the United States in large-scale transoceanic wars of protracted duration, either without prior congressional sanction or under circumstances in which the participation of Congress was at best feeble and uncertain. The consequence was to deprive Congress of any substantial role in major decisions of peace versus war and to render any formal declaration of war either meaningless or at best a declaration after the fact.

The first instance of this kind came in the fall of 1941, when President Roosevelt, as a result of the *Greer* incident, involving a bloodless encounter southwest of Iceland between an American destroyer and a German submarine, ordered the American navy into action against German submarines operating in the Atlantic. This step, which amounted to the commencement of an undeclared naval war against Germany, came as the climax of a long series of unneutral acts against the Nazi state by the United States: the destroyer-base deal, the Lend-Lease Act, and the conversion of the Western Hemisphere Neutrality Patrol into naval support for the Allied convoy system. Some of these actions had involved congressional legislation, but in the final analysis the decision to resort to de facto naval war was Roosevelt's alone. The exchange of formal declarations by Germany and the United States the following December merely imposed legal status upon a war already well begun.

From a constitutional point of view, President Truman's decision in June 1950 to intervene in South Korea in order to counter the Communist North Korean invasion was more remarkable than Franklin Roosevelt's 1941 institution of de facto naval war against Germany. On twenty-four-hours' notice, and without any possibility of formal consultation with Congress, President Truman commenced what was to become one of the bloodiest wars in American history. The president claimed that he had acted in support of the United Nations Participation Act of 1945 and of American obligations under the United Nations Charter, and that accordingly he had no need for congressional sanction for his decision. Technically, from the official American point of view, the war in Korea was a police action, fought under the United Nations flag, and not a de jure war in the legal sense of the term.

As several senators and representatives pointed out on the floor of Congress, the president's argument was constitutionally unconvincing. The United Nations Charter carried no specific obligation to go to war in support of its decisions, nor had the United Nations police force, which had been considered in the Charter, been brought into being.

Moreover, there was immediate precedent at hand for the legal principle that a treaty obligation alone could not commit the United States to war without a decision to that end by Congress. Article V of the North Atlantic Treaty (1949), to which the United States had subscribed only the previous year, carried legal language that pointedly refrained from any direct commitment by any of the signatories to go to war in pursuance of any obligation under the pact. Instead, the pact merely declared that an armed attack against one of the parties in Europe or North America was to be considered "an attack against them all," and obligated each high contracting power merely to consult and to take "such action as it deems necessary, including the use of armed force." This phraseology had been incorporated into the North Atlantic Treaty at the specific instance of the United States, on the ground that, under the American Constitution, Congress alone can decide upon war, so that a treaty obligation to that end would be without force and effect.

It was for this reason that Robert Taft of Ohio, in an embittered speech on the Senate floor, charged that President Truman had "usurped power and violated the Constitution of the United States" by his Korean intervention. But in spite of the constitutional doubts expressed by Taft and several other senators, Congress regularly appropriated ample funds to support the war. In reality it had little choice in the matter unless it wished to see an American army far from home overwhelmed in the field.

In 1951, while the Korean War was still in progress, Truman announced that he was sending four army divisions to Germany in support of the new American obligations to defend the Continent, in accordance with the North Atlantic Treaty and the Lisbon and Ottawa agreements. It was obvious that a large-scale American army on the Elbe opposite Soviet-occupied East Germany constituted a heavy American commitment to go to war in the event of a Soviet invasion of Western Europe, regardless of any constitutional limitation upon the war power. Indeed, the American divisions thereafter were commonly described as a "trip wire" for the very purpose of committing the United States to war should such an invasion occur.

Truman thus precipitated a so-called great debate in the Senate on the constitutionality of his action. Several senators, among them Paul Douglas of Illinois and Tom Connally of Texas, argued flatly that the president in fact possessed the power under the Constitution to move troops overseas, both in pursuance of American treaty obligations and by virtue of his constitutional powers as commander in chief of the armed forces. On the other hand, Robert Taft and John Bricker of Ohio attacked the president's action as grossly unconstitutional.

The outcome of the debate was a substantial victory for the president. The Senate concluded its discussion with the adoption of a weak resolution expressing its "approval" of the president's action, but declaring it to be "the sense of the Senate" that in the future the president ought to obtain the approval of

Congress prior to the assignment of troops abroad, "in the interests of sound constitutional processes and of national unity."

For a time, at least, the Korean War and the great debate very nearly settled completely the question of the scope of the president's power to resort to de facto hostilities as an instrument of foreign policy. President Dwight D. Eisenhower on occasion expressed a certain deference to the power of Congress to declare war. Thus, in 1955 he sought and obtained a congressional resolution authorizing him to use armed force to defend the offshore Nationalist Chinese islands, should he decide that it was in the interest of the United States to do so. But in 1958, when confronted with what he regarded as a major Middle East crisis, he landed troops in Lebanon without any prior notice to Congress, in a move reminiscent of similar presidential "police actions" in the Caribbean fifty years earlier.

In 1962 President John F. Kennedy moved armed forces into the fighting in Vietnam, although the initial American commitment was on a small scale. In the fall of that year, in the Cuban missile crisis, Kennedy employed the navy, again without any congressional authorization, to impose a maritime "quarantine" upon Cuba, a step that avoided war in the formal de jure sense, only because the president deliberately avoided use of the word "blockade." (In international law imposition of a blockade is legally an act of public war.)

The third major "presidential war" of the twentieth century began in 1965, when President Lyndon B. Johnson commenced large-scale American intervention in the civil war in Vietnam. Nominally the president took this step in pursuance of the so-called Tonkin Gulf Resolution of August 1964, by which Congress, acting after an alleged attack upon American destroyers off Vietnam, had authorized the president to use the armed forces in Southeast Asia in defense of American national interest in that region.

In no sense had Congress considered the Tonkin Gulf Resolution to be a constitutional grant of authority for a full-scale war. President Johnson, however, proceeded to wage one. For some time the president's massive intervention in South Vietnam had a large measure of congressional support. But as the war waned in popularity, numerous leading figures in Congress, among them J. William Fulbright, chairman of the Senate Foreign Relations Committee, charged repeatedly on the floor of Congress that the president, without proper authorization from Congress, had involved the United States in a grossly unconstitutional "presidential" war.

Notwithstanding the increasing unpopularity of the Vietnam War, President Richard M. Nixon, even while "winding down" the American ground commitment in Vietnam, at the same time expanded the war into neighboring Cambodia. He did this both with a series of ground thrusts and with a "secret aerial war," which he carried on in Cambodia in the face of persistent denials to Congress and the country at large that any such involvement existed.

The wording of the third article of the Tonkin Gulf Resolution was such that it would have enabled Congress to terminate any authority for the Vietnam conflict under that provision, had it chosen to act. But in spite of rising clamor from its own members, Congress long persisted in refusing to take any such step. President Nixon finally gave in to public sentiment and political pressures and brought American involvement in the war to a close in January 1973, after protracted negotiations and a "Christmas bombing" attack on North Vietnam.

It was the congressional control over appropriations that enabled Congress, at long last stirred into action by an aroused public opinion, to impose sharp limitations upon executive foreign policy in Southeast Asia. The Constitution declares, in Article I, Section 9, that "No money shall be drawn from the Treasury, but in Consequence of Appropriations made by Law . . . ," and thus far no president has ventured overtly to breach this injunction. Beginning in 1970, Congress inserted provisions in all military appropriation bills prohibiting any American military assistance for the government of Cambodia, except where necessary to effect the withdrawal of American troops from Southeast Asia, or to secure the release of prisoners of war.

In June 1973, following the withdrawal of American forces from Vietnam, Congress voted to cut off all funds for further United States military operations in Cambodia. President Nixon vetoed this measure, but he thereafter accepted a compromise resolution fixing the fund cutoff for operations in Cambodia at 15 August. Meanwhile, the United States Court of Appeals for the Second Circuit ruled in July that the constitutionality of the American air war in Cambodia amounted to a "political question," and therefore was not subject to justiciability in the federal courts. The Supreme Court thereafter refused to intervene, thus in effect sustaining the circuit court finding. The attempt to impose limits upon presidential war making through the courts thus ended in failure, but control through the appropriations process was presently reaffirmed.

In the spring of 1975 President Gerald R. Ford, dismayed by the prospect of the imminent conquest of South Vietnam by communist forces, appealed to Congress to adopt a large supplemental emergency military appropriation for South Vietnam, to replace military supplies lost in that government's recent defeats. But Congress adamantly refused to adopt any such measure. Congress also stalled on an appropriation bill for nonmilitary assistance for South Vietnam, for which the president asked. The war in Vietnam shortly ended in a total communist victory, public opinion and the congressional stance on appropriations having rendered any last-minute assistance to Saigon impossible.

Meanwhile, Senator Jacob Javits of New York, aroused by successive revelations of congressional weakness with respect to its control over the war power, introduced a war powers bill to limit executive war making. This measure, which passed the Senate in 1972 and again in 1973, finally became law in October of that year over President Nixon's veto.

The War Powers Act amounted to a modest attempt to reassert some congressional control over war making. It provided that in the absence of a declaration of war by Congress, the president could lawfully initiate hostilities only under four limited conditions: to repel an attack on the United States, to protect American armed forces overseas, to protect the lives of Americans abroad, or to fulfill the military obligations of the United States as set forth in a specific statute. Once commenced, presidential hostilities must be reported to Congress immediately, and could not be continued for more than sixty days without formal authorization by Congress.

Whether the War Powers Act constitutes any very serious check upon established presidential war-making prerogative is doubtful. As critics have pointed out, its language is so broad that it permits the president to initiate almost any kind of military action he considers to be in the national interest. Moreover, it is difficult to imagine a circumstance in which Congress, in the face of a large-scale de facto presidential war once begun, would find itself possessed of any substantial discretion as to whether hostilities should be continued. While the War Powers Act appears to confirm presidential war-making prerogatives, it also provides means for curbing them, especially if public opinion and Congress are opposed to presidential actions. President Ford's swift military action in May 1975, after only nominal consultation with a few congressional leaders, to rescue an American merchant vessel that had been seized by Cambodian communist forces, appears to expose the act's weakness, but the precedent is not yet clear.

Presidential authority under the treaty power is also extensive, although the controls exercised by Congress are substantial. Generally in the making of treaties it is the president who proposes and the Senate that disposes. Yet, in fact, presidential prerogative has to some considerable extent subverted the treaty-making process, through use of "executive agreements."

Early in Washington's administration the principle became established that the Senate plays no role in the negotiation of treaties, as distinct from their ratification. The Constitution stipulates that the Senate gives both "advice and consent" to treaties. But Washington's attempt to consult the Senate with respect to a pair of Indian treaties resulted in dramatic failure, as the chamber insisted upon referring the questions posed by the president to a committee for consideration. Washington thereupon abandoned further attempts at consultation. Since that time the Senate has not been consulted during the treaty-making process, although presidents have on occasion employed individual senators as emissaries in the negotiation of treaties. In other words, the Senate "consents" but it does not "advise."

Precedent has established also that the president may at his discretion decide not to submit a negotiated treaty to the Senate for approval. Thus, President Jefferson "pigeonholed" the Monroe-Pinkney Treaty (1806) with Great Britain, deeming its provisions too unsatisfactory for consideration. The president also may withdraw from the Senate a treaty already submitted to it, as Cleveland did in 1894 with a projected treaty for annexation of Hawaii. Indeed, even after Senate approval the president may decide against an exchange of ratifications with the foreign state in question, thereby aborting the treaty process at the last moment.

The Senate's role in "consenting" to treaties is nonetheless substantial. While it has not often defeated treaties outright by voting them down, it has nonetheless done so on a number of prominent and even spectacular occasions. Thus in 1870 the Senate killed President Ulysses S. Grant's treaty that annexed Santo Domingo; earlier, in 1844, it had voted down President John Tyler's projected treaty for the annexation of Texas. In 1935 it killed American adherence to the Protocol of the Permanent Court of International Justice; and in the most celebrated instance of all, in March 1920, the Senate refused to ratify the Treaty of Versailles.

The Senate may also "bury" treaties simply by refusing to report them to the floor for a vote. It did this in 1904 with a treaty ceding the Isle of Pines to Cuba, refusing to take any action until 1925, when it at length reported out the treaty and approved it. At present writing, the United Nations Covenant on Human Rights, submitted to the Senate in 1948, remains unapproved.

At its discretion the Senate may also strike out or amend a provision in a treaty submitted to it, thereby obliging the president to obtain the consent of the other signatories to the altered text. Thus the Senate struck out Article XII of Jay's Treaty, opening the British West Indies to American trade on terms the Senate considered so onerous as to make the concession worthless.

On numerous occasions the Senate has attached reservations to its ratification of a treaty, laying down certain stipulations as to the treaty's meaning and effect. Such reservations have with some exceptions generally been considered to constitute amendments to the text of the treaty, particularly if they involve any alteration of the obligations of the contracting powers to one another. Thus the Senate in 1926, in approving American adherence to the Protocol of the Permanent Court of International Justice, attached to its ratification the Swanson resolution, which would have reserved to the United States a right to nullify the Court's power to render advisory opinions in cases where the United States "has or claims an interest." Refusal by the other parties to the protocol to accept this reservation effectively killed American adherence.

A resolution setting forth the Senate's "understanding" of the meaning of a treaty, on the other hand, does not technically constitute an alteration of its provisions and thus need not be submitted to the other signatories for acceptance. Thus, in ratifying the Kellogg-Briand Pact (1928), by which the signatories renounced war as an instrument of national policy, the Senate adopted a resolution stating what it understood to be "the true interpretation of the treaty": that it did not impair a signatory's right of self-defense. The Senate was careful to make clear that the resolution in no sense constituted a "reservation," so that it did not require new negotiations with the other signatories involved.

In the courts, treaties have equal standing with acts of Congress as "the supreme law of the land." It follows that a treaty may repeal or nullify a prior act of Congress, while an act of Congress may in like fashion have the effect of repealing the provisions of a treaty, although the repeal may constitute a clear violation of the obligations of the United States under international law. Thus, in the *Chinese Exclusion Case* (1889) the Supreme Court held valid the Chinese Exclusion Act of the previous year, even though the law's provisions violated the American guarantee of free Chinese immigration in the Burlingame Treaty of 1868. "The last expression of the sovereign will," said the Court, "must control."

Treaties, however, do not necessarily take effect as internal law binding upon private parties in the courts unless Congress enacts supporting legislation to execute their provisions.

In this respect treaties thus may be classified as "self-executing" and "non-self-executing." Thus, a treaty cannot appropriate money, since the Constitution expressly stipulates that "no Money shall be drawn from the Treasury, but in Consequence of Appropriations made by Law." On two notable occasions the House of Representatives has balked temporarily at appropriating money required to execute a treaty: in 1795, in connection with Jay's Treaty, and in 1868, in connection with the Alaska Purchase Treaty with Russia. In each instance the House finally yielded, although in the latter case it did so only after massive bribery of House members by the Russian minister to Washington.

Although the courts have not formally decided the matter, it seems probable that a treaty cannot of itself create a state of de jure war, since the Constitution expressly reserves to Congress the power to declare war. The North Atlantic Treaty, as already observed, recognizes this as a constitutional fact of life, as do also the Rio Pact of 1947, the Anzus Pact of 1951, and numerous other defense treaties to which the United States is a party. Nor can a treaty's provisions be enforced internally in the courts as criminal law, except through supportive legislation pursuant to the provisions of the treaty.

On the other hand, the courts have on occasion ruled that a treaty may control the rights of private parties in either the state or federal courts without benefit of supportive legislation by Congress. Thus, in *Fairfax's Devisee* v. *Hunter's Lessee* (1813) the Supreme Court in effect invalidated Virginia's Revolutionary War legislation confiscating the estates of British nationals. The Court held that British land titles were protected against such legislation by the Treaty of Peace of 1783 and Jay's Treaty of 1794. Again, in *Kolovrat* v. *Oregon* (1961) the Court upheld the right of a Yugoslav citizen to inherit property in Oregon pursuant to a treaty guarantee, despite the provisions of an Oregon law that prohibited inheritance by foreign nationals where no reciprocal provisions as to inheritance existed with the foreign state in question.

Under some circumstances a treaty may serve as the basis for an expansion of congressional power, a possibility that has given rise to some considerable controversy. In *Missouri* v. *Holland* (1920) the Supreme Court by a 7-to-2 vote held constitutional the Migratory Bird Act of 1918, which Congress had adopted in pursuance of a 1916 treaty with Great Britain for the protection of certain wildfowl that migrated regularly between Canada and the United States. A similar law, enacted in 1913 without benefit of any treaty, had been held by the lower federal courts as lying outside the powers of Congress, and hence in violation of the Tenth Amendment.

But in an opinion that emphasized the sweeping character of national sovereignty, Justice Oliver Wendell Holmes pointed out that by the wording of Article VI, Paragraph 2, acts of Congress are the "supreme Law of the Land" only when made in accordance with the Constitution, whereas treaties are declared to be such when made "under the Authority of the United States." A treaty, then, could constitutionalize legislation in pursuance of its provisions, which otherwise would lie outside the bounds of congressional power. Holmes conceded that there might conceivably be certain limits upon the treaty power. But in a matter of great national importance, he added, the presumption of constitutionality for a statute in pursuance thereof was extremely strong.

For a time, the dictum in *Missouri* v. *Holland* remained a "sleeping lion." It attracted little attention, and no new expansion of federal power took place in consequence of it. But in the period after World War II a serious controversy developed over the constitutional limits of the treaty power. In *Oyama* v. *California* (1948) the Supreme Court declared unconstitutional a California alien land law that prohibited ownership of land by persons ineligible for citizenship, in this instance Japanese. The Court rested its decision principally on the ground that the act in question violated the equal protection clause of the Fourteenth Amendment. But four of the nine justices, led by Justice Black, argued in concurring opinions that the act also violated Article 55 of the United Nations Charter, by which the United States as a signatory had pledged itself to promote respect for and observance of human rights, "without distinction as to race, sex, language, or religion." In *Fujii* v. *State* (1950) a California district court reached the same conclusion.

The concurring *Oyama* opinions raised two crucial constitutional questions: First, was Article 55 of the United Nations Charter internally self-executing in the absence of supportive congressional legislation? Second, even if it was not self-executing, might not Congress revive the doctrine in *Missouri* v. *Holland,* and use Article 55 as the basis for an expanded federal civil rights statute, of a sweep and extent that otherwise would lie outside the constitutional competence of Congress? These questions worried conservatives generally and Southerners in particular, who feared that Congress might now enact powerful civil rights legislation under the United Nations Charter or like treaties, or that the courts now would proceed to enforce the Charter as internal law without regard to any supportive legislation.

Most constitutional experts, among them Zechariah Chafee of the Harvard Law School, and Manley O. Hudson, a noted authority on international law, now declared that in their opinion the United Nations Charter was not self-executing and that it could not be enforced directly in the courts without supportive legislation. On the other hand, Professor Quincy Wright of the University of Chicago, and Oscar Schacter, deputy director of the United Nations General Legal Division, disagreed, holding that the Charter was indeed self-executing internally.

Neither group of experts, however, was prepared to argue that Congress could not enact supportive legislation for the Covenant under the *Missouri* doctrine. Beyond the United Nations Charter there also loomed the United Nations Covenant on Human Rights, then in the process of preparation, and the prospect that Congress might also eventually legislate to implement the document, should it win ratification by the United States.

The consequence was widespread agitation by conservative interest groups for a constitutional amendment to limit the scope of the treaty power. In 1951 and 1952 the legislatures of Georgia, Colorado, and California petitioned for such an amendment; so, also, did the House of Delegates of the American Bar Association.

In response, Senator John W. Bricker of Ohio, in February 1952, introduced a constitutional amendment to accomplish this end. The heart of the Bricker amendment, as it soon became known, was the "which clause" providing that "a treaty shall become effective as internal law only through legislation which would be valid in the absence of a treaty." Other provisions would have required treaties to conform to the Constitution and would have given Congress general authority to regulate executive agreements with foreign states.

In the extensive debate in and out of Congress which followed, supporters of the Bricker amendment argued that its adoption was imperative if the federal character of the American constitutional system were to be preserved. On the other hand, opponents charged that the amendment was unnecessary, that it would destroy the supremacy of federal treaty law in relation to the states and thus return the nation to the chaotic situation that had existed in this respect under the Articles of Confederation, and that it would seriously impair the conduct of foreign relations.

At length, in February 1954, the opponents of the amendment prevailed, as the Senate voted 60 to 31 (one short of the required two-thirds majority) in favor of a modified form of the amendment. Thereafter agitation for the Bricker amendment gradually died down, since it became evident that no extraordinary expansion of federal sovereignty through the instrument of the treaty power was in prospect.

The Supreme Court itself presently quieted a portion of the prevailing concern about the sweep of the treaty power. In *Reid* v. *Covert* (1957) it held that treaties, like acts of Congress, were subject to the supremacy of the Constitution, so that a treaty in violation of a constitutional provision was void. Justice Black observed that to hold otherwise would be to allow amendments to the Constitution to be adopted by a procedure "not sanctioned by Article V."

Reid v. *Covert,* however, had to do with the guarantees of the Bill of Rights, which *Missouri* v. *Holland* had not hinted could be nullified by treaty. It apparently still remains true that both through the courts and through supportive legislation treaties may on occasion invade the reserved powers of the states, as indeed the Constitutional Convention of 1787 appears to have intended.

In the course of the twentieth century the

executive agreement—although it is nowhere recognized in the Constitution—has become an increasingly important instrument for the conduct of foreign policy. The number of such agreements has steadily increased over the years. In 1941 the number in force was calculated to be well over 1,250; by 1970 the State Department reported the number in force to be 3,973 as compared with 909 active treaties, while in 1973 the department announced that between 1941 and 1973 the United States had concluded 5,590 executive agreements, as compared to 368 treaties. If the variety of lesser agreements, local understandings, and the like is included in the count, the number of executive agreements unquestionably amounts to several thousand a year.

Executive agreements are of two kinds: those to which Congress is a party, either before or after the fact, and those into which the president enters solely upon his own authority, without either submitting the agreement to the Senate for ratification as a treaty, or for approval by the two houses of Congress. The former, the congressional-executive agreement, has become well recognized as an entirely legitimate alternative to the treaty-making process.

Submission of an international agreement to Congress for approval gives the executive branch advantages over the procedure of gaining approval from the Senate. It gets around the two-thirds majority requirement; it makes virtually certain that the House of Representatives will later enact necessary appropriations under the agreement and also other supportive legislation, and it eliminates any question as to whether the agreement is internally self-executing, since Congress itself has already acted.

Assent by Congress to congressional-executive agreements may be forthcoming in advance of the negotiation and conclusion of the agreement, or it may be obtained by the president subsequent to its negotiation, upon its submission to Congress. Thus Congress, in enacting the Lend-Lease Act (1941), authorized the president to enter into contract agreements with certain nations the defense of which the president deemed "vital to the defense of the United States." In like fashion, the European Recovery Program (1949), or Marshall Plan, set up a mechanism for the economic relief of Europe and authorized the president to negotiate agreements with cooperating states pursuant thereto.

In effect this procedure virtually reverses the customary one whereby a treaty resulting from negotiations with a foreign state is then submitted to the Senate for approval. As the implementation of foreign policy has come to involve on occasion the expenditure of hundreds of millions or even billions of dollars, advance legislative authorization has become more and more common. It is one more instance of the control Congress exerts over foreign policy through the appropriations power.

On the other hand, the joint resolution of 1947 ratifying the headquarters agreement with the United Nations involved approval of an agreement already entered into, the agreement itself being incorporated into the statute. The Bretton Woods Monetary Agreement also received formal congressional approval by joint resolution, in 1945, as did the agreements for American membership in the World Health Organization (1948), the International Refugee Organization (1947), and the earlier International Labour Organization (1934).

Congressionally sanctioned executive agreements pose no serious constitutional problems. As early as 1882 the Supreme Court in *Cotzhausen* v. *Nazro* held that an international postal convention, when approved by Congress, was valid law.

By contrast, executive agreements with foreign states entered into by the president solely on his own authority, without any submission either to the Senate or to Congress, have frequently been the subject of some controversy, although they have a certain recognized standing in the courts. There have been many such agreements dealing with matters of substantial, or even vital, national importance. Thus, as early as 1817, President James Monroe negotiated with Great Britain the Rush-Bagot Agreement, providing for a limitation of naval armaments on the Great Lakes. A more dramatic instance occurred in 1905, when President Theodore Roosevelt resorted to an executive agreement with the president of the Dominican Republic establishing a financial protectorate over that state, after the Senate had refused to approve a treaty to that end. Indignant but helpless, the Senate finally capitulated, and in 1907 approved a treaty substantially similar to that it had rejected two years earlier.

Equally controversial were several executive agreements that Franklin Roosevelt negotiated during World War II. The destroyer-base deal (September 1940) was essentially an unauthorized executive agreement, although the president had the benefit of a strained and dubious legal opinion by Attorney General Robert H. Jackson resting the agreement upon prior statutory authorization. Not without reason, the noted constitutional authority Edward S. Corwin labeled the agreement an exercise of "unrestrained autocracy in the field of our foreign relations."

Even more controversial was the Yalta Pact (1945) between Franklin Roosevelt, Winston Churchill, and Josef Stalin, in which the three men entered into a series of wide-ranging understandings with respect both to Germany and to certain occupied or partially occupied allied states, notably Poland and China. Technically, Yalta was a military field agreement, not unlike an armistice, so that the president's constitutional capacity to enter into it without subsequent senatorial or congressional assent could be regarded as derived properly from his powers as commander in chief. Yet, in its form and consequences, Yalta was meant to be a treaty, committing the United States, as it did, to a variety of postwar territorial arrangements.

In a few instances the Supreme Court has accorded the force of internal law to executive agreements lacking senatorial or congressional sanction. In *United States* v. *Belmont* (1937), which gave domestic effect to the Litvinov agreement case, the Court passed favorably upon the title of the United States government to a bank account in New York originally owned by a Russian national, which had been confiscated by Soviet decree and subsequently assigned to the United States by the agreements.

"In respect of what was done here," Justice Sutherland's opinion declared, "the executive had authority to speak as the sole organ" of the national government, in a matter "vested exclusively" within it. Because of its nature, the agreement was not a treaty "as that term is used in the treaty making clause of the Constitution," and hence "did not require the advice and consent of the Senate." It was nonetheless a valid international compact, enforceable in the courts as valid law, and state laws might not be "interposed as an obstacle thereto." Six years later, in *United States* v. *Pink* (1942), the Court again affirmed the enforceability of the Litvinov agreements as internal law on the same grounds.

For many observers the extraordinary power that the executive can exercise over the conduct of foreign policy is a principal element in what Arthur Schlesinger, Jr., has named the "imperial presidency" and constitutes a major threat to the democratic foundations of the American constitutional system. The repercussions of the Vietnam War and the revelations of the activities abroad of the Central Intelligence Agency inspired a strong movement in Congress and among the public to reassert sleeping constitutional and legislative checks upon the vast power that the president possesses in the field of foreign affairs.

Whether limitations of consequence are likely to be imposed upon the president is open to some doubt. In the conduct of foreign policy the present "living constitution" is in part the consequence of steady growth over a period of nearly two centuries, bulwarked by numerous Supreme Court decisions.

It is also arguable that the vast discretionary power in foreign policy, which the president has assumed within the last forty years or so, is a reflection of overweening realities that confront the United States in the late twentieth century. These include the destruction of the isolation that once enveloped the United States; the disappearance of the old system of the European balance of power; the rise of superpowers, including the United States; the heavy international military commitments of the United States; the disappearance of the former comfortable "time cushion" in international emergencies; and the potential of modern technology in nuclear warfare. It is debatable whether a presidentially elitist or a more democratically constituted foreign policy would best possess the flexibility, resourcefulness, decisiveness, and speed in implementation to deal properly with the realities of the contemporary world order.

BIBLIOGRAPHY

On the Constitution and foreign policy, see C. A. Berdahl, *War Powers of the Executive in the United States* (Urbana, Ill., 1921); E. S. Corwin, *The President: Office and Powers, 1787–1957* (New York, 1957), which is very valuable on constitutional prerogative in foreign policy; Louis Henkin, *Foreign Affairs and the Constitution* (Mineola, New York, 1972), an excellent comprehensive analysis of the constitutional law of foreign policy, with good footnotes; Louis Henkin, "The Treaty Makers and the Law Makers: The Law of the Land and Foreign Relations," in *University of Pennsylvania Law Review,* 107 (1959), which is useful on relationships between treaties and acts of Congress; Jacob K. Javits, *Who Makes War: The President Versus Congress* (New York, 1973), which has an attractively written historical analysis of the control of the war power, with some technical inaccuracies; Charles A. Lofgren, "War-Making Under the Constitution: The Original Understanding," in *Yale Law Journal* (March, 1972), the best short analysis of the original intent of the framers with respect to the war power; James A. Robinson, *Congress and Foreign Policy Making* (Homewood, Ill., 1962), a concise accurate study of foreign policy as Congress influences it; John Stevenson, "Constitutional Aspects of the Executive Agreement Procedure," in *Department of State Bulletin,* 65 (1972), which presents useful statistics and valuable constitutional insights; and Quincy Wright, *The Control of American Foreign Relations* (New York, 1922), the classic modern analysis of the subject.

[*See also* Congress and Foreign Policy; Executive Agreements; Politics and Foreign Policy; Presidential Power in Foreign Affairs; Treaties.]

CONTAINMENT

Barton J. Bernstein

> If . . . I was the author in 1947 of a "doctrine" of containment, it was a doctrine that lost much of its rationale with the death of Stalin and with the development of the Soviet-Chinese conflict. I emphatically deny the paternity of any efforts to invoke that doctrine today in situations to which it has, and can have, no proper relevance.
>
> —George F. Kennan (1967)

THE containment doctrine, with its ambiguities and imprecision, has been the guiding principle in American foreign policy since shortly after World War II. In its most general form, containment denotes the American effort, by military, political, and economic means, to resist communist expansion throughout the world. Yet, precisely because of the looseness of the doctrine and the differing interpretations, its acknowledged author, George F. Kennan, then an influential foreign service officer and now a respected private scholar, has often opposed important tactics that policymakers have defined as the implementation of containment: the global rhetoric of the Truman Doctrine in 1947, establishment of the North Atlantic Treaty Organization in 1949, the heavy military emphasis of United States policy in the 1950's, the extension then of alliances to Asia and the Middle East, and the prolonged military involvement in Vietnam.

While agreeing on the desirability of resisting communist expansion, Kennan and others have disagreed on whether the doctrine remained relevant, and how and where to implement it. Their disputes have often rested on fundamental differences about the capacity of American power, about the extent of American interests beyond Western Europe, and especially about the nature of the communist threat. The last issue has raised many questions. Is the threat subversion, revolution, military aggression, economic encirclement, or some combination? With the exception of Yugoslavia, was world communism controlled by Josef Stalin even after the successful Chinese revolution in 1949? After the death of Stalin in 1953 or after the obvious Sino-Soviet split in the early 1960's, did the nature of the communist threat change? Was the threat then primarily China and wars of national liberation in the Third World, not the Soviet Union and the developed world?

Beyond these important issues, scholars, as well as politicians and policymakers, have raised other questions: whether the doctrine in 1947 was new or necessary, whether it was ultimately self-defeating, whether it was active or passive, and whether it did or should have endured as American policy into the mid-1970's. Many of the questions about containment, if it is interpreted as the general course of American foreign policy, become the basic questions about that policy itself, from Harry S. Truman to Gerald R. Ford.

KENNAN'S PUBLIC STATEMENT OF CONTAINMENT

Writing mysteriously as "X," George Kennan, then the head of the State Department policy-planning staff, first publicly articulated the doctrine of containment in "The Sources of Soviet Conduct," in *Foreign Affairs* (July 1947), the influential journal of the Council on Foreign Relations. When his identity quickly leaked out, his analysis was interpreted as official policy, because of his position in the State Department and because the essay seemed to justify a recent bold departure in American foreign policy: Truman's call on 12 March 1947 for economic and military aid "to support free peoples who are resisting attempted subjugation by armed minorities or by outside pressures."

Kennan's essay offered both a diagnosis of and a prescription for treating the Soviet threat. His prescription attracted the most attention: the need to confront "the Russians with unalterable counterforce at every point where [the Soviet Union] shows signs of encroaching upon the interests of a peaceful world." There would be perpetual crises, presumably frequent confrontations. Such a policy "must be . . . long-term, patient but firm and vigilant." Kennan predicted that it would increase enormously the strains in Soviet society, compel Soviet foreign policy to be cautious and circumspect, and produce the gradual mellowing or breakup of the Soviet system. Containment promised the liberation of Eastern Europe and an American victory in the long run, without preventive war. History was on the side of the West. His faith that the future belonged to democratic capitalism directly repudiated the Marxist faith that capitalism would crumble from its own contradictions.

Kennan's diagnosis of Soviet policy was central to his optimistic forecast and to much of his doctrine. Soviet policy was, he asserted, relentless but not adventurous—"a fluid stream which moves constantly wherever permitted to move toward a given goal." This patient but insatiable expansion, he explained, was the logical outgrowth of communist ideology. Soviet hostility to the West, in turn, was a result largely of the "neurotic world view" of Soviet leaders and of their need to create a foreign enemy to justify dictatorship at home. Their "world view" was both paranoid and functional; it misunderstood Western actions but also it helped them stay in power.

Kennan's message was clear: Soviet hostility was not a reasonable response to America's wartime policy or to earlier American actions, nor could negotiations ease or end this hostility and produce a settlement of the Cold War. His analysis became the new orthodoxy: the Soviet Union was "committed fanatically to the belief that with the United States there can be no permanent *modus vivendi,* that it is desirable and necessary that the internal harmony of our society be disrupted, our traditional ways of life be destroyed, the international authority of our state be broken, if Soviet power is to be secure."

THE BACKGROUND OF THE MR. "X" ESSAY

Kennan, a member of the first generation of State Department specialists on the Soviet Union, was born in Milwaukee in 1904 of a well-to-do family, attended Princeton University in the early 1920's, and perhaps because of his provincialism amid the glitter of the eastern elite, developed the sense of the outsider. A man of rarefied intelligence and of strained sensibility, he was in many ways a latter-day Jamesian character. He was sensitive to the slightest rebuff, to minor breaches in etiquette, and yet, judging from his *Memoirs,* when he returned to the United States during the 1930's, remained curiously untroubled by the economic depression in his own nation.

In the diplomatic service Kennan happily found what he termed "protective paternalism" and seemed to delight in the ordered tasks, the requirements of discipline, the acts of civic responsibility, the applications of intelligence, and the distance from the United States. When the United States opened diplomatic relations with the Soviet Union in 1933, Kennan became third secretary in Moscow. He later recalled that his four years in Moscow were "unavoidably a sort of liberal education in the horrors of Stalinism," and his hostility to Marxism and the Soviet system grew. They offended his taste, his sensibility, and his values.

A fierce critic of the Soviet system, Kennan deplored America's welcoming the Soviet Union in 1941 as an "associate in defense of democracy," for this alliance, he complained, would identify the United States with Soviet oppression in Eastern Europe. By 1944 Kennan was already counseling that Soviet-American diplomatic collaboration was impossible. Fearing that the United States lacked "the political manliness" to stop the Soviets from carving out a sphere of influence in Eastern and Central Europe, he proposed, in despair, that the United States might as well divide Germany, partition Europe into spheres, and define "the line beyond which we cannot afford to permit the Russians to exercise unchallenged power or to take purely unilateral action." This was the containment doctrine in embryonic form.

In 1944 and 1945 Kennan's analysis was unacceptable to many policymakers, including his immediate superior, W. Averell Harriman, the American ambassador to the Soviet Union. They had defined American interests in universalist terms to include Eastern Europe, but believed that Soviet-American cooperation was possible—that the Soviets would withdraw or reduce their influence and accede in this area to free elections. These policymakers concluded that American economic power and atomic energy might compel the Soviets to accede to American wishes in this border area. Unlike Kennan, they believed that Soviet policy was alterable, that accommodations could be reached—on American terms.

In early 1946, when Stalin warned of future capitalist wars, called for Soviet military strength, and refused to join the World Bank and the International Monetary Fund, the Department of State asked for an analysis of Soviet policy, evoking from Kennan his famous "long" telegram of 22 February 1946, an early statement of his "X" essay. "The more I thought about this [opportunity]," he later wrote, "the more it seemed obvious that this was 'it.' For eighteen months I had done little else but pluck people's sleeves, trying to make them understand the nature of the phenomenon with which we in the Moscow embassy were daily confronted and which our government and people had to learn to understand if they were to have any chance of coping successfully with the problems of the world."

Kennan's telegram—explaining that Russia was expansionist, malevolent, warlike, and uncompromising—neatly expressed the emerging conclusions among policymakers in Washington. The response was, Kennan recalls, "nothing less than sensational." It lifted him from the relative obscurity of chargé d'affaires in Moscow, won the affection of Secretary of the Navy James Forrestal, brought Kennan a position at the newly created National War College, and gave him fame and popularity within the higher echelons of the Truman administration. Kennan had not offered new thoughts or insights, but, rather, at a critical juncture had phrased in telling words the emerging analysis within the administration.

According to some revisionist historians, his message arrived as policymakers were moving away from "liberation" in Eastern Europe and the hopes of using "atomic diplomacy" to roll back Soviet influence there. The Soviets, while delaying elections in Bulgaria in August 1945, had not yielded further to implied threats. The result was a virtual stalemate in this area. While pledged to universalism, and wanting democratic governments and an economic open door in Eastern Europe, the United States was not prepared to go to war to achieve its goals there.

Two weeks after the "long telegram," on 5 March 1946, Winston Churchill, former British prime minister, delivered his famous "iron curtain" address. The Soviet Union, he asserted, did not want war, only the "fruits of war and the indefinite expansion of [its] power and doctrines." The implication was that the Soviet Union was insatiably expansionist and would use subversion and aggression to take over Europe and Asia. Churchill's clarion call to the West had the endorsement of President Harry S. Truman, who had read the speech in advance and presumably welcomed it as part of the administration's strategy of reorienting the American public for a "get-tough" policy toward the Soviet Union.

That strategy included exploiting the dispute in Iran, where the Soviet Union had not yet withdrawn its troops from Azerbaijan, an oil-rich northwestern province once part of czarist Russia's sphere of influence. In early 1946 the United States pushed this issue into the United Nations forum, and insisted upon keeping the matter there even after the Soviet Union promised in late March to remove its troops in a few weeks. American success in this venture established for many policymakers that firmness could compel the Soviets to withdraw from recently occupied areas beyond Eastern Europe and to accede to American demands.

In the summer of 1946 Truman requested an analysis of Soviet policy. Simplifying Kennan's analysis in the "long telegram," the resulting study stressed the influence of Marxist ideology on Soviet action. The Kremlin leaders "adhere to the Marxian theory of ultimate destruction [of capitalist states] by every means at their disposal." Efforts at accord or mutual understanding would be "highly dangerous" for the United States, since concessions would raise Soviet demands. Warning that the Soviet

Union might start war to spread communism, the report called for "resisting [Soviet] efforts to expand into areas vital to American security" and being "prepared to wage atomic and biological warfare." Such strength, the report concluded, might make it possible to avoid actual war.

By late summer the Soviet Union's refusal to endorse the American plan for international control of atomic energy confirmed to policymakers that the Soviets were deceitful, suspicious, and uncompromising. How, Americans asked sincerely, could the Truman administration's offer, which they incorrectly deemed magnanimous, be rejected? Concessions were impossible. Compromise would not work. Kennan privately suggested that the United States use implicit "atomic diplomacy" to force the Soviets to accept the plan. He proposed, in the words of an associate, tactics "designed to convince the Russians of our serious intent and of the consequences if they chose to continue their present course." His proposal included the public announcement of "the construction of a new bomb-proof General Staff headquarters in a remote region"—a possible preliminary to war.

Amid the growing East-West tension, with his own expanding reputation as a prescient Soviet expert, Kennan found additional opportunities to refine and advance his views in Washington and in other influential quarters. In January 1947 Secretary Forrestal, Kennan's benefactor, asked him to comment on a manuscript on Soviet policy, and Kennan went beyond the assignment to present on 31 January his own lengthy interpretation. His paper for Forrestal—based on an early January speech before the Council on Foreign Relations in New York—became the "X" essay. It was speedily cleared by the State Department, for Kennan's thoughts were compatible with emerging American policy. Upon publication of the essay, he became the recognized philosopher-diplomat of containment. He had synthesized the emerging wisdom and dignified it within an acceptable intellectual framework.

THE TRUMAN DOCTRINE

Four months before publication of "The Sources of Soviet Conduct" and while it circulated within the administration, President Truman launched what became known as the Truman Doctrine. Speaking before Congress on 12 March 1947, he called for a global crusade against encroaching communism and requested $400 million in military and economic aid, as well as military and economic advisers, to halt what he described as communist aggression and subversion in Greece and communist threats to Turkey. The alternatives in beleaguered Greece, he contended, were totalitarianism or freedom. The world was at a critical turning point: the struggle was between the forces of light and darkness, of humanity and evil. America's commitment could turn back the hordes of oppression and guarantee freedom.

Although Truman never explicitly labeled the Soviet Union as the malefactor, his slightly veiled references left no room for doubt. Most policymakers then assumed that Stalin was supporting and planning the revolution in Greece, the intended recipient of most of the American aid. According to the later testimony of Milovan Djilas, a Yugoslavian revolutionary, Stalin opposed the revolution in Greece and tried to stop communist nations from supplying the Greek revolutionaries. Stalin was sometimes a counterrevolutionary, who believed, Djilas wrote, "that the creation of revolutionary centers outside Moscow could endanger its supremacy in world communism. . . ." American policymakers were apparently blinded by their own ideology, by their belief that the communist world was then monolithic, and by their conviction that Stalin was an ardent revolutionary and would extend communism whenever possible.

The Truman administration seized the opportunity to declare the Cold War in the "Truman Doctrine" speech. Until March, partly because of some pro-Soviet attitudes in the United States and fears of a disastrous rift in the Democratic party, policymakers had wavered publicly on whether the United States could reach an accommodation with the Soviet Union or whether the Russians were an implacable adversary. Resolving his earlier public ambivalence in March, Truman called for a global crusade against communism while limiting his specific legislative requests to Greece and Turkey.

Kennan, then in Washington at the National

War College and active in the State Department's planning of the program, objected to the tone and ideological content of the message, and to some aspects of the aid program. Judging that the Turkish problem was one of morale that the Turks themselves could solve, he opposed military aid to Turkey. Truman's message, Kennan believed, went too far in its ideological analysis and in its global promises—the stark portrayal of two opposing ways of life and the open-ended commitment to aid free peoples everywhere. He feared that the Soviet Union might be provoked by the tone and crusading commitment to declare war.

Kennan's anxieties eased when the administration, in presenting its request to Congress, retreated from the promise of a global crusade and limited its commitment to Greece, Turkey, and Western Europe. Like most policymakers, Kennan feared the results of a communist victory in Greece and linked that to what later became known as the domino theory. The triumph in Greece would destabilize the Middle East and weaken the morale of Western Europe, so that the people there might "trim their sails and even abet" the victory of communism. For Kennan, the commitment to Greece was necessary, reasonable, and desirable; it was within American capabilities; it would halt "our political adversaries"; and its "favorable consequences will carry far beyond the limits of Greece itself." According to Kennan, other European nations, then beset by communist threats internally or near their borders, would gain hope and have confidence in the United States.

CRITIQUES OF MR. X'S DOCTRINE

Despite Kennan's doubts about some aspects of the Truman Doctrine, most commentators viewed Truman's speech and the "X" essay as parts of the same program—containment. Most unfriendly critics focused on the Truman Doctrine. They charged the United States with bailing out British imperialism in the Middle East, establishing American imperialism there, risking war against the Soviet Union, exaggerating the crisis, militarizing policy, abandoning negotiations, misinterpreting Soviet action, misunderstanding the civil war in Greece, supporting totalitarianism there, escalating the Cold War, and trying to scare the American people. Both right-wing critics like Senator Robert A. Taft, a leading Republican, and left-wing critics like Henry A. Wallace, who had recently left Truman's cabinet because of disagreements on foreign policy, agreed that the Soviet Union was not a military threat. A self-styled heir of Franklin D. Roosevelt's foreign policy, Wallace argued publicly for a settlement of the Cold War and the avoidance of the arms race.

Shortly after Kennan's essay appeared, Walter Lippmann, the respected columnist and sympathetic critic of American foreign policy, published in a series of columns a penetrating critique of the containment policy, later collected as *The Cold War: A Study of U.S. Foreign Policy* (1947). Interpreting the "X" essay as the intellectual rationale for the Truman Doctrine, Lippmann focused on the essay. It was, he contended, fundamentally wrong on two major grounds: it misunderstood the sources of Soviet behavior and offered recommendations for American policy that were a diplomatic and strategic "monstrosity."

Whereas Kennan had stressed Marxist ideology as the major source of Soviet actions (belief in the "innate antagonism between capitalism and socialism"), Lippmann argued on the basis of Russian history that expansion—the quest for a sphere of influence in Eastern Europe and power in the Mediterranean—was an inherited czarist ambition, not a communist innovation. By emphasizing the continuity of Russian history, Lippmann minimized the role of communist ideology. Yet, curiously, in explaining Soviet behavior, he did not stress the long history of Western hostility and American opposition to the Soviet system. Unlike later revisionist historians, Lippmann was not placing the burden for Soviet-American antagonism on American, or Western, actions.

Lippmann agreed with Kennan that Soviet power would expand unless confronted by American power, but he objected on pragmatic grounds to Kennan's plan for the next generation or beyond: resistance with "counterforce" wherever the Soviets threatened, until the pressure destroyed or mellowed the Soviet system. Lippmann argued that this plan was too optimistic: America did not have the patience, the economic power, or the armed forces to contain the Soviet Union wherever it showed signs of encroaching and until it collapsed. Kennan's doctrine was strategically dangerous to the United States; it gave the Soviet Union the initiative, allowed the Soviets to choose for confrontation the areas near their border where they were stronger, and would ultimately lead to excessive demands upon American forces. Lippmann warned that the United States, compensating for inadequate military strength, would recruit and organize a "heterogeneous array of satellites, clients, dependents, and puppets," who might plunge the United States into crises or compel it to abandon them and risk charges of appeasement and "sell out." Kennan's strategy required the United States to create "unassailable borders" near the Soviet Union, which would be an unnatural alliance for the West. For Lippmann, the doctrine of containment, as represented by the "X" essay, failed the test of realism. The essay did not recognize the limits of American power and thereby threatened to involve the United States in dangerous alliances, and ultimately to sap American will and morale when the policy of confrontation did not bring prompt victory.

Lippmann's alternative strategy—later known as "disengagement" when Kennan publicly advocated it a decade later—called for the withdrawal from Germany and eventually from continental Europe of the armies of the United States, the Soviet Union, and Great Britain. This policy, Lippmann argued, would be the "acid test" of Soviet intentions, and, if successful, would reduce tension, eliminate troubling issues, move the two great powers toward a modus vivendi, contribute to a better life for many Europeans, and conserve American resources.

More important than this specific proposal, Lippmann was counseling the continuation of negotiations, the use of diplomacy, in order to achieve at least a partial Soviet-American settlement. The Truman Doctrine and "X" 's diagnosis, the columnist asserted, erred because they rejected diplomacy. "The history of diplomacy," Lippmann wrote, "is the history of relations among rival powers, which did not enjoy political intimacy, and did not respond to appeals to common purposes. Nevertheless, there have been settlements. . . . For a diplomat to think that rival and unfriendly powers cannot be brought to a settlement is to forget what diplomacy is all about."

REFLECTIONS ON KENNAN'S ORIGINAL MEANING

Twenty years later, in his *Memoirs* (1967), Kennan lamented publicly for the first time that his "X" essay had been misunderstood and that he had been mistaken for the architect of those very features of the Truman Doctrine that he had opposed. He had not intended to offer a doctrine, he claimed, but wanted to show that war with the Soviet Union was neither inevitable nor necessary, that there was no need to conclude from the failure of American concessions to the Soviets that there must be an eventual war between the two great powers.

Kennan regretted that he had not explained his meaning of "counterforce" and, thus, had seemed to endorse the militarization of American foreign policy. In 1967 he claimed that by counterforce he had meant "not the containment by military means of a military threat, but the political containment of a political threat." Some scholars have regarded this belated explanation as disingenuous, as an effort to rewrite his own recent past. Certainly, it is curious that, as a master stylist who sought clarity, he chose a metaphor that was so clearly military to express what he claims was a nonmilitary meaning. Even some friendly critics suggest that Kennan's use of language revealed that he intended to propose more than just a political or economic response—also a military one.

Until 1955, despite Kennan's many speeches and articles, including the reprinting of the "X" essay in his *American Diplomacy* (1951), he never publicly clarified his meaning, never explained that his intentions had been grossly distorted. Even in 1967, he did not adequately explain his years of public silence before correcting the record. He did provide, however, a 1948 letter to Lippmann, which Kennan never sent, in which he clarified his understanding of the communist threat and of the American response. In that unsent letter Kennan wrote that he did not favor the stationing of military forces near the Soviet border to halt Soviet aggression, for the Soviets "don't want to invade anyone. . . . They don't want war of any kind. . . . They far prefer to do the job with stooge forces."

In clarifying his understanding of the Soviet threat, Kennan revealed in this letter that he considered the real communist threat internal but often military: "The violence is nominally domestic, not international, violence. It is, if you will, a police violence. . . ." The implication of this analysis, which he seemed to deny in 1967, was that small-scale American interventions might be necessary to deal with these "police" threats. For, presumably, Kennan did not think that the United States should rely in every case on words of support, friendly advice, and economic assistance, even if they were inadequate. In most cases, he assumed, they would be sufficient. But what if the "stooge forces" were not conquered so easily? Applying this logic in the 1960's, others could argue that the Truman Doctrine and the counsel of "X" dictated the commitment of American troops to Vietnam—a conclusion and policy that Kennan opposed by 1966.

In 1947, communism was, for Kennan, monolithic. It was in the service of Josef Stalin. "Any success of a local Communist party," Kennan later explained, "any advance of Communist power anywhere [was] an extension . . . of the political orbit, or at least the dominant influence, of the Kremlin." Looking back on the 1940's, even in 1967, Kennan maintained that the Chinese Communist party had been "an instrument of Soviet power"—a conclusion disputed by some experts who trace the Sino-Soviet rift back to this period and contend that Stalin opposed the revolution of Mao Tse-tung.

Placing himself in 1967 closer to Lippmann's views than the text of his 1947 essay may have justified, Kennan emphasized that "X" did not mean to bar negotiations, only to postpone them until issues could be settled. Whereas in 1947, Kennan had seemed to locate that time in the distant future, in 1967 he implied that he had thought it was quite near when he wrote the essay. Nor, he claimed, did he want a permanent division of Europe, only a temporary division until the possibilities for negotiations developed.

Commenting twenty years later on "X" 's analysis of Soviet motivations, Kennan lamented, "much of it reads exactly like one of those primers put out by alarmed congressional committees or by the Daughters of the American Revolution, designed to arouse the citizenry to the dangers of the Communist conspiracy." This belated reassessment indicates how far in two decades Kennan and the American consensus had shifted. In 1947, however, his tough-minded, hostile analysis of Soviet policy won him respect within the administration and among scholars of the Soviet Union. Few then dissented or criticized him, even though he virtually neglected Russian history and Western hostility in explaining the sources of Soviet conduct.

THE SUPPLENESS OF CONTAINMENT

Although Kennan did not endorse the Truman Doctrine's global rhetoric, he, as well as many of its critics, applauded the Marshall Plan. Whereas the doctrine's military emphasis and ideological tone troubled many, the Marshall Plan with its promise of economic aid was attractive. To many Americans and Europeans, though not to Kennan or other policymakers, the plan seemed to offer a rapprochement to the Soviet Union, even an end to the division of Europe that the Truman Doctrine threatened. For Lippmann, the program of economic assistance was not a part of containment; but to Kennan and others in the administration it was simply another tactic in the implementation of containment.

Kennan, then head of the policy-planning staff of the State Department, had worked on the Marshall Plan in early 1947 and was among those who conceived of it as a way of shoring up Western Europe, improving its morale, halting communism there, prying the Eastern bloc out of the Soviet orbit, and weakening the Soviet Union. This American program of massive economic assistance promised to contain communism and Soviet expansion, maybe even to speed the liberation of Eastern Europe and hasten the destruction of the Soviet system—precisely the promise of the "X" essay. By Truman's own admission, the Marshall Plan and the Truman Doctrine were "two halves of the same walnut."

To the public, the Marshall Plan seemed generous and friendly, partly because the United States invited the Soviet Union, as well as the Eastern bloc nations, to participate in the program. Kennan and other policymakers knew that Soviet membership was unlikely, for they had devised the plan to be unacceptable to the Soviets. It required that European nations provide data on their economy, open their land freely to American agents, and move toward economic multilateralism. As policymakers knew, the Soviets would neither relax secrecy, upon which they believed their security partly rested, nor adopt multilateralism, which would have required them to reorganize their economy and abandon state trading. As Kennan later acknowledged, the Marshall Plan also anticipated that the Soviets would be a donor nation—an expectation that would make the plan even more unacceptable to Stalin.

By reintegrating Eastern European trade back into Western European channels, the plan promised to weaken Soviet power in the Eastern bloc and reorient it to the West. How long—Vyacheslav Molotov, the Soviet foreign minister, had asked earlier—could, say, Rumania or Bulgaria remain independent of the West after the introduction of American capital? Or, for that matter, how could the East industrialize, following Soviet plans, if it joined the Marshall Plan and once more played the role of supplier of raw materials and agricultural products to the West? To halt this "rollback" of its influence, the Soviet Union blocked Eastern European nations from joining the American program.

The Marshall Plan, like the Truman Doctrine, contributed to the division of Europe and probably to the hardening of Soviet policies in her bloc. When the United States successfully helped drive communist parties out of Western coalition governments in 1947 and 1948, the price was increased Soviet suspicion and stepped-up suppression of dissent in the East. As a result of the Marshall Plan, "as a defensive reaction," according to Kennan, the Soviet Union ended democracy in Czechoslovakia with the brutal coup in February 1948.

Containment, as conceived by Kennan and other policymakers, also required various forms of covert action abroad. In early 1948 he urged the government to create a permanent covert capability, including paramilitary activity and political and economic warfare. Under the National Security Council (NSC) paper 10/2, in June 1948, President Truman authorized the Central Intelligence Agency to handle such operations. They included both the blocking of Left forces in the West (especially in Italy and France) in 1948, and assistance to anticommunist forces behind the "iron curtain." Put bluntly, covert activity could offer containment and, ultimately, liberation. It could speed the weakening of Soviet power, as forecast in Mr. "X" 's essay.

Containment, mixed with occasional hopes of "liberation," continued as the policy of the Truman administration. It was, in short, a counterrevolutionary policy that tried to prevent revolutions of the Left, block subversion, eliminate instability ("the breeding ground of communism") in the West, and stop Soviet expansion. Containment, like most other competing American doctrines then, interpreted revolutions as communist and Soviet inspired.

Analysts then and later questioned the mainsprings of this anticommunism. Why did policymakers conclude that American security was threatened by revolution abroad? Did they simply fear that the Soviet Union might benefit and hence that the United States would lose? No. Nor did they fear Soviet military aggression in the short run, for well into 1947 no policymaker expected the Soviet Union to expand militarily. In the long run, leaders were less sanguine. Some revisionist historians have analyzed the fears of policymakers in a larger ideological context: American leaders believed that the removal of markets and resources from the world economy would disrupt international trade, impair production, and weaken the international economy and, in turn, the American economy, which depended upon the international capitalist system and expanding trade. In this view, for some analysts, policymakers believed that American freedoms depended upon prosperity at home, and that the spread of communism abroad, by threatening the American economy, also threatened the American political system and its traditional freedoms. These policymakers also preferred the creation of democratic governments abroad, and believed that they were useful, if not essential, to the flourishing of the American political economy at home.

The containment policy did prove sufficiently supple for the United States to give Tito's Yugoslavian government economic aid in 1949, a year after he had broken with Stalin and the Cominform. The policy, despite its counterrevolutionary implications, also proved sufficiently flexible in practice that policymakers greatly modified, and practically abandoned, it in one notable case (China) where the cost of armed intervention, in American dollars and lives, would have been exorbitant to block the revolution. Earlier economic assistance and military advisers had not been able to check the erosion of Chiang Kai-shek's political and military power. By early 1949, policymakers recognized that they could not halt the communist revolution unless they were willing to commit millions of American soldiers and billions of dollars. Whatever the sources of American anticommunism, whatever the reasons for trying to halt communism, policymakers were aware of the relationship of means and ends; they knew that some commitments to allies and some interventions were too costly. China was such a case.

The administration dramatically applied the doctrine of containment to Asia in 1950, when the United States stressed negotiations for a peace treaty with Japan and military bases there; provided economic aid in May to the French, who were trying to prevent a communist triumph in Indochina; and intervened in June in Korea, in the civil war between the communist north and the American "client state" in the south. That intervention, and the policies following it, ended for more than a decade the hopes of policymakers that the Soviet Union and China might split, that Chinese nationalism might overthrow Mao or make him another Tito.

DISPUTES OVER THE APPLICATION OF CONTAINMENT: NATO AND NSC–68

In 1948–1949, when Western European governments feared armed insurrection, Soviet military expansion, and the power of a revived West Germany, the United States constructed the North Atlantic Treaty Organization to maintain stability, improve morale, block revolution, restrain Soviet pressure, and ease fears about the revival of West Germany. Kennan understood these purposes, but he still objected to the treaty, partly because he deemed it unnecessary. The United States would defend its vital interests (Western Europe) without a treaty, he declared; there was no need to request from signatories a reciprocal pledge that they would go to the aid of the United States. A simple American pledge would suffice.

This attack on legalisms did not cut to the core of Kennan's objections. "The Russians had no idea," he later explained, "of using regular military strength against us. Why should we direct attention to an area where we were weak and they were strong?" He forecast correctly that the pact would mean "a general preoccupation with military affairs, to the detriment of economic recovery and of the necessity for seeking a peaceful solution to Europe's difficulties." In a lame effort to avoid what the Soviets might regard "as an aggressive encirclement of their country," Kennan proposed the exclusion of Greece and Turkey, and probably Italy, as outside the North Atlantic area. His criticisms found no favor with Dean Acheson, the new secretary of state.

Containment, as Kennan recognized, was taking on a life of its own. He was its uneasy sire, torn between pride and distress; he could not restrict it to the paths he wished to follow. Although popularly regarded as its preeminent philosopher and spokesman, he was being relegated within the councils of policy to the outer orbit reserved for critical scolds, for men whose judgment no longer commanded respect. Kennan and Acheson were differing on important issues involving the implementation of containment. Their differences, in important measure, were rooted in the very ambiguities of the "X" essay, especially its definition of "counterforce" and the nature of the communist threat. NATO was partly a military response to the potential insurrections that Kennan, in his unsent letter to Lippmann, had described as political, but which others labeled as military.

Kennan believed that the military needs of containment could be met within the limits of the current defense budget (about $13.5 billion): the development of highly mobile, small, unified forces to deal with the likely military threats of localized, limited conflicts. In 1949–1950 his analysis conflicted sharply with that of Paul Nitze, whom Acheson would soon name as the new director of the policy-planning staff, for Nitze was concerned with the overall threat of Soviet arms and wanted a greatly expanded budget to provide both a limited-war capacity and, more importantly, overall strategic superiority against the Soviets.

Joined by Acheson, Nitze stressed "the Soviet purpose of world domination," and they disregarded Kennan's fears that policy should not be set down in a single document, that it would lead to distortion and a freezing of policy. In part, perhaps, Kennan had learned a lesson from the reception of the "X" essay and its hardening into dogma, albeit an ambiguous one. But more important, he believed that Nitze and Acheson were overmilitarizing American policy and misunderstanding Soviet aims. Acheson later characterized the Nitze-Kennan debate as "stultifying," for he concluded that the question of emphasis in Soviet aims—whether the Soviet Union placed world domination or survival of the regime first—made little practical difference. For Acheson there was still a considerable "degree of risk of all-out war which the Soviet government would run in probing a weak spot for concessions."

Kennan, looking forward to the future, claimed that he was thinking of disengagement in Europe and stressed that there was no Soviet military threat to Western Europe. Defeated by Acheson, Kennan watched unhappily as NSC-68, the security document embodying the Nitze-Acheson plan, moved to the president's desk. NSC-68 would cost between $38 and $50 billion, and promised, ironically, to provide the global capabilities that the Truman Doctrine had outlined, that the administration had retreated from in 1947, and that Lippmann had believed the "X" essay was promoting. NSC-68, when it was accepted after the outbreak of the Korean War, was the dramatic turning point, the bold new departure, in American foreign policy.

THE KOREAN WAR: FROM CONTAINMENT TO LIBERATION TO CONTAINMENT

The Korean War led to the endorsement of NSC-68, vast expenditures for arms in Asia and in Europe, and the overextension of American power. American intervention in Korea was the most dramatic test to that date for containment. Although questions about the origins of the war linger, Truman and his advisers speedily concluded that North Korea had attacked South Korea, that Stalin had approved and planned the attack, and that the invasion was a test of American credibility and a possible preliminary to Soviet probes elsewhere—in Europe, perhaps in Germany. "This could be the Greece of the Far East," Truman declared.

The president quickly expanded the American commitment and sent ground forces to assist the embattled South Koreans. His was a popular decision in the United States, even though he did not ask for a declaration of war. Kennan, among other advisers, agreed that "We would have to act with all necessary force to repel this attack. . . ." He had already urged that the United States should prepare for limited war, and Korea became the test case of his own counsel. The Kremlin, he concluded, had unleashed its puppets to try to block America's peace treaty with Japan and to exploit the opportunity in Korea created by America's withdrawal of troops. A major concern of Soviet policy, he reaffirmed in 1951, was "to make sure that it filled every nook and cranny available. . . . There was no objective reason to assume that the Soviet leaders would leave the Korean nook unfilled if they thought they had a chance of filling it at relatively little risk to themselves and saw time running out." Containment, then, could mean "counterforce" by military means—precisely what Kennan claimed the "X" essay did not counsel; and the military test was in Asia, not Europe, which had been Kennan's preeminent concern.

In July 1950 Kennan agreed with others in the government that the air force should operate beyond the thirty-eighth parallel, but thought that American war aims should be sharply limited: restoration of the status quo ante. Unfortunately, the Truman administration wanted to achieve more and would not negotiate in July 1950, when the Chinese accepted an Indian proposal for a settlement of this nature. Casting aside Kennan's counsel, policymakers rejected India's proposal, partly because it "would leave South Korea defenseless [before] a renewed North Korean attack." Even before American ground troops crossed the thirty-eighth parallel in October and moved toward the debacle near the Chinese border,

Kennan urged caution lest the United States overextend its lines and "frighten the Russians" into war. Unlike many policymakers then, he was content to limit the commitment of American power, not to try to "liberate" North Korea, but simply to stop what he defined as a civil war ("'aggression' . . . was as misplaced here as it was to be later in . . . Vietnam"), and thereby to restrict containment. Kennan lost to Acheson and Truman, who wished to move beyond containment to "roll back" and "liberation." Korea, they then said, could not be "half slave and half free."

When in the fall and early winter of 1950–1951, Red China sent in "volunteers," who pushed back American troops and killed thousands of GI's, American policymakers promptly abandoned "liberation" and shifted back to containment. Some even denied that their war aims had ever included unification of the split nation and the vanquishing of communism there.

LATER APPLICATIONS OF CONTAINMENT: EISENHOWER TO FORD

The ensuing stalemate led many frustrated Americans to question their nation's involvement in Korea, the tactics and purposes of limited war, and the policy of containment itself. John Foster Dulles, a Republican spokesman and State Department adviser who would become Dwight D. Eisenhower's secretary of state, issued the most forceful challenge. In "A Policy for Boldness," in *Life* (19 May 1952), Dulles castigated containment as negative and called for a new policy: one that would "liberate" the "captive peoples" of Eastern Europe and not shrink from the use of nuclear weapons in meeting communist military aggression. Sketching the strategy that would later be fleshed out and bear the name of "massive retaliation," Dulles proposed that the United States might retaliate anywhere ("where it hurts") "by means of our choosing." Such a strategy, he pledged, would deter communist aggression and eliminate limited war initiated by Soviet "stooges." His critiques and proposals, with some softening and hedging, became the Republican party's foreign policy plank in 1952: it promised victory in the Cold War and liberation of Eastern Europe.

Despite the bold rhetoric of massive retaliation and liberation, the Eisenhower administration generally subscribed in its actions to the containment doctrine and even expanded its application to create new alliances in Asia and the Middle East. The administration avoided both nuclear war and significant limited war, and restricted liberation to words of encouragement, even when revolution erupted in Eastern Europe. In Korea, after bombing some irrigation dams and obliquely threatening nuclear escalation, the Eisenhower administration accepted the division of the country and the return to status quo ante—Truman's original war aims. Despite the much-heralded "unleashing" of Chiang Kai-shek in 1953, the Eisenhower administration soon "releashed" him and restricted his actions. Having learned lessons from Truman's involvements in Greece and Korea, Eisenhower would not commit troops to the war in Indochina but used other tactics to prevent a communist victory in his time—the establishment of a client state that received about $2 billion in military and economic aid. Expanding commitments in Asia and the Middle East, along the general lines of NATO, the administration created security pacts, which, critics charged, extended American alliances and power beyond their natural limits. Under Eisenhower, the government used subversion and sponsored revolutions and small armed military interventions to overthrow suspected communist governments and to maintain stability. Eisenhower's major failure, judged by the standards of containment, was the rise in Cuba of a communist government allied with the Soviet Union.

The most marked shift from the earlier policy of containment was Eisenhower's decision (endorsed by Kennan) that negotiations with the communists were desirable and that some important differences in Europe might be settled. In 1955, for the first time since Potsdam in 1945, a president of the United States met with a Soviet premier. Although Eisenhower, Soviet Premier Nikolai A. Bulganin, and Nikita S. Khrushchev, the head of the Soviet Union's Communist party, did not resolve important issues, their summit meeting at Geneva did ease East-West tensions. Kennan, among others, wanted the two nations to go further. In late 1957, echoing Lippmann's plea in 1947, Kennan proposed disengagement—the creation of a unified, independent Germany, withdrawal of foreign troops from Germany and Eastern Europe, and the elimination of nuclear weapons in that area. The Soviet Union had changed under Khrushchev, Kennan declared. There were new "realities." The Eisenhower administration, while implicitly recognizing some of these "realities," would not endorse the plan and even considered giving nuclear weapons to West Germany. Dean Acheson, denying that the Soviet Union had changed and warning against Khrushchev's talk of peaceful coexistence, condemned Kennan for preaching a "new isolationism" and counseling a "futile and lethal attempt to crawl back into the cocoon of history."

Promising victory in the Cold War, John F. Kennedy's administration castigated Eisenhower for allowing communism in Cuba and for failing to provide an arsenal that would give the United States "flexible options"—a capacity ranging from limited conventional war, through limited nuclear war, to holocaust. The Kennedy administration, while seeking to roll back communism in Cuba, generally endorsed the containment doctrine and acted to enforce it by blocking communist expansion, including national liberation movements in Africa and Asia. The result was an escalated arms race and efforts to strengthen the faltering NATO alliance, but after the Cuban missile crisis Kennedy achieved a limited test ban treaty and moved toward détente—a policy opposed by Kennan.

Under Lyndon B. Johnson, national liberation movements in Asia became the focus of administration energies, as the United States abandoned the surreptitious warfare that Kennedy had initiated and openly applied the policy of military containment in Vietnam—a policy that Kennan challenged in 1966. Containment, he suggested, could be extended from Europe in the Stalin years to China in recent years, but the doctrine was ill-suited for Indochina. The costs were too high, Kennan explained to a congressional committee in 1966: "If we had been able, without exorbitant cost in American manpower and resources . . . to do better in Vietnam I would have been delighted, and I would have thought that the effort was warranted." He also thought that Vietnam might well follow an independent, not a Russian- or Chinese-directed foreign policy. While warning against "a precipitate and disorderly withdrawal [which could be] a disservice to our own interests . . . and even to world peace," he recommended liquidation of American involvement "just as soon as this can be done without inordinate damage to our own prestige or to the stability of conditions in that area."

Undeterred by this unwelcome counsel, the Johnson administration publicly justified American intervention in Indochina as necessary to stave off communism, to defeat wars of national liberation, to establish the value of counterinsurgency, to affirm American credibility, to protect the security of the "free world," to halt the loss of dominoes, to maintain access to raw materials, and, variously, to contain the Soviet Union or China, and sometimes both. The limited war proved to be one the United States could not win, as Kennan had lamented, and the cost in American lives and dollars, as well as the disruptions and protests at home, tore apart the nation. The war divided members of the elite, produced the defection of policymakers and old cold warriors, and ultimately compelled Presidents Richard Nixon and Gerald Ford to withdraw American armed forces from much of Southeast Asia. Their decisions did not necessarily represent the abandonment of containment in principle, for that loose doctrine, at least since the fall of China in 1949, had always operated on the assumption that some interventions were too costly and too dangerous.

By the mid-1970's, scholars were unsure whether American policy still subscribed to containment. The détente with the Soviet Union, the recognition of communist polycentrism, the Sino-Soviet split, the erosion of Soviet influence in Eastern Europe, the uneasy settlement in Southeast Asia, the rapprochement with China, the movement toward restoration of relations with Cuba, and the Soviet-American strategic arms limitation agreements—all marked the distance that American foreign policy had moved. Yet, American assistance, despite public denials, in the overthrow of Salvador Allende's elected communist government in Chile, the continued fear of Soviet influence in the Middle East, the efforts to maintain worldwide military alliances, and the desire to thwart national liberation movements—all these suggested that the policy of containment, modified at times, endured as a guiding principle in the conduct of American foreign policy through the end of the Ford administration in 1977.

BIBLIOGRAPHY

The literature on containment is enormous, for it includes material on George Kennan; analyses of the application of his doctrine to various problems since 1945; and also studies of various events, trends, doctrines, and policymakers that are linked, by some interpretations, to containment.

Many of Kennan's wartime and early postwar writings are in Department of State, *Foreign Relations of the United States;* see primarily *1944, IV: Europe* (Washington, D.C., 1966); *1945, V: Europe* (Washington, D.C., 1967); *1946, VI, Eastern Europe; the Soviet Union* (Washington, D.C., 1969); and *1947, III, The British Commonwealth; Europe.* Four major volumes by Kennan reveal his thinking after 1944: *Memoirs, 1925–1950* (Boston, 1967); *Memoirs, 1950–1963* (Boston, 1972); *American Diplomacy, 1900–1950* (Chicago, 1951); and *Russia, the Atom, and the West* (New York, 1958). Kennan's position on Vietnam appears in U.S. Senate, Committee on Foreign Relations, *Supplemental Foreign Assistance Program, Fiscal Year 1966—Vietnam,* 89th Cong., 2nd Sess.

Among the important analyses of Kennan and the doctrine of containment are the following: Walter Lippmann, *The Cold War* (New York, 1948—the 1972 edition, edited by Ronald Steel, has a useful introduction and bibliography); Thomas Paterson, ed., *Containment and the Cold War: American Policy Since 1945* (Reading, Mass., 1972); Charles Gati, ed., *Caging the Bear: Containment and the Cold War* (Indianapolis, 1974); Robert Tucker and William Watts, eds., *Beyond Containment: U.S. Foreign Policy in Transition* (Washington, D.C., 1973); C. Ben Wright, "Mr. 'X' and Containment," in *Slavic Review,* 35 (1976) and "George F. Kennan Replies," *ibid.;* and Wright's rejoinder, *ibid.* (June 1976).

Relevant revisionist volumes on the Cold War are Gabriel Kolko, *The Politics of War* (New York, 1968); Gabriel Kolko and Joyce Kolko, *The Limits of Power* (New York, 1972); Barton J. Bernstein, ed., *The Politics and Policies of the Truman Administration* (Chicago, 1970); Thomas Paterson, *Soviet-American Confrontation* (Baltimore, 1973); William A. Williams, *The Tragedy of American Diplomacy,* 2nd rev. ed. (Cleveland, 1972); and Walter LaFeber, *America, Russia, and the Cold War, 1945–1975* (New York, 1976), which has a substantial bibliography.

For orthodox interpretations of the Cold War, see Adam Ulam, *The Rivals* (New York, 1971) and *Expansion and Coexistence: Soviet Policy, 1917–1973* (New York, 1974); Raymond Aron, *The Imperial Republic* (Englewood Cliffs, N.J., 1974); and Alexander George and Richard Smoke, *Deterrence in American Foreign Policy* (New York, 1974).

The issue of postwar "atomic diplomacy" is disputed in Barton J. Bernstein, ed., *The Atomic Bomb* (Boston, 1976). John Gaddis, *The United States and the Origins of the Cold War, 1941–1947* (New York, 1972), analyzes the impact of Churchill's "iron curtain" speech and America's Iran policy in 1946. The summer 1946 report, "American Relations With the Soviet Union," drafted by George Elsey, is in the Clark Clifford papers, Truman Library. Charles Bohlen, *The Transformation of American Foreign Policy* (New York, 1969), adds information on the Marshall Plan. Milovan Djilas, *Conversations With Stalin* (New York, 1962), expresses his disappointment with Stalin's counterrevolutionary ways. Ray Cline, *Secrets, Spies, and Scholars* (Washington, D.C., 1976), discusses the origins of CIA covert warfare.

Dean Acheson, *Present at the Creation* (New York, 1969), disputes Kennan on NATO and the Korean War. "NSC-68" is available in *Naval War College Review* (1975). Analyses of the Korean War are available in Glenn D. Paige, *The Korean Decision, June 24–30, 1950* (Glencoe, Ill., 1968); and in Barton J. Bernstein, "The Week We Went to War: American Intervention in the Korean Civil War," in *Foreign Service Journal* (January 1977 and February 1977) and in his "Policy of Risk: Crossing the 38th Parallel and Marching to the Yalu," *ibid.* (March 1977).

Material on opposition to national liberation movements is available in U.S. Senate, Select Committee . . . With Respect to Intelligence Activities, *Alleged Assassination Plots Involving Foreign Leaders,* 94th Cong., 1st Sess.; Richard Barnet, *Intervention and Revolution* (New York, 1968); and Noam Chomsky, *At War With Asia* (New York, 1972). Official and quasi-official views are available in Dwight D. Eisenhower, *Memoirs,* 2 vols. (New York, 1965); Roger Hilsman, *To Move a Nation* (Garden City, N.Y., 1967); Lyndon B. Johnson, *The Vantage Point* (New York, 1971); and Walt Whitman Rostow, *The Diffusion of Power, 1957–1972* (New York, 1972). For analyses of the Nixon-Ford policy, see Bernard Kalb and Marvin Kalb, *Kissinger* (Boston, 1974); and John Stoessinger, *Henry Kissinger* (New York, 1976).

[*See also* THE COLD WAR; INTERVENTION AND NONINTERVENTION; THE MARSHALL PLAN; NUCLEAR WEAPONS AND DIPLOMACY; REVISIONISM; THE TRUMAN DOCTRINE.]

THE CONTINENTAL SYSTEM

Marvin R. Zahniser

THE continental system was the name given to those measures of Napoleon Bonaparte taken between 1806 and 1812 that were designed to disrupt the export trade of Great Britain and ultimately to bring that country financial ruin and social breakdown. This term likewise refers to Bonaparte's plan to develop the economy of continental Europe, with France to be the main beneficiary.

Although the continental system was formally inaugurated with publication of Napoleon's Berlin Decree in November 1806, its historical antecedents can be traced as far back as the Anglo-French commercial wars that began late in the seventeenth century. The maxims of mercantilist thought nourished the propensity of France and Britain to institute blockades and carry on commercial war. A common argument of the mercantilists stated that trade, shipping, industry, and the world's bullion resources were fixed quantities that could not be significantly increased or decreased by human effort. This concept led inexorably to the conclusion that nations could increase their wealth and resources only by depriving other nations of their sources of wealth, such as trade. Commercial wars, therefore, if successfully prosecuted, promised a meaningful augmentation to a nation's wealth and diminution of that of the enemy.

Profit was generated, in part, by increasing the volume and value of a nation's exports and in compelling competitors to purchase one's exports on disadvantageous terms while purchasing the least possible amount of the competitor's goods. A favorable balance of trade indicated that a nation's profits and wealth were increasing; this could be gauged by the flow of bullion into the country.

With every nation perceiving that its own advancement could be made only at the expense of others, each country began to pursue trade and tariff policies that differed little in war or peace. War simply stimulated nations such as France and Great Britain to accept even fewer goods from the enemy while pressing their own exports upon the other by every conceivable device. In addition, it was presumed sound economic policy both in war and peace to protect native industries by appropriately stringent tariff legislation.

The major break in this policy came in 1786 with negotiation of the Anglo-French Commercial Treaty (Eden's Treaty). England was largely satisfied with the treaty, but it provoked bitter criticism and complaints in France. Revolutionary France soon began to drift back to the pre-1786 commercial policies. In 1791 the Constituent Assembly adopted a tariff with rates high enough to indicate the new trend. France finally denounced Eden's Treaty early in 1793, an indication of the growing strain in French-British relations and of French determination to protect their industries against British competition. With the execution of Louis XVI in mid-January and the outbreak of war on 1 February 1793, Britain and France resumed their long-standing attempts to strangle each other economically.

Rigid exclusionist policies of early revolutionary France were slightly eased during the ascendancy of Robespierre; they were adopted and strengthened by the government of the Directory (1795–1799). For example, in the notorious decree of 18 January 1798 (29 Nivôse, Year VI), the principle was laid down that the cargo of a ship would determine its nationality; and any vessel carrying goods from England or its possessions was subject to confiscation, both ship and cargo. Ships touching at English ports could not enter French ports. The severity of this measure produced a virtual French self-blockade. Likewise, the Directory supported the Navigation Act, passed by the Convention on 21 September 1793. This act prohibited foreign vessels from importing into France products other than those of their own nation or engaging in the French coastal trade. It is clear that these laws of the revolutionary regimes had essentially the same purpose as their predecessors of the past two hundred years—to damage Great Britain by excluding British goods and ships and to foster French industry, agriculture, and the merchant marine by protecting them from British, and other, competition.

The harshness of the French measures was in part prompted by the disturbing reality that British sea power was annihilating the French merchant marine, bottling up the French fighting navy, taking possession of French colonies one by one, building an enormous carrying trade, and threatening to control neutral trade to its own advantage. Before 1789 there had been 2,000 French merchantmen; by January 1799 the Directory admitted that not a single merchant ship on the high seas was flying the French flag. On the other hand, Great Britain's merchant marine was prospering handsomely during these war years. Between 1793 and 1800 the number of ships under British registry rose from 15,000 to nearly 18,000.

British naval power was much less decisive than British mercantile superiority, overmatching the French fighting navy by a two-to-one ratio. France believed it possible to reduce Britain's naval superiority by rapid shipbuilding and under Bonaparte launched major attempts to do so. For example, between 1803 and 1806 French naval expenditures leaped from a projected triennium total of 240 million francs to more than 400 million francs, an indication of French hopes and ambitions.

Coming to power through the coup d'état of 18 Brumaire, Year VIII (9 November 1799), First Consul Bonaparte, himself a mercantilist, became heir to French commercial traditions and current practices. He also inherited an unpalatable oceanic situation in which the French merchant marine had disappeared and the fighting navy was bottled up and decaying. Bonaparte was soon to turn his enormous energies toward remedying these situations, but he wished for a period of internal consolidation before proceeding with his larger plans. Fortunately for him, the Second Coalition of 1799 soon dissolved. Russia, coming to fear British power in the eastern Mediterranean more than French ambitions, in effect withdrew from the coalition. When Austria was forced to sign the peace of Lunéville in 1801, the Second Coalition disappeared. In March 1802 peace was concluded with Great Britain at Amiens. For the first time since 1792 no great European power was at war with another.

Peace proved to be only an interlude. Great Britain viewed with great anxiety Napoleon's activities during the months of peace: dispatching an army to Haiti as the first step in establishing an American empire; reorganizing the Cisalpine Republic with himself named president; and reorganizing the Helvetic Republic as the Confederation of Switzerland with himself as mediator. Bonaparte also supervised the reorganization of Germany, resulting in consolidated and enlarged German states that now relied on Bonaparte to maintain their position. Great Britain was unwilling to countenance this continuing expansion of French influence. Picking a fight over Malta, Great Britain declared war in May 1803 and began the search for coalition partners. Austria signed an alliance with Great Britain in 1805; the Third Coalition was completed when Alexander I brought Russia into the alliance.

Great Britain did not wait for the Third Coalition to form before instituting its own measures. In June and July of 1803 Britain declared that the mouths of the Elbe and Weser rivers were under blockade, thus cutting off the entire trade of Hamburg and Bremen. On 9 August 1804 Britain also declared all French ports on the English Channel and the North Sea under blockade. In the spring of 1805 Britain placed major restrictions on the carrying trade of the United States (in the *Essex* decision), a response to increasing American attempts to trade directly between the Continent and the enemy's colonies (the reexport trade). In June 1805 and July 1806 Britain also took other measures that underlined its determination to see American trade with enemy colonies carried on only with British approval.

Between 1803 and 1805 Napoleon expended enormous energy in planning to gain temporary naval superiority in the English Channel and thus be able to ferry a conquering army to the British Isles. After two years of frustration and lost hopes, Napoleon temporarily abandoned his invasion plans in August 1805 in order to meet the continental challenge of the Third Coalition. As part of his strategy, he ordered the Cádiz squadron to attack Naples. Admiral Pierre de Villeneuve, under a cloud and fearful that he was going to be recalled in disgrace, put to sea on 19 October with a combined Franco-Spanish fleet of thirty-three vessels. Two days later the blockading force of twenty-seven British ships, commanded by Horatio Nelson himself, engaged the French fleet off Cape Trafalgar. When the battle of Trafalgar had ended, only one third of the Franco-Spanish squadron regained harbor; Great Britain did not lose a single ship. Any lingering hopes of Napoleon that England could be invaded and subdued by land armies had now to be abandoned. More indirect and subtle methods had to be devised to erode and eventually to destroy British power.

As Napoleon analyzed England he perceived certain weaknesses which, if shrewdly exploited, could serve to disrupt its economy, provoke social unrest, and eventually bring England to the conference table in a more compliant mood. Napoleon believed that the British economy was vulnerable because he thought its wealth was founded primarily on trade, rather than on agriculture and industry. He also believed that by disrupting British export trade to the Continent and by forcing England into trade channels on disadvantageous terms, there would be a drain on Britain's bullion reserves; dislocation of industry, banking, and the mercantile communities; and destruction of the overextended credit system. Strikes and other forms of social unrest would surely follow, placing the British government in a highly weakened position vis-à-vis France. Since his own measures could be framed in such a way that French industry and agriculture would be protected, Napoleon felt certain of domestic support in pursuing a regulated blockade. Napoleon gradually perceived that only a coordinated and Continent-wide refusal to accept British goods would produce the intended effects.

Napoleon was also propelled toward a trade war by the English blockading measures and by a series of his own military victories. While the English actions infuriated and challenged him, victories at Ulm and Austerlitz (October and December 1805) and the crushing defeat of Prussia at Jena (October 1806) led him to believe that he could compel, if not persuade, other continental nations to support him in enforcing anti-English trade measures. Napoleon himself later pointed to Jena as the antecedent to inauguration of the continental system, for that battle placed him in control of the Weser, Elbe, Trave, Oder, and the coastline as far as the Vistula.

On 21 November 1806, some three weeks after his triumphal entry into Berlin, Napoleon issued his Berlin Decree. Announcing his decree as a measure of retaliation against Great Britain's blockade declaration of 16 May (Fox's blockade), Napoleon proclaimed the British Isles to be blockaded and all trade or communication with them prohibited. War was likewise declared on all British goods. Trading in British goods was prohibited, and all goods coming from England or its colonies, or belonging to England, were declared fair prize. Further, every vessel sailing directly from any port of England or its colonies was now to be refused entrance to any port on the Continent. A peculiarly hard provision declared all British citizens in territory occupied by France to be prisoners of war and their property to be confiscated.

Contemporaries and some historians have scoffed at the Berlin Decree because Napoleon had no ships to blockade the British Isles. This position misses the point that, like England, which also engaged in declaring paper blockades, Napoleon felt he would stand on firmer legal ground in dealing harshly with foreign merchantmen, both neutrals and allies, if he could demonstrate they had violated his duly proclaimed blockade.

Others, following the arguments of Alfred T. Mahan, have expressed surprise that the

Berlin Decree, and subsequent decrees designed to strengthen the system, fell so harshly upon neutrals like the United States. Since France and its colonies were dependent on neutral carriers to supply their needs, Napoleon, it is claimed, should have wooed neutral trade rather than have treated it in such a peremptory and cynical fashion. Such an argument does not properly weigh several factors in Napoleon's thinking. First, he reasoned that since England controlled the high seas, neutral commerce could only come to the Continent on terms acceptable to Great Britain. As Napoleon saw it, neutral trade was therefore ultimately British trade. Also, Napoleon was anxious to encourage hostility between England and the neutrals, hoping that the neutrals would, as his foreign minister said in 1810, "cause their rights to be respected." Neutrals who refused to trade with England would inevitably become part of France's continental system. Last, Napoleon believed the continental economy much more self-sufficient than Great Britain's. While the Continent might suffer some losses through denying itself neutral or English goods, the vulnerable British economy would experience catastrophe and ruin. If the French colonies suffered because neutral trade was denied them, one must remember that they survived only through British tolerance.

Napoleon's Berlin Decree gave Great Britain the excuse it needed to strengthen those measures designed to force neutral, that is, primarily American, trade into English ports. England had already blockaded all French ports on the English Channel and the North Sea. By a series of orders-in-council in 1807, the most significant being that of 11 November, England prohibited intercourse between enemy colonies and the northern countries. Further, England forbade direct trade between enemy ports and other ports except when those "other ports" were either European British ports (such as Malta) or ports of the vessel's own nation. Thus trade was prohibited between enemy and neutral ports other than in the ports native to the neutral ships. England planned to enforce these regulations by compelling neutral vessels into British ports for inspection, by demanding payment of customs duties, and by issuing licenses authorizing the vessel's journey. Finally, mere possession of the required French "certificate of origin," showing that the vessel's goods were of non-British origin, brought English confiscation of ship and cargo.

Napoleon retaliated in his two Milan decrees (23 November and 17 December 1807) by announcing that any vessel submitting to any of the three basic British regulations (examination of cargo and papers, call at a British port, or payment of duty on the cargo) was thereby denationalized, becoming a proper lawful prize. French privateers, quite obviously, would be the chief enforcers of these decrees. Napoleon again demonstrated his cavalier attitude toward neutral trade some four months later when in the Bayonne Decree (17 April 1808) he ordered confiscation of all ships flying the American flag and entering the ports of France, Holland, Italy, and the Hanse towns. Since the United States had declared an embargo, Napoleon cynically reasoned, ships flying the American flag must be British vessels in disguise. Under the Rambouillet Decree of March 1810, he seized scores of American ships and imprisoned hundreds of the captured crewmen.

This last measure underscored the cruel position in which the wars of the French Revolution and the continental system placed the United States. Articulation of the continental system merely sharpened a major question confronting the United States after 1793: Would England or France be the primary benefactor of American trade? Federalist administrations essentially had answered that question through negotiating Jay's Treaty (1794) with Great Britain, but American ratification of the treaty contributed to a quasi war with France between 1798 and 1800. The war led to internal unrest, the eclipse of the Federalist party, a widespread assault upon the civil liberties of dissenters, and a national hope that such a war would not again soon be necessary.

During the four years prior to enunciation of the continental system, and the responsive British measures, American commerce prospered remarkably. British, continental, West Indian, and South American markets all contributed their share to this era of great commercial prosperity. It was President Thomas Jefferson's and Secretary of State James Madison's mistake to believe that this lucrative interlude could and should continue. Nor did many American merchants seem to grasp fully that the continuing flow of trade and relatively open markets was entirely at the discretion of the belligerents. When the belligerents began to decree the regulation of neutral trade, many Americans reacted with shock, indignation, and a determination that the measures be repealed or modified.

Jefferson and Madison's perspective on how to resist the continental system and related British measures is complex and interesting. Both were sympathetic to the larger purposes of the French Revolution yet outraged by the rise of Napoleon Bonaparte and his bold aggressions against those nations resisting his program of conquest. Yet both wished to keep their indignation within bounds, partly because they fervently hoped to persuade Bonaparte to help the United States deprive Spain of the Floridas at some opportune moment. Also, they struggled to keep some perspective on Napoleon; in essence, they viewed him as temporary scum floating on the beneficial and permanent wave of the French Revolution. They believed that such a person should not be allowed to disrupt permanently the spirit of American and French comradeship arising out of their revolutions, so close in time and in their larger purposes.

Also, Jefferson and Madison shared with Bonaparte the view that Great Britain was the greatest enemy of their respective nations. After all, they reasoned, Great Britain was seizing American sailors and forcibly pressing them into service, in effect denying many Americans their right to life and liberty. And quite clearly Britain was the major culprit on the maritime trade issues, for she exercised effective naval power in regulating American trade while Bonaparte had power only to harass the trade lanes with commerce destroyers or to close continental ports to American trade. Finally, British ill will was demonstrated by the continuing intrigue with American Indians in the Northwest Territory.

Paul Varg has likewise commented extensively on the conviction of Jefferson and Madison that a practical accommodation with Great Britain on the difficult maritime and trade issues would have constituted a betrayal by the United States of its self-appointed role as defender of the rights of small powers in war situations. While they wished to be practical statesmen, they also intended to be regarded as prophets by future generations. Defense of neutral rights seemed one way to ensure their future historical stature. Thus a certain principled rigidity was introduced into American-British diplomacy that was not operative in defining the American-French relationship.

As they contemplated measures to counter the economic systems established by France's continental system and a series of British orders-in-council, Jefferson and his successor, Madison, were confronted by a puzzling domestic situation. Jefferson in particular was regarded by fanatical New England Federalists as a devotee of everything French and a tool of Napoleon. His persistent hostility to Great Britain, and to the advancement of American trade, was also presumed. The presumption that Jefferson and Madison acted from unworthy motives when dealing with both England and France became especially troubling when such views were held precisely by those who would be severely affected if the United States pursued a course of economic retaliation. Another complicating factor was that these same Federalist merchants expressed willingness to endure most maritime hardships imposed by Great Britain, mainly because such conformance would guarantee the continuance of their trade and profits, but partly because they shared England's horror of Napoleon and the French Revolution that had spawned him. The fact that these merchant-Federalists were largely located in New England also raised Jeffersonian anxiety that coercive commercial measures would be interpreted as politically inspired punishment for the one geographical section having continuing Federalist strength.

Thus, whatever policy or series of policies Jefferson and Congress adopted in reaction to the continental system or to British measures, certain difficulties lay ahead. Submission would disturb militant patriots and those who believed neutral rights should be defended on principle; resistance would alienate those with a vested economic or political interest in continued trade. It is therefore interesting to note how decisively Jefferson pressed for an embargo, a measure certain to have profound internal consequences. Jefferson and Madison, however, were intellectual cousins to Bonaparte and to British statesmen in believing that severe economic measures were the best means to bring an offending nation to heel. In this sense, the continental system, the British orders-in-council, and the embargo (and subsequent American measures) were all grounded in common postulates about the persuasive power of economic warfare and in the assumption that nation-states will respond in a rational way if enough economic pressure is mounted against them. As events turned out, only the American economic measures had their desired impact, but even then repeal of the offending orders-in-council came too late to prevent war between the United States and Great Britain.

Jefferson's embargo policy provoked real consternation in England and New England, primarily because of the hardships it imposed on Anglo-American trade. But it also aroused deep anger because it quite clearly complemented Napoleon's continental system. Since the United States was not free to trade with France, given British control of the high seas, an American self-blockade was clearly designed to injure England. Jefferson's objective, of course, was not to aid Napoleon but through economic coercion to persuade Great Britain to modify its regulations concerning neutral trade. If the chief culprit, England, modified its regulations, Jefferson and Madison felt confident that Napoleon would likewise be forced to ameliorate the continental system. Such a modification would in turn attract American trade to the Continent and to French colonies.

American domestic pressures against the embargo, however, became so severe that Congress moved toward repeal in the last days of Jefferson's presidency. Pressures came from many directions, some anticipated and some not. Jefferson's support began to erode within his own party; this circumstance was reflected in the difficulties of enforcing embargo measures at the state level, even where the governors were Republicans. Madison's administration, together with a wavering and troubled Congress, was subsequently never able to devise a series of measures to persuade France and England to ameliorate significantly their virtual warfare on neutral trade. The Non-Intercourse Act (1809), which became effective three days before Madison entered office, was an embargo measure with a difference: commerce was restored with every nation except France and England, but provision was made that trade with those nations would be resumed as soon as they repealed their noxious decrees and orders.

When this measure proved unavailing, Macon's Bill Number 2 was enacted in May 1810. This mischievous law reopened trade with France and England but provided that should either nation repeal its restrictive commercial measures, trade with the other power would be interdicted. Napoleon, who with great regret had learned of the repeal of the embargo, saw an opportunity to stop American trade with England once again. He therefore informed Madison that as of 1 November 1810 he was conditionally revoking his Berlin and Milan decrees pertinent to American trade and called upon the United States to invoke nonintercourse against Great Britain. Madison understood that Napoleon's action was conditional upon England's revocation of certain orders-in-council.

With his eyes open, Madison decided to take the biggest gamble of his political life and presume that Napoleon intended to revoke his decrees before his precondition was met. With questionable haste, Madison issued a proclamation in November stopping trade with England within three months if she had not cancelled her orders-in-council. England refused to do so pending evidence that Napoleon had repealed his decrees. Since Madison could not prove Napoleon had acted, England refused to alter its measures. Bitter and embarrassed, Madison nevertheless encouraged Congress to renew nonintercourse against England, which Congress voted to do in March 1811.

Through Napoleon's shrewd diplomatic tactic and through Madison's untimely willingness to gamble, the United States once again became a reluctant partner in strengthening the continental system. The results of this episode, and the bitterness engendered by it, helped to pave the way for the War of 1812, for many Americans believed England had been inflexible and overly legalistic when there had been a chance to be constructive and conciliatory. England found Madison's willingness to see the United

States reinforce the continental system evidence of the administration's ill will toward England and softness toward France.

It therefore seems fair to say that the continental system, as manipulated by Bonaparte, played a crucial role in bringing about the War of 1812. The acts committed by Napoleon under the mantle of the continental system were serious enough even to have provoked war with the United States; Madison and Congress backed away from this prospect, however, believing that England was enemy enough.

The whole complex of maritime belligerent measures, of which the continental system was the centerpiece, had significant consequences for the United States other than the War of 1812. Because of trade interruptions of varying length, the American carrying trade was hurt, as were American hopes to nourish a promising trade with Latin America. Also, domestic objections to Jefferson's and Madison's seemingly pro-French policies were sizable and significant enough ultimately to raise the threat of a New England secession from the Union. On the positive side some argue that American exclusion from continental markets proved to be a healthy stimulus to American manufacturing enterprises even though other sectors of the economy suffered unduly.

Imposition of the continental system demonstrated once again the cruel situation in which neutral powers are placed when great belligerent powers are determined that neutral resources will be channeled to the enemy only upon disadvantageous terms. Jefferson's and Madison's unsuccessful attempts to bluff and to pressure France and Britain underlined that truism of statecraft. Also, the experiences with Napoleon and the continental system reinforced the American belief that Europe was the home of political and moral corruption, and of self-serving politicians. Washington's advice on avoiding unnecessary entanglements with foreign powers was therefore given emphasis through American experiences with Napoleon's economic system.

While Napoleon had substantial success in disrupting American-British trade, he found it difficult to achieve the larger objective of excluding British and British-controlled neutral trade from the Continent except on terms disadvantageous to Britain. The continental system continued to spring leaks. Portugal and Spain—particularly following the insurrection in Spain in 1808—served as ports of entry for goods from Britain and its colonies. In addition, Great Britain used depots along the coast of Europe as smuggling centers. British merchants crowded into these centers in great numbers in order to conduct business as usual. From Helgoland in the North Sea, smuggled British and neutral goods made their way to Leipzig, Basel, Strasbourg, and Frankfurt. In the Baltic, Göteborg became the center for goods forwarded to Prussia, Poland, and Russia. Gibraltar, Sardinia, Sicily, the Dalmatian and Ionian islands, and Malta most of all, served as the depots for British goods in the Mediterranean. After England gained a foothold in Turkey in 1809, Belgrade and Hungary were supplied with British goods forwarded from Salonika and Constantinople.

The continental system was likewise undermined by Napoleon's need for money. Growth of an enormous smuggling trade deprived Napoleon's empire of desperately needed tax revenues. Searching for monies to pursue his campaign against Austria in 1809, Napoleon recognized the necessity to stem this tax loss and accordingly established a system of licensed trade in 1809 and 1810. For a time, Napoleon himself tried to supervise directly the granting of these licenses. At first a secret operation, the license system was formalized through the Decree of St. Cloud on 5 July 1810. Licenses were sold for substantial, varying fees. In establishing the license system, Napoleon virtually negated the rationale of his system. He angered his allies and associates by granting licenses in such a way that French economic needs and promotion of the French merchant marine were given first consideration. Needed British goods now flowed freely and legally into French ports. Coupled with the license system came the Trianon Decree of 5 August 1810, which raised tariffs on colonial goods to an exorbitant degree, so high in fact that smugglers saw nothing but good in the measure. Napoleon's need to build his war chest thus led him to abandon the continental self-blockade, but he did so in such a way that he made it appear the French empire had no higher purpose than the enhancement of

French interests. He also confused both allies and enemies, for while the license system was designed in part to negate the smuggling trade, the new tariff rates furnished considerable incentive for the smuggling to continue.

Napoleon never formally ended the continental system, but inauguration of the license system in 1809 and adoption of the Trianon tariff rates in 1810 marked its virtual abandonment. The defection of Russia in 1810 was the single greatest blow to the continental system, one that made further enforcement efforts ludicrous. Following Napoleon's downfall, one of the first acts of the restored Bourbon regime was to sweep away the various edicts of the continental system. All that remained were the milder enactments of the commercial legislation passed between 1791 and 1793 and the continuing firm conviction that French trade and industry must be sheltered from foreign competition.

The continental system revealed the scope and some of the limitations of Napoleon's thinking and planning. It was Europocentric in its focus, was dependent upon the Grand Army for its success, was nationalistic and traditional in its emphasis upon the promotion of French interests, and was parochial in assessing how far sea power could assist England in escaping Napoleon's net. He pursued his plan with method and a certain cunning but had to modify it drastically when resistance grew too great. Unfortunately for Napoleon the continental system was politically counterproductive in that it fostered increasing hostility to French hegemony within Europe.

In terms of its primary goal, the continental system was a failure. Britain suffered but devised a successful smuggling system, formed new markets in Latin America and East Asia, and traded freely with the colonies of France. The war that Napoleon helped to provoke between England and the United States played no part in determining his larger destinies.

BIBLIOGRAPHY

Ulane Bonnel, *La France, les États-Unis, et la guerre de course, 1797–1815* (Paris, 1961), describes in lucid fashion the effects of the continental system upon the United States. Anne C. Clauder, *American Commerce as Affected by the Wars of the French Revolution and Napoleon, 1793–1812* (Philadelphia, 1932), is an old but useful analysis of trade statistics and maritime regulations. Alfred W. Crosby, Jr., *America, Russia, Hemp, and Napoleon: American Trade With Russia and the Baltic, 1783–1812* (Columbus, Ohio, 1965), is an important study for understanding why the continental system never effectively excluded neutral and British commerce from Europe. Eli F. Heckscher, *The Continental System: An Economic Interpretation* (New York, 1919), is especially useful in understanding the historical background to the continental system, and provides a detailed analysis of continental response to the blockade. Alfred T. Mahan, *The Influence of Sea Power Upon the French Revolution and Empire, 1793–1812,* 2 vols. (London, 1892), demonstrates the difficulties Napoleon experienced in effectively countering the naval power of England. Bradford Perkins, *Prologue to War: England and the United States, 1805–1812* (Berkeley–Los Angeles, 1963), a well-balanced account that looks beyond American-English relations, is strong on domestic political factors that shaped foreign policies. Louis M. Sears, *Jefferson and the Embargo* (Durham, N.C., 1927), the standard account of the embargo, supports Jefferson's position on several disputed issues. Paul A. Varg, *Foreign Policies of the Founding Fathers* (East Lansing, Mich., 1963), provides an astute analysis of the practical and ideological components in the thinking of Jefferson and Madison concerning foreign affairs. And Marvin R. Zahniser, *Uncertain Friendship: American-French Diplomatic Relations Through the Cold War* (New York, 1975), discusses why Jefferson and Madison were reluctant to confront France, despite the severity of her economic measures.

[*See also* Blockades and Quarantines; Embargoes; Freedom of the Seas; Neutrality; Trade and Commerce.]

DEBT COLLECTION

Richard W. Van Alstyne

IT was during the early twentieth century that debt collection first appeared as a problem in American foreign relations. Dictatorships in the several Caribbean republics that had managed to live on loans granted by European banking and speculative interests were involved. Their incapacity or unwillingness to pay brought threats of armed intervention from European governments, notably the British, German, French, and Italian. The classic instance is that of Venezuela, whose irresponsible ruler, Cipriano Castro, had aroused the anger and contempt of foreign powers, including the United States. In 1902 the British and German governments, joined nominally by Italy, blockaded Venezuela and seized the country's customs, the revenues from which would then be utilized toward redemption of the debts. This method, which proved effective but which also aroused American susceptibilities over the Monroe Doctrine, soon brought from the administration of Theodore Roosevelt an important policy statement, namely, that the United States would henceforth be responsible for the behavior of the Latin American republics toward Europe: "What we will not permit the Great Powers of Europe to do, we will not permit any American republic to make it necessary for the Great Powers of Europe to do."

In due course the United States assumed fiscal supervision over several Caribbean countries. In the Dominican Republic (1905) the United States appointed a receiver general of customs to act as paymaster and apportion the proceeds from the customs among the foreign creditors. It was not until 1940 that the Dominicans regained complete control over their own customs, but even then they were making payments on past debts. In 1911 a refunding operation in Nicaragua was completed under the direction of the Taft administration. New York bankers agreed to take over the Nicaraguan external debt and grant additional credits upon an assurance that an American-appointed collector general would be put in control of the customs. Four years later in Haiti a violent revolution led to an armed American intervention and the appointment of both a receiver general and a financial adviser to bring about order and pay off the foreign debts. Subsequently a high commissioner from the United States took up residence in Port-au-Prince, followed by another financial adviser nominated by the United States but representing the foreign bondholders. Because Haiti had a market in France for its coffee, cotton, and sugar, redemption of its bonds, held chiefly in that country, proceeded on an orderly basis.

The finances of Cuba and of the Republic of Panama were meanwhile kept under surveillance as of 1903, so that no occasion arose for European intervention in those countries. The Platt Amendment (1901) reduced Cuba to formal protectorate status, and the Panama Canal Zone Treaty (1903) effected the same end regarding Panama. The two other countries where debt collection became of primary concern, Guatemala and Honduras, were left to the British government, which had only partial success in recovering the sums owed its bondholders. Meanwhile South American aversion to collecting debts by armed intervention found expression through the Drago Doctrine (1903), propounded by Luis María Drago, minister of foreign affairs in Argentina. The United States accepted this view "in principle"; but since it had already found effective means of superintending the affairs of the Caribbean republics, Drago's proposal was really irrelevant.

Debt collection was merely a phase of a larger program of control that passes under the general heading of the Monroe Doctrine. This program began with the Theodore Roosevelt administration, received further refinement and extension during the administrations of Taft and Wilson, and then was gradually allowed to taper off during the years between the two world wars. Its most ambitious statement came from State Department counselor Robert Lansing in June 1914. Both Wilson and Secretary of State William Jennings Bryan gave their ready assent.

> Should not a new doctrine be formulated, declaring that the United States is opposed to the extension of European control over American territory and institutions through financial as well as other means, and having for its object, not only the national safety and interests of this country, but also the establishment and maintenance of republican constitutional government in all American states, the free exercise by their people of their public and private rights, the administration of impartial justice, and the prevention of political authority from becoming the tool of personal ambition and greed? . . .

Reduction of all Latin America to financial vassalage, so confidently proposed in Lansing's memorandum, was never put to the test. Debt collection and its concomitant, fiscal and political supervision, were limited to the petty, semianarchical republics of the Caribbean.

A completely different and far more disturbing problem involving international debts arose soon after the outbreak of World War I. Accustomed to financing their normal purchases of American foodstuffs and raw materials through the regular processes of international trade, Britain and France in 1915 found themselves obliged to enter the American money market for a $500 million loan. During the next year and a half the two Allies borrowed additional sums aggregating well over a billion dollars, paying commercial rates of interest and putting up collateral securities safeguarding repayment. The total British borrowing alone came to $1.065 billion. These operations greatly worried the British treasury, for it realized that Britain was surrendering its historic position as the world's greatest creditor nation to become a debtor. For its part every segment of the American economy benefited: the banking syndicates that made the loans; the western wheat farmer and cattle grazer who were rewarded with rising prices; and copper and other metal producers, Southern cotton growers, machinists, and munitions manufacturers. To illustrate, the wholesale price index in the United States rose from 100 in 1913 to 146 in December 1916 and to 172 in April 1917.

This then was the situation at the time the United States itself entered the war. The Allies were straining their credit resources in borrowing dollars to pay for their wartime purchases in the United States at steadily rising prices. Before the end of the third year of war they were paying $3 billion more for the same amount of goods than they would have paid in 1913. Clearly it was quite out of the question for them to continue their purchasing program through private sources.

Promptly in April 1917 the United States Treasury assumed the role of banker to the Allies. The British ambassador received a check for $200 million, and by selling its own bonds to the American public the United States government obtained money to finance both its own wartime purchases and those of the Allies. Congress passed four Liberty Loan acts, and the Treasury purchased the notes of the Allies at par and bearing the same rate of interest (about 4.25 percent) as it was paying its own bondholders. In this manner Allied purchases in the United States of commodities of all sorts needed for the war continued without interruption. Including Russia, seven European governments became debtors to the American government between April 1917 and November 1918, and the credits allowable amounted to approximately $8 billion.

The Allies also loaned large sums to each other—Britain especially, but also France and even Italy—borrowing United States dollars that they passed on to the smaller allies. In this manner the various governments in a measure avoided bidding against one another in the American market. For example, Britain passed on in excess of $3 billion, and France advanced nearly $2 billion to its debtors. France also borrowed direct (in pounds sterling) from the British treasury. Britain and France were both borrowers and lenders; the other Allies, such as Belgium and Russia, were borrowers only. But in its accounting practices the United States charged Britain and France respectively the total sums they borrowed, not merely the amounts they used for their own direct needs.

In round numbers these war debts at the time of the Armistice (11 November 1918) totaled $7 billion, the extra billion not having been drawn upon; but dollar loans continued on through 1920 in excess of $3 billion. These loans were employed on various reconstruction, relief, and rehabilitation projects, so that at the end of the lending period the grand total of European expenditures resting on United States government credits exceeded $11 billion (accumulated interest included). Many of these post-Armistice loans had little, if any, relationship to the war. The most remarkable of such loans was the $9 million credit to Finland, one of the new independent countries that broke away from the Russian empire. The exception is worth noting because Finland had nothing to do with the war, although as in other such cases, no distinction was made between war debts and nonwar debts. All the debts were treated as interest-bearing commercial loans, extended in dollars and repayable in dollars (expressed in gold or its equivalent having a fixed value). When this proved a difficult, not to say insuperable, problem for the war debt countries proper, and when ill feelings and resentments arose against the debtors, politicians found it worth their while to draw comparisons between the Finns, who never failed to meet their installments on time, and the larger powers who faced serious balance of payments problems. But Finland always had an exportable surplus and therefore never had any difficulty in buying dollars on the open market to hand the United States Treasury. Making comparisons of this sort was both inequitable and irrelevant.

Meanwhile a deadlock was not slow in developing between the United States and its principal debtors—Britain, France, and Italy. Added to these complications were the demands levied by the Allies upon Germany for reparations. Recognizing that debts and reparations were closely tied together, and that repayment in each and every case rested on capacity to pay, the three Allies wanted a general agreement reached at the Paris Peace Conference in 1919. The proposed basis was that they had all participated in a common war against the enemy and that their resources would be pooled and the intergovernmental debts scaled down accordingly. This had been the policy of the British government during the long French Revolutionary and Napoleonic Wars (1793–1816). Britain financed its allies directly through subsidies, and at the end of these wars it virtually wiped the slate clean. No problem of war debts arose in the post-Napoleonic period; hence neither Britain nor its continental debtors had to cope with a balance of payments problem. Repeated approaches—especially by Italy, the most impoverished of the debtor nations—to secure some similar accommodation at the Paris Peace Conference met with rebuffs. In November 1920, however, a flat refusal by President Wilson even to discuss the question brought the matter to a dead halt. The United States had contracted with each of the debtors separately, and fulfillment of each contract according to the original terms was expected. From the legal standpoint none of the debtors could challenge the rectitude of the American position. The economics of the problem, however, was something entirely different.

Historically the United States had always been a debtor nation, borrowing large amounts of capital from European private banks and other investors and using the funds for development purposes of many kinds. With some exceptions—notably the 1840's, when several of the American states defaulted on their bonds—these obligations were met without difficulty, for the country enjoyed an export surplus and was able to acquire foreign exchange accordingly. From 1915 to 1918 the United States changed from the traditional status of a borrower to that of a creditor on a large scale. Moreover, the change was unique in that it consisted in the main of war loans by the government, which obtained the funds by borrowing from its own citizens. While required in dollars, repayment could not be made in dollars unless they were first earned. But the earning of dollars could only be realized by selling goods or furnishing services on the part of the debtors. Or, as one writer suggested, if the

French government would buy from French vintners enough wine to equal the dollar value of its debt, and then deliver the wine gratis to the American government for sale to whoever would buy, it could readily pay off its debt. The illustration is accurate, but in view of the American Prohibition laws it must have been suggested with tongue in cheek. A serious point, however, is that not only must the debtor pay in goods, but the creditor must accept the goods (or services) offered. This raises further questions. The war debts could not be kept out of American domestic politics; they were linked directly to the Liberty Bonds that had to be redeemed in cash. Hence they aroused the emotions of the taxpaying public and provided an easy issue for party politics. Whether the leaders in the American government, Democrat or Republican, understood the intricate nature of the debts is not clear. All the available evidence is that they did not; at least no effort was ever made to elucidate the problem so that it could be removed from politics.

The gulf between the American insistence on adherence to the original agreements and the European proposals for general all-around cancellations opened wide in 1922. A request from Secretary of the Treasury Andrew W. Mellon that Congress grant the Treasury Department plenary powers to negotiate met with a stiff rebuff. Instead, in February 1922 Congress established the World War Foreign Debt Funding Commission and empowered it to negotiate sinking fund agreements, the debtor countries to deposit bonds maturing in twenty-five years and bearing interest at not less than 4.25 percent. Faced with this uncompromising attitude, the British government, in August 1922, addressed an identical note to its own several debtors explaining its predicament, expressing its regret, but saying that it had no alternative but to make the same terms with them that it was forced to make with the American government. It could not

> . . . treat the re-payment of the Anglo-American loan as if it were an isolated incident. . . . It is but one of a series of transactions, in which this country appears sometimes as debtor, sometimes as creditor, and if our undoubted obligations as a debtor are to be enforced, our not less undoubted rights as a creditor cannot be left wholly in abeyance.
>
> The policy favoured by His Majesty's Government is . . . that of surrendering their share of German reparation, and writing off through one great transaction, the whole body of inter-Allied indebtedness. But, if this be found impossible of accomplishment, we wish it to be understood that we do not in any event desire to make a profit out of any less satisfactory arrangement. In no circumstances do we propose to ask more from our debtors than is necessary to pay our creditors.

This statesmanlike note, composed by the earl of Balfour and indirectly addressed to the United States, met with a steely negative from the latter. Senator Porter J. McCumber said, "We will never cancel our war debts"—a typical response from a senator who was about to give his name to a new tariff bill. The contradiction between tariffs on the one hand and international debts on the other went virtually unrecognized. A creditor nation must be prepared to receive payments in goods; there is no other way. Editorially the *New York Times* condemned the time-honored protectionist policy of the Republican party, then in full control; but more basic than politics was the fact that American agriculture and industry had greatly expanded during the war and were fearful of losing out to European competitors struggling to regain their former trading positions. Put rather too simply, it was a case of sacrificing either the tariff or the debts, and American opinion was not prepared to do either.

Officially the American government ignored the economics of the problem, merely reiterating that it had made a loan agreement with Britain that had no relation to the agreements with other governments. Accordingly, both the British and the French sent representatives to Washington to emphasize the impracticability of redeeming their debts under the terms laid down by Congress. Subsequently the British signed an agreement capitalizing their debt at $4.6 billion to be paid in installments over a period of sixty-two years, bearing interest at 3 percent to 1931 and 3.5 percent thereafter. All told, twelve other governments made similar agreements, although at lower interest rates. Under the Bolsheviks, Russia repudiated all of its war debts. Italy and France were to pay no interest during the first five years from the dates of their agreements (1925 and 1926 respectively) and would start paying interest at 1 percent thereafter, increasing gradually to a maximum of 3.5 percent. Congress ratified these agreements and thus to an extent retreated from its earlier intransigence. But all the payments had to be made in dollars, which somehow the debtor governments had to acquire.

Meanwhile a moral barrier sprang up between the United States and Europe. Prohibitionists dwelt on the enormous sums spent in Europe on "drink," but more emphatic were the protests against armaments. Taught to regard an arms race as a certain road to war, Americans reproached France especially for supporting an army that was admittedly the largest in Europe. Senator William E. Borah of Idaho, chairman of the Senate Committee on Foreign Relations, was chief spokesman for this viewpoint. To Borah the American taxpayer was bearing the cost of the French army, "and we are under the same obligation to the taxpayer to deal with this situation as we are to protect him from the unnecessary burdens of his own government." The ultimate in simplistic argument was reached by James T. Begg, a bombastic Ohio congressman who demanded that European nations who refused to disarm be "made to pay every dollar of the debt . . . as fast as possible." And since France was the guilty party, "I shall expect France to walk up and pay and that in the immediate future."

On their part the French were not slow in showing their wrath. After the State Department had clamped an embargo on private loans to French companies, the Chamber of Deputies in France refused ratification of the funding agreement. Of all the belligerents France had suffered the most during the war; farms, coal mines, and industry north and east of Paris had been laid waste by the armies of both sides. Consequently the French found it difficult to make payments of any kind on foreign loans, while having a real need for new capital for reconstruction. Added to these injuries was the American tariff, which—as Herbert Adams Gibbon, a war correspondent and a noted postwar writer, pointed out—hit hard at French specialties (notably silks and perfumes) that were capable of earning dollars; nor have we "realized how heavily handicapped France has been by these extraordinarily high duties and by our refusal to allow entry of French wines and spirits."

Italy was similarly handicapped. Cordell Hull, then a congressman but later the secretary of state who was to do yeoman service in getting the tariffs down, pointed this out in 1925. "The United States," declared Hull, "is now at the crossroads with respect to this entire problem as it relates to the tariff. She can adhere to her existing high tariff policy and scale down our foreign debt correspondingly or she can return to a level of moderate tariff rates and favor the removal of economic barriers everywhere and thereby make it possible for foreign debtor governments to pay. . . ."

Occasionally some prominent man in private life, such as Dudley Field Malone, spoke out: "European nations will never pay . . . their war debts because it is an economic impossibility. . . . The sooner this fact is recognized in Washington and the United States cancels the foreign debt . . . the better it will be for this country as well as Europe." But President Calvin Coolidge, betraying his economic illiteracy, voiced the common opinion: "They hired the money, didn't they?" A cartoonist in *Punch* saw his opportunity in a picture entitled "Uncle Sam's Tonic Talk"—"Uncle" in dress clothes standing on a platform and lecturing to representatives of Britain, France, and Italy. "My poor dear friends," he asks, "what have you learned from the great war? Nothing!" "Oh, sir! at least we've learned what we owe you."

None of the presidents from Wilson to Franklin D. Roosevelt or the high officials under them evinced any enlightenment. Herbert Hoover stuck to his rigid belief in the sanctity of contracts, and in October 1930 his secretary of state, Henry L. Stimson, rejected the idea of a connection between the Allied war debts and German reparations. But by this time the depression had entered its serious stage, and voices were being raised at home and abroad for a drastic reduction of the debts just as German reparations had been twice reduced. Senator Alben W. Barkley of Kentucky returned from a trip to Europe to announce publicly that the American tariff was a handicap, that there was no possibility that Britain could continue to pay, that "in every circle with which I came in contact, official and unofficial, there was a profound feeling bordering on despair and even bitterness." Europeans could not understand "our demand that they pay us what they owed us and buy the goods we send them while at the same time denying them the ability to do either by preventing them from selling anything to us." Barkley's reference was to the new Smoot-Hawley Act (June 1930), the effect of which was to reduce foreign trade to a trickle. President Hoover had brushed aside warnings of the evil consequences of the bill. Senator Reed Smoot (Utah), the principal author, had been a member of the World War Foreign Debt Funding Commission, but to his mind no "good American" would advocate cancellation of the debts or oppose his tariff bill.

Actually tariffs, debts, reparations, and loans were so closely related as to be almost inseparable. The basic economic consequence of the war was to advance the United States to a position of supremacy. Despite the difficulties surrounding the war debt settlements, dollar loans poured from private American banks and investment syndicates on a vast scale, accelerating after 1924 but coming to an almost complete stop in 1930. European governments, municipalities, and private corporations sought and received these loans, paying high interest rates (in dollars) and meeting their war debt installments from the proceeds of these loans. Germany was a leading recipient of American loans and was thus able to pay reparations to the Allies, who in turn were able to pay their American creditors. The source of these extraordinary loans was the profits of American industry in the sale of its products both at home and abroad, and in the abundance of speculative capital-seeking outlets. An open door—or rather, open doors—appeared as if by magic to dazzle the American investor. Latin America, Australasia, Africa, and East Asia obtained dollar loans. The lending process was a continuation (better yet, extension) of the Open Door policy pursued in China: an attempt by means of loans to capture the world's markets, but without serious consideration as to how these loans were to be repaid. Actually interest was being paid out of principal, not out of returns on the investment. As secretary of commerce under Coolidge, Herbert Hoover encouraged loans of this type, particularly to South American countries. Criticism, scrutiny, and hints to the naive individual investor to exercise caution were alien to Hoover's peculiar laissez-faire cast of mind.

When the bubble burst in 1930, total United States private long-term foreign investments stood at $15.17 billion, triple the figure in 1919. Germany still routinely made payments on its reparations account, and at least some of the Allied governments were forwarding their installments to Washington. But the principal of the war debts (including the postwar loans) carried on the books of the United States Treasury stood at $11.64 billion, which was $120 million more than the total shown at the time the thirteen governments had signed the settlement agreements. Supposing that all thirteen had continued to pay principal and interest through the entire sixty-two-year period, the grand total would have exceeded $22 billion. Meanwhile the fascist dictatorship under Benito Mussolini had installed itself in Italy; and in Germany, the Nazis, now on the high road to power in that country, had promised to repudiate reparations.

By June 1931 Germany, the greatest of the world's debtors, was near collapse; and while continuing to maintain that debts and reparations were unconnected, Hoover, after assuring himself of sufficient congressional support, proposed a year's moratorium on all intergovernmental debts. Hoover was now ready to admit that debt redemption on the part of any country depended upon its capacity to pay, although probably as a political gesture, he again declared his disapproval of cancellation. Hoover's opponent, Franklin D. Roosevelt, declined to take a position but did not miss his opportunity to ridicule the Republicans for their absurd policy "of demanding payment and at the same time making payment impossible." Meanwhile the Lausanne Agreement (1932) between Germany and its creditors put an end, for all practical purposes, to reparations payments. Then Belgium, followed by France, defaulted. Britain and Italy managed to make partial payments through December 1932. It was at this time that Finland became conspicuous. "Sturdy little Finland" earned a high mark with the American public for meeting its semiannual installment of $166,538 punctually and in full. Britain offered a token payment in 1934 but, on being informed that this would not save it from the stigma of being a defaulter, decided to make no further gesture. Spurred by Senator Hiram Johnson, most vociferous among the diehards, Congress (April 1934) made certain there would be a stigma. It passed the Johnson Debt Default Act, closing the door to any foreign government in default on its debts. Private investment houses were forbidden under this ill-tempered measure from doing business with any defaulting foreign government. The act had no practical effect; no foreign nation offered to resume payments, and none of those at whom the act was pointed was in the market for further American credits.

A witty adaptation by a *New York Times* writer from Lewis Carroll's immortal tale is a fitting conclusion:

"But we were going to speak about the war debt payments," said Alice, half angry, half in tears.

The White Rabbit stared at her.

"Why, Alice," he said, "what good would it do if we talked about them from now until doomsday?"

BIBLIOGRAPHY

Ralph Hidy, *The House of Baring in American Trade and Finance, 1763–1861* (Cambridge, Mass., 1949), is a fine, analytical narrative of the contribution of this great banking firm to early American development. John T. Madden, Marcus Nadler, and Harry C. Sauvain, *America's Experience as a Creditor Nation* (New York, 1937), is a comprehensive, scholarly treatise on the economics of foreign lending, both private and governmental. Harold G. Moulton and Leo Pasvolsky, *World War Debt Settlements* (New York, 1926), gives the documents and describes the problems of the several debtor nations; and *War Debts and World Prosperity* (Washington, D.C., 1932), is the indispensable study of the subject, with many statistical appendices. Ernest Minor Patterson, *The World's Economic Dilemma* (New York, 1930), is an excellent survey of the 1920's. Richard W. Van Alstyne, *American Diplomacy in Action* (Gloucester, Mass., 1968), a reissue of the Stanford University Press edition of 1947, contains chapters on the Caribbean republics and their relations with the United States; and "Private American Loans to the Allies, 1914–1916," in *Pacific Historical Review,* 2 (1933), is a pioneer study of this subject. Benjamin H. Williams, *Economic Foreign Policy of the United States* (New York, 1929), written during the period of the war debt controversy, is a perceptive and fair-minded account (although it is outdated by subsequent events) and deals with the diplomacy of investment on a broad scale.

[*See also* Congress and Foreign Policy; Economic Foreign Policy; Intervention and Nonintervention; The Monroe Doctrine; The Open Door Policy; Reparations; Trade and Commerce.]

DECISION-MAKING APPROACHES AND THEORIES

James N. Rosenau

ALTHOUGH concern for the dynamics whereby individuals and groups reach decisions relevant to the conduct of world affairs can be traced as far back as Thucydides, it is only since World War II that systematic efforts to develop theories of decision making in foreign policy have been undertaken. To a large extent these efforts have been initiated and sustained by American scholars, but the resulting formulations are not primarily theories of decision making in American foreign policy. Rather they tend to be general formulations, presumably applicable to any society, or at least to any Western, industrialized society. The ensuing discussion is thus cast at a somewhat abstract level, with the relevance of the several approaches to the United States context being noted only in those cases where the analysts have done so themselves. Notwithstanding the lack of explicit applications to decision making, however, useful insights into American practices can be derived from all the approaches and theories.

Interest in the dynamics of foreign policy decision making expanded rapidly after World War II as it became increasingly evident to scholars that the billiard ball model of world politics—in which each state is considered to respond similarly to similar external stimuli, irrespective of its internal structure—was no longer an appropriate description of international relations. Prior to World War II, decision making was not regarded as particularly important, since all states were viewed as responding to the same rules of international conduct. As publics became increasingly vocal, nation-states increasingly numerous, and international affairs increasingly differentiated, it became imperative to account for those points at which different officials in different nation-states undertake different kinds of actions. The choice point—the moment at which a course of action is initiated, reaffirmed, modified, or terminated—thus became a focus of concern. When individuals, groups, or nations reach a choice point in their affairs, they either make decisions or they fail to make decisions (failures that are in themselves decisions)—decisions as to goals, as to alternative means to achieve chosen goals, and decisions as to the allocation of the resources necessary to employ the means selected.

For a number of analysts, in short, everything that happens in foreign affairs came to be seen as linking back to decisions made, explicitly or implicitly, rationally or nonrationally, effectively or ineffectively. Accordingly, a series of formulations emerged that properly can be viewed as theories of decision making or, in some cases, simply approaches to decision making. Some of the following theories and approaches differ widely in their scope and in the variables considered to be central, but they all share a preoccupation with the processes of choice.

THE DISTINCTION BETWEEN INTELLECTUAL AND SOCIOPOLITICAL PROCESSES OF DECISION MAKING

In order to assess the utility of the various approaches to decision making, it is crucial to differentiate between approaches that focus exclusively on the processes of reasoning, whereby the contents of decisions develop, and other approaches that concentrate on the clash of social, economic, political, and bureaucratic forces that undergird the reasoning processes. For some analysts decision making is an intellectual process that occurs within individuals, while for others it is a sociopolitical process that occurs between individuals in groups, agencies, and institutions.

To be sure, both processes are always operative. Individual officials constantly think through the problems they confront while they are also caught up in sociopolitical dynamics that constantly influence the reasoning in which they engage. Nevertheless, no extant theory or approach has achieved a solid and adequate union between the two types of processes, perhaps because in one case the reasoning of individuals is treated as merely the end product of either rational calculation or complex sociopolitical processes, while in the other it is viewed as intervening importantly between the forces that give rise to decisions and decisions themselves. It follows that each reader will have to develop his own conception of the relative importance of intellectual and sociopolitical processes if the utility of the various approaches and theories noted below is to be assessed.

THE DISTINCTION BETWEEN RATIONAL AND NONRATIONAL DECISION MAKING

Another aspect of the various approaches and theories is the extent to which the steps that precede decision are conceived to result from rational or nonrational calculations. This distinction tends to correspond to, but is not identical with, the difference between intellectual and sociopolitical processes. Those who focus on sociopolitical processes posit decision making as founded on nonrational considerations (that is, those that are dominant in the unfolding of the social and political processes of a nation), but those who concentrate on the intellectual processes differ in this regard. Some assume rational actors, while others proceed from the premise that nonrational factors can and do pervade the perceptions, estimates, and choices of decision makers.

Again both types of decision making are operative in the real world; or, more accurately, both the rationality and nonrationality assumptions yield important insights into the dynamics of foreign policy. The rationality assumption—that actors decide by clearly articulating their goals, the alternative policies through which they might reach their goals, and the costs and benefits likely to be associated with each alternative—permits assessments of what ought to be done if foreign policy is to be effective. The nonrationality assumption—that an endless array of factors prevents officials from clearly articulating their goals, identifying a full range of alternative means to achieve them, estimating the costs and benefits of each, and then selecting the policy most likely to minimize costs and maximize benefits—allows assessments of what is done in foreign policy. Again none of the extant approaches and theories adequately incorporate both assumptions into their schemes. Instead, one or the other assumption is treated as primary, thus again compelling the reader to assess the conditions under which he or she is best advised to presume the existence of rational or nonrational methods of framing, sifting, and selecting policy alternatives.

THE DISTINCTION BETWEEN DECISION MAKING AS CHOICE AND AS CHOICES

The role ascribed to change through time serves as another important distinction among the various approaches and theories. Some focus exclusively on a single point in time—the one in which a choice is made—while others posit decision making as a series of choices, each of which is affected by the changes that have occurred since, and perhaps because of, the choices that preceded it. Stated differently, those analysts who concentrate on a single choice point treat decisions as dependent variables, whereas those who do not hold time constant and allow for feedback from prior choices view decisions as independent as well as dependent variables.

To allow for response is to recognize that

nonrational factors may be relevant to decison making. Officials may seek to maximize the flow of feedback from prior choices in order to enhance their rationality as they enter the next round of choices, but the analyst who focuses on the interaction of such decision sequences is bound to proceed on the assumption that unanticipated, and thus nonrational, developments intervene between any two decision points. If this were not so, if initial decisions were totally effective, there would be no need for reconsideration and subsequent decision making. It follows that analysts who treat decision making as rational action confine themselves to choices made at a single point in time. Not all those who hold time constant, however, presume rationality, so that the correspondence between the rational-nonrational and the single-serial dimensions is not exact.

THE DISTINCTION BETWEEN DEDUCTIVE AND INDUCTIVE MODELS OF DECISION MAKING

A final distinction is that between analysts who derive their understanding of the processes of choice by the sorting of and generalizing about observed phenomena, and analysts who start with axioms of how choices are made and then trace what decisions will necessarily follow from the initial postulates when the conditions that occasion them vary. For the former, empirical data serve as the basis for theorizing about decision making, while for the latter the dictates of logic constitute the analytic foundations. Analysts who proceed deductively from logical models thus tend to posit rational actors and to focus exclusively on the reasoning process whereby the advantages and disadvantages of different decision alternatives are calculated. They do not deny that decision makers in the real world, lacking perfect information, cannot conform to the dictates of logic inherent in their models, but argue instead that considerable insight into the dynamics of choice can nevertheless be gained by tracing how decisions would be made if officials were fully informed and their calculations founded on the requirements of rational behavior.

Not all those who posit rational actors, however, proceed deductively. As noted below, at least one major approach to decision making presumes rationality even as it is also grounded in empirical inquiry. Thus, while there is substantial overlap between the rational-nonrational and the deductive-inductive dimensions, again it would be erroneous to treat them as identical.

In sum, comparison of the various approaches to and theories about foreign policy decision making is facilitated by asking the same four questions about each one: Does it focus on intellectual or sociopolitical processes? Does it treat those who make the decisions as rational or nonrational actors? Does it allow for the passage of time and the processes of feedback? Is it founded on a deductive or an inductive methodology? Five approaches or theories have been sufficiently explicated in recent years to warrant consideration in the context of these questions. They are discussed roughly in the order that they came to command the attention of analysts in the field.

THE SNYDER-BRUCK-SAPIN APPROACH TO FOREIGN POLICY DECISION MAKING

First published as a monograph (1953) and later as a book (1962), the work by Snyder, Bruck, and Sapin was the first to focus the attention of students of world politics on decision-making phenomena. Earlier formulations had elaborated both the intellectual and sociopolitical processes of decision making (for example, Barnard, 1938; Lasswell and Kaplan, 1950; and Simon, 1947), but the monograph by the three (then) Princeton analysts was the first to apply decision-making concepts to the field of foreign affairs. Its impact was instant and widespread, perhaps because most practitioners in the field had become increasingly restless with the billiard ball model of world politics and were eagerly looking for cogent reasons to abandon it. A number of such reasons were clearly articulated by Snyder and his colleagues. They persuasively argued that states do not respond automatically and similarly to stimuli from their external environments, that rather the actions of states follow from the decisions of concrete, identifiable individuals, and that therefore what states do in foreign affairs is to a large extent a consequence of how they go about deciding what to do. The authors stressed that it follows that the only way in which the behavior of states can be explained is by reconstructing the world as it is experienced and assessed by those who are the duly constituted authorities responsible for making decisions that commit the polity to courses of action. A variety of external considerations helps explain the outcomes of state action, whether foreign policies succeed or fail. But the action of a particular state can only be understood if it is analyzed from the perspective of the officials who made the choices that gave rise to the policies under examination.

In reconstructing the world as it is perceived by decision makers, Snyder and his colleagues posited them as exposed to stimuli from three major sources: those that originate in the external setting (that is, abroad), those that flow from the internal setting (that is, at home, in their societies), and those that emanate from within their own decision-making organizations (that is, the bureaucracy and the government). A number of stimuli considered central were identified within each of these three areas, but no attempt was made to assess their relative importance as sources of foreign policy. Identification of domestic factors located in the internal setting and of bureaucratic factors located in the policy-making organization was in itself such an innovative formulation, requiring extensive elaboration and justification, that the question of their relative strength as causal agents was never raised.

The way in which the stimuli converging upon officials were conceptualized underlay the definition of decision making offered by Snyder and his colleagues: *"Decision-making is a process which results in the selection from a socially defined, limited number of problematical, alternative projects of one project intended to bring about the particular future state of affairs envisaged by the decision-makers"* (1962, p. 90, italics in original). Each of the terms in this definition was elaborated at some length, with particular emphasis being given to the intellectual process whereby alternative projects are framed, selected, and implemented.

While this brief summary of the Snyder monograph does not begin to capture its cogency and complexity, it is sufficient to permit an assessment in terms of the four questions noted above. Such an assessment is perhaps particularly important in this case because the monograph has been widely misunderstood (although, interestingly, some of the ways in which it has been misunderstood served to stimulate subsequent developments in decision-making analysis). Much of the misunderstanding arises from the fact that Snyder and his colleagues outlined an approach that inductively treats decision making as both an intellectual and sociopolitical process in which both rational and nonrational actors participate, partly as a consequence of feedback that operates through both the intellectual and sociopolitical dimensions whereby choices are made. These apparent discrepancies are best resolved by stressing that the Snyder monograph neither offers nor purports to offer any theory. No hypotheses or predictions are developed as to the kinds of decision that are likely to result from varying conditions. Indeed, "factors" and "determinants of action" are identified rather than variables with a specified range of variation, so that any outcomes to which the factors and determinants give rise are cited merely as descriptive examples rather than as systematic products of varying circumstances. Although concerned with empirical phenomena, the monograph is only an "approach." Its authors explicitly and repeatedly refer to it as such, claiming that it was premature to theorize, that the main components of the decision-making process had to be carefully identified before viable theories could be developed.

It is precisely because they offered an approach rather than a theory that Snyder and his colleagues were able to outline both the intellectual and the sociopolitical dimensions of the decision-making process and to treat both rational and nonrational actors as participants in it. Not bound by the theoretical requirements in which variations in independent variables must be linked to those of dependent variables, they could freely identify, describe, and analyze all those phenomena that struck them as relevant. For example, the fact that the intellectual process was dependent on sociopolitical inputs could be noted, even emphasized, without an accompanying specification of how the former changed when the latter varied. Similarly, to trace diagrammatically, using single- and two-way arrows, the interaction between the internal and external settings and the decision-making organization is not to delineate the dynamics of such relationships. It is merely to stress their existence and, in effect, this is all the monograph did.

Much the same can be said about the treatment of rationality and nonrationality, although in this case the authors appear to have unintentionally allowed for rational action. Not confined by the requirements of theory, they were able to highlight the impact on decision makers of nonrational factors embedded in the domestic setting and the governmental bureaucracy. And, indeed, calling attention to the operation of such factors was one of the prime conceptual breakthroughs initiated by Snyder and his colleagues. Similarly, concerned with only the outlining of a general approach, they could take note of the various stages through which decisions pass before a final choice is made and, in so doing, derive the foregoing definition of decision making. In so doing, also, they tend to presume that decision makers engage in rational calculation when they frame, winnow, and select policy alternatives. This does not appear to have been their intention, since they gave so much credence to the impact of nonrational stimuli arising out of the internal setting and the policymaking organization. Yet, as their basic definition indicates, their discussion of decision making as an intellectual process clearly springs from the premise that somehow officials detach themselves from the nonrational factors playing upon them and systematically develop policy alternatives, carefully assess the costs and benefits of each alternative, and then select the one that appears most likely to move them most effectively toward their goals. In effect, therefore, their format allowed them to posit nonrational actors who engage in rational behavior, a contradiction that proved to be functional since it provoked subsequent theoretical efforts at clarification.

To stress the discrepancies created by their lack of theory is not to downgrade what Snyder and his colleagues accomplished. Their monograph was, and still is, a pioneering document; it probably introduced more fresh thinking and a greater number of new concepts into the analysis of foreign policy than any other work previously or subsequently published. Even the diagrams, for all their atheoretical quality, served to uncover and focus attention on relationships that had been ignored and that, in turn, led to the uncovering of still other phenomena that are regarded as central to any inquiry into the behavior of states. Indeed, as the ensuing discussion reveals, the Snyder-Bruck-Sapin monograph was as much a facilitator of later breakthroughs as it was a major breakthrough itself. As noted elsewhere (Rosenau, 1967), it did not lead to a myriad of empirical studies, but it did open theoretical doors through which others have walked.

DISJOINTED INCREMENTALISM

A consequence of the Snyder monograph was fostered by its passages that portrayed foreign policy decision making as a rational process in which officials consider all alternatives and select the one likely to obtain the best results. Ignoring those parts of the monograph that allowed for the operation of nonrational factors, several critics stressed that both logically and psychologically it was impossible for decision makers to conduct their deliberations in a rational way. Critics cited substantial empirical evidence indicating that every stage of the policymaking process was marked by the intrusion of nonrational considerations. In the course of demonstrating that reality fell far short of rationality, one analyst was led to evolve what he viewed as a more empirically accurate scheme for comprehending the intellectual processes whereby officials make foreign policy choices. Calling the model "disjointed incrementalism," Lindblom developed in a series of works a conception of decision making that allowed for, even highlighted, the factors that intrude upon and distort rational calculation (1959, 1965, 1968; and Braybrooke and Lindblom, 1963). These factors include the fact that officials are not omniscient, that they cannot possibly grasp situations in their entirety so that all possible alternative policy choices can be identified, that they cannot possibly acquire all the information necessary to a complete evaluation of each policy alternative, that they lack the time and resources to adequately consider and compare each alternative, and that they are incapable of separating values from facts in the way that is necessary to rationally calculate the link between means and ends in the process of framing and selecting policy alternatives. Lindblom argues that officials, inevitably burdened by these limitations, tend merely to cope with problems, "to stave them off or nibble at them" rather than solve them, to move incrementally at the margins of problems on a day-by-day basis rather than encompassingly at their core on a thoroughgoing basis.

Disjointed incrementalism thus deviates from rational decision making in a number of ways. Where rationality requires a readiness to engage in a total reconsideration of prevailing policies and a capacity to turn in a radically different direction, incremental decision making involves comparing, evaluating, and choosing among policies differing only marginally from existing policies. Where rational actors consider a wide range of alternatives, their incrementalist counterparts ponder only a restricted number. Where the former seek to anticipate all the consequences to which a given alternative may lead, the latter focus on only a few important consequences. Where the rational model posits means as being geared to ends, incrementalism allows for a continual redefinition of the problem, with ends also being adjusted to means as countless adjustments are made to changing circumstances. Where rationality presumes a single "best" solution to a problem, incrementalism permits acceptance of a variety of solutions. Where rational officials seek to promote future goals, incrementalists aspire to alleviate present dilemmas.

It follows that disjointed incrementalism is also more of an approach than a theory of foreign policy decision making—an inductive means of describing and comprehending the intellectual process whereby nonrational actors constantly experience feedback from prior actions in the course of responding to stimuli from their external environments. Indeed, given the emphasis upon the disjointedness of situations and ad hoc means of coping with them, it is an approach that defies theory-building; or at least it is hardly surprising that Lindblom does not propound any hypotheses as to the kinds of decisions that are likely to be made under varying circumstances. To do so would be to discern an underlying order in a world he conceives to be marked largely by discontinuities.

GAME THEORY

Not long after the concept of decision making became a central focus of foreign policy analysts, and partly on account of another innovative article by Snyder (1955), the possibilities of applying game theory to international politics came to be appreciated. Originally developed several decades earlier through the collaboration of a mathematician and an economist (Von Neumann and Morgenstern, 1944), game theory focuses on situations in which the actions of the actors are partly dependent on what each actor perceives that the others are likely to do. Such situations, in which interdependent perceptions are central, pervade human experience, from interactions between two persons to those that mark bargaining among large groups. They are situations in which strategy is a more important component than chance or skill. Since strategy is so much a part of the moves that states make on the world stage, it is hardly surprising that the potentiality of game theory for the study of foreign policy began to command attention as analysts became increasingly focused on the dynamics of decision making. The emergence of a bipolar world after World War II and the advent of nuclear capabilities at both poles hastened the realization that game theory could be as usefully applied to world politics as it had been earlier to the world of business. Indeed, the first major application of game theory to international politics focused on the military realm and the question of avoiding a nuclear holocaust (Schelling, 1960). Both the strategy of deterrence and the resulting balance of terror that have dominated world politics since World War II can be readily traced to the application of game theoretical precepts.

Since game theory is extensively considered elsewhere in this volume, its premises and procedures need not be elaborated here. In comparison to the other approaches to decision making, however, game theory is distinctive in several important respects. It is the only approach that is thoroughly founded on deductive reasoning. It posits rational actors and is exclusively concerned with the intellectual process whereby they make choices, with the impact of sociopolitical variables being treated as subsumed by the values that the actors attach to policy options. That is, each actor is conceived to have a set of well-defined and mutually consistent basic objectives derived from whatever considerations are deemed important and—on the basis of the "utility function" expressed by the values attached to each objective—to make choices exclusively in terms of maximizing his utilities. What the various actors will do at any point in a sequence of interaction, therefore, can be logically deduced from whatever would maximize their utilities at that point (which includes how the utilities have been altered by feedback from decisions made at previous points in time).

It follows that game theory is indeed theory. All the deductive models of various types of strategic situations that have been developed contain concise predictions of how rational actors will behave under various conditions and, accordingly, how the ensuing interaction among them will turn out. In its most advanced form game theory is highly mathematical and sophisticated, with the expectations of interactive behavior being precisely specified. To be sure, a few empirical inquiries designed to test game theoretical propositions have been undertaken, but these rely mainly on experimentation in simulation laboratories and do not negate the essential point that game theory has enriched the comprehension of foreign policy decision making primarily through the clarity and incisiveness of the deductive models it has generated. In other words, the fact that empirically actors do not behave rationally has not impeded the development of valuable insights, since the unqualified assumption of rationality has allowed game theorists to uncover behavioral dynamics that are otherwise obscured by the many nonrational factors that pervade decision making in the real world.

ALLISON'S THREE MODELS

Another major development in the analysis of foreign policy decision making—one that occurred explicitly with reference to policymaking in the United States—fully emerged with the publication of Graham Allison's *Essence of Decision* (1971). In this work Allison uses press accounts, interviews, and other empirical materials to reconstruct the 1962 Cuban missile crisis three times: once from the perspective of a rational actor model, the second time in terms of what he calls the "organizational process" model, and lastly in the context of what he labels the "governmental politics" or "bureaucratic" model. The last two of these are conceived to distort rational policymaking because, in one instance, the foreign policy organization falls back on standard operating procedures to cope with challenges from abroad and, in the other instance, officials bargain with each other and make choices on the basis of the various constituencies they feel obliged to serve. These two models give rise to distortions of rationality because in both the nature of external challenges is subordinated to, and interpreted through, factors that either sustain the foreign policy organization or meet the requirements of interagency bargaining—factors that may be rational from the perspective of maintaining organizational and governmental processes but that are nonrational in terms of making decisions that relate the whole society to the outside world.

The viability of the three models is revealed by the fact that three Cuban missile crises emerge from Allison's analysis. The motives and behavior of the actors, their perceptions and the information on which they rely, the sequence of events and the outcomes of their interactions, as well as a number of other aspects of the situation, all take on very different dimensions as the analysis moves from one model to the next. Consequently, if for no other reason, Allison's study has become a landmark because it so clearly demonstrates how the analysis of decision making is crucially dependent on the theories the observers bring to bear, explicitly or implicitly, on the foreign policy phenomena they are assessing.

There is, however, another reason why Allison's work constitutes a major development in decision-making analysis, namely, it focuses attention on the importance of organizational and governmental variables as sources of the choices officials make. The existence of these variables had been identified previously—it will be recalled that Snyder and his colleagues included them in their scheme—but they had never before been so exclusively and thoroughly explored and applied. Reinforced by the writings of Halperin (1974), Allison's work gave rise to a continuing interest and research into the role of bureaucratic behavior in foreign policy.

The intense preoccupation with the bureaucratic politics model is in some ways distressing. It tends to discount stimuli from the external environment beyond what may be reasonable. To some extent officials undoubtedly interpret events abroad in terms of their bureaucratic squabbles, but this tendency may be less pronounced than the Allison-Halperin type models presume. Conceivably the very same officials also assess situations with other, more encompassing interests in mind; or at least it seems likely that their behavior results from a combination of factors, of which bureaucratic considerations are only one set, albeit an important set. Furthermore, the stress on bureaucratic factors inhibits theorizing, since the bargaining that sustains bureaucratic infighting is presumed to spring from such unsystematic motives as personal ambition and impetuous demands of a constituency. Indeed, neither the bureaucratic model nor its several variants are theoretical. Like the Snyder-Bruck-Sapin framework, all of them are only approaches and lack concrete, testable hypotheses. All of them have been explored through elaborate case studies, which are a legitimate form of inquiry but which suffer in this instance because the various cases are not comparable.

It follows that Allison's models of decision making derive from inductive forms of inquiry. Two of them posit nonrational actors whose choices are essentially responses to the sociopolitical processes in which they participate. In all three models decision making is conceived to evolve across time, with feedback from prior choices being given due consideration. In effect, the organizational process and bureaucratic models are similar to, but less encompassing than, the Snyder-Bruck-Sapin approach; and, like that approach, they suffer from treating the intellectual and sociopolitical processes and the rational and nonrational actors who, respectively, sustain them as separate and distinct, rather than seeking to bring them together into a coherent, integrated, and empirical theory.

THE CYBERNETIC PERSPECTIVE

The most recent theoretical developments in the study of foreign policy decision making explicitly seek to overcome the weaknesses of previous efforts by focusing on the cybernetic and cognitive processes through which officials reduce complexity and control uncertainty. Several analysts have converged on one or the other of these processes (Axelrod, 1973; George, 1969, 1972; Holsti, 1976; Rosenau, 1970; Shapiro and Bonham, 1973), and Steinbruner has sought to bring them together into a coherent whole. Although only the outline of a theory, his synthesizing work (1974) seems likely to become a landmark.

Steinbruner seeks to explain foreign policy choices by tracing the interaction of the cognitive capabilities of the mind and the structure of the policymaking organization. Cognitive theory is conceived to have yielded three types of findings that explain how officials reduce the vast uncertainty with which they are confronted in their external environment: those pertaining to the dynamics of reinforcement, whereby beliefs acquire strength and information is stored; those stemming from a need to achieve a minimum degree of consistency among beliefs and perceptions; and those that spring from the tendency toward agreement and conformity in small group interactions. These cognitive processes are, in turn, conceived to coincide with and sustain the cybernetic mechanisms through which any actor, be it an individual or organization, adapts to the challenges from and the uncertainty in its environment. The cybernetic model posits actors not as rationally considering all alternatives or responding to all stimuli, but rather as focusing only on those stimuli that feedback indicates may undermine or alter critical variables of concern to the actor beyond tolerable limits. Thus foreign policy decision-making organizations tend to proceed on the basis of a highly focused span of attention and a highly programmed set of responses. When faced with external challenges, the organizations are assumed to have only a limited repertory of action programs on which to fall back. These programs rest on standard operating procedures that have worked in the past and that only undergo change when feedback highlights unwanted movement toward unacceptable arrangements in the environment. Accordingly, "the basic cybernetic process of decision works out in an organizational setting" through a "major focus on processes which remove or avoid uncertainty, thus reducing the burdens of processing information, and which divide problems into segments, thus avoiding conflict within the organization. The consequence is a dissection of complex problems—a decision process which disaggregates values, utilizes information selectively, and does not perform outcome calculations" (Steinbruner, p. 78).

In effect, Steinbruner's formulation of the cybernetic model has much in common with Lindblom's disjointed incrementalism. The major differences are that the former is more highly developed, that it builds in cognitive processes more fully, and that it offers more extensive explanations for the ways in which external challenges are met than does the latter. Moreover, by focusing on the explanatory power of cognitive and adaptive mechanisms the cybernetic model has the potential of evolving into genuine theory. Steinbruner does not offer an integrated set of hypotheses, preferring instead to highlight the components of the model through examples of United States policymaking practices; but the groundwork for generating either deductive or inductive theory is laid in his work, theory which might well be able to account for how the intellectual and sociopolitical processes converge to shape the behavior of nonrational actors.

CONCLUSION

The study of decision making in foreign policy has undergone a veritable explosion in the last several decades. Although the processes of decision are extraordinarily complex and unraveling them poses severe methodological problems, the analyst now has available a variety of schemes, approaches, theories, and concepts with which to probe how and why officials make certain choices. Already these various lines of inquiry have yielded substantial insights into the dynamics of foreign policy behavior, and, if the past is any guide, they seem likely to continue to enrich understanding and to provide the basis for further theoretical breakthroughs.

BIBLIOGRAPHY

On decision-making approaches and theories, see Graham T. Allison, *Essence of Decision* (Boston, 1971); Graham T. Allison and Morton H. Halperin, "Bureaucratic Politics: A Paradigm and Some Policy Implications," in *World Politics,* 24 (1972); Robert Axelrod, "Schema Theory: An Information Processing Model of Perception and Cognition," in *American Political Science Review,* 67 (1973); Chester I. Barnard, *The Functions of the Executive* (Cambridge, Mass., 1938); David Braybrooke and Charles E. Lindblom, *A Strategy of Decision: Policy Evaluation as a Social Process* (New York, 1963); Richard M. Cyert and James G. March, *A Behavioral Theory of the Firm* (Englewood Cliffs, N.J., 1963); Alexander L. George, "The 'Operational Code': A Neglected Approach to the Study of Political Leaders and Decision-Making," in *International Studies Quarterly,* 13 (1969); "The Case for Multiple Advocacy in Making Foreign Policy," in *American Political Science Review,* 66 (1972); Morton H. Halperin, *Bureaucratic Politics and Foreign Policy* (Washington, D.C., 1974), with the assistance of Priscilla Clapp and Arnold Kanter; Ole R. Holsti, "Foreign Policy Decision-Makers Viewed Psychologically: 'Cognitive Process' Approaches," in James N. Rosenau, ed., *In Search of Global Patterns* (New York, 1976); Harold D. Lasswell and Abraham Kaplan, *Power and Society: A Framework for Political Inquiry* (New Haven, 1950); Charles E. Lindblom, "The Science of 'Muddling Through,' " in *Public Administration Review,* 29 (1959); *Intelligence of Democracy* (New York, 1965); *The Policy Making Process* (Englewood Cliffs, N.J., 1968); Martin Patchen, "Decision Theory in the Study of National Action: Problems and a Proposal," in *Journal of Conflict Resolution,* 9 (1965); James A. Robinson and R. Roger Majak, "The Theory of Decision-Making," in James C. Charlesworth, ed., *Contemporary Political Analysis* (New York, 1967); James A. Robinson and Richard C. Snyder, "Decision-Making in International Politics," in Herbert C. Kelman, ed., *International Behavior: A Social-Psychological Analysis* (New York, 1965); James N. Rosenau, "The Premises and Promises of Decision-Making Analysis," in James C. Charlesworth, ed., *Contemporary Political Analysis* (New York, 1967); *The Adaptation of National Societies: A Theory of Political Behavior and Its Transformations* (New York, 1970); Thomas C. Schelling, *The Strategy of Conflict* (Cambridge, Mass., 1960); Michael J. Shapiro and Matthew Bonham, "Cognitive Process and Foreign Policy Decision Making," in *International Studies Quarterly,* 17 (1973); Herbert A. Simon, *Administrative Behavior: A Study of Decision-Making Processes in Administrative Organization* (New York, 1947); Richard C. Snyder, "Game Theory and the Analysis of Political Behavior," in *Research Frontiers in Politics and Government,* Brookings Lectures, 1955 (Washington, D.C., 1955); Richard C. Snyder, H. W. Bruck, and Burton M. Sapin, *Decision-Making as an Approach to the Study of International Politics* (Princeton, 1954); "Decision-Making as an Approach to the Study of International Politics," in Richard C. Snyder, H. W. Bruck, and Burton M. Sapin, eds., *Foreign Policy Decision Making: An Approach to the Study of International Politics* (New York, 1962); John D. Steinbruner, *The Cybernetic Theory of Decision: New Dimensions of Political Analysis* (Princeton, 1974); Sidney Verba, "Assumptions of Rationality and Non-Rationality in Models of the International System," in Klaus Knorr and Sidney Verba, eds., *The International System: Theoretical Essays* (Princeton, 1961); and John Von Neumann and Oskar Morgenstern, *Theory of Games and Economic Behavior* (Princeton, 1944).

[*See also* THE BEHAVIORAL APPROACH TO DIPLOMATIC HISTORY.]

THE DEPARTMENT OF STATE

Jerry Israel

THE FIRST chief clerk of the Department of State, Henry Remsen, upon his resignation in 1792, left the following instructions:

> . . . such of the Foreign Letters as are not filed away in the cases, are for the present put on my desk in two pigeon holes at the right hand side. The Consular returns are at the bottom of said desk right hand side . . . the drafts of foreign proceedings . . . are filed in said desk left hand pigeon hole. The letters from our ministers and *charge des affaires* now in commission Mr. Jefferson keeps. . . . A little attention will be necessary in separating the foreign from the domestic letters, as they are sent to the Office by Mr. Jefferson to be filed. My rule in making the separation was by reading them. The domestic letters to be filed in the Office down stairs, the foreign letters in the Office up stairs [Leonard White, *The Federalists: A Study in Administrative History* (New York, 1948), 50].

Nearly two centuries later, commenting on the move from "Old State" to headquarters in "New" and finally, "New, New State," the diplomat Henry Serrano Villard wrote:

> . . . even this fantastically outside complex is inadequate. Spilling over into nine rented buildings, using nearly 1.5 million square feet of space, the State Department premises are already too small; if AID (Agency for International Development), ACDA (Arms Control and Disarmament Agency) and USIA (United States Information Agency) are added, the total is twenty buildings with 2,547,377 square feet. Offices are overcrowded, tenants must double up, conference rooms must be lopped off, new outlets sought [Henry S. Villard, *Affairs of State* (New York, 1965), 21–22].

The irony of these comparisons of simple and complex styles is that Villard's larger department was if anything less rather than more involved in the making of American foreign policy, the State Department's primary responsibility. Along these lines, in modern times one notes the competitive foreign policies of departments such as Commerce, Agriculture, Defense, Labor, Treasury, Interior, and Health, Education, and Welfare, plus the role of the Central Intelligence Agency, Federal Reserve Bank, and Post Office Department, not to mention semiofficial business, scientific, cultural, and journalistic groups. In addition, there is the superior and sometimes competitive power of the president and groups or individuals he may especially empower outside the State Department.

Henry A. Kissinger noted the paradox of an increasingly specialized, bureaucratized society having negative consequences for American policy and policymakers. Calling for a return to the individual and intellectual approach to problems and policy, not uncharacteristic of the formative age of Jefferson and Remsen, Kissinger has written of policy "fragmented into a series of *ad hoc* decisions which make it difficult to achieve a sense of direction or even to profit from experience. Substantive problems are transformed into administrative ones. Innovation is subjected to 'objective' tests which deprive it of spontaneity. 'Policy planning' becomes the projection of familiar problems into the future. Momentum is confused with purpose. There is greater concern with how things are than with which things matter."

Borrowing from the example of Remsen and the explanation of Kissinger it is possible to observe, at least until the mid-twentieth century, that amidst efforts to institutionalize the apparatus of the State Department, what machinery there was rested on a precious few long-lived cogwheels. Working backward not quite all the way from Kissinger to Remsen, one traces a remarkable continuity within the careers of just three men: Wilbur J. Carr, with forty-five years of service (1892–1937); Alvey A. Adee, with forty-six years in Washington (1878–1924) and seven before that for the Department of State in Madrid; and William Hunter, with fifty-seven years (1829–1886) as chief of bureau, chief clerk, and second assistant secretary (the latter two being key administrative posts held also by Carr and Adee).

As late as 1929, the Department of State was small and its central leadership even more scant. When Henry L. Stimson took office as Herbert C. Hoover's secretary of state, there were—including everybody from the secretary to chauffeurs, clerks, stenographers, and janitors—six hundred people.

Yet Stimson, not unusually for the department, surrounded himself with an able, tight-knit group of assistants including Carr, Joseph Cotton, Francis White, and Nelson T. Johnson. Like Cotton, some assistants were new to foreign policy; others, like Carr and Johnson, had seen extended service in the consular and diplomatic corps. They blended together, however, to advise the secretary and the president on critical policy matters in Latin America, Europe, and Asia.

The history of the State Department until very recently was tied, it appears, to the history of the few men who have served as secretary of state, or on his staff. The role of the individual has become increasingly institutionalized, and with that change has come a larger and yet often less effective Department of State than it was in its humbler days.

THE CALIBER OF LEADERSHIP

It is tempting to start at the very beginning with Jefferson, James Madison, James Monroe, and the Virginia dynasty. Indeed it must be noted that these Founding Fathers and "systems builders" used the State Department's highest official, not the vice-president, as counselor and successor. Yet it remained for one of the second generation of American revolutionaries, John Quincy Adams, to achieve the golden age of American diplomacy and thereby establish the model, perhaps yet unequaled, of a great secretary of state. Adams dominated events in which the United States signed the Treaty of Ghent (1814), which concluded the War of 1812, issued the Monroe Doctrine, and strengthened American maritime power by agreeing with England to clear the Great Lakes of warships and by obtaining rights to fish off Labrador and Newfoundland. Under Adams' leadership at State, the United States extended its landed empire by annexing Florida, removing Russia from the west coast of North America, settling the Canadian boundary from the Great Lakes to the Rockies, and by claiming, for the first time, the Pacific coast. Even amidst Adams' successes, however, the State Department and its secretary retained the highly personal and political character developed under the Virginia dynasty.

Adams himself used the post of secretary of state to dangle in front of Henry Clay in 1824 in what their political rivals, the Jacksonians, called a "corrupt bargain." While personally worlds apart, Adams and Clay were closer together in support of an "American system" of economic regulation and internal improvements than has been generally noted. Nonetheless a pattern of granting political favors or rewarding factions with high office in the State Department was well established and would continue into the twentieth-century appointments of William Jennings Bryan (by Woodrow Wilson in 1913) and Cordell Hull (by Franklin Roosevelt in 1933). Perhaps no period was more replete with political partisanship in the State Department than the years between Adams and the Civil War. First used by the followers of Andrew Jackson as patronage rewards, or the spoils of victory, the department's leadership positions were given—especially in the administrations of James K. Polk, Franklin Pierce, and James Buchanan—to proponents of Southern slave expansion who styled themselves "Young Americans."

By 1860, and certainly after the Civil War, the rapid advance of the industrial economy of the United States and the transfer of power from planters to industrialists and financiers was closely mirrored in the composition of State Department leadership. In fact, resisting the divisive trends of the Young Americans, some department leaders such as Daniel Webster and William Learned Marcy had begun in the 1840's to develop interest in a new wave of expansionism directed toward California, Hawaii, and Asia. Foremost among postwar figures was William Henry Seward, next to Adams, the greatest secretary of state of the nineteenth century.

Seward, like John Quincy Adams, was also an intellectual. He had read widely and well in the classics and contemporary works. His ties to Adams were as strong a link as was the more mundane relationship between Hunter and Adee, whose careers overlapped those of their more famous superiors. After Adams' death in 1848, Seward mourned, "I have lost a patron, a guide, a counsellor, and a friend—one whom I loved scarcely less than the dearest relations, and venerated above all that was mortal among men."

Seward's State Department years saw the outline developed for a vast, coordinated American worldwide empire with its great continental base producing goods for the consumers of Latin America, Africa, and Asia. While Seward's master plan was not fulfilled during his tenure in office, it was followed carefully by such capable, if less visible, successors as William M. Evarts and Hamilton Fish.

With Evarts, in particular, the State Department began to take on its modern cast as an organization intent, in its own way, on "the fostering, the developing, and the directing of . . . commerce by the government." In October 1880, under Evarts' supervision, the State Department received congressional approval and appropriations for the publication of monthly consular reports, a step urged by local chambers of commerce throughout the country. Also characteristic of the years ahead, Evarts was a lawyer. Indeed, like many future secretaries of state, he was a dominant figure in the American bar at the time—a profession gaining increased significance in modern American business and government.

THE LEGAL MIND

A list of the secretaries and undersecretaries of state of the twentieth century reads like a hall of fame of attorneys: Elihu Root, Philander C. Knox, Robert Lansing, Charles Evans Hughes, Henry L. Stimson, Edward R. Stettinius, Dean Acheson, John Foster Dulles, and William P. Rogers, not to mention Huntington Wilson, William Phillips, Joseph C. Grew, Nicholas deBelleville Katzenbach, and Elliot L. Richardson. Indeed a number of men have served both at the State and the Justice Department, and the number of men who have been both secretary of state and attorney general is significant. The modern business flavor; cross-examining perception; studied, organized knowledge; attention to detail; and developed cynicism of the legal mind—as found, for example, in a Root or a Stimson—are important to note as traits common to the personnel of the Department of State. More precisely, those in leadership positions at State have often been Ivy League–trained, Wall Street lawyers whose careers have paralleled the growth of the American industrial system and policy. Such lawyers have been uniquely prepared to deal on a large scale with the organization of railroads, banks, and other developing enterprises at home and abroad.

Dulles' law firm, Sullivan and Cromwell, was involved in the making of American foreign policy as early as the Panamanian revolution of 1903, in part engineered in a New York hotel room by Phillip Cromwell. Stimson's clients included the Continental Rubber Company, the United States Printing Company, the National Sugar Refining Company, the Bank of North America, the Mutual Life Insurance Company, and the Astoria Power and Light Company. In such representations, Stimson, like his colleagues, was accustomed to high finance. In foreign policy matters, once in the service of State, a Stimson, Root, or Dulles would easily fall into the conditions and attitudes emerging from a successful legal practice. Such men could easily talk as though they had the will and power to arrange a set of conditions for society. They were concerned, as always, with the important things: money, boundaries, goods, and, perhaps for the first time, guns.

Corporation lawyers derived their power from their relationship to the developing corporate economy they helped to construct. They had the power of expertise in legal matters. They also had the power of individuals who had a broader perspective of the total system and could thereby give advice to those functioning in narrower channels. By controlling various scientific, educational, and cultural projects through foundations and associations, they also could dramatically influence opinion and events in noneconomic aspects of American life. They served, in particular, as key people in educating persons who were going to be decision makers in foreign policy matters, which were less directly tied than domestic concerns to political and congressional sanctions. By taking the leadership at State and other departments (for example, Treasury), corporation lawyers came to dominate American foreign policy by the beginning of the twentieth century. They moved comfortably within expansionist objectives outlined by Seward. The primary concern of State Department officials became the articulation of a managed, professional structure by which to achieve this well-defined strategy.

MANAGEMENT EFFICIENCY

Developed—like all cabinet-level executive departments of the federal government—along the lines of precedent and personality rather than constitutional or legislative sanction, the State Department until the twentieth century had little organizational rhyme or reason. From Jefferson and Remsen through to Evarts and Adee, the department, in its aptly named Foggy Bottom headquarters, functioned by tradition, and often did so rather poorly. For example, in 1906 an inspector of American consulates in the Orient found two consuls who were decrepit; two otherwise unfit for duty; one morally suspect; one charged with coercing a sultan into paying a debt for which he, the consul, was collector; one charged with drunkenness and the issuance of fraudulent papers; and one, "a coarse and brutal type," against whom eighty-two complaints were registered. Pressure to restructure the consular service, the branch of the department charged directly with the responsibility of looking after American citizens and business interests abroad, came, in great part, from those business interests themselves. Nearly a decade of lobbying went into the executive order of November 1905 and the passage in April 1906 of a consular reorganization bill. The purpose of the pressure and the proposals produced by it was the same, ". . . in a word, to put the entire diplomatic system on a business basis, and to manage it in the future in accordance with the principles of sound common sense." Such principles included more effective training programs. Selective language training in the Foreign Service began in 1895 through the assignment of officers as "student interpreters" to the American legations in Persia, Korea, and Siam. In 1902 ten student interpreter posts were created at Peking for Chinese language training.

Training in consular responsibilities dates from 1907, when seven new consuls were given thirty-day courses of instruction. The purpose was "to give novitiates in the consular service some practical training in the running of a consular office before sending them off to their posts." In 1924 additional training for diplomatic and consular officers began with the establishment of a foreign service school, which sent new officers to divisions of the department for several months before their assignment abroad. In the 1930's the renamed Foreign Service Officers' Training School provided junior officers with training in consular and commercial work after their two-year probationary tour abroad.

Increasingly, some officers were also sent to universities for graduate study. While all training was suspended during World War II, it was resumed after the war with the establishment of the Foreign Service Institute. In theory the intention was to copy a business model by creating the most efficient system with the most efficient people. Such changes included revised entrance examinations and consular associations, in addition to the foreign service schools.

The reforms were perhaps best represented in the internal system of ratings and inspections used to rule on promotions. Forms, which eventually swelled to some 212 questions by the 1920's, and departmental retention and promotion rating codes were used to provide uniform standards for personnel decisions. The most significant concern expressed by the forms and rating codes was to be a measuring device of the "efficiency of the individual." It was hoped that such evaluations would purge the "decrepit, unfit, morally suspect, drunken and coarse and brutal types, *etc.*," from the consular service.

Deeply felt personal, status, and career differences separated the department's consular service from the diplomatic, which officially represented the government of the United States in international relations. Diplomats often considered themselves professional policymakers and were more bound to State Department traditions. Managers and planners, usually emerging, like Carr, from the consular side, were held in low esteem. One diplomat observed those "administrative types who inflate themselves with all sorts of rich and resonant titles like Career Evaluators, and General Services Specialists, and even Ministers of Embassy for Administrative Affairs. These glorified janitors, supply clerks, and pants-pressers yearn to get their fingers in the foreign affairs pie, and when they do, the diplomatic furniture often gets marked with gummy thumbprints."

It must be noted, however, that truly significant organizational reform in the Department of State did not stop at the consular-diplomatic demarcation. Diplomats such as Phillips and Grew remarked at how much of their work concerned the same business interests and pressures directed at the consuls. New departures were taken with a view to improving the efficiency of the State Department, not just one part of it.

Of most direct contact with the business-consular developments of the early twentieth century were modifications in the preparations of commercial reports. The Bureau of Statistics, a province of influential geopoliticians such as O. P. Austin, was renamed the Bureau of Foreign and Domestic Commerce. Although control of it was shifted to the Commerce and Labor Department in 1903, a corollary agency, the Bureau of Trade Relations, was immediately established. The State Department advanced this effort to collect and analyze business data with the creation of the Office of the Economic Adviser in 1921. This position came to be held by important advisers such as Herbert Feis.

The State Department's approach to filing and record-keeping, somewhat more detailed than in Remsen's day, was reworked several times in the twentieth century to provide greater systemization. Thus were created in turn the Numerical Files of 1906–1910 and the more comprehensive and efficient Decimal Files for 1910 and after. The Division of Information, created in 1909, took responsibility for preserving the department's data and publishing selected annual excerpts in the already established House of Representatives publication series Foreign Relations of the United States. This series entered what has been called its "modern era" in 1921, under the supervision of Gaillard Hunt and another agency he headed called the Division of Publications.

Of greatest precedence on the diplomatic side was the creation in March 1908 of the Division of Far Eastern Affairs and the structuring of the whole State Department into a number of similar geographically grouped "divisions" in the years that followed. Before World War II, when the Department of State still numbered well below a thousand employees in all, these regional divisions were small, usually manned by only a few "desk officers" dealing with American embassies and legations overseas. Their purpose was to provide better machinery for the coordination of policy at all levels. In time the five regional divisions (Europe, East Asia, Near East and South Asia, Inter-American, African) and a sixth desk, the Bureau of International Organization Affairs (responsible for relations with the American mission to the United Nations), grew dramatically in size and complexity. An assistant secretary headed each bureau and supervised the close contact with American embassies in the respective areas of responsibility. Below the assistant secretary were office directors, each responsible for a small group of countries. The country desk officer was the "low man on the totem pole," concerning himself with policy toward a single foreign nation.

The culmination of all these administrative changes came in two efforts to make the various components of the State Department into "interchangeable" parts. First was the Rogers (Foreign Service) Act of 1924 and second was the movement known as "Wristonization" in the 1950's. The pressures and reasoning producing the Rogers Act, merging the consular and diplomatic services into a single foreign service, were similar to those that resulted in the previously mentioned separate and more piecemeal reforms on both sides of the department. As Representative John Rogers remarked, business forces were united and once again exerting influence. "Practically every chamber of commerce and trade organization in the United States and many of the American chambers and trade organizations functioning in other parts of the world have gone on record as favoring this particular reorganization of our foreign service." Rather than a radical departure, the Rogers Act was a culmination of the well-defined premises of efficient control and a transition to still further forms of administrative systemization. In place of the separation and distinction between the broadly separated categories of political interest in the diplomatic service and commercial interest in the consular service, there would be one unified Department of State.

With the increased size of the department, by the 1950's a movement developed to merge still further the civil service staff of the State Department with the Foreign Service. With a shortage of personnel for positions, and especially training programs and a distrust between the "line" desk officers and the "staff" administrators, a committee was charged by Dulles with the task of additional State Department reorganization. Chairman of the committee was Henry M. Wriston, president of Brown University, and hence the merger of the two staffs became known as Wristonization.

This reform was not only another in a series, but it also gave the first real evidence that the other similar ones that had preceded it might not, after all, have been effective. Throughout the century, optimism had prevailed. Thus Huntington Wilson had boasted in 1908, "I am happy to tell you that one of my pet hobbies, the politico-geographical division, has at last received final recognition by the creation of the Division of Far Eastern Affairs . . . so I now have much better machinery for my direction of the Far Eastern business." Or after the Rogers Act, Grew felt the State Department had "a new order . . . established, a new machine developed." But the Wriston committee described well the catalogue of State Department problems after a half century of such administrative reforms. In sum, there was a marked decline in public confidence in the State Department; a similar decline in morale in the diplomatic ranks; and failure to carry through on various legislative mandates such as the Foreign Service Act of 1946, which provided for inducting officers into all levels of the Foreign Service so as to make it more flexible and successful.

Although Wristonization itself was another management panacea, it drew attention to the fact that the State Department's "management of human resources has been irresolute and unimaginative." Even though the question of personnel management had been under repeated study, "substantially nothing has been accomplished." The committee remarked that while "all modern personnel management organizations utilize machines to facilitate the mechanical tasks of keeping personnel records; the Department however has not effectively utilized such a system." In particular, Wriston's committee criticized the "occasional tinkering" and "token" programs of recruitment and training. Congress had intended the Foreign Service Institute to be "for the State Department, what the Naval War College, the Army War College, and the National War College are for the Armed Services—an advanced training ground for officers destined for high command." Instead of educational leadership and scholarship, the institute had been given little attention. Such was characteristic of the State Department's general lack of a clear concept of training requirements, career planning, and development.

The Wriston committee missed the perhaps larger significance of the protracted failure of management reforms and put all its faith in a still bigger and, it hoped, better structure. While many civil servants had been seriously involved in foreign affairs and thus would benefit themselves and the State Department by merger with the foreign service officers, a larger number of straight administrative employees (office personnel, for example) were trapped by the move into being diplomatic officers, for which they had neither ambition nor preparation.

Forgetting, or perhaps choosing not to remember, that similar organizational reform enthusiasms had failed to deter and might be blamed for the bad situation now at hand, the brightest people in and out of the Department of State continued to talk of what could be done to increase management efficiency and policy effectiveness. Thus one had come almost full circle from Remsen to Kissinger. The larger and more complex the State Department and the world became, the less important was the role of the department in making foreign policy. Instead of individual advice, the department became expert in institutional adjustments and its influence shrunk proportionally. A Rand Corporation think-tank study, *United States Policy and the Third World* (1967), never once mentioned, nor obviously conceived of, the State Department.

As State's structure increased and its power vanished in the mid-twentieth century, its once high and mighty place became almost laughable. Thus satires of departmental memoranda about such things as waste-power removal were not uncommon, nor were genuine titles such as chief of the administrative management and personnel division of the Bureau of Educational and Cultural Affairs. While some flirted with participative management and Dean Rusk instituted a department suggestion box, few shared the Kissinger or Villard view that perhaps the goal might once again be "top-notch organization in which the human equation is not sacrificed to the Moloch of bureaucracy."

LEADERSHIP OR MANAGEMENT?

One recent State Department publication notes the "startling contrast between the age when Benjamin Franklin in Paris penned his diplomatic dispatches by candlelight for arrival in the New World perhaps months later and 1972 when a flash report from Vietnam might arrive on the Secretary of State's desk minutes after an event." Can, in short, the modern secretary of state, however talented and qualified, break free as Kissinger suggests from the management ethos?

The obstacles to such freedom are rather clear in the recent history of the State Department. A secretary's duties are extremely heavy. He is a senior personal adviser to the president and the only cabinet officer primarily charged with looking at the nation as a whole in its relations with the outside world. The secretary of state is also the ranking diplomat in dealing with foreign governments at the same time that he serves as an administration spokesman on American foreign policy to Congress, the country, and abroad. He is chief of the State Department and as such is responsible to the president and accountable to Congress. Finally, he is also in direct line to presidential succession. The modern secretary of state is thus adviser, negotiator, reporter of trouble, spokesman, manager, and coordinator. One thinks of days filled with calls, conferences, talks with senators, ambassadors, delegations of private citizens, newspapermen, and bankers, not to mention the increasingly frequent global troubleshooting all the time while running a department.

Secretary Stimson's biographer reports one day, even in the more serene pre–World War II world, as follows:

> . . . a conference at ten o'clock with Silas Strawn, the United States delegate to a conference at Peking on Chinese tariffs. At 10:30 a press conference followed at 10:45 by an appointment with Dr. McClaren of the Williamstown Institute. Between 11:00 and 12:00 receiving the Spanish Ambassador and a representative from the Bolivian delegation. They were followed by Senator Howell at 12:00, Congressman Keyes at 12:40 and General Allen at 12:55. After lunch at 2:30 he began to sign the official mail, a task he had finished by 3:30 when Congressmen Robinson, Thatcher, Walker, Newhill, Kendall and Blackburn called upon him and talked for an hour. Elihu Root, Jr. appeared at 4:30 and remained until 5:00. Just before going home the Secretary called James M. Beck, then a congressman, in New York. That evening he attended a dinner given by the Chilean Ambassador in honor of the Chilean Minister of Finance.

How against these activities does one formulate the basic strategies and plans of action required? Even if time and attention be found, more myriad problems await in terms of the delegation of authority to bureaus that distrust each other's prerogatives or to individuals anxious for good assignments and promotions. Each bureau, each office within a bureau, each officer, is improvising from day to day, unaware, unprepared, or uninspired in the work of partners, neighbors, and colleagues.

Against this setting, several recent secretaries of state have stood out in the effort to orchestrate the department's activities. Most notably mentioned by those in the State Department, George C. Marshall, accustomed to command, and Dean Acheson, experienced on the Hoover

Commission for government reorganization, brought about a sense of planning amidst the chaos. Yet their task was so difficult because the role of the State Department was, in the last analysis, so weak. Primacy in coordinating foreign policy itself, the lifeblood of the State Department's leadership in the days of Adams and Seward, had been challenged and the counterattack had few bases for claims to legitimacy. The Constitution says nothing of the State Department and refers only to "executive" and "presidential" responsibilities. The Congress has never helped. The original legislation setting up the State Department also recognized the president as supreme. Even when granting power to the secretary of state it has always been understood that he "shall act under the direction of the President." Such direction has wandered from giving State considerable room to those who have wanted State out of foreign affairs.

Some analysts of American diplomacy go even further to suggest that the State Department, while it never had a constitutional or legislative claim to primacy, did, at one time in the nineteenth century, come to hold such a position by tradition and that the department itself gradually allowed such power to erode. One of the first four departments to be established (along with War, Treasury, and Justice), the State Department came to view itself as the first among equals. This, in turn, led to an attitude of general superiority in the federal establishment—an attitude that regardless of ability, the State Department had a special dispensation to control foreign policy. If other valid interests arose in other departments, the State Department worked for too long not to foster them but to cut them off. Thus began a movement to place control of foreign policy in more reasonable and responsive hands. The "legal mind" and "administrative efficiency" movement made State more introspective and took it further from the center of integrated policy.

As the State Department failed to keep abreast and federal agencies multiplied, new voices emerged to decide, negotiate, and implement foreign policy. When the State Department cried "foul," but showed little aptitude, foreign policymaking moved elsewhere. The emergency experience of World War II, in particular, put personal presidential policy in the forefront. Self-defensively, the State Department took to eulogizing its establishment, and the American people had to be reminded frequently after the war that "the Department of State, under the direction of the President, in cooperation with Congress is responsible for the advancement of our foreign policy objectives."

Such leadership moved most directly, in reality however, to the National Security Council. Created by the National Security Act of 1947 (the same statute that established the Central Intelligence Agency), the National Security Council was, in fact, charged with the responsibility of "effectively coordinating the policies and functions of the departments and agencies of the Government relating to the national security." It was provided with a staff and set about operating, close to the White House, as an interdepartmental committee with functions most immediately related to questions of foreign policy. Thus was created what the State Department had once been, a coordinating, orchestrating mechanism for the various elements of policy at the highest level. The State Department, at least in the contemporary United States, was not a part of the primary machinery by which the nation would set about to meet the demands of increased world leadership.

Despite this, each decade, most notably the 1970's, has produced renewed drives to revitalize Foggy Bottom. The program "Diplomacy for the 1970's," embarked on by the Department of State under William P. Rogers and his chief assistant, Elliot L. Richardson, was perhaps the most publicized and professional. Yet, it must be noted that when one scratches underneath the rhetoric of the program, it is, in short, still another management reform package, not unlike in design, if not in definition, the earlier programs that had failed and, in part, led to disaster for the department.

The Rogers-Richardson proposals had, at least, the knowledge, which had begun with Wristonization, that structural reforms were not universally productive. Indeed, they noted, "substance can suffer at the hands of technique; spirit can be alienated from operation." The lessons of the participative managers, more serious than the mere superficiality of a suggestion box, were also deeply ingrained. A prime focus of "Diplomacy for the 1970's" was a new era in management-employee relations. Openness and creativity were encouraged. There was even concern, for the first time, for ensuring equal employment opportunities and new openings for women. The role of the Foreign Service wife was redefined.

Still, characteristically, the new proposals clung to the same brass rings. First was the commitment to a belief that this was the only real, significant reform where all the acknowledged previous attempts were specious and superficial. All previous reformers of management guidelines had believed similarly about their proposals, from Huntington Wilson's geopolitical divisions through Wriston's merger. Second was a still unshattered faith in techniques, no matter what the preamble, to solve problems. Demonstrating this faith was a program called "Policy Analysis and Resource Allocation" (PARA), under the aegis of the Secretary's Planning and Coordination Staff (S/PC). One of the tasks of the program was to provide a structural way back into the top echelons of decision making for the department by writing annual reviews designed to serve as common denominators for discussion in the department, the Inter-Agency Group of the National Security Council, and the White House. In turn, Policy Analysis and Resource Allocation was to feed into an even more centralized executive council known as the Secretariat. The authors of "Diplomacy for the 1970's" proudly acclaimed this Secretariat, at the "heartbeat" of Department operations, as "thoroughly modernized" and ready with "up-to-date techniques and equipment for high-speed telecommunications and automated information handling." Thus Secretary Rogers urged development of a new operations center and improved information management known as Secretariat Automated Data Indexing System (SADI).

Into this nerve center of the Department of State in 1973 moved Kissinger, who had challenged the hegemony of efficiency while an outsider. It is difficult to perceive how a Kissinger or certainly a Remsen, Adams, Seward, Adee, or Evarts could function in the kingdom of PARA and SADI, that is, an environment where "substantive problems are transformed into administrative ones." What was the remaining role of leadership and policy in a department that could issue forth "Airgram 5399" concerning the use of the title "Ms.," which reads in part: "The Department has added 'Ms.' to the personnel title codes . . . maintained in the automated master personnel file. All documents which access these codes and which are printed by the computer may now employ this form of address."

The juxtaposition of Airgram 5399 and Remsen's original instructions put one in mind of a recent debate between two diplomatic historians about the utility of speedy publication of foreign policy files by the Department of State. While both scholars supported such a policy, their reasons differed dramatically. The first argued the administratively defensible position that quick access to such documents and the resulting historical monographs, sure to follow, would teach contemporary diplomats how to do a better job. More reflectively, the second historian suggested that while scholarship and research demanded quick access, better policy would emerge not from monographs, but from "wisdom."

Leadership, the quality of greatness inherent in the work of an Adams or a Seward, is still possible. The Department of State is not beyond its reach. Yet one must conclude that its achievement slips further and further out of reach in the wake of those variables the department has come to identify as progress in the twentieth century: complexity, bigness, and accelerated change.

BIBLIOGRAPHY

Samuel Flagg Bemis, ed., *American Secretaries of State and Their Diplomacy* (New York, 1928), consists of good, short sketches, and *John Quincy Adams and the Foundations of American Foreign Policy,* 2 vols. (New York, 1949), is a good biography; Katherine E. Crane, *Mr. Carr of State* (New York, 1960), gives a favorable view of a key middle manager; Alexander DeConde, *The American Secretary of State* (New York, 1962), has useful analyses; Robert E. Elder, *The Policy Machine: The Department of State and American Foreign Policy* (Syracuse, N.Y., 1960), is a landmark political science study; Norman S. Graebner, ed., *An Uncertain Tradition: American Secretaries of State in the Twentieth Century* (New York, 1961), is one of the most-used sources for general, interpretive information; Waldo Heinrichs, *American Ambassador: Joseph C. Grew and the Development of the United States Diplomatic Tradition* (Boston, 1966), besides being a biography of an important man, traces the evolution of foreign policy implementation; Frederick Ilchman, *Professional Diplomacy in the United States, 1779–1939* (Chicago, 1961), is the most careful and documented study available; James McCamy, *The Administration of American Foreign Affairs* (New York, 1950), is perhaps the first serious, analytical such volume, and *Conduct of the New Diplomacy* (New York, 1964), a revision of the author's point of view, is based on the intervening decade; Elmer Plischke, *Conduct of American Diplomacy* (Princeton, 1950), is the standard classroom text; and Graham H. Stuart, *The Department of State: A History of Its Organization, Procedure and Personnel* (New York, 1949), is an older source of itemized changes.

[*See also* CONGRESS AND FOREIGN POLICY; ECONOMIC FOREIGN POLICY; ELITISM AND FOREIGN POLICY; INTELLIGENCE AND COUNTERINTELLIGENCE; INTERNATIONAL LAW; INTERNATIONAL ORGANIZATION; NATIONAL SECURITY; PRESIDENTIAL ADVISERS; PRESIDENTIAL POWER IN FOREIGN AFFAIRS; PUBLIC OPINION.]

DÉTENTE

Arthur A. Ekirch, Jr.

DÉTENTE refers to the relaxation of tensions in international affairs. At the Congress of Vienna after the Napoleonic Wars, and later during the nineteenth century, détente was often practiced by the nations on the Continent that made up the so-called Concert of Europe. For much of American history, however, the concept of détente had little reality as the United States remained relatively isolated from world politics. In recent times détente has come to refer to the easing of the strained post–World War II diplomatic relations between the United States and the Soviet Union. In this latter sense, détente initially attracted public attention in the 1950's during Dwight D. Eisenhower's administration. Later it was revived as a conscious American policy under President Richard M. Nixon who, in 1972, visited both the People's Republic of China and the Soviet Union. Between 1953 and 1972 a number of close students of American foreign policy, including George F. Kennan, one of the architects of the Truman administration's policy of containment, also advocated scaling down the Cold War, especially in relation to the fighting in Vietnam.

As an alternative to a resolution of the Cold War by military means, détente became a serious possibility for the first time in the early 1950's as a result of a number of important worldwide political changes. In January 1953 Eisenhower succeeded Harry S. Truman as president of the United States. Although a military hero, Eisenhower owed his election, at least in part, to his reputation for moderation and to his promise to go to Korea to help conclude what had become an unpopular, uncertain military struggle against both the North Koreans and the Communist Chinese. In March 1953 the death of Josef Stalin, the Russian dictator, further opened the way for a reconsideration of Soviet-American postwar relations. It was widely assumed that Soviet officials would be preoccupied with the domestic struggle to choose his successor who, it was hoped, would be less ruthless and unreasonable than Stalin. In another important political shift Winston Churchill, the British Conservative party chief, author of the divisive phrase "Iron Curtain," had already come back into power as an advocate of better relations between the West and the Soviet Union. To this end Churchill in May 1953 planned a meeting on the model of World War II's summit diplomacy, "on the highest level," of the leaders of the great powers.

Finally 1953 also marked the effective conclusion of the Korean War by the signing of the armistice of July 27. This agreement signified only a stalemate in the Far East, for the Chinese Communists remained embittered against the United States for its predominant role in Korea and policy of refusing to have mainland China, as distinct from Chiang Kai-shek's government on Taiwan, admitted to a seat in the United Nations. Nevertheless the political events of 1953, climaxed by the end of the Korean War, brought a break in the Cold War.

Officially the Eisenhower administration adhered to the Truman policy of containment. The new secretary of state, John Foster Dulles, accordingly gave strong verbal support to the 1952 Republican campaign promises of a "massive retaliation" to Soviet military aggression and of liberation for the peoples of Eastern Europe who remained under Russian domination. The Eisenhower "New Look" in military affairs, calling for economy in conventional arms while strengthening America's ability to deliver nuclear weapons to targets abroad, was, however, like the rhetoric of Dulles, more militaristic in theory than in practice. The Eisenhower new look with its capacity for nuclear war—although this presumably served as a deterrent in the Cold War—did not offer a feasible tactic for fighting small wars. Thus, rather than all-out military victory, it pointed the way to some sort of peaceful accommodation in the Cold War.

In the midst of these worldwide developments, pressure mounted for an alternative strategy to the negative policies of containment and confrontation. An uncommitted bloc of Asian and African states within the United Nations stood as a moderating Third Force, opposed to having the world torn apart by the Cold War rivalry of the United States and the Soviet Union. Therefore, in response to what seemed a new direction in world affairs, Eisenhower and Prime Minister Anthony Eden (Great Britain), Premier Edgar Faure (France), and Premier Nikolai Bulganin (Soviet Union), supported by Nikita Khrushchev, the real Soviet spokesman, met at Geneva in July 1955. The previous evacuation of Russian troops from garrisons in Austria and Manchuria, as well as new Russian disarmament proposals, encouraged the leaders of the Western nations and paved the way for the harmonious tone of the discussions at Geneva. Soviet statesmen were reassured, in turn, by Eisenhower's pledge to the world that the United States would never take part in an aggressive war.

The conciliatory mood of Geneva was shattered, however, at least temporarily, by the Soviet Union's harsh tactics in suppressing the Hungarian Revolution in October 1956. At the same time a major war broke out in the Middle East when British and French troops seized the Suez Canal in conjunction with Israel's attack on Egypt. Although the United States and the Soviet Union backed the United Nations in bringing the Suez crisis to an uneasy armistice, the events of 1956 coupled with the Soviet Union's success a year later in launching *Sputnik* (the first man-made satellite to circle the earth) aroused American fears and renewed the old Cold War antagonisms. It seemed clear that the United States and the Soviet Union continued to be rivals, ideologically and politically. Each nation also competed for economic, military, and scientific predominance in an increasingly bipolarized Cold War world.

Nevertheless it was possible to draw a line in the Cold War, which both sides respected. The United States did not intervene to aid Hungary's fight for freedom, and the Soviet Union avoided carrying its exploitation of the troubles in the Middle East and other areas to the point of a general war. In 1957 Kennan, in his Reith Lectures in Great Britain, suggested the feasibility of a political settlement in Europe. As a first step he urged that Soviet and American forces be pulled back to make possible a neutral zone in the heart of the Continent. Kennan's proposal of an orderly disengagement with a nuclear free zone in Europe won considerable popular support in the West and also the continued backing of Adam Rapacki, the Polish foreign minister. Kennan, however, was also bitterly criticized by such staunch cold warriors as Dean Acheson, secretary of state in Truman's second administration.

Despite continued Soviet-American tensions surrounding Germany and the city of Berlin, President Eisenhower adhered to his declaration that "we are certainly not going to fight a ground war in Europe." He resisted accordingly the demands—reinforced by H. Rowan Gaither of the Ford Foundation and by the Rockefeller reports—for a bipartisan national program entailing the expenditure of vast sums for missiles and other arms to build up America's military strength. Although Americans were disturbed by the growing signs of the Soviet Union's power, the international scene offered some reassurance. Soviet attacks on Chinese Chairman Mao Tse-tung's "Great Leap Forward" program of enforced collectivization in 1958 indicated a break between the Russian and Chinese versions of communism. The Chinese leaders, on their part, were critical of the Soviet Union's new emphasis on the production of consumer goods instead of military hardware.

In the Cold War thaw that accompanied the changing climate of world opinion, Khrushchev accepted an invitation to visit the United States. The Soviet leader's pleasant tour of the country and private meetings with Eisenhower at the president's rustic vacation retreat at

Camp David, Maryland, in September 1959 held out the hope that the United States and the Soviet Union might reach an understanding over the key European problem of Berlin and the two Germanies. But the "spirit of Camp David" unfortunately proved short-lived. On 5 May 1960, the eve of the first summit conference of heads of state since 1955, Khrushchev announced to the world the sensational news that the Soviets had shot down, deep over their own territory, an American U-2 reconnaissance plane. Washington's unconvincing denials had to be reversed when Khrushchev revealed that the Russians had captured not only the wrecked plane but also Francis G. Powers, the pilot. The Central Intelligence Agency's scheduling of such a provocative overflight of Soviet territory two weeks before the summit conference seemed to indicate either its indifference to the success of the meeting at Paris or its fear that a détente might put an end to all such future flights.

Although the summit conference began as scheduled in Paris on 16 May 1960, Khrushchev disrupted the meetings and took back his invitation to Eisenhower to visit the Soviet Union after the president refused his demand for an apology. Eisenhower's projected trip to Moscow might have been the climax of his administration's efforts to reverse the direction of American foreign policy and de-escalate the Cold War. Instead the U-2 incident served as a major factor in destroying the possibility of a détente in 1960. Khrushchev, embarrassed by the breach of Soviet national security by the U-2 flights, did his best to humiliate the American government and Eisenhower. Although he may have botched the chance for a real peace, Eisenhower refused to reply in kind to Khrushchev's jibes or to exploit the American government's knowledge of the Soviet Union's inner military weaknesses.

Nevertheless, as a result of the debacle at Paris, Eisenhower was again hard pressed to answer the demand for more armaments voiced by military leaders and so-called cold warriors at home. At the same time Fidel Castro's new radical regime in Cuba and the threat of the Soviet Union's superiority in long-range, intercontinental ballistic missiles aroused popular American fears and gave the Democrats an issue in the forthcoming presidential campaign. Thus the original high hopes that had characterized so much of the Eisenhower era lay buried in the wreckage of the U-2 affair and the unfortunate Paris summit meeting. In a sense it was true that, in their initial efforts to advance a détente, Khrushchev and Eisenhower had both fallen victims to those forces in the Soviet Union and the United States that still sought a military, rather than diplomatic, solution to the Cold War.

The prospects of détente, uncertain at best in the 1950's, declined in the 1960's. In 1961 President John F. Kennedy, ignoring Eisenhower's farewell warning of the dangers to peace and freedom from "the military-industrial complex," called for a new build-up of American conventional military forces to boost the country's slumping economy and protect its foreign image. Meanwhile the diplomatic crises over the Soviet government's decision in the summer of 1961 to build the Berlin Wall, and a year later over its construction of missile-launching sites in Cuba, threatened an awesome confrontation between the world's greatest nuclear powers.

When President Kennedy persuaded the Russians to withdraw their missiles from Cuba in 1962, the world breathed more easily. The danger of nuclear war, which had inspired Pope John XXIII's encyclical, *Pacem in terris,* in April 1963, was also eased with the signing by the United States, Great Britain, and the Soviet Union of the Moscow Agreement, the long-proposed nuclear test-ban treaty prohibiting further nuclear testing in the atmosphere, outer space, or under water. At this time too Kennedy in a series of notable speeches before his assassination on 22 November called for a new American attitude toward the possibility of reaching an understanding with the Soviet Union by relaxing the hatreds and conflicts of the Cold War.

From the start, however, the Kennedy administration had committed itself to doctrines of limited war and counterinsurgency as alternatives to a nuclear conflict. The prospective use abroad of the stronger conventional military forces demanded all along by American Cold War strategists seemed to offer a relatively easy means of countering communist tactics of guerrilla warfare in such remote areas as Laos and Vietnam. In any case America's growing military intervention in support of the South Vietnamese government, carried to a climax in the Lyndon B. Johnson administration, postponed, even if it did not destroy, the achievement of some sort of détente between the United States and the Soviet Union. Although the war in Vietnam dragged on with heavy casualties until 1975, an important break occurred on 31 March 1968, when Johnson announced that he would not run for reelection and would order a partial halt in the bombing of North Vietnam.

The Republicans' 1969 return to the White House in the person of Richard M. Nixon, vice-president under Eisenhower, introduced a new dimension to the concept of détente. Encouraged by Henry A. Kissinger, his chief foreign policy adviser, Nixon rejoiced in the opportunity to practice realpolitik in the manner of a Metternich or a Bismarck. Thus the war in Vietnam was continued and even expanded. But under the announced Nixon policy of the Vietnamization of the war, forced by public opposition to the conflict, American ground troop levels were cut back, and the administration began to explore a negotiated settlement. The president himself, while still a private citizen, in an article in *Foreign Affairs* (1967), had hinted at the possibilities of détente. "One of the legacies of Vietnam," he then wrote, "almost certainly will be a deep reluctance on the part of the United States to become involved once again in a similar intervention on a similar basis. . . . Any American policy toward Asia," Nixon added, "must come urgently to grips with the reality of China."

After a tour of Asia in the summer of 1969, the president announced his so-called Nixon Doctrine. Here Nixon seemed to return to the old Eisenhower-Dulles policies by offering a shield of nuclear power to allied nations whose survival was deemed vital to the United States. The United States would honor its treaty commitments, but threatened nations were expected to use their own manpower for their own defense. In his "State of the World" message to Congress on 18 February 1970, the president reemphasized these points, while Congress in an amendment to an earlier defense appropriations bill (HR 15090), which the White House approved, prohibited a commitment of American ground troops to Laos and Thailand. On a visit to West Berlin in February 1969, Nixon had already called for an end to Cold War tensions in that city. Although the president, in support of the North Atlantic Treaty Organization, resisted any reduction of American troops on the Continent, the new turn in American diplomacy pointed toward negotiation rather than confrontation in relations with the Soviet Union.

Accustomed to thinking of Nixon as one of the most militant cold warriors, the American people were surprised by the rapid succession of events in 1971 and 1972—events that heralded a revolution in American foreign policy. In the fall of 1971 the first of a series of massive grain sales to the Soviet Union was announced. As a result principally of wheat sales on easy terms, American exports to the Soviet Union jumped from $162 million in 1971 to $550 million in 1972 and $1.19 billion in 1973. In February 1972 the president, after a preliminary trip there by Kissinger, visited the People's Republic of China. Three months later he went to the Soviet Union. The Paris Accord for a ceasefire in Vietnam on 27 January 1973, ending America's longest war, followed logically in the wake of the president's summit diplomacy. Coming after America's combat ground troops had already been systematically reduced, the events in Vietnam seemed almost an anticlimax. Whether construed as a tactic in the new Nixon-Kissinger diplomacy of détente, or whether considered as a major step toward ending the Cold War, the termination of America's fighting in Vietnam was most welcome.

President Nixon's dramatic and personalized foreign policy was a major factor in his 1972 reelection. But the president's diplomatic successes were overshadowed in his second term by the news of the Watergate scandal and cover-up, which in the summer of 1974 forced his resignation. Still, as Gerald Ford, Nixon's successor in the White House, made clear, détente within the limits of national security remained at the core of America's foreign policy. In a "State of the World" message to Congress on 12 April 1975, the new president declared: "The United States and the Soviet Union share an interest in lessening tensions and building a more stable relationship. . . . But we cannot expect the Soviet Union to show restraint in the face of United States weakness or irresolution. As long as I am President, we will not permit détente to become a license to fish in troubled waters. Détente must be and I trust will be a two-way street."

In the summer of 1975 President Ford traveled to Helsinki to join thirty-four other world leaders who affirmed the spirit of détente by accepting the post-1945 boundaries of Europe. In the Middle East, where the dangers of a Soviet-American confrontation remained strong, Secretary of State Kissinger was successful in negotiating a disengagement agreement between Egypt and Israel. Central to the hope of improved United States relations with the Soviet Union were the continuing Strategic Arms Limitation Talks (SALT) between the two countries. Although détente was criticized for its alleged indifference to defense and national security interests, SALT at least was more open to attack for having done so little to halt the proliferation of strategic nuclear weapons and by its failure to reach an agreement to put a ceiling on the arms race. It appeared that the United States was still determined to try to maintain its predominant world position, both strategically and economically. Thus détente did not mean that the United States government was ready to accept a unilateral peace policy.

This became apparent in the 1976 presidential campaign when President Ford tried to drop the word though not the policy of détente. Under strong political pressure from Ronald Reagan and the right wing of the Republican party, and from East European ethnic groups that resented Soviet domination of their homelands, Ford was forced to adopt a more nationalistic public stance. Nevertheless, as both Secretary Kissinger and Soviet leaders recognized, the principle of détente remained of value. Confronted by the rising Chinese power in Asia and possible restiveness among the satellite nations in Eastern Europe, the Soviet Union welcomed a relaxation of its Cold War tensions with the United States. At the same time the American people, following the debacle in Vietnam, were seized by a more somber, even isolationist, mood. In the 1970's, a decade in which it seemed probable that the worsening economic position of the United States would necessitate some retrenchment in the nation's commitments abroad, détente offered the practical advantage of encouraging Soviet-American trade and a growing market for American manufacturers and agricultural products.

In some ways détente marked merely another turn in the Cold War, a shift from the doctrinaire containment policy of Truman and Acheson to the more flexible diplomacy of Nixon, Ford, and Kissinger. On the other hand it was possible that détente might come to be seen not only as an end to the Cold War but as a vital first step toward a durable peace.

BIBLIOGRAPHY

On détente, see the following works: Stephen E. Ambrose, *Rise to Globalism: American Foreign Policy Since 1938* (Baltimore, Md., 1971), a broad survey covering the imperialistic and militaristic aspects of American diplomacy; Henry Brandon, *The Retreat of American Power* (New York, 1973), a generally sympathetic account of American foreign policy by an English journalist; Robert H. Ferrell, ed., *America in a Divided World, 1945–1972* (New York, 1975), a useful compilation of the more important diplomatic documents; Lloyd C. Gardner, ed., *The Great Nixon Turnaround: America's New Foreign Policy in the Post-Liberal Era* (New York, 1973), excerpts from speeches and state papers, which help to explain Nixon's thought and policies; Marshall I. Goldman, *Détente and Dollars: Doing Business With the Soviets* (New York, 1975), a detailed, factual account of the mechanics of Soviet-American trade; Paul Y. Hammond, *Cold War and Détente: The American Foreign Policy Process Since 1945*, rev. ed. (New York, 1975), a textbook by a political scientist interested especially in national security issues; George F. Kennan, *Russia, the Atom and the West* (New York, 1958), an early work that expresses Kennan's changed views on the Cold War; Walter LaFeber, *America, Russia, and the Cold War, 1945–1971*, 2nd ed. (New York, 1972), a popular textbook, good for its clarity and interpretation; George Schwab and Henry Friedlander, eds., *Détente in Historical Perspective* (New York, 1975), the transcript of a scholarly symposium that relates détente to both world wars and also to current controversies; Richard J. Walton, *Cold War and Counterrevolution: The Foreign Policy of John F. Kennedy* (New York, 1972), a strong criticism that helps to correct the early adulatory Kennedy biographies and memoirs; and Lawrence S. Wittner, *Cold War America: From Hiroshima to Watergate* (New York, 1974), a provocative interpretation, good on the domestic background of world events.

[*See also* Arbitration, Mediation, and Conciliation; Balance of Power; The Cold War; Containment; Disarmament; The Nixon Doctrine; Peacemaking; Power Politics; Realism and Idealism; Revisionism; Summit Conferences.]

DISARMAMENT

Merze Tate

FUNDAMENTAL among often stated objectives of American foreign policy has been the promotion of peace by means of disarmament. Generally speaking, American statesmen have believed that the competitive increase of national armaments constitutes one of the principal causes of international discord and strife. A recognition of this condition and a desire to remove the threat of war have led American statesmen to support international efforts to reduce and limit armaments and at times to play a constructive and leading role in arms limitation. Some officials state that the record of progress in arms control indicates that the movement depends on American initiative.

Several presidents from George Washington to James E. Carter have either expressed their opposition to large armaments or considered their limitation as a means of reducing the danger of war. American officials, however, have been more interested in the restriction of naval armaments and nuclear weapons systems than land forces, because such limitation could be dealt with by measures affecting a limited group of powers or just one other power. This procedure was clearly responsible for the qualified success of the Washington and London naval conferences of 1921, 1930, and 1931, and the Soviet–United States negotiations on ballistic and antiballistic missiles.

American policy with respect to naval armaments has been guided solely by the desire for adequate defense. This approach led to the Rush-Bagot Agreement (Great Lakes Disarmament Agreement) of 29 April 1817, limiting battleships on the Anglo-American water frontier. It embodied both quantitative and qualitative restrictions by limiting the naval force to be maintained "on Lake Ontario, to one vessel, not exceeding one hundred tons burden, and armed with one eighteen pound cannon. On the upper lakes, to two vessels, not exceeding like burden each, and armed with like force," and "on the waters of Lake Champlain, to one vessel not exceeding like burden, and armed with like force." By 1825 government vessels had practically disappeared from the lakes. Later, two periods of temporary misunderstanding threatened to subvert the Rush-Bagot Agreement and the boundary for decades was far from peaceful. But after the Washington Treaty of 1871 and the Geneva award, tranquillity pevailed on the longest unarmed frontier in the world.

From 1818 until the close of the century the United States government did not discuss armaments limitation and took no official stand on the question. The Hague Peace Conference of 1899 was the first international meeting called to explore the means of ensuring world peace. Although President William McKinley stated that "it behooves us as a nation to lend countenance and aid to the beneficent project," he was of the opinion that the active military force of the United States "in time of peace was so conspicuously less than that of the armed powers" of Europe that the question could have for us little practical importance.

At The Hague, Captain Alfred T. Mahan, the American delegate, worked closely with Admiral Sir John Fisher, the British naval delegate, to prevent a limitation of naval forces. The new expansionist policy of the United States meant that "the vital interests of America now lie East and West, and no longer North and South," and that this nation would be compelled to take a leading part in the struggle for Chinese markets, which would "entail a very considerable increase in her naval forces in the Pacific." Moreover, in consequence of the Monroe Doctrine, the United States looked upon the limitation of armaments as a European problem. But the American government was interested in extending the use of arbitration, and its delegates advocated peaceful means of settling international disputes.

In the second Hague Conference (1907), the United States reserved the right to introduce the question of reduction or limitation of armaments, although the discussion was initiated by Britain's Sir Edward Fry. Since not one of the European great powers was willing to reduce or even limit its army, or navy, neither Hague conference brought about international agreement on arms limitation.

But this failure did not mean that the United States government was averse to entering into agreements for the limitation of navies. Considering the rise of three new naval powers—the United States, Germany, and Japan—and the increasing rivalry in the construction of the revolutionary new battleships, the dreadnoughts, both houses of Congress in June 1910, without a single dissenting vote, resolved:

> That a commission of five members be appointed by the President of the United States to consider the expediency of utilizing existing international agencies for the purpose of limiting the armaments of the nations of the world by international agreement, and of constituting the combined navies of the world as an international force for the preservation of universal peace, and to consider and report any other means to diminish the expenditures of government for military purposes and to lessen the probability of war.

If this proposal had been acted upon, it might have marked the first step on the path to the establishment of international sanctions.

President Woodrow Wilson was willing to accept and even to assist in bringing about a holiday in naval construction. In the spring of 1914 he sent his intimate adviser, Colonel Edward M. House, on a fruitless mission to Germany to help win the consent of Kaiser Wilhelm II to the naval holiday that Winston S. Churchill, then first lord of the British admiralty, had proposed. But, in addition to temporary cessations in the building of battleships, the American government had advocated a "permanent policy to guard against extravagant and needless expansion." Before World War I, Secretary of the Navy Josephus Daniels held that the "wise naval policy for the United States was to find a golden mean." He believed that it ought not to be difficult to secure an agreement by which navies would be adequate without overburdening the national economy with taxation.

After World War I, with a fleet built and building superior to that of the greatest naval power, the United States was willing for the sake of economy and peace to limit that fleet by international agreement. Although isolationist in refusing to join the League of Nations or the World Court, the United States, in the hope of garnering some credit in foreign affairs, took the initiative in summoning the first two interwar disarmament conferences, the Washington and the Geneva naval conferences of 1921 and 1927. Partly as a result of American activities in this field, from 1921 to 1931, what may be called a legislative system of dealing with the military strength of nations was brought into existence.

Deliberations at the Washington Naval Conference (1921–1922) among the five leading naval powers (the United States, Great Britain, France, Japan, and Italy) were dominated by the conviction that the greatest threat to world peace lay in the disturbed conditions and international rivalries in the Pacific. In calling the conference the United States was anxious to stabilize the Far Eastern situation in a way favorable to American interests. By persuading Great Britain and Japan to give up their 1902 defensive alliance, a powerful combination that might have thwarted or frustrated American policies in the Orient was eliminated.

Limitation of battleships and aircraft carriers was realized at the Washington Naval Conference because of a combination of circumstances: the policies of the three great naval powers apparently were not in conflict, yet all had an economic interest in stabilizing armaments. The United States was in a superior economic position and under a system of unbridled competition could easily outstrip its rivals. Satisfied with its own territorial, political, and national security status, the initiator of the conference was willing to make the greatest sacrifices in ships in order to reach an understanding at a level that would represent economy and security for all. Since there were no political disputes outstanding between Britain and the United States, Anglo-American agreement on naval parity in the two types of vessels—capital ships and aircraft carriers—was possible. Thus the conference did not have to consider the defense of the British Empire's communication lines and the naval forces of the minor powers, or to raise the question of the interdependence of armaments generally. Acceptance of the principle of limiting capital ships based on the approximate status quo, however, led to competition in other categories of vessels.

The American proposal was an attempt to apply the total or global tonnage method of limitation rather than limitation by categories; consequently, France and Italy could adhere to some features of it, thus making a five-power agreement possible. Japan accepted a position of capital ship inferiority in accordance with the 5:5:3 ratio on condition that Great Britain and the United States agree not to build new fortifications in the Pacific during the ten-year life of the treaty. In return for the naval supremacy and security in the western Pacific this gave them, the Japanese promised to evacuate Siberia, restore Shantung, and respect the sovereignty of China. No attempt was made to provide machinery for the prevention or settlement of international disputes in the Pacific. Both Great Britain and the United States were willing to accept and trust Japan's word, which was the only sanction of the agreements. Taken together, the Washington Five-Power Naval Treaty (6 February 1922) and the Nine-Power Treaty (also signed 6 February), guaranteeing the territorial integrity and the independence of China, were based on certain assumptions in regard to the Far East, which in the long run proved fallacious.

Yet in 1921 the Washington Naval Conference was a memorable occasion, for it was the first successful attempt to restrict and reduce armaments. All earlier parleys had failed because concrete plans had been avoided and only general views and platitudes had been exchanged. In this conference the United States had proposed a definite program for the limitation of naval armaments. No ulterior motives, such as those attributed to Czar Nicholas II of Russia and his ministers at the Hague Peace Conference (1899) and to the British Liberal government in 1907, could be ascribed to the Washington Conference. With its enormous financial and natural resources, the United States occupied a position of commanding advantage in any armaments race; therefore, it was in a peculiarly strong and unassailable position to take the lead. While asking others to make some sacrifices, the United States was ready to make even larger ones. In a sense it was practicing self-denial in accepting a position of theoretical parity with its closest rival.

The naval limitation provisions of the Five-Power Treaty were avowedly aimed at giving Great Britain, the United States, and Japan maritime superiority in their own waters. But Japanese control of the Far East was buttressed by the agreement providing for the limitation of fortifications on certain stipulated Pacific islands. This removed the chance of England and the United States having the use of either Hong Kong or Corregidor as naval bases in the event of war in the Pacific. Under the established 5:5:3 ratio, Japan, in addition, was given naval mastery in all Pacific and Asian waters between the Aleutian Islands and Indochina, because distance more than counterbalanced the numerical advantage of the Anglo-American fleets.

By means of the abrogation of the Anglo-Japanese Alliance, the Washington settlement resulted in a sweeping adjustment of the political alignment in the Pacific region; it freed the United States, especially the West Coast area, from the fear of a Japanese attack; and it also relieved the Japanese of uneasiness about naval bases in the Pacific, and so, temporarily, reduced the tension in the Far East. No action, however, was taken to revise American immigration and tariff policies, both deep sources of irritation to the Japanese.

Considering the history of the intervening years since the Washington treaties were signed, it is difficult to hail the conference as a diplomatic victory for the United States. Instead of securing the national interests vis-à-vis Great Britain and Japan, a double surrender was made. In consenting in advance to scrap excess tonnage in capital ships, the United States relinquished the most effective means of obtaining British consent to parity in all other categories. Likewise, in pledging not to add to the existing fortifications on Guam, Tutuila, the Aleutians, and the Philippines, the United States surrendered its power to act in the Far East not only to preserve the open door and the territorial integrity of China but to protect its outlying possessions. When war came, the Philippines, Guam, and Wake were Japan's. Even Hawaii was at its mercy had Japan realized it. Air power, which so profoundly altered the strategy and use of naval strength, was left out of consideration. No understanding was reached with regard to land forces. Nor was real progress in limitation or reduction of naval armaments achieved, for the reduction in the treaty extended only to dreadnoughts and aircraft carriers. Consequently, the naval race was transferred from capital ships to big cruisers, and in this category a new competition ensued.

Yet the limitation of capital ships and aircraft carriers produced a favorable psychological effect and prompted the naval committee of the House of Representatives to call for another conference to consider the problems involved in limiting the number of cruisers, destroyers, and submarines. In England both the Labour and Liberal parties by 1926 were demanding a conference for similar reasons. In order to thwart the pressure groups that were urging the United States to increase its number of auxiliary vessels, President Calvin Coolidge chose to call a conference of the signatories of the Washington Treaty to ascertain whether future limitation in the classes of naval vessels not covered by that treaty was possible.

Since Coolidge considered that any achievements of the conference of the five great naval powers would contribute to the cause of armaments reduction, he did not intend to embarrass the efforts of the League of Nations Preparatory Commission. Underlying his invitation was a lack of faith in the League's ability to deal successfully with disarmament. He was also convinced that it was entirely appropriate for the naval powers to handle the problem of limitation of naval armaments separately. The Washington Conference had already established a precedent for such five-power deliberation. As the initiator of the conference, the United States was ready and willing to enter into an agreement to extend the 5:5:3 ratio of the Washington Five-Power Treaty to auxiliary categories in the navies of the United States, Great Britain, and Japan, leaving to discussion at Geneva the ratio of France and Italy, and taking into account those two countries' special conditions and requirements in regard to the types of vessels in question.

President Coolidge's sponsorship of a five-power conference ran counter to the axiom that disarmament "to be successful must be general." It challenged the French thesis that all categories of armaments must be considered together in any conference that seeks to achieve a measure of disarmament within the limits of security. Furthermore, the American proposal seemed to indicate an intention to abandon Secretary of State Charles Evans Hughes's earlier method of considering naval armaments as but one thread in the tangled web of political relationships. The new approach was to be narrowly technical, and the only political astuteness that entered into the calling of the conference came from the desire of the Republican party to present to American voters a record of some achievement in the field of foreign policy.

At the Geneva Three-Power Naval Conference of 1927, Great Britain and the United States agreed on accepting parity, but no formula could be found to achieve it. While the British conceived of parity as strategic equality, Americans demanded mathematical parity—equality in ship for ship, gun for gun, and ton for ton. The approach to disarmament was purely technical, and naval experts who "viewed the world through a porthole" were at the helm. No proposal was advanced like that Hughes proposed at Washington, which translated idealism into practical propositions. At Geneva the United States had no concessions to make, no dramatic scrapping of vessels built and building as in the conference of 1921. The British proposition to limit the number of cruisers with 8-inch guns—preferred by the United States, which had fewer worldwide bases than Britain, and therefore had to patrol its cruisers within a greater radius—was viewed with skepticism by the American delegates and could not be interpreted as a concession. Great Britain had been the first to initiate extensive construction of these new cruisers and had, therefore, set the pace in a new, dangerous, and expensive form of competition. Great Britain's action could be interpreted in a fashion similar to its proposal to limit dreadnoughts at the second Hague Conference—a desire to force a halt in competition at the moment of its own great preponderance.

Neither strategic equality nor mathematical parity would give practical equality. "There is no 'technical base,' " wrote Charles P. Howland, editor of the publications of the Council on Foreign Relations, "for establishing ratios of armaments among nations; it is impossible to determine what type of ships or how many of them are 'needful' unless there is an understanding of the purpose for which they are intended." In other words, geographical, historical, commercial, and political considerations made it inevitable that the purposes of the British and American fleets would be different. Thus, as Howland observes, "at Geneva each side argued for a definition of 'equality' or 'parity' which, if accepted, would give it superiority" (*Survey of American Foreign Relations, 1928* [New Haven, Conn., 1928]).

Failure of the British and Americans to reach an agreement in 1927 was more unfortunate than was realized at the time and of greater import for its effects on the Far Eastern situation than the temporary misunderstanding between the two nations. Up to that time Japanese naval disarmament policy had been essentially pacific and accommodating. But the want of hearty cooperation between Great Britain and the United States encouraged Japan's unscrupulous and adventurous militarists to attack Manchuria, which began a series of international aggressions leading ultimately to Nazi Germany's invasion of Poland on 1 September 1939.

In the final analysis, however, the Geneva Three-Power Naval Conference was not a complete failure since it actually paved the way for the relatively successful London Conference of 1930. A shift in American attitude was doubtless the result of Herbert C. Hoover's election to the presidency. His tenure coincided with that of Prime Minister Ramsay MacDonald who, like Hoover, was interested in peace and the reduction of armaments and willing to make concessions. Moreover, the signing of the Kellogg-Briand Pact (1928) created an atmosphere in which discussions of naval limitations could be resumed. If the United States and Great Britain were sincere in their adherence to the pact, armaments could no longer be employed for the furtherance of national policies.

Accordingly, Hugh Gibson, the American representative on the League of Nations Preparatory Commission for the Disarmament Conference, announced on 22 April 1929 that the United States would

> . . . be prepared to give consideration to a method of estimating equivalent naval values which takes account of other factors than displacement tonnage alone. In order to arrive at a basis of comparison in the case of categories in which there are marked variations as to unit characteristics, it might be desirable in arriving at a formula for estimating equivalent tonnage, to consider certain factors which produce these variations, such as age, unit displacement, and calibre of guns. [League of Nations, *Documents of the Preparatory Commission,* Series VIII: *Minutes of the Sixth Session (First Part) of the Preparatory Commission for the Disarmament Conference* (Geneva, 1929), p. 57]

This pronouncement, which came to be known as the "yardstick proposal," overcame the obstacle of British-American disagreement on the question of gun calibers. The American preference for cruisers with 8-inch guns and the British desire for 6-inch guns had been the stumbling block at the Geneva Three-Power Naval Conference of 1927. Consequently, the yardstick was hailed as a new invention in the mechanics of naval limitation, and it permitted an adjustment of the apparently insoluble Anglo-American cruiser problem.

On 22 April 1930 the naval powers supplemented the Washington Five-Power Treaty of 1922 with the London Naval Treaty. While the United States and Great Britain had resolved the problem of naval "equality," difficulties arose with Japan from the endeavor on the part of the United States to extend the 5:3 ratio to auxiliary categories, which Japan countered with an increasingly persistent effort to gain recognition of a higher ratio. The Japanese government finally accepted a 5:3 ratio in cruisers with 8-inch guns, 10:7 in cruisers and destroyers with 6-inch guns, and parity in submarines. But more portentous was Japan's announcement that five years thereafter, when the naval powers were to meet again, it might demand equality in all categories. As negotiated, the London Naval Treaty of 1930 limited the fleet of the United States to 1,123,000 tons; that of Great Britain to 1,151,000; and that of Japan to 714,000; thus establishing a ratio of 100 for the United States to 102.4 for Great Britain and 63.6 for Japan. The slightly larger figure for Great Britain was due to the fact that the British cruiser fleet would be constituted largely of smaller vessels, weaker in gun power than those of Japan and the United States. The latter two powers had the option, however, of duplicating the exact size and gun caliber of the British cruisers.

The impossibility of meeting the conflicting demands of France for "absolute requirements" (which would provide a superiority over Italy, or a substitute for these), some agreement on the part of Great Britain to guarantee French security, and Italy's insistence on parity posed a danger to the British Empire. Consequently, a so-called escape or escalator clause made the treaty limits purely conditional and therefore acceptable to Great Britain, who might exceed the tonnage totals agreed upon should they become insufficient to ensure her traditional two-power standard—a fleet equal in tonnage to that of the next two continental naval powers combined.

The London Naval Conference of 1930 clearly illustrates that disarmament is a question of politics. When political differences between nations are settled, the technical adjustment of their respective armaments becomes possible. Thus the British government in 1930 was prepared to accept fifty instead of seventy cruisers for a strictly limited period as its minimum requirement, provided that other powers met its standard and that in the fifty allotted to Great Britain there was a proper proportion of new construction suitable for extended operations.

Moreover, in 1930 the United States was prepared, as it had not been in 1927, to admit that the only basis for an Anglo-American agreement was equality in combat power. Its government was also willing to withdraw from the position it had adopted with regard to merchant ships at the Geneva Three-Power Naval Conference. Senator Joseph T. Robinson of Arkansas, a member of the United States delegation to the London Conference, insisted that there was no scientific process by which the potential combat value of converted merchant ships could be assessed or their efficiency, in comparison with cruisers, established. This was similar to his contention that no scientific basis existed for measuring the difference in value between large 8-inch-gun cruisers and vessels carrying 6-inch guns. Thus the problems, which at Geneva had appeared insoluble, were resolved at the London Conference by the simple method of not taking them into consideration. But that was possible only because political harmony had been achieved.

Through the discussions in the League of Nations Preparatory Commission, the United States delegation maintained a fairly consistent policy, defining armaments strictly as those forces and instruments immediately ready for war and contending that trained reserves should be counted in any plan for disarmament. The United States favored the limitation of naval armaments by categories and approved qualitative restrictions only when accompanied by quantitative limitations. However, the United States opposed budgetary limitations and any regulation that would tend to restrict industrial potential—the peacetime capacity of a people to prepare for a national emergency.

The League of Nations Conference for the Reduction and Limitation of Armaments received constructive plans from both Hoover and Franklin D. Roosevelt. After the Kellogg-Briand Pact, Hoover proposed a one-third reduction in all armies and battle fleets. Roosevelt, on the supposition that modern weapons of offense are vastly stronger than those of defense, proposed the abolition of the former type, and authorized Norman H. Davis, head of the American delegation to the conference, to announce United States willingness to consult with other states in the event of threatened conflict. But the Senate, not yet ready to abandon neutrality for international cooperation, refused to follow the president in his policy of collective security.

Between the signing of the London Naval Treaty of 1930 and the London Naval Conference of 1935 there were increased political tensions in the Mediterranean and undeclared wars in Ethiopia and Asia. Japan's conquest of Manchuria and its threat of hegemony in the

Far East conflicted with both American and British interests there. Fearing that the United States and Great Britain might some day challenge its imperialistic ventures, Japan demanded parity; equality, from the Japanese point of view, would mean only a 10:5 ratio in the face of a combined Anglo-American naval force.

In such a charged international atmosphere the chief difficulty of the conference of 1935 arose over the question whether disarmament should rest on the principle of equality of armament or equality of security. Japanese demands for a so-called "upper limit" amounted to changing the 5:5:3 ratio to 5:5:5. Neither Britain nor the United States was willing to accede to this proposal, for it would have given their rival more than equality of security, which Japan already had in the China Sea and the western Pacific Ocean. Thereupon Japan withdrew from the conference, and the system of combined quantitative and qualitative limitation of naval armaments ended. Although the United States preferred a combination of the two methods, its officials were forced to the conclusion that qualitative even without quantitative restriction would offer distinct advantages, and would certainly be better than no limitation at all. Thus the second London Naval Treaty differed from its predecessors by giving more prominence to restrictions upon the size of ships and the caliber of their guns. Having maintained an unbroken peace for over a century, Great Britain and the United States were firmly resolved that they should have no competitive building and were able to agree because their national policies were not in conflict. But an escalator clause was again included in the text. Considered together, the Washington, Geneva, and London naval conferences achieved no general limitation of armaments, contributed little to permanent peace, and did not serve to prevent a second world war.

Since the United States government at times has played a leading role in the movement for the voluntary limitations of armaments, it also formulated policy and suggested the administrative machinery for the disarmament of Germany and Japan after World War II. The State Department's draft treaties for disarmament and demilitarization of those two countries made no provision for restricting, eliminating, controlling, or decentralizing German and Japanese war potentials.

The Morgenthau Plan to confine Germany exclusively to agriculture and light manufacturing was rejected and instead it appears that American officials adopted the program of those who would permit the Reich to retain a large industrial structure in order to avoid disastrous consequences to the German and the whole European peacetime economies. Indeed, within thirty years after World War II, the two Germanys and Japan were among the most highly industrialized and prosperous countries in the world. Furthermore, by the mid-1970's West Germans were second only to the British in European holdings in the United States. The Japanese held 25 percent of foreign investments in the United States.

The United States also committed itself to seek international arrangements that would prevent nuclear war and promote peaceful uses of atomic energy. Financier Bernard M. Baruch, as Truman's representative, presented the American proposals to the United Nations Atomic Energy Commission on 14 June 1946. The American plan—ultimately to hand over a monopoly on atomic development to an international authority and gradually disclose information and vital knowledge of uranium and other ores from which fissionable materials could be developed—entailed sacrifices of national sovereignty greater than the United States or any power had yet embraced. But the most drastic infringement of sovereignty in the proposal was the provision for the abolition of the veto power in the Security Council of the United Nations so far as concerns the punishment for the violation of the atomic agreement. Andrei A. Gromyko, chief Soviet delegate to the United Nations, presented the Soviet plan on June 19. The Soviet Union insisted on retention of the veto and proposed the immediate outlawing of atomic weapons and that each nation assume responsibility for preventing its citizens from violating the agreement.

Prolonged debate ensued in the Atomic Energy Commission, and thirty years later nuclear weapons were still national instruments. The real issue was a matter of confidence. With good faith, either the American or the Russian plan for the control of atomic energy or a synthesis of the two could have been made to work, but suspicion and mistrust prevailed during the Cold War. Moreover, in the same period and even after, no agreement on the reduction of armed forces in Europe could be reached between the eastern Soviet-oriented bloc and the members of the North Atlantic Treaty Organization.

After extended policy review, a decision was taken by the United States government in 1967 to pursue with the Soviet government the possibilities for an agreement on strategic arms placing reliance on national technical means. The Strategic Arms Limitation Talks (SALT) began in November 1969. The Interim Agreement on Strategic Offensive Arms that imposed a five-year freeze on various offensive missiles and the Treaty on the Limitation of Anti-Ballistic Missile Systems, signed at Moscow on 26 May 1972, were the outcome of the first phase of SALT.

These treaties were the first arms control agreements to make explicit provision for verification by national technical means. Under Article XII of the ABM Treaty and Article V of the Interim Agreement, each party agreed to use for purposes of ensuring compliance "national technical means at its disposal in a manner consistent with generally recognized principles of international law." Moreover, each party undertook not to interfere with the means of verification of the other, or "to use deliberate concealment measures which impede verification by national technical means." These provisions represented an important step forward.

Meanwhile, an attempt was made to negotiate a treaty that would limit offensive weapons. The central issue in the nuclear bargaining was how to strike a compromise between the Soviet advantage in numbers of nuclear launchers permitted by the temporary five-year accord and the three-to-one advantage in multiple nuclear warheads and bomb-dropped weapons that the United States held.

At the Moscow summit of June–July 1974 President Richard M. Nixon and Soviet leader Leonid Brezhnev failed in their efforts to extend the temporary accord and add to it a new MIRV (multiple independently targeted reentry vehicle) pact to check the multiple rocket competition. The technical problems of such a package (the "various asymmetrics" in the nuclear forces of the two sides) and the uncertainties of volatile MIRV technology proved too difficult to resolve. The encouraging factor was that in the atmosphere of détente the representatives of the two major nuclear powers could announce their adherence to the objectives and principles of the treaty banning nuclear weapons tests in the atmosphere, in outer space, and under water and of the treaty on the nonproliferation of nuclear weapons, the limitation of underground testing and the acceptance of the concept of defensive missile control to run initially until 1985.

The objective of the American offer at Moscow in July 1974 was to agree on a quantitative ceiling for multiple warheads giving an advantage to the United States, which held a commanding lead in this field, in return for a Soviet advantage in total numbers of missile launchers. Since neither side disclosed the numbers of warheads or launchers proposed as a trade-off, it is not possible to judge whether the American demands or the Russian counterdemands were too high to permit bargaining. It appears, however, that in several central issues at the 1974 Moscow summit the strategic superiority advocated by the American Joint Chiefs of Staff and defended by Secretary of Defense James R. Schlesinger prevailed, rather than Secretary of State Henry Kissinger's strategy of détente.

In spite of the reported gains made in agreements to control nuclear arms, some responsible American officials demanded a United States nuclear capacity inferior to none and continued to warn that the Soviet Union was superior to the United States in nuclear weapons, especially intercontinental ballistic missiles.

Disarmament, both by the direct method of restriction and by the indirect process of organizing collective security, has failed tragically because all peoples have coveted national security but have envisioned different means of achieving it. A method advocated by some is to gain strategic superiority.

In the Soviet-American negotiations on the quantitative and qualitative limitation of nuclear weapons, of intercontinental ballistic and antiballistic missiles, and the testing of the same, the strategic approach and the jargon have been similar in many respects to those of the naval conferences of the preatomic age, with arguments about offensive and defensive weapons, parity, numerical equality, combat equality, nuclear weapons balance, strategic equality, and strategic superiority. Every nation defines the requirements and pursues strategic superiority to suit its own particular situation. As long as the approach to the problem is based upon fears and suspicions there can be little hope of disarmament.

BIBLIOGRAPHY

Bernard G. Bechhoefer, *Postwar Negotiations for Arms Control* (Washington, D.C., 1961), gives a thorough and authoritative treatment of the subject up to date of publication; Lincoln P. Bloomfield, *Disarmament and Arms Control,* Headline Series, no. 187 (New York, 1968), is brief but excellent; Trevor N. Dupuy and Gay M. Hammerman, *A Documentary History of Arms Control and Disarmament* (Dunn Loring, Va., 1973), contains a collection of documents related to arms control and disarmament from all periods of history; Henry W. Forbes, *The Strategy of Disarmament* (Washington, D.C., 1962), is useful for the period between the world wars for an analytic approach to the negotiations; Merze Tate, *The United States and Armaments* (Cambridge, Mass., 1948), a general treatment of United States disarmament policy and negotiations to 1947, also includes the disarmament of Germany and Japan and proposals to control atomic energy; U.S. Arms Control and Disarmament Agency, *Arms Control and Disarmament Agreements, 1959–1972* (Washington, D.C., 1972); U.S. Library of Congress, Legislative Reference Service, *Disarmament and Security: A Collection of Documents, 1919–55,* U.S. Senate Committee on Foreign Relations, Subcommittee on Disarmament (Washington, D.C., 1956); U.S. Arms Control and Disarmament Agency, *Arms Control and Disarmament Agreements, Texts and History of Negotiations* (Washington, D.C., February 1975); and U.S. Arms Control and Disarmament Agency, *Verification: The Critical Element of Arms Control,* Publication 85 (Washington, D.C., March 1976).

[*See also* THE COLD WAR; DÉTENTE; NAVAL DIPLOMACY; NUCLEAR WEAPONS AND DIPLOMACY.]

DISSENT IN WARS

Russell F. Weigley

"THESE men are not being supported as we were supported in World War One": so the Vietnam War appeared in contrast to the crusade of 1917–1918 to a speaker addressing a reunion of the First Infantry Division in 1969 and reported by the military journalist Ward Just. American military men who fought in Vietnam widely believed that wartime dissent of unprecedented intensity uniquely denied them the support of their compatriots at home. Wartime dissent might never have become a lengthy subject had not the Vietnam War raised the issue to unaccustomed prominence and created a wider debate, ranging well beyond disgruntled military men, over the extent to which the threat of dissent against subsequent use of force might cripple American foreign policy. General Maxwell D. Taylor, former chairman of the Joint Chiefs of Staff and ambassador to South Vietnam, wrote: "As I see the lesson, it is that our leaders of the future are faced with a dilemma which raises questions as to the continued feasibility of a limited war option for future Presidents faced with a compelling need to use military force in support of a national interest" (*Swords and Plowshares* [New York, 1972], p. 404).

Yet the intensity of dissent during the Vietnam War was not so unprecedented as many critics of home-front attitudes thought. An exceptionally perspicacious military man of an earlier generation, General George C. Marshall, the army chief of staff during World War II, said that the strategic planning for that supposedly popular war had to seek success in short order, because "a democracy cannot fight a Seven Years' War." More than those who saw uniqueness in the dissent that marked the Vietnam War, Marshall probably approached the heart of the issue of dissent in any democratic, and particularly American, war: because democratic public opinion is impatient, popular support of a war depends on the war's not dragging on indefinitely. If not simply a short war, to minimize dissent a war should be distinguished by continuous visible progress toward achieving popularly understood and approved goals.

In a 1973 study of dissent during the Korean and Vietnam wars, as reflected in public opinion polls, John E. Mueller similarly concluded in more precise fashion that dissent against war tends to increase with the duration of the war, or more specifically, that it can be expressed by the logarithm of the duration of the war and the casualties of the war. Thus Mueller found that despite the apparent evidence afforded by the uncommon noisiness of dissent against the Vietnam War, the Korean War received less public support than the Vietnam War—until the latter conflict surpassed it both in duration and in its toll of American casualties.

To be sure, Mueller did not have available to him public opinion polls concerning earlier prolonged wars, and both the Korean and the Vietnam wars differed from many earlier American wars in that they failed to produce results generally recognizable as victory for the American armed forces and the defeat of the enemy. The historian may suspect that if polls such as those cited by Mueller had been taken during the American Civil War, they would show that the war was more popular in the North in November 1864, at the time of Lincoln's second election to the presidency, than earlier in the same year, in May 1864, when Lieutenant General Ulysses S. Grant was just beginning his slugging campaign in the Wilderness and at Spotsylvania—despite the accumulation of weary months and horrifying casualties in the interval. The intervening months brought morale-building military victories, and especially the triumphs of Mobile Bay, Atlanta, and Cedar Creek not long before the presidential election. Korea and Vietnam never afforded any such satisfying battlefield successes. The historian therefore would suggest that the effects of time and casualties on the popularity of a war might be at least partially offset by military victories, and especially by military progress toward some readily comprehended goal—for example, the destruction of the enemy armed forces pursued by Grant and his lieutenants in 1864.

Still, while in the end dissent in the North during the American Civil War was largely drowned out by a tide of military victories, nevertheless until nearly the end the prosecution of the Civil War was plagued by more internal opposition than was the later waging of World War II. It was easier to rally public support for retaliation against the Japanese after Pearl Harbor and for suppression of Adolf Hitler than to bind domestic political dissidents to the Union with the bayonet. The roots of opposition to a war can be found in the duration of the war, its casualties, and its measure of military success. But one cannot ignore the commonsense view that the war's political aims and circumstances have much to do with its popularity. Of course the generation and expression of dissent even in wars of politically controversial origin are handicapped because wars tend to appear as national crises so dramatically overpowering that they inherently require the whole nation to rally round the national standard.

Mueller's analyses of recent wars and national emergencies tend to indicate, nevertheless—and the longer historical view would seem to confirm—that such a rally-round-the-flag phenomenon is fleeting. Even in the midst of wars, politics as usual soon tends to resume. The resumption of habitual political battles can then readily fuel dissent, especially because in the development of American partisan politics it has required a considerable accumulation of experience and a considerable sophistication for partisan rivals of wartime administrations and congresses to learn to disentangle opposition to the incumbent political party from opposition to the war, and the process of disentanglement has never been complete. And as common sense would have it, the more politically controversial the origins of the war, the greater is likely to be the intensity of wartime dissent, especially if the political controversy involves conscientious opposition to the morality of the war, as in the Mexican and Vietnam wars.

Moreover, once initial patriotic enthusiasm subsides, the dissent fueled by partisan rivalries and the circumstances of the origins of a war can draw upon a still more fundamental source of restiveness, the traditional American hostility toward the armed forces and a traditional ambivalence, at the least, toward the very institution of war.

Once these persistent sources of dissent against war interact in wartime with the hardships, inconveniences, and simple nuisances inevitably attendant upon any war, and with the more or less severe political controversies of any war, the rise and expression of dissent become so likely, and in most wars have become troublesome enough, that wartime administrations have been perennially tempted to suppress dissent by the use of law and armed force, diluting the constitutional guarantees of free expression of dissent on the plea that the national crisis demands it. Supporters of wars have also been tempted to use informal extralegal means to eliminate dissent. Thus the record of such temptation and of consequent actions against dissent forms part of the history of dissent in American wars, although on the whole the ability of administrations and populace to resist these temptations is fairly heartening to believers in the American constitutional system.

THE REVOLUTIONARY WAR

Despite the quotation from General Marshall, the United States did manage to fight and survive a seven years' war at the very outset of national existence, the Revolutionary War. It is possible that the Revolutionary War was exceptional because it was so directly and unequivocally a war for national survival, with independence itself at stake. Modern nationalism is such a strong force that its survival may transcend ordinary rules concerning the depth of democratic support for war. It is at least as likely, however, that the safe emergence of the United States from the Revolution was largely a matter of fortunate historical accident.

Among British and Loyalist leaders there had developed a widespread impression by 1780, which lasted until October 1781, that for them the War of the American Revolution was almost won. In the southern colonies, 1780 witnessed the virtual completion of the reconquest of Georgia and South Carolina, and the following year Lieutenant General Charles Cornwallis pursued the remnant of the revolutionary forces in the area all the way northward across North Carolina and planted the royal standard in that province. The remaining resistance south of Virginia, although highly and perplexingly troublesome, was mainly of the irregular sort that later generations would call guerrilla warfare. Farther north, at British headquarters in New York, General Henry Clinton received consistently optimistic reports from his agents throughout the Middle Colonies. Typical was the conclusion of the prominent New Yorker William Smith (1728–1793) that "the Rebels were a minority who governed by the army & that this [the revolutionary army] reduced, the Loyalists would overturn the usurpation" (Thomas Fleming, *The Forgotten Victory: The Battle for New Jersey, 1780* [New York, 1973], p. 36). If it was the sole remaining prop supporting rebellion, the rebel army itself appeared well on the way to collapse. There had been a mutiny in the Massachusetts line as early as the beginning of 1780; in the Connecticut line in May 1780; in the large and critical Pennsylvania line at the beginning of 1781; and in the New Jersey line in response to the Pennsylvania mutiny. During this period General George Washington, the commander of the Continental army, repeatedly warned Congress that his army was on the verge of dissolution—from loss of supplies, pay, popular support, and internal morale. If Washington felt obliged to put on a show of pessimism in order to try to wring maximum assistance from a frugal Congress, accounts from other sources inside his army agreed with those of Clinton's informers that his exaggerations were small and that his army might collapse under the slightest British pressure, or simply expire. ". . . why need I run into the detail," Washington wrote John Laurens on 9 April 1781, "when it may be declared in a word that we are at the end of our tether, and that now or never our deliverance must come."

Deliverance, of course, came. Clinton did not muster the energy or the self-confidence to pursue his opportunities with even the slightest vigor; he was thinking instead of how to woo back to British allegiance the faltering revolutionaries without in the process antagonizing Loyalists who were crying for condign punishment of the rebels as a reward for their own loyalty—that is, the very flagging of the Revolution paradoxically contributed to Clinton's perplexities and thus to his irresolution. Meanwhile, Lord Cornwallis, the other principal British military commander in America and Clinton's nominal subordinate in the South, lapsed into the opposite kind of bad generalship—recklessness. Cornwallis presented the revolutionary army with the opportunity to join forces with the French navy in a manner that entrapped him at Yorktown in October 1781. Although Cornwallis' blunders were egregious, Washington and his French allies were able to capitalize upon them on account of a most remarkable run of good fortune in weather and timing, to say nothing of what was to prove the only major French naval success against a British fleet in the whole second Hundred Years' War. The surrender of Cornwallis has no suggestion of inevitability about it but appears rather as historical accident. The United Kingdom in 1781 was no democracy, but the British government was far enough from a despotism and representative enough that it was having its own troubles in sustaining the war. The setback at Yorktown proved sufficient to push Britain into the hands of the peacemakers. Until Yorktown the American revolutionary cause had been in much more parlous condition than the British cause, and except for the supreme good fortune of Yorktown it was the American cause that had been more likely to founder.

Dissent in the Revolutionary War is otherwise difficult to measure on any scale similar to those applicable to later wars, when there was an established American government from which to dissent and more or less established channels of dissent. During the Revolution the prosecutors of the war on the side of the United States were themselves the dissenters from the accustomed American order of politics. The war was more confusedly an American civil war than the later war of 1861–1865, in which the antagonists were more clearly marked off from each other by geographical lines. Just as the Revolutionary War was both a war for independence from Great Britain and a revolution seeking social change at home, so both thrusts of the war provoked their own sets of dissenters, with some who otherwise supported independence, for example, dropping out when the struggle set a course toward social revolution. In Pennsylvania, where the revolutionary movement most drastically changed the previous political order with the radically democratic Constitution of 1776, the sense of the revolutionaries that they must use the force of their new system of laws to compel the laggard to fall into their procession became most desperate, and it precipitated the most troublesome controversy in any province over test oaths of loyalty to the new regime. But everywhere the revolutionary governments felt obliged to curb dissent with legal penalties of confiscation of property and political ostracism. Furthermore, the patterns of dissent were not easily predictable; loyalty oaths excited most controversy in Pennsylvania where the Revolution became most radical, but dissent against the Revolution took its most ambitious military form—and apart from the incursions of the British army required the nearest approximation of full-blown military campaigns to repress it—in the Carolinas where the movement toward independence changed little in the previous social and political order. The sources of dissent and its manifestations were at least as varied as the motives that separately guided each colony into statehood.

THE QUASI-WAR AND THE WAR OF 1812

After the American Revolution, dissent in the next war presents a special case; the war did not last long enough, or amount to enough as a military operation accompanied by casualties, for the effects of duration to have much play, but in its origins the war was perhaps the most politically controversial in the history of the country. It was the Quasi-War with France of 1797–1800. With the American political system still in process of formation, and partisan political opposition still widely regarded as illegitimate, it was hardly more a war against France, however, than a war conducted by the Federalists, who controlled the executive branch and the Congress, against the Jeffersonian Republican opposition. French depredations against American maritime commerce and the XYZ affair precipitated naval conflict with the French. Yet the causes of the war never ran deep enough to generate even a brief initial enthusiasm—despite the XYZ affair—in more than a few localities. Moreover, the Federalists used the war to push through Congress authorizations of substantial increases in the army, although President John Adams remarked that as for an enemy army for this force to fight, "At present there is no more prospect of seeing a French army here than there is in Heaven." Stephen G. Kurtz's conclusion is that the new army, whose officers were carefully screened to assure their Federalist partisanship, was to be the tangible instrument for suppressing Jeffersonianism—a political army to cow the opposition. Against this threat to the antimilitary tradition and against the Quasi-War that nourished the threat, dissent became so sharp that Kurtz also concludes that fear and resentment of the political army ranked with the notorious Alien and Sedition Acts as a cause of disaffection from the Federalists and thus of the Republican "revolution" in the election of 1800.

Historians can perceive a deeper stream of causation leading to the War of 1812 than to the Quasi-War. In 1812 there was a fuller, more widespread patriotic spirit generated by the conviction that long-standing British refusal to grant the United States the rights of independent nationhood at sea represented a threat to the very independence of the Republic. Nevertheless, to the Federalists, now reduced to the role of opposition, the War of 1812 appeared as much a partisan war conceived for the political benefit of the rival party and for the ruination of themselves as the Quasi-War had seemed to the Republicans. By

1812 the Federalist party had become a sectional party; except for enclaves of strength in the Carolinas, Philadelphia, and New York City, it was a New England party, and its interests and those of New England had come to seem indistinguishable. For commercial New England, the War of 1812 was the hideous culmination of a perverse Republican policy of countering British and French depredations against maritime commerce by terminating American overseas commerce altogether. For New England, no cause of the old revolution had loomed larger than the Boston Port Act; now the Republican strangulation, not just of Boston's but of all New England's commerce, naturally suggested a Boston Port Act much magnified. Thus, if the Boston Port Act had offered just cause for withdrawing from the British Empire despite all the benefits and ties of loyalty that the empire represented, then some New England Federalists saw Republican restrictions upon commerce as cause for seceding from the American Union. Republican trade restrictions and the ensuing war seemed all the more perverse to the Federalists because unlike the Republicans, the Federalists saw Great Britain as the defender of all people's rights against a revolutionary France whose excesses had descended into Napoleonic tyranny, while the Republicans responded to both French and British maritime depredations with an increasingly anti-British policy leading at last to a war whose only beneficiary was likely to be Napoleon.

The vote of the New England members of the House of Representatives, except for frontier Vermont, on the war resolution of 4 June 1812, was nineteen against war, nine for, and three not voting—surely a clear alignment against the war, although not nearly so one-sided as some accounts might suggest. Connecticut and Massachusetts soon rejected federal calls for their militia, and Rhode Island and New Hampshire supplied only a handful of militiamen for federal service in 1812. Federalist Governor Caleb Strong of Massachusetts proclaimed a fast day to mourn a war "against the nation from which we are descended," and New England Federalist leaders generally made no secret of their displeasure with the war. Nevertheless, New England's passive dissent threatened to turn into active resistance to the Republican administration only when the badly conceived war proved to be badly fought as well. Then twenty-six New England Federalists met in late 1814 at the Hartford Convention, "to protest," in the words of James M. Banner, Jr., "against the inept Republican management of the war with Great Britain and the whole system of Republican administration since Jefferson's election . . . to force the federal government to provide defensive help."

Early in the conflict, New England profited from it. Hoping to encourage New England's disaffection, Great Britain at first did not apply its naval blockade of the United States to New England. In the spring of 1814, however, with Napoleon defeated and Great Britain free to devote major military attentions to the American war, the British decided that making New England bear some of the brunt of the conflict would be a more productive encouragement to dissent. On 31 May 1814 the blockade was extended to the whole United States coast. Worse, British invasion of New England followed. In July an expedition from Halifax took Eastport in the District of Maine; by early September, Lieutenant General John Sherbrooke had entered the Penobscot, taken possession of the whole Maine coast east of that river, and claimed the coast as far as New Brunswick. Towns around Cape Cod were raided, and under British guns Nantucket declared its neutrality. What brought the Hartford Convention movement to a head, according to established scholarship, was the inability of the government in Washington to provide respectable defense against these British attacks. The Federalist state governments and the Republican federal government still quarreled over who was to control the militia, the New England states insisting that in the crisis they must retain command of their militia for their own defense but that the federal government should pay the costs of defense. When early in 1815 Congress authorized compensation of state forces by the federal government, it met what Banner calls the Federalists' "central demand"; Harrison Gray Otis (1765–1848), perhaps the most influential Massachusetts Federalist, thought that passage of such an act earlier would have forestalled the Hartford Convention altogether.

This issue of defense was certainly more central to the Hartford Convention than the plots of secession that have sometimes been charged against the convention. The convention was engineered by the moderate leadership of the New England Federalist party, of whom Otis was one example and George Cabot, the president of the convention, another, in order to press for effective action for defense and against Republican mismanagement. At the same time New England Federalists kept the political initiative in their section in their own hands—those of pragmatic politicians—and out of the hands of moralists, often led by the clergy, who increasingly couched their opposition to the Republicans in absolutist moral terms and were in fact likely to move toward extreme action, even including disruption of the Union. A convention of party leaders was an affair the pragmatists could control, and they did, confining the Hartford Convention to resolutions on behalf of federal support for state self-defense and proposals for constitutional amendments to pare the power of the Republican dynasty in Washington. This outcome fulfilled George Cabot's prediction that he could tell exactly what the convention would produce, namely, "a great pamphlet."

A delegation including Otis carried the Hartford resolutions to Washington, leaving Boston just after they learned of Andrew Jackson's victory at the battle of New Orleans and arriving in the capital just in time for the celebrations of the Treaty of Ghent that ended the war in February 1815. Holding the convention and passing its resolutions were probably necessary to divert the New England extremists and maintain, for the time being, a viable Federalist party in New England. But enough secessionist overtones were imputed to the Hartford Convention that Federalism was forever damned elsewhere for disloyalty in time of war.

THE MEXICAN WAR

The conventional wisdom surrounding what happened at the Hartford Convention consequently came to be that failure to support a war effort is likely to mean the death of a political party. Thus in 1846–1848, when the Whig party found itself opposed to the Mexican War, the party pragmatists argued that although they might challenge the policy of going to war, they must not fail to vote funds and supplies to support the army that was fighting it. A rival faction of Conscience Whigs nevertheless took the logical and principled position that if the war was wrong, supporting the fighting of it was also wrong, and that therefore opposition must be thoroughgoing at whatever risk to party fortunes. The resulting divisions within the Whig party very nearly produced the fatal effect that the pragmatists hoped to avoid.

During the Mexican War the sources of Whig dissent were partially the same as those of Federalist dissent during the War of 1812. In both instances, New England was the stronghold of dissent, although opposition spread more widely from 1846 to 1848. In both instances, the grievances of New England against the administration in Washington included the administration's policies of westward territorial expansion, which implied a permanent diminution of New England's political power. In the Mexican War, of course, westward territorial expansion was immediately at issue. In both instances, fear of the diminution of New England's power sprang not only from direct political interests but from distaste for the whole southern and western economic and cultural system that the dissidents saw represented in the administration in Washington and in the administration's war. During the Mexican War such distaste for southern and western values was reinforced by the rise to prominence of the slavery issue, which had been merely a cloud on the horizon—although already perceptible—during the War of 1812. In August 1846 the Wilmot Proviso tied the slavery issue inextricably to the issues of the Mexican War by proposing to forbid slavery in any territory to be acquired from Mexico. In both instances, opposition to the war could draw upon and be reinforced by the self-conscious Christianity of New England tradition. New England dissent from the War of 1812 had in fact led to the founding of peace societies, which later helped mobilize opposition to the Mexican War.

In the 1840's the Christian antiwar tradition was readily mobilized against a conflict even more iniquitous than the War of 1812, in that the Mexican War could well be regarded—and is still regarded by some historians—as an act of aggression by the strong United States against weak Mexico. The mobilization of this Christian antiwar tradition in its New England centers at a time when New England happened also to be experiencing its first great literary renaissance gave an unprecedented literary aspect to dissent against the Mexican War, as illustrated by James Russell Lowell's *The Bigelow Papers* (1848) and Henry David Thoreau's essay "Civil Disobedience" (1849).

For all that, organized dissent against the Mexican War never attained a climax as notable, albeit ambiguous, as the Hartford Convention. The military campaigns of the war proved to be short and unvaryingly successful, which in turn proved an insurmountable handicap to effective dissent. Military success in fact diverted the pragmatic, political Whigs from the issue of whether to vote supplies to the more expedient issue of how to capitalize on the military fame of the victorious generals, Zachary Taylor and Winfield Scott, who chanced also to be Whigs.

Nevertheless, opposition to the Mexican War tended to grow more intense the longer the war lasted. When the conflict began in May 1846, only two members of the Senate and fourteen members of the House voted against the bill declaring that war existed "by the act of the Republic of Mexico." Congress authorized the president to call volunteers and appropriated $10 million for the conduct of the war. By the time the Thirtieth Congress assembled for its first session in December 1847, however, to be greeted by President James K. Polk's message that no peace had yet been obtained and there was no immediate prospect of one, Congress appeared much less ready to vote more men and money, and certainly the Whigs were more determined to pin upon Polk and the Democrats responsibility for a war begun, as they interpreted it, not by Mexico but by American aggression. Furthermore, the Whigs had captured at least nominal control of the House, although their own divisions made their election of Robert C. Winthrop of Massachusetts as Speaker (1847–1849) a very near thing, because the most dedicated Conscience Whigs refused to support Winthrop as too willing to sustain the war. The House then defeated a resolution declaring the war just and necessary. Opposition to slavery inevitably still influenced much of the opposition to the war, but even a southern Whig, Alexander H. Stephens of Georgia, could say, "The principle of waging war against a neighboring people to compel them to sell their country is not only dishonorable, but disgraceful and infamous." Playing upon the fact that hostilities had begun when Mexican troops attacked Taylor's forces after they had crossed south of the Nueces River, which Mexico claimed as the southern boundary of Texas, Congressman Abraham Lincoln of Illinois introduced his "spot" resolutions calling on the president to say candidly whether the spot where the war began was Mexican or American soil.

Some powerful Democrats, too, had grown outspokenly critical—the elderly Albert Gallatin, who called it a war of subjugation; Thomas Hart Benton; even John C. Calhoun, who feared the war was becoming one for the conquest of central Mexico, which would bring into the Union a racially inferior people incapable of free government. Fortunately for the president, in the midst of congressional debate there arrived the Treaty of Guadalupe Hidalgo (1848), negotiated in Mexico by Nicholas P. Trist, which ended the war with the annexation of Texas confirmed and California and New Mexico added to the United States, in exchange for a payment of $15 million and the assumption by the United States of American claims against Mexico. Although Polk had earlier repudiated Trist as his negotiator, and although some Democrats thought Trist's terms too generous toward Mexico, Polk submitted the treaty for ratification lest the increasingly noisy dissent prove able to paralyze him and make a good treaty henceforth impossible. Under public pressure to end the war as swiftly as could be done, the Senate ratified the treaty.

The opposition Whigs became the immediate political beneficiaries of discontent with the war. Some Conscience Whigs split off from the party to join with various northern Democratic factions disgruntled over the pro-Southern tendencies of all Polk's policies and to form the Free-Soil party for the election of 1848; but this third party hurt the Democrats more than the Whigs. Choosing Zachary Taylor as their presidential nominee, the Whigs carried the White House. The expedient course of the party pragmatists in supporting war measures if not the war itself apparently had accomplished far more than merely warding off the fate of the Federalists. But the Whig success of 1848 was deceptive. Wartime strains upon the relations between Conscience Whigs and pragmatists had so weakened the party that it could not survive another bout with the slavery issue. The slavery crisis of 1850 broke open the cracks imposed on the party structure by the war and destroyed the party.

THE CIVIL WAR

The foregoing events obviously threw into question the conventional wisdom derived from the War of 1812 about what opposition to both war measures and war alike would do to an opposition party. Discarding the expediential course of the Whigs in the Mexican War, then, most of the Democratic party leadership in the role of opposition to the new Republican party during the Civil War chose to revert to a relatively uncomplicated kind of dissent. In general, its opposition to the Republican administration of Lincoln and to the Republican Congress in their conduct of the war was not disentangled from opposition to the war itself.

Democratic policy might have been different if the great Democratic paladin of the Middle West, Stephen A. Douglas, had not died almost at the outset, on 3 June 1861. Douglas had said that "The shortest way to peace is the most stupendous and unanimous preparation for war." But it would have been difficult for Douglas to hold his party to such a policy. The style of American politics at mid-nineteenth century was one of rough-and-tumble conflict, with the business of the opposition regarded as straightforward opposition to virtually everything the party in power stood for. In this context the maneuverings of the Whigs during the Mexican War could more readily be perceived as having been too subtle and devious by far. Furthermore, the war at hand was a civil war, and the Democratic party and politicians of the North had long been the comrades and allies of the leaders of the Confederacy, against which the federal government was now contending. It was too much to expect a prompt wholehearted embrace of old political enemies in common cause against old friends. This matter was especially crucial; historical studies of the Copperhead dissent that was to develop have attempted to tie it to various economic and social interests—assuming, for example, that poor agriculturalists might have objected to the business alliances of the Republicans. But the one consistent gauge of any district's tendency toward Copperheadism seems to have been the Southern ties of segments of its population.

Aggravating the latter dissent, and displeasing others who initially supported the war, as hostilities continued Republican policy came to include emancipation of the slaves. Therefore the issues of race and slavery again became intermingled with dissent in war, and the Democrats became the spokesmen for all of white America's deep fears of racial equality, toward which Republican war policies could be interpreted as tending.

Finally, American parties, although diverse coalitions, were by no means without ideology. The ideology of the Democratic party was well summed up in its favorite wartime watchword, "The Union as it was, the Constitution as it is." This maxim rightly implied that the methods taken by the Lincoln administration to prosecute the war—centralizing methods threatening to transform the old loose federation of states into a consolidated nation—seemed to many Democrats so subversive of a proper Union and the true Constitution that a victory for Lincoln's Union would be scarcely more appetizing than the independence of the Confederacy.

The Democratic position was so close to a plague-on-both-your-houses attitude that it is not surprising that under the tensions of civil war, Republicans were likely to suspect nearly the whole Democratic leadership of Copperheadism. Furthermore, after Douglas' death the core of the Democratic membership in the House, thirty-six congressmen, subscribed to a pact of party unity conceived and drawn by Congressman Clement L. Vallandigham of Ohio, who was candidly an obstructionist. After the summer of 1861, the Democratic congressional delegations offered much more nagging of the administration and parliamentary foot-dragging than willingness to sustain the war. Most Democratic leaders would have protested sincerely that they were not disloyal to the Union—the old Union. Much recent scholarship has been at pains to deny that even the leaders of the Copperhead faction among the Democrats were disloyal to the Union. But the insistence of these Peace Democrats that the only Union worth preserving was the old noncentralized Union makes this a distinction of limited practical application.

By the fall elections of 1862, the prolonged war and the disappointingly few victories—none in the crucial eastern theater—were reflected in the Democratic gains in the congressional and state elections. By that time too, the Emancipation Proclamation added abolition to the Union war aims and aggravated discontent with Lincoln's leadership. In New York State the Democrats elected Horatio Seymour to the governorship. During his campaign Seymour had called emancipation "a proposal for the butchery of women and children, scenes of lust and rapine, and of arson and murder." As governor he employed a states' rights rhetoric reminiscent of Jefferson Davis, and his scornful opposition to conscription contributed to the New York City draft riots of July 1863. In the Midwest the Republican governors of Indiana and Illinois believed that the newly elected Democratic majorities in their legislatures were in league with an empire of secret societies planning a coup d'état to ensure the victory of the Confederacy. The governors collected evidence that Indiana alone had 125,000 members enrolled in antiwar secret societies and that in Illinois 300 secret lodges met every Tuesday night. The Confederate government believed these and similar reports and sent agents to cooperate with the secret societies. Thus can a fratricidal war generate hysteria; for the threat of the secret societies was a chimera. No substantial danger ever emerged from their alleged plotting. The Confederate agents who made contact with them found the Copperhead malcontents unwilling to take risks or action, and no coup d'état ever had a chance of success because the overwhelming bulk of Northern sentiment—including that of the rank-and-file Democrats who continued to serve in or send their sons and brothers into the Union armies—remained determined to restore the Union by war, war-weariness notwithstanding.

This fact proved fatal to the Democratic party's immediate antiwar policies and highly injurious to the party for many years to come. By the presidential election of 1864, the Democratic party formed its ranks for the campaign around the principles that while the Union ought to be restored, Lincoln's centralizing war was the wrong way to restore it, and that in addition to being wrong the war was a practical failure. The Democratic platform of 1864 called for a cessation of hostilities "to the end that at the earliest possible moment peace may be restored on the basis of the Federal Union of the States." The assumption that peace could come first and be followed by restoration of the Union was one that was not supported in any of the attitudes of the Confederate leaders. Furthermore, to adopt the assumption would imply that all the sacrifices accepted thus far to seek reunion through war had been needless. Northern voters were not willing to concede that they had sustained so large an error so long, and at so high a price. In late August, Lincoln himself believed that war-weariness would defeat his bid for reelection; but the best remedy for war-weariness, a succession of military victories, intervened. On November 5 the electorate chose Lincoln for a second term by a margin of 55 percent, a respectable victory by the standards of American politics.

The Confederacy had its own problems of war-weariness and dissent. There were many contributing factors, but above all, Southern support for the war and for the Confederacy crumbled away as the South lost the battles. In contrast, Northern support for the war solidified itself as the North at last won battle after battle. For partisan politics the consequence of this latter fact was that on 25 February 1865 *Harper's Weekly* could without much exaggeration proclaim: "We are at the end of parties." The Democratic party had so identified itself with the idea of the war as a failure as well as a wrong that the Union victory left the party appearing impossibly myopic. So much had the Democratic leadership identified itself with opposition to the Civil War that during the war large numbers of War Democrats had felt obliged to join the Republican party. So much had the Republican party identified itself with the Union and the war that victory in the war represented such a complete vindication of the party that the memory of the war would go far to assure Republican supremacy in northern politics for a generation. Heeding the implied warning, in no subsequent war has a major party been willing to risk joining its fortunes with those of dissent.

THE SPANISH-AMERICAN WAR AND THE FILIPINO INSURRECTION

In the small wars between 1865 and 1917, dissent would not have been likely to assume proportions highly troublesome for the administrations waging the wars even without such an object lesson. The wars with the Indians had become too remote from the interests of most voters, especially because they could be fought by a small professional army with a large enrollment of immigrants. Any given uprising and campaign was too brief to allow dissent to accumulate, with intervals of peace allaying such public concern as it developed. An Indian rights movement did generate growing support among eastern philanthropists, intellectuals, and some religious denominations, but never on a scale to slow down seriously the military conquest of the Plains tribes. The constraints both upon the army and upon the government's Indian policy, causing occasional spasms of congressional or executive peacemaking efforts, were more largely those of fiscal economy than of philanthropic concern.

Similarly, the war with Spain was brief enough and inexpensive enough in casualties that it was over before the customary initial patriotic enthusiasm had dissipated. Criticisms of the war effort came afterward and concerned the conduct of the war more than the war itself. The Filipino insurrection, the name most often applied to the Filipino-American War (1899–1902), which followed from the consequences of the Spanish-American War, was more unpleasant in every sense. It raised up anew the moral outcry against American expansionism at the expense of weaker peoples, which had agitated the opponents of the Mexican War. Suppressing the insurrection was a process prolonged enough (two and a half years for the main insurrection on Luzon alone) and costly enough in casualties that it gave play to two of the principal wellsprings of dissent in war. Furthermore, the fighting involved guerrilla warfare in a difficult tropical climate, a type of combat that the European-style American army attuned to European-style regularized war has consistently found distasteful since its first major exposure to it in the Seminole Wars of 1816–1818 and 1835–1842, as has the society that supports the army. The strains imposed upon the army's patience by such irregular warfare in turn provoked acts of terrorism and atrocities against the Filipinos that still further exacerbated the moral dissent at home.

Nevertheless, dissent against the suppression of the Filipino insurrection never became a major political force. The outcry against this war, like the more general anti-imperialist movement of which it was a part, was the Indian rights movement writ somewhat larger. It was a movement centering in the eastern, or at least urban, aristocratic, and upper-middle-class intellectual and literary communities, with only occasional outposts in larger constituencies, such as Samuel Gompers in the labor movement; but it had no mass support. The inclusion of distinguished literary and academic figures gave it a high visibility, disproportionate to its strength. In the later era of public opinion polls, the evidence was to suggest—and more impressionistic evidence suggests it was already true—that except during a large-scale war touching numerous lives, foreign policy tends to be too remote from the concerns of most citizens and voters (again resembling the later Indian wars) for the "foreign policy public" to be very large. The opponents of imperialism and of the war in the Philippines were in this light the representatives of a schism within the elite segment of the population concerned with foreign policy that had propelled the nation into the Spanish-American War and overseas expansionism in the first place. The misgivings within that elite were severe enough to bring American territorial expansion overseas to an abrupt halt, with the elite foreign policy public in general soon reverting to its more traditional opposition to that kind of expansionism. Meanwhile, although the opposition party (still the Democrats) flirted with anti-imperialism, the party pursued at most an ambivalent course and after its Civil War experience did not again embrace outright dissent against the war. Dissent remained anything but a mass movement. Although it seemed prolonged at the time, the suppression of the major part of the Filipino insurrection within three years made the affair brief by contrast with the later Vietnam War, with the forces involved and the American casualties also much smaller.

THE WORLD WARS

The unhappy experience of the Democratic party during the Civil War was surely not the only cause of the reluctance of major parties to embrace dissent in subsequent wars. The discipline and cohesion that modern industrial societies impose upon their populations, in contrast to less-centralized and more loosely organized agricultural societies, had already helped maintain the united front of the North during the Civil War, and that discipline of industrialism had grown immensely stronger by the time of the great world wars of the twentieth century. In World War I the unity of the populace of every major power in support of nationalist war and patient endurance of the populace through prolonged war confounded the expectations of numerous prophets who had forecast that modern wars would be so costly that they could last only a few months. By World War II the public discipline of the great powers had become even more impressive. Democratic America certainly was no exception to this pattern; if anything, it was the democracies that displayed the greatest social cohesion. In both world wars, dissent in the United States was confined to minuscule fringe groups, mainly of socialists, radical leftists, and pacifists, and conscription focused far more attention upon the conscientious objector than it had done in the Civil War. This change occurred not only because the government and the public demonstrated increasing sensitivity to the demands of the pacifist conscience, but also because the conscientious objector was much more nearly alone as a dissenter than he had been in 1861–1865.

Before the entrance of the United States into World War I on 6 April 1917, it is true, there had been dissent aplenty over the course in foreign policy that proved to be leading to war, most conspicuous among the protesters being the Progressive elements of President Woodrow Wilson's own governing coalition. Although after the war the intractable realities of international politics were to cause among this coalition a speedy disillusionment with support for the war, nevertheless from Wilson's war message onward throughout the war itself, all but a small fraction of this group were enthralled by the president's promise that the fight was for a reformation of the whole world, and they joined ranks behind the war effort. Not surprisingly, however, the considerable dissent that had surrounded Wilson's foreign policy before the war contributed to an expectation that there would be more dissent during the war than actually materialized. This expectation in turn contributed to passage of stringent espionage and sedition acts seeking among other things to suppress any utterances that might discourage recruiting or the united prosecution of the war. These acts were enforced not only by an enlarged body of federal investigative agents but also by the federally sponsored American Protective League of private citizens. Abetted thus by what amounted to vigilantes, attacks upon civil liberties and particularly upon free speech became absurdly disproportionate to a mere trickle of dissent. No cases involving wartime suppression of dissent reached the Supreme Court until after the war. Then Justice Oliver Wendell Holmes's characterization of *Abrams* v. *United States* (1919) as involving merely a silly leaflet by an unknown man came close to what is likely to be the historian's view of all the targets of the espionage laws; but in *Abrams,* Holmes spoke for the minority of the court, and he himself had seen "a clear and present danger" in the earlier and not much different *Schenck* case (1919).

A greater sophistication and tolerance marked the government's attitude toward dissent in World War II—always excepting the relocation of more than 100,000 Japanese from the Pacific Coast. Tolerance could well be afforded. Although American entry into World War II was also preceded by much debate over the nation's course in foreign policy, the Japanese attack on Pearl Harbor assured that from the beginning of direct American participation there would be still less dissent than there had been in 1917–1918. Although such a leading Republican spokesman as Senator Robert A. Taft of Ohio suspected Franklin D. Roosevelt of exploiting the war emergency to fix the changes of the New Deal permanently upon American institutions, he and most other Republicans permitted themselves only the most cautious criticism of the conduct of the war, which they carefully distinguished from criticism of the war itself. ". . . every problem," said Taft, "must be approached in a different spirit from that existing in time of peace, and Congress cannot assume to run the war"—a far cry from the attitudes even of congressmen of Lincoln's own party during the Civil War, let alone the opposition. In World War II as in World War I, a certain amount of trouble did develop between the government and the labor movement, over labor's threats to strike to ensure itself a due share of war prosperity; but this friction can hardly be said to have involved dissent over the war. In World War II, national unity survived even though the American participation lasted nearly four years and was by American standards costly in casualties, unlike the American participation in World War I. The most evident explanation for this national unity was the nature of the enemy and of the circumstances with which the war began. But the historian seeking the sources of unity should also keep in mind that once the initial defeats were overcome, it would be hard to find a long war marked by so consistent a record of military success as favored America and surely helped sustain American morale in World War II.

THE KOREAN AND VIETNAM WARS

One of the meanings of the worldwide restlessness that marked the 1960's may well be that the notable social discipline characteristic of the populations of industrialized countries in the first century of the Industrial Age was breaking down. If so, a fundamental shift in social organization may underlie the contrast between the unity with which the United States fought the two world wars and the reversion to major dissent and internal conflict in the Korean and Vietnam wars. But more immediate explanations for the contrast readily present themselves. The most frequently voiced explanation is that the world wars fitted much better than the more recent wars the traditional American image of the nature of war. From the colonists' first struggles with the Indians, in which each side fought for the very survival of its culture, this argument goes, Americans came to regard wars as total struggles for absolute victory or defeat. The very aversion to war and the military that was so much a part of American tradition implied that when the nation went to war, it must be under the most extraordinary circumstances, and that so immoral an instrument must be employed only against such moral enormities as demanded absolute destruction. The American Civil War reinforced these preconceptions as the North fought for and achieved complete victory over the Confederacy. The argument concludes that after such a history, Americans could well sustain their unity against the Axis Powers during World War II, but they could not readily accept a limited war such as the Korean War, in which negotiations with the enemy to bargain for objectives far short of his destruction accompanied the very fighting of the war.

Allowing for some oversimplification—not every American war had been fought for the enemy's destruction, as witness the conflicts of 1846–1848 and 1898—such an explanation captures much of the American attitude toward war and goes far to account for the frustrations of the Korean War. Dissent against the Korean War also was much encouraged by a peculiarly uneasy political atmosphere troubling the United States in 1950 even before the war began. World War II had produced not a satisfactory peace but a Cold War with communism and the Soviet Union, in which the United States government held out the prospect of no more triumphant an outcome than containment. So low an expectation was itself a drastic departure from popular expectations of what America might accomplish in the world. Moreover, from 1945 to 1950 the containment policy did not even produce a satisfactory restriction of communism. China, with all its historic attractions to the American imagination, fell to the communists. Then there broke out the prolonged, costly, and militarily stalemated war in remote Korea, a war which itself could be perceived as springing from the mistakes of Harry S. Truman, whose Democratic administration had allowed China to be "lost" and had then supposedly invited communist attack on

South Korea by excluding that country from America's publicly proclaimed Pacific defense perimeter.

During the Korean War the opposition party, the Republicans, did not revert to the risks of outright partisan opposition, although they came close to that in such statements as Senator Taft's denunciation of the war as "an unnecessary war . . . begun by President Truman without the slightest authority from Congress or the people." Here Taft touched also on another source of public dissatisfaction in the post-1945 limited wars, the unwillingness of presidents for various reasons to ask Congress to declare war. In such puzzling circumstances of undeclared war for limited but not clearly defined objects, it was not surprising that Republican objections came to focus on the theme that the war should either be fought to win or be terminated. This theme linked the Republicans with General Douglas MacArthur, the Far East commander whom President Truman felt obliged to relieve because of his insubordinate public calls for extension of the war in pursuit of "War's very object . . . victory."

The upshot of MacArthur's activities was the dramatic Truman-MacArthur crisis; but given the anomalies of the Korean War in terms of the American tradition of war, Korea would have provoked much the same partisan and popular discontent even if there had been nothing like that particular eruption. The concept of limited war was difficult for the sponsoring administration itself to master. The theorizing that was to make limited war a familiar conception at least to foreign policy and strategy intellectuals during the next decade still lay in the future. The Truman administration kept the Korean War limited not out of a sophisticated understanding of the conception but largely because of a misapprehension, namely that the war was a communist feint to divert American attention in preparation for a major Soviet offensive in Europe, and that accordingly American military resources must remain as much as possible concentrated in Europe and the United States. After China entered the war and destroyed the possibility of using the war to reunite all of Korea, the Truman administration lost its own enthusiasm for prosecuting the war, such as it had been able to summon up, and the administration became so eager for peace that it spared the enemy most military pressure as soon as it announced a disposition to negotiate. In these circumstances the negotiations dragged on inconclusively until the inauguration of a new government in Washington. With the very sponsors of the war so vague about its nature and objectives, so unskillful in its management, and so lacking in conviction that it was worth fighting, it is little wonder that public discontent with the prolonged bloodletting and the absence of clear military success made the Democrats extremely vulnerable in the elections of 1952. The electorate responded to Republican criticism of every aspect of the conduct of the war, and especially to the Republican candidate General Dwight D. Eisenhower's promise that somehow he would end it. With the help of the East-West thaw that followed the fortuitous death of Soviet Premier Josef Stalin, President Eisenhower did end the war.

Dissent in the Vietnam War seemed to be still deeper and more widespread. Dissent certainly became a more conspicuous feature of the public scene, expressing itself in mass protest marches, demonstrations, and displays of civil disobedience. Public opinion polls indicate, however, that opposition to the Vietnam War grew stronger than opposition to the Korean War only after the Vietnam War had surpassed the Korean War in duration and in American casualties. The conspicuous public displays of dissent reflected not so much a greater opposition to the war in Vietnam than the war in Korea, but rather a shift in liberal opinion. Except for the extreme left wing, liberals had usually supported the Korean War as part of the staunch anticommunism that tended to mark their reaction to Stalinist Russia. By the 1960's, a less intransigent Soviet Union, the disruption of virtually all appearances of a monolithic international communism, and a rethinking of Cold War postulates in a more relaxed international atmosphere than that of the Truman years made liberals much less willing to support another war against a small Asian communist state than they had been in 1950–1953, especially when the Asian regime being supported by the United States was a distasteful blend of dictatorship and chaos. The conspicuousness of dissent against the Vietnam War was largely a product of the defection of many of the liberals from the foreign policy coalition of the establishment, for this group is an especially articulate one, in direct line of descent from the literary and academic dissenters against suppression of the Filipino insurrection. The conspicuousness of dissent against the Vietnam War was also much enhanced by employment of the methods of dramatizing dissent that liberals had learned from association with the civil rights movement of the late 1950's and early 1960's. Measured against the apparent volume and the new tactics of dissent, the tolerance of the government for controversy displayed an advance over World War I, despite conspiracy trials directed against dissenters and the illegal methods of attempting to discredit Daniel Ellsberg, who leaked the so-called Pentagon Papers to the press.

The liberal defection during the Vietnam War from the coalition that had supported the Truman administration during the Korean War also reinforced the moralistic quality that dissent from the Vietnam War shared with dissent during the Mexican War and the Filipino insurrection. The liberal protest against the Vietnam War was another moral protest against an allegedly aggressive onslaught by the great and powerful United States against a weak and ill-armed adversary that was said to be seeking only the self-determination that America's own Declaration of Independence championed. Like dissenters during the Mexican War and the Filipino insurrection, liberal protesters against the Vietnam War charged that the war was betraying the highest ideals of the United States itself. Some of the more horrifying of the military expressions of modern technology, such as defoliation techniques and napalm, combined with an indiscriminate use of aerial and artillery bombardment by the American forces in Vietnam, gave special intensity to this moral protest.

Yet public dissent against the Vietnam War was not primarily moralistic. The conspicuous character of left-wing protest demonstrations against the war gave a misleading impression of the degree and the nature of the unpopularity of the war as compared with the Korean War. The left-wing protesters, especially the young among them, through the very tactics that made their protests conspicuous, antagonized moderate and conservative citizens. At any rate, the larger public discontent—including that discontent that most directly contributed to the electoral defeat of the original Democratic sponsors of the war and the triumph of their Republican opponents in 1968, much on the model of 1952—was not a moralistic dissent. It was again an expediential discontent that the issues of the war were puzzling in contrast to the great crusades of the world wars and that the Vietnam War was not being won.

In summary, dissent in war is not a new phenomenon in American history, born during the Vietnam War. All American wars have provoked dissent. Dissent is implicit in historic American attitudes toward war itself and is nourished when war becomes prolonged, costly in casualties, and indecisive. Because the American electorate has always shown only a limited patience for war, those troubled by dissent are mistaken when they interpret it as a new constraint upon the use of military force in American foreign policy. The constraint has been present from the beginning of American history.

BIBLIOGRAPHY

Thomas B. Alexander and Richard E. Baringer, *The Anatomy of the Confederate Congress: A Study of the Influences of Member Characteristics on Legislative Voting Behavior, 1861–1865* (Nashville, 1972), approaches the subject indirectly but provides as satisfactory an index to dissent in the Confederacy as can be found. James M. Banner, Jr., *To the Hartford Convention: The Federalists and the Origins of Party Politics in Massachusetts, 1789–1815* (New York, 1970), despite its very local emphasis, is the best study of New England dissent in the War of 1812. K. Jack Bauer, *The Mexican War, 1846–1848* (New York, 1974), the most recent full-scale study of the Mexican War, is based on primary sources, and includes a good brief treatment of partisanship and dissent. John Morton Blum, *V Was for Victory: Politics and American Culture During World War II* (New York, 1976), is the best survey of the American home front in World War II. Robert McCluer Calhoon, *The Loyalists in Revolutionary America, 1760–1781* (New York, 1973), examines the Loyalists less in isolation and more in the whole context of the Revolution than do previous works, therefore comes closest to treating the problem of Loyalism as a problem of dissent in war. Richard O. Curry, "The Union As It Was: A Critique of Recent Interpretations of the 'Copperheads,' " in *Civil War History,* 13 (1967), is an introduction to Civil War dissent by way of a survey of the relevant literature. Alexander DeConde, *The Quasi-War: The Politics and Diplomacy of the Undeclared War With France, 1797–1801* (New York, 1966), concerns a small war, but a formative one in shaping the limits and acceptability of dissent. Stephen G. Kurtz, *The Presidency of John Adams: The Collapse of Federalism, 1795–1800* (Philadelphia, 1957), is another study of the Quasi-War, with grim implications that the legitimacy of dissent in war might have failed to become an American tradition. Stephen G. Kurtz and James H. Hutson, eds., *Essays on the American Revolution* (Chapel Hill, N.C.–New York, 1973), includes a number of the essays that incorporate the most recent scholarship and touch on dissent (John Shy's essay on the conflict as a "revolutionary war" especially has pertinent passages). Joan M. Jensen, *The Price of Vigilance* (Chicago, 1968), a history of the American Protective League of World War I, applies more recent scholarship to some aspects of the Peterson and Fite work cited below. Ward Just, *Military Men* (New York, 1970), includes profiles of American soldiers during the Vietnam War, and is useful for its portrayal of how the military perceived dissent. Samuel Eliot Morison, Frederick Merk, and Frank Freidel, *Dissent in Three American Wars* (Cambridge, Mass., 1970): in the perspective of the Vietnam War, Morison examines the War of 1812, Merk the Mexican War, and Freidel the Spanish-American War and imperialism. John E. Mueller, *Wars, Presidents and Public Opinion* (New York, 1973), is the most valuable effort to use public opinion polls to analyze the extent and nature of dissent in the Korean and Vietnam wars, which is the source of much of the interpretative framework of the present essay. H. C. Peterson and Gilbert C. Fite, *Opponents of War, 1917–1918* (Madison, Wis., 1957), is a standard work. Richard Polenberg, *War and Society: The United States, 1941–1945* (Philadelphia, 1972), offers a good introduction to issues of dissent and personal liberty. David Rees, *Korea: The Limited War* (New York, 1964), is written from the perspective of a British journalist applied to dissent in what Americans saw as a new kind of war. Daniel B. Schirmer, *Republic or Empire: American Resistance to the Philippine War* (Cambridge, 1972), is the fullest study of dissent during the Filipino insurrection, despite a perhaps inordinate focus on Massachusetts. John R. Schroeder, *Mr. Polk's War: American Opposition and Dissent, 1846–1848* (Madison, Wis., 1973), offers the most comprehensive study of Mexican War dissent.

[*See also* AMERICAN ATTITUDES TOWARD WAR; ANTI-IMPERIALISM; BIPARTISANSHIP; THE COLD WAR; CONGRESS AND FOREIGN POLICY; CONSCRIPTION; CONSENSUS HISTORY AND FOREIGN POLICY; ELITISM AND FOREIGN POLICY; IDEOLOGY AND FOREIGN POLICY; IMPERIALISM; ISOLATIONISM; MILITARISM; NATIONALISM; PACIFISM; PEACE MOVEMENTS; PHILANTHROPY; PUBLIC OPINION.]

DOLLAR DIPLOMACY

Eugene P. Trani

IN his final message to Congress on 3 December 1912, President William Howard Taft looked back at the foreign policy followed by the United States during his administration and noted: "The diplomacy of the present administration has sought to respond to modern ideas of commercial intercourse. This policy has been characterized as substituting dollars for bullets. It is one that appeals alike to idealistic humanitarian sentiments, to the dictates of sound policy and strategy, and to legitimate commercial aims."

Taft's remarks gave formal definition to the term "dollar diplomacy," a phrase synonymous with the diplomacy his administration pursued between 1909 and 1913. During those years the goal of diplomacy was to make the United States a commercial and financial world power. The Taft administration concentrated on assisting American businessmen in the protection and expansion of investment and trade, especially in Latin America and the Far East.

In a narrow sense dollar diplomacy was not new. Protection of American commercial interests around the world had been part of the diplomacy of the United States since earliest days. Efforts to trade with British and Spanish colonies in the Western Hemisphere, defense of the rights of neutrals to trade in wartime, and support of the most-favored-nation concept were all predecessors of dollar diplomacy. Yet dollar diplomacy was the subject of much controversy during the Taft administration and in the years that followed.

Much of the contemporary controversy over dollar diplomacy stemmed from the fact that Taft, the handpicked successor of Theodore Roosevelt, had embarked on a policy that differed from the one Roosevelt had followed. Roosevelt was an expansionist and had supported the American move into world affairs. For a variety of reasons Roosevelt believed expansion necessary for the United States, with benefits for the rest of the world. He viewed foreign affairs in strategic terms, with Europe as the center of world power. He felt an affinity for Britain and based much of his diplomacy on cooperation between Washington and London. To be sure, Roosevelt supported the expansion of American business throughout the world, but he was much more concerned with the balance of power and improving the Anglo-American relationship. As a result, Roosevelt mediated the Russo-Japanese War (1904–1905) and the conflict between France and Germany over Morocco in 1906.

Taft came to office with a different view. Ever the lawyer, he viewed foreign policy in terms of legal institutions. He thus came to support arbitration treaties. He had differences with Roosevelt over Europe, feeling that the United States had little or no interest in events there. Taft kept the United States out of the second Moroccan crisis in 1911, and, while supporting mediation, he was not willing to mediate the Italo-Turkish War (1911) nor the first Balkan War the following year. Taft believed that the most important relations with Europe occurred in what is currently referred to as the Third World, backward nations where the United States and Europe shared interests.

Taft's view of the role of American business in foreign policy also differed from Roosevelt's. Taft long had been concerned with foreign trade. He recognized that by 1909 the United States was producing more goods than Americans could consume and therefore had to increase exports. It was perhaps symbolic that during the Taft administration, in 1910 to be exact, the United States began to export more manufactured goods than raw materials, changing the focus of trade from industrial nations in need of raw materials to lesser developed countries that required finished products. In this regard the developing areas of Latin America and East Asia seemed particularly important. A concentration on economic opportunities in Latin America and East Asia, especially China, would have many benefits. Such a policy would help the American economy by solving the problem of overproduction. It would benefit recipient nations, bringing economic progress, which in turn would mean political stability; and stability would guarantee American strategic interests in underdeveloped areas. It was not surprising that in Taft's first annual message (7 December 1909) he stated: "To-day, more than ever before, American capital is seeking investment in foreign countries, and American products are more and more generally seeking foreign markets."

While Taft had ideas as to the diplomacy the United States should follow, he had no interest in serving as his own secretary of state, further distinguishing his administration from Roosevelt's. The man whom Taft chose to carry out his foreign policy, after refusals by Elihu Root and Henry Cabot Lodge, was Philander C. Knox, a wealthy conservative Pennsylvania lawyer then in the Senate. Knox had been attorney general between 1901 and 1904; and this fact, in the president's view, more than made up for his lack of experience in foreign affairs, since Taft wanted lawyers in his cabinet. Knox had been what is now known as a corporation lawyer, the Carnegie Steel Corporation being one of his clients. He was thus sympathetic to big business.

Knox shared Taft's views concerning the goal of American diplomacy—protection and expansion of economic interests. A State Department memorandum of 6 October 1909 pointed out that all developed countries were seeking trade, and noted that trade was essential to American prosperity. There could be no more important task than expanded investment and trade. Diplomacy had to support American financiers and businessmen by finding opportunities abroad. The State Department anticipated the activities of the Bureau of Foreign and Domestic Commerce in the 1920's, when Herbert Hoover was secretary of commerce. But locating commercial opportunities abroad was not enough for Knox and Taft. As the 1909 memorandum indicated, the United States would insist that Americans compete with Europeans in the developing countries by buying bonds, floating loans, building railroads, and establishing banks.

So it was that the State Department during the Taft years turned to dollar diplomacy. The policy gained support throughout the diplomatic corps, a fact that was especially important as Knox concentrated on policy and allowed subordinates to run day-to-day operations. Francis M. Huntington Wilson, first assistant secretary of state, presided over the daily activities of the State Department and carried out a reorganization of the department into geographical bureaus. Huntington Wilson, Willard D. Straight, and Thomas C. Dawson, the latter two the initial heads of the Division of Far Eastern Affairs and the newly created Latin American Division respectively, all shared the views of Taft and Knox on trade and investment.

When the administration talked about dollar diplomacy in Latin America, it was almost always referring to the Caribbean, which had strategic implications because of the soon-to-be-completed Panama Canal. Concerned over the general instability of the Central American governments, Taft and Knox set a goal of stable governments and prevention of financial collapse. Fiscal intervention would make military intervention unnecessary. As Knox told an audience at the University of Pennsylvania on 15 June 1910: "True stability is best established not by military, but by economic and social forces. . . . The problem of good government is inextricably interwoven with that of economic prosperity and sound finance; financial stability contributes perhaps more than any other one factor to political stability."

Such statements did not mean that Taft and Knox were unwilling to use military power in the Caribbean. They did use it. They thought that fiscal control would lessen the need for intervention. They believed that the United States and nations of the Caribbean would both benefit. For the United States an increase in trade, more profitable investments, and a secure Panama Canal would result. For the local inhabitants, the benefits would be peace, prosperity, and improved social conditions.

Taft and Knox believed that the way to control the finances of the Caribbean countries was to take over customhouses, following the example of the Roosevelt administration in the Dominican Republic. According to the Taft-Knox doctrine, it was important to get the Caribbean nations to repay European debts by means of loans from American businessmen or at least from multinational groups in which Americans participated. In Nicaragua, Honduras, Guatemala, and Haiti, the United States pushed refunding schemes. The State Department believed that these sorts of reforms would end political instability in the Caribbean.

Nicaragua proved the classic case of dollar diplomacy in the Caribbean. While the American economic interest in Nicaragua was small, the country had been an alternate route for the transisthmian canal. The United States was sensitive to activities in Nicaragua. The longtime dictator José Santos Zelaya had never been popular in Washington and was seen as the cause of much instability in Central America, the result of his efforts to dominate the area. When Knox took control of the Department of State, he ordered withdrawal of the chargé d'affaires from Nicaragua, began to press private business claims against the Zelaya government, and sought, albeit unsuccessfully, to discourage a Franco-British consortium from making a loan. In cooperation with Mexico, the United States also sent warships to stop Zelaya from filibustering in Central America.

In October 1909, the situation became complex with the outbreak of civil war in Nicaragua. Insurgency centered on the eastern coast in Bluefields, a city dominated by foreign businessmen and planters. These foreigners and conservative politicians in Nicaragua followed the lead of General Juan J. Estrada. Foreign money, some of it American, bankrolled the revolutionaries. While declaring itself neutral, there was little question as to which side the American government supported. Formal neutrality disappeared when Zelaya executed two Americans captured while fighting with the rebels. The United States broke off relations, asserting that the revolutionaries represented "the ideals and the will of a majority of the Nicaraguan people more faithfully than does the Government of President Zelaya."

Washington made known that Zelaya's resignation in late 1909 was not enough. Huntington Wilson pushed for expulsion of the liberal party from power, hoping the rebels would take control. American forces landed at Bluefields to make sure fighting did not damage American interests. Successes followed for the insurgents, and by the end of August 1910 they had taken the capital, Managua.

The United States expected fiscal reform in Nicaragua, and refused to recognize the new government until it had agreed to American control of the customhouses and to the refunding of the debt owed to British bankers by means of a loan from American financiers. Dawson went to Nicaragua to negotiate the terms of recognition.

This did not end the difficulties, for the American demands were unpopular. The United States went ahead with its financial program, even though the Senate delayed action on the treaty (known as the Knox-Castrillo Convention) worked out between Washington and Managua in June 1911, which called for refunding of Nicaragua's internal and external debts, and administration of the customs by a collector approved by American officials. While the Senate debated, bankers went ahead with the rehabilitation of Nicaraguan finances, making a loan with the national railroad and the national bank as collateral. American citizens also began to collect Nicaraguan customs and to serve on a mixed claims commission, all in anticipation of Senate action. Much to the distress of Taft and Knox, the treaty died in a Senate committee in May 1912, along with a similar treaty with Honduras.

Another revolution broke out in Nicaragua in July 1912, and this also brought American intervention. Approximately 2,700 marines landed to protect American citizens and property and to suppress the revolution, which was over by early October. Although the majority of the marines was soon withdrawn, a legation guard remained as a symbol of intervention until 1925. The Taft administration went out of office in March 1913, convinced that the policy it had followed in Nicaragua was correct.

Intervention had proved necessary, the administration admitted, but it was only for a short time and continued fiscal intervention would make further military intervention unlikely.

The Taft-Knox policy toward Nicaragua, and for that matter toward the rest of Central America, was unquestionably offensive to Latin Americans. Even a goodwill visit through the Caribbean by Knox could not overcome suspicions. Knox said the United States did not covet an inch of Latin territory, but such utterances were not accepted south of the Rio Grande.

In the years after 1912, political leaders in both Latin America and the United States attacked Taft's policy toward Central America. Elihu Root believed that dollar diplomacy rekindled Latin fears and suspicions of the United States that he had worked so hard to overcome while secretary of state from 1905 to 1909. In 1913 President Woodrow Wilson made clear that he would not support special interests trying to gain advantages in Latin America. The Bryan-Chamorro Treaty, finally approved in 1916, contained provisions similar to the second treaty Knox had worked out with President Adolfo Díaz of Nicaragua in early 1913. Even so, Wilson and Secretary of State William Jennings Bryan were much less interested in protecting American businesses in Latin America than Taft and Knox. Dollar diplomacy as a policy was at an end in Latin America. Criticism of the policy continued. Presidents Herbert Hoover and Franklin D. Roosevelt both renounced dollar diplomacy as they attempted to construct what became known as the Good Neighbor policy in dealing with Latin America. In the long run, of course, American businessmen did increase trade and investment in Latin America, but it was World War I, not dollar diplomacy, that decreased European economic interests in that part of the world.

If the results of dollar diplomacy were meager in Latin America, where the United States was the dominant power, they were a disaster in China, the target for the Taft-Knox policy in East Asia. Of course, the situation in the Far East was difficult. In the late nineteenth century and the first decade of the twentieth century much change had taken place. With victories over China in 1895 and Russia in 1905, Japan had become the major power in the Far East. Theodore Roosevelt had supported Japan's new prominence in East Asia. He decided that Japan did not threaten American interests there. He saw the Japanese as a barrier to Russian expansion; a preserver of the balance of power in East Asia; protector of the Open Door; and stabilizer of China, a nation for which he had little respect. Roosevelt had backed Japan in its war with Russia and in 1905 had mediated the peace.

Roosevelt had hoped to arrange a balance of power between Russia and Japan after the war. But the Japanese victory was so decisive and other events in Japanese-American relations so important that he gave up on the Open Door in China, especially in Manchuria, which the Japanese began to close after 1905. Because of the need to protect the Philippines, which Roosevelt believed was the "heel of Achilles" of the United States, and the war scare that resulted from the Japanese immigration crisis, Roosevelt accepted Japanese expansion on the mainland of Asia. He came to feel that the Open Door was not worth war with Japan. The United States should do what it could to preserve interests in China, but should recognize Japan as the dominant power on the Asian mainland. In short, he gave a green light to Japanese expansion. One of the best expressions of this belief appeared in a letter to Knox on 8 February 1909, shortly before Roosevelt left office. He noted that Japanese-American relations were of "great and permanent importance." While immigration to the United States had to stop, the United States should "show all possible courtesy and consideration." The Taft administration had to understand that "Japan is vitally interested in China and on the Asiatic mainland." Since the Pacific coast of the United States was defenseless and "we have no army to hold or reconquer the Philippines and Hawaii," the country had to avoid war. Roosevelt felt that American interests in China were insignificant in American Far Eastern policy.

Even as his administration came to an end, forces were at work that would change Roosevelt's policy in East Asia. In 1908 Root had established the State Department's first geographic unit, the Division of Far Eastern Affairs. Headed by Willard Straight, the division opposed Japanese expansion in China, and this opposition was to dominate the division in the years between 1909 and 1941.

Roosevelt's East Asian policy thus was reversed. With urging from the State Department and because of a combination of motives—economic expansion, suspicion of Japan, faith in the future of China—the Taft administration decided to challenge Japan in China. During the Taft years the Open Door notes, which had frequently changed in meaning after 1900, assumed new importance in the Far Eastern policy of the United States.

In Far Eastern policy, department officials now proved important. Taft and Knox did not need convincing. Both believed China was the country of the future in the Far East and that if the United States desired influence with that emerging nation it had to increase its financial interests there. If the president and secretary of state had any doubts about such policy, they were overcome by State Department advice. Huntington Wilson, who had served in Tokyo, and Straight, who had been consul in Mukden, Manchuria, were both hostile to Japanese ambitions in China. They had tried unsuccessfully in the last days of the Roosevelt administration to enlarge the Open Door to include investment and trade. With Taft and Knox they had more success.

The Taft administration came to see investment in railway development and loans to the Chinese government as the means to increase influence in China. Knox demanded that American financiers be given the opportunity to join the British, French, and German consortium in lending money to China to finance railroad construction in the Yangtze Valley, the so-called Hukuang Railway loan. When the demand met with European hostility, Taft appealed to the Chinese head of state: "I have an intense personal interest in making the use of American capital in the development of China an instrument for the promotion of the welfare of China, and an increase in her material prosperity without entanglements or creating embarrassments affecting the growth of her independent political power and the preservation of her territorial integrity." The State Department persuaded a group of investors to assume part of the loan. Knox grudgingly got his way, but only at the price of irritation in Britain, France, and Germany. In the long run this project was a failure.

From the Hukuang loan the State Department turned to Manchuria. The result was the Knox neutralization policy, which more than any other proposal epitomized dollar diplomacy in China. In the fall of 1909 Knox proposed that American, Japanese, and European bankers lend China enough money to repurchase the Chinese Eastern Railroad, held by Russia, and the South Manchurian Railroad, in the possession of Japan. Manchuria would be neutralized and open to all commercial activities. Washington feared that southern Manchuria was being closed to non-Japanese influences. Knox realized that the Japanese would be difficult, but he thought the proposal would be supported in Europe. Britain, France, and Germany eventually decided to defer to the wishes of Japan and Russia, and in January 1910 the latter two nations rejected the plan. Only the Chinese showed interest, but that soon turned to concern when Russia and Japan agreed in July to cooperate in guaranteeing the status quo in Manchuria. Knox had only succeeded in driving the former enemies into a virtual alliance to prevent American interference in Manchuria. A companion proposal by Straight, who had left the State Department to head the American consortium planning a railroad that ran parallel to portions of the South Manchuria line, met a similar fate.

By the fall of 1910 Knox recognized defeat in his railroad plans for Manchuria. Throughout the rest of his term as secretary of state, he continued to work for increased American involvement in China, but through plans that did not contest the Japanese and Russians in Manchuria. He became involved in plans for a multinational currency reform loan, but the Chinese Revolution that began in 1911 put an end to that scheme. The government that overthrew the Manchu then negotiated with a six-power consortium for a reorganization loan. Negotiations dragged on until the Taft administration left office.

Dollar diplomacy in China stimulated international controversy. The Taft-Knox policy succeeded in causing distress, irritation, and even anger in London, Paris, Berlin, St. Petersburg, and Tokyo. Knox's clumsy attempts to help China only weakened the empire, since Japan and Russia agreed on a policy. The policy aroused controversy in the United States, where bankers were reluctant to participate. Roosevelt opposed the policy, writing to Taft in late 1910 that the Open Door in China could only be maintained by general diplomatic agreement. He noted that "as has been proved by the whole history of Manchuria, alike under Russia and under Japan, the 'Open Door' policy, as a matter of fact, completely disappears as soon as a powerful nation determines to disregard it, and is willing to run the risk of war." Roosevelt was convinced that Japan was one such nation, and that the United States ought not to try to bluff the Japanese on the mainland of Asia, especially since Americans would never agree to fight a war there. Later, Wilson withdrew government support from American investors planning the reorganization loan, charging that the loan violated Chinese sovereignty and threatened China with intervention. The American investors backed out of the loan, and the last of the dollar diplomacy schemes came to an end. In the long run, Wilson reversed his position, approving participation in a consortium in 1918. But Japan remained the dominant power in China until World War II, and Roosevelt's policy seemed valid in retrospect. Taft and Knox failed in their goal—to dislodge Japan from the Asian mainland.

There were other areas to which the Taft administration tried to apply dollar diplomacy, such as in Turkey. Breaking sharply with the traditional American policy toward the Ottoman Empire, which centered on protecting the rights of American citizens, the Taft administration attempted to share in the mining, irrigation, and railroad concessions then being negotiated by the Turkish government. Taft hoped that the United States would obtain a larger share of the commerce of the Near East. He was to be disappointed. The United States found the European powers too entrenched, and dollar diplomacy failed in Turkey. But Central America and China were the most spectacular examples of the doctrine.

The controversy over dollar diplomacy lasted well after 1913. In fact, historians are still debating the concept. Generally recognized by students of international relations as a failure, dollar diplomacy has engendered controversy concerning its motives and the people responsible for carrying it out. The dispute over motives has been sharp. Some writers, especially New Left historians, have argued that the policy was primarily economic, while others have contended that it was dominated by strategy, especially in Latin America. Others have noted the desire of the Taft administration to "do good" in Latin America and Asia. The most balanced account of dollar diplomacy, that of the historians Walter and Marie Scholes, has combined these motives and also noted that Taft's diplomacy anticipated United States foreign policy after World War II. Taft and Knox chose private capital as their instrument, whereas President Harry S. Truman used public capital. In both instances, the most important consideration was preservation of vital American interests abroad by helping underdeveloped countries establish viable governments and integrating them into the twentieth century.

Debate as to responsibility for the policy has taken two directions. Historians have argued over the roles of Taft, Knox, the State Department, and American businessmen. Straight has especially been the subject of debate. One recent account has convincingly argued that Straight's role in the Far East has been exaggerated. The most reasonable conclusion would seem that there was a common purpose among the advocates of dollar diplomacy.

Another direction of the debate over dollar diplomacy has been whether it was only one aspect of a continuous policy followed in the twentieth century by the United States—to expand American economic opportunities abroad. It is clear that Taft's predecessor, Theodore Roosevelt, and his successor, Woodrow Wilson, as well as the rest of the American leaders in the twentieth century, supported the expansion of American business. But no president in this century, other than Taft, has made such a policy the principal goal of his diplomacy. As a result, the term "dollar diplomacy" remains synonymous with the diplomacy of 1909 to 1913.

DOLLAR DIPLOMACY

BIBLIOGRAPHY

Samuel Flagg Bemis, *The Latin American Policy of the United States* (New York, 1943), is dated, but still valuable; Naomi W. Cohen, "Ambassador Straus in Turkey, 1909–1910: A Note on Dollar Diplomacy," in *Mississippi Valley Historical Review,* 45 (1959); Paolo E. Coletta, *The Presidency of William Howard Taft* (Lawrence, Kans., 1973), gives a comprehensive study of Taft's administration; Raymond A. Esthus, "The Changing Concept of the Open Door, 1899–1910," in *Mississippi Valley Historical Review,* 46 (1959), is important to see how the Taft administration tried to change the meaning of the Open Door policy; Lloyd C. Gardner, "American Foreign Policy 1900–1921: A Second Look at the Realist Critique of American Diplomacy," in Barton J. Bernstein, ed., *Towards a New Past: Dissenting Essays in American History* (New York, 1968), argues the importance of economic motives; Michael H. Hunt, *Frontier Defense and the Open Door: Manchuria in Chinese-American Relations, 1895–1911* (New Haven, 1973), disputes Straight's importance in the formulation of America's East Asian policy; Jerry Israel, *Progressivism and the Open Door: America and China, 1905–1921* (Pittsburgh, 1971), stresses continuity in America's Far Eastern policy; Helen Dodson Kahn, "Willard D. Straight and the Great Game of Empire," in Frank J. Merli and Theodore A. Wilson, eds., *Makers of American Diplomacy: From Theodore Roosevelt to Henry Kissinger* (New York, 1974), portrays Straight as architect of dollar diplomacy in East Asia; Ralph E. Minger, *William Howard Taft and United States Foreign Policy: The Apprenticeship Years, 1900–1908* (Urbana, Ill., 1975), gives extensive treatment to Taft's involvement in foreign affairs before he became president; Dana G. Munro, *Intervention and Dollar Diplomacy in the Caribbean, 1900–1921* (Princeton, 1964), cites the importance of strategy as the motivation of dollar diplomacy in the Caribbean, and is very comprehensive; Walter V. Scholes and Marie V. Scholes, *The Foreign Policies of the Taft Administration* (Columbia, Mo., 1970), is the best study of the diplomacy followed by Taft; Robert Smith, "Cuba: Laboratory for Dollar Diplomacy, 1898–1917," in *Historian,* 28 (1966), is a revisionist account of relations with Cuba; Paul A. Varg, *The Making of a Myth: The United States and China, 1897–1912* (East Lansing, Mich., 1968); and Charles Vevier, *The United States and China, 1906–1913: A Study of Finance and Diplomacy* (New Brunswick, N.J., 1955), gives a generally balanced treatment.

[*See also* CONSORTIA; ECONOMIC FOREIGN POLICY; INTERVENTION AND NONINTERVENTION; THE OPEN DOOR POLICY; TRADE AND COMMERCE.]

THE DOMINO THEORY

Ross Gregory

PERHAPS no facet of foreign policy has followed a more hectic course than the domino theory in the few years it occupied center stage in American politics and society. Announced in 1954 as rationale for United States policy in Southeast Asia, it received for several years even less notice than problems in that area. As attention of the troubled postwar world shifted from Europe to the so-called undeveloped countries, and as the conflict in France's former colony of Indochina developed into America's Vietnam War, the domino theory became in the 1960's a familiar part of American verbiage in foreign policy and focal point of the controversy over the conflict in Vietnam. For supporters it stood as the most convincing means of justifying an increasingly unpopular policy; to critics it represented at least misapplication of a onetime valid proposition, at worst a device used to foster a generation of mistaken American policy during the years of the Cold War.

President Dwight D. Eisenhower had introduced the term on 7 April 1954 when, speaking at a press conference, he explained why Indochina should not be allowed to fall under communist control:

> First of all, you have the specific value of a locality in the production of materials that the world needs.
>
> Then you have the possibility that many human beings pass under a dictatorship that is inimical to the free world.
>
> Finally you have broader considerations that might follow what you would call the "falling domino" principle. You have a row of dominoes set up, you knock over the first one, and what will happen to the last one is the certainty that it will go over very quickly. So you have a beginning of a disintegration that would have the most profound influences.

At inception the domino theory thus applied to events developing beyond, not inside, Indochina. In subsequent messages the president and his secretary of state, John Foster Dulles, explained that the war against the French in Indochina was in truth not a struggle for independence but part of an international communist movement directed by the Soviet Union and Communist China. Fall of Indochina likely would lead to collapse of such nearby states as Burma, Thailand, Malaya, Indonesia; and eventually all of Asia would stand in the path of an advancing communist menace. By these means the government rationalized assistance already being extended to the French; the same argument later would promote a fateful broadening involvement in a small, seemingly insignificant nation, thousands of miles from the United States.

For all the derision it was to receive, the domino theory evolved from an old and frequently valid idea. In broadest and most general meaning it pertained to nothing more than a chain reaction, a succession of events set in motion by a single, or common, force. The record of the past showed virtually countless examples of such chain reactions or nations fearing they would develop. Leaders of the Roman Empire had rushed legions to frontier outposts to suppress uprisings that might spread to other parts of the empire. The rulers of post-Napoleonic Europe had intervened to put down nationalist revolutions in several places from fear that such developments would threaten their domain and upset the order of the Continent. Application of a domino theory thus invariably called for conservative action, prevention of change, maintenance of the status quo, although proponents could direct it as easily against right-wing movements as toward the left.

Perhaps most interesting is the fact that the Soviet Union, in the American estimate the ultimate mover of a succession of dominoes, endorsed a similar principle. Following World War II the Russians had moved to establish in adjacent East European states governments first "friendly" to the Soviet Union and eventually nothing short of satellite communist regimes. In ensuing decades the Kremlin kept an eye on its European neighbors, watchful that no nation chart a course contrary to Soviet interests or wishes. When in 1956 nationalist leaders in Budapest turned on their rulers, and threatened Russian dominance and perhaps the communist system in Hungary, Soviet forces brutally suppressed the uprising. Reminiscing in 1970 on his action, Soviet Premier Nikita Khrushchev stressed the danger of a spread of events: ". . . if the counter-revolution did succeed and N.A.T.O. took root in the midst of the Socialist countries, it would pose a serious threat to Czechoslovakia, Yugoslavia, and Rumania, not to mention the Soviet Union itself." A dozen years later, events in Czechoslovakia reaffirmed Soviet adherence to a domino principle.

In applying its version of the domino theory, the United States had drawn heavily on past experience. Still fresh in the minds of American leaders were origins of only recently ended World War II, a conflict that had started when Adolf Hitler had conquered one country after another until Germany controlled nearly all of Europe. Adherents to the domino theory were to embellish the doctrine by associating it with German aggression and by reminding critics of the disastrous consequences of yielding to Hitler's threats of war—the so-called Munich syndrome. The United States could avoid a similar disaster in Asia, so the reasoning went, by application of power early and strong enough to prevent collapse of the first domino and beginning of a chain reaction.

The immediate force behind the domino theory had been the struggle that had developed between the United States and the Soviet Union at the end of World War II. Rich, powerful, and secure, the United States had expected defeat of Germany and Japan to lead to a world of independent states willing to practice liberal political and economic policies. Soviet leaders, notably Premier Josef Stalin, had a much different view of the world. Insecure, burdened with enormous wartime damage, distrustful of capitalist nations and fearful of economic encroachment from the West, the Soviet Union had acted to protect and expand its interests by establishing, between 1945 and 1948, communist regimes in virtually all of Eastern Europe. The United States had responded with alarm. The administration of President Harry S. Truman angrily concluded that in the Soviet Union the United States faced a revolutionary and imperialistic foe, which promoted policy contrary to American interests and principles and threatened all Europe and possibly the world. Truman thereupon applied, without using the term, a domino theory by instituting the policy of containment, a policy that began in 1947 with economic and military aid to Greece and Turkey. "It is only necessary to glance at a map to realize that the survival and integrity of the Greek nation are of grave importance in a much wider situation," Truman asserted. "If Greece should fall under the control of an armed minority, the effect upon its neighbor, Turkey, would be immediate and serious. Confusion and disorder might well spread throughout the entire Middle East." Eventually all Europe, behind Winston Churchill's definition of an "iron curtain," came within the scope of an American policy designed to check the nation-by-nation advance of Soviet and communist power in Europe.

Within a short time the Truman administration had applied the same policy, and the same theory, to Asia. The critical year in Far Eastern affairs was 1950, during which time the recently established communist regime in China signed a military pact with the Soviet Union, thus confirming an American suspicion that the Chinese were acting under Soviet direction. In the same year communist forces in North Korea, prompted by the Russians, attacked their countrymen in the South. Convinced that the Soviet conspiracy now had extended to the East, Truman moved to offer resistance on all fronts. "The Communists in the Kremlin are engaged in a monstrous conspiracy to stamp out freedom all over the world," he said. "The attack on Korea was part of a greater plan for conquering all of Asia." The president then sent American troops to Korea, bolstered defense of the Nationalist Chinese regime on Formosa, and extended military aid to the French in Indochina. Thus Truman took the first step in adapting a domino theory to the Far East. It remained for Eisenhower only to apply the concept directly to Indochina and give it a catchy, simplistic title.

Unfortunately the United States directed a theory that in other cases had had validity to an area where it did not apply. A chain reaction of sorts had developed in Eastern Europe, where the Soviet Union had both the means and motive to act as a prime mover. An enormous Soviet army was at hand, and Eastern Europe stood beyond the reach of American military power—save, perhaps, an unthinkable nuclear assault. The region was important to the Soviet Union for reasons other than ideology. The United States persisted in applying the model of Eastern Europe to Indochina even though conditions vastly differed. The source of conflict in Indochina was not the presence of Russian, or even Chinese, power or of either nation's effort to impose its will, but the existence of a decadent French colonial regime. French colonialism had prompted Vietnamese nationalists to take up arms in a war for independence, which lasted between 1946 and 1954. Although prominent resistance leaders, such as Ho Chi Minh, were communist, the movement had self-determination as an objective and not the fostering of Russian, Chinese, or international communism. The major error of American policy during the Cold War stemmed from a conclusion that communist movements were the same everywhere: all were subservient to the Soviet Union (or later to China), all were imposed upon the native populace, and all were inherently hostile to American interests.

These ideas were later to become a great deal more clear than they seemed at the time Eisenhower proclaimed the domino theory. Americans knew little about Southeast Asia in 1954: the countries stood close together; the people seemed much the same, were in a similarly low state of political development, and were vulnerable to any movement that showed strength and determination. The State Department had not much more understanding than the American people. Dulles ruled the department with an iron hand; those individuals with expertise in Asian affairs, who often disagreed with the secretary, were either removed from service or placed in insignificant posts. Eisenhower and Dulles were clear on one point—the need to resist communism. Consequently after the French were forced out of the area, the administration continued military and economic assistance to South Vietnam, the area denied to Ho Chi Minh by the Geneva Conference of 1954. Saturated with rhetoric of the Cold War and with visions of a communist monolith, Americans found little reason to object. In any event it did not seem a large matter, for the conflict soon cooled and Americans all but forgot Indochina and Vietnam.

The brief administration of John F. Kennedy corresponded with a transition in Vietnam from the quiet of the late 1950's to the tumult of the mid-1960's. The Kennedy administration found reason to reaffirm commitment to the domino theory. Kennedy had come to office bursting with confidence and ambition, expecting to promote a foreign policy that would be more realistic, flexible, and successful than that of his predecessor. Whatever he hoped to change soon became forgotten as he faced one crisis with communists after another—in Cuba, Berlin, Asia, and Cuba again—each of which, in his estimate, challenged his ability to endure the difficult tasks of Cold War diplomacy.

Kennedy treated the problem of Indochina within the context of this interpretation. Although he earlier had questioned the wisdom of Eisenhower's policy, and although by 1961 there existed reasons for questioning the legitimacy of a separate regime in South Vietnam and the domino theory as well, Kennedy refused to acquiesce in the advance of communist forces in Indochina or anywhere else. Fighting had increased in South Vietnam during the early 1960's, a change that had threatened survival of the American-sponsored regime of President Ngo Dinh Diem. Faced with the prospect of continuing the war at its existing level and likely losing, Kennedy chose to increase American military involvement. The approximately 1,500 American military personnel on hand when Kennedy took office had grown to some 15,000 at the end of his administration. If he had doubts about this course, he did not allow them to show. Asked his opinion of the domino theory, only weeks before his assassination in November 1963, Kennedy replied: "I believe it. I think that the struggle is close enough, China is so large, looms so high just beyond the frontiers, that if South Viet-Nam went, it would not only give them an improved geographic position for a guerrilla assault on Malaya, but would also give the impression that the wave of the future in Southeast Asia was China and the Communists. . . . I believe it."

It was during the presidency of Kennedy's successor, Lyndon B. Johnson, that the domino theory received the most forceful endorsement and the closest critical scrutiny. Johnson's limited exposure to East Asia—he had visited the area as vice-president in 1961—had left him convinced of the need to continue the war in Vietnam. Much a creature of American politics, he did not wish to risk the domestic consequences of having to announce that another nation had fallen under communist control. Moreover, he had inherited Kennedy's group of activist advisers, the bulk of whom believed that the conflict in Vietnam had far-reaching international implications. Determined not to accept an American defeat, assured by advisers that the war was legitimate and possible to win, Johnson of course proceeded to escalate the conflict to an almost unbelievable level in the late 1960's, when the United States had in Vietnam more than half a million men and thousands of war machines.

Johnson's policies prompted protest marches, riots on campuses and in the streets, bombings, and a division of the country sharper than at any time since the Civil War. Critics found many reasons to attack the war; perhaps at the time moral objections were most impressive, but they also launched a multisided assault on the principle of the "falling dominoes." For example, one group argued that the theory had rested on the existence of a unified communist movement, and that if such a movement ever had existed, it did no longer. The rift between China and the Soviet Union, which began in the late 1950's, had split communism into two and eventually many camps. Since that time communist nations had been able to act with considerable independence. The status of countries in East Asia thus depended not on events in neighboring states or on commands from Moscow or Peking, but on conditions and problems within each country. Most critics conceded—indeed many welcomed the prospect—that Vietnam and possibly all of Indochina would come under control of revolutionary regimes, but they doubted that the movement would spread or foster the interests of China or the Soviet Union. Curiously, the sharpest critics accepted a form of domino theory by insisting that defeat in Vietnam would begin an overdue retreat of American political and economic repression throughout the world. As one individual, Gabriel Kolko, concluded: "Vietnam . . . became the focus of the futile American effort to . . . translate its seemingly overwhelming technological and economic might into a successful inhibition of local revolutionary forces, thereby aborting the larger pattern of world revolution and advancing America's own economic and strategic interests" (*Pentagon Papers,* V [1972]). However much they might disagree among themselves, most individuals in academic circles, the press, and large groups of the American populace had come to treat the domino theory, and the war, as objects of derision.

The sharper the attack on the theory, the more the Johnson administration felt compelled to defend it. "The Communists have taught us that aggression is like hunger," the president said in July 1966. "It obeys no law but its own appetite. The leaders of free Asian nations know this better than anyone. If South Vietnam falls, then they are the next targets." Speaking in May 1967, William P. Bundy, assistant secretary of state for East Asian and Pacific affairs, insisted that "the extension of hostile control over other nations or wide areas of Asia, specifically by Communist China, North Korea, and North Vietnam, would in a very short time create a situation that would menace all the countries of the area and present a direct and major threat to the most concrete national interests of this country."

In fact, many officials had come to question their own words—to doubt either that the theory was valid or as important as the problems the war had caused for the United States. Intelligence agencies for some time had been advising that the much-feared chain reaction might never develop; the war had begun to have a shattering effect on the economy, national unity, and personal and political reputations, any of which might be a more pressing matter than whatever happened in Southeast Asia. In a memorandum prepared within the Department of Defense in 1965, one official, John McNaughton, assigned 70 percent of "U.S. aims" to avoidance of a humiliating defeat and only 20 percent to keep South Vietnam "and . . . adjacent territory from Chinese hands." Its credibility in question, the administration began offering new, expanded interpretations of the domino theory. Failure in Vietnam would damage American reputation, and cause one nation after another to doubt the word and reliability of the United States; it would encourage "wars of liberation" over all the world. The theory thus had changed a great deal from what it had meant at the time of its introduction in 1954. By the late 1960's it had become a strained device for defending an unpopular policy, for making a war of doubtful importance to the United States appear an undertaking of enormous meaning.

President Johnson even appeared to doubt his own words, for at the same time he defended the war, he also sought ways to lower the level of conflict and to find an escape for the United States. He had made little progress by 1968, when he decided not to run for reelection. Johnson left office in 1969, a discredited president.

The new president, Richard M. Nixon, had traveled an irregular path during a long career in American politics. Identified in earlier years as a vigorous opponent of communism and defender of the domino theory, he now took note of changes in East Asia, changes which probably nullified—though Nixon would not concede the point—a domino theory. His most dramatic move in foreign policy—renewal of discourse with China—constituted an outgrowth of those changes and Nixon's belief that the world had moved, as he put it, from an age of confrontation to an era of negotiation. He nonetheless would not sanction an abrupt reversal of policy in Indochina; he refused to repudiate the theory and occasionally vigorously defended it. In 1970 Nixon said:

> Now I know there are those who say the domino theory is obsolete. They haven't talked to the dominoes. They should talk to the Thais, to the Indonesians, to the Singaporans, to the Japanese, and the rest, and if the United States leaves Vietnam in a way that we are humiliated or defeated . . . this will be immensely discouraging to the 300 million people from Japan clear around to Thailand in free Asia; and even more important it will be ominously encouraging to the leaders of Communist China and the Soviet Union who are supporting the North Vietnamese [Papers of the Presidents, Nixon (1970), 546–547].

As with his predecessor, however, Nixon had to concern himself more with the war itself than with possible external consequences in Asia. His primary objective was to find a formula that would allow American departure while avoiding appearance of a defeat. In time he identified that formula as Vietnamization, the strengthening of South Vietnamese forces to that point where they could handle their own defense—a policy that represented not repudiation of the domino theory, but an assertion that the first domino still stood upright. Nixon could argue that the armistice, negotiated by Secretary of State Henry Kissinger in January 1973, left a South Vietnamese regime in power and thus constituted attainment of his objective. To many observers the armistice carried another meaning: If South Vietnam, or even all Indochina, did fall to communist control in the future, the United States would interpret the collapse as neither disastrous to American interests nor the beginning of a chain reaction in Asia.

With the armistice of 1973 and de-escalation of the Vietnam War, the domino principle lapsed into limbo. Government officials still had made no effort to discredit the idea, and it was altogether likely that a general domino theory, prompting action to prevent a succession of events, would have as much usage in the future as it had had in the past. What seemed impossible was resurgence of the narrow definition of the doctrine to justify renewal of an American war in East Asia. The government did invoke the theory on a limited basis in 1975, with reference to a progression of events within Indochina, when President Gerald R. Ford asked for funds to increase shipments of military supplies (Ford quickly denied any intention of sending troops) to South Vietnam and Cambodia. The following year Secretary of State Kissinger warned of a new domino effect in Africa when he asked for aid to American-supported forces in Angola. But Congress refused to act in either case and the people seemed little moved by the political consequences of events in Indochina or Angola. The future might bring a different attitude, but in the mid-1970's the domino theory lingered for most Americans as a bad memory of a sorrowful and fruitless war, of a troubled time in the nation's life—a memory to be filed alongside An Loc, Da Nang, "Search and Destroy," and other verbiage of the Vietnam War.

BIBLIOGRAPHY

There is no study of the domino theory, but references appear in most books about the Vietnam War and recent foreign policy. The most detailed material is in *The Senator Gravel Edition: The Pentagon Papers,* 4 vols. (Boston, 1971), the controversial study by the Department of Defense not originally designed for public consumption. A fifth volume of the same publication, subtitled *Critical Essays Edited by Noam Chomsky and Howard Zinn* (Boston, 1971), contains radical scholarship on the war. Virtually everything Presidents Truman through Nixon have said in public about the domino theory appears in *Public Papers of the Presidents of the United States,* 33 vols. (Washington, D.C., 1961–1974). A fascinating, if long-winded, recent account of the war, focusing on decision making in the Kennedy and Johnson administrations, is David Halberstam, *The Best and the Brightest* (New York, 1969). Other worthwhile studies include Ellen Hammer, *The Struggle for Indochina* (Stanford, 1954); and Bernard Fall, *Two Vietnams: A Political and Military Analysis* (New York, 1967). See also Richard J. Barnet, *Intervention and Revolution: America's Confrontation With Insurgent Movements Around the World* (New York, 1968); Ralph K. White, *Nobody Wanted War* (New York, 1970); and Hans J. Morgenthau, *A New Foreign Policy for the United States* (New York, 1969). A Soviet domino theory appears in *Khrushchev Remembers* (Boston, 1970).

[*See also* AMERICAN ATTITUDES TOWARD WAR; THE COLD WAR; CONTAINMENT; DISSENT IN WARS; PUBLIC OPINION.]

ECONOMIC FOREIGN POLICY

Joan Hoff Wilson

HISTORIOGRAPHICAL BACKGROUND

COMMERCE and commercial expansion have always been a part of American diplomacy. Only recently, however, have historians begun to concentrate on the relationship between economic and ideological or political considerations in the formulation of foreign policy. There are a number of reasons why this development has taken so long to occur in the field of diplomatic history and why it has become a divisive force among diplomatic historians.

First, a peculiar time lag has characterized the writing of foreign policy studies. It was not until the 1920's that the initial generation of professional diplomatic historians appeared. Most of them concentrated on American documents, and many wrote diplomatic history as though it were simply an exercise in the exchange of formal communiqués between countries. (The most notable exception to this generalization was the economic foreign policy work of Benjamin H. Williams.) While this approach finally produced a number of sophisticated monographs based on multiarchival (transnational) research in foreign and domestic governmental archives, it often seemed to inhibit or prevent any questioning of American ideological motivation or close scrutiny of the socioeconomic impact of United States policies and interventions on other countries.

Second, when diplomatic historians finally did begin to catch up with prevailing historiographical trends after World War II, they did so with a vengeance. Long before then other students of American history had divided into two general groups. The basic division occurred around the turn of the century and produced two broad categories of historians—those who emphasized consensus and unity or continuity in the development of political theory and institutions of the United States, and those who stressed the diversity and conflict in the country's history. The former, known as "conservative evolutionists," initially encouraged transnational diplomatic research because it stressed or sought European origins for many American ideas and actions. The latter, known as "progressive historians," were much more ethnocentric and introspective, concentrating almost exclusively on domestic documents and internal developments that seemed unique to the American experience. Another important difference between these two schools of historical thought was that the first tended to be uncritical of American capitalism, while the second, although not necessarily Marxist, was suspicious of big business and, hence, often anticapitalist in orientation.

This split over how to interpret American economic development did not significantly affect writings about the foreign affairs of the United States until the 1940's and 1950's, although it had permeated other fields of American history since at least 1900. As is often the case when an attempt is made to bridge a time (or in this case, historiographical) gap, exaggeration and hostility can be generated in the process.

Among those who specialize in United States diplomacy the result has been to create two distinct camps. While both increasingly share new interdisciplinary and quantitative methods, they differ sharply in their interpretation of data. Their strongest disagreement has centered on the relationship between the political economy of the United States and its foreign policy. The degree to which domestic economic and ideological considerations have affected past and present American foreign policy decisions is at the heart of the major interpretative battle currently raging among diplomatic historians.

On opposite sides of this polemic are historians who tend to overemphasize the role of economics in the formulation of foreign policy and are justly accused of being economic determinists. At the other end are those who righteously claim to have objectively defined national self-interest, but in doing so they conveniently eliminate the need to examine American economic and ideological motivation—or at least place this motivation on a moral level far above that of other countries. It is at these extremes that the controversy over economic foreign policy is most bitter and counterproductive because both are based on the dubious assumption that "foreign policy formulation is a completely rational, calculated process."

In the middle of this historiographical dispute, of course, are those foreign policy scholars who are attempting to present a balanced picture of when and where economic and ideological influences have been important factors in foreign policy decisions or major diplomatic concepts. Generally speaking, even in this less-charged atmosphere, those diplomatic historians who write from anticapitalist assumptions are also usually critical of the modern corporate state as it has evolved in the United States. Therefore they attribute more economic motivation and ideological characteristics to American foreign affairs than do those diplomatic historians who begin with a predominantly procapitalist point of view.

At the heart of the problem is an honest disagreement over the relative merits of capitalist ideology, that is, corporate liberalism, as it is reflected in American foreign policy. Stated in a more polemical fashion, it is a disagreement over the desirability of perpetuating an American foreign policy that, at least for most of the twentieth century, appears to have been aimed at exporting capitalism and democracy indiscriminately all over the world, by whatever means necessary.

Critics of the influence that capitalist ideology has had on the formulation of foreign policy are often called revisionist or New Left historians because so many of them since World War II have been influenced by the writings of Charles A. Beard and William Appleman Williams, the founder of the so-called Wisconsin school. But not all of them are advocates of left-of-center politics. There are many who identify with the New Right and who, in recent years, have also relentlessly attacked the corporate liberalism of American foreign policy. Murray H. Rothbard's writings contain excellent examples of this New Right libertarian or nonsocialist critique of United States diplomacy.

Using many of the same interdisciplinary methods as their opponents, this revisionist point of view is represented in varying degrees by such diplomatic historians as Walter LaFeber, Lloyd C. Gardner, Gabriel Kolko, Robert Freeman Smith, N. Gordon Levin, Jerry Israel, Ronald Radosh, Richard H. Miller, Marilyn Blatt Young, Barton J. Bernstein, and Carl P. Parrini. These historians usually assume that "diplomacy is essentially a response to forces generated by America's economic and social structure."

Rather than viewing the foreign conduct of the United States basically as an altruistic or defensive response to action taken by other nations, these revisionists believe that American diplomatists are so imbued with, or conditioned by, corporate liberalism that they automatically formulate foreign policy that is in the best economic interest of the United States. Therefore, their writings abound with value judgments based on various levels of economic and ideological analyses. At its best this emphasis on economic foreign policy has contributed to the writing of diplomatic history that avoids excessive chauvinism, superficial anecdotes, and the presentation of foreign affairs as a simplistic exchange of diplomatic notes.

In contrast, orthodox or traditional diplomatic historians claim that this stress on economic foreign policy is misplaced and that they use a more objective, value-free approach to interpreting American foreign policy. Their present position has been influenced by two very different types of historical writing. One is not usually considered diplomatic. It began with that first generation of post–World War II entrepreneurial historians like Joseph A. Schumpeter, Allan Nevins, Fritz Redlich, Thomas C. Cochran, and Edward Chase Kirkland. This probusiness faction within the historical profession existed long before 1945, but it has been most influential since the establishment of the Social Science Research Council, which appointed a Committee on Research in Economic History in 1941 to investigate the role of the American government in economic development.

Between 1948 and 1958 orthodox diplomatic historians were increasingly impressed by the monographs produced under the auspices of the Harvard University Research Center in Entrepreneurial History and of the Committee on Historiography of the Social Science Research Council. Generally speaking, early entrepreneurial historians concentrated their efforts on the positive aspects of American economic development by describing business structures and developing organizational theories. They tended to avoid making any value judgments about individual businessmen or the corporations that they studied. Such entrepreneurial studies often create the illusion of total objectivity when in fact thay are based on strongly probusiness assumptions.

In the hands of skillful diplomatic historians who recognized its deceptive amorality and conceptual limitations, this entrepreneurial research ultimately gave rise to a sophisticated type of organizational methodology. It has been usefully employed to understand how governmental bureaucratic structures and business, as well as other interest groups, contribute to the formulation of foreign policy. At its best this approach prevents the writers of foreign policy from falling into the trap of economic determinism by exploring the complex and often irrational aspects of decision making within the public and private bureaucratic structures of authority that permeate any highly developed society like the United States. Since 1966 the Research Seminar on Bureaucracy, Politics, and Policy of the Institute of Politics in the John F. Kennedy School of Government at Harvard has, under the original leadership of Ernest R. May, Morton H. Halperin, and Richard E. Neustadt, stimulated a number of seminal socioeconomic, psychoorganizational works in diplomatic history.

The other influence at work on orthodox scholars has been the writings of diplomat-historians like George F. Kennan and Herbert Feis, as well as the political scientist Hans J. Morgenthau. These three men greatly influenced the establishment of the school of liberal criticism of American foreign policy after World War II. This school views twentieth-century United States diplomacy, particularly since 1945, as a perversion of an earlier, more realistic type of foreign policy practiced by the Founding Fathers and by most American leaders in the nineteenth century. These liberal realists are critical of diplomacy to the degree that it abandons a sense of balance of power or realpolitik approach to foreign affairs. They usually deny, however, that systematic economic expansion has ever been central to the formulation of American foreign policy. In other words, they either arbitrarily separate economic and political matters when discussing foreign affairs, or they define national interest in such a way as to make economic considerations a subordinate factor in foreign policy decisions.

Their writings have also been characterized by a tendency to deny that American foreign policy has ever been as ideologically motivated as that of its worst enemies. While they differ in their degree of criticism, some of the better-known proponents of this implicitly probusiness, yet noneconomic, defense of United States foreign policy, include Lewis Mumford, Samuel Eliot Morison, Arthur M. Schlesinger, Jr., Herbert Feis, Robert James Maddox, John W. Spanier, Norman A. Graebner, Warren F. Kimball, Dana G. Munro, Joseph M. Siracusa, Robert W. Tucker, and Robert A. Divine.

Despite their disagreement over the relationship between ideological motives and economic self-interest in the formulation of foreign policy, there are points of agreement between the revisionist and the orthodox diplomatic historians. Both are critical of American foreign policy in the Cold War era, especially as it appears to be increasingly counterrevolutionary and indifferent to the national and cultural aspirations of foreign peoples. Both are searching for a comprehensive synthesis to explain American foreign policy in this and previous centuries. Finally, both have increasingly used the latest quantitative, collective biographical and organizational techniques, as well as traditional archival research methods.

In terms of their historiographical evolution there is only one major point on which the revisionists and orthodox diplomatic historians deviate from the split that occurred among students of history in general around the turn of the century. The conservative evolutionists stressed not only the continuity of American history, but also its growth from certain European traditions, while progressive historians originally emphasized the conflict and the unique past of the United States. Orthodox and revisionist diplomatic historians have reversed positions on this question of the country's uniqueness. Revisionists now tend to deny that the foreign policy of the United States has ever been that different from the imperialist patterns set by Western Europe in the course of the nineteenth century; they argue that its dominant economic position in this century has only reinforced this aggressive predisposition. Proponents of diplomatic orthodoxy, however, now often maintain that the United States has always tried to deal with foreign nations from a uniquely moral and politically superior base, regardless of its particular stage of economic development.

DIPLOMATIC DEFINITIONS AND DOCTRINES

It is not enough, however, to understand how this historiographical controversy over economic foreign policy evolved among diplomatic historians after World War II. One must also come to terms with the language employed by both sides—for example, the definition of the term "ideology." In the broadest sociological sense it has been defined as an " 'ordered system of cultural symbols' that may or may not correspond to reality, depending on the function it is performing" for the individual, group, or country involved. Such a definition is intended to encompass political and socioeconomic viewpoints. The major difficulty encountered by historians in the field of economic foreign policy is how to determine the relationship between ideology and self-interest. It is the interaction of the whole (ideology) with one of its parts (economic, as opposed to political or cultural, motivation in this case) that continues to be one of the most inadequately researched and interpreted aspects of recent diplomatic history. This is true of both revisionist and orthodox historians.

Part of their problem stems from the complexity of determining what constitutes self-interest. Most sociopsychological studies have for some time refuted the idea that economic self-interest alone can explain the behavior of individuals or organizations. Such studies maintain that it is fallacious to equate economic self-interest with every type of action taken by businessmen or corporations or countries. Such an assumption reflects a lack of understanding of the psychology of motivation and a simplistic notion of what constitutes self-interest. On the other hand, it makes no more sense to go to the other extreme, either ignoring economic self-interest because it is so difficult to determine or pretending that it does not exist.

The best guideline is that which allows the historian to view businessmen as responding not only to what they perceive to be their best self-interest, but also to self-interest as it is "reinforced or at least not countered by a series of ideological and political considerations." In other words, "although self interest stimulate[s] action, just how much it did so depend[s] on a number of attitudinal and political considerations." The key consideration in writing about economic foreign policy is to ascertain the degree to which ideology and economics are mutually reinforcing, rather than to emphasize their incompatibility or consider them as separate, opposite entities.

This reinforcement may take many forms, depending on which social science model of the American power structure is employed. The most flexible model is what is known as the "establishment orchestration model." It allows for a variety of interaction between business groups and the government, including formal lobbying and also informal influence through organizational and class-group identification. In other words, both government and business have become increasingly bureaucratized in this century, and their convergence has resulted in "collage" decisions and actions representing "coalitions, bargains, . . . compromises, and . . . confusion."

Those in bureaucratic policy positions share

basic values that they view "not as self-serving, but as in the public interest" and indeed, except on rare occasions, "the majority of the 'visible, audible and active' members of the general public appear to endorse and support the action of the major officials of government. . . ." Thus, the established orchestration model is based on a multicausal decision-making process "rather than one based exclusively on economic dominance." A "basic 'belief system' may be a more important force than sheer economic interest," according to this theory about how the American power structure operates. It does not deny that such bureaucratized positions and structures were originally shaped under the strong influence of the political economy, but it also suggests that they become self-perpetuating. Hence, decision making is a much more complex process than economic determinists would have us believe. At the same time, this is far from the rational image of foreign policy decisions that is most often presented to the public.

Another thing to remember about this frequently irrational decision-making process is that although modern bureaucracies often take on autonomous, anonymous functions and characteristics that far surpass their original purpose, they still exist as "an expression of the [current] social, political, and economic organization of a society." This means that the various public and private bureaucratic agencies that influence foreign policy should not be viewed in isolation, because they usually reflect a similar set of ideological assumptions, namely, those of American corporatism.

In order to understand what historians in the field of economic foreign policy mean by such terms as corporatism, corporate liberalism or corporatist ideology, it is necessary to review organizational trends in the United States. Since the last quarter of the nineteenth century, many kinds of Americans—reformers, businessmen, government leaders, and all types of interest groups—have engaged in a search, semiconscious at best, for a new political and economic order. The first phase of this quest for more efficient governmental and economic organization led to the appearance of federal regulatory agencies and departmental restructuring, along with the revitalization of specialized trade associations and such broadly based, influential national economic groups as the National Association of Manufacturers, the American Bankers Association, the Chamber of Commerce of the United States, the American Farm Bureau Federation, the Farmers' Union, and the American Federation of Labor.

It was an agonizing search for a new sense of order among human values and for more efficient organizational and industrial techniques. And it took many different forms among government officials, businessmen, farmers, and social reformers, especially during the Progressive era of the early twentieth century. Viewed as part of the pervasive thrust toward greater rationalization of society, which was common to all industrialized nations at the turn of the century, this search for a new order in the form of socioeconomic organization followed corporatist lines in the United States.

Ideally, corporatist ideology projects a view of society as organized into functionally independent economic units, including labor, agriculture, and management, that are supposed to remain voluntarily decentralized yet simultaneously self-governing and self-regulating. In theory these industry-wide units work together harmoniously in the public interest out of a sense of community, of social responsibility, and of devotion to efficiency. A blend of democratic liberalism and capitalism, this ideal of corporatism was proffered by some reformers as an ideological and economic means of preserving individual initiative while taking advantage of the latest technological advances.

In practice, however, there were two courses open to reformers who wanted to implement a corporatist economy in the United States in the early twentieth century. One stressed completely cooperative economic organization and regulation along neoguildist and voluntary associational lines. The other stressed federally directed and enforced organization along rigidly bureaucratic and statist lines. The American corporatism that first grew out of these different means of implementation was an ambiguous and often contradictory structure of federal regulatory agencies and antitrust procedures purporting to preserve liberal democratic concepts of private property, individualism, voluntary effort, and local control.

Concurrently, there was a significant increase in monopolistic or oligarchic economic practices and large-scale, national economic organizations at all levels of society, which often came to dominate and utilize the federal regulatory apparatus in their own interests. Often private economic groups, without regard for the public interest, monitored themselves by controlling or influencing the Federal Trade, Interstate Commerce, and Tariff commissions. Also, well-intentioned efforts designed to eliminate machine politics sometimes ended up turning government over, not to the people, but to an elite group of professional urban planners and self-perpetuating, nonelective bureaucrats, many of whom were businessmen—all in the name of efficiency and order.

It is the degree to which economic coordination in the form of business influence took place between public and private organizations as a result of Progressive reforms that must be determined by historians, regardless of whether they are writing about the foreign or domestic policies after 1900. In retrospect it appears that more potential existed for such coordination before and during World War I than ever actually materialized. This was partially due to the standard rivalry between government departments like the State and Commerce departments. It was also due to competing business interests that staffed many of the new government regulatory and coordinating agencies coming out of the Progressive period and out of the war itself.

The first step, therefore, in unraveling the relationship between public and private economic groups in the formulation of economic foreign policy is to try to identify those private business interests and then to determine the degree to which they were able to overcome their differences and to work together within public groups, such as wartime or other types of regulatory government agencies. Within the American governmental bureaucracy in the twentieth century, successful economic coordination has taken place only to the degree in which public and private interest groups have been successful in blurring or merging their functions. This coordination has not always been in either the country's or the public's best interest. The second step is to determine the private channels by which business interests affect governmental decisions. In contrast to public meetings and statements or editorials in business journals, these private contracts can consist of friendships, shared ideological and social standards, or personal influence based on positions of power.

The principle of associational, decentralized corporatism, which involved informal cooperation and a delicate balance between private and public segments of the political economy, was significantly undermined in the course of the first decade after World War I as the distinctions between, and the responsibilities of, the private and public sectors became increasingly blurred. This neoguildist brand of corporatism was repudiated and finally abandoned in the panic of the Great Depression for an equally ambiguous, pluralist brand of liberal welfare statism under the New Deal. Neither version of corporatism has yet resulted in an economic and political order compatible with proclaimed American humanitarian, democratic, and rural ideals of the nineteenth century. But it is the New Deal brand of statist corporatism that those writing about American economic foreign policy are referring to when they use the terms corporate liberalism or corporatist ideology.

Other terms, the meanings of which are important in the writing of economic foreign policy, are related to the manner in which the United States acquired territory and international commercial power during the nineteenth and twentieth centuries. Those who believe in what has been called the "concept of empire in American diplomatic history" take the view that such an empire, whether formally or informally established, was necessary to ensure domestic prosperity. Thus, to say that the United States was expansionist during the nineteenth century arouses little controversy. To say that the United States was aggressively imperialistic in acquiring a continental empire in the course of the nineteenth century immediately raises a controversial semantic issue among foreign policy historians.

Since almost all of these territorial acquisitions were contiguous, the initial generation of professional diplomatic historians viewed the process as most business, government leaders and the public did, that is, as the natural and inevitable consequence of the rapid American economic development across the continent. Therefore, they deemed it expansionist and not imperialist. In fact, there was little talk in early diplomatic studies about American imperialism or aggression, except for such "aberrations" as the noncontiguous territory acquired as a result of the Spanish-American War (1898). This is an obvious example of a "basic 'belief system'" at work. Even anti-imperialist groups at the turn of the century believed in an ever-expanding domestic economy that would continue to grow naturally without undue domestic government aid or military intervention abroad.

It was in such an atmosphere of value consensus, where American political and economic goals appeared equally humanitarian and where imperialism was considered a pejorative term—an evil form of control of one nation over another practiced primarily by European monarchies—that the American ambassador to Chile, William S. Culbertson, could write to President Herbert Hoover in 1930:

> In spite of competition or even propaganda, American business will more than take care of itself. Our efficiency in production and distribution will excell [sic]. Furthermore, American capital will be the controlling factor in public and private finance in these [South American] countries simply because the greatest reservoirs of savings are to-day in the United States. Opposition and criticism may divert or slow down these tendencies, but they cannot defeat the final result, namely, that American civilization, material and cultural, is bound to impress itself upon, and I believe, benefit these peoples. If anti-American critics wish to describe this as our "imperialism" let them make the most of it. It is the natural result of our expanding life which, having achieved commendable results at home, is seeking new opportunities over-seas [Presidential Papers, Hoover Library].

The same set of assumptions can still be found in the following statement by diplomat-historian Dana G. Munro, writing in 1974 about United States policy decisions for the Caribbean in which he participated during the 1920's:

> We thought that the United States must try to promote orderly government in the Caribbean because disorder would invite interference by other powers. . . . We thought that the first requisite for progress in the Caribbean was the development of orderly republican government. . . . We realized, however, that there were great obstacles to the holding of free elections in many of the Caribbean countries, and we were inclined to support constituted governments against any attempt to overthrow them by force, in the belief that only the maintenance of peace would permit the sort of progress that was necessary for the development of democratic institutions. . . . We were interested in economic development in the Caribbean because the poorer countries were not likely to have better governments so long as the masses of the people lived in ignorance and poverty. . . . One obvious way to improve both economic and political conditions was to improve the government's financial administration. . . . The State Department had always thought that its efforts to promote peace and economic progress in the Caribbean would be welcomed by intelligent and peace-loving people in the countries concerned [*The United States and the Caribbean Republics, 1921–1930* (Princeton, 1974)].

These positive attitudes about an ever-expanding domestic and foreign economy, if only the United States were granted the right to compete with other nations on the basis of equal access to international markets, and about the benevolence of American intentions abroad in terms of self-determination, humanitarianism, and progress have been referred to in the writings of William Appleman Williams as the Open Door policy. Originally the Open Door notes of Secretary of State John Hay were intended to apply only to China. But ultimately the equal economic opportunity concept was applied to the world, according to Williams.

In essence, this definition of the Open Door policy is a shorthand way of referring to the corporatism ideology of American foreign policy. Viewed from this perspective, imperialism is not something practiced only by malevolent European nations but by any country that extends its power in a formal or informal way over a weaker one. Under the Open Door, imperialism exists whenever American economic domination of a country or area of the world takes place through trade and investment. No formal annexation is necessary. Such a definition of imperialism, with its emphasis on both informal and formal power relationships, is accepted by revisionist diplomatic historians. They agree with Williams that it is the most accurate way to describe the intent of American foreign policy for most of the nineteenth century and the result of diplomatic actions of the United States throughout the twentieth century.

It should be noted, however, that the Open Door policy has been utilized very selectively by the United States. It has been advocated mainly in those areas of the world outside of the Western Hemisphere where the country has faced serious economic competition, but has almost never been encouraged where the opposite is true. In principle the policy represents the exact opposite of such traditional diplomatic concepts as balance of power and spheres of influence because it ostensibly substitutes peaceful economic expansion for political and military confrontations between rival nations.

In practice, equal opportunity in world trade and in finance inevitably benefits the strongest competitor, which, from 1920 to the late 1960's, was the United States. Consequently, wherever American trade and investment interests gain the upper hand, they usually begin to practice what can only be called a Closed Door policy, aimed at establishing economic spheres of influence. Recently, the term "multilateralism" has sometimes been used to embody both the Open Door and Closed Door concepts.

For example, it was thought by many government and business leaders immediately following World War I that a properly functioning worldwide Open Door policy might be an effective substitute for the League of Nations because it would provide the peaceful means for nations to compete in developing areas. Even before the Great Depression killed the innocence and benevolence of this Open Door concept by encouraging economic nationalism, it had been tainted by numerous military and economic interventions in Central America and other parts of the world.

After the 1930's, endless pursuit of economic expansion on the part of the United States could no longer be explained away as a spontaneous, inevitable development proving the superiority of capitalist free enterprise over all other economic systems. On the contrary, the Open (and Closed) Door has been accompanied, especially after World War II, by an increasingly complex series of economic incentives and agreements between government and business that ultimately became the military-industrial complex of the Cold War era. In turn this has resulted in political and military commitments between the United States and other nations, often based on ideological hostility to communism.

Once the indiscriminate exportation of capitalism and democracy by the United States began to meet serious ideological opposition from the communist bloc countries and developing nations in the post–World War II period, diplomatic historians divided over whether implicitly negative terminology, like the Open Door, should be applied to American foreign policy. Such an interpretation would mean running the risk that the United States might be charged with acting out of narrow economic self-interest in international affairs. So the problem now facing all diplomatic historians is how much emphasis to place on ideology and economics as they interpret past and present formulation of foreign policy and its impact on other nations.

HISTORICAL EVOLUTION OF AMERICAN ECONOMIC FOREIGN POLICY

Writers of American history in the nineteenth century and the first half of the twentieth century were not deeply divided over the relationship between domestic and foreign policies. The economic philosophies of the Founding Fathers were accepted as being integrated with their other ideas. It was generally agreed, given the republican origins of the United States, that the country would not act one way at home and another way abroad. Nevertheless, as a developing nation from 1776 through most of the nineteenth century, it was an accepted fact, according to historian Paul Varg, that "economic necessity narrowed the field of [foreign policy] decision making." Moreover, until the onset of the Cold War, historians felt little need to defend the viability of capitalism.

This confidence was prominently displayed in the pride that Americans took in themselves and their country's growth. As a result, from the pens of Benjamin Franklin, James Madison, Alexander Hamilton, Thomas Jefferson, John Quincy Adams, and from practically all of the presidents and secretaries of state following the Mexican and Civil wars came expressions of desire for an American continental and foreign empire. The Founding Fathers, in particular, were convinced that "a reciprocal relationship could be developed between [American] expansion and the . . . ideals of justice, political representation, and opportunity largely inherited from deeply revered pre-1750 Anglo-American law and religion." In other words, for much of its history the leaders and people of the United States believed that its domestic and foreign goals were perfectly compatible.

Consequently there was often more talk about expanding a democratic, free enterprise empire than actually took place. (It is also ironic to note how much of the continental expansion in the nineteenth century was the result of federal and state subsidies to transportation industries and the ruthless extermination or removal of native Americans.) Nonetheless, a future secretary of state like William Henry Seward could declare in 1850 without fear of serious rebuttal: ". . . there is not in the history of the Roman Empire an ambition for aggrandizement so marked as that which has characterized the American people." Yet his grand designs for an empire, like those of so many other proud, confident Americans, were not fully realized until the twentieth century.

In fact, it was not until World War I that the combination of nationalism, economic development, and international power transformed many earlier statements about an American empire into reality. Emerging from that war as the leading creditor nation of the world, the United States was, for the first time in its economic history, in a position to realize the most fantastic dreams of earlier expansionists. It was at that precise moment that expansionism assumed all the overtones of imperialism as previously defined.

Most important, beginning with World War I, the United States had to face the increasing threat of foreign ideologies: first, as represented by imperial Germany; then by Bolshevik Russia; and still later in the 1920's by nationalist revolutions in China and Latin America. These developments "literally forced Washington policy makers to formulate an ideological alternative based on the American brand of democracy and capitalism. . . . Therefore, in these two postwar conditions—hostile foreign ideologies and unprecedented economic opportunity—are found the dual foundations of modern American diplomacy."

But something happened to the United States in the process of formulating an ideology based on nineteenth-century ideals to fit twentieth-century realities. Its domestic and foreign policy goals began to diverge or at least not appear to be in perfect harmony. Where were the humanitarian ideals of justice, and political and economic opportunity in Latin America after a half century of American economic domination and in the authoritarian regimes that the United States found itself supporting after World War II? What had happened to the relationship between domestic and foreign affairs? Were they still supposedly mirror images of one another? Or had even that relationship changed?

Apparently so, if we are to take the words of Dean Acheson at their face value. In 1944 he said:

> If you wish to control the entire trade and income of the United States, which means the life of the people, you could probably fix it so that everything produced here would be consumed here, but that would completely change our Constitution, our relations to property, human liberty, our very conception of law . . . you find [instead] you must look to other markets and those markets are abroad [*Herbert Hoover: Forgotten Progressive* (1975), p. 262].

Later in 1969 Acheson reflected in his memoirs that for the United States to try to confine itself to the Western Hemisphere would change "the spacious freedom of American life" and would "undermine its cultural, moral, political, and constitutional bases."

It now appeared in the Cold War era that if the United States continued to base its economic foreign policy on the traditional principle of open-ended expansion at home and abroad, its political foreign policy would have to be increasingly supported by military and ideological intervention in world affairs. Such actions often contradicted previously proclaimed humanitarian goals. One alternative suggested by recently rehabilitated critics of the Cold War—cited in the works of Ronald Radosh, Thomas G. Paterson, Justus Doenecke,

Murray Rothbard, Leonard Liggio, and Joan Hoff Wilson—is the moderation and control of American economic expansion in the interests of domestic self-sufficiency and extensive political reform inside the United States. To do so would mean abandoning the goals of an ever-expanding economy and of self-appointed policeman for the world that the country had pursued in the course of the twentieth century.

Not all historians writing about Cold Warriors in the United States after World War II agree. Some still refuse to use the term "ideology" to describe Washington policy, although they will admit that "American leaders sincerely believed that opening channels of international trade would raise living standards throughout the world and lessen the danger of future wars." They will even talk about economic expansion, self-determination, collective security, and multilateralism without ever viewing them as components of an American Open Door ideology. For these diplomatic historians it is important to emphasize that the revival of postwar trade stemmed neither from "narrow considerations of economic self-interest," nor from fear that domestic institutions would collapse without it.

To date, the most controversial examples of this disagreement over how to interpret the economic foreign policy of the United States have occurred in works on the origins of the Cold War. In their most extreme forms they have been either "deludingly objective, ideologically chauvinistic, or economically reductionist." The most productive efforts by both orthodox and revisionist diplomatic historians in applying traditional, as well as socioeconomic and organizational, methodologies to arrive at a new synthesis for understanding the general thrust of American foreign policy since 1900 have been in studies about World War I and the 1920's.

Building on the writings of Joseph Brandes, N. Gordon Levin, Carl P. Parrini, Joseph S. Tulchin, and Joan Hoff Wilson, a new generation of historians has provided further insights into the question of whether the American political economy after 1920 required the creation of a new world economic order dominated by the United States. Unfortunately much of their research remains in the form of articles and unpublished doctoral dissertations. Melvin P. Leffler, Robert H. Van Meter, Michael J. Hogan, Burton I. Kaufman, Robert Neal Seidel, and Frank Costigliola are but a few of these historians whose work deserves high praise for not becoming bogged down in the futile debate between economic determinists and defenders of the establishment. They are, indeed, seriously and productively examining the "complex impact of ideological and economic motivation as it is affected by structural relationships and role playing within government agencies and business organizations," and as it applies to the concept of isolationism in the 1920's.

Interpretations about the economic foreign policy of the United States have evolved from those expressing confidence and integration with national humanitarian goals to those defending or criticizing its future viability and relationship to those goals. Ideology and economics remain essential elements in the formulation of foreign policy, as do domestic considerations. Equally true is that rationalizations about the complex nature of these relationships will remain a tendentious topic among diplomatic historians for some time to come.

BIBLIOGRAPHY

Frederick C. Adams, *Economic Diplomacy: The Export-Import Bank and American Foreign Policy, 1934–1939* (Columbia, Mo., 1976), presents detailed information on a subject not previously researched by historians.

Irvine H. Anderson, Jr., *The Standard-Vacuum Oil Company and United States East Asian Policy, 1933–1941* (Princeton, 1975), is one of the most recent studies to document the influence of a single company on the attitudes of government officials toward a major area of the world. Richard J. Barnet, *Roots of War: The Men and Institutions Behind U.S. Foreign Policy* (Baltimore, Md., 1973), synthesizes the role of economics, elite groups, and institutions in the formulation of foreign policy during the Cold War. Raymond Bauer, Ithiel de Sola Pool, and Lewis Anthony Dexter, *American Business and Public Policy: The Politics of Foreign Trade* (New York, 1963), contains a standard, pseudo-objective, entrepreneurial study of economic self-interest and its relation to the commercial diplomacy of the United States. Joseph Brandes, *Herbert Hoover and Economic Diplomacy* (Pittsburgh, 1962), is an important reevaluation of Hoover's economic foreign policy, though written before the opening of the Hoover papers. John C. Donovan, *The Cold Warriors: A Policy-Making Elite* (Lexington, Mass., 1974), provides a provocative sociological-historical portrait of the military-industrial bureaucrats who designed post–World War II diplomacy. Herbert Feis, *The Diplomacy of the Dollar, 1919–1932* (New York, 1966), remains an excellent brief summary of the economic foreign policy of the 1920's by a man who was a State Department adviser. John Lewis Gaddis, *The United States and the Origins of the Cold War, 1941–1947* (New York, 1972), is an ambiguous study of the role of economics and other factors in the determination of American foreign policy during and immediately following World War II. Lloyd C. Gardner, *Economic Aspects of New Deal Diplomacy* (Boston, 1971), is a pioneering, but disjointed and inadequately documented, revisionist study of foreign policy under the first two administrations of Franklin D. Roosevelt; and *Architects of Illusion: Men and Ideas in American Foreign Policy, 1941–1949* (Chicago, 1970), argues about American economic motivation based on domestic needs. Michael J. Hogan, *Informal Entente: The Private Structure of Cooperation in Anglo-American Diplomacy, 1918–1928* (Columbia, Mo., 1977), is a most-balanced account of economic relations between England and the United States.

Burton I. Kaufman, *Efficiency and Expansion: Foreign Trade Organization and the Wilson Administration, 1913–1921* (Westport, Conn., 1974), is a significant study of the growth of government bureaucracy in the area of economic foreign policy marred only by a tendency to exaggerate the influence of Prussian models on American organizational structure. Joyce and Gabriel Kolko, *The Limits of Power: The World and United States Foreign Policy, 1943–1945* (New York, 1972), is one of the most detailed revisionist accounts of American economic aims at the end of World War II. Gabriel Kolko, *The Roots of American Foreign Policy: An Analysis of Power and Purpose* (Boston, 1969), contains a polemical interpretation of economic dominance over diplomacy, including the United States Vietnamese policy. Bruce Kuklick, *American Policy and the Division of Germany: The Clash With Russia Over Reparations* (Ithaca, N.Y., 1972), offers the best analysis to date of "multilateralism" as the key to the economic origins of American-Soviet antagonisms in the mid-1940's. Walter LaFeber, *New Empire: An Interpretation of American Expansionism* (Ithaca, N.Y., 1963), is an early revisionist account of the ideas and forces behind American economic expansion in the last half of the nineteenth century. N. Gordon Levin, Jr., *Woodrow Wilson and World Politics: America's Response to War and Revolution* (New York, 1968), is the best interpretative account of Wilson's economic foreign policy. Dana G. Munro, *The United States and the Caribbean Republics, 1921–1930* (Princeton, 1974), presents a traditional defense of American economic and political expansion by a man who participated in the process. Carl P. Parrini, *Heir to Empire: U.S. Economic Diplomacy, 1916–1923* (Pittsburgh, 1969), is a revisionist study documenting the conflicting economic policies of the United States and the Allied powers during and immediately following World War I. Thomas G. Paterson, *Soviet-American Confrontation: Postwar Reconstruction and the Origins of the Cold War* (Baltimore, 1974), is a balanced account of the economic and political aspects of the early Cold War years. Bradford Perkins, " 'What's Good for the United States Is Good for the World, and Vice Versa': Reflections of a Diplomatic Historian," in *Society for Historians of American Foreign Relations (SHAFR) Newsletter* (March 1975), attempts to reconcile the basic differences between revisionist and orthodox diplomatic historians over the role played by economics in the formulation of American diplomacy. E. E. Schattschneider, *Politics, Pressures and the Tariff: A Study of Free Enterprise in Pressure Politics, as Shown in the 1929–1930 Revision of the Tariff* (New York, 1935), is a pioneering work on the influence of business on the commercial policy of the United States. Robert F. Smith, *The United States and Cuba: Business and Diplomacy, 1917–1960* (New York, 1960), is a highly critical account of American economic relations with Cuba; and *The United States and Revolutionary Nationalism in Mexico, 1916–1932* (Chicago, 1972), analyzes how American economic interests opposed national aspirations in Mexico. Dick Steward, *Trade and Hemisphere: The Good Neighbor Policy and Reciprocal Trade* (Columbia, Mo., 1975), gives a relatively sympathetic account of Cordell Hull's attempt to eliminate trade barriers with Latin America. Robert W. Tucker, *The Radical Left and American Foreign Policy* (Baltimore, 1971), is the most significant critique of New Left interpretations of the economic basis of American foreign policy to appear since the debate between revisionists and orthodox diplomatic historians began. Mira Wilkins, *The Emergence of Multinational Enterprise: American Business Abroad From the Colonial Era to 1914* (Cambridge, Mass., 1970) and *The Maturing of Multinational Enterprise: American Business Abroad From 1914 to 1970* (Cambridge, Mass., 1974), are two highly detailed and descriptive accounts of the growth of American business activity which avoid any systematic interpretative analysis of the impact of these multinational companies on United States foreign policy. William Appleman Williams, *The Tragedy of American Diplomacy* (New York, 1972), remains the most seminal and controversial of New Left interpretations of foreign policy. Benjamin H. Williams, *Economic Foreign Policy of the United States* (New York, 1929), is a much overlooked, but highly valuable, compilation of economic data about American diplomacy for the first quarter of the twentieth century. Joan Hoff Wilson, *American Business and Foreign Policy, 1920–1933* (Lexington, Ky., 1971), presents a middle-of-the-road account that attempts to demonstrate the extent to which business influenced major diplomatic decisions in the 1920's and early 1930's; and *Ideology and Economics: U.S. Relations With the Soviet Union, 1918–1933* (Columbia, Mo., 1974), constructs a structural-functional synthesis between the two opposing schools of diplomatic thought, and details the institutional and economic aspects of ideological opposition to recognition of the Soviet Union.

[*See also* DEBT COLLECTION; DOLLAR DIPLOMACY; FOREIGN AID; THE MARSHALL PLAN; THE MOST-FAVORED-NATION PRINCIPLE; THE OPEN DOOR POLICY; PHILANTHROPY; TRADE AND COMMERCE.]

THE EISENHOWER DOCTRINE

John A. DeNovo

ON 5 January 1957 President Dwight D. Eisenhower appeared before a joint session of Congress to request a new declaration relating to the Middle Eastern policy of the United States. After two months of sometimes acrimonious discussion, Congress approved a joint resolution giving the president most of what he wanted. Almost immediately the president's Middle Eastern proposal came to be known popularly as the Eisenhower Doctrine.

The resolution stated that the United States regarded "as vital to the national interest and world peace the preservation of the independence and integrity of the nations of the Middle East." It authorized the president to devise programs of economic and military cooperation and assistance with "any nation or group of nations in the general area of the Middle East desiring such assistance" in the interest of maintaining their independence. For this purpose the president could draw on $200 million previously appropriated by Congress to carry out the Military Security Act of 1954. The most controversial provision appeared at the end of Section 2 of the resolution. It stated that if the president deemed it necessary in connection with preserving the independence and integrity of these nations, he could, subject only to the treaty obligations and the Constitution of the United States, "use armed forces to assist any such nation or group of nations requesting assistance against armed aggression from any country controlled by international communism. . . ."

Ambiguities in both the intent and language of the resolution make it difficult to define the Eisenhower Doctrine precisely. The resolution did not delimit the Middle East or enumerate the nations constituting that region; neither did it define "international communism" nor provide criteria for determining when a country was "controlled" by international communism. There was no clarification of whether "armed aggression" might include a civil uprising if supplied and supported from outside a country. The vagueness appears to have been intentional on the part of the administration. With even Secretary of State John Foster Dulles describing the doctrine as "an attitude, a state of mind, a point of view," it is no wonder that various observers attached different connotations to it. This was the case while it was under discussion, when it was referred to during the crises of 1957 and 1958, and in subsequent commentaries of historians and publicists.

The narrowest construction finds the essence of the doctrine in the American commitment to use armed forces in the Middle East under certain conditions: first, a Middle Eastern nation or group of nations (presumably the Baghdad Pact) must be the victim of armed attack by a nation controlled by international communism; second, the victim must request American aid; and third, the response was to be at the discretion of the president, who would be limited only by treaty and constitutional obligations. A second and broader interpretation views the Eisenhower Doctrine as supporting a policy of economic and military assistance to receptive Middle Eastern nations striving to maintain their independence and sovereignty. The pledge to use American armed forces in case of overt military attack would provide a shield behind which nations could counter subversion or indirect aggression from within by strengthening their economies and defense forces.

If one understands the Eisenhower Doctrine as "only an outline of a policy," as Harry N.

Howard, a former State Department official and professor at American University, has described it, or, in Dulles' words, "a state of mind," a still broader construction follows. In this sense the United States was telegraphing a declaration of intent with the purpose of deterring the Soviet Union and its new Middle Eastern allies, Egypt and Syria, from engaging in military action or even in unacceptable indirect aggression, a concept left undefined. These three interpretations are obviously not mutually exclusive.

Like previous presidential dicta elevated to the status of "doctrines," such as James Monroe's of 1823 and Harry S. Truman's of 1947, the Eisenhower Doctrine grew out of a set of concrete circumstances at a particular time. Thus, the premises of Eisenhower, Dulles, and their supporters in Congress and among the public can be understood only against the background of the Cold War in the Middle East between the end of World War II and the Middle East war of 1956. During that decade the United States had already experimented with tools prescribed in the Eisenhower Doctrine: economic and military assistance programs, and pledges of military assistance to deter aggression.

Only since World War II has the United States ranked stability in the Middle East and balance among the major powers there as an important goal of its foreign policy. During the war the United States increased its presence in that area, while supplying its British and Soviet allies and holding back Axis penetration into the eastern Mediterranean and Persian Gulf regions. Immediately after the war, Anglo-American resistance to Soviet pressure on Turkey and Iran was a prominent feature of the developing Cold War. In 1945 the Soviet government had pressed the Turks to allow the Soviets to use naval facilities in the zone of the Turkish Straits and had also demanded cession of the Turkish provinces of Kars and Ardahan. With strong Western support, the Turks successfully resisted these Soviet demands. The first great postwar international crisis arose early in 1946 over the failure of the Soviet Union to remove its troops from northwestern Iran (Azerbaijan) within the six months following the end of the Japanese War, as required by treaties with Britain and Iran. By 1947, American officials erroneously perceived leftist elements in the Greek civil war to be under the firm direction of the Soviet Union, and, in connection with the campaign for the Greek-Turkish aid bill in the spring of 1947, the Truman administration articulated its doctrine of containment of the Soviet Union. Using such instruments as military and economic assistance and the embryonic Sixth Fleet, the United States asserted an unprecedented strategic stake in the eastern Mediterranean and its environs.

During this period Soviet pressure was confined chiefly to three northern tier nations of the Middle East—Iran, Turkey, and Greece. The concern of the United States, however, was expanding into the regions to the south, the Arab East, largely because of the clash between Zionism and Arab nationalism, with the United States supporting the Zionist program for Palestine. The outcome was the establishment of the state of Israel in 1948 and the first Arab-Israeli War of 1948–1949. To strengthen the fragile truce that emerged, the United States joined with Great Britain and France in issuing the Tripartite Declaration of May 1950, stating their intent to forestall an arms race that might threaten the territorial status quo.

Europe, however, remained the primary concern of the Truman administration during the late 1940's as it further articulated the concept of containment. Massive economic assistance was integrated into the containment strategy through the European Recovery Program (Marshall Plan), and the North Atlantic Treaty (1949) added a military dimension. Measured by the economic recovery of Western Europe and the expectations of greater security through collective action, containment seemed to be a success by 1951. The Truman administration then turned its efforts toward institutionalizing containment in the Middle East, where the British were also keenly interested in a regional defense pact. The two Western powers hoped to link the United States, the United Kingdom, France, Turkey, and the Arab states in a defensive system relying on Egyptian bases. Egypt, however, would have no part in the scheme, and the Arab states generally rejected being drawn into the Cold War to serve Western interests, which seemed antithetical to their own well-being. The archenemy of the Arab world was Israel, created and sustained by the very Western powers now soliciting Egypt's adherence to a Middle East Defense Organization (MEDO). Thus, MEDO had to be shelved, but it was not forgotten.

During a tour of the Middle East in 1953, shortly after joining the Eisenhower cabinet, Secretary Dulles again explored the idea of a regional defense organization. When the new leaders in Egypt, who had assumed power after the revolution of 1952, proved even more resistant, Dulles turned to an alternative plan based on the Middle Eastern countries closest to the Soviet Union geographically; their experiences had made them wary of their northern neighbor's intentions. The upshot was the formation in 1955 of the Baghdad Pact, consisting of Turkey, Iran, Iraq (the only Arab participant), Pakistan, and Great Britain. Dulles' conception of the northern tier barrier to Soviet expansion into the Arab East actually alienated most of the Arab world, which looked upon the venture as yet another attempt by the West to divide the Middle East for its own purposes. Egypt's Gamal Abdel Nasser regarded Iraq's adherence to the Baghdad Pact as a betrayal of pledges given by its prime minister, Nūrī as-Sa'īd.

The Soviet Union had not been particularly active in the Middle East during the early 1950's, but by the middle of the decade local conditions afforded new possibilities for jumping over the northern tier barrier and taking the part of Arab nations in their struggle against their twin anathemas, Zionism and Anglo-French colonialism. Now that ardent Arab nationalists associated the United States with Western colonialism, the Soviets saw further opportunities for the weakening of American influence.

Nasser provided the opening in 1955, when he turned to the Soviet bloc for arms unobtainable from the Western powers, which invoked the restrictions proclaimed in the Tripartite Declaration of 1950. Fears of Israeli expansion at Egypt's expense undoubtedly played a part in Nasser's plans. The barter agreement announced in September 1955, whereby Egypt would exchange Egyptian cotton for arms from Czechoslovakia, set in motion a sequence of events leading to the second Arab-Israeli War and the Anglo-French invasion of Egypt in late October and early November 1956. Massive pressure from the United States and the Soviet Union, working through the United Nations, forced the withdrawal from Egypt first of the British and French and subsequently the Israeli forces. The United States, however, received little credit from Nasser and his admirers in the Arab world for its role. Instead, the Soviet Union appeared to the Arabs as the savior and friend of their cause. Conditions were ripe for further extension of Soviet influence in the Arab East. For the Soviets, the temptation to extend their influence was irresistible as long as the risks were slight. Secretary Dulles' and President Eisenhower's belief that Soviet intentions were aggressive led to the president's request to Congress for the Middle East resolution early in 1957.

Hastily, without advance consultation with the National Security Council or its North Atlantic Treaty Organization allies, the Eisenhower administration sought a congressional resolution to buttress the president's conduct of foreign relations in the Middle East. The rationale for the proposed resolution was the hardened set of precepts formed during the first decade of the Cold War. The basic assumption was that Moscow was continuing to orchestrate a worldwide conspiracy to extend communist ideology and Soviet power wherever and whenever circumstances pemitted. According to that view, the Soviets were prepared to supplement their array of tactics for the subversion of weak nations with overt military attack whenever the price was not too high. Associated with this notion was a conception of the international balance of power that saw the strongest nations or combinations competing to extend their power and influence in weak areas considered to be power vacuums. If the United States was to make military aggression in these power vacuums too risky for the Soviet Union, it would have to strengthen the barrier to Soviet penetration, preferably with allies, but unilaterally if necessary. This was the doctrine of deterrence: forestalling prospective "aggressive" Soviet actions before they could occur. If the United States signaled in advance what Soviet action it would regard as intolerable, the warning would dissuade the Soviets from adventures based on miscalculations about probable responses by the United States. Proponents of this strategy could point to its putative success in deflecting Soviet moves against Iran and Turkey in 1946 and 1947, and mainland China's potential moves against Taiwan via Quemoy and Matsu in 1955.

Specifically, Eisenhower and Dulles believed by the end of 1956 that the capacity of Britain to maintain the power balance in the Middle East had been gravely compromised by the fiasco of the invasion of Egypt two months earlier. Under the circumstances, the Baghdad Pact could not alone play the deterrent role; Britain, though a member, was crippled, and the United States was not formally a member. Washington fretted over the anticipated economic decline forecast by the closing of the Suez Canal and the sabotage of pipelines in Syria, which diminished the flow of oil for Western Europe and revenues for Middle Eastern governments. The administration feared that the Soviets would be tempted to take advantage of these weaknesses by invading the Middle East. Already the Soviets were capitalizing on Egyptian and Syrian dependence by offering them additional arms and promising economic assistance and cultural exchanges. Contending that greater responsibility now devolved on the United States, the administration argued the urgent need for a dramatic show of solidarity and intention on the part of the president and Congress.

Such were the diagnoses and prescriptions of Eisenhower and Dulles when they met for four hours with congressional leaders of both parties on 1 January 1957. So that everybody would know that the United States was "fully determined to sustain Western rights in the region," it must fill "the existing vacuum" before the Soviet Union did. The president requested that at its impending session Congress should make its first business the authorization of a special economic fund and, if necessary, the use of American military forces. Some skeptical senators and representatives present anticipated the doubts that soon were to be expressed in Congress and the public forum regarding both the administration's assessment of the problem and its proposed remedy in the form of a special congressional resolution.

Four days later, President Eisenhower addressed a joint session of Congress to present his appeal. He asserted that the Soviet Union wanted to dominate the Middle East in order to weaken Western civilization. It would be intolerable to allow the Soviet Union to control the geographical crossroads of the world and the birthplace of three monotheistic religious traditions. The United States must, therefore, provide concrete evidence of its determination to strengthen the will and capacity of those in the Middle East who understood the menace of communism. Later that day, the administration's bill, designated House Joint Resolution 117, was introduced in Congress.

In his memoirs Eisenhower recalled that Congress "did not move as one man to endorse the administration's proposal. Far from it." Instead of the speedy action requested by Eisenhower, two months passed before Congress completed action on the resolution. Even though the House Foreign Affairs Committee reported out the administration's resolution without amendments on 26 January 1957, some members complained that Dulles had failed to establish the administration's contention that communist armed aggression was imminent. Nevertheless, the House passed the administration's version on 30 January by the lopsided margin of 355 to 61. The size of the affirmative vote probably did not signify conviction so much as it reflected a reluctance to deny a president the tools he deemed essential for carrying out his foreign policy.

The Senate was less pliable, and reservations were more evident. Some senators, doubting that the Middle East was as close to Soviet armed aggression as the administration contended, believed that the problems of the area were mainly of intraregional origin and only indirectly related to communism. They pointed out that the Arabs did not feel threatened by a communist menace; their enemies were Western colonialism and its offspring, the state of Israel. It seemed unlikely to many senators that the Soviets would consider overt military action. Why should they when they were having their way just by posing as the Arab's friend and capitalizing on the local resentment against Western nations? The real problem was the circumstances that allowed the Soviets to advance further even without engaging their armed forces. According to this dissenting view, the conditions that permitted Soviet subversion would have to be ameliorated.

Critics regarded the economic and military aid contemplated by the administration as a token, far too modest to induce the rapid improvements in living conditions required to lessen political tensions. They considered the proposed military and economic aid nothing more than bait to attract governments to fall into line with American plans for regional defense arrangements within the framework of the containment policy. The Eisenhower Doctrine could be construed as the administration's substitute for what had theretofore been unobtainable: a regional defense system encompassing both the northern tier nations and the Arab East.

Ultimately, the Senate made modest changes in the resolution to assuage some of the doubts expressed by its members. These alterations merely prescribed that the president should exercise his discretion with due respect for the treaty obligations and Constitution of the United States. This revised resolution then passed the Senate on 5 March by a vote of 72 to 19, and the House immediately accepted the Senate version. The president signed the bill into law four days later.

As Congress began to consider the proposed resolution, President Eisenhower on 7 January appointed James P. Richards, a South Carolina Democrat who had served as chairman of the House Foreign Affairs Committee, to be his special agent on a mission to the Middle East. Richards' task would be to explain the Eisenhower Doctrine to Middle Eastern leaders, ascertain which countries would participate, and work out the programs of economic and military assistance authorized by the resolution.

While Richards bided his time in Washington awaiting congressional action on the resolution, foreign reactions to the administration's proposal began to crystallize within a few days after the president's address to Congress. On 10 January Charles Malik, the foreign minister of Lebanon, hailed the doctrine, which both the Soviet Union and Communist China denounced a few days later. Meeting in Ankara, members of the Baghdad Pact on 21 January approved the Eisenhower approach. Caustic comments emanating from Cairo and Damascus asserted that it was Western imperialism and Zionism, not communism, that was producing the strife troubling the Middle East. There was general Arab resentment at the suggestion that there was a "power vacuum" in their region. At a Cairo meeting on 19 January, leaders from Egypt, Syria, Saudi Arabia, and Jordan proclaimed that they would never allow foreign spheres of influence in their region: Nationalism was the basis of Arab policy. Egypt shortly received new arms shipments from the Soviet bloc, while Syria accepted several motor torpedo boats and Soviet technicians.

Thus, before Richards could entice the Arab countries, the Eisenhower Doctrine had actually hardened the divisions within the Middle East. The northern tier regimes, leagued together in the Baghdad Pact, were the more enthusiastic, although in Iraq there were misgivings about the possible introduction of American troops into the area. Hemmed in by Syria and Israel, Lebanon applauded. Syria and Egypt, the critical areas in terms of Soviet penetration, drew more closely toward Moscow. King Saud of Saudi Arabia, no lover of communism, was caught in a peculiar position. Although he enjoyed strong ties with the United States, he was first and foremost an Arab and hoped to use his considerable prestige to conciliate discordant Arab factions. Initially, at the Cairo meeting of 19 January, he stood with the critics of the Eisenhower proposal, but upon his return in February from a successful state visit to the United States, he put in a cautious good word for the United States during another Cairo meeting with leaders from Egypt, Syria, and Jordan. They remained unconvinced.

Richards finally departed from Washington on 12 March with a small staff of experts from the State and Defense departments, the International Cooperation Administration, and the United States Information Agency. During the next two months he visited fifteen countries: Afghanistan, Ethiopia, Iran, Iraq, Lebanon, Libya, Pakistan, Saudi Arabia, Turkey, Greece, Yemen, Sudan, Israel, Tunisia, and Morocco. Notable by their absence from his itinerary were Egypt and Syria, where Soviet influence was deepest, and Jordan, where pro-Nasser Arab nationalism was strong. Richards negotiated agreements for economic and military assistance with nine countries (Iran, Turkey, Pakistan, Iraq, Afghanistan, Lebanon, Libya, Saudi Arabia, and Ethiopia). These agreements totaled approximately $119 million, slightly over half of which was for economic programs.

Somewhat misleading were both Richards' optimistic assessment, presented in a radio-television address on 9 May after his return, and the president's subsequent claim that thirteen of the fifteen nations visited had endorsed the purposes and objectives of the resolution. Responses varied, there being most approval for the economic aid and least for American readiness to engage its armed forces under certain conditions.

While Richards was still in the Middle East, a political crisis in Jordan came just short of testing American readiness to use its armed forces. Deep political divisions within Jordan threatened the government of young King Hussein. The incumbent cabinet represented the strongly pro-Nasser Palestinian element from the left bank of the Jordan, which approved of Soviet support for Egypt and Syria in behalf of the Arab cause. Hussein was alarmed by the pro-Soviet influence in his own civil service and armed forces, and charged that Egypt was supporting a communist plot to take over in Jordan. Prime Minister Suleiman Nabulsi had denounced the Eisenhower Doctrine, and when he announced on 3 April that Jordan would establish diplomatic relations with the Soviet Union, accept Soviet aid if offered, and reject American aid, the king decided to move against the leftist domination of the government.

Jordan's internal crisis was of serious concern to its immediate neighbors and to the large powers. If Jordan collapsed, there would probably be a grab for its territory involving military action that might not remain limited. While Hussein was engaged in the tricky business of forcing Nabulsi and his dissident generals out of the government and gambling, successfully it turned out, on support from Bedouin elements in the army, further encouragement came from President Eisenhower and Secretary Dulles. On 17 April 1957 Eisenhower stated that United States policy toward Jordan was governed by the Tripartite Declaration of 1950 and the Eisenhower Doctrine. A week later the president's declaration that Jordan's independence and integrity were vital to the United States seemed to invite Hussein to request military assistance under the doctrine. Even without such a formal request, the United States ordered the Sixth Fleet, including the carrier *Forrestal,* into the eastern Mediterranean and sent air reinforcements to bases in Turkey. The crisis suddenly broke when a pro-Royalist government was set up in Amman. Within a week, the United States announced a $10-million emergency grant to aid Jordan's economic development and political stability, and within the following two months an additional $20 million was forthcoming.

The Jordanian crisis of April 1957 did not put to the ultimate test that part of the doctrine that gave the president discretion to send armed forces into a Middle Eastern country. Jordan's problem was fundamentally a struggle for political control between internal factions. Certainly the elements believing in Nasser as the guiding force capable of uniting the Arabs drew support from Egypt and Syria, but neither Egypt nor Syria was "controlled" by "international communism." If Israel had occupied Jordan's west bank territory, the requirement of armed aggression would have been present, but Israel was obviously not controlled by "international communism." In any case, there was no armed invasion of Jordan, and Hussein did not publicly request American armed forces. In his first report to Congress (31 July 1957) Eisenhower conceded that "no action" had been required under the provision assigning him discretionary authority to employ American armed forces. Yet, under the broad construction of the doctrine as an instrument of deterrence, Eisenhower did claim that the resolution had served its purpose as a warning of consequences to would-be aggressors. Of course, the weakness in the president's argument was the unprovable assumption that a communist-supported armed attack on Jordan would have taken place had it not been for the deterrent of the doctrine.

A second major Middle Eastern crisis during the summer and fall of 1957, with Syria at its center, proved to be an equally indecisive test of the Eisenhower Doctrine. On 12 August, Syrian officials charged that they had uncovered an American plot to overthrow the government of Prime Minister Shukri Kuwatly. During the summer the government of Syria had completed a military agreement with the Soviets, which granted arms seemingly far beyond Syria's defense needs. Political and command changes agreeable to the Soviet Union soon followed. These developments alarmed Syria's immediate neighbors—Turkey, Iraq, Jordan, and Lebanon. In this acrimonious atmosphere, accusations and counteraccusations flew.

Since the Syrian government appeared to its neighbors to be slipping under Soviet domination, they wanted action before that process was completed. At this juncture, Lebanon asked the United States for support in the event of an attack by Syria. The United States did not favor military action unless Syria actually invaded, but Washington did take measures to reassure Syria's nervous neighbors by sending planes from Western Europe to Adana in Turkey, by ordering the Sixth Fleet into the eastern Mediterranean, and by alerting the Strategic Air Command. Loy Henderson, the experienced deputy under secretary of state, hurried to the Middle East on 22 August to confer with Turkish, Iraqi, Jordanian, and Lebanese leaders. Reporting after his return early in September, Henderson concurred in the apprehension of Syria's neighbors that the Soviet Union would topple their regimes by exploiting the crisis in Syria. To forestall the danger, the bordering countries talked of joint military action against Syria. Henderson advised, however, that intra-Arab rivalries precluded unified military action against Syria. By mid-September, all the Arab governments except Lebanon had backed away from the idea of collective action. Only the Turks remained determined, and they increased their forces on the Syrian border.

When Secretary Dulles summarized Henderson's findings in a statement on 7 September, he announced that the president had reaffirmed his intention to carry out the Eisenhower Doctrine. The United States was accelerating deliveries of economic and military items already programmed. At a press conference on 10 September, Dulles reiterated the three requirements prescribed in the congressional resolution: before United States armed forces could be used, the president had to find that a country was dominated by international communism; there must be an act of aggression; and the victim must request the intervention of American forces. According to Dulles, the administration had not yet determined that Syria was under the control of international communism, and the president would have to make that decision. Dulles thought the situation might become clearer in a week or so.

That same day, Soviet Foreign Minister Andrei Gromyko advanced the Soviet version, which charged Turkey and the United States with conniving in a plan to attack Syria. On 11 September, Premier Nikolai Bulganin warned Prime Minister Adnan Menderes of Turkey that the Soviet Union would attack Turkey if that country moved on Syria. The propaganda battle continued during the next six weeks. In an interview of 7 October with James Reston of the *New York Times,* Nikita Khrushchev menacingly referred to the imminence of flying rockets. A few days later, Dulles responded in kind with an assertion that Soviet territory would not be allowed to remain a "privileged sanctuary" for an attack on Turkey. When Syria pressed the United Nations General Assembly to take up its charges, American representative Henry Cabot Lodge reviewed the American version of the crisis.

Then, quite abruptly, the crisis dissipated. There was no coup against the Syrian government, no Soviet attack on Turkey, no engagement of United States forces. The popular conclusion among pro-Nasserites was that although a coup had been planned, it had not taken place because Soviet pressure had forced the United States to back down. The Eisenhower administration's interpretation claimed that the staunch position of the United States under the doctrine had deterred Soviet-inspired Syrian attacks against its neighbors.

In the wake of the crisis, Soviet prestige soared; so did Nasser's. And the Soviet presence in Syria remained strong, while the standing of the United States in the Arab world plummeted even lower. The crisis also hastened the political union between Egypt and Syria. The United Arab Republic was formed the following February, and the Arabs hoped it would be the first stage toward achieving their dream of an Arab federation. In his required semiannual report to Congress, which covered the period of the Syrian crisis, Eisenhower made no specific reference to the confrontation over Syria. While extolling the efficacy of the congressional resolution as a deterrent, he obliquely mentioned that the final provision in section 2, permitting him to dispatch armed forces, had not been invoked during the second half of 1957.

Lebanon became the focus for another episode in the Middle Eastern competition between the East and the West in 1958. President Camille Chamoun's maneuvers to extend his tenure, in contravention of the Lebanese constitution, sparked civil strife in that small country beginning in May. As Chamoun was losing support among his people, he turned to the United States for assistance under the Eisenhower Doctrine. Some intervention in domestic Lebanese affairs, which was not displeasing to the Soviets, was occurring both across the Syrian frontier and from Egypt. Thus, the internal dispute acquired an international dimension. Although Washington was uneasy, it did not originally think the situation called for the application of the Eisenhower Doctrine. On 20 May, Secretary Dulles told the press that it seemed unlikely there would be an armed attack from a country the United States would regard as subservient to international communism; but he also called attention to the provision in the resolution saying that the independence of Middle Eastern countries was vital to the United States: ". . . that is certainly a mandate to do something if we think that our peace and vital interests are endangered from any quarter." The United States supported Lebanon's complaint to the United Nations against "massive intervention" by the United Arab Republic, but the United Nations Observer Corps sent to investigate found little evidence for the charge. During a 1 July press conference, Dulles referred to the applicability of the United Nations Charter's Article 51 permitting "collective self-defense if an armed attack occurs. . . ." Dulles did not think the words "armed attack" precluded "treating as such an armed revolution which is fomented from abroad."

Just as the turmoil in Lebanon seemed to be coming under control, an unexpected development intervened. On 14 July a bloody revolution in Iraq overthrew the pro-Western government. The king and most of the royal family were murdered. Chamoun was convinced that the Iraqi revolution was part of a plot organized by Nasser and the Soviets and that it would next sweep over Lebanon. Washington and London, also caught off guard by the revolution, also feared that the Iraqi revolution was Soviet inspired. When Chamoun reiterated his request for American troops and Hussein sought British help for Jordan, the United States and Britain immediately decided to take no chances with the possibility of swift Soviet-Nasserite takeovers. On 15 July the United States began landing marines and army forces whose numbers eventually reached between 14,000 and 15,000 on the Lebanese beaches, while the British airlifted forces to bolster Hussein in Jordan.

Whether or not the decision to send troops was misguided, Eisenhower's main goal apparently was to ensure that Lebanon be able to select its president in accordance with its own constitutional procedures. The United States also believed its credibility required a demonstration that it had both the will and the power to carry out the broadest implications of the Eisenhower Doctrine. In late January, Dulles had told the Ankara meeting of the Baghdad Pact Council that American commitments for defense of the Middle East under the doctrine "were no less efficacious than membership in the pact itself."

With the Soviet Union exploiting the crisis for its propaganda value, the United Nations rescued the United States and Britain. An Egyptian resolution, supported by all the Arab states, called for withdrawal of foreign troops. On 18 August both the United States and Britain announced their intention to withdraw troops on request of the inviting governments. By 25 October, American forces had withdrawn as smoothly as they had arrived, and British forces were out of Jordan by 2 November.

Although the Lebanon landings have sometimes been called the one and only real test of the Eisenhower Doctrine, that contention seems unwarranted. Only a strained construction of the congressional resolution would have justified basing the dispatch of troops on that authority, for there had been no overt armed attack on Lebanon from a country controlled by "international communism." In fact, the administration only referred vaguely to the doctrine when justifying its course in Lebanon. In attempting to legitimize its action, the administration appealed mainly to provisions in the

United Nations Charter and to principles of international law. In messages of 15 July announcing the landings to Congress and to the American public, Eisenhower declared that American forces were being sent to protect 2,500 American lives and to assist Lebanon in preserving its integrity and independence, "which have been deemed vital to United States national interests and world peace." He referred to collective security for self-defense as an inherent right recognized by Article 51 of the United Nations Charter. Events in Lebanon "represent indirect aggression from without."

On balance, the United States probably lost more than it gained in the Arab East as a result of the Lebanese operation. Soviet advances of the previous three years remained unimpaired. The best that could be said was that Lebanon had not become a Soviet puppet, if indeed that had been a serious contingency. But Lebanon was definitely no longer in the Western camp. Its new premier, Rashīd Karāmī, dissociated himself from the Eisenhower Doctrine and proclaimed Lebanon to be a neutral state in the Cold War conflicts. After the revolution, Iraq repudiated the Baghdad Pact, not an unmixed loss in view of the contentions that had arisen because of Iraq's isolation from the mainstream of Arab nationalism. Egypt and Syria remained bitter over American hostility to Nasserism. As might have been expected, the Baghdad Pact nations (excluding Iraq) had immediately endorsed the American incursion into Lebanon, but Dulles' five-year effort to integrate the Arab nations into a regional defense structure had failed. Intraregional problems and tensions were no less serious than prior to the enunciation of the doctrine. Among the Arab states only weak Jordan, obviously a client-state, stood firmly with the United States. Saudi Arabia, though leaning toward the West, had been unwilling to compromise its standing in the Arab world by unqualified endorsement of Washington's policies.

Nonetheless, not even vehement castigators of United States imperialism could ignore certain restraints shown by the United States in its Lebanese operation: there had been no violence in connection with the American landings; there had been no subversion of Lebanese constitutional processes for selecting their new president; there had been no counterrevolutionary invasion of Iraq; and, instead of remaining, American forces had withdrawn with dispatch and without conditions. Even though the Eisenhower administration had not specifically invoked the doctrine, the Soviets had been unwilling to challenge American forces by engaging their own armed forces in behalf of their clients. Nasser and his supporters now had evidence that there were limits on the reliance they could place on Soviet aid to advance Arab aspirations.

The Eisenhower Doctrine was seldom mentioned after 1958 except in the periodic reports the president was required to make to Congress. Although the doctrine has not become enshrined among the national dogmas, it could conceivably someday experience the kind of revival the Monroe Doctrine has had. The Eisenhower Doctrine was overshadowed by Truman's, which a decade earlier had both expressed and set the tone for the emerging global foreign policy of the United States. The Monroe Doctrine, the distillation of the first half-century of American experience in foreign affairs, had contrasted two worlds—the republican Western Hemisphere versus monarchical Europe—and thereby reaffirmed official abstention by the United States from the politics of the European continent. The Truman Doctrine, while retaining the notion of two opposing systems, had broadened both the geographical and ideological scope. No longer was it just the Western Hemisphere against Europe. Now it was the forces of light, characterized as "the free world," juxtaposed against the forces of darkness embodied in "communism," which strove to move from its centers of power to engulf the whole world. This new formulation dictated not abstention from European politics, but involvement. The Eisenhower Doctrine was essentially a regional application of Truman's rhetorical proclamation of the obligation of the United States to assist countries struggling to preserve their independence.

Whether the Eisenhower Doctrine proves to be a durable feature of American foreign policy, it is significant for the issues that were raised as it was introduced, debated, and applied (or misapplied) to the Middle Eastern crises of 1957 and 1958. There were, for example, the constitutional implications of the doctrine. Strong American presidents since Theodore Roosevelt have arrogated to the office vast power in the conduct of foreign relations. In a dangerous era of rapid communication and frightening military technology, Congress found it increasingly difficult to deny the chief executive wide latitude to defend national interests around the world. More often than not, Congress has gone along with the president. Although some members of Congress grumbled when Eisenhower sought a blank check to act in the Middle East, the Senate's changes in the resolution imposed merely modest restrictions. As the crises of 1957 and 1958 demonstrated once again, presidential decisions could still lead the nation close to a state of war without specific congressional approval. The issue was not new, of course, and it would continue to bedevil American politics. There was the usual partisan aspect in the debate over the respective authority of Congress and the president. Like Truman, Eisenhower could count on considerable bipartisan support, but both presidents found criticism strongest among the opposition party. Thus, Senate Democrats raised more questions about Eisenhower's proposal than did Republicans.

The controversies surrounding the Eisenhower Doctrine also reveal the prevailing American ideas about international politics in the 1950's and the proper relationship of the United States to the rest of the world. Most Americans rejected the pre–World War II tradition of political "isolationism" and accepted the Eisenhower-Dulles assessment of international politics. They were heirs of the so-called Munich syndrome, which exerted such a powerful influence on the perceptions and actions of Western statesmen after World War II. From the aggressions of Hitler, Mussolini, and the Japanese in the 1930's they had learned "the lessons" of recent history. If the bell tolled for one nation overrun by an authoritarian system, the knell was a warning of other victims to follow. This was an early version of what later came to be called the domino theory, and the Eisenhower-Dulles reaction, like Truman's, was to be ready to counter power with power. Given the weakened condition of the Western allies of the United States, it fell to the strong, wealthy, and determined United States to fill the breach. The cause of the United States was still the cause of mankind. Supporters of the Eisenhower Doctrine believed they were serving these larger interests.

The conviction that the power of the United States would be used for good causes was another facet of the ingrained American national self-image, and this was part of the administration's rationale for the doctrine. Spokesmen emphasized certain strains in the national tradition bearing on the proper role of the United States in the world. Thus, American policy in the Middle East, as they saw it, was anti-imperialist, dedicated to upholding the principle of national self-determination and the rights of small nations: it was committed to constitutional government and individual rights, including property rights. A few Americans were troubled, for they knew that the American record had not always matched its reiterated rhetorical pledges in support of these benign principles. The opponents of the Eisenhower Doctrine in the Middle East and the Soviet Union, quick to seize on these contradictions between American theory and practice, were at least as hyperbolic in their criticism as were its Washington supporters in their defense.

BIBLIOGRAPHY

D. Eisenhower, *The White House Years: Waging Peace, 1956–1961* (Garden City, N.Y., 1965); Alexander L. George and Richard Smoke, *Deterrence in American Foreign Policy: Theory and Practice* (New York, 1974); Townsend Hoopes, *The Devil and John Foster Dulles* (Boston, 1973); Harry N. Howard, "The Regional Pacts and the Eisenhower Doctrine," in Parker T. Hart, ed., *The Annals of the American Academy of Political and Social Science,* 401 (1972); Richard H. Nolte, "United States Policy in the Middle East," in Georgiana G. Stevens, ed., *The United States and the Middle East* (Englewood Cliffs, N.J., 1964); Richard P. Stebbins *et al.,* eds., *The United States in World Affairs,* volumes for 1957, 1958, and 1959 (New York, 1958–1960); Robert W. Stookey, *America and the Arab States: An Uneasy Encounter* (New York, 1975); U.S. Department of State, *United States Policy in the Middle East, September 1956–June 1957: Documents* (Washington, D.C., 1957); *American Foreign Policy: Current Documents, 1957* (Washington, D.C., 1961); U.S. House of Representatives, *Economic and Military Cooperation With Nations in the General Area of the Middle East,* Hearings Before the Committee on Foreign Affairs, 85th Cong., 1st sess., Jan. 1957 (Washington, D.C., 1957); U.S. Senate, Foreign Relations Committee, *The President's Proposal on the Middle East,* Hearings Before the Senate Committee on Foreign Relations and the Committee on Armed Forces, 85th Cong., 1st sess., Jan.–Feb., 1957 (Washington, D.C., 1957); and Paul E. Zinner *et al.,* eds., *Documents on American Foreign Relations,* volumes for 1957, 1958, and 1960 (New York, 1958–1961).

[*See also* The Cold War; Congress and Foreign Policy; Containment; Intervention and Nonintervention; Presidential Power in Foreign Affairs.]

ELITISM AND FOREIGN POLICY

Richard S. Kirkendall

A THEORY of wide-ranging importance in historical and political thought, elitism as applied to foreign policy seeks to explain how that policy is made. According to elitist theory, the explanation is found in the machinations of a small group. The theory has appeared frequently during the past sixty years in public debate and in historical writing. Versions of it have been especially prominent in periods of intense concern over foreign affairs and have customarily been championed by critics of reigning policies or of policies that appeared to be moving to the top. Most of the theorists have viewed policy from the Left, although not all have done so. Many have stressed the power and influence of business groups, but they have not been seen as the only members of the "power elite."

Although always present in some form, elitism emerged as a recognizable and clearly defined part of Western political thought late in the nineteenth century and early in the twentieth. The leading contributors were Gaetano Mosca, Vilfredo Pareto, and Roberto Michels. They attacked classical democratic theory and also Aristotle and Karl Marx. Majority rule, they insisted, is impossible. Every society is divided into those who rule and those who are ruled, and the rulers constitute only a small minority of any society. Aristotle's classification, which divided political systems into three types (rule by one, rule by the few, and rule by the many), does not fit reality, for no man is capable of ruling by himself and the many also lack the capacity to govern. And Marx, with his emphasis upon class struggle, which in the end, after the victory of the working class, leads to social harmony in a classless society, was also wrong. History features a struggle among elites; the struggle will never end, and a classless society will never be created. Also, to the pioneers in the development of elitist theory, Marx placed too much emphasis on economics, not enough on politics.

Classical elitist theory did not maintain merely that the active, identifiable people in a society make the decisions. The theory went beyond that to insist that the majority exerts little or no influence on the governing process. Even in societies with elections and other democratic mechanisms, the ruling minority functions largely free of control by the masses of people.

A version of elitism became prominent in American thinking about foreign policy during World War I. To be sure, elitist theories had already been expressed occasionally in foreign policy discussions, especially in the debate over imperialism in the late nineteenth century and early twentieth century. A few critics of imperialistic schemes, including socialists such as Daniel De Leon and Eugene V. Debs and reformers like William Jennings Bryan, blamed the phenomenon on "the greed of the commercial and money-making classes," "the trusts and the money power . . . crying out for new fields to exploit," and "the desires of the syndicates to extend their commerce by conquest." Most anti-imperialist leaders at the time could not endorse such a radical view, but an English theorist, John A. Hobson, supplied an elaborate version of it in *Imperialism* (1902), arguing that the capitalist drive for greater profits than were available at home and for security for investments explained imperialism. He concluded that it was "the endeavor of the great controllers of industry to broaden the channel for the flow of their surplus wealth by seeking foreign markets and foreign investments to take off the goods and capital they cannot sell or use at home." Ernest R. May has suggested that some Americans "already disillusioned by the Philippine war and concerned about the growing power of trusts probably found Hobson's arguments especially attractive."

Thus, a few individuals employed elitist theories in efforts to explain the change taking place in the nation's relations with other parts of the world, but the theories gained greater prominence after 1914 as the United States became more heavily involved in European affairs. A sharp departure from past relations between the United States and Europe, American intervention in the European war demanded an explanation. Men of the Left, much opposed to what was happening, supplied an explanation that stressed the influence of an economic elite. This theory was called upon to explain the pressure for military preparedness and for American intervention, the decision to intervene, and the effort to bring the United States into the League of Nations. The theory was expounded by Progressives such as Senators Robert M. La Follette of Wisconsin, George W. Norris of Nebraska, William E. Borah of Idaho, and Hiram W. Johnson of California; by socialists, including Debs, Victor L. Berger, and Scott Nearing; by men even further left, such as William D. "Big Bill" Haywood of the International Workers of the World, and by spokesmen for the Non-Partisan League and other radical groups.

The theory blamed a small group of economic men for the sudden emergence of a very ambitious American foreign policy. It seemed to be a capitalist plot. Particular individuals, such as J. P. Morgan, the Rockefellers, and the Du Ponts, were singled out for attack; defined groups, especially the international bankers and the munitions makers or Wall Street, became targets of attack. According to the theory, they were dominated by economic interests, which led them to demand a large role for the United States in world affairs, including fighting in a bloody European war.

This interpretation of history with its emphasis on economics resembled Marx more than Mosca, Pareto, and Michels. Also unlike those European theorists, the Americans did not regard elite domination as inevitable. The "interests" had dominated in this episode, at least until the defeat of the League; the "people," according to the critics, had opposed intervention in the war for it meant suffering rather than profit for them. Yet, they could and should control foreign policy. La Follette, Debs, and other foes of the course of American history at this juncture attempted to alert the people to what was actually taking place in an episode that Wilson insisted was designed to make the world safe for democracy and to abolish war from human affairs. The men on the Left tried to inspire the majority to play its proper role and destroy the power of the elite. They assumed that the people could become people of power.

This elitist theory was not the dominant American interpretation in the period, but it, or variants of it, gained adherents as time passed. Several historians in the 1920's, who were participants in a revisionist movement that challenged official explanations of the war and of American intervention, criticized intervention. The leading American revisionists of the decade—John Kenneth Turner, Harry Elmer Barnes, Frederick Bausman, and C. Hartley Grattan—pictured Wall Street and "Big Business" as very influential and suggested that capitalism should be abolished or at least reformed so that the nation could stay out of future wars. Yet, these historians did not emphasize economic factors alone or only economic groups. They found noneconomic forces at work, especially British propaganda, a pro-British bias, and Wilsonian idealism, and they gave considerable weight to the activities of political men, above all President Wilson and his ambassador to Great Britain, Walter Hines Page. In other words, the theory propounded by these writers stressed the role of a small group of political men and also a small group of economic men. The people were not responsible; they, in fact, had been deceived by Wilson and others.

World War I revisionism became prominent in the 1930's as many Americans grew alarmed once again about the course that American foreign policy might take. Economics and economic elites received much attention from historians writing in the midst of the Great Depression. Barnes, Grattan, and Charles A. Beard, who emerged as the leading revisionist in the mid-1930's, stressed the influence of bankers and munitions makers in the decision to go to war in 1917. Blaming American commercial interests, Beard saw them as the interests of the few and not of the country as a whole, and he hoped to avoid economic entanglements that would lead the nation into new wars and divert it, as he saw things, from pursuit of the real national interest: reform at home.

Elitism implied that men, not impersonal forces, make history; but Grattan, now more radical than he had been in the 1920's, blamed the system—capitalism, rather than the people at the top—for American intervention in 1917. The bankers, Wilson, and everyone else involved had acted properly. They had behaved in accord with the logic of capitalism; the result was war.

These historians were not engaged in academic exercises. They were passionately involved in contemporary public affairs and, using history as a weapon, hoped to persuade the American people to avoid involvement in world affairs that could lead to war. Their work was a significant part of the revival of isolationism in the 1930's.

Elitist theories figured prominently in the thinking about foreign policy of politicians, journalists, and the public. Many people viewed ambitious foreign policies as products of business influence upon the policymakers, and explained American participation in World War I as a consequence of the behind-the-scenes activities of international bankers, such as the House of Morgan, and munitions makers, the "merchants of death." Eager for the profits of war, they willingly accepted the sacrifices that it meant for others. A Senate investigating committee, headed by North Dakota Republican Gerald P. Nye and composed mainly of isolationists, publicized this historical interpretation. The Neutrality Acts of 1935, 1936, and 1937, the major illustrations of isolationist strength at the time, were designed to keep the United States out of future wars by placing restrictions on three dangerous parts of the American elite: munitions makers, international bankers, and presidents of the nation.

A proposed constitutional amendment that came to the fore in 1937–1938 also expressed elitist theory. Sponsored by Congressman Louis Ludlow of Indiana, the amendment would require a popular referendum before Congress could declare war. The proposal assumed that only small groups would press for American intervention in foreign wars. The people would not. Although the proposal gained support, it never came to a final vote in the House.

As elitist theories began to influence policy, two revisionists grew unhappy with them. Walter Millis argued that the American people, rather than their leaders, had made the war of 1917–1918; and Beard challenged the emphasis upon bankers and munitions makers involved in conspiracies with political leaders. Beard argued that the people as a whole had become dependent on purchases by the Allied powers; the people had developed an economic interest in the Allied cause by 1917, and that explained American intervention. Still regarding it as a mistake, he now insisted that intervention had merely delayed facing an inevitable domestic crisis, a crisis that had come in 1929. He continued to fear the influence of bankers and politicians, but he also feared farmers and other large groups with an interest in foreign trade. Thus, Beard called for a sharp reduction in dependence on such trade so as to avoid involvement in undesirable wars. Determined to stay out of war, he would scrap the capitalist system if necessary.

This emphasis upon the people was only a stage in a move toward emphasis on political men, but before Beard made that move, a major contribution came from another historian, Charles C. Tansill. The work of Beard, Barnes, Grattan, and other revisionists was affected by their interest in reform or even revolution at home; Tansill's was not. He was dominated by concern about American relations with Great Britain and by an anti-British point of view. He rejected the emphasis upon business leaders and their economic interests in explanations of American behavior, and he stressed instead the political leaders—Wilson, Edward M. House, and Robert Lansing—and their pro-British bias.

By the time Tansill made his contribution, war was raging in China and approaching rapidly in Europe, and fear of American involvement was mounting inside the United States. As the nation intervened economically following the outbreak of war in Europe, some isolationists blamed international bankers and munitions makers for the growing sentiment for American involvement. Scott Nearing stressed the role of a ruling class in the shaping of foreign policy and portrayed Roosevelt, like Wilson before him, as a spokesman for that class; and Barnes called attention to the work of economic as well as political leaders. Isolationists, however, gave even greater attention to noneconomic factors than they had in the mid-1930's. Many, including Tansill and Grattan, emphasized political rather than economic motives and the dangers of presidential, not economic, power. According to this version, Roosevelt was leading the American people into war in order to maintain and enlarge his power and conceal his failures at home.

Beard was a leading proponent of this interpretation in the months before the Japanese attack on Pearl Harbor. Before the 1930's, in his explanations of American foreign policies, he had emphasized forces outside the United States. Now, however, he stressed domestic forces, and the one given greatest attention was not an impersonal force and was not a small economic group, such as the commercial interests he had stressed only a few years earlier. He focused instead on the central figure in the political elite, Franklin D. Roosevelt.

Soon after the war Beard developed this interpretation more fully. Bankers and munitions makers no longer appeared in his pages as the movers and shakers. Instead, Roosevelt was portrayed as the man of power who had deceived the American people, promising them peace while leading them into war. He had provoked the Japanese into an attack in order to get the war he desired.

Beard's work on World War II, which was the last work of his life, marked the beginning of a new revisionist movement, though not one that gained the strength of revisionism in the 1930's. Leading contributions were made by Tansill, who focused attention on Roosevelt, and by Paul W. Schroeder, who portrayed Secretary of State Cordell Hull as a key figure but also gave more weight to public opinion than most revisionists had. Like the earlier writers, these historians sought to explain moves that seemed to be serious errors and found the explanation at home, not in events abroad.

These historians did not emphasize economics. The influence of the economic interpretation fell off during the 1940's and 1950's. It still had a few adherents, including Henry A. Wallace in the 1948 presidential campaign; and Wallace, Roosevelt's vice-president from 1941 to 1945, used the elitist version of the interpretation and added a group—the military chiefs—that had not been stressed before. As the candidate of the new Progressive party, he waged an unusually strenuous and hard-hitting campaign that focused on foreign policy and charged that Truman's containment policy was a creature of Wall Street and the military, was imperialistic, and was leading to atomic war. Echoing Beard and other revisionists of the 1930's, Wallace maintained that reform at home depended on peace in the world, and that the groups opposed to reform—big business and the big brass—also promoted international conflict. Their power had to be destroyed so that policies could be changed. Little more than a decade earlier, a similar theory had been the basis of the Neutrality Acts. Now, Wallace received only slightly more than 1,150,000 votes, about 2.5 percent of the total in a "low turnout" election.

A noneconomic form of elitist theory made much more sense to many people in the late 1940's and early 1950's. This theory was propagated by Senator Joseph R. McCarthy of Wisconsin, among many others. Speaking for Americans who were very unhappy with many developments in international affairs, McCarthy supplied a conspiracy theory to explain recent history. His version of what had been happening ignored encouraging developments, such as the recovery of Western Europe and the frustration of communist parties there, and instead focused attention on discouraging events, such as Russian domination of Eastern Europe, the communist victory in China, and the Korean War. His explanation pinned the blame on disloyal men in the Democratic administrations, especially in the State Department, not on complex forces. He suggested that this was the only way to explain the frustration of a superior people who had always succeeded in the past. "How can we account for our present situation unless we believe that men high in the government are concerting to deliver us to disaster?" McCarthy asked. "This must be the product of a great conspiracy on a scale so immense as to dwarf any previous venture in the history of man." "The reason why we find ourselves in a position of impotency is . . . the traitorous actions of those who have been treated so well by this nation." He proclaimed: "It has not been the less fortunate or members of the minority groups who have been selling this Nation out but rather those who have had all the benefits the wealthiest nation has had to offer. . . ." Here was a simple explanation for discouraging events, which suggested that problems could be solved without great expenditures. Expressing what some have called "the illusion of American omnipotence," McCarthy suggested that solutions would follow once traitors had been removed from office and replaced by true Americans.

The theories of McCarthy, Wallace, and Beard had little impact on historians and political scientists in the 1940's and 1950's. They tended to view American policies, such as entry into World War II and containment, as necessary and valuable. "We have only to contrast this action with the shilly-shallying of American policy toward the Manchurian invasion of 20 years ago, or toward Mussolini's attack on Ethiopia, to appreciate the extent to which Truman had learned the lessons of history," Henry Steele Commager exclaimed shortly after the United States intervened in Korea; and many of this historian's colleagues agreed.

In their explanations of American actions, professional students of American foreign policy in the period stressed external forces, such as German, Japanese, and Russian aggression, yet they did not deny the existence and importance of elites. These scholars did not, however, take a consistently negative view of these groups, and they did not emphasize the role of economic men. They stressed ideas and political motives, and they insisted that many elites, not just one or a very small number, participated significantly in the policymaking process. Pluralism, a theory developed in postwar years by David B. Truman, V. O. Key, Earl Latham, and Robert A. Dahl, became very prominent. The pluralists argued that American society was divided into many groups; that power was distributed among them, although some had more than others; and that the groups competed with one another in the political arena. Only a few members of each group participated actively in politics, but the behavior of those who did was affected significantly by the others. The former at least tried to anticipate how the latter would react to their moves.

Public opinion occupied an important place in the theorizing of these years. To many scholars it seemed to be a force of substantial importance that had to be taken into account by both statesmen and historians. Thomas A. Bailey, a prominent historian who was especially important in this area of diplomatic history, published pioneering work that portrayed public opinion as the most powerful force and one that often exerted an undesirable influence. The so-called "Realists" (George F. Kennan, Hans Morgenthau, and Walter Lippmann), a group with great influence on academic thought, were deeply troubled about the power of public opinion, viewing it as an important source of unrealistic or moralistic, legalistic, and utopian behavior. Regarding foreign policy as enormously important, these writers believed that a well-educated and experienced elite should play the key role in the shaping of policy. The task of reconciling the requirements of democracy and the needs of foreign policy seemed very difficult, if not impossible, to many scholars and commentators. Public opinion seemed to threaten the development of sound policy.

Many of the leading theorists of the postwar years agreed with Beard and Tansill that one man, the president, deserved special attention, but these theorists tended to view the presidents, especially Roosevelt and Truman, quite favorably. Success seemed to depend upon presidential action, and scholars frequently published treatises exalting the president and criticizing the impact of public and congressional views. "The source of an effective foreign policy under our system is presidential power," Senator J. William Fulbright wrote early in the 1960's, reflecting two decades of thought and scholarship. "I think that we must contemplate the further enhancement of Presidential authority in foreign affairs," he added. "The prospect is a disagreeable and perhaps a dangerous one, but the alternative is immobility and the paralysis of national policy in a revolutionary world, which can only lead to consequences immeasurably more disagreeable and dangerous."

ELITISM AND FOREIGN POLICY

At the end of his second term and under fire for what seemed to his critics to be an inadequate defense policy, President Dwight D. Eisenhower called attention to an elite that he regarded as potentially very dangerous. He labeled the group the "military-industrial complex." "This conjunction of an immense military establishment and a large arms industry is new in the American experience," Eisenhower explained. "The total influence—economic, political, even spiritual—is felt in every city, every statehouse, every office of the Federal Government." And he went on to warn against "the acquisition of an unwarranted influence . . . by the . . . complex. . . ."

Although this elite seemed to be very dangerous, Eisenhower did not advocate its destruction. He believed that if its proposals for a vast expansion of military spending were accepted, the American economy would be severely damaged. Yet, he assumed that the United States needed the group, and he also assumed that it could be controlled. His message was part of his effort to limit its influence.

Before the end of the 1960's, Eisenhower's concept, a contribution of a conservative man, had become important in liberal thought. It helped liberals understand how containment, a policy that they had favored, had led to disaster in Vietnam. For example, Republican Senator Thruston B. Morton of Kentucky charged that President Lyndon B. Johnson had been "brainwashed" by the "military-industrial complex" into believing that the United States could achieve military victory in Southeast Asia. To many liberals it seemed that the complex had become too powerful and a major source of the nation's difficulties. They stressed its costs and its power. According to Democratic Senator William Proxmire of Wisconsin, "there is today an unwarranted influence by the military-industrial complex resulting in excessive costs, burgeoning military budgets, and scandalous performances," and John Kenneth Galbraith argued that the main goal of American politics must be *"to get the military power under firm political control."*

It seemed that the military-industrial complex had become a threat to the nation, rather than its defender. The power group prevented the United States from facing and solving its most serious problems. The liberal arguments often resembled the conservative philosophy of the Truman-Eisenhower years, with its emphasis on the economic dangers of government spending and the importance of economic strength for national security, but they had a liberal twist. They stressed the need to divert spending to domestic programs. Maintaining that foreign and military policies had been given top priority for three decades, the liberals called for change because the commitments abroad were both generating problems at home, such as inflation, and hampering efforts to grapple with domestic difficulties. Charles Beard and Henry Wallace would have found much to endorse in such arguments.

Coupled with the attack upon the military-industrial complex was liberal disenchantment with the presidency. The prominent historian, liberal publicist, and political adviser Arthur M. Schlesinger, Jr., provides a major illustration. Once he had championed presidential power, but in the 1970's he launched an attack upon what he called the "imperial presidency." He contrasted this type with the constitutional presidency, which shared the making of major decisions, such as the decision for war, with other institutions, above all Congress; he defined the imperial president as one who monopolizes the power to carry the country into war, and he called for a sharing of decision-making power by Congress and the presidency. Again, Beard could have applauded the new liberalism.

By the time Schlesinger wrote, a much more thoroughgoing critique of American policy and its sources had emerged, and this critique also included an emphasis on the workings of an elite, although not quite the same one that the liberals defined. The radical critique had debts to two intellectuals who had come into prominence, at least in their own circles, in the 1950's. One was the sociologist C. Wright Mills, who challenged pluralist theory from the Left, from a point of view that owed much to Marx as well as to Mosca and Pareto, but denied that political power is based only on property ownership and that the masses can make history. Mills maintained that American life was dominated by a "power elite" composed chiefly of the leaders of the three major sets of institutions—the federal government, the military, and the corporations. He did not deny that there were many other groups with power in some issue areas. What he did insist was that the groups he emphasized, which were interlocked and harmonious, made the major decisions, including the most important ones in foreign affairs.

The historian William A. Williams exerted an even larger influence on radical thinking about foreign policy. In a series of publications beginning in the 1950's, Williams argued that American foreign policy since the late nineteenth century had been imperialistic; that the explanation was the ideas that American economic and political leaders shared about the needs of capitalism; that the aim was not the control of territory but domination of markets, raw materials, and opportunities for investment; and that the result was conflict with other nations, including Russia, and with revolutionary movements. Far removed from realism, Williams' thought resembled Beard's of the 1930's, including the suggestion that overseas expansion involved efforts to avoid making major changes at home, changes that were needed and that, if made, would enable the nation to free itself from overseas entanglements.

Elitist theory constituted one of the important links between Mills and Williams, and a significant number of scholars, in varying degrees of explicitness, called upon it to help them explain the development of American foreign policy. The writers included Victor Perlo, G. William Domhoff, Richard J. Barnet, John C. Donovan, Walter LaFeber, Thomas J. McCormick, Carl P. Parrini, Robert F. Smith, Lloyd C. Gardner, Gar Alperovitz, David Horowitz, Athan Theoharis, Barton J. Bernstein, Thomas G. Paterson, Gabriel Kolko, and Stephen E. Ambrose. Many of them had studied at the University of Wisconsin with Williams and his mentor, Fred Harvey Harrington, and were recognized as the Wisconsin school of diplomatic history. Most of them were part of a New Left that became prominent in American intellectual life in the second half of the 1960's.

These new revisionists did not give equal attention to all parts of Mills's power elite. They emphasized the corporate leaders and gave considerable attention to political men. Some of these writers gave more weight to political men, especially presidents, and their personal characteristics, than others did. For example, the change from Roosevelt to Truman seemed much more important to Alperovitz or to Theoharis than it did to Kolko or Gardner. Some interpretations pictured a politician like Truman as largely an agent or servant of the ruling elite. "It was no accident . . . that a politician of his kind became President," Bert Cochran wrote in *Harry Truman and the Crisis Presidency* (1973), a study drawing heavily on revisionist scholarship. "Where the business elite was looking for reliability, not greatness, the political system was weighted to favor the middle-of-the-road trimmer." And some, above all Kolko, challenged theories of the great importance of the military chiefs. In the New Left view the military was clearly subordinate to corporate executives and other men at the top.

New Left revisionism recognized differences and conflicts among members of the power elite but often interpreted them as differences and conflicts over tactics only. For example, the split on the League of Nations was, Parrini argued, merely a conflict over means, not ends. Truman did break with Roosevelt's policy for Eastern Europe, Bernstein maintained, but the change was only a shift in tactics.

The elite were united by their relationship with American capitalism. The emphasis upon a casual link between American capitalism and modern American foreign policy was the fundamental and distinctive characteristic of New Left revisionism. Some of these scholars argued that the needs of an enormously productive capitalism actually dictated a policy of global imperialism; other revisionists maintained that the leaders merely believed that they must be imperialistic to serve and protect capitalism. All revisionists agreed, however, that somehow American foreign policy was rooted in American capitalism. For example, this meant that while many other scholars emphasized Soviet aggression and threats of it, the New Left stressed the dynamics of American capitalism in their explanations of the Cold War.

New Left historiography also attacked theories that suggested that public and congressional opinion exerted a large influence on foreign policy. The revisionists saw the elites as quite free to use American power as they wished. In this area, the research of Theoharis and Richard Freeland and the theorizing of

Bernstein were very important. Challenging the view that the Truman administration was largely an innocent victim of McCarthyism, Theoharis and Freeland argued that the rhetoric used by Truman and his aides to build support for their policies was heavily responsible for the emergence of strong, militant, and irrational anticommunism that in the end created serious problems for the administration. More traditional scholars seemed to Bernstein and others to give too much weight to public opinion and not nearly enough to the ability of leaders in the American system to change and manipulate it. Some revisionists maintained that the people were easily manipulated because they too had come to believe that the United States must expand into other parts of the world. Thus, all the leaders had to do was to persuade the people to endorse the use of particular tactics. There was little debate of basic issues, especially in the first twenty years after World War II.

Like the revisionists of the 1930's, this revisionism was not confined to academic quarters. The scholars who contributed to it hoped to promote fundamental changes in the United States and its policies; and their arguments, and arguments that resembled theirs, figured prominently in the public debates of the late 1960's and early 1970's. A New Left became a part of public life and denounced the imperialistic character of American policy and the role of the power elite in the shaping of it. Unlike the scholars, some of the activists employed violence in pursuit of their interest in fundamental changes, regarding it as necessary owing to elite domination of American institutions and willingness to employ force in defense of them. The activists called for mass action to destroy the old order and for "participatory democracy" as the basic feature of the new order.

New Left revisionists did not rise to dominance in American intellectual life, and New Left activists failed to take control of American politics, but both demonstrated that elitism had become an important way of explaining the development of American foreign policy. In the past sixty years Americans frequently have turned to elitist theory when baffled by or unhappy with the movement of international affairs. Many who have done so have been on the Left side of the political spectrum, though not all have been. There have been liberal, conservative, and antiradical as well as radical versions of the theory. The broad appeal of it and the likelihood that foreign policies will continue to be deeply troubling to many people seem to guarantee that the theory will continue to be important. Faced with a need to explain, many theorists and activists seem certain to find the explanation they seek in the power of small minorities.

BIBLIOGRAPHY

Kenneth Prewitt and Alan Stone, *The Ruling Elites: Elite Theory, Power and American Democracy* (New York, 1973), is a recent, sympathetic, and helpful introduction to elite theory. Two books on the turn-of-the-century debate over imperialism, Ernest R. May, *American Imperialism: A Speculative Essay* (New York, 1968) and E. Berkeley Tompkins, *Anti-Imperialism in the United States: The Great Debate, 1890–1920* (Philadelphia, 1970), are useful. A superb study is Warren I. Cohen, *The American Revisionists: The Lessons of Intervention in World War I* (Chicago, 1967), which should be supplemented by Manfred Jonas, *Isolationism in America 1935–1941* (Ithaca, N.Y., 1966), an analysis of isolationist ideas. Edward A. Purcell, Jr., *The Crisis of Democratic Theory: Scientific Naturalism and the Problem of Value* (Lexington, Ky., 1973), is a distinguished work on recent American social and political thought. Robert Tucker, *The Radical Left and American Foreign Policy* (Baltimore, Md., 1971), provides a sophisticated appraisal. The following are also helpful: Alexander DeConde, *Diplomatic History in Transformation* (Washington, D.C., 1976); Wayne S. Cole, "The United States in World Affairs, 1929–1941," in William H. Cartwright and Richard L. Watson, Jr., eds., *Interpreting and Teaching American History* (Washington, D.C., 1961); Daniel M. Smith, "Rise to Great World Power, 1865–1918," in Cartwright and Watson, eds., *The Reinterpretation of American History and Culture* (Washington, D.C., 1973); the essays by Robert Ferrell, Lloyd C. Gardner, David S. McLellan, and Barton J. Bernstein, in Richard S. Kirkendall, ed., *The Truman Period as a Research Field: A Reappraisal, 1972* (Columbia, Mo., 1974); and Barton J. Bernstein, "Cold War Orthodoxy Restated," in *Reviews in American History,* 1 (1973).

[*See also* AMERICAN ATTITUDES TOWARD WAR; ANTI-IMPERIALISM; THE COLD WAR; CONGRESS AND FOREIGN POLICY; CONSENSUS HISTORY AND FOREIGN POLICY; DECISION-MAKING APPROACHES AND THEORIES; IDEOLOGY AND FOREIGN POLICY; IMPERIALISM; ISOLATIONISM; THE MILITARY-INDUSTRIAL COMPLEX; PRESIDENTIAL POWER IN FOREIGN AFFAIRS; PUBLIC OPINION; REALISM AND IDEALISM; REVISIONISM.]

EMBARGOES

Jerald A. Combs

THE word "embargo" can properly be used to describe any government restriction on trade. Usually, however, it refers specifically to a prohibition on the departure of ships or exports from a nation's own ports, with "boycott" or "nonimportation" being used to describe prohibitions of imports or ship entries, and "nonintercourse" to describe a total prohibition of trade with a nation. To avoid confusion, this is the way these terms will be used in this essay.

In eighteenth-century Europe an embargo was generally a prelude to a formal declaration of war. A civil embargo prohibited a nation's own ships from leaving port, a hostile embargo affected all ships in the port, foreign or domestic. Neutral ships caught in the embargo might even be forced into the service of the belligerent nation. The right to do so was called the power of angary. By imposing an embargo before declaring war, a nation could keep friendly ships from falling into the hands of the enemy and hold enemy ships hostage for future contingencies.

European powers rarely resorted to an embargo as a weapon in itself rather than as a prelude to war, although there were two exceptions to this in the sixteenth century—a French grain embargo against Spain and a threatened Turkish wheat embargo against Venice. In most cases, European nations had little incentive to consider a broader use of embargoes since geographical proximity made conventional military attacks easy and effective. Besides, the seventeenth and eighteenth centuries constituted the age of mercantilism, an age which believed that national power depended upon exports exceeding imports. Thus most diplomats expected an embargo of long duration to hurt the embargoing nation more than its enemy. An extreme example of this philosophy was Great Britain's famous blockade of Napoleonic France, which was not designed to starve France but to compel it to accept British imports or receive no trade at all.

The United States was the first modern nation to make a significant use of the embargo as a substitute for, rather than a prelude to, war. Being three thousand miles from the centers of European power, the United States was not in imminent danger of invasion if it resorted to economic warfare. Also, for most of its early history, the United States had a small army and only a moderate-sized navy. Finally, America had been a colony whose major physical ties to the mother country had been those of trade. Since the American colonies were primarily of value to England as economic entities that provided between a third and a sixth of the entire trade of the empire, it stood to reason that the colonists would think first of commercial measures if they were seeking to pressure the mother country. They were convinced especially that the West Indies were dependent upon imports of American food and lumber for survival. They reasoned, then, that an embargo would be a formidable weapon against any nation with colonies there.

Yet Americans were reluctant to resort to a complete embargo. They had economic interests and mercantilist ideas of their own that militated against such a measure. In the decade preceding the American Revolution, the colonists wielded economic weapons against many of Britain's unpopular measures, but in each case it was a boycott rather than an embargo. In fact, when George Mason proposed that Virginia embargo certain exports to protest the Townshend Acts of 1767, his fellow members of the Virginia legislature specifically rejected the idea, adopting nonimportation and nonconsumption resolutions instead. Similarly, the Continental Congress, meeting in 1774 to respond to the Coercive Acts, quickly adopted nonimportation. But the Virginia delegation insisted that any embargo be delayed until September 1775, by which time the Virginia planters could sell off the tobacco crop. Congress agreed. Then when actual warfare broke out in April, the members moved immediately to forbid all exports without congressional permission. The embargo was soon lifted when Congress found that it was hurting America more than Britain. After a lengthy debate, America's ports were thrown open to all nations except Britain, and Congress was soon begging the French for naval help to get American ships out of port.

Despite this failure, most members of Congress were still convinced that the United States could wield economic weapons effectively. They remembered that the British had repealed the Stamp Act and Townshend Acts at least partly in response to the boycotts, and they were convinced that, during and after the war, foreign nations would pay a high price to divert American trade from Britain to themselves. When Benjamin Franklin was appointed minister to France, Congress instructed him and his colleagues to offer only American trade as bait for France to enter the war as an ally of the United States. Though quickly enough disabused of the hope that France would accept so little for so much, Americans continued to believe that once the war was over, European powers would scramble over one another to offer concessions for access to American markets and produce. But when peace was restored Europeans returned to their mercantilist systems, and the United States was closed out of most colonial markets. The Americans once again considered commercial retaliation.

Since the Articles of Confederation left trade regulation in the hands of the individual states, it was found impossible to coordinate any retaliatory policy. The Constitutional Convention at Philadelphia was called in part to correct the situation. Southerners were fearful that the commercial Northeast, using its greater population for voting advantage in Congress, would wield the weapon of commerce too freely. The South demanded that any navigation law should require a two-thirds vote of each house for passage. Ultimately a compromise was reached. Congress would be permitted by the Constitution to levy taxes on imports; taxes on exports would be constitutionally prohibited. Exports could be embargoed, but they could not be taxed.

Despite this evidence of Southern opposition to export taxes, there were still several Southern leaders who believed devoutly that commercial weapons such as embargoes could be America's primary diplomatic weapons. The leaders in this movement were Secretary of State Thomas Jefferson and James Madison. When the first Congress met in 1789, after ratification of the Constitution, Madison, a member of the House of Representatives, began a campaign for a broad use of commercial weapons that, with Jefferson's help, would last for more than twenty years. Angry at Britain for closing American ships out of the British West Indies and for refusing to sign a trade treaty with the United States, Madison told Congress that America could force Britain into a more amenable posture by threatening to divert American trade from Britain to France. He did not propose anything so drastic as an embargo at this point; he merely called for higher duties on imports from unfriendly nations than from friendly nations. The shipping interests and their congressional representatives had been strong supporters of commercial retaliation against Britain during the hard times of the Confederation period, but now, in a time of rising prosperity, they had changed their minds. Led by Secretary of the Treasury Alexander Hamilton, they defeated Madison's proposals in session after session. Hamilton and his supporters thought British trade too valuable to the United States to risk its use as a diplomatic weapon, and they feared that British retaliation would hurt America far more than America could hurt Britain.

When war broke out between Great Britain and Revolutionary France in 1793, Madison and Jefferson saw a new chance for the use of their commercial weapons. Buoyed by the American populace's strong pro-French feelings, Jefferson issued a report to Congress from the State Department heavily critical of Britain, and Madison responded by introducing discriminatory duties against England in the House. Hamilton and his followers in Congress rallied against the proposals, with Fisher Ames of Massachusetts complaining that "Madison & Co. now avow . . . that we will make war, not for our commerce, but with it; not to make our commerce better, but to make it nothing, in order to reach the tender sides of our enemy, which are not to be wounded in any other way." Ames and his fellow Federalists argued for military preparedness and negotiation rather than commercial retaliation. They succeeded for a time in putting off Madison's proposals, but when the British suddenly swooped down on American ships trading with the French West Indies and captured more than 250 of them, Madison and the Republicans introduced even more stringent measures, such as sequestering British debts and embargoing all trade with England.

Compelled by the public's outrage to do something, the Federalists agreed on a short-term general embargo as the least harmful alternative. By embargoing all ships, foreign and domestic, in American harbors, the measure would ostensibly affect all nations alike, thus avoiding a direct challenge to Great Britain. Also it could be defended as a traditional precautionary step in case of war, and the Federalists could deny that it had anything to do with the Republican campaign for commercial coercion. Thus, with mixed motives, Congress passed a joint resolution in March of 1794, laying a hostile embargo for thirty days. This was later extended for another month, and President Washington was empowered to resume the embargo if the public safety required it.

The Federalists now resumed their crusade to strengthen the army and navy and thwart the rest of the Republican program for commercial retaliation against Britain. They sidetracked the bill for sequestering British debts, and Vice President John Adams cast the tie-breaking vote in the Senate against a total prohibition of British trade, imports as well as exports, which had passed the House. Meanwhile, the Federalists persuaded Washington to send John Jay to England as a special envoy to negotiate with the British and head off the war crisis. When Jay returned with a treaty promising not to interfere in any way with Anglo-American trade in exchange for a minimum of British concessions, the Republicans cried that using America's commercial weapons would have been far more effective than exchanging them for so little. After a bitter battle, the Federalists got the treaty ratified by the narrowest of margins, and on the heels of that victory, elected John Adams to the presidency over his Republican rival, Thomas Jefferson.

Adams, however, found the French as bitter about the Jay Treaty as the Republicans. The French counted on Americans as carriers of their commerce, since the British had swept the seas clear of most French ships. The Americans, by compromising with the British rather than fighting for America's neutral rights, hurt French trade as badly as their own. The French responded by capturing American ships, claiming the right to do to the Americans whatever the Americans allowed the British to do to them. The Federalists and Adams were less reluctant to oppose the French Revolutionaries than they had been to resist the British, but they used the same techniques they had used in the Jay's Treaty crisis, military preparations and negotiation. Their only concession to Republican theories of commercial retaliation was an embargo on French trade passed in July of 1798, after negotiations had broken down over the XYZ affair. Even this was clearly a precautionary war measure rather than a substitute for a military response. Ultimately Adams made peace with France, splitting the Federalist party and enabling Jefferson to defeat him for the presidency in 1800. The embargo would soon receive its supreme test as a substitute for war.

The truce of Amiens (1802) brought a temporary peace to Europe, which allowed the new president to concentrate on domestic programs and to purchase Louisiana. Then the Napoleonic Wars resumed, and Jefferson found himself in the same predicament faced by his predecessors. Once again the belligerents interfered with American trade and captured American ships. In the early years British offenses were more numerous and blatant than those of the French, often taking place within sight of the American coast and involving the impressment of American seamen and the raiding of American commerce. Jefferson began his program of retaliation with the Nonimportation Act of 1806, barring certain British imports. It was more a gesture to demonstrate American determination on the eve of negotiations than an all-out attempt to coerce Britain. However, the Republican negotiators, James Monroe and William Pinkney, did no better than their Federalist predecessor, John Jay. Jefferson and his secretary of state, Madison, rejected the treaty their negotiators sent back from Britain because it failed to prohibit impressment. The envoys were instructed to renegotiate the treaty, eliminating the excessive appeasement of Britain. Such a task, Monroe and Pinkney realized, was hopeless.

Meanwhile, another catastrophe drove Jefferson and Madison toward stronger measures. A British vessel, H.M.S. *Leopard,* fired on an unsuspecting American naval ship, the U.S.S. *Chesapeake.* The British attackers then mustered the crew of the *Chesapeake* and removed four men who were alleged to be British deserters. This violation of American sovereignty brought a loud outcry even from many Federalists, and Jefferson could easily have had a declaration of war. He delayed six months until he received news of a British order-in-council barring all nations from trading with any part of Europe except the Baltic area. At the same time he learned that France had begun capturing American ships in enforcing Napoleon's Berlin Decree. Jefferson then called upon Congress not for war, but for an embargo. In that call he and his followers in Congress defended the move on two separate grounds. On the one hand it would be a proper precautionary move in case of war, on the other it might in itself coerce Great Britain. Thus he appealed to two very different groups. Those who wanted war should have been put on their guard by the fact that the administration secured a rejection of the original plan to embargo foreign as well as domestic ships and then specifically refused to place a time limit on the measure. But the two disparate groups were united for the time being by the ambiguity of the measure. The Senate passed the Embargo Act in a single day by a vote of twenty-two to six; a few days later the House did the same by a two-to-one margin.

As the months wore on, America's ardor for war cooled. Jefferson was soon left with no alternatives but to continue the embargo as the sole coercive weapon or to abandon the measure entirely in a humiliating retreat. He decided to continue the embargo. Now, as he introduced supplementary measures designed to close the loopholes in the law, the Federalists leaped to the attack. Between the embargo and the supplementary laws there was no connection, declared Barent Gardenier, representative from New York. One was a prelude to war, preventing ships from going out and being captured, the other a measure of coercion in itself. Gardenier and his fellow Federalists insisted that only French influence could inspire so foolish and wicked a measure as a permanent embargo. Jefferson was strong enough in Congress to override these objections and force through stringent enforcement acts, including elaborate bonding procedures, precautionary seizures, and general search warrants. But the unpopularity of the embargo, especially in New England, led to widespread defiance, smuggling, and criticism. As a result, the Federalists' electoral vote in 1808 was triple that of 1804, and their share of the House of Representatives was doubled.

The embargo was no more successful abroad than it was popular at home. France, of course, was unaffected by the embargo, since its trade had already been substantially cut off by the British blockade. British trade was affected. The embargo substantially reduced American exports to Britain, and the Nonimportation Act of 1806, which unlike the embargo was directed explicitly at Great Britain, reduced British exports to the United States. This affected Britain's foreign exchange, and gold began leaving the country. The price of gold rose from 8 shillings per ounce in 1807 to 110 shillings per ounce in 1813, embarrassing the Treasury and precipitating discontent over wages and prices. In most other areas, the Embargo Act and the Nonimportation Act did not wound Britain severely. The stoppage of cotton exports was actually welcomed by many British merchants who had warehouses so full they had been worried about a glut. It did harm many workers in the textile industry, setting off a riot of weavers in Yorkshire; but these were not people with much political leverage. Meanwhile, the revolutions in Spain and the Spanish colonies in Latin America opened new markets and sources of supply for Britain, which helped compensate for the loss of trade with the

United States. The Nonimportation Act of 1806 was no more effective than the embargo, since it exempted cheap textiles and manufactured goods, those things the United States needed most from Britain but also the goods Britain most needed to export. The sight of British ships arriving in American ports with these goods was galling to the American merchants whose own ships were rotting at the wharves. They were not much consoled that the embargo forced British vessels to leave in ballast. In the West Indies, too, the embargo failed. It hurt the French West Indies more than the British, since the British had ships to supply their islands, while the French did not.

As the failure of the embargo abroad became apparent and disaffection at home continued to rise, the Republicans were forced to retreat. During Jefferson's lame duck period, he abandoned direction of Congress, and the Nonimportation Act and the Embargo Act were replaced by the Nonintercourse Act of 1809. This act reopened trade with all nations except Britain, France, and their dependencies. But the purposeful vagueness as to just which nations would be considered British or French dependencies, and the lack of a navy to enforce these regulations outside American territorial waters, made the new law an invitation to smuggling. It too was soon abandoned and replaced by Macon's Bill Number Two (1810), throwing trade open to all nations with the promise that America would cut off trade with the enemy of any nation respecting America's neutral rights. When Napoleon promised to respect those rights, Madison, Jefferson's successor, cut off trade with Britain, despite the fact that Napoleon never actually lived up to his promises. When economic weapons again failed to coerce Britain, Madison recommended and Congress declared war. Actually, Britain had finally abandoned some of its orders-in-council before the American declaration. But news of the repeal failed to reach the United States before Congress voted. When the news did arrive, Madison refused to consider peace unless impressment also was eliminated. So the war went on.

Ironically, two months before America declared war, Congress had laid yet another embargo on Great Britain. It was specifically a measure to prepare for war, and it expired shortly after the war began. But Madison was not satisfied. He pushed another embargo through Congress in 1813. This had little effect on the Southern states because the British were already blockading them; but in New England, which the British left unblockaded as a mark of favor to the section most opposed to the war, the embargo hit hard, increasing discontent and leading to threats of secession. Madison and his followers refused to admit the uselessness of the measure until the defeat of Napoleon in 1814 opened the markets of Europe to the British and destroyed what little leverage the embargo had.

In the euphoria of what Americans considered a victorious and glorious defense against Britain in the War of 1812, the humiliation of this period and of the early fighting were almost forgotten. Republican partisans cast the blame for the failure of the embargo on the Federalists and the New Englanders who had defied the law, saying that only such subversion prevented the measure from coercing Britain. But this rhetoric did not erase America's bitter memories of commercial warfare, and it would be many years before the United States tried it again. Even then it would be with far less sanguine hopes than the followers of Jefferson and Madison had had.

For years after the War of 1812, peace in Europe gave the United States a chance to spend its diplomatic energies on westward expansion, where it did not need economic weapons. Population pressure and diplomatic maneuvering were often adequate, and where they failed, outright military action was possible, since these areas were physically contiguous. Not until the Civil War was the weapon of embargo once again taken up, this time by the Confederacy. The South was convinced that "cotton was king" and essential to both British and French industry. After the North instituted a blockade of the entire Confederacy, the South decided to enhance that blockade by embargoing exports of cotton. Southerners were urged not to plant cotton until the war was over, and over two-and-a-half-million bales were burned. Unfortunately for the South, the bumper crop shipped in 1860 had already given Great Britain an oversupply of cotton, and cotton factors actually welcomed the shortage as a chance to reduce their supplies. Shortages did begin to occur by 1862. Four hundred thousand workers lost their jobs. Many of these workers advocated British intervention on behalf of the South to restore the cotton supplies; but their political impotence, the increasing supplies of cotton from Egypt, and the growing realization that the South would lose the war doomed their efforts. As the war went on, even Southerners found the embargo too painful, and they cooperated in running more than a million and a half bales of cotton through the Northern blockade. Once again an embargo had proved to be a disastrous failure.

From the Civil War on, America's use of the embargo would be very different. Gone was the confidence that an embargo could substantially affect an enemy. Now it would be used more as a gesture than a weapon. It might be used to indicate moral disapproval, or to keep the United States out of foreign wars. It might be used as a warning of firmer measures to come, or as a futile substitute for war when war was impolitic. But Americans would no longer regard it as a potent weapon in their armory.

The embargo was not revived until 1898, when Congress by joint resolution granted the president authority to bar the export of coal or war matériel from American seaports during the Spanish-American War. This embargo was merely an adjunct to war, not an important weapon of itself. Theodore Roosevelt stretched the authority of this law in 1905 to keep weapons from falling into the hands of revolutionaries in the Dominican Republic, where the United States had taken control of the customs. In 1912, when the government of Francisco I. Madero protested American shipments of arms to Mexican rebels, Congress gave President William Howard Taft more specific authority to handle the situation than Roosevelt had had. It amended the 1898 resolution to provide that when there existed in any Western Hemisphere country conditions of domestic violence promoted by American arms, the president should proclaim that fact and this would make exports of arms or munitions illegal except as the president provided. In effect this gave the president the right to provide arms to whichever side he favored. Taft used this authority to embargo all arms to Mexico, but when a revolt broke out against the reviled Victoriano Huerta, Woodrow Wilson lifted the embargo so that arms could be shipped to Huerta's opponents. When the United States recognized the Venustiano Carranza government, the embargo was restored, but American arms were made available to Carranza's forces near the American border. When Pancho Villa began raiding in the area and General John J. Pershing was sent across the border after him, this exemption to the embargo was removed. Thus the United States had begun a regular use of arms embargoes as a means of controlling or manipulating domestic revolutionary situations in the Western Hemisphere as well as using them to prevent aid to nations with which it was at war.

During this same period, United States businesses began serious overseas operations and another kind of embargo made its appearance—the capital embargo. Throughout most of American history, capital embargoes have applied only to loans involving the public sale of foreign bonds and have been quite informal. The government has only to recommend against a loan and foreign bonds will not find purchasers, since prospective buyers know that the government will not enforce payment if the borrowing country should default. Thus Taft's secretary of state, Philander C. Knox, discouraged a loan to China during the Revolution of 1911, and Wilson discouraged a consortium seeking to reorganize a loan to China in 1913. Wilson also advised against loans to the belligerents during World War I, but reversed that policy in 1916. In March 1922 the State Department made its informal policy official by announcing the hope that American corporations contemplating loans would check with the department first.

Just prior to World War I, Wilson dusted off the idea of a broader use of the embargo as a means of pressuring the British to lessen their interference with American shipping to the European continent. In September 1916 he persuaded Congress to pass a law permitting him to ban imports and deny clearance for any departing vessels. After his reelection in November of that year, he hinted to the British that he might use that authority to embargo arms or deny clearance to vessels refusing to carry goods for firms blacklisted by the British. Since the British blockade had already cut off trade to Germany, any embargo would hurt only the Allies, thus paralleling the situation in Jefferson's day. Wilson never actually exercised his authority; he remembered too well the lesson of history. He was more concerned with German submarine warfare, an issue he considered far more important than the British blockade or blacklist. He did not want to find himself in Jefferson's or Madison's position, locked in a dispute with both belligerents at the same time. With the entry of the United States into the war, Congress embargoed all supplies to the Central Powers by passing the Trading With the Enemy Act of 1917. This embargo was wielded against the neutral powers of Europe, driving them into agreements to limit trade with the Central Powers in exchange for vitally needed products from the United States. These agreements, along with blacklisting and bunker control directed against firms within neutral countries suspected of trading with the enemy, tightened the economic noose that the Allied blockade and American embargo placed around the Central Powers and contributed substantially to the Allied victory in World War I.

After World War I, there arose in the United States a general revulsion against American involvement in world politics, and the policy of embargo came to play an important part in the debate over the shaping of a new foreign policy for the United States. As a kind of prelude, Congress made two minor gestures in 1922. It expanded the arms embargo of 1912, which had previously applied only to Western Hemisphere countries, and permitted the president to embargo arms to countries where the United States exercised extraterritorial jurisdiction whenever there existed conditions of civil violence. This law was directed primarily at China. Also in 1922, the State Department recommended against credits to Soviet Russia because that nation refused to pay its war debts. But neither this capital embargo nor the refusal to recognize the Bolshevik regime hindered American trade with the Soviets.

Consideration of a broader use of the arms embargo began later in the 1920's. Some influential Americans wanted the president to have authority to embargo arms and munitions to any aggressor nation. They saw this measure as a chance for the United States to cooperate with the League of Nations. They were fearful that America's traditional policy of neutrality, which insisted on a neutral's rights to trade with all belligerents, would undermine any system of collective sanctions the League might undertake. Conversely, American cooperation in those sanctions would strengthen the League and the system of collective security immeasurably. Thus they argued for a discretionary embargo, which would allow the president to embargo arms to aggressor nations but to supply arms to the victims of that aggression.

The movement for cooperation with the League ran head-on into a growing countermovement inspired by disillusionment with World War I and a belief that American involvement in the war had been manipulated by munitions makers and other so-called merchants of death. This countermovement, too, called for an arms embargo, but its advocates insisted that the embargo be impartial. The purpose should be to keep the United States out of any future wars, not to deter future wars by the threat of collective sanctions against aggressors. This debate created a groundswell for some sort of arms embargo. By the mid-1930's, only a few congressional voices, along with the weapons manufacturers themselves, still called for adherence to America's traditional policy of enforcing a neutral's right to trade with belligerents in any commodities whatever.

Although the debate over arms embargoes began in 1928, the first Neutrality Act was not passed until 1935. Henry Stimson, secretary of state in the late 1920's, favored a discretionary embargo to strengthen collective security, but received little support from President Herbert Hoover. Without strong administration backing, the measure failed. Hoover was particularly adamant against imposing economic sanctions on Japan for its aggression in Manchuria, sanctions strongly favored by Stimson. Instead, Hoover forced Stimson to retreat to an ineffective policy of refusing to recognize any gains Japan might make, a policy ironically known as the Stimson Doctrine.

Franklin D. Roosevelt came to the presidency pledged to Stimson's policy of discretionary embargoes. Such an embargo actually passed the House in 1932, but when it encountered opposition in the Senate, Roosevelt consented to an impartial embargo, a complete negation of collective security. When his own advisers, including Secretary of State Cordell Hull, objected to his concession, Roosevelt agreed to drop the whole matter, and the embargo died.

The issue was revived during the next congressional session, however. Bolivia and Paraguay were engaged in the Chaco War, and the administration wanted to cooperate with the League of Nations in an arms embargo against both nations. Roosevelt could simply have supported a general impartial embargo on all warring nations. One was already before the Senate. But he still hoped for a discretionary embargo, and so he settled for a specific resolution embargoing arms to Bolivia and Paraguay only. This was the first time the United States had adopted an embargo avowedly for the purpose of stopping a war between two countries, and in that way it could be seen as a step toward collective security. In fact, it strengthened the concept of an impartial embargo, since arms to both countries were stopped. That concept was further strengthened by the widely publicized Nye Committee hearings and the publication of several best-selling books promoting the idea that American economic interests, particularly the munitions makers, had been responsible for America's entry into World War I. Primary among these books was *The Road to War* by Walter Millis. Perhaps even more important in the movement for an impartial embargo were the growing crises in Europe and Asia, as Japan, Germany, and Italy engaged the other powers in an arms race and embarked on campaigns of territorial expansion. Many hoped that the United States could escape the coming conflagration by embargoing arms and thus not repeating the supposed error of becoming involved in World War I.

The result of this growing movement was the Neutrality Act of 1935. Rejecting an administration bill allowing discretionary embargoes, Congress instead passed a mandatory impartial embargo on arms to belligerents, closed American ports to belligerent submarines, and prohibited Americans from taking passage on belligerent liners. The administration managed to limit the act to six months' duration, and then to use it for its own purposes. When Italy attacked Ethiopia, Roosevelt, to show America's displeasure with Italy, put the Neutrality Act into effect and declared a further "moral embargo" on any trade with the belligerents that was not covered by the Neutrality Act. Although supposedly impartial, the actions hurt only Italy. The United States had no trade with Ethiopia, and a prohibition against American passengers on belligerent liners could hardly harm the still-undeveloped African nation.

Although these actions may have given America some spiritual satisfaction, they had little effect on the course of world events. American businesses defied the moral embargo, and the League of Nations embargo omitted oil from the list of prohibited exports. Since oil was Italy's most vital need, the conquest of Ethiopia continued apace. This failure notwithstanding, Congress renewed the Neutrality Act in 1936, adding a provision prohibiting loans to belligerents. The administration and the business community managed to stave off a movement for an impartial general embargo rather than a mere arms embargo, but that movement gained considerable strength as the year wore on.

When civil war broke out in Spain later in 1936, Congress honored the administration's request to embargo arms to that country. As Germany and Italy began to provide massive support for Francisco Franco, considerable pressure was put on the American government to lift the embargo and supply the Loyalists. But the embargo remained. The advocates of collective security had been defeated again.

In 1937 pressure to expand the arms embargo to a general embargo applying to all belligerents frightened many businessmen, and they sought a way to sidetrack the issue. Presidential adviser Bernard Baruch came up with a suggestion of "cash-and-carry," arguing that so long as American goods were purchased and transported by belligerents, the capture or sinking of the goods would not affect the United States. In return for other concessions, the administration succeeded in making the cash-and-carry principle discretionary, to be instigated with the rest of the Neutrality Act only at the option of the president. Roosevelt was also willing to accept cash-and-carry because he realized it would favor Britain and France; Great Britain controlled the seas and could ensure that only allied ships would reach the United States to take advantage of the offer. The Neutrality Act of 1937 passed Congress just one day before the expiration of the Act of 1936 and was flown to the presidential yacht in the Gulf of Mexico for Roosevelt's signature.

The Neutrality Act of 1937 was the high-water mark for advocates of an impartial neutrality; the decline of the movement had already begun. Sentiment was heavily against Franco's forces, and many regretted the embargo on arms to his opponents. Then, in 1937, Japan renewed its war against China. By rights, Roosevelt was supposed to embargo arms and loans to both nations and, if he chose, to establish the cash-and-carry policy. But both of these actions would favor Japan, since China needed the arms and credits, while Japan needed neither. Also Japan was a seapower capable of taking advantage of the cash-and-carry policy. Roosevelt avoided this dilemma by pointing to the technicality that no official declaration of war had been made. Thus he refused to invoke the Neutrality Act, enabling private loans and arms to continue to flow to China. Roosevelt followed this action with his famous quarantine speech and then imposed a moral embargo on exports of aircraft to Japan. Although the country remained strongly isolationist and Roosevelt was forced to retreat from his quarantine policy, in general people accepted his tacit ignoring of the Neutrality Act. The United States was beginning to use embargoes as sanctions against aggressors rather than as a means of avoiding conflicts.

In 1938 Roosevelt failed to secure revision of the Neutrality Act. It was not until Germany invaded Poland in 1939, setting off World War II, that the act was revised. Even then Roosevelt had to disguise his actions by claiming that the arms embargo actually endangered the peace of the United States. He also offered to bar American ships from designated war zones. He was thus able to persuade Congress to place arms on the same cash-and-carry basis as other commodities. He then went on to greater aid measures, such as the destroyer deal and lend-lease.

But while Roosevelt turned from embargoes toward measures of positive aid to Europe, in Asia his administration moved toward a more pointed use of embargoes against Japan. Japan relied heavily upon American oil and metals to fuel its war effort in China. Any threat to stop those exports would have a significant impact on Japanese plans. The swing of public opinion and the revision of the Neutrality Act in 1939 allowed Roosevelt to take some action on behalf of China. So in May 1939 the United States notified Japan that it was withdrawing from the 1911 Treaty of Commerce. By terms of the treaty, in six months the United States would be free to limit or terminate exports to Japan. Roosevelt hoped this would give the Japanese pause. But the war in China continued. The American government hesitated to implement sanctions for fear that they would drive Japan to replace the embargoed items by invading new sources of supply. This would most likely be Southeast Asia, where French, British, and Dutch colonies were supplying those same vital materials to America's allies in Europe. First the six-month period of grace passed, then a year, with no sanctions applied.

In July 1940 a cabinet change in Japan signaled a more aggressive Japanese policy in Southeast Asia. With that, the United States imposed an embargo on aviation gasoline and high-grade scrap iron to Japan. This embargo affected only a fraction of exports to Japan, and the American government went to some lengths to justify the embargo on the grounds of American domestic needs rather than any displeasure with Japan. Still, the embargo signaled the Japanese that the United States would oppose any moves against Southeast Asia.

Instead of backing down, Japan accelerated its search for more secure sources of vital raw materials. Japan pressured concessions from the Dutch East Indies, coerced Vichy France into allowing Japanese occupation of northern Indochina, and began negotiations for an alliance with Germany and Italy. The United States responded with a complete embargo on scrap iron, but this was followed the very next day by the formal announcement of the Axis pact. The United States continued to expand its embargo, extending it to tools, iron, steel, copper, bronze, and many other critical metals. When the United States intercepted Japanese messages detailing plans for further expansion in Southeast Asia and reports arrived that Japanese transports were moving on southern Indochina, Roosevelt decided on a last-ditch gamble to stop Japanese expansion. He issued an order freezing all Japanese assets in the United States. Only a special license from the American government could release Japanese assets to pay for American exports, including, most critically, oil. When the British and Dutch joined the embargo, Japan was cut off from its vital sources of raw materials. With only a two-year supply of petroleum, Japan had either to give up the war in China or secure its own sources of supply. Japan first tried diplomacy. But the negotiations with the United States failed and Japan declared war. During World War II, the 1917 Trading With the Enemy Act was used to impose a complete embargo on the Axis powers.

The embargo weapon was not picked up again until 1948, when the Cold War was in full swing. In March of that year, the Department of Commerce announced restrictions on exports to the Soviet Union and its European allies. These restrictions were formalized in the Export Control Act of 1949. Originally this act was intended as a temporary measure to keep arms and strategic materials out of the hands of potential enemies, but the outbreak of hostilities in Korea made the Cold War more rigid and the measure was given permanence. It has been renewed every few years, the most recent extension of it being the Export Administration Act of 1969. In 1951 America attempted to strengthen these embargoes with the so-called Battle Act. According to this act, the United States would refuse assistance to any nation that did not embargo strategic goods, including oil, to the Soviet Union and nations subject to its influence. Under pressure from its allies, the United States accepted many exemptions from this act and it has not been notably effective.

For many years, the embargo on the Soviet Union was quite severe. The embargo on Eastern European countries was less stringent in hopes of driving a wedge between the Soviet Union and its allies. Two of the most independent East European nations, Poland and Rumania, have had particularly mild treatment. With the growing détente of the 1970's, trade restrictions on the Soviet Union and its allies were increasingly lightened, most notably in the wheat deal of 1973.

In Asia, the United States imposed embargoes on North Korea, China, and North Vietnam. These were severe embargoes established under the Trading With the Enemy Act. The embargo of China and North Korea began in 1950, during the Korean War. Secretary of State John Foster Dulles insisted that the embargo continue after the war, but America's allies protested, arguing that such trade should be under the same regulation as that to Eastern Europe. The United States used the Battle Act to prevent this but in 1957 gave way to allow its allies to trade with China and North Korea. The United States, however, maintained its own unilateral embargo until 1969, when the administration of Richard M. Nixon lifted some of the restrictions. The economic effect of the embargo on China was minimal, since China of its own choice restricted its imports to what it could pay for with its few exports. China found all the imports it needed in Europe anyway.

America's postwar embargoes in the Western Hemisphere have taken a different form from those in either Europe or Asia. At the Buenos Aires Conference of 1936, the United States had reluctantly signed a treaty prohibiting any nation from intervening in the affairs of any other nation in the Western Hemisphere. Only the Organization of American States (OAS) could undertake such interventions. Thus the United States embargo of oil, trucks, and spare parts to the regime of Rafael Trujillo in the Dominican Republic in 1961 was part of an OAS embargo. When the United States fell out with Cuba, it again sought the cover of the OAS for its anti-Castro actions. In 1962, a month after the OAS, at the urging of the United States, had expelled Cuba from the inter-American system, the OAS put an embargo on all trade with Cuba except certain humanitarian items. The embargo had little effect on the Cuban economy except to make it more expensive for the Soviet Union to maintain its ally in the Western Hemisphere. Like the embargoes of the Soviet Union, Eastern Europe, and China, the Cuban embargo was an ineffective gesture of dislike and frustration rather than a significant diplomatic weapon. As of 1977, several OAS members had abandoned the embargo, and the United States seemed to be moving in that direction also.

American postwar embargoes in Africa have had yet another basis. The United States has participated in embargoes against South Africa and Southern Rhodesia in response to demands from the United Nations. In both cases the United States has supported these embargoes as a moderate alternative to the more militant actions demanded by a majority of United Nations members. From 1951 to 1962, the United States embargoed any arms to South Africa that might have been used domestically to support apartheid and in 1962 extended that embargo to all arms. America has voted consistently against attempts by the United Nations to expand these economic sanctions, however. In Southern Rhodesia, where black majority rule is the issue, the United States followed the lead of Great Britain in the United Nations, joining first a 1966 embargo on oil, arms, and spare parts along with a boycott of major Rhodesian products, and moving to a complete embargo in 1968. While responding to these initiatives of the United Nations, the United States has voted against proposals demanding that Britain use force against Rhodesia. The United States cast its first veto ever in the Security Council to defeat such a measure in 1970. In 1971 a coalition of conservative legislators led by Harry F. Byrd, Jr., sponsored an amendment forbidding the United States to boycott products from non-Communist countries unless it also boycotted such products coming from Communist nations. As the United States was importing much of its chromium from Russia instead of its usual supplier, Rhodesia, the Byrd amendment opened the door once again to imports of Rhodesian chromium. Although South Africa and Portugal had tacitly defied the embargo to the point that by 1972 Rhodesia's exports and imports were almost back to the pre-embargo level, the American action was the first formal defiance of United Nations economic sanctions. This congressional action seriously embarrassed the United States in the United Nations, but Congress held to its policy despite President Ford's announced opposition to the Byrd amendment. In 1977 the Carter administration secured the repeal of the amendment.

Overall, America's wielding of the weapon of embargo has not been notably successful except as a direct adjunct of war. Jefferson's embargo brought serious domestic disaffection and helped bring on the War of 1812. King Cotton diplomacy was a colossal failure. As the United States became an industrial power in the twentieth century, the nation was itself more dependent on foreign trade than its potential opponents. Thus embargoes stood to hurt the United States more than its enemies. Because of this and the historical failures of the embargo, the American government has wielded the weapon more carefully, and usually as a supplement to military operations or as a symbolic gesture when the course of outright military attack was for some reason closed to it. Thus it was used effectively during World War I and World War II, but when it was used against Japan in 1941 to forestall war, the Freeze Order drove Japan to the precise action it was hoped the measure would deter. Ironically, the United States is now a more likely victim than an effective wielder of economic sanctions, as the Arab oil embargo of 1973 demonstrated.

This is not to say, however, that the economic power of the United States is useless in diplomatic affairs. It is just that this power has been exercised more effectively in forms other than embargoes. On the public level, the granting or withholding of economic and military aid has been used effectively, and in the private sector American-based multinational corporations have been enormously influential.

BIBLIOGRAPHY

There is no general work summarizing American embargo policy. An overall view of the policy must be gathered from various works on other topics. Jerald A. Combs, *The Jay Treaty: Political Battleground of the Founding Fathers* (Berkeley, 1970), deals with the early struggle between Madison and Hamilton over economic retaliation, culminating in the embargo of 1794 and Jay's Treaty. Robert A. Divine, *The Illusion of Neutrality: Franklin D. Roosevelt and the Struggle Over the Arms Embargo* (Chicago, 1962), is an excellent account of the Neutrality Acts of the 1930's. Herbert Feis, *The Road to Pearl Harbor: The Coming of the War Between the United States and Japan* (Princeton, 1950), is a full account of America's attempt to use economic sanctions to deter Japanese expansion yet avoid military action. Felix Gilbert, *To the Farewell Address: Ideas of Early American Foreign Policy* (Princeton, 1961), is a brilliant exposition of American ideas of economic warfare during the nation's formative years. Merrill Jensen, *The Founding of a Nation: A History of the American Revolution, 1763–1776* (New York, 1968), has the best account of pre-Revolution economic action. Ernest R. May, *The World War and American Isolation, 1914–1917* (Cambridge, Mass., 1959), deals with Wilson's consideration of the embargo against the Allies before World War I. John Bassett Moore, *A Digest of International Law* (Washington, D.C., 1906), is good for early American precedents. Frank L. Owsley and Harriet C. Owsley, *King Cotton Diplomacy: Foreign Relations of the Confederate States of America,* 2nd ed. (Chicago, 1959), is the most complete work on King Cotton diplomacy. Bradford Perkins, *Prologue to War: England and the United States, 1805–1812* (Berkeley, 1961), is the best modern work on the economic measures leading to the War of 1812. M. M. Whiteman, *Digest of International Law* (Washington, D.C., 1963), is good for later American embargoes.

[*See also* BLOCKADES AND QUARANTINES; THE CONTINENTAL SYSTEM; ECONOMIC FOREIGN POLICY; FREEDOM OF THE SEAS; INTERNATIONAL LAW; INTERVENTION AND NONINTERVENTION; THE KING COTTON THEORY; TRADE AND COMMERCE.]

ETHNICITY AND FOREIGN POLICY

John Snetsinger

THE consistent and substantial support of Israel by the United States, and the diplomatic consequences that have flowed from that relationship, have quickened scholarly interest in the subject of ethnicity and foreign policy. The world was plunged into a potentially catastrophic energy crisis as a direct result of the 1973 Arab-Israeli war. Almost immediately students of American diplomacy began to focus on the Middle Eastern policy of the United States, the Jewish community in the United States, and the interrelationship between the two.

The special friendship that exists between Israel and the United States clearly indicates how one ethnic group can effectively influence foreign policy. Although none have approached the Jewish achievement in recent years, other ethnic minorities have sought, with varying degrees of success, to apply pressure and to shape a specific area of diplomatic policy that interests them. From the earliest days of the republic, ethnic minorities have played a role in the conduct of foreign policy.

Reasons for the link between American diplomacy and ethnicity are found in the manner in which the country was settled. In Europe it was common to have a single national or religious identification shared by the public. In the emerging American republic, however, the composition of the population reflected a high degree of national, religious, and racial diversity. One wave of immigrants after another swelled the American population with persons of vastly dissimilar backgrounds.

These immigrants and, in many instances, their descendants have retained ancestral loyalties. It has been and remains common for ethnic minorities, such as Italian-Americans, Jewish-Americans, and Polish-Americans, to embrace their new American loyalties while at the same time clinging to their ancestral ties.

The process through which American foreign policy is formulated works to the advantage of ethnic groups interested in assisting some cause of their homeland. All forms of government, including dictatorships, ultimately rely upon the support of public opinion to sustain their activities abroad. In a democracy, however, the link between the nation's diplomacy and the desires of the citizenry is more direct than in nondemocratic states.

Astute politicians must not only be aware of broad-based national sentiment concerning a diplomatic issue, but they must also give a hearing to ethnic minorities who have a particular interest in certain areas of the country's foreign policy. Organized ethnic minorities can bring pressure on the government for specific policies that are peculiarly their own and that may favor their original homeland vis-à-vis another nation, or a particular political movement within the homeland, or simply reflect an attitude that is common to similar American immigrant groups.

The extent to which ethnic minorities are able to shape foreign policy is a uniquely American phenomenon. No other nation absorbed such extensive waves of immigration as did the United States. Sixty percent of the world's international migration between the early nineteenth century and 1930 came to the United States. An indication of the result of this migration is the fact that in 1950 approximately 34 million out of the total population of 150 million were either immigrants themselves or had at least one immigrant parent.

So apparent and consistent are the desired

diplomatic policies of some ethnic minorities that politicians can frequently anticipate what actions will solidify support for themselves among these groups. Even though the resulting positions may flout foreign policy objectives outlined by the federal government, politicians have made attempts to please the large ethnic blocs within their constituency. Mayor William H. ("Big Bill") Thompson, for example, placated citizens of Irish extraction when he threatened that he would "punch the snout" of the king of England should the monarch dare to enter Chicago. More recently, New York City mayors Robert F. Wagner, John V. Lindsay, and Abraham D. Beame pursued a policy designed to meet with the approval of the city's three million Jews by refusing to welcome Arab rulers on goodwill tours of the United States.

Mayors and other local officials may irritate foreign leaders, but the extent to which such actions affect American diplomacy is relatively slight. More serious consequences can arise when ethnic minorities place sufficient pressures on the national government to alter the direction of foreign policy. Since 1900, for example, the development of a close understanding between the United States and Great Britain has been blocked on several occasions by persistent anglophobia that centered among those citizens of Irish and German ancestry. These two minorities opposed early American intervention to aid Britain in both world wars. Partly on account of such opposition, the United States not only postponed early wartime alliances with Britain, but peacetime rapprochement also was handled in every instance with extreme caution.

Those Americans of Irish descent have been a particularly active minority in attempting to influence foreign affairs. The United States Senate failed to ratify a treaty with Britain that allowed construction, but not fortification, of a canal across the Central American isthmus. Opposition on the part of Irish-Americans to the pact, which had been negotiated in 1901 by Secretary of State John Hay and Britain's Sir Julian Pauncefote, was a major factor that blocked this agreement. President Woodrow Wilson's failure to press for Irish independence as part of the World War I peace settlement resulted in bitter Irish-American attacks against the president and the Treaty of Versailles (1919), and played a key role in obstructing the treaty's acceptance by the United States.

Whether to ratify the Treaty of Versailles was, in fact, an issue that resulted in several emotionally charged campaigns. Various ethnic minorities, each specially motivated to seek a negative Senate vote on ratification, assailed Wilson's handiwork. German-Americans could not accept the relatively harsh punishment meted out to Germany. Since the Versailles agreement failed to provide for the expanded Italy hoped for by Italian nationals, initial Italian-American enthusiasm for Wilson soon turned to denunciation. Exclusion of the Adriatic city of Fiume from Italy's control was considered to be one of the treaty's most objectionable points.

Not only the larger and more influential ethnic minorities resisted Wilson's endeavors to secure United States acceptance of the treaty, but also Armenian-Americans, Syrian-Americans, Greek-Americans, and Lithuanian-Americans, among several other groups, combined forces with the foes of ratification for a variety of reasons. Millions of Americans viewed Wilson as the man who had betrayed dreams of nationalistic glory for their land of origin.

Over the years scholars have clashed on the issue of whether Anglo-Americans, who have constituted the population base of this nation, can legitimately be considered another of the nation's ethnic groups. There is no doubt, however, that Americans of English ancestry have had a significant impact on formulating diplomatic relationships with Great Britain. Since the earliest days of the Republic, the Anglo-Americans have influenced American foreign policy. By placing pressure upon President Wilson, who was himself of English ancestry, the Anglo-Americans exerted a powerful influence in stimulating American intervention in World War I.

Few ethnic groups have been as successful in influencing foreign policy as were Polish-Americans during World War I. The re-creation of Poland following the war is linked to the Wilson administration's interest in securing the Polish-American vote.

There are countervailing pressures that can neutralize or even eliminate the opportunity an ethnic group has to affect foreign affairs. If public sentiment is clearly defined as opposed to the policy being sought, or if nonethnic special-interest lobbies in the United States wage a campaign against an ethnic minority's goals, or if other ethnic groups commit themselves to work in behalf of an alternate policy, the influence that an ethnic minority can command is mitigated.

The first of these balancing factors has frequently proven critical to ethnic minorities desiring to convince a president and Congress that specific policies should be accepted. Ethnic groups can exert disproportionate pressure in a specific area if their demands arouse no broad opposition from the public at large. Part of the Jewish-American success in winning American support for the creation of a Jewish state following World War II resulted from the existence of this condition.

It was fortunate for the Zionists that, throughout the struggle to obtain official United States backing for the Jewish state, the American public was either mildly sympathetic or at least apathetic. The basic Zionist aim of establishing a Jewish state was consistently favored by those in the polling samples with an opinion, although at times the margin of support was as narrow as a few percentage points.

Perhaps as significant as the opinions expressed was the fact that so large a percentage of the public did not follow the Palestine controversies. Only 45 percent of those questioned in one poll (National Opinion Research Center poll, May 1946) could identify Britain as the country that had the mandate for Palestine. As late as the fall of 1946, 49 percent admitted that they had not followed the discussion about establishing a Jewish national homeland (American Institute of Public Opinion poll, 11 September 1946). Outside the Jewish community the Zionist program did not raise very intense political issues.

Significantly, the one aspect of the Zionist program that received clear-cut public disapproval was never adopted by the American government. Following Israel's birth in May 1948, the new nation asked for positive action by the American president on three specific issues. One was for President Harry S. Truman to extend de jure recognition to Israel. Great urgency was also attached to the request for a hundred-million-dollar American loan to the Jewish state. Truman responded favorably to both requests. Truman was also asked to lift the American arms embargo on the Middle East, allowing Israel to purchase weapons. On 5 December 1947 the American arms embargo had been imposed at the request of the United Nations Security Council. Truman was persuaded by the State Department to believe that any unilateral revocation of the embargo would be regarded as exhibiting a striking disregard for United Nations efforts to pacify the Middle East. Another compelling reason for presidential inaction derived from the public response to the embargo. Although the Zionist program generally met with either mild public approval or indifference, one nationwide poll (National Opinion Research Center poll, 1 July 1948) indicated that 82 percent of the electorate opposed any change in the status of the embargo.

A second balancing factor, which can challenge the potential influence of an ethnic minority, is made up of the variety of nonethnic special-interest lobbies that are themselves determined to have foreign policy conducted along the lines they desire. For example, economic interests within the United States might seek policies that are diametrically opposed to the programs sought by ethnic groups. In a democracy, ethnic minorities make up just a small percentage of those pressure groups hoping to influence foreign policy.

A third factor that works against the policy-making influence of a particular ethnic minority consists of other ethnic groups taking on the role of the adversary. Wilson was faced with a variety of ethnic groups, each of which insisted that the president fully endorse the claims of their homeland. America's ethnic populations themselves collided on how the map of the world should be redrawn. Wilson's attempts to compromise instead left most of the groups dissatisfied, and in part led to his inability to have the Treaty of Versailles ratified.

The situation of having one ethnic group lined up against another occurred when Italian dictator Benito Mussolini sent his troops into Ethiopia in an effort to expand his colonial empire. Supporting their ancestral home, most Italian-Americans defended the action and many lobbied against any American plan to establish a discriminatory embargo against Italy. Since President Franklin D. Roosevelt opposed Mussolini's actions during the Ethiopian campaign, large numbers of Italian-Americans turned against the president and the Democratic party.

On the other side, black Americans rallied to Ethiopia's support on the basis of their ethnic identification with the black African nation. American blacks called for the United States to stand up firmly against Italy. Lester Taylor, the chairman of the New African International League, wired the State Department: "Black citizens are surprised and filled with misgivings at the lukewarm attitude of this government." In the Ethiopian crisis of 1935, there was a tendency for the two ethnic groups, Italian-Americans and black Americans, to cancel out whatever political influence the other hoped to wield on this issue.

One reason why Jewish-Americans have been so successful in obtaining support for Israel is because until very recently they were virtually unchallenged by any other ethnic pressure group in American politics. Political parties have not worried about alienating an Arab vote, since there has been no significant Arab population in the United States. In the past few years, however, a pro-Arab lobby has begun to emerge in the United States. With articulate spokesmen such as the Democratic senator from South Dakota, James Abourezk, an Arab-American, the Arab position will probably receive a public hearing in the future that it has not had in the past.

It seems likely that the pro-Arab lobby in the United States has been influenced by the emergence of an aggressive Arab nationalism in the Middle East. Whether this new pressure group will eventually prove successful in countering the demands of Jewish-Americans on foreign policy issues remains to be seen.

Where none of the three countervailing pressures exist, an ethnic minority can dominate a policy area. Placing foreign policy in the context of electoral politics, the candidate or officeholder has everything to gain and nothing to lose by endorsing the goals of the particular ethnic group. He can obtain the political support of the members of the group who consider the issue in question to be of significance; at the same time he alienates no voters.

Truman's political advisers made just this argument in obtaining the president's support for the new state of Israel during the 1948 presidential election. White House staff members Clark Clifford and David Niles suggested to the president that he could obtain the support of Jewish voters by taking a pro-Israel stand; at the same time he would not lose any significant number of votes.

The degree of success an ethnic minority can obtain is often directly related to how strongly committed their own members are to the cause being promoted. Irish-Americans represent a significant percentage of the electorate, but by the mid-1970's they neither shared a common view on policy toward Ireland, nor did they approach the issue with a high degree of intensity. Accordingly, their ability to influence American policy toward Ireland is questionable.

Jewish effectiveness in influencing American diplomacy is due in part to the fact that for Jewish-Americans continued American support of Israel remains an issue of critical importance. A poll taken by Elmo Roper in 1945 indicated that only one Jew in ten was against establishing a Jewish state in Palestine. Recent surveys indicate that an even higher percentage of Jewish-Americans now support Israel as well as an American policy of strong support for that beleaguered nation.

Politicians without a strong commitment to Israel run into serious problems with Jewish voters. Lyndon B. Johnson and Hubert H. Humphrey received, respectively, 90 and 83 percent of the Jewish vote in their 1964 and 1968 presidential races. Both men, as well as the Democratic party, which they represented, had solid pro-Israel reputations in the Jewish community.

Although George McGovern represented the same Democratic party that most Jewish-Americans politically associate themselves with, the 1972 nominee suffered from the belief among some Jews that he was "soft" on Israel. McGovern received 66 percent of the Jewish vote, a significant drop of 24 percent and 17 percent from the totals compiled by the Democratic standard bearers of 1964 and 1968.

Candidates soon learn which ethnic groups will deliver their votes to the political figures who support the desired foreign policy programs. The ultimate weapon possessed by ethnic minorities is the ballot. If a group can reward its friends and punish its enemies on election day by bloc voting, it will soon find that it has more friends than enemies. If, as is the case with Jewish-Americans, the group not only votes in proportions far higher than the national average, but also is concentrated in strategic states (New York, California, Illinois), the ethnic minority can exert pressure in a given field that is totally disproportionate to its size.

Political parties do not always wait for ethnic groups to initiate action in behalf of a particular foreign policy. Parties may themselves opportunistically seek the votes of ethnic groups by pledging to respond to a particular foreign policy request that may not have emotionally stirred the group for many years.

The electoral process itself encourages the parties, or individual candidates, to find issues that when exploited can unite an ethnic group either for or against a policy. By stirring up an issue, and then lining up on the "right" side, a party or a candidate can work for a bloc vote that otherwise would have been impossible to obtain.

Since the 1880's both the Democratic and Republican national committees have organized their election year nationalities divisions with the single purpose of attracting the ethnic vote. Many of the issues that have been artificially produced have been negative in nature. For example, politicians played to the Irish-American vote for generations by promising to work for an anti-British foreign policy.

This persistent campaign policy has openly encouraged and exploited the emotions of ethnic voters. Anxious to win votes during a heated election, political parties have made pledges that no president or party could fulfill. The Republican platform plank of 1952 promised to liberate the captive peoples of Eastern Europe—one example of an unattainable campaign pledge to ethnic minorities.

By the mid-1970's the critical question raised regarding ethnicity and foreign policy was not whether ethnic minorities actually affected the conduct of American diplomacy. Such influence was once again clearly demonstrated when negotiations on a major trade agreement between the United States and the Soviet Union collapsed in 1975. Jewish-Americans had successfully lobbied in favor of a congressional amendment that involved the status of the Jewish community within the Soviet Union. Rather than accept what they considered to be an intrusion into their internal affairs, the Soviet Union backed out of the entire agreement.

The substantive question now is whether such influences upon the conduct of foreign affairs is an obstruction to sound policymaking or makes a legitimate contribution. The traditional approach has been for students of American diplomacy to condemn the interrelationship between ethnic pressure and the direction of foreign policy. Diplomatic decision making, it is often said, should be determined solely on the basis of what is best for the national interest of the United States. This prevailing sentiment was expounded by political scientist G. Lowell Field in a 1964 essay. Field states that he is interested in discovering remedies "for the curse of ethnicity in American politics."

According to Field, ethnicity poses a "danger to prudent national decision-making." Besides suggesting the disbandment of the nationalities divisions of the Republican and Democratic parties, Field favors the "ostracism . . . [of] any political leader who obviously directs special appeals for the support of particular foreign policies to ethnic groupings with an undue emotional involvement."

Field argues that in the "proper moral climate" an ethnic group should be embarrassed when politicians make "this kind of appeal, just as a judge would be embarrassed by efforts to get him to participate in the decision of a case involving a close relative." It is simply illegitimate, Field says, to promote or even "tolerate situations—like those in which foreign policy hearings are conducted by the major parties before their national conventions—in which it appears that the feelings of ethnic minorities are legitimate grounds for deciding whether or not such intervention by American power is possible or desirable" (Louis L. Gerson, *The Hyphenate in Recent American Politics and Diplomacy* [1964], pp. xiii–xxvii). Taking decision making in foreign policy out of domestic politics and consigning it to the experts is a suggestion not limited to academia. In 1961 Senator J. William Fulbright insisted that foreign policy should not be determined in a deliberative forum in which parochial domestic interests would have influence. "The question I put," wrote Fulbright, ". . . is whether in the face of the harsh necessities of the 1960s we can afford the luxury of 18th century procedures of measured deliberation."

Fulbright doubted that a successful foreign policy could originate "by continuing to leave vast and vital decision-making powers in the hands of a decentralized, independent-minded, and largely parochial-minded body of legislators. . . . I submit that the price of democratic survival in a world of aggressive totalitarianism is to give up some of the democratic luxuries of the past." Foreign policy, Fulbright argued, should be determined by the experts in the executive branch of government and should not be a political football in Congress. Although Fulbright's thesis was that Congress should play less of a role in foreign policy formulation, the implementation of such a concept would clearly hinder the ability of ethnic groups to lobby for their particular interests.

Until recent years there was an assumption that the political assimilation of ethnic minorities was desirable. It seems likely that changes of attitude toward ethnicity and foreign policy in the past several years stem in part from the widespread abandonment in American society of the concept that ethnic groups benefit from assimilation. Ethnic minorities are now urged to emphasize their distinctiveness and to retain and identify with the culture of their land of origin, their religion, or their race. To lobby in favor of certain policies as a member of an ethnic group is seen as a more legitimate function than it was two decades ago. Proponents of assimilation have been attacked by ethnic group leaders who have argued that assimilation would strip ethnics of their most meaningful identification factor.

By the mid-1970's those who approved of the link between ethnic minorities and foreign policy no longer argued from a defensive position. They argue that the policymakers can themselves be highly partisan and political on specific foreign policy issues. For example, Jewish-Americans have long contended that the Middle East desk at the State Department has traditionally been staffed by people who are pro-Arab. Since some persons in the State Department contend that the national interest lies in protecting American commercial interests in the Middle East, ethnic bias is not the only possible explanation of the State Department position. Similarly, supporters of America's pro-Israel stance are not necessarily Zionists but can instead insist that the national interest is best served by supporting democracies, such as Israel, wherever they exist. Why, the critics of official Washington ask, should it be assumed that the State Department's interpretation of national interest is any more creditable than the views of State Department critics?

Ethnic leaders have suggested that nothing could be more appropriate in a democracy than to bring interest groups into the decision-making process. Following an era in Washington marked by governmental disdain for the public, the concept of broadening the public's role in decision making has substantial appeal.

Promoting good relations with foreign nations is basic to American diplomacy. One way to foster such friendly ties would be to make conspicuous a link between specific ethnic minorities and United States foreign policy toward their homeland. Ethnic leaders have argued that the goodwill that can be won by emphasizing the interrelationship between the ethnic group and policy toward the land of origin provides a compelling argument for encouraging such a relationship.

Among world powers, only the United States, with its diversity of ethnic populations, has had such obvious opportunities. Individual representatives, as well as an entire ethnic community, can be effectively used for diplomatic purposes. When President John F. Kennedy visited his ancestral home in Ireland and when he frequently referred to his Irish background, the resulting benefit to Irish-American relations was enormous. Similar goodwill is gained when a prominent ethnic is given a diplomatic assignment.

One example of using an entire ethnic group to obtain a foreign policy goal was presented in Italian-American relations during the late 1940's. Washington became concerned that the Italian electorate might vote the Communist party into control of the national government. Encouraged by United States officials, Italian-Americans mounted a mail campaign in which relatives in Italy would be persuaded to vote against the communists. Italian-Americans responded enthusiastically.

Events of recent years have shown that American policies toward the emerging nations of Africa have frequently failed to develop much respect or support from the African governments themselves. Perhaps one remedy for the increasingly anti-American image would be to have the black population in the United States play a role in policy formulation. It is possible that making American blacks conspicuous in policymaking would in itself drastically improve the American image among black African nations. Apparently this is one of the major reasons why President James E. Carter appointed black congressman Andrew Young to be the United States ambassador to the United Nations.

The role that has been played by black Americans in the making of policy has been minimal. Until recently, black voting was systematically discouraged—and a solid voting bloc is an essential ingredient when ethnic groups successfully influence diplomacy. It is possible that in the future, blacks could play a prominent role as one of the ethnic minorities that most successfully influences foreign policy.

One generation ago, both blacks and whites widely accepted the proposal that blacks should avoid any kind of cultural or political identification with their African heritage and should instead seek to assimilate into the American mainstream. Recently the same argument has been vigorously opposed by the majority of black people and their leadership. Full citizenship for blacks, it is now believed, can best come not from an abandonment of ancestral ties, but rather from the opportunity to identify with their African past.

One way in which black Americans could blend their ancestral loyalties with their life in the United States would be for them to assume a substantive role in United States diplomacy toward Africa. Ethnic leaders of other minorities could argue that the same concept applies to their particular group. Should blacks play a larger role in the conduct of American diplomacy, it could alter United States policy toward the white supremacist governments of South Africa and Rhodesia in the direction of greater official American hostility toward both nations.

The right of ethnics to lobby for policies they desire no longer seems questionable. Why is the attempt by ethnic minorities to influence the direction of foreign policy any less legitimate than the lobbying efforts of any number of economic interest groups? Why should it be any less legitimate to vote from ethnic considerations than for economic or social reasons? These are questions that are asked by spokesmen for ethnic minorities involved in foreign affairs issues.

An argument made against ethnic influence on foreign policy is that such influence is likely to spring from emotional loyalties rather than rational objectives. The goals of United States foreign policy can be summarized as military security, protection of economic interests, and minimization and peaceful settlement of international disputes. Ethnicity certainly has no obvious relation to any of these goals, and to the extent that it might be in conflict with them, it is an improper influence.

What this argument ignores is that the rational objectives articulated by professional policymakers usually omit such "emotional" factors as fairness to downtrodden or impoverished peoples. This has usually been the case with respect to colonial or dictatorial governments friendly to the United States. Such governments, especially in strategically located or mineral-rich countries, have consistently been supported by the United States for the reasons previously suggested.

Thus, the articulation of arguments for a contrary policy—based on justice, commitment to democracy, and other ideals—is typically left to the affected ethnic groups. An example in the recent past is the dictatorship in Greece, in the creation of which the United States played a considerable and unsavory role. American support was drastically curtailed, in large measure, on account of the persistent efforts of Greek-Americans. Similarly, the ethical commitment to displaced Jewry after World War II was argued mainly by Jewish-Americans, while the State Department and the public at large took little interest. Any ethical commitment to Palestinian Arabs, who had been consistently under foreign domination, was overlooked. There was no Arab-American lobby to promote the cause of the victimized Palestinian Arabs.

It is argued that to insist that the formulation of foreign policy should remain separate from the right of ethnics to influence it, would be to abandon a central attribute of a vital democratic state. Ethnic participation in foreign policy is defended as being consistent with the

American political ideals of democracy and freedom.

Those opposed to ethnic participation counter by saying that the result of openly sanctioning such political bartering would be a foreign policy in which a president or Congress would risk national survival simply to uphold a political pledge. The safeguard against such a disaster would likely be the general public itself. The political reality would seem to be that the public would simply not tolerate a president or a Congress embroiling the United States in some ill-conceived adventure designed to placate a particular group. Although it would have been popular with a variety of ethnic voters, the Republican party did not "liberate" Eastern Europe from communism following the 1952 election. Republican campaign pledges proved to be insincere, since there was little likelihood that the new administration was actually going to war in order to terminate communist control of Eastern Europe. Presented with the opportunity to intervene in the 1956 Hungarian revolt against the Soviet Union, the administration quickly indicated it would stay uninvolved in that effort to throw off Soviet domination.

Political scientist Lawrence Fuchs, arguing in favor of a close interrelationship between minority group pressure and American diplomacy, suggested "that foreign policy is too important to be left to the experts." Fuchs's advice was written in 1959, but it seems more relevant now than when he wrote it. Opponents of ethnic participation in foreign policy remain unimpressed. They still believe that there is grave danger ahead if foreign policy is taken away from the specialists and allowed to become even more of a political football.

The question of the appropriateness of mixing ethnicity with foreign policy will no doubt continue to be debated, but even diehard assimilationists must concede that ethnicity is probably an inevitable concomitant of the American political process, and that group pressure by ethnics provides a measure of political accountability in an area where lack of accountability can have dire consequences—as in the recent past.

BIBLIOGRAPHY

Louis Gerson, *The Hyphenate in Recent American Politics and Diplomacy* (Lawrence, Kan., 1964), is the first overall study of ethnicity and American foreign policy. Gerson writes from the perspective that it is inappropriate for ethnic groups to pressure and shape an area of foreign policy that is of particular interest to themselves.

For specific studies of how individual ethnic minorities can affect an aspect of foreign policy, see Louis Gerson, *Woodrow Wilson and the Rebirth of Poland, 1914–1920* (New Haven, 1953), which traces the Polish-American pressure on the Wilson administration that proved to be effective in bringing about an independent Poland. See also John Snetsinger, *Truman, the Jewish Vote and the Creation of Israel* (Stanford, 1974), which attempts to explain the critical role Jewish-Americans played in bringing into existence the state of Israel.

World War I created unprecedented opportunities for ethnic minorities eager to sponsor claims of their ancestral homeland. Accounts of the attempts by several of these groups to influence Wilson's peacemaking diplomacy are collected in Joseph P. O'Grady, *The Immigrants' Influence on Wilson's Peace Policies* (Lexington, Ky., 1967).

Until recently, almost all scholarly material on ethnicity and foreign policy was written with the editorial view that ethnic pressure on foreign policy goals was undesirable. An exception was Lawrence Fuchs, "Minority Groups and Foreign Policy," *Political Science Quarterly,* 76 (1959). Sympathetic treatment of the ethnic's involvement in foreign affairs is far more common today. An important work that adopts this approach is Patrick Moynihan and Nathan Glazer, eds., *Ethnicity* (Cambridge, Mass., 1975). Moynihan and Glazer emphasize the impact ethnicity has had on American diplomacy; they state "that immigration is the single most important determinant of American foreign policy."

Mark Levy and Michael Kramer have compiled some valuable statistical data on ethnic group voting patterns in *The Ethnic Factor: How America's Minorities Decide Elections* (New York, 1973).

[*See also* INTERCULTURAL RELATIONS; NATIONALISM; NATIVISM; POLITICS AND FOREIGN POLICY; PUBLIC OPINION.]

EXECUTIVE AGENTS

Kenneth J. Grieb

EXECUTIVE agents have been employed in the conduct of United States foreign policy throughout the history of the nation, dating from the earliest days of the Republic to the present era. The term executive agent denotes an individual appointed by the president, acting without legislative consultation or sanction, for the purpose of carrying out some specific function of limited duration. Executive agents, as distinct from regular diplomatic representatives who are either selected with the advice and consent of the Senate or hold regular diplomatic positions in the Foreign Service Corps by virtue of a career appointment and report to the secretary of state, receive instructions from and are directly responsible to the chief executive. The use of executive agents derives indirectly from the constitutional stipulation that the appointment of heads of regular diplomatic missions requires Senate approval, a procedure that frequently proves cumbersome and time-consuming. Special missions responding to temporary circumstances that necessitate prompt action require distinct procedures. Congress recognized this situation by providing the president with a "contingent fund" for special expenses, and salaries of agents are normally drawn from this fund. In practice such individuals tend to be considered the personal representatives of the president, as distinct from regularly accredited diplomats who are responsible to the secretary of state (though theoretically to the president through the secretary) and are regarded as representatives of the government of the United States. If this is a fine distinction that appears somewhat technical to the layman, it is an important differentiation in terms of function and operation, and one to which diplomats and governments are closely attuned.

That presidential envoys are employed for a wide variety of purposes reflects the flexibility of the office, which in the strictest sense is a pragmatic device available to the executive whenever expediency requires some fresh or supplemental channels. Because of this the functions of agents and the nature of their office vary with circumstances and with presidents.

Given the flexible nature of the instrument and its dependence on executive initiative, it is scarcely surprising that executive agents tend to be employed most extensively by strong chiefs of state. Presidential dynamics is thus a key element in the use of agents and their powers, for chief executives who prefer to act independently and conduct their office in a vigorous manner utilize this device to assume some degree of personal control of foreign policy. Consequently, the greatest use of such envoys has occurred during administrations such as those of Woodrow Wilson and Franklin Delano Roosevelt, both rated as "strong" executives by historians. Whether the agents supplement or supersede regularly accredited diplomats is dependent upon the president, and is generally indicative of his vigor and relations with the State Department.

It is no accident that the two presidents making the most extensive use of agents, Wilson and Roosevelt, both sought to conduct personal diplomacy, attempted to circumvent relatively weak secretaries of state appointed because of domestic political considerations, and mistrusted the personnel of the regular foreign service. Both employed executive agents as a means of accomplishing their goal of placing the conduct of key aspects of foreign policy directly in their own hands. Since there is obviously a limit to the number of situations to which a president can effectively devote personal attention, the appointment of this class of envoys can also provide an indication of the importance attached to a particular problem, nation, or region.

Selection of the individuals affects not only the operation of the institution, but also the degree of controversy surrounding its use. Since the very nature of the position renders it a dependency of the president, the chief executive is free to select the individuals according to any criteria he chooses. Full congressional debates regarding the constitutional powers involved have been rare, though a notable exception occurred in the Senate in 1831. Even in this discussion, the question was not whether the president had the right to appoint such agents, but rather what functions they could perform and their relation to regular diplomatic representatives. If the president seeks simply to secure the temporary services of an individual with recognized expertise in a given realm, whose talents would not otherwise be at the disposal of the government and whose abilities are especially suited to a specific task, this will normally evoke little dispute. Similarly, agents assigned to discrete or minor tasks seldom breed controversy.

The situation changes when the chief of state sends a personal representative to supersede a regularly accredited head of mission. In this instance, the agent clearly displaces an individual appointed with the consent of the legislature, allowing more direct control by the executive. If the agent is dispatched to an important theater of foreign policy on a highly visible or important mission, the likelihood that such an action will arouse the ire of Congress is increased. A president who relies upon agents because of suspicion of the objectives of the regular diplomatic personnel or as a means of placing the matter in the hands of an individual more ideologically compatible with his own views, assumes a greater risk of controversy. This is particularly true if the individuals employed as agents are politicians associated with the chief executive, who are likely to be controversial figures whose employment can be expected to antagonize the opposition party. Although the resultant disputes often focus on the agents, the basic issue involves the policies pursued by the president.

The controversy regarding the activities of Wilson's surrogates in Mexico is a case in point. The issue was not the use of agents per se, but rather the uses to which they were put. Wilson was clearly employing this device to circumvent the regular diplomatic officers, who disagreed with his policy. This was particularly evident in the type of individuals he dispatched on such missions, for they were invariably "deserving Democrats" who were politically associated with the president or Secretary of State William Jennings Bryan. Wilson felt that the most important qualifications for a prospective appointee were loyalty and similarity of outlook, which he considered more significant than knowledge of the area involved or the possession of any diplomatic skills. It is scarcely surprising that the appointment of partisans to carry out partisan policies provoked political controversy. Franklin D. Roosevelt, by contrast, though he also employed executive agents extensively and was himself scarcely less of a storm center than Wilson, managed to minimize such disputes through the selection of men of stature and experience who were clearly well qualified, and by employing them only on missions that obviously required special procedures.

The most common use of executive agents has been in dealing with nations or governments with which the United States did not at the time maintain normal diplomatic relations. In these circumstances, recourse to some special type of temporary representative is plainly necessary for the transaction of any business, including the inauguration of formal diplomatic intercourse. Inevitably, such agents were common during the early days of the Republic, when the United States had not yet been accorded recognition by many of the world's nations, and during the nineteenth century when the United States maintained regular diplomatic missions in only a small portion of the world's capitals. Indeed, the first representatives of the United States in the immediate aftermath of independence had the status of simple diplomatic agents, though they were technically congressional rather than executive agents, since they were dispatched during the days of the Continental Congress and the Articles of Confederation, prior to the existence of a separate executive branch. These individuals were appointed by the Committee of Secret Correspondence and later the Committee of Foreign Affairs, and only appointments to regular diplomatic missions were considered by the full Congress. Thus the use of agents whose designation was not subject to confirmation by Congress actually predates the existence of the executive branch.

Four of the nation's first five chief executives—George Washington, John Adams, James Madison, and James Monroe—all found it necessary to employ executive agents extensively. Among the earliest was Colonel David Humphries, whom Washington dispatched in 1790 to conduct negotiations leading to the establishment of diplomatic relations with Portugal. A series of similar emissaries was employed during the 1820's to arrange the nation's first treaty with Turkey. Executive agents were also utilized extensively in the intermittent negotiations with the Barbary States from the 1790's to the 1820's, and in establishing initial contact with the newly independent former Spanish colonies in the Western Hemisphere. In Latin America, individuals such as Joel R. Poinsett conducted reconnaissance missions and represented United States interests during the period when the ability of the new republics to maintain themselves was still in doubt and when formal recognition was delayed by the negotiations with Spain regarding the purchase of Florida. Temporary representatives proved convenient for this type of mission and have served as the instrument of this class of exchanges throughout the existence of the United States. In the 1970's Henry A. Kissinger played a pivotal role in establishing relations with the People's Republic of China.

Agents have also been employed extensively as a means of dealing with nations or governments with which formal diplomatic contacts have been severed or temporarily suspended. This is another situation in which the device is well suited to a particular need, for preliminary negotiations are often a necessary prelude to the renewal of formal ties. Such exchanges are obviously of temporary character and must be handled through some vehicle other than a regularly accredited representative, for the appointment of an individual with the latter status would in itself constitute de facto recognition of the government in question. Missions of this type have included efforts to protect American citizens and their rights in areas controlled by unrecognized governments or rebel factions, simple negotiations regarding the procedures for the renewal of regular relations, and attempts to impose preconditions as a price for full recognition. If the break is of recent origin and short duration, the appointment of special agents is often unnecessary, since members of the regular diplomatic service still on the scene can serve as the vehicle for such exchanges. In instances where the use of such individuals proves inconvenient or where they have been withdrawn as part of the break, the appointment of an executive agent is necessary.

Agents of this nature also date from the initial days of the nation, when President George Washington dispatched Gouverneur Morris to England in 1790 in a futile effort to open negotiations seeking a commercial treaty and the establishment of regular diplomatic relations. They have most often been employed in dealing with the newly emerging nations of the so-called Third World, where governmental instability is more frequent. This is particularly true in the Western Hemisphere, where the United States is more likely to attempt to exact concessions as a precondition for recognition. Such efforts have frequently included attempts to secure pledges of elections or the resignation of a government that has recently seized power. Wilson's dispatch of John Lind, a former Democratic governor of Minnesota and a political associate of Bryan, to Mexico in 1913 was one example of this type of mission. Lind, who had no prior diplomatic experience and no previous contact with Mexico, was appointed "adviser to the American embassy in Mexico City," but in reality served as the "personal representative of the president of the United States." In this manner he superseded the regularly accredited diplomats in that country, and acting as Wilson's spokesman and "confidential agent" conducted negotiations with the incumbent government of General Victoriano Huerta, which included the presentation of demands that stipulated Huerta's surrendering his office. This is an instance in which Wilson, who was suspicious of the regular foreign service personnel, chose to employ his own representative, on the ground that he preferred someone who was an adherent of his policies as his instrument.

In some instances more formal negotiations are employed, such as the so-called Bucareli Conference in 1923, when executive agents designated as "commissioners" representing the United States and Mexico held an extended "exchange of impressions" whose "sole object" was "to report afterwards to their respective high officials." Because the conferees were executive agents, the sessions did not technically constitute recognition of the Mexican government of General Álvaro Obregón, but did prove to be the vehicle for eventual recognition, through a resulting "memorandum of understanding" that enabled the satisfactory settlement of the questions regarding damage claims and oil land. Executive agents are frequently used in comparable situations, but it must be noted that although a useful vehicle for this type of negotiations, such envoys are but one mechanism for completing the necessary arrangements.

At times, executive agents have even been employed to conduct negotiations with nations with which the United States was at war, in an effort to conclude an early peace. Executive agents offer the only appropriate vehicle for such delicate discussions. The outstanding example of this type of mission was that of Nicholas P. Trist, chief clerk of the State Department. He was dispatched by President James K. Polk to Veracruz to accompany the military expedition of General Winfield Scott, which had landed at that port and was advancing toward the Mexican capital. Since the United States had entered the war for limited and clearly delineated objectives, and had already established effective control of the territory it desired, Polk hoped that Trist's presence would enable negotiations to be conducted simultaneously with the military campaign and might render the completion of the latter unnecessary. The use of an executive agent was essential both because Mexican reaction was uncertain and to maintain secrecy as a means of circumventing a mounting domestic sentiment to extend the original war aims. Trist's mission resulted in an incongruous combination of intermittent combat and negotiations, which failed to produce results until after the military expedition had fought its way into Mexico City.

During the early twentieth century, executive agents were frequently employed as the instruments of intervention in the domestic affairs of Latin American nations. In some instances this constituted a conscious attempt to avoid military intervention, through mediation between internal factions or the imposition of a political settlement. Admittedly this entailed political intervention, but such action was far less controversial than the landing of troops to terminate an internal conflict or to protect American citizens. Such roles were particularly prominent in the Caribbean region, with which the United States was especially concerned because of its significance for the security of the nation and because of the necessity of protecting the approaches to the Panama Canal.

The mission of Henry L. Stimson to Nicaragua in 1927 illustrates the use of an agent to mediate between internal factions. Civil war broke out in that Central American republic within a few months of the withdrawal of a United States Marine detachment which had kept the peace while serving as a "legation guard." The United States considered it necessary to act to preserve peace in Nicaragua, owing to the presence in that country of an alternative canal route. Stimson went to Nicaragua as the "personal representative" of President Calvin Coolidge to mediate between the Liberal and Conservative party forces in an effort to secure an agreement providing for a cessation of hostilities and the transfer of the dispute from the battlefield to the ballot box. The special envoy negotiated with the leaders of both factions, notwithstanding the fact that this entailed dealing with both the rebels and the incumbent government, which had been installed with the support of the United States and was still recognized.

The mission of General Enoch H. Crowder to Cuba in 1921–1923 constituted a similar effort to substitute political intervention for military action. Crowder was dispatched to Cuba in January 1921 by the Wilson administration in an effort to forestall hostilities over a disputed election when Liberal ex-President José Miguel Gómez challenged the reported victory of his former vice-president, Alfredo Zayas y Alfonso, who now had the support of the Conservative party. Crowder was continued in his position as the "president's personal representative" by Warren G. Harding. Crowder's open intervention and the implied threat of force prevented a civil war, but failed to satisfy the opposition. When a compromise agreement proved impossible, Crowder remained in Cuba as a virtual viceroy, in effect an American governor of Cuba, overseeing and dictating to that nation's government. Such methods did serve to prevent an insurrection, but constituted forceful intervention. It is interesting to note that Crowder's position became far less imposing when in 1923 his title was changed from the "president's personal representative" to ambassador to Cuba.

In addition to mediation and political intervention, executive agents have also been employed as a means of establishing and maintaining contact with rebel movements during times of turmoil when it is apparent that such factions have established effective control of substantial territory. Although such agents may participate in mediation efforts, their primary purposes are to promote the protection of American lives and property within rebel-controlled territory, to exert some influence upon the policies of the insurrection leaders, and to furnish information regarding the revolution to Washington. The most notable example of this practice occurred in Mexico during the Wilson administration. At this point Mexico was torn by civil war, and Wilson dispatched numerous "personal representatives" and "confidential agents" to that country, usually maintaining such individuals at the headquarters of two or three of the factions simultaneously. This resulted in a confusing welter of overlapping jurisdiction, with agents at times reporting on each other's activities. It was necessary to utilize executive appointments, for only in this manner could Wilson maintain representatives in more than one of the camps and attempt to influence the factions without technically conferring recognition upon them.

Agents have been employed on similar missions at other times, as for example the mission of William M. Churchwell, who in late 1858 was dispatched to confer with Mexican leader Benito Juárez. Arriving early in 1859, at a time of civil war when several factions claimed control of the nation and Juárez had been driven from the capital, Churchwell's mission paved the way for formal United States recognition of the Juárez regime.

Presidents have also found executive agents a convenient device to conduct negotiations or investigations of special delicacy in situations that would render it inexpedient to inform Congress and the public in advance by requesting confirmation of a formal appointment. In some instances this reflects the necessity for secrecy. The mission of Robert D. Murphy to French North Africa during World War II illustrates this situation. Although ostensibly an American consul, Murphy was in fact dispatched as Roosevelt's "personal representative" to determine the loyalty of French officials in North Africa to the German-dominated Vichy government, and to conduct negotiations to arrange for their cooperation with an Anglo-American invasion of North Africa. Clearly the success of a mission of this character depended on secrecy, which could not be maintained through a congressional confirmation proceeding.

Executive agents are also useful to the president when a disagreement with Congress precludes a request for advance approval. President Grover Cleveland's dispatch of former Congressman James H. Blount on an investigatory mission to Hawaii in 1893 was such an instance. A revolution had led to the installation of a new government dominated by American landowners and settlers, which promptly negotiated a treaty of annexation with the United States. Despite considerable sentiment for approval of the treaty, Cleveland withdrew it from the Senate and dispatched Blount, whose report confirmed that United States naval forces had aided the rebellion. The knowledge that the United States had been implicated in the revolt led to rejection of the annexation accord.

President Ulysses S. Grant's use of his private secretary, General Orville E. Babcock, as his "personal representative and special agent" in Santo Domingo in 1869 constituted an instance of the executive employing an agent to conduct confidential negotiations in the face of congressional disapproval. Grant was convinced of the advisability of acquiring Samaná Bay as a naval base, and dispatched Babcock ostensibly on a mission of investigation. Babcock negotiated a series of protocols providing for a lease on the bay and a virtual protectorate over the Dominican Republic, even though this action exceeded his instructions. The accords meticulously stipulated that they constituted merely the "basis" for a "definitive treaty" to be negotiated subsequently by a duly accredited envoy, and consequently had the character of an agreement between the two presidents, acting personally, rather than between their respective governments. Grant later sent his secretary back to Santo Domingo to "sit in" on the formal treaty negotiations as an "unofficial observer," who was "fully possessed of the President's views." Despite the fact that the negotiating powers were technically vested in the regularly accredited American minister in that capital, Babcock conducted the negotiations, while the minister merely signed the accord. The effort proved futile, as the treaty was rejected by the Senate.

Executive agents also serve as channels of direct communication with other heads of state in instances when particular circumstances require the bypassing of normal diplomatic channels, either as a matter of expediency, or as means of emphasizing the special importance of the talks. Usually this involves the dispatch of a prominent individual of considerable stature who is closely associated with the chief executive. Frequently the envoy is one of the president's principal advisers. The result is an emissary who plainly is speaking for the president, and whose mere appearance as a negotiator consequently demonstrates the importance attached to the question.

Woodrow Wilson resorted to this type of agent, to bypass normal diplomatic channels, in sending Colonel Edward M. House to Europe during 1916, to offer a plan designed to terminate World War I or, failing in that, to bring the United States into active participation. The dispatch of House enabled direct negotiations with British Prime Minister Sir Edward Grey, while ensuring that only the two executives and the emissary were aware of the precise contents of the proposal until the completion of the negotiations. Since House was a close ally of Wilson, his dispatch on a mission automatically endowed it with considerable importance, for in this instance the "president's personal representative" was indeed an individual who could be presumed to speak fully for him.

President Franklin D. Roosevelt also employed a close personal associate as a special envoy when he sent Harry Hopkins to Moscow to initiate discussions regarding Lend-Lease aid to the Soviet Union shortly after Nazi Germany invaded Russia in 1941. Again the president chose to use a separate channel, both to ensure confidentiality and to demonstrate his concern through the selection of an individual so closely associated with him that his mere appearance on the mission constituted a symbolic commitment, which accordingly assuaged the suspicions of Soviet Premier Josef Stalin.

Roosevelt also attempted similar methods in dealing with Generalissimo Chiang Kai-shek of China, who proved highly resistant to pressures exerted through normal diplomatic channels. As a consequence, Roosevelt resorted to a number of special officials in addition to the regular ambassador, ranging from a "political adviser" to Chiang (Owen Lattimore) to a "personal representative" (General Patrick J. Hurley). Hurley later became ambassador to China, though his influence as special representative was greater. President Harry S. Truman resorted to similar tactics when he dispatched former Chief of Staff General George C. Marshall to China during 1945–1946, in an effort to convince the nationalist and communist factions to negotiate an agreement to terminate the civil war. President Richard M. Nixon sent his personal foreign policy adviser, Henry A. Kissinger, on several missions, particularly for negotiations in Moscow regarding the Strategic Arms Limitation Treaty (1969).

Executive agents have also been utilized in dealing with international organizations, where they function as "unofficial observers" rather than as full delegates. Harding employed such individuals to establish contact with some agencies of the League of Nations and several other European conferences, as a means of circumventing the isolationist sentiment in the United States. Such unofficial observers are normally members of the regular diplomatic service, who are stationed at nearby posts and function in a dual role.

The principal variants in the institution of executive agents are the type of mission, the particular individual involved, and the method of reporting to the chief executive. Of necessity, the purpose of the mission is one of the primary determinants of the activities of the agent and the importance of the effort. The personality and prominence of the agent are other significant factors. Dispatch of a prominent individual who also functions within the government, particularly if he is closely associated with the chief executive, endows the mission with an importance of its own. It is scarcely surprising that such individuals are most frequently employed in missions to the heads of governments of important powers or allies. The use of members of the regular foreign service can also affect the institution, for although such individuals come to their missions with greater diplomatic expertise, their appointment is less dramatic, and consequently has less impact than that of the dispatch of a prominent individual or political figure. Accordingly regular diplomatic officers tend to be employed as executive agents principally on missions requiring some degree of secrecy, as their movements are less conspicuous.

The channels through which executive agents file their reports and receive their instructions are also significant determinants of their activities. Some agents are of such stature, or are so closely associated with the chief executive, that they report directly to him, bypassing the Department of State. Such individuals obviously have greater latitude, and acquire the stature of spokesmen for the chief executive. Yet the impact of their labors is somewhat limited by this very fact, since the Department of State and its diplomats in the field are often unaware of the details of the mission until after the fact. In some instances this lack of communication has caused serious difficulties. At the least it prevents the regular diplomatic officers from providing assistance or advice, and it can delay the implementation of the resulting agreements. On the other hand many agents, usually those from the regular diplomatic corps or those not closely associated with the president, file their reports through the Department of State. Indeed, some of these individuals, though executive agents, are not in fact the president's "personal representatives," but rather officials on special mission under the control of the Department of State, just as regular diplomats.

During the second half of the twentieth century, the employment of executive agents has tended to become institutionalized, reflecting a trend throughout the government. The growth of the bureaucracy, which has expanded rapidly as the government assumes more extensive functions, has necessitated a considerable structuring which has affected even so flexible an institution as that of executive agents. The formalization of a White House staff with distinct foreign policy advisers is the result of a gradual development over an extended period. Many presidents have employed their own advisers, but the institution first came into prominence under Woodrow Wilson, through his use of Colonel House.

The use of specific presidential foreign policy consultants and personal envoys expanded during World War II and the postwar years. Franklin Roosevelt's use of Harry Hopkins and a "brain trust" contributed to the development of a separate White House office, though in large measure this merely reflected the growth of the government with the increasing complexity of its functions in the modern world. By the 1950's the result was an entirely separate White House staff of considerable size. The existence of White House foreign policy advisers and the creation of the National Security Council as a separate body provides the president with a staff of specialists of his own, distinct from the State Department and the regular foreign service. This has strengthened the hand of the president in foreign affairs, enabling him to conduct his own policy through what virtually amounts to an alternate foreign office. That it is housed in the building formerly occupied by the State Department is symbolic both of the increased size of the two institutions (the State Department moved to larger quarters) and of the change in the relationship between the chief executive and the State Department.

The use of this power has varied with each chief executive, and has inevitably led to rivalry and controversy with the State Department. Under this arrangement the president has at his disposal a body of trained specialists who can serve as personal envoys, who can speak for him in the direct execution of policy and the conduct of negotiations. Executive agents dispatched abroad are frequently drawn from this group. The current trend toward summitry, or personal negotiations between heads of state, and "hot lines" directly connecting them renders the use of presidential advisers as executive agents to conduct direct negotiations not only convenient, but highly desirable in dealing with key allies or important questions. The dispatch of such an agent in itself constitutes an indication that the matter has been brought to the personal attention of the president, and hence assumes a certain symbolism of its own. Inevitably the use of executive agents tends to downgrade the importance of regularly accredited diplomats, who are considered representatives of the government (that is, the bureaucracy as represented by the State Department) rather than of the president himself.

This development is obviously fraught with difficulties, particularly since instant communications enable regular envoys to be in constant touch with Washington. The question of whom they reach in Washington, however, has endowed the special agent with a status as a demonstration of concern by the chief executive. In some respects this pattern is an inevitable result of the burgeoning of bureaucracy caused by the complexities of the modern world. Nixon's use of Kissinger to conduct important negotiations is a clear example of this situation. Since heads of state feel neglected if approached by someone other than the man who has the president's ear, the mere appearance of Kissinger tended to facilitate serious exchanges and promote accord. In this sense the use of executive agents is expanding, and the institution has been adapted to serve yet another purpose—that of enabling prompt action through bypassing the necessarily complex channels of modern governmental bureaucracy.

The increasing use of executive agents has caused considerable controversy regarding their role in presidential control of foreign policy. To many, the reliance upon such agents has led to the circumvention of the State Department and Congress, thereby contributing to the expansion of presidential power at the expense of the legislature. Although the Constitution clearly vests authority and responsibility for the conduct of foreign affairs in the president, congressional controls are provided through placing the sole war-making power in the hands of the legislature, and the requirement of Senate "advice and consent" to treaties and to the appointment of the ambassadors and ministers who represent the nation abroad, as well as to the selection of the secretary of state. Hence while the State Department is clearly part of the executive branch, the legislature has a greater role in its functioning than in the case of presidential advisers and agents. The growth of the National Security Council to the point that it has become virtually an alternate State Department functioning wholly under the president's control has provided the chief executive with a separate foreign affairs staff and enabled him to act independently in foreign affairs.

If such agents are employed to supplement normal diplomatic intercourse and execute a policy upon which a broad national consensus exists, they will arouse little concern. The institution becomes far more debatable, however, when a particular chief executive employs it on a large scale in an effort to concentrate control of foreign policy exclusively in his own hands or to bypass objection to a controversial policy. The result has been a decline in the morale of the State Department and its foreign service officers, as their functions have been partially usurped by a presidential office, leaving them with largely routine duties.

Presidents have shared the resulting concern. President John F. Kennedy attempted to alleviate the difficulty by appointing a "permanent executive agent" or roving troubleshooter by designating veteran diplomat Averell Harriman as "ambassador at large." The selection of a diplomat closely attuned to the State Department as the president's personal envoy provided a link between the two foreign affairs staffs. Yet the mere institutionalization of the position made it part of the bureaucracy, and this arrangement proved functional only because of the stature of Ambassador Harriman. President Nixon's concern about the resulting dichotomy between the White House foreign affairs staff and the State Department was evident when he shifted Kissinger from the White House to the State Department. Kissinger's appointment as secretary of state was yet another attempt to merge the two staffs and enable cooperation between them. Yet this too is clearly dependent on the stature of the incumbent, and it is significant that Kissinger gained his prominence while a member of the White House staff, rather than moving from the diplomatic corps to the White House.

Whatever the result of this continuing evolution, it is clear that executive agents have played and will continue to play an important role in American foreign relations. The institution has proven sufficiently flexible to be adaptable to a wide variety of uses and functions, and this has rendered it valuable. It remains primarily a supplement to normal diplomatic intercourse, to be employed in critical circumstances requiring special attention.

BIBLIOGRAPHY

Samuel Flagg Bemis and Robert H. Ferrell, eds., *The American Secretaries of State and Their Diplomacy* (New York, 1928–), an extensive series containing a volume on each of the individuals who served as secretary of state throughout American history, offers some comments on the relationship of special agents to the regular diplomatic establishment, and brief descriptions of some of the missions. Samuel Flagg Bemis, *The Latin-American Policy of the United States* (New York, 1943, 1967), is a general survey, useful since agents were frequently employed in Latin America. Kenneth J. Grieb has written the following works: *The Latin-American Policy of Warren G. Harding* (Fort Worth, Tex., 1976), which contains a discussion of several missions during an administration that employed them frequently in Latin America; "Reginald Del Valle: A California Diplomat's Sojourn in Mexico," in *California Historical Society Quarterly,* 47 (1968), a full discussion of one of Woodrow Wilson's agent's mission to Mexico; and *The United States and Huerta* (Lincoln, Neb., 1969), a detailed examination of an era during which Woodrow Wilson employed numerous agents in Mexico, containing a full discussion of the various missions. Larry D. Hill, *Emissaries to a Revolution* (Baton Rouge, La., 1973), examines Woodrow Wilson's use of agents in Mexico throughout his administration. Dana G. Munro, *Intervention and Dollar Diplomacy in the Caribbean, 1900–1921* (Princeton, 1964), includes a brief consideration of some missions in this area. Charles Seymour, ed., *The Intimate Papers of Colonel House,* 3 vols. (Boston–New York, 1926), provides the personal records of House's missions. Robert E. Sherwood, *Roosevelt and Hopkins: An Intimate History,* 2nd ed. (New York, 1950), details the relationship between the two title figures and contains chapters referring to Hopkins' service as an executive agent. Henry M. Wriston, *Executive Agents in American Foreign Relations* (Baltimore, Md., 1929; Gloucester, Mass., 1967), the most extensive study presently available, deals mainly with the nineteenth and early twentieth century; the discussion is rather cumbersome because of a broad interpretation of the term, but useful for consideration of purposes of agents, early precedents, and congressional debates.

[*See also* ARBITRATION, MEDIATION, AND CONCILIATION; CONGRESS AND FOREIGN POLICY; THE DEPARTMENT OF STATE; EXECUTIVE AGREEMENTS; INTELLIGENCE AND COUNTERINTELLIGENCE; INTERNATIONAL ORGANIZATION; INTERVENTION AND NONINTERVENTION; PRESIDENTIAL ADVISERS; PRESIDENTIAL POWER IN FOREIGN AFFAIRS; RECOGNITION POLICY.]

EXECUTIVE AGREEMENTS

Diane Shaver Clemens

PERHAPS the most significant neglected subject in the history of American foreign policy is the executive agreement. The most sensitive policies, especially war and peace, are arranged and executed by the president through this extraconstitutional means. The phrase itself began to be used about 1930; subsequently the device increasingly accounted for major policy until both the Korean and Vietnam wars could be initiated and concluded by executive agreements.

The very attempt to define an executive agreement as distinct from a treaty has resulted in a chaos produced by those who most use the device and profit from such lack of clarity. For example, in 1953 Senate hearings Secretary of State John Foster Dulles evasively informed Congress, "It is difficult, if not impossible, to define an executive agreement." In 1954 Democratic Senator Guy M. Gillette requested a more definite State Department definition only to be informed, "A treaty is a contract which must be submitted to the Senate for ratification, an executive agreement is one which does not have to be submitted to the Senate." Gillette mused: "I cited at the time something I heard as a boy. I was told the way to distinguish a male pigeon from a female was to put corn in front of the bird; if he picked it up, it was a he; and if she picked it up, it was a she." In 1941 Wallace McClure, a State Department civil servant, in the first book defending the president's displacement of Congress, wrote that "for controversial international acts the Senate method [ratification] may well be quietly abandoned, and the instruments handled as executive agreements." By 1961 a foreign service textbook taught that the executive agreement is "a final device, and perhaps one of the most important that may be resorted to in order to overcome the Senate two-thirds rule."

In this essay the definition of the Senate Judiciary Committee in 1953 will be used: "Every agreement and understanding formal and informal, made by any official of the executive branch with any foreign power or international organization and not submitted to the Senate as a treaty." This definition includes understandings or agreements of the United States not only with other nations, but also, as recent history reveals, with factions of other nations, and even between different United States agencies that operate both at home and abroad. (According to Senator John Sparkman, chairman of the Senate Foreign Relations Committee, the agency-to-agency agreement is the means by which the executive branch has contrived since 1972 to avoid the obligation imposed upon it by congressional restraining legislation in the Case Act.) Executive agreements must also include those presidential orders and proclamations which can lead to and obligate the United States to significant commitments with foreign parties without the advice and consent of the Senate or without congressional legislation. In the latter category, there is frequent overlap between executive agreement and action.

Before widespread use of the phrase "executive agreement," the form of such presidential engagements included instruments such as the modus vivendi, convention, compact, exchange of notes, pacts, acts, protocols, procès-verbaux, compromis, declarations, proclamations, and, finally, even armistices. The significance of such arrangements prior to recent history lies in their insignificance; such agreements were considered temporary in nature, related to matters of comparatively trivial importance and not policy-setting in a major way, and never exceeded congressional will. Thus international agreements were limited in scope and delimited by the Constitution. Only after World War II did the concept reverse itself; suddenly the executive made policy unilaterally, executed it in matters of war and peace, abrogated constitutional responsibility, and justified this imperious course as inherent in an alleged independent constitutional authority of the president.

Executive agreements, as the term now is commonly used, fall into three distinct categories and are of certain discrete types. The first two categories cause little difficulty since they derive from the Constitution and are affirmed by Supreme Court interpretations.

I. AGREEMENTS IMPLEMENTING LEGISLATION

These agreements are those made pursuant to a treaty, in implementation of it or contingent upon future congressional action. For example, agreements with Turkey in 1976 for reopening American bases were dependent on Congress' approval of economic and military funds to aid Turkey. In the case of extradition, demands upon the United States result from treaty provisions, with the president the appropriate respondent for the nation. This has not been interpreted as conferring independent authority on him. Hence, the State Department refused in 1910 to exchange notes with Mexico because the department admitted no authority even to interpret articles in an extradition treaty. Such interpretations, wrote Secretary of State Philander C. Knox, could be disregarded by the federal courts, were not binding, and ought rather to be submitted to Congress either for legislation or formal ratification in a new treaty. In this vein, the Supreme Court found in 1936 that there is "no executive prerogative to dispose of the liberty of the individual."

Arbitration agreements arising from treaties have resulted in even more rigid Senate control over executive negotiations by often imposing the rule that the "compromis" agreement itself (already provided for by treaty) be submitted as if it too were a treaty. This illustrates how complete is the Senate's power to tie the hands of the executive in foreign affairs at its will. The word and concept of treaty entertained by the Founding Fathers was all-encompassing with the intent that all foreign relations of a permanent or significant nature be conducted by the president upon the advice and consent of the Senate.

II. AGREEMENTS AUTHORIZED BY CONGRESS

The second category of executive agreements also stirs little debate. Congress (either the House of Representatives or both houses acting together) explicitly has authorized the president to carry out the intent of its legislation. For example, trade, commerce, and tariff have until recently accounted for most of the congressionally authorized executive agreements. History is replete with Supreme Court decisions on whether or not the president may properly be the recipient of liberal rather than finely designed instructions from Congress. The Court has ruled that if authorization provides a sufficiently tight and intelligible guideline, Congress has not delegated power but only requested the president to act as agent or administrator. Negotiations following from congressional instructions include raising and lowering of tariffs, most-favored-nations clauses, trade, fishing rights, and the abrogation or interruption of commerce. Other executive agreements common to this category include postal conventions, trademark and copyright agreements, money orders, exchange of documents with foreign nations, and matters of immigration.

Monetary and financial affairs of the nation are handled by acts of Congress. Congress authorized credit bonds in World War I, with the president concluding contracts. In World War II, under lend-lease, the president supplied the Allies with war matériel through executive agreements with thirty-nine countries.

Presidential Encroachments. Supreme Court tests have come mainly on issues of trade and commerce and have reaffirmed the power of Congress rather than that of the president in such international understandings. Presidents have nonetheless exceeded such authority. For example, when the Senate failed to ratify a treaty with the Dominican Republic in 1905 to give the United States control over custom houses, President Theodore Roosevelt "put the agreement into effect," as he stated. The Senate capitulated after two years and legitimized his action. He claimed in his autobiography that anyhow he "would have continued without any action by Congress." In 1905 he made a secret agreement blessing the Japanese military protectorate in Korea—an executive agreement that came to light only twenty years later. Similarly, there was Theodore Roosevelt's high-handed boastful creation of the Panamanian republic at the expense of Colombia.

The executive branch continuously encroached upon congressional constitutional obligations, especially in innocuous areas such as citizens' claims against foreign governments. Important encroachments include recognition of foreign governments, the unauthorized use of congressional monies, and the creation of military missions abroad separate from any treaty obligation or congressionally sanctioned agreement.

Claims against the United States cannot be collected without a treaty; however, claims by Americans have since 1936 fallen almost exclusively into what the executive branch has come to term "presidential diplomatic authority." From what began as congressional authorization for the president to settle particular claims there emerged a new source of executive power purportedly sustained by Supreme Court decisions (*U.S.* v. *Belmont* [1937] and *U.S.* v. *Pink* [1941]), which upheld the Litvinov assignment following the Roosevelt administration's recognition of the Soviet Union. Here the United States accepted Soviet seizure of considerable American assets in the Soviet Union in exchange for comparatively small Russian assets held by private American citizens and institutions. Although the Supreme Court did not rule on the right of executive recognition as such, that and other acts of magnitude were nourished by the supportive obiter dictum of Justice George Sutherland in the famous *Curtiss-Wright* case (1936). The issue of claims had become significant in the nineteenth century and early twentieth century, but only if policy matters of import were involved. In such a case, the president acknowledged that, were war a conceivable consequence, he could not act on a claim. Thus in 1860 the government refused to collect claims against Nicaragua; and in 1911 President William Howard Taft, when confronted with probable confiscation of American investments in Mexico, responded by assembling troops but warned that he could protect property only "if Congress shall direct."

Executive authority to settle claims, the legal adviser to the State Department has argued, rests on the power to recognize foreign governments, a power that in practice has reposed with the executive and that must be viewed as a mode of executive agreement in itself and certainly a formidable generator of others. Yet the constitutional base for such a power is flimsy or nonexistent. The Constitution authorizes the president "to receive ambassadors." In this matter of diplomatic etiquette the executive came to discover, especially by the 1930's, an independent power beyond the reach of Congress; indeed by clandestine negotiation the administration of Richard M. Nixon in 1972 recognized the government of the People's Republic of China. Yet historically when the matter of recognition of an independent Texas posed a vital policy question, President Andrew Jackson believed the decision was best left to Congress. Abraham Lincoln refused "to inaugurate a novel policy . . . without approbation of Congress" and left the matter of recognition of Haiti and Liberia to the legislative branch. Yet contemporary history reveals that the president unilaterally has set the course of policy through recognizing not only the People's Republic of China, but South Vietnam and the Soviet Union as well. Recognition of the Soviet Union by Franklin Roosevelt in 1933 was a momentous decision. What Alexander Bickle called "a little snippet of a phrase"—to receive ambassadors—thus emerged as one of the most potent executive instruments in taking liberties with the Constitution.

III. EXECUTIVE AGREEMENTS BASED ON THE PRESIDENT'S INDEPENDENT POWER

Illustrations of these liberties are various. In foreign aid, where the power of the purse should make the executive dependent on annual legislative appropriations, a dramatic change has taken place since Franklin Roosevelt's destroyers-for-bases agreement in 1940. Before the enactment of the Marshall Plan in 1947, German contributions in the form of raw materials to the war-torn economy of Europe were actually financed through American funds channeled into the German economy through the American military government of occupation. This procedure was never presented to a wary Congress, still mindful of World War I when victor had paid reparations owed by the vanquished. In 1953, unknown to Congress and using the mutual defense agreement as a cover, President Dwight D. Eisenhower started subsidizing the Ethiopian army in exchange for a major National Security Agency installation at Asmara; this aid led to expansion of Ethiopia's army and a secret commitment to protect the government even from internal threats. In the same year Eisenhower presumed to underwrite expenses for bases supportive of General Francisco Franco's fascist regime in Spain. A similar commitment of aid and bases was made to Thailand until the president built a formidable military establishment beyond congressional purview. Bilateral assistance agreements were negotiated and executed with South Vietnam, Portugal, South Korea, and other countries. These agreements, in order to evade the legal obligation to report them to Congress under the Case Act of 1972, were tortuously construed to be internal agreements between the Defense Department and the Agency for International Development.

Clearly by the 1960's the third category of executive agreements had emerged—those negotiated solely on the presumed authority of the president acting without congressional approval.

Intention of the Constitution and Precedent. The Constitution defines only two sole powers of the president in the area of foreign relations: (1) once a war is declared, to conduct it as commander in chief, and (2) to receive ambassadors. The other powers (treatymaking and appointment of ambassadors) he holds conjointly with the Senate. On the other hand, the Constitution clearly delegates power for foreign affairs to the Senate, as Article II, Section 2, states: "He [the president] shall have Power, by and with the Advice and Consent of the Senate, to make Treaties. . . ." "Treaties" had a broad and all-comprehensive meaning for the framers of the Constitution. Alexander Hamilton said that "it was understood by all to be the intent of the provision to give that power ample latitude—to render it competent to all the stipulations which the exigencies of national affairs might require; competent to the making of treaties of commerce, treaties of peace, and every other species of convention usual among nations."

The role of the president in this treatymaking process came almost as an afterthought. The framers of the Constitution—thirty of whom had been members of the Continental Congress, which stood for parliamentary supremacy and for no executive—provided in their Committee of Detail draft that "the Senate . . . shall have power to make treaties." As debate proceeded, James Madison pointed out that the Senate represented just the states. To retain separation of power and balance, the president should be added as "an agent." Thus on 7 September 1787, ten days before the adjournment of the Constitutional Convention, the president became an adjunct to the envisioned parliamentary control. Prior to that day, a suggestion to give the president the power of the treaty was defeated. Patrick Henry explained, "The President, as distinguished from the Senate, is nothing."

The minutes of the Constitutional Convention, the *Federalist Papers,* the ratifying conventions, and the explanations of the participants as well as an analysis of the syntax and punctuation of the Constitution itself, demonstrate that the framers of the Constitution intended the Senate to be involved actively in the making of a treaty from its inception (that is, formal agreement between nations to negotiate a treaty) through its modification and negotiation to its ratification or rejection. The words and intentions of the framers were forgotten or ignored by the mid-twentieth century. As Secretary of State Dean Acheson asserted, "The negotiation of a treaty is given to one branch and the ratification to another." The role of the Senate?—"exercising its constitutional power to make a treaty by ratifying it." Woodrow Wilson held an exalted view when he wrote in 1908: "One of the greatest of the President's powers . . . [is] his control, which is very absolute, of the foreign relations of the nation. The initiative in foreign affairs, which the President possesses without any restriction whatever, is virtually the power to control them absolutely."

In short, the "Advice" portion of Article II, Section 2, has been disregarded. A popular explanation and argument for the president's not seeking "advice" is attributed to the precedent allegedly set by George Washington. The tale has it that Washington went to the Senate for advice regarding his first treaty, and when no advice was forthcoming Washington supposedly left the Senate chamber, exclaiming "he would be damn'd if he ever went there again." In reality Washington and the Senate understood their respective obligations. The Senate and the president resolved this problem by written correspondence, keeping each other fully informed.

Bases for Executive Agreement. Since the Constitution was written, the president has discovered the distinction between constitutionality and opportunity. By doing it, he instituted policy and avoided Congress. Only since World War II has it been argued that such action was legal and that the president had the constitutional authority to make foreign policy by interchanging the executive agreement with the prescribed treaty. Whereas Hamilton had contrasted the British sovereign's exclusive authority in foreign affairs to the president's restricted power ("The one can do alone what the other can do only with concurrence of a branch of the legislature"), by the 1950's sovereignty seemingly shifted to the executive alone, measured by presidential actions or by what the State Department deemed as precedent. For example, by means of alleged precedent (125 cases, according to State Department arguments for executive action in the Vietnam War), the war-making powers have become appropriated by the president.

The apologists for an elevated use of such a simple business device as the executive agreement will be referred to as "sovereignists," since their position essentially rests on a claim by Justice Sutherland. In *Curtiss-Wright* he said that in the conduct of foreign affairs the president possessed a source of power transferred directly from the sovereignty of George III and not dependent upon the Constitution at all, a power that made the president the "sole organ" of the nation in the field of international relations. Besides Sutherland's claim, there are a number of other arguments conjured up to support the sovereignists' view. The main arguments are the following: (1) the president is recognized in international law as the responsible authority for the nation; (2) the president is chief diplomatic officer and derives power from that; (3) he has independent executive authority under Article II of the Constitution; (4) because the Constitution refers to "compacts" among states, this wording confers upon the president the right through executive agreement to make compacts among international states; (5) by precedent and usage the president has established new boundaries; (6) the Supreme Court has sanctioned the president as "sole organ" and put the executive agreement on a par with, similar to, and interchangeable with the treaty; and (7) as commander in chief the president can repel attacks, engage in reprisals, fight limited wars, and determine jeopardy to the national security.

1. INTERNATIONAL LAW

From the international point of view, if a nation contracts an obligation with another, that obligation is binding. International law books tend therefore to state: "In international law . . . treaties and executive agreements are alike, and both constitute equally binding obligations on the nation." The problem is that international law or opinion regarding it has no independent legal standing in American law. The Constitution provides for American law and recognizes no higher law. Even by its own standards international law is applicable only when consented to by both parties and when the obligation incurred is considered moral and nonjusticiable. Examples of executive agreements having a bilateral consent are the House-Grey memorandum of World War I and the Nixon-Thieu exchange of notes in 1973. In the former, the United States proposed to call a peace conference with demands favorable to the Allies and to threaten war on Germany if she refused attendance; in the latter, Nixon, after the Paris peace accords had been achieved, promised further American military intervention were Thieu threatened. Such agreements might claim legal validity if one were an international citizen rather than a citizen of a nation state. The degree to which even these bilateral agreements were actually binding is measured by the ease with which they were quickly dropped. Moreover, one can consult recent international law for a current indication of a ruling on executive agreements. Article 46 of the Vienna Convention on the Law of Treaties (1969), the latest codification of acceptable international law, is relevant. It recognizes that a nation is not committed to an international agreement if that agreement manifestly violates a fundamental provision of internal domestic law that a third party could ascertain. This concept was adopted by the nations unanimously 93 to 0.

2. CHIEF DIPLOMATIC OFFICER

The diplomatic center of the nation is located in the presidency. Here the secretary of state is the president's principal officer and the Department of State the executive agency. Further, the president has come in the twentieth century to negotiate through summit conferences personally with other nations' leaders as did Woodrow Wilson and Franklin D. Roosevelt in the world wars. President James Carter initiated summit diplomacy early in his administration with an economic conference in London.

Through the executive agreement major policies are developed entirely within the executive branch. Yet to attain standing in American law, such agreements must ultimately be approved by Congress. The president remains the "agent" as Madison said, or the officer.

3. INDEPENDENT EXECUTIVE AUTHORITY

The executive function of the nation resides in the president. Although in foreign relations Congress can appoint someone other than the president to act in its name, the details that would burden Congress and prevent it from substantive policy decisions are assigned to the president in his administrative, housekeeping function. As Henry Steele Commager explained this assignation, it was a "useful method for disposing of routine business that did not rise to the dignity of a treaty."

The word "executive" was historically not employed by English law; the term was a post-Revolutionary creation that came into usage in various state constitutions in order to repudiate the notion of royal prerogative. In the conferment of power through the Constitution, the Founding Fathers conceived that, as Madison stated, it was necessary "to fix the extent of the Executive authority." A study of the evolution of the constitutional clause, "the executive Power shall be vested in a President," shows clearly that the purposes of this clause were to settle the issue of whether the executive should be plural or singular and to give the executive a title. Executive powers were limited by painstaking enumeration, and this wording was a descriptive, not an enabling, sentence. As Chief Justice William Howard Taft stated in *Myers* v. *United States* (1926): "The vesting of the executive power in the President was essentially a grant of the power to execute the laws." The Founding Fathers took great care to point out that this power bore no resemblance to that of the British king. That this wording has been construed as bestowing inherent authority of any import distorts the Constitution.

4. "COMPACT" ARGUMENT

The sovereignists try to support the concept of "inherent" power by claiming that the Constitution makes a distinction between a "Treaty, Alliance, or Confederation" (which no individual state may enter) and an "Agreement or Compact" (which states may make either with each other "or with a foreign Power," subject to congressional approval). From this the sovereignists argue that the Constitution could not have denied the president that which it allowed the states: ". . . the conclusion is inescapable that the Federal Government was intended to have the power to make 'agreements' or 'compacts.' " Explicit authorization was for the states to make "agreements" and the inescapable fact, if there was any, was that the president was not mentioned at all. Such agreement among states had been common under the Articles of Confederation and continued under the Constitution with the permission of Congress. It does not follow that this constitutional grant to the states to make agreements with the consent of Congress gives an unmentioned president the power to make agreements in the field of foreign affairs without the consent of Congress.

5. PRECEDENT AND USAGE

Another source claimed by sovereignists derives from adaptation by usage. Raoul Berger has described this as "a label designed to render palatable successive usurpations whereby the President has taken over treaty functions confided to Senate and President jointly, and war functions exclusively granted to Congress and withheld from him, and thus disrupted the constitutional distribution of powers considered inviolable under the separation of powers." Berger's argument explains how an unsanctioned practice repeated often enough in effect takes on the force of a constitutional amendment. For example, if the president has successfully accumulated enough instances of usage of power where none before existed, then eventually a new power base is assumed, transferring authority from Congress to him. Thus executive power is also plenary and the president becomes his own legislator. The Constitution postulates separate powers that cannot be transferred or delegated to another branch; nor can they accrue to another branch through precedent. By the executive's criterion, bank robbery, repeated successfully, becomes lawful. In the twentieth century the effect of such precedents and assertions has been to give the nation a president who claims (and exercises) the power to make war.

6. COURT DECISIONS

In the executive's search for justification of its unilateral conduct of foreign policy, it has referred us to no weightier body of authority than the rulings and opinions of the justices of the Supreme Court. Constantly twisting the statements of the Court to fit its view, the executive has cloaked its expansion of power by distorting the Court's decisions. In this spirit, the executive has specifically claimed that the Court has ruled that the executive agreement is of equal dignity with a treaty; that the executive is "sole organ" of the nation in the international arena; that Congress may delegate extensive powers to the president; that the president could legally substitute an executive agreement for a treaty at will; and finally, that the president inherited directly from George III of England, without the help of the Constitution, all the sovereign prerogatives of the monarch in external affairs. Richard Nixon thus confidently asserted, "It is quite obvious that there are certain inherently governmental actions which, if undertaken by the sovereign in protection of the interest of the nation's security, are lawful but which, if undertaken by private persons, are not."

The most readily accepted justifications for executive agreements have come from a few repeatedly cited Supreme Court cases. Sovereignists thus claim that treaties are the "supreme law of the land," purporting that in *Altman & Co.* v. *U.S.* (1912) and *U.S.* v. *Pink* (1941) executive agreements were ruled to be of "similar dignity" to a treaty. They further maintain that in *U.S.* v. *Belmont* (1937) the Court held that an executive agreement supersedes state law. Thus the conclusion rendered by the sovereignists has been that an executive agreement is equivalent to a treaty. The next step has been to conclude that the business of the United States is better done by the tested executive agreement than by the Constitution's prescribed treaty. By the 1960's sovereignists therefore widely stated that the treaty was obsolete and should be put aside in favor of executive agreements.

Other justifications used by the sovereignists are based on Supreme Court decisions which they claim designate the president as solitary agent for the government in foreign affairs. In particular the *Curtiss-Wright* decision (1936) provided the most extreme logic in attempting documentation for presidential authority. Thus they seized upon the gratuitous proclamation on the part of Justice Sutherland that in foreign affairs the chief executive has an inherent power not granted by the Constitution but inherited from the British king. From this the justice derived ". . . an exclusive power of the President as the sole organ of the federal government in the field of international relations—a power which does not require as basis for its exercise an act of Congress."

The argument that an executive agreement is the same thing as a treaty and therefore that the Senate or House can be bypassed in foreign policy by the president stems from the *Altman* case. Congress had authorized the president to make commercial compacts and, in separate legislation, given the courts jurisdiction in writs of errors in cases of treaties. The complainant claimed the Court had no jurisdiction over the congressionally ordained compacts because a compact, instead of a treaty, was involved. The Court ruled that the intent and purpose of Congress in the enabling legislation was to make use of the term "treaty" in the broadest international sense, including commercial international agreements. It decided that the compact in question was not a treaty in the domestic or constitutional sense, but for purposes of Court jurisdiction in this particular case the compact would be treated with "similar dignity," thus allowing the Court to hear the suit. Considering the facts of the case, it is hardly likely that a Court action, provided for by congressional legislation in the case of treaties, and which considered compacts to be like treaties, would rule that Congress had no jurisdiction over compacts. Moreover, it was not the Court's intention to do so. In its interpretation, the Court viewed treaties in the broadest possible sense, with compacts subsumed under this category. The narrow procedural ruling that compacts were of "similar dignity" to the treaty was affirmation that compacts could not be removed from this category and attain any independent status. The sovereignists reverse this interpretation entirely, attempting to remove compacts from congressional control and create the separate category the Court denied. The Court understood Darwin—a genus divided into species did not suddenly transmogrify the various species into new genuses.

The *Belmont* case (1937) is cited as evidence that the president can, on his own authority, make an executive agreement that is then law. The issue in the *Belmont* case involved the Litvinov assignment, an executive agreement subsequent to recognition of the Soviet Union by the United States. The United States took possession of all Soviet assets in the United States through the assignment. The question to be decided by the Court was whether federal law or state law should prevail, since the state of New York backed banker August Belmont when he refused to relinquish Russian funds. The Supreme Court repeated the *Curtiss-Wright* phrase, "sole organ . . . of the government," and authorized the executive to collect funds under the agreement. The Court at no point ruled on the president's authority to recognize the Soviet Union as a basis for the subsequent executive agreement (the Litvinov assignment) or on the legality of the agreement; it ruled only that federal law superseded state law in this instance. For the purpose of this ruling, the agreement was categorized with compacts and postal conventions, which generally are direct results of congressional authorization. Clearly there was no intent or ruling to suggest the president had authority that Congress or the Constitution had not given him. Constitutional scholars have pointed out that the Court could not have ruled otherwise; if it had, this would have meant that a private bank, with the backing of a state such as New York, could take the property of the United States government.

In 1941 yet another case resulted from the Litvinov assignment. The federal government again attempted to collect further assets from a New York insurance company (*U.S.* v. *Pink*), citing as precedent the *Belmont* case and declaring that the Litvinov assignment was a compact with "similar dignity" for purposes of federal jurisdiction in the suit. Justice William O. Douglas wrote that the "Litvinov Assignment was an international compact which did not require the participation of the Senate." This opinion has been interpreted by sovereignists to mean that the president has authority on his own initiative to make international compacts. On the contrary, the Court again chose not to comment on the power of the president to recognize foreign governments, which was not an issue in the case. It did find a new rationale for the legality of the Litvinov assignment, not on the basis of presidential power but on the power of Congress to legitimize the compact, which, it can be argued, Congress tacitly had done in 1939 by creating a commissioner for claims. Justice Douglas quoted Sutherland verbatim, finding the president once more to be the "sole organ" who, in this nonbinding obiter dictum, possessed a "modest implied power" to remove obstacles standing in the way of full diplomatic recognition of another nation. This was hardly a sanction to make international agreements. Justices Harlan F. Stone and Owen J. Roberts took offense even at these remarks and declared: "We are referred to no authority which would sustain such an exercise of power as is said to have been exerted here by mere assignment unratified by the Senate." If one is still in doubt whether this case supports elevation of the executive agreement, one need only consult Article VI of the Constitution itself. Only "Laws" and "Treaties" are the "supreme Law of the Land," and an executive agreement is not a treaty because it lacks the "Advice and Consent" of the Senate, nor is it a law because it is not "made" by Congress.

President as Sole Organ. The reference to the president as the "sole organ" in international affairs in the *Pink, Belmont,* and *Curtiss-Wright* cases has had the most far-reaching consequences in claims of presidential power. The wording itself, extravagantly embroidered upon in *Curtiss-Wright,* was a distortion of a ruling that Justice John Marshall had made in the early days of the republic.

Under the terms of Jay's Treaty (1795) the British government requested the extradition of one Jonathan Robbins, wanted for murder. The issue was whether the president or the Court would be the proper authority to execute the treaty. Marshall held that the president's responsibility to execute the law of the land compelled him to act in accordance with the treaty since the president was the "sole organ of the nation in its external relations" until such time as Congress should see fit to authorize another representative. "Congress, unquestionably, may prescribe the mode and Congress may devolve on others the whole execution of the contract. . . ." This is hardly Court sanction for the president to execute policy on his own initiative. "Far from excluding Congress from this 'sole organ' area," wrote constitutional scholar Edward S. Corwin, "Marshall regard[ed] the exercise of even this power [as 'sole organ'] as subject to Congressional control." But Sutherland, who is responsible for transplanting Marshall's decision into the *Curtiss-Wright* case, failed to comprehend and accurately construe the role Marshall had ruled upon. As a result the misstatement has been taken out of the context in the *Curtiss-Wright* case, and used by sovereignists to prove the opposite. Thus it has been advanced repeatedly that the president is sovereign and can at whim or will decide whether he prefers a treaty or an executive agreement in conducting his foreign relations. This view ignores the existence of a Constitution with enumerated powers, none of which confers any sole power on the president to conduct foreign relations, beyond the ceremonious welcome of foreign ambassadors.

Justice Sutherland's Obiter Dictum. The *Curtiss-Wright* case requires careful examination. It resulted from Congress' authorizing the president to prohibit arms shipments to the belligerents in the Bolivia-Paraguay war. He did so, and the Curtiss-Wright Corporation, which was held in violation of this prohibition, sued the government, claiming that the president did not have the right to exercise this congressionally delegated authority because Congress could not delegate such power to the president. The question was whether the president could be given the power to halt arms shipments and prosecute violators. The Court held that Congress had properly delegated the president to act within the congressional rules and that he had accordingly done so. And this was all that the Court ruled.

The case took a bizarre turn when Justice Sutherland seized this occasion to deliver opinions, deemed by scholars as a "mischevious and demonstrably wrong" obiter dictum, "ill-considered and aberrant" to the case at hand. His appropriation of the powers of the crown of England to the president was without foundation in law or history, for in the American system there is no law outside the Constitution, and the historical transfer of power during the Revolution was from the crown to the American people, who delegated it to their various state governments (for a time, then, sovereign themselves), thence to the Continental Congress and the legislature of the Confederation. Thus it is simply incorrect to say, as Sutherland does, that "the external sovereignity of Great Britain . . . immediately passed to the Union" and its agent, the president. This transferrence, be it noted, was limited to external affairs. Sutherland did not attribute the same latitude to the president in internal affairs, which everyone would have recognized as patently absurd. Yet to attempt to split the powers conferred by the Constitution into external and internal realms is impossible. Nevertheless, this artificial distinction positing an external realm of authority, where the president is sovereign, has gained an extraordinary following in recent years.

Even Sutherland contradicted himself. In referring to "the exclusive power of the President as sole organ," he qualified that power with the stipulation that it "of course, like every other government power, must be exercised in subordination to the applicable provisions of the Constitution." Thus, as Elbert M. Byrd summarized it: ". . . the opinion is self-contradictory in the extreme, for an inherent power doctrine cannot be reconciled with a doctrine of delegated powers subject 'to the applicable provisions of the Constitution.' "

Sutherland's view was embraced by the sovereignists of the 1940's, who indeed saw the Constitution as a quaint document, framed in archaic language by gentlemen-farmers for a small unarmed seaboard nation of rustic bumpkins—a document that could suffice to fill the needs of a now imperial nation only by thorough "reglossing" in the light of contemporary experience. (For example, the influential, often-cited McDougal and Lans are prominent examples of such a view.) Later courts, however, ruled contrary to Sutherland's opinion. In *Ex Parte Quirin* (1942), the Court, with little notice from the academic world, owing to the war, ruled that "Congress and the President, like the courts, possess no power not derived from the Constitution." In 1952 in *Youngstown Sheet and Tube Co.* v. *Sawyer* (Steel Seizure Case), Justice Robert H. Jackson was astounded that the executive could hold the doctrine of external sovereignty seriously—namely, claim that since the president had involved the nation in war through an executive agreement with the Korean president, he could therefore seize the domestic steel mills. Jackson's ruling did not direct itself to external policy, but did find the seizure illegal, stating that history did not leave presidential power open to question: "The purpose of the Constitution was not only to grant power, but to keep it from getting out of hand."

A particularly pertinent case, *Reid* v. *Covert* (1957), involves a decision on a status of forces executive agreement with Britain that permitted a private citizen abroad to be tried by a military court. The Court nullified those portions of the agreement that violated the enumerated constitutional rights of the citizen. The case is important, for it emphasizes what sovereignists ignore—that executive agreements do not have the same force as ratified treaties and that neither may bargain away rights specifically granted to American citizens by their Constitution. Similarly an earlier case, *Missouri* v. *Holland* (1920), established that an executive agreement with Canada concerning migratory birds could not, as a treaty could, be enforced within a particular state. When the same agreement became a treaty and was ratified by the Senate, Missouri and its game warden bowed to what was now the law of the land. Finally, in *Powell* v. *McCormack* (1969) the House argued that its exclusion of Representative Adam Clayton Powell on grounds not enumerated in the Constitution was justified by precedent of similar exclusions. In rejecting this argument the Court observed: "That an unconstitutional action has been taken before surely does not render that same action any less unconstitutional at a later date." Taken all together the preceding cases demonstrate that doctrines of inherent powers have been denied whenever the issue of enumerated powers could be raised; that falsifications of history, erroneous obiter dicta, and bold actions do not set legal precedent.

Nevertheless major issues of foreign policy, the making of executive agreements, presidential deployment of troops and military equipment outside the limits of the United States without congressional consultation, and the demonstrated presidential ability to wage war in the absence of a declaration of war, or even a joint resolution by Congress, are matters that have never been tested before the Supreme Court and which by their nature may be unjusticiable. In abuse of such political power impeachment is the sole immediate recourse of the people through their Congress. Thus must be prefaced a discussion of the president's claims to authority in the commander-in-chief clause of the Constitution, from which, through the instrument of the executive agreement, have come events of a frequently world-altering nature.

7. SOLE AUTHORITY OF THE PRESIDENT ACTING AS COMMANDER IN CHIEF

In 1951 Truman claimed that "under the President's constitutional powers as Commander-in-Chief of the Armed Forces" he had authority—"repeatedly recognized by Congress and the courts"—to send troops anywhere in the world. Lyndon B. Johnson and Richard M. Nixon made similar and expanded claims. The State Department supported these claims, enhancing popular belief and enlisting the support of scholars and news commentators. Thus was created the myth of the "imperial presidency."

The chief mechanism for presidential war making in the post–World War II years has been the executive agreement. The Constitution confers only one power in military affairs on the president alone: he is designated "Commander in Chief of the Army and Navy of the United States, and of the Militia of the several States, when called into the actual Service of the United States." The power to declare war lies solely and independently in the hands of Congress, with no qualifications. The wording of the Constitution is clear enough: "The Congress shall have Power . . . to declare War, grant Letters of Marque and Reprisal, and make Rules concerning Captures on Land and Water." Given executive encroachment even in this area of congressional jurisdiction, Congress felt it necessary to restate the obvious in the War Powers Act of 1973: "The term 'war powers' may be taken to mean the authority inherent in national sovereignities to declare, conduct, and conclude armed hostilities with other states. In the U.S. Constitution the war powers [such as those stated above and others in Article I, section 8] are expressly reserved to the Congress."

The phrase "declare war" was substituted for "make war" in the last draft of the Constitution in order not to prevent the president from repelling a sudden attack until Congress should act. Congress should "provide for the common . . . Defence," "raise and support Armies," and appropriate funds and specify how those funds should be spent. In the minds of the Framers such authority extended to the deployment of troops. Finally, Congress shall "make all Laws which shall be necessary and proper for carrying into Execution" all the above. The commander in chief, on the other hand, has the obligation to uphold these constitutional provisions and obey and enforce the laws. As the Founding Fathers saw it, the commander in chief may do nothing more, independently or on his own authority, than conduct campaigns.

Professor Berger clearly demonstrates the limited role the Founding Fathers envisioned for the president in the making of war:

> Viewed against repudiation of the royal prerogative no more can be distilled from the ["repel sudden attacks"] remark than a limited *grant* to the President of power to repel attack when, as the very words "sudden attack" imply, there could be no time to consult with Congress. Despite the fact, therefore, that the replaced "make" is a verbal component of warmaking, the shift to "declare" did not deprive Congress of the war powers expressly enumerated and "naturally connected" with the power to "declare war." Instead the change merely removed the power to *conduct* a war once declared. . . . [I]f the warmaking power did not remain in Congress, the exception for presidential power "to repel sudden attacks" was superfluous.

Writing from his presidential experience, Jefferson had recognized the possibility where cases of extreme urgency and peril might justify an executive to take extraordinary action beyond the law "when the laws become inadequate to their own preservation, and where the universal recourse is a dictator, or martial law." The executive taking such measures would then be bound to "throw himself on the justice of his country and the rectitude of his motives." Abraham Lincoln, who was faced with just such a case of extreme urgency, took sweeping measures in the opening months of the Civil War, but when Congress convened he sought and obtained sanction for his acts.

The twentieth century has witnessed a remarkable departure from constitutional government. There is no "precedent" set in the nineteenth century allowing the president to plunge the nation into war to repel an attack on some foreign nation. Presidential power has not been what the sovereignists say.

Contrary to contemporary State Department memoranda, the undeclared hostilities with France from 1798 to 1801 are not precedent for executive wars "without obtaining prior Congressional authorization." President John Adams took no independent action while Congress moved step by step. Moreover two Supreme Court decisions reaffirmed the language of the Constitution: "Congress is empowered to declare a general war or Congress may wage a limited war" (*Bas* v. *Tingy* [1800]), . . . and "the Congress may authorize general hostilities . . . or partial war" (*Talbot* v. *Seeman* [1801]). When the president's actions exceeded congressional delegation (*Little* v. *Barreme* [1804]), they were found illegal. Fifty years later the Court held against the broad power of the president as commander in chief, finding it to be one "purely military" (*Fleming* v. *Page* [1850]). In the war with the Barbary States Jefferson initiated defense measures which were, as he told Congress, "unauthorized by the Constitution without the sanction of Congress to go beyond the line of defense." He left the matter with Congress to pursue hostilities and to end them with a treaty.

Most of the instances the State Department has dredged up to justify unilateral presidential use of force have involved the protection of American citizens and are instances not involving bloodshed or collision of force. For this ostensible "protective" function, the president has exercised his own proclaimed authority for military intervention to achieve political ends. In 1893 the executive made an agreement with American citizens in Hawaii to land troops for their protection. The day following the landing the queen was deposed, an American became president, and Hawaii was proclaimed first a protectorate and then a republic until it could be respectably annexed, an apt example of the marriage between military adventurism and the executive agreement disguised as a quasi-treaty with a "foreign" government. In 1965 the United States conspired with the military junta of Colonel Benoit in the Dominican Republic to have the latter request American assistance to protect Americans against the "threat" from the democratic faction of Juan Bosch, this following the assassination of dictator Rafael Trujillo (in which the Central Intelligence Agency is said to have had at least an indirect hand). President Lyndon B. Johnson sent 21,000 troops, reserving another 9,000 offshore for the "rescue" that kept the junta in power. After exhaustive and conclusive study, Senator J. William Fulbright wrote that "the decision to intervene" was motivated by American determination "to defeat the rebel, or constitutionalist, forces whose victory at that time was imminent."

American presidents have taken it upon themselves to deploy troops around the world and occupy foreign territory, not in consultation with Congress, but in concert with policies of foreign powers. After World War I Woodrow Wilson sent a considerable armed force to Siberia on his own presumed authority. By 1927 Calvin Coolidge had 5,000 men in Nicaragua. In 1941 Franklin D. Roosevelt occupied Iceland (jointly with the British), Greenland, and Dutch Guiana for their protection while the United States was officially neutral. By 1958 Dwight D. Eisenhower espoused this presidential prerogative and sent 14,000 troops to Lebanon. Such exercise of power, natural as it may be to the "imperial president" and to those who matured under the shadow of the Axis conquests, is alien to the intentions of the makers of the Constitution. James Madison and James Wilson (leader of the "strong executive" faction at the Constitutional Convention) confirmed that rights of "war and peace" were not included in "executive powers." Illegality is not legitimized by repetition.

The executive cannot claim that a state of war grants him extraordinary power. *Ex Parte Milligan* (1866) confirmed that the Constitution must be applied in war and peace. During World War II, in *Ex Parte Quirin* (1942), the Court held that the Constitution "invests the President as Commander in Chief with power to wage war which Congress has declared, and to carry into effect all laws passed by Congress for the conduct of war and for the government and regulation of the Armed Forces." Once again the authority flows from Congress and is not inherent in the executive.

GROWTH BY NUMBER AND SIGNIFICANCE

Presidential power as contrasted with the constitutional power of Congress developed slowly in the nineteenth century. The first fifty years under the Constitution yielded twenty-seven executive agreements and sixty treaties, an average of 1.2 treaties per year to only .54 executive agreements. The latter number steadily rose; from 1839 to 1889, 4.3 executive agreements per year; from 1889 to 1939, 10.5; 1940–1954 saw 125 annually, with the number doubling each five years. By 1939 there were about two executive agreements for each treaty; after 1939 that ratio increased to fourteen per treaty. By 1972 the legal adviser to the State Department reported that between 1946 and 1972, 368 treaties became effective and at least 5,590 executive agreements were in operation. Of course, some of these agreements were authorized by legislation and others stemmed from treaties such as the North Atlantic Treaty Organization pact. Nevertheless, it is startling to see how the executive agreement has replaced or even defied Congress. The shift from the housekeeping function of the device to its embodiment of substantive policy decisions is reflected in these figures alone.

Historically, the executive agreement evolved slowly. Interestingly enough, the first provision for one was made by Congress. This was an authorization by the Second Congress in the act establishing the first post office and requiring the postmaster general to develop international communication through postal service. Many years intervened before such a device would begin to take on a heftier meaning.

The first executive agreement customarily cited as an example of an "arrangement," which was "sort of a treaty" executed by the president, was the Rush-Bagot Agreement (1817). To effect the wish of Congress in 1815 to strip the Great Lakes of armaments, James Monroe concluded an agreement with Great Britain. Since his action involved liaison with a foreign power, his authority was in doubt. He asked the Senate whether "this is an arrangement as the Executive is competent to enter into, . . ." to which the Senate responded by endorsing the arrangement by a two-thirds vote. This pact constituted a continuing obligation of a substantive nature akin to a treaty and should reinforce rather than detract from the necessity to follow constitutional procedure.

After 1823, the Monroe Doctrine set a course for American policy toward Latin America in perhaps the first famous commitment made by the executive branch. President Monroe warned Europe that any "interposition" would be viewed as "an unfriendly disposition toward the United States." Asked by the Colombian government for clarification of his pronouncement, Monroe responded, "You understand that by the Constitution of the United States the ultimate decision of this question belongs to the Legislative Department of the Government." Theodore Roosevelt extended the Monroe Doctrine in 1904 by adding his own corollary, which proclaimed the right of the United States to intervene without reference to Congress. The president, as Roosevelt put it, "without consultations with anyone . . . took Panama," intervened in the Caribbean with force, and installed provisional governments there. Later, Franklin D. Roosevelt perceived similar authority to make policy and, under the name "The Good Neighbor Policy," embarked upon still another commitment to Latin America. Yet when John F. Kennedy used such presidential prerogative in his Alliance for Progress, Congress monitored his proposals and exercised its prerogative to refuse substantial foreign aid. In recent decades the American wish to maintain loyal neighbors has led several presidents (Eisenhower, Kennedy, Johnson, and Nixon) to authorize the overthrow or subversion of governments in Guatemala (Jacobo Arbenz Guzmán), Cuba (ironically both Fulgencio Batista and Fidel Castro), the Dominican Republic (Juan Bosch), and Chile (Salvador Allende). The American presidents then contrived to recognize and prop up the new regimes (Castro's excepted) through the mechanism of the executive agreement.

In the last months of the first William McKinley administration, Secretary of State John Hay put into operation the Open Door policy in Asia. In 1900 the president sent 5,000 troops to China to help quell the Boxer Rebellion. By intervention he avowed to protect American life and property as well as to prevent the possibility that China "would be sliced up by the European powers." In 1857 the United States had not dared to move with such stern authority; when the British asked for American military intervention against Peking, Secretary of State Lewis Cass replied: "The President has no authority, for the exercise of that great attribute of sovereignty is vested in Congress." In spite of public policy opposed to spheres of influence, the presidency under Theodore Roosevelt and Woodrow Wilson made executive agreements creating such spheres. The Taft-Katsura memorandum of 1905, a "confidential, informal agreement," arranged a free hand for Japan in Korea in exchange for Japanese acquiescence in American control of the Philippines, thus violating the Korean–United States Treaty of 1882. While acknowledging that it was "indeed impossible" for the president to enter into an understanding "without the consent of the Senate," Taft pledged verbally that "without any agreement at all the people of the United States were so fully in accord with the policy" that it was tantamount to a treaty. The Root-Takahira agreement of 1908 reaffirmed the oral understanding of 1905 in a written agreement. In addition to respect for each other's territories, the status quo in China would be maintained. By 1917, in the secret Lansing-Ishii agreement, the status of China was renegotiated. While lauding the Open Door, the United States in a secret protocol recognized that Japan's "territorial propinquity" to China gave it "special interests" there. Japan interpreted this as support for what became her "Monroe Doctrine for Asia."

The Constitution is not specific (Article IV, sec. 3) on how the United States could annex territory. The first significant occasion, the Louisiana Purchase, would later provide President Harry S. Truman and Chief Justice Frederick M. Vinson with a claim on the basis of precedent for unilateral presidential initiative independent of Congress. The historical facts do not support this claim. Congress wanted Louisiana, confirmed negotiations, and sanctioned every step. It was not Congress but President Thomas Jefferson who was fearful lest this be "an act beyond the Constitution." Jefferson's envoys negotiated treaties with France, and he submitted them to the Senate for consent and to the House for approval for funds. This can hardly be twisted into a precedent for territorial annexation by executive agreement without Congress. Subsequently, John Tyler used authority of a joint resolution (when the treaty failed) to legitimize his agreements for the annexation of Texas. McKinley followed this model in the annexation of Hawaii. Lesser territorial questions have been settled by various executive agreements, for example, congressionally authorized agreements to claim bits of land still unoccupied and unpopulated. The status of San Juan Island in Puget Sound was arranged by modus vivendi until settled by arbitration; the status of Samoa for twenty-five years following joint occupation depended on executive agreements until Congress ratified them.

The critical point in the displacement of treaties and congressional acts came with the advent of World War II. When Franklin D. Roosevelt decided in 1940 to exchange American destroyers for British bases, the fact that the United States was still officially neutral led him to seek legal justification. A surge of support ensued from executive, legal, and academic circles. By 1944 extensive claims were being made for the executive agreement, the most cogent ones by Myers S. McDougal and Asher Lans, and by State Department official Wallace McClure. With the imminence of war, the controversy provoked by this failed to loom as large as the issue merited. Edward S. Corwin condemned the new interpretation of the executive agreement as "an endorsement of unrestrained autocracy in the field of our foreign relations." The seminal question was put by legal educator Philip B. Kurland: "Should the Constitution really be read to mean that by calling an agreement an executive agreement rather than a treaty, the obligation to secure Senate approval is dissolved?"

The absurd position to which the treaty was relegated can be seen in the following incident. Senator Fulbright had demanded to know from the State Department why an important trade agreement with Canada had not been submitted to the Senate as a treaty for ratification, only to be told that the president could choose the procedure. Economic negotiations might preferably be submitted as a treaty especially if the foreign power were "a less developed member country" for whom "the status of these agreements would be enhanced if the United States . . . followed the formal treaty process in making them." Fulbright complained: "The Senate is asked to convene solemnly to approve by a two-thirds vote a treaty to preserve cultural artifacts in a friendly neighboring country. At the same time, the Chief Executive is moving American military men and material around the globe like so many pawns in a chess game."

The presidency has not been entirely free of congressional retaliation in efforts to constrain the executive behemoth. During the early history of the United States, the Supreme Court affirmed in many cases the president's constitutional obligation in foreign affairs to act only in accordance with congressional authorization. Since the Korean War, the Supreme Court has fallen silent: it has failed to confirm the unbridled power exercised in later years, and, it should be noted, it has also declined to hear cases challenging sweeping actions of presidents in taking the nation into undeclared wars that might have led it to deny the validity of the exercise of that power.

Between 1871 and 1898 the Senate ratified no important treaty. Woodrow Wilson chafed at what he feared was the Senate's "treaty-marring power." Theodore Roosevelt virtually made foreign policy by executive agreement. The Senate objected and held firmly onto arbitration treaties for fear that the president would bind the United States without specific approval by the Senate of the agreements. World War I gave rise to a new round of executive agreements: loans, rationing, supplies, shipping, a regional agreement with Murmansk in July 1918, and the Covenant wherein Wilson laid out policy for the postwar world. His negotiating of the peace treaty unilaterally, believing the Senate "virtually committed," led to a rebellious Senate which finally defeated the treaty and the League of Nations. Compromise could have been reached between the Senate and the president, but Wilson's "all or nothing" attitude got him nothing.

Presidential incursions into the international arena then waned until Franklin D. Roosevelt began to elevate the executive agreement to the high plateau where it now resides. On his own authority, Roosevelt contrived to aid the British as a nonbelligerent: thus he entered into an agreement, the Atlantic Charter of August 1941, formulating the goals for which Britain's war was being waged; he forged the second alliance in the history of the United States on his own initiative by means of the United Nations Declaration, 1 January 1942; and he attended two tripartite wartime conferences at Teheran and Yalta, which made secret preliminary decisions on the disposition of issues and territory after the war.

A number of armistices and surrenders have occurred by executive agreements, such as the "Declaration for the Suspension of Arms and Cessation of Hostilities" signed with Britain before the Peace of Paris (1783) which ended the American Revolution. In 1898 an armistice was concluded with Spain, which included nonmilitary principles such as Spain's withdrawal from Cuba and the cession of Puerto Rico, the Philippine Islands, and Guam to the United States. In World War I the armistices with Germany and Austria were by executive agreement as were those in World War II, starting with Italy in September 1943. That the president as commander in chief has the authority to order and agree to a cessation of hostilities is not generally disputed; these agreements, however, entailed political matters of substance and long duration. In 1953 the Korean War was ended by an armistice still in effect, negotiated in a series of executive agreements, including the "Agreement on Prisoners of War." In this case, contested issues normally reserved for a peace treaty have become issues negotiated under an armistice on a daily basis for the past 24 years. In Vietnam, the negotiations of Secretary of State Henry Kissinger with North Vietnam to end the fighting were conducted with little congressional consultation, and their exact nature has not been revealed.

Serious confusion has arisen in recent years as to the distinction between an executive agreement and a treaty. The differences are real. Yale professor of law Edwin Borchard has spelled out the differences between a treaty and an executive agreement. (1) A treaty, like a constitutional amendment, can deal with any subject of international negotiation; an executive agreement is limited to congressionally delegated authority or to powers normally exercised by the commander in chief or principal diplomatic officer. (2) A treaty can do what Congress cannot. It can confer powers on Congress it did not have (*Missouri* v. *Holland* [1920]). An executive agreement cannot do what Congress cannot. (3) A treaty must be ratified; an executive agreement does not require ratification. (4) A treaty binds the United States and usually cannot be repealed by Congress; an executive agreement is binding only to the extent both parties see fit to abide by it. The executive is morally bound, but the agreement can be repealed by Congress, by either party, or by repeal of authorizing statutes. (5) A treaty has special significance; it can repeal an act of Congress. An executive agreement cannot repeal an act of Congress. (6) A treaty is the "supreme law of the land"; an executive agreement, except in a few instances when it supersedes state law or when pursuant to an act of Congress, is not the supreme law of the land. In fact, executive agreements have been declared unconstitutional. (7) A new treaty is required to modify an earlier treaty; an executive agreement cannot alter a treaty. (8) A treaty is submitted to the Senate for approval; an executive agreement has no procedure for approval. (9) A treaty lasts, with unimportant exceptions, for the term provided therein; there is no binding time period for an executive agreement, which may be broken unilaterally and which is not binding upon any future successor. (10) A treaty may not be secret and must be published; executive agreements have developed because they can be made secretly.

BALANCE TO THE IMBALANCE

"Congress," former Justice Arthur Goldberg said, must "act to correct departures from the spirit and letter of the Constitution." As the president became more "sovereign," Congress made a number of moves to restore its rightful power. A furor arose over the commitments that Roosevelt made to Josef Stalin at Yalta, particularly the Far Eastern agreement for Soviet entry into the war against Japan. Cries of "sellout" led to release of the Yalta documents and caused Eisenhower to promise repudiation of any agreement in violation of American principles. Nothing substantial occurred, however, when the government familiarized itself with these agreements, perhaps because so many of them had been redone at Potsdam—the same way they had been made at Yalta—in bilateral and trilateral bargaining between Truman and Stalin (and Great Britain). Besides, an agreement by one president does not legally bind the next.

The mode of entry into the Korean War, although that war was informally supported by Congress, coupled with concern and publicity over Roosevelt's wartime agreements, gave rise to public and congressional wariness with the war. When British Prime Minister Clement Attlee visited Washington in 1950, twenty-four senators introduced a sense of the Senate resolution that the president report to it fully and not enter into any binding agreements with Attlee. The Bricker Amendment, although it failed, loomed large in the early 1950's as an effort to curb once and for all the executive agreement. Traversing through a number of changes, the amendment reached the Senate floor in February 1954. Sixty senators voted in favor and thirty-one were opposed, defeating the proposal by only one vote. The intention, as spelled out in one draft, was clear: "All executive or other agreement between the President and any international organization, foreign power, or official thereof shall be made only in the manner and to the extent to be prescribed by law. Such agreements shall be subject to the limitations imposed on treaties or the making of treaties by this article." Alarmed by this undermining of the executive, Eisenhower fired back that such a proposal was tantamount to a "Constitution demolished brick by brick by Bricker."

The Indochina war finally provoked Congress to redress the imbalance of power that had swung so far in favor of the president. In August 1972 the Case bill became law. Senator Clifford Case had revived a fourteen-year-old bill requiring all executive agreements to be transmitted to the Senate within sixty days; extremely sensitive agreements would go to the Senate Foreign Relations Committee. Yet even this did not stop secret and unilateral policymaking by the president: the Nixon-Thieu agreement, the thirty-four separate interagency agreements to funnel nearly $2 billion to South Korea, as well as other unaccountable presidential deals. The Senate fought for its lawful position. In 1971 it voted fifty to six to force Nixon to submit agreements with Portugal and Bahrein as treaties. When Nixon refused, Case amended the foreign aid bill to block assistance until this should be accomplished. Senator Samuel J. Ervin proposed a congressional veto over all executive agreements within sixty days. Senator Fulbright sought to make action by one house sufficient to veto presidential action.

From the Ninety-first Congress to the

Ninety-third Congress, other moves were initiated to halt executive agreements that might commit the nation to executive wars. Recognizing that "the constitutional balance of authority over war making has swung heavily to the President in modern times," the War Powers Act was passed in November 1973, providing that the president must consult with Congress before as well as during an emergency action; that the president must make a formal report if there is no declaration of war; and that he must do so within 60 days. Some opposed the bill on the undeniable grounds that it authorized the president to do on his sole authority what the Constitution did not—commit American troops overseas on his own initiative. In its first test the War Powers Act was ignored. President Gerald R. Ford, on his own authority, attacked Cambodia to rescue the crew of a freighter, the *Mayaguez,* seized for unlawfully violating Cambodian waters as a belligerent. (By 1977 the crew entered a multimillion-dollar suit against the United States government and the shipping line working for it.) Ford's actions did not include the congressional consultation envisioned under the law; as some of his predecessors, he had a few brief conversations with friendly congressmen and a post facto informing of the nation.

Secretary of State John Foster Dulles did intimate in 1953 that conversations with select members of Congress had indicated that executive submission of a plan for worldwide bases was not necessary because Congress had winked approvingly through these chats. Constitutionally, this was not formal approval, and the Supreme Court already had ruled: "Congress cannot delegate legislative power to the President" (*Field* v. *Clark* [1892]).

KOREA AND VIETNAM: WAR BY EXECUTIVE AGREEMENT

The war-making power lies in two places: Congress, which alone can declare war and appropriate funds for the support of the armed forces; and in a foreign power whose sudden attack upon the United States would require the president to act for the immediate defense of the nation. By 1950 a drastic reinterpretation of both tenets of the Constitution had occurred—a plenary president waged war in a foreign country on behalf of a puppet government and intervened in a civil war. Truman, by executive agreement, first with President Syngman Rhee of South Korea, and then with the United Nations, took upon himself the constitutional burden of going to war with North Korea, which Truman had charged with invading South Korea. The decision was surprising because the president and his advisers had concluded prior to the invasion that South Korea was not vital to American strategic concerns. Truman did not seek congressional authorization. After deciding to aid South Korea, he turned instead to the United Nations. It first pronounced a "breach" of the peace and asked for North Korea's withdrawal, directing members "to render every assistance." Truman and the military consulted among themselves and ordered air and sea support. A second United Nations resolution called for "urgent military measures . . . to repel the armed attack." Truman committed ground troops to South Korea. When he announced American involvement, the president cited the United Nations resolution as his authorization. Consulting only the executive branch, Truman maintained that his "constitutional powers as Commander-in-Chief . . . repeatedly recognized by Congress and the courts" allowed him to send troops wherever he pleased. Asked what evidence proved this, Truman replied, "I haven't got it with me just now."

In fact any use of American troops by the United Nations was implicitly forbidden by the United Nations Participation Act, Section 6, which empowered the president to negotiate agreements with the United Nations under Article 43 of the United Nations Charter. This article stated that military contributions by members should be based on special agreements negotiated by the Security Council of the United Nations and ratified by the individual nations. Section 6 stipulated that this authorization could not be construed as authorization to make armed assistance available except as set forth in the agreements envisioned in Article 43. Such an agreement with South Korea was never negotiated and never approved by Congress; thus the president had no statutory authority to do what he did.

The commander-in-chief clause of the Constitution remained on paper. No war had been declared, no attack on the United States had been made, and Truman was not a wartime commander in chief. As for precedent, which the executive also claimed as authority, precedent included only minor incidents involving protection of citizens under circumstances of local disorder, and hardly addressed itself to Truman's action. Other precedents, moreover, when closely examined, are not instances of constitutional and therefore applicable action.

Sovereignists further argue that Congress has ratified American intervention by voting military appropriations. This proposition in the Korean and Vietnam wars has never been tested by the Supreme Court. However, other instances have. In *Ex parte Endo* (1944) the Court denied the contention that an appropriation act ratified the activities it supported: ". . . the appropriation must plainly show a purpose to bestow the precise authority which is claimed." And Justice Roberts asserted: "If Congress is to ratify by appropriation any part of the programme of an executive agency the bill must include a specific item referring to that portion of the programme." Appropriation of funds is simply that and justifies nothing without specifically prescribing a definite course of action with standards and guidelines sufficient to meet the requirements of ample Court rulings. Most fundamentally, the Constitution does not provide for the nation to be engaged in a state of war by congressional appropriation. Court rulings have established that the president cannot designate funds in advance to any course of action without statutory authority. Truman did.

The history of American involvement in Indochina is also the story of decision making by executive agreement. By executive agreement the United States in 1950 recognized the French-supported government of Bao Dai in Vietnam and extended military and economic aid. Defense accords were signed between France and the United States, after which the executive branch financed eighty percent of France's expenditures in its war against the Viet Minh. The "failure" of the United States to come to France's aid at Dien Bien Phu resulted from both inability to force an executive agreement with Britain (for purposes of creating the appearance of multilateral action) and from concern that Congress would have to be consulted.

In return for attendance at and verbal acquiescence to the decisions made at the Geneva Conference in 1954, the United States wrung agreements from reluctant allies for a collective security pact. Thus from executive agreements the Southeast Asia Treaty Organization emerged, embodying a policy accepted by the Senate. This treaty committed the United States only to abide by "constitutional processes" if a member nation (or protocol client, such as the South Vietnamese government) were attacked and to "consult" if there were an indirect threat. Nevertheless Secretary of State Dean Rusk in 1966 made it clear that the executive intended to act beyond the treaty even while invoking it: ". . . if the United States determines that an armed attack has occurred against any nation to whom the protection of the treaty applies, then it is obligated to 'act to meet the common danger' without regard to the views of action of any other treaty member." (Pakistan, a member nation, was on record as opposing American intervention in Vietnam.)

Military advisers and, finally, troops went to Vietnam by executive agreements never submitted to Congress; Bao Dai arranged that with the United States. The arrangements were renewed when Bao Dai was ousted in favor of Diem in 1955. When Diem was overthrown in 1963 the agreements were extended. In one of the many attempts to justify the legality of ground troops in Vietnam (ordered into offensive action in 1965), the Secretary of State cited bilateral assistance agreements never seen by Congress. An important piece of evidence was a letter from President Eisenhower to Bao Dai's Prime Minister, Diem, in October 1954 offering foreign aid in a nonmilitary context in exchange for internal reform. This was hardly a "sacred promise," as Lyndon Johnson was later to call American commitments, to send more than a half million fighting men. Substituting the executive agreement for an act of Congress, the executive had at last involved the United States in the longest war in its history.

At various points the executive had tried other ploys to achieve the aura of constitutionality. The Southeast Asia Treaty Organization was wrenched out of context and intent for this purpose; still the Constitution (even had the Southeast Asia Treaty Organization been what the State Department claimed) does not provide for war by treaty. The Tonkin Gulf resolution was contrived by the executive under false pretenses and later repealed by Congress. It must, of course, be noted that in the interim the resolution could only sanction a limited reprisal and had little legal significance despite what was claimed for it. By no method can Congress transfer to the executive its power and authority to make war. Had Congress decided upon a clear Vietnam policy, it could at most have authorized the president to make rules for it in conformity with standards supplied to guide him. The Tonkin Gulf resolution did none of this. Though foreign aid agreements and the resolution were indeed cited as mandates, eventually the president chose to pursue his case on other grounds. As Lyndon Johnson explained to a press conference on 18 August 1967, he had wanted the Tonkin Gulf resolution only because it was "thought desirable" and "not necessary to do what we did and what we are doing." He stood by the claim that "We are well within the grounds of our constitutional responsibility." Richard M. Nixon invoked especially his power as commander in chief repeatedly: "The legal justification is the right of the President of the United States under the Constitution to protect the lives of American men. . . . As Commander in Chief I had no other choice."

Congress moved in 1969 and 1970 to halt the escalation by American forces in Laos, Thailand, and Cambodia. The Defense Procurement Authorization Act was amended in 1971: "the policy of the United States [is] to terminate at the earliest possible practicable date all military operations of the United States in Indochina." This amendment along with cancellation of the Tonkin Gulf resolution expressed congressional will. Nevertheless, the war continued until the Paris agreement of 1973, itself a secret executive agreement. Intensive bombing of Cambodia then began. Kissinger affirmed that the peace settlement changed nothing; there were "no inhibitions" to renew bombing at presidential discretion. "That is legally correct," he said. "We have the right to do this." The bombing was rationalized by an executive agreement with Lon Nol (leader of one of the Cambodian factions) in which he requested American air strikes. The bombings ceased only when Congress, goaded at last to exercise one yet unappropriated power, cut off funds as of August 1973 for any further American military action in Southeast Asia.

The development of executive agreements is intertwined with the ascendancy of presidential power. According to the Constitution there is no need for such presidential leeway. As agent of Congress, the executive has been authorized to obey its laws and act in its behalf in foreign affairs until it designates another party. When and if Congress declares war, the president becomes commander in chief. The executive agreement, as it has been called only in the last forty years, is no substitute for constitutional government. The following constraints upon the president are absolute: (1) the Constitution, which, despite the "sovereignists" interpretations, is quite thorough and explicit; (2) Supreme Court decisions upholding the narrow construction of presidential war powers; and (3) congressional restraining legislation, which has become necessary in an effort to legislate the Constitution.

BIBLIOGRAPHY

Raoul Berger, "Executive Privilege v. Congressional Inquiry," in *UCLA Law Review,* 12 (1965), and *Executive Privilege: A Constitutional Myth* (Cambridge, Mass., 1974); William W. Bishop, Jr., *International Law: Cases and Materials,* 3rd ed. (Boston, 1971); Edwin Borchard, "Shall the Executive Agreement Replace the Treaty?" in *Yale Law Journal* (Sept. 1944), and "Treaties and Executive Agreements—A Reply," *ibid.,* 54 (1945); Elbert M. Byrd, Jr., *Treaties and Executive Agreements* (The Hague, 1960); Edward S. Corwin, *The Constitution and What It Means Today* (Boston, 1963); Royden James Dangerfield, *In Defense of the Senate: A Study in Treaty Making* (Norman, Okla., 1933); Richard A. Falk, ed., *The Vietnam War and International Law,* II (Princeton, 1969); David N. Farnsworth, *The Senate Committee on Foreign Relations,* Illinois Studies in the Social Sciences, XLIX (Urbana, Ill., 1961); Green Hayworth Hackworth, *Digest of International Law,* V (Washington, D.C., 1943); Louis Henkin, *Foreign Affairs and the Constitution* (Mineola, N.Y., 1972); W. Stull Holt, *Treaties Defeated by the Senate* (Gloucester, Mass., 1964); F. M. Kail, *What Washington Said: Administration Rhetoric and the Vietnam War: 1949–1969* (New York, 1973); George McTurnan Kahin and John W. Lewis, *The United States in Vietnam* (New York, 1967); Wallace McClure, *International Executive Agreements* (New York, 1941); Myres McDougal and Asher Lans, "Treaties and Congressional-Executive or Presidential Agreements: Interchangeable Instruments of National Policy," in *Yale Law Journal,* 54

(1945); David Rees, *Korea: The Limited War* (Baltimore, Md., 1970); Edgar E. Robinson, ed., *Powers of the President in Foreign Affairs, 1945–1965* (San Francisco, 1966); Arthur Schlesinger, Jr., *The Imperial Presidency* (New York, 1973); Glendon A. Schubert, Jr., *The Presidency in the Courts* (Minneapolis, Minn., 1957); Richard J. Walton, *Congress and American Foreign Policy* (New York, 1972); and Quincy Wright, *The Control of American Foreign Relations* (New York, 1922). *The Constitution of the United States of America: Analysis and Interpretation,* Senate Document 39, 88th Congress, 1st Session (Washington, D.C., 1964); Hearings: *On Availability of Information From Federal Departments and Agencies Before a Subcommittee of the House Committee on Government Operations* (85th Congress, 2nd Session, 1958); *On Transmittal of Executive Agreements to Congress Before Senate Foreign Relations Committee* (92nd Congress, 1st Session, 1971); *On War Powers Legislation Before Senate Committee on Foreign Relations* (92nd Congress, 1st Session, 1971); and *Congressional Oversight of Executive Agreements, Separation of Powers Subcommittee of the Senate Judiciary Committee* (92nd Congress, 2nd Session, 1972).

[*See also* ALLIANCES, COALITIONS, AND ENTENTES; CONGRESS AND FOREIGN POLICY; THE COLD WAR; THE CONSTITUTION AND FOREIGN POLICY; EXECUTIVE AGENTS; IMPERIALISM; INTERNATIONAL LAW; INTERVENTION AND NONINTERVENTION; MILITARISM; THE MONROE DOCTRINE; PRESIDENTIAL POWER IN FOREIGN AFFAIRS; RECIPROCITY; RECOGNITION POLICY; TRADE AND COMMERCE; TREATIES.]

EXTRATERRITORIALITY

Jules Davids

A VITAL function of American diplomacy is the protection of persons, property, and trade interests of United States citizens, both native-born and naturalized, in foreign countries. The problem of guaranteeing such protection, especially in the Islamic and Oriental countries, was responsible for the eventual development of a system of extraterritoriality. Although differences in cultures, religions, and legal systems between Western Christian countries and those of Africa, the Near East, and Asia motivated Western countries to secure legal and economic exemptions for their nationals, the roots of extraterritoriality can be traced to ancient times. During antiquity, legal rights and obligations in Egypt, Greece, and Rome were deemed an integral part of membership in the community and could never be extended to aliens—the "strangers within the gates." Merchants and traders, however, traveling to distant lands were often permitted to reside and to establish trade factories, to manage their own affairs, to build temples, and to live according to their own customs, ceremonies, and rites.

The Egyptian-Graeco-Roman heritage laid the foundations for the modern system of extraterritoriality that took form in the seventeenth century. Egypt was the first society to establish a "consular" agency. As early as 1294 B.C., Phoenician merchants were allowed to reside in Egyptian cities, where they lived under their own laws and enjoyed freedom of worship. The Egyptians later permitted foreign merchants to select local judges of their choice—or judges of their own nationality—to settle trade disputes, based on their own laws and customs. But the Egyptians, the ancient Greeks, and the Romans deprived foreigners and strangers—who were regarded as enemies and treated with cruelty—of all protection under their own laws. Such protection was granted exclusively to citizens. About the end of the seventh century B.C., the Greeks created the "proxenial institution." This agency granted Phoenician traders the right to appoint officials at ports where they congregated and allowed them to manage their own commercial affairs. These officials essentially provided the services of modern consuls, for they acted as intermediaries between their country and the city in which they resided; supplied information to their own government; helped their fellow countrymen abroad with regard to trade and other matters; and were given consular jurisdiction in litigations and disputes. The Romans, on their part, faced with complex mercantile transactions, also appointed, in 256 B.C., a *praetor peregrinus* to settle quarrels that arose among foreigners.

During the Middle Ages, the principle of extraterritoriality, which granted aliens the right to be exempt from native laws, and to live in accordance with their own customs, subject to their own laws, was firmly established. Acknowledgment of separate laws for different communities of individuals was recognized as early as the twelfth century. Italian cities secured guarantees to their own jurisdiction not only from Egypt, but from the Greek Christian rulers at Constantinople and the Barbary States of North Africa. Byzantine rulers readily granted to the Genoese, Venetians, and Pisans, who formed their own settlements within the Byzantine Empire, the right to retain their own laws and customs. Significant immunities were later also obtained by mercantile organizations, such as the Hanseatic League, which secured the rights of local jurisdiction.

The status of foreigners in Islamic countries presented special difficulties, chiefly because the law was essentially religious and its jurisdiction limited only to the true believer. While the foreigner found himself excluded from Muslim society, the question of dealing with disputes that arose in commercial relations with the Barbary States remained. Unwilling and unable to deal with the infidel legally, Muslim rulers, relying on custom and usage, simply permitted foreigners to settle their disputes by their own magistrates and in accordance with their own laws. The first such treaty, which granted extraterritorial jurisdiction in Morocco, appears to have been concluded with Pisa in 1388. This agreement gave consuls the right to settle disputes between foreigners, and in cases involving foreigners and natives, it permitted an appeal to the cadi, or local judge. A more significant advance in the adoption of the principle of extraterritoriality occurred in 1535 in the Ottoman Empire, when Sultan Suleiman the Magnificent negotiated a treaty of peace, amity, and commerce with France that contained charters or articles—capitulations—which defined in detail the privileges of foreigners within the empire and formalized the rights that had previously been conferred on the Italian city-states. Subsequent treaties were closely modeled on this treaty. During the next three centuries, capitulary rights were granted to Britain, the Netherlands, Italy, and Denmark, as well as Germany, Russia, Spain, Portugal, and the United States, by Turkish rulers.

Before the Declaration of Independence, colonial Americans, engaged in trade in the Mediterranean and with the Barbary States, were dependent upon the British for protection from Barbary piracy. France had led the way in securing definite rights or protection not only to foreigners but also to natives in the employ of foreigners. The first treaty granting these privileges was concluded between Morocco and France in May 1767; other nations soon gained similar rights through a most-favored-nation clause. When the United States declared its independence in 1776, England withdrew its admiralty passes. To prevent the plundering of American ships, a committee of the Continental Congress immediately urged the negotiation of a treaty with France to obtain a royal pledge to protect and defend American vessels as effectively as England had previously done. Although Louis XVI promised in the Treaty of Amity and Commerce between the United States and France, signed on 6 February 1778, to interpose with the Barbary States "for the benefit, convenience, and safety" of his American ally, this agreement proved of little value.

After the American Revolution, the United States Congress took the initiative to establish direct contacts to secure the protection of American ships and seamen in the Mediterranean area. In May 1784 Thomas Jefferson, John Adams, and Benjamin Franklin were commissioned to negotiate treaties with the Barbary States. When an American ship, the *Betsey,* was seized by Moroccan pirates and taken to the port of Tangier, the commissioners authorized Thomas Barclay, U.S. consul general at Paris, to go to Morocco and act as their agent to conclude a treaty with Morocco. Barclay's mission was successful. In 1786 he signed an agreement with Sultan Sidi Mohammed, which was ratified by Congress on 18 July 1787. This treaty established the basis for American extraterritorial rights in Morocco; it was modified and renewed in 1836, again in 1886, and remained in effect until 1956. Commenting on its commercial value when the first treaty was negotiated, Barclay reported, "Our trade to the Mediterranean is rendered the securer for it, and it affords us ports where our ships can refit, if we should be engaged in a European war, or in one with other Barbary states." The United States soon negotiated treaties with the other North African states: with the dey of Algiers in 1795, with the sultan of Tripoli in 1796, and with the dey of Tunis in 1797. But contrary to Barclay's expectations, neither the treaty with Morocco nor those concluded with the Barbary States provided protection to American commerce. Tripoli declared war on the United States in 1801 and hostilities ensued with the Barbary pirates until 1816, when new treaties were imposed upon Algiers, Tripoli, and Tunisia. Following the War of 1812, the United States ceased to be harassed by piracy in the Mediterranean. Meanwhile, prompted by developing interests and problems of missionaries and trade in the Ottoman Empire, the American government initiated direct contacts with Turkey. While efforts to arrange a treaty of amity and commerce were initiated in 1799, it was not until 1830 that a Turkish-American agreement was concluded that extended capitulation privileges to the United States.

By the end of the eighteenth century, a significant change occurred in the concept of extraterritoriality. Before the Treaties of Westphalia of 1648, which ended the Thirty Years' War and established the basis for the modern European system of nation-states, the notion of territorial sovereignty had not yet taken definite and concrete form. Sovereignty was generally viewed as personal rather than territorial, and it was related to the theory of the personality of laws—namely, that a foreigner carried his own law wherever he went. The belief prevailed that it was the ruler's duty to protect those who swore personal allegiance to him. Such allegiance was usually rendered by military service, or in the case of Oriental nations by the payment of tribute as well. In China, for example, the sovereign will of dynastic emperors extended to the furthest limits of the empire's territorial borders, and as widely as the rulers could exact military assistance, the payment of tribute, and the performance of the kowtow. Following the Treaties of Westphalia, however, the concept of territorial sovereignty collided with the notions of personal sovereignty and the personality of laws, especially when the national right of territorial jurisdiction became a basic tenet of Western international law.

The recognition of territorial sovereignty in the West had a profound impact on the Ottoman Empire and in the Orient, where the principle that law was personal rather than territorial persisted for a long period of time. It affected, in particular, the relationships between Christian Europe and those states, such as the Islamic and Asian countries, which were viewed as outside the pale of "civilization." Since these states were considered beyond the sphere of international law, where pagan religions and different laws and customs prevailed, it was held that European subjects and citizens had to be protected from the barbarities of uncivilized peoples, at least until such time as they conformed to the standards of law and justice that Europeans considered to be just and equitable. Westerners, in particular, singled out the alleged deficiencies of judicial systems in the Levant, in Asia, and in Africa to justify the necessity of extraterritorial privileges. Viewing "backward" peoples with contempt, Europeans chafed at the idea of being subservient to the laws of inferior civilizations. Such subservience, they felt, did violence to their dignity, pride, and concepts of justice. On their part, Muslims and Chinese held foreigners in disdain because of their belief in the superiority of their own virtues and civilization.

Modern extraterritoriality, which reflected the differences in values, in ethical and religious concepts, and in judicial systems between Western Christian civilization and Islamic and Oriental societies, originally was designed to provide a protective shield for foreign nationals. From the earliest times, foreign ambassadors, government officials, and diplomatic representatives were granted a special status and exemption from local jurisdiction. This privilege later became known as the right of *exterritoriality*. Diplomatic immunities were acknowledged in Western countries and in most non-Western states, as well. *Extraterritoriality* was distinguished from exterritoriality, since it applied not simply to foreign diplomats and government officials, but to foreign nationals residing abroad, who were given special rights and immunities. These privileges were specifically defined in treaties, and were not reciprocal. Although initially the bestowal of extraterritorial rights did not connote any loss of territorial sovereignty—but symbolized instead the beneficence of the grantor state—such was not the case following the Treaties of Westphalia. The imposition of extraterritoriality clearly came to represent the superiority of Western Christian countries over inferior, backward, and "uncivilized" peoples. In this sense, modern extraterritoriality served not only as a protective shield but also as an instrument to further penetration and imperialistic expansion.

From the 1780's to the twentieth century, both the European powers and the United States pressed vigorously to conclude treaties that contained extraterritorial rights, with countries in Africa, the Near East, and the Far East. Although the system of extraterritoriality was developed most extensively in China, the United States became a party to a network of treaties, not only with the Barbary States, but with Siam, Japan, Turkey, Egypt, and Ethiopia, among others, in which American extraterritorial privileges were obtained. Much of the day-to-day conduct of United States diplomacy, from the birth of the American republic to World War II, was connected with problems relating to treaty rights and extraterritoriality. These differed, of course, from country to country, but certain common features can be discerned.

Although the Ottoman Empire first nurtured a capitulatory system that established the basis for extraterritorial privileges, it was in China that the extraterritoriality system was developed most extensively. China's experience exemplified in an acute form problems that other states had in granting special rights to foreigners. Both China and the Islamic countries were confronted, in a sense, with a similar situation—namely, how to deal with the barbarian or the infidel. When contacts with Westerners first occurred, each acknowledged a special status to foreigners, exempting them from their own laws. As early as the ninth century, the Chinese allowed Arabs to reside and trade along the coast of the Chekiang province, and to govern themselves under their own headman. Later, when the Portuguese arrived in Macao in 1557, the emperor let them do as they wished; they were permitted to live according to their own customs and laws. However, while it was Chinese policy to treat all barbarians equally, to permit them to enjoy the blessings of Chinese civilization, and to grant to all the privilege of trade, barbarians were required to accept the conditions of trade laid down by the Chinese. Whereas the Muslims exempted foreigners from Muslim law for religious reasons, the Chinese did so on other grounds: in part, because they believed that foreigners were inferior and lacked the capacity to understand the complex rules of Chinese society—in part, because such exemption allowed the Chinese to free themselves from the difficulty of trying to govern aliens who had strange customs, language, and traditions; and, in part, because the Chinese felt the barbarians should be given a chance to observe their civilized way of life and by so doing eventually become assimilated.

The origin of extraterritoriality in China has been traced to the T'ang dynasty (A.D. 618–907). Both its motivation and its development, however, differed substantially from that which prevailed in the Islamic states. In contrast to the Muslims, neither custom nor usage nor religion appears to have influenced the Chinese in granting extraterritorial privileges to barbarians. The capitulatory system in the Ottoman Empire, moreover, did not hinder commercial relations between Christian and Islamic countries, and, unlike China, extraterritoriality was secured through common consent. The Chinese, on their part, always insisted upon complete control over foreign residence, and Westerners ultimately secured the acknowledgment and extension of extraterritorial rights only by the threat of, or resorting to, force.

In China, the tribute system, rather than religion, established the basis of relationships with barbarians. Foreigners who wanted to trade with China were compelled to abide strictly by the rules and regulations set forth by the emperor. Down to the first Anglo-Chinese or Opium War (1839–1842), Western merchants accepted China's institutional framework and adapted themselves to Chinese requirements of trade. This meant adhering to the Canton system, which confined all foreign trade to the Canton area—the "factory" section of the city and at Whampoa and Macao—and its supervision by the Co-Hong, a Chinese merchants' guild. To the Chinese, the Canton system, in effect, preserved a tribute-and-trade nexus that coincided with their traditional practice of dealing with barbarians.

The Opium War shattered this institutional arrangement. In the 1840's it was replaced by the Western "treaty system," built on treaties signed by China with England, the United States, France, and Russia. The British-dictated Treaty of Nanking of 1842 led to the collapse of the Co-Hong system, the opening to trade of the ports of Canton, Amoy, Foochow, Ningpo, and Shanghai, and the altering of relations with China. The "treaty system" that emerged was to be pivoted on two significant stipulations: a most-favored-nation clause, which automatically extended concessions granted by China to one nation to other treaty powers, and the right of extraterritorial jurisdiction.

Before the Opium War, the British and

other Europeans had willingly acknowledged, for the most part, China's jurisdiction in the punishment of crimes—both civil and criminal. But a gap steadily widened between the British and Chinese on the interpretation and procedures of the law, on matters of responsibility, on evidence, and on punishment. On occasion, the British resisted compliance, particularly by refusing to surrender their nationals who were accused in homicide cases. Westerners were also alarmed by the Chinese practice of torturing prisoners and by the corruption of Chinese magistrates and judicial authorities. However, Americans, more so than the British, readily submitted to China's laws and jurisdiction to avoid interference with trade. This was pointedly disclosed in the famous Terranova case in 1821, when Americans surrendered Francis Terranova, an Italian seaman on board the *Emily* of Baltimore, who was accused of killing a Chinese boatwoman peddling fruit. He had struck her with a jar, accidentally it seems, causing her to fall out of her small boat and drown. After a trial at Canton, from which all foreigners were excluded, he was condemned to death, strangled, and his body returned to the *Emily*. At the time, a group of American merchants declared: "We are bound to submit to your laws while we are in your waters, be they ever so unjust. We will not resist them."

The position of the United States changed drastically after the signing of the Treaty of Nanking, and the supplementary Bogue Convention of 1843, which gave British consuls limited jurisdiction to deal with crimes committed by British nationals. Although England first took the initiative in asserting jurisdiction over British subjects in China nearly a decade before the Chinese formally agreed to the principle of extraterritoriality, no direct steps were taken to establish a court of justice, with criminal and admiralty jurisdiction, at Canton. Because this measure was opposed by the Chinese and lacked approval of Parliament and the public, England hesitated to take any action. As a result, the imposition of an extraterritoriality system in China mainly was effected by the United States.

Caleb Cushing, who was appointed the first official American envoy to China in 1843, was responsible for obtaining China's full recognition of the principle of extraterritoriality. In numerous dispatches to Washington, he expounded at length on the subject, explaining its justification. Cushing argued that jurisprudence of Western Christendom alone guaranteed equitable treatment of foreigners. "This fact," he boldly claimed, was "the result of evidence of the superior civilization and respect for individual rights consequent thereon, which prevail in Christendom." Cushing insisted that the United States demand extraterritorial rights in China for American citizens, not as a matter of concession on China's part, but as a principle of established international law.

Cushing's major achievement was the negotiation of the Treaty of Whanghsia, signed on 3 July 1844, which granted the United States the right not only to determine punishment of American offenders, but to exercise absolute extraterritorial jurisdiction in both civil and criminal cases. By giving explicit definition to extraterritoriality, the Cushing treaty proved to be of enormous value to foreigners, for by the most-favored-nation clause the privileges granted to the United States were automatically bestowed on the other treaty powers. For the next 100 years, extraterritoriality, which constituted a fundamental treaty right, not only provided protection to Americans and other foreigners, but also served as a vehicle for the expansion of Western trade and influence.

From the mid-nineteenth century to World War II, American diplomacy in China was greatly occupied with problems relating to the administration of judicial affairs, shipping regulations, piracy, and claims. Other matters that explicitly concerned extraterritorial rights dealt with the buying and leasing of land; crimes against American persons and property; ensuring the guarantee of fair trials, whether in Chinese courts or consular courts; the safety of travel inland; and the right to trade, to worship freely, and to propagate the faith. At the same time, extraterritoriality became a cloak for the development of successful foreign commercial enterprises, and a means to secure control over much of China's foreign trade. It also offered a protective shield to Christian missionary activities, buttressed the creation of international settlements, and stimulated the use of foreign gunboats. By the twentieth century, the protection of Americans and other foreign nationals was provided not only by gunboats, but by the presence of foreign troops.

The setting up of the machinery and administrative apparatus of the extraterritoriality system in China and other countries produced many problems. Weaknesses and abuses gave rise to serious friction and were a constant source of complaint. For example, few American consuls in China, down to 1906, had adequate knowledge or competence to handle legal disputes. The State Department provided neither suitable training nor proper compensation. Many consuls were attached to various American mercantile firms; their meager consular fees and dependence on commercial houses seriously affected judicial administration. Bias and prejudice for one's own nationals could not be eliminated. Moreover, the complexity of laws and procedures, the difficulties of appeal, as well as securing witnesses or producing evidence for trials and offenses committed by foreigners in the interior, made the handling of cases onerous. The creation of a mixed court in Shanghai in 1864 sought to remedy these judicial problems; a Chinese magistrate presided and a foreign consular "assessor" sat with him as a cojudge. Although the removal of consular appointments from politics and the establishment of the United States Court in Shanghai in 1906 helped to improve the situation, the abuses of extraterritoriality persisted.

Initially, in the 1840's, the Chinese were not aware of the implications of extraterritoriality or of other concessions granted to foreigners. Nor were they disturbed by consular jurisdiction, since it did not affect directly China's political structure. It was felt that extraterritoriality could be helpful in the segregation of aliens; as long as foreigners were confined to the treaty ports there would be minimum contact with the people. But as foreign control over the Chinese economy steadily increased, these expectations rapidly disappeared. First applied to about 350 foreigners in five treaty ports, the extraterritoriality system by the beginning of the twentieth century was extended to about ninety treaty ports and some twenty-five ports of call for steamships, and embraced approximately a third of a million foreign residents. Westerners attained an unassailable position independent of Chinese laws. At the same time, their wealth and position gave them a privileged status, as powerful in its way as the Chinese upper class itself.

In the Islamic countries, a problem that created serious difficulty was the protégé system. Under bilateral treaties, European consuls obtained the privilege not only of almost complete jurisdiction over the persons and properties of their own nations, but also the right to offer this protection to anyone else whom they employed. These protégés were not subject to local law and were also exempt from all personal or direct taxation or forced levies. The system lent itself to abuses, since many local citizens who were not employed by European and American consuls or representatives gladly paid large sums of money to secure these exemptions.

A celebrated case involving the abuse of the protégé system concerned Felix A. Matthews, the American consul general at Tangier, appointed in 1871. On several occasions he was accused of selling protection rights to Moroccans, ranging "to upwards of 100 wealthy Moorish subjects," according to the British minister, Sir John Drummand Hay, at a time when the United States "have no trade and there is only one United States citizen in Morocco." These charges were vehemently denied, and the case against Matthews was dismissed by the State Department on the grounds that they were "wholly unsubstantiated." But when a second investigation was made in 1886, Matthews was found guilty, reprimanded, and compelled to resign. The new American consul, however, after again examining the protégé situation, exonerated him from all charges, and Matthews was reappointed to the Tangier post in 1890 and served three more years.

Foreign consuls found the practice of selling protection an excellent way of augmenting their incomes. As early as 1859, the Moroccan government demanded more careful regulation of the protégé system. Complaints were voiced not only against the corrupt practice of selling exemption from taxation, but also against the unwarranted interference by consuls in the local courts. Efforts to remedy the situation were made in 1877, when the sultan sought to limit and control the extent of protégé protection, and to obtain the return to his jurisdiction of any Moroccan subjects who, after naturalization in a foreign country, had returned to live in Morocco. But the discussions with the Tangier diplomatic corps brought no agreement, and the United States, while expressing its willingness to remedy the abuses of protection, insisted that naturalized citizens were equal to native-born citizens and therefore not subject to Moroccan jurisdiction if they returned to that country. The American government consistently maintained that no distinctions could be made between American citizens based on religion, race, or method by which citizenship was acquired.

At the Conference of Madrid in 1880, at which thirteen countries were represented, the subject of protégés was the main item on the agenda. While Britain, followed by most other powers, favored granting concessions to Moroccan demands, France, supported by Italy and Germany, urged that no abridgment be made on the right of protection that had been previously accorded. The conference adopted the French point of view, and the Convention of Madrid not only validated the protégé system, but by clarifying, defining, and legalizing the situation, strengthened it. This was accomplished by converting the former bilateral treaties and simple consular agreements to an international convention, which now was sanctioned by all interested powers. After the Madrid Convention of 1880, an orgy of protection selling began. More significant, however, was that the protection problem became linked to political penetration. In varying degrees, the European powers used both the legal and illegal issuance of protection to increase their influence in Morocco, and this practice reached its zenith in the early years of the twentieth century.

During the latter decades of the nineteenth century, imperial rivalries steadily exerted a profound impact on extraterritoriality in North Africa, the Near East, and Asia. As European powers pressed to partition Africa and carve out their colonial empires, the danger of the dismemberment of Morocco, of the Ottoman Empire, and of China became increasingly ominous. In 1871 the sultan of Morocco, fearful that his country might be partitioned by European countries, offered to place his entire nation under an American protectorate. Not yet ready for overseas expansion, the United States declined; but the State Department expressed its regret about "any attempt on the part of foreign powers of a dismemberment of the Empire of Morocco." Although refusing to accept the offer from "His Majesty to confer upon the United States a protectorate over his domains," the State Department proffered its friendly offices to prevent such an act. To forestall dismemberment or the establishment of hegemony in a region by any one power, and at the same time ensure the maintenance of treaty rights and extraterritoriality, the United States espoused the creation of international settlements, such as the International Settlement in Shanghai that had been set up in the 1850's, and a policy of the Open Door.

The United States strengthened the basis for extraterritorial rights not only in China, but in Japan. This was accomplished by Townsend Harris, a New York businessman and merchant who was appointed the first American consul at Shimoda, Japan, in 1855. Three years later, in July 1858, he succeeded in concluding a treaty of amity and commerce that greatly extended the privileges secured by Commodore Matthew C. Perry with Japan in 1854. Perry's treaty, which opened Japan, contained no extraterritorial provisions, but Harris persuaded the Japanese to grant Americans jurisdiction in both civil and criminal matters. Agreements with the Netherlands, Russia, England, and France promptly followed. With a few minor changes these conformed to the Harris treaty.

Though critical of the inefficiency of Japanese judicial administration, the Western powers were negligent—as they had been in China and elsewhere—in improving the system of extraterritoriality. Gross interference occurred in the enforcement of Japanese laws, especially with regard to hunting regulations, adopted by the Japanese in 1871; in quarantine regulations, drawn up in 1873; and on the control and regulation of the opium trade. The British minister, Sir Harry Parkes, adamantly insisted that British subjects could only be tried and punished for violation of British laws. He declared, on authority of Parliament's orders-in-council, that the Japanese government could not enact laws applicable to British nationals. The United States and the Netherlands opposed this position, claiming that there was no danger in recognizing all Japanese laws as long as the power to try and punish foreigners remained in the consular courts. Although England modified its policy, Parkes's persistent attempts, and those of other Western representatives, to control the lawmaking power of Japan convinced Japanese leaders and the public of the need to abolish the extraterritoriality system.

During the 1880's the Japanese government raised the matter of treaty revision. A concerted attempt was made to secure tariff autonomy and the repudiation of extraterritorial privileges. These efforts provoked vigorous opposition, especially on the part of England. Despite this resistance, Japanese leaders took steps to obtain full judicial autonomy by completing the codification of their laws. At the same time, they pressed for an immediate end to consular jurisdiction over matters relating to police administration, partnerships between Japanese and foreigners, and custom affairs. In January 1882 a Preparatory Conference for Treaty Revision, attended by the ministers of twelve treaty powers, was convened at Tokyo. Japan proposed the abolition of extraterritorial jurisdiction in five years and the employment of foreign judges in Japanese courts during the transition period. The Western powers, in return, were offered an extension of foreign rights to residence and land tenure within treaty ports and the opening of the country to all foreigners. These proposals were studied and exchanges of views took place. By 1885 a general agreement was reached that the treaties should be revised. The next year, on 1 May, an Official Conference of the Treaty Powers opened at Tokyo, and, after many lengthy sessions, a draft jurisdictional convention was approved.

Although the prospects of early treaty revision looked bright, they were quashed by the strong popular opposition that arose against Westernization and the proposals advanced by Japan's leaders. Widespread agitation was especially directed against the suggested system of mixed courts and the humiliating promise to submit the constitution of the courts and the codified laws to the Western powers for their approbation. Unsuccessful in reaching a general agreement, the Japanese attempted to abolish extraterritoriality and to obtain tariff autonomy by bilateral treaties. Toward this end the United States was first approached, and, in February 1889, the American minister, Richard D. Hubbard, concluded a treaty with Japan that included the abolition of consular courts in five years. His successor, John Franklin Swift, strenuously opposed the treaty's adoption, and Secretary of State James G. Blaine withheld it from the Senate. Meanwhile, Japan undertook negotiations separately with other countries, and new treaties, practically the same as the American-Japanese agreement, were signed with Germany and Russia. England's delay in joining the movement toward treaty revision and the insistence of the Japanese public that the principle of absolute equality of treatment be obtained in whatever arrangements were made with the Western powers were major stumbling blocks in securing treaty revision.

The deadlock was finally broken in 1890, when, to the great surprise and relief of Japan, the British came forward with a favorable response to the Japanese overtures and agreed to treaty revision, on condition that Japanese jurisdiction over foreigners would be postponed for five years and that the newly codified Japanese laws would be in actual and satisfactory operation for one year before the expiration of that period. Discussions lasted for the next three years, and a compromise was reached that was acceptable to England and Japan. In July 1894 an Anglo-Japanese Treaty of Commerce and Navigation was signed. The agreement specified that foreigners would be treated on an equal footing with Japanese in regard to travel, residence, and trade. Consular jurisdiction and foreign settlements were abolished. The implementation of the treaty was made contingent upon the satisfactory operation of Japan's newly codified laws, and provision was made for its termination at the end of twelve years.

By waiting for the outcome of the British negotiations, the United States lost the opportunity to be the first power to relinquish extraterritorial rights in Japan. Further delays were caused by Washington's objection to a reciprocal clause in the Anglo-Japanese treaty that provided for the right of entrance, travel, residence, and property ownership. This raised the problem of Japanese immigration into the United States. However, after Japan agreed to include a clause in an American treaty mutually to exempt laws relating to laborers and labor immigration, a new treaty was signed in November 1894. The Senate delayed ratification until provisions satisfactory to both parties were worked out. Early the next year, the American-Japanese treaty was ratified by both nations. Other agreements were quickly concluded with Italy, Germany, Russia, France, and Austria-Hungary. Japan fulfilled all of the conditions that had been specified within the prescribed period of time, and in 1899 extraterritorial jurisdiction in the Japanese Empire was at last abolished.

The ending of extraterritoriality in Japan coincided with Japan's astonishing victory in the Sino-Japanese War of 1894–1895, and its emergence as a major world power. Although constituting the first significant breakthrough in the problems concerning extraterritoriality, the retreat of the Western powers in Japan did not immediately have an impact on the countries in North Africa, the Near East, or the rest of Asia. Political and economic competition between and among the European powers in these regions intensified, rather than weakened, efforts to maintain and broaden extraterritorial rights. In Morocco, particularly, a decisive shift occurred from concern with persons and property to an interest in economic exploitation and trade. The Moroccan crisis that almost triggered conflict between France and Germany, and was a prelude to World War I, was occasioned by Germany's desire to prevent French economic control of that country. The intervention of President Theodore Roosevelt in this dispute led to the Algeciras Conference in 1906. While the Act of Algeciras effected a compromise, which guaranteed equality of economic opportunity and the Open Door, France and Spain secured privileged positions with the Moroccan police force.

The interests of France, Spain, and Britain converged especially on Tangier, which overlooks one of the most important waterways in the world, the Strait of Gibraltar. England and Germany, for different reasons, strongly favored internationalization of Tangier, but France resisted this proposal, insisting on French and Spanish preponderance. Following the Act of Algeciras, France swiftly took steps to establish a protectorate over Morocco. Germany attempted to counter this move by dispatching a German gunboat, the *Panther,* to Agadir to "protect German interests." This action, in 1911, precipitated a second Moroccan crisis. But again a compromise was reached. In a Franco-German accord, concluded in November 1911, Germany conceded France a free hand in Morocco in exchange for a sizable slice of French Congo territory. After firmly establishing its position in Morocco, and working out arrangements with Germany and Spain, France agreed to cooperate in the creation of an international regime for Tangier, modeled on the International Settlement of Shanghai. A technical commission, representing France, Spain, and Britain, worked on a draft for a future constitution for the municipality and on arrangements for the administration of the city. A proposed statute was finally approved by most of the Algeciras powers by November 1914.

China, like Morocco, was unable to resist the encroachment of the Western powers. For more than a half-century after the Opium War, China was wracked by insurrections, economic dislocations, and the spread of European and Japanese imperialism. Compelled to accept the West's goods and ideas, China's humiliation, by the turn of the twentieth century, reached its nadir with its defeat in the first Sino-Japanese War, the crushing of the Boxer Rebellion, and the signing of the Boxer Protocol in 1901. The latter provided for a huge indemnity and the permanent quartering of foreign troops in the capital as legation guards.

The rise of nationalism and reform movements, however, steadily gained momentum. As they did so, the "unequal treaties" and extraterritoriality in China and the capitulatory system in the Islamic countries increasingly became targets of attack. To counter the agitation in China, the Western powers and Japan signed a series of treaties in 1902 and 1903. While not renouncing their extraterritorial rights, these agreements indicated the willingness of these powers to help China in its efforts to effect judicial reform so that extraterritoriality, in time, could be ended. The continuation of internal strife, which led to the abdication of the Manchu dynasty and the creation of the Chinese Republic in 1912, delayed progress on judicial reforms.

With the outbreak of World War I, the Western powers found themselves on the defensive. Turkey was the first country to take advantage of the conflict by declaring its intention to rid itself of the capitulatory regime. In September 1914 the Turks announced that the capitulations were "an impediment to the progress and development of the Ottoman Empire." Asserting that the capitulatory rights were "in complete opposition to the juridical rules of the century and to the principle of national sovereignty," they proclaimed that Turkey's relations with all states would be based on the "general principles of international law" after Turkey abrogated the capitulatory agreements, effective 1 October 1914. The United States promptly denied Turkey's right to abolish the capitulations unilaterally, claiming that such action could only be taken by agreement among all the nations concerned. Despite the protests of the American government and other powers, Turkey made it clear that it considered the capitulations dead.

When China, in 1917, entered World War I on the Allied side, steps were immediately taken to cancel the extraterritorial privileges of Germany and Austria. At the Paris Peace Conference, the Chinese delegation set forth a program that called for the return of all foreign concessions, settlements, and leased territories; the gradual abolishment of extraterritoriality; and complete tariff autonomy. But China's efforts to rescind the "unequal treaties" were unsuccessful. To the dismay and anger of the Chinese, Woodrow Wilson endorsed Japan's claims to Shantung, which had been obtained in 1914 by the expulsion of the Germans. On 4 May 1919 Chinese students staged massive demonstrations in Peking denouncing the unjust verdict. Delegates at the Paris Conference refused to reconsider the Shantung question or China's arguments on the abolition of extraterritoriality. As a result, the Chinese declined to sign the Treaty of Versailles.

After World War I, extraterritoriality was viewed as a key symbol of foreign domination. At the Washington Conference in 1921–1922, the Chinese delegation again made a strong bid for recognition of its full sovereignty. But the major powers—the United States, Britain, France, and Japan—balked at agreeing to treaty revisions with China. Although the Nine-Power Treaty (1922) confirmed China's independence and its territorial and administrative integrity, the agreement upheld the existing privileges of the signatory powers in the country. It did not bind them to defend the Open Door or Chinese independence, nor did it provide the machinery for the "security pledge." The Washington Conference, therefore, did little to alleviate China's sense of injury to its self-respect. China secured only a promise of a study on the question of extraterritoriality, and real tariff autonomy was postponed to an indefinite date.

Although the Western powers and Japan resisted the relinquishment of extraterritorial rights in China, stressing that significant treaty revisions had to await China's progress in the field of legislation and adoption of adequate judicial reforms, the extraterritoriality system deteriorated during the interwar years. Turkey's abolition of the capitulatory regime was officially affirmed by the European powers in the Treaty of Lausanne, signed in July 1923. Since the United States was not a party to this agreement, American rights were not terminated until 1931, when a separate treaty was concluded. Following the establishment of the French protectorate in Morocco, many countries, with the exception of the United States and England, surrendered their capitulatory rights. With the signing of the Tangier Statute in 1923, the protégé system was also eliminated. England was the last of the signatory powers to renounce formally its right of protection and all capitulatory rights, in a 1937 accord with France. But the United States refused to accept the Tangier Statute of 1923 or the modification in 1928 that officially established the basis for the internationalization of the city. At the time, Americans had few interests either political or economic in Tangier, and Washington decided it would be more advantageous to remain outside the international settlement, thus retaining both its diplomatic status and its extraterritorial rights.

Meanwhile, the impact of the Bolshevik Revolution made itself felt in China, spurring the growth of nationalism and radicalism in the country. Affirming its desire to deal with China on the basis of equality, the Soviet Union renounced extraterritoriality, and in May 1924 a Sino-Soviet agreement officially relinquished Russia's privileges. As turmoil and civil strife gripped China in the 1920's, students, intellectuals, and the labor class in the large cities, infused with patriotic ardor, clamored to end China's semicolonial status.

Although the Washington Conference adopted a resolution that provided for the establishment of a fact-finding commission to investigate extraterritoriality in China within three months after its adjournment, the chaotic conditions in the country and a petty squabble between France and China over Boxer indemnity payments led to the delay of the convening of the Commission on Extraterritoriality until January 1926. After almost a year of investigation and the assembling of a mass of detailed information on China's judicial system and practices of extraterritoriality, the members unanimously concluded that until more effective judicial reforms were carried out the abolition of extraterritoriality by the twelve treaty powers was unwarranted. While the *Report of the Commission on Extraterritoriality* was a historically significant document, it failed to perceive that a fundamental economic and social revolution was taking place in China.

In the meantime, the Nationalist revolution, which had moved into a more active phase, coalesced under Chiang Kai-shek's leadership, and by 1928 defeated the northern government. Pledged to put an end to the extraterritoriality system, the Kuomintang adopted a provisional constitution in October, and immediately took steps to establish a new basis of relations with foreign powers. At the end of the year, China reached agreements with five states—Belgium, Denmark, Italy, Portugal, and Spain—that provided for tariff autonomy, an acceptance, in principle, of ending extraterritoriality, and a promise that rights would be relinquished when other states had done so.

In May 1929 the Kuomintang government announced that it intended to promulgate civil, criminal, and commercial laws to replace the extraterritoriality system. Three months later it issued a set of regulations that ended the provincial and local handling of matters of a diplomatic nature and prescribed new procedures for dealing with aliens. But the Nationalists withheld a unilateral abrogation of extraterritoriality. They expressed the hope, instead, that the system could be abolished by mutual consent with the Western powers and Japan by 1 January 1930. Since the United States and Britain insisted upon a gradual relinquishment of extraterritorial rights—and only if China gave evidence of an improvement of its judicial system that ensured "effective enforcement of jurisprudence"—the Kuomintang declared its dissatisfaction with this response. On 28 December the Western powers were informed that beginning 1 January 1930 "all foreign nationals in the territory of China who are now enjoying extraterritorial privileges shall abide by the laws, ordinances, and regulations duly promulgated by the Central and Local Government of China." This mandate was qualified two days later, when China stated its intent was merely to abolish extraterritoriality in principle. With the understanding that 1 January would be regarded simply as the date from which the process of gradual abolition would be said to have commenced, Washington, London, and Tokyo agreed to negotiate further with China "within a reasonable time."

For almost a year and a half, the United States and Britain attempted to work out an acceptable agreement with China. By June 1931 the points in dispute were resolved, and England consented to the exchange of texts of a draft treaty. The next month the State Department prepared a similar draft. But final agreement was left in abeyance, pending an examination of the treaty terms by London, Washington, and Tokyo. Then, the Japanese struck in Manchuria on 8 September 1931. The treaties had not yet been ratified and were indefinitely suspended. Efforts to resume negotiations and to arrive at final agreements on the abolition of extraterritorial rights were made in the mid-1930's. But the outbreak of the second Sino-Japanese War in July 1937 once again resulted in a halt to the discussions.

The issue of extraterritoriality was not further considered until World War II. After the bombing of Pearl Harbor and America's entry into the conflict, the State Department decided that it would be advantageous to end extraterritoriality. On 11 January 1943 China simultaneously concluded with the United States at Washington, and with Britain at Chungking, a "Treaty for the Relinquishment of Extraterritorial Rights in China and the Regulation of Related Matters." By these treaties, together with exchanges of notes, the United States and England surrendered not only their extraterritoriality rights, but also their unilateral privileges in China that had previously been acquired by the "unequal treaties."

The long-standing grievances relating to extraterritoriality, concessions, settlements, legation quarters, and the right to station foreign warships in Chinese waters and foreign troops on Chinese soil were thus ended. Other treaty powers quickly followed the American and British example. Belgium, Brazil, the Netherlands, Norway, and Sweden concluded new treaties with China on the bases of equality and reciprocity during the war; Denmark, France, Portugal, and Spain did so soon afterward. Japan and Italy lost their treaty rights as a consequence of the war. In addition to ending extraterritoriality, the United States, in 1943, repealed Chinese exclusion laws that had been in effect since 1882. At the same time, Congress placed Chinese immigration on a quota basis and made Chinese immigrants eligible for naturalization.

Some vestiges of extraterritoriality persisted after World War II. For example, American extraterritorial rights were not ended in Morocco until 1956, when Moroccan independence was attained; and the final economic integration of Tangier was secured only in October 1960. Extraterritorial jurisdiction continues to exist in the Panama Canal Zone, where, on the basis of the Hay-Bunau-Varilla Treaty of 1903, the United States exercises "all the rights, power and authority within the zone" that it "would possess if it were the sovereign of the territory . . . to the entire exclusion of the exercise by the [Panama] Republic of any such sovereign rights, power or authority." Although in 1965 President Lyndon B. Johnson indicated a willingness to negotiate a new treaty and a Joint Statement of Principles in 1974 affirmed this desire, it was not until 1978 that the Carter administration was able to persuade the Senate to ratify treaties recognizing Panama's sovereignty and jurisdiction in the Canal Zone by the year 2000. Military status of forces agreements negotiated after World War II with Japan, Korea, Formosa, and the Philippines, among others, embody in a new form extraterritorial jurisdiction affecting American military personnel abroad.

For the most part, the extraterritoriality system that prevailed in the nineteenth century, and was maintained, especially in China, down to World War II, is now a relic of the past. The assessment of its evolution, development, and decline must be viewed within its historical context and its practical applications. From ancient times to the mid-nineteenth century, extraterritoriality served a useful function. To foreigners, it afforded a measure of safety and protection in an alien environment, enabling them to live in accord with the manner of existence that they enjoyed in their homelands. To states that extended special rights and privileges to "strangers within the gates," it eased many troublesome problems in dealing with foreigners and facilitated their segregation and control.

In its modern form, extraterritoriality became closely linked to Western expansion and imperialism and served as an instrument to promote political and commercial penetration in weaker countries in Africa, the Middle East, and East Asia. By the twentieth century, it provided not only a diplomatic and juridical shield for foreign nationals and missionaries, but it also contributed to economic exploitation. Increasingly, the extraterritoriality came to be viewed as intrinsically harmful, for it represented a derogation of sovereign powers and symbolized inferiority.

BIBLIOGRAPHY

Jules Davids, ed., *American Diplomatic and Public Papers: The United States and China,* ser. I, "The Treaty System and the Taiping Rebellion, 1842–1860," 21 vols. (Wilmington, Del., 1973); vols. 8–11 contain documents on consular regulations, judicial affairs, and major cases and problems relating to extraterritoriality in China. Wesley R. Fishel, *The End of Extraterritoriality in China* (Berkeley, Calif., 1952), is an excellent, well-balanced account of the abolition of extraterritoriality in China. Green H. Hackworth, *Digest of International Law,* 2 vols. (Washington, D.C., 1941); these volumes published by the State Department include the original texts of diplomatic documents on extraterritoriality. Frank E. Hinckley, *American Consular Jurisdiction in the Orient* (Washington, D.C., 1906), is an old work but still useful as a survey of American consular jurisdiction in Turkey and East Asia. Frances Clifford Jones, *Extraterritoriality in Japan and Diplomatic Relations Resulting in Its Abolition, 1853–1899* (New York, 1960; originally published 1930), is the best detailed study of the extraterritoriality system in Japan. George W. Keeton, *The Development of Extraterritoriality in China,* 2 vols. (London, 1928), comprehensively surveys extraterritoriality in China from a historical and legal point of view. Shuh Shun Liu, *Extraterritoriality: Its Rise and Decline* (New York, 1969; originally published 1925), views extraterritoriality from the perspective of the Chinese; he traces its origins and development, the problems of consular jurisdiction, and the reasons for its decline in China. Graham H. Stuart, *The International City of Tangier*, 2nd ed. (Stanford, 1955), explores the background to the creation of the international city of Tangier and its problems from the standpoints of geography, history, and diplomacy. Nasim Susa, *The Capitulatory Regime in Turkey: Its History, Origins, and Nature* (Baltimore, 1933), emphasizes custom and usage as the major reason for the granting of capitulary rights to foreigners by the Islamic states. Payson J. Treat, *Diplomatic Relations Between the United States and Japan, 1853–1895*, 2 vols. (Stanford, 1932); based primarily on archival sources, this study thoroughly surveys American-Japanese relations and includes extensive material on Japan's efforts to secure treaty revision and the abolition of extraterritoriality.

[*See also* IMPERIALISM; INTERNATIONAL LAW; INTERVENTION AND NONINTERVENTION; THE MOST-FAVORED-NATION PRINCIPLE; PROTECTION OF AMERICAN CITIZENS ABROAD; TRADE AND COMMERCE; TREATIES.]

Encyclopedia of American Foreign Policy: studies of the principal movements and ideas. 3 vols.

Scribners. 1978. 1201p. ed. by Alexander DeConde. index. LC 78-5453. $99; library ed. $79.

POL SCI/REF

This encyclopedia does not attempt to survey the entire range of U.S. foreign policy; rather, the focus is on analyzing basic concepts and recurring issues that affect foreign policy. The 95 essays are arranged alphabetically; each is about ten pages long, including a brief bibliography. Most of the contributors are American historians, respresenting diverse ideological positions. The essays are extensive and scholarly, but not ponderous, and will be of lasting value to students of U.S. history and government. There are both predictable ("The Cold War," "The Nixon Doctrine," "The Marshall Plan," "Détente," etc.) and refreshingly innovative ("Elitism and Foreign Policy," "Missionary Diplomacy," "American Attitudes toward War," "The Most-Favored-Nation Principle," etc.) entries. There are no single entries for major episodes in American history, such as the Vietnam war, but information on such broad topics is scattered throughout the encyclopedia. The third volume contains a substantial biographical section and a detailed index. The craftsmanship involved in this unique encyclopedia makes it highly recommended. For academic libraries. —*Thomas A. Karel, Rider Coll. Lib., Lawrenceville, N.J.*